LEE'S FERRY

from

Mormon Crossing to National Park

The last ferryboat accident at Lee's Ferry, June 27, 1928 (*Harper Goff drawing*).

LEE'S FERRY

from

Mormon Crossing to National Park

by

P. T. Reilly

Edited by Robert H. Webb
With contributions by Richard D. Quartaroli

Utah State University Press
Logan, Utah

Utah State University Press
Logan, Utah 84322-7800

Typography by WolfPack
Cover design by Karen Groves

Library of Congress Cataloging-in-Publication Data

Reilly, P. T.
Lee's Ferry : from Mormon crossing to national park / by P.T. Reilly;
edited by Robert H. Webb; with contributions by Richard D. Quartaroli.
p. cm.
Includes bibliographical references and index.
ISBN 0-87421-261-8 (alk. paper)
ISBN 0-87421-260-X (pbk. : alk. paper)
1. Lees Ferry (Ariz.)—History. I. Webb, Robert H. II. Quartaroli, Richard
D. III. Title.
F819.L44 R45 1999
979.1'33—dc21 98-58050
CIP

Contents

Illustrations		VII
Editor's Preface		IX
Author's Preface		XII
Acknowledgments		XV
1	In the Beginning	1
2	John D. Lee and Lonely Dell	25
3	The Ferryman	54
4	The Widow and Her Mite	71
5	Building the Oasis	85
6	Brother Johnson's Green Acres	108
7	The Controversial Emetts	145
8	The Antagonists	180
9	Charles H. Spencer	215
10	The Aftermath	249
11	Water	275
12	Change and Reversion	310
13	The Polygamists	340
14	Paradise Canyon Ranch	372
15	A Change in Priorities	412
16	Big Brother Takes Over	439
Epilogue		460
Chapter Notes		469

Appendices

    1   Children Born at Lee's Ferry   515
    2   Deaths at Lee's Ferry   517
    3   Proprietors, Ferrymen, and Custodians   518
    4   Postmasters   520
    5   Schoolteachers   521
    6   USGS Resident Hydrographers at Lee's Ferry   522
    7   Lee's Ferry Ownership   525
    8   The National Park Service   527

Illustrations

The last ferryboat accident at Lee's Ferry   frontis
Map of Lee's Ferry and vicinity   XVII
John D. Lee   12
The mouth of the Pahreah River   40
The drowning of Bishop Roundy   66
Emma Batchelor Lee French   79
Franklin H. French and sons   79
Warren M. Johnson   86
Warren M. and Permelia Johnson family   109
Christmas dinner at Lee's Ferry, 1889   119
Prayer before the rescue of Franklin Nims   121
Map of the Lee's Ferry cemetery   129
Buffalo Bill Cody and entourage on ferryboat   134
The Johnson house at Lee's Ferry   135
James S. Emett   146
Emett family at the Johnson ranch house   154
Galloway, Mesken, James, French, Fluke   157
Nathaniel Galloway in Glen Canyon   158
Ferryboat at the lower crossing   159
Map of historical roads, Lee's Ferry vicinity   162
Sadie Staker   171
Sadie Staker and students   175
Charles Spencer, Howard Mayrant, and wagon train   219
Launching the *Canopy*   224
The Spencer barges and the *Violet Louise*   239
The *Charles H. Spencer* docked at Lee's Ferry   247
Charles H. Spencer   250
The Caffalls, Bill Langton, and Charles H. Spencer   255
Theodore Roosevelt chopping wood at Lee's Ferry   257

Jerry and Pearl Johnson family at the ranch house 264

Frank and Jerry Johnson 269

The *Navajo* on the dugway at Lee's Ferry 283

Owen Clark, Sid Wilson, and Don Blockberger 299

Ferryboat with automobiles at the lower crossing 306

Ferryboat with automobile and passenger 307

Jim Klohr 313

Shine Smith, Buck Lowrey, and Clyde Eddy 325

Adolpha Johnson 330

Navajo Bridge nearing completion 334

Dedication of Navajo Bridge 338

Owen Clark 341

Streamgager's residence at Lee's Ferry 359

"Buck" Lowrey at Vermilion Cliffs Lodge 367

Leo Weaver 375

George Wilson at Marble Canyon gas station 383

Bowerses, Weavers, Decker, Dodge, and Forsythe 385

Ed Fisher and David Lowrey 396

Shine Smith and Isabella Moseley at Wilson cabin 402

Shine Smith 403

Norman D. Nevills 414

Art Greene's airboat 429

P. T. Reilly, boatman, and Edwin McKee 461

Editor's Preface

I FIRST MET P. T. AND SUSIE REILLY IN THE EARLY 1990S. I WAS ATTEMPTING to learn about long-term changes in rivers in northern Arizona and southern Utah, and I had embarked on a large repeat-photography project in Grand Canyon. I first heard of P. T. in 1985, when Ron Smith, then owner of Grand Canyon Expeditions in Kanab, Utah, showed me a nearly unbelievable photograph Dwain Norton took of Reilly rowing a boat (Susie was a passenger) past a nearly submerged Boulder Narrows in Marble Canyon. Among those who knew river history, Reilly had a near-legendary status as a boatman. After being told repeatedly to see P. T. about his extensive photography of Grand Canyon, I finally called and scheduled a visit.

P. T. was an imposing man. He quizzed me repeatedly about Grand Canyon geography; fortunately, I knew something about the place. I felt that if I had not genuinely cared about Grand Canyon, he would not have given me the time of day. But he did, and he generously shared his photography. No coaxing was required to get story after story of river trips before Glen Canyon Dam. Fascinated, I got him to write up some of his stories.[1] My river crews and I matched about fifty of his photographs, and the observations from his diaries were extremely important in documenting changes that have occurred over the years in the Colorado River.

I heard the news a month after P. T. died on October 24, 1996. I knew he was ill, but I did not have the time to visit him one last time. I owed a debt to P. T. and Susie for their help and graciousness during my visits, and I wanted to repay them. When I was asked to edit P. T.'s book on the history of Lee's Ferry, I jumped at the task. I could only hope that my help in bringing his manuscript into publication would in small measure repay him for his help to me.

Of course, I had heard about the manuscript. I was dying to see it, but he wouldn't let me. I thought his history would answer a number of questions I had about the local environment and changes in the Paria and Colorado Rivers. How often did the river freeze? P. T. told me what was published in other sources and said his book wouldn't help. When did the Paria River change course in its delta? Again, no real answer from P. T. The answers were in the manuscript that I wasn't allowed to see until one day, in September 1997, a large package arrived in the mail.

My job was to turn a thousand page manuscript, written as two volumes, into a book. I couldn't ask the author questions—what did you mean in that passage, P. T.?—and the book didn't seem finished. Two previous books had been published on Lee's Ferry;[2] how was this one different? P. T. Reilly was a well-published historian; how could I change a single word in his life's work? With tremendous help and support from Susie and the Cline Library at Northern Arizona University, I prepared the final manuscript for this volume.

I quickly realized that Reilly's book differed significantly from the previous two, which I had first read years ago. Both previous books always seemed to me to be about Lee's Ferry, the place; P. T.'s book is most definitely about Lee's Ferry, the people. My changes to P. T.'s original text were designed to preserve and enhance his stories of people and their activities in this remarkable place. P. T. was thorough; he interviewed nearly everyone alive who had relatives at or lived at Lee's Ferry. He scoured the archives of the Church of Jesus Christ of Latter-day Saints, as well as other major archives. Much of the history of northern Arizona and southern Utah swirled through this little transportation bottleneck. My task was to make the constant ebb and flow of people to and from this place, by river and by land, accessible.

The biggest problem was to establish continuity in the story line without losing facts or lessening the impact. P. T. had adopted a strictly chronological style that fragmented the lives of many of his major characters, particularly Jerry Johnson, Charles Spencer, and Leo Weaver. Finally, the style changed from beginning to end, reflecting the long period over which P. T. wrote the manuscript.

My editorial changes to the text are silent. The spelling of two geographic names was sacrosanct. I retained the punctuation of Lee's Ferry, despite the official Board on Geographic Names designation of Lees Ferry. Similarly, and for reasons that P. T. explains in an endnote, I retained Pahreah instead of Paria, although I insisted on calling it the Pahreah River instead of Pahreah Creek. I found several small errors of dates and facts that were quietly corrected. P. T. seemed to want to mention the names of everyone who he could document at the ferry; I chose to eliminate many of the nonessential characters, particularly the names of hydrographers who measured streamflow in the Colorado and Pahreah Rivers (we now call them hydrologic technicians). Because numerous relevant books and articles had been published after the manuscript was completed, I tried to insert the best ones into the endnotes for academic thoroughness. Reilly's endnotes were to some extent unfinished. Although I have corrected and updated them, they are in some cases still incomplete or inconsistent in form. However, in all cases the sources should be traceable from the information provided.

To me, the largest problem with the book was that P. T. Reilly did not insert himself into the history of Lee's Ferry. I asked Richard Quartaroli to finish the book with an appropriate epilogue. Richard, a river historian, supplied the ending that the book needed. I thank Richard for his help with proofreading the text; Karen Underhill for her help with the photographs used in the text, and Clio, an on-line group of river historians, for advice on certain individuals mentioned in the text. I can only hope that this book is what P. T. Reilly would have wanted to see in print.

ROBERT H. WEBB

JULY 1998

Author's Preface

Although I was familiar with Lee's Ferry as a place name in Western history, I never visited it until May 7, 1947. On that occasion I had spent a week listening to river legend roll glibly out of the mouth of Norman Nevills. The recitation began at Mexican Hat, Utah, and ended on the beach at Two Mile at the lower ferry crossing—a distance of 192 miles. Here the boats were removed from the river, placed on trailers, and more "history" was dispensed during the ride back to the Hat. In his individually distinctive style Norm provided many names but few dates, and even the customers perceived that he seldom allowed historical fact to interfere with a good story. As a professional boatman for Nevills, I found the long rides back to Mexican Hat to be splendid opportunities to discuss in more depth the sites he had sketched for the passengers. I soon learned that no authoritative study in this field had been made after Powell, and even Norm's versions varied from trip to trip. This was especially true of the Lee's Ferry area.

During the years that followed, it seemed that I constantly was landing or starting a trip at Lee's Ferry. I talked to Jeremiah Johnson twice in the late 1940s but did not know of the role he played in ferry history and consequently learned little from him. In the next decade, Otis R. "Dock" Marston confided to me that he considered the pre-1909 discovery of Rainbow Bridge and the true record of Lee's Ferry to be the major offshoots of Colorado River history. I began making inquiry of local citizens and found that general knowledge was on the same level as that dispensed by Nevills. I consulted libraries and archives but found little relief. Nothing had been compiled; the story probably existed but was widely diffused.

The Huntington Library published the diaries of John D. Lee in 1955 and I obtained one of the first sets. I poured through these books, especially Volume 2, and received a basic understanding of Lee and the Mormon pioneer movement. This motivated me to study the *Mountain Meadows Massacre*, which had been published five years earlier. Thus it really was Juanita Brooks who inspired me to consult original source material and unearth the story that had been neglected for so long.

One source led to another; old journals, newspapers, and letters were read and many references ultimately led to the Church of Jesus Christ of Latter-day Saints. I tracked the children and grandchildren of John D. Lee, Warren M. Johnson, James Emett, and everyone else who had lived or worked at Lee's Ferry. All contributed to my knowledge and made it possible for me to accumulate the lore of nearly forgotten people and events. It would not be possible to repeat this research today because most of the informants have died and not all source material remains available.

It became apparent quite early that Lee's Ferry came into existence because the mouth of the Pahreah was the easiest place for pioneer wagons to cross that barrier of barriers—the Colorado River and its canyons. Therefore, the history of the ferry begins with the pioneers' period and the colonists' umbilical tie to Mother Utah. Succeeding phases involved the great herds and flocks of livestock that crossed there; the promoters and miners; the river gagers, engineers, and dam builders; dude operators, river tourists, and fishermen; and the people who lived there.

As I delved into ferry history, I perceived that a number of historical questions remained unsolved, and any comprehensive study demanded answers. Other issues important to ferry development had not been recognized or defined. A few problems, such as the so-called "Lee cabin" and the supposed incorporation of the *Nellie Powell* into its building, had been discussed by several interested people but were not explained satisfactorily. Hearsay and misinterpretation allowed errors of fact to be repeated as actual truth by just about everybody, including government representatives. Clarification clearly was needed.

Neglected phases of ferry history pertained to the roles of Jacob Hamblin and John D. Lee, their deteriorating friendship, Utah's political troubles and their effect on the ferry, the selection of Warren M. Johnson as ferryman, the Roundy drowning, ferry ownership by Emma B. Lee, her sale to the church, evolution of ranch development, the significance of the John R. Nielson mining boat, George M. Wright's strike, the Jim Emett–Bar Z conflict, Charlie Spencer's promotion, the Edison Company venture, the Geological Survey, the Arthur P. Davis–E. C. LaRue struggle that led ultimately to the latter's resignation from the Survey, the polygamy and dude eras, the rise of commercial river running, and the purchase of the property by the National Park Service. Since these matters had a direct bearing on ferry history, and should be studied, I set about finding answers.

The motivation to write more than a dry presentation of historical facts and dates was provided by Frank T. Johnson, who dwelt extensively on his boyhood at the ferry. I interviewed him many times, spent days with him, and we became good friends. Frank stated that he thought the flavor of the old ranch was gone and it would be impossible to recapture the spirit of pioneer times. This was a challenge that bid me recreate each era in its own terms, to present the problems inherent to them, to record the now nearly forgotten people who were born, lived, worked, or died at Lee's Ferry. Life is a continuum, but too often individual segments end with the people who lived them and are lost forever.

It would be easy to dismiss devout men such as John D. Lee and Warren M. Johnson as religious zealots who willingly placed what they considered to be the progress of their church ahead of the welfare of themselves and their families, but they sincerely believed the Kingdom of God was at hand and they had a responsible part in helping to build it. The terms of their reactions may not be understood today but they were very real in the 1870s. It was my aspiration to give substance to those attitudes.

P. T. REILLY

n.d.

Acknowledgments

I AM GRATEFUL TO THE MANY INDIVIDUALS AND INSTITUTIONS WHO HAVE made this work possible. It is regrettable that some who shared their experiences, personal records, and photographs are unable to see the result of their assistance because they have passed on to the Great Beyond.

A work of this nature could not have been compiled without my having been given access to the source material in the Historical Department of the Church of Jesus Christ of Latter-day Saints. The cooperation and help provided by the efficient staff is freely acknowledged and appreciated.

Thanks also are extended to other institutions who opened their materials and research facilities: the Arizona Department of History and Archives, the Arizona Historical Society, the Bancroft Library, Brigham Young University Library, the California State Archives, the Denver Public Library, Dixie College, the Harrison Western Research Center, the Huntington Library, the Los Angeles County Museum, the Museum of Northern Arizona, the National Archives, the National Park Service (at Grand Canyon, Pipe Spring, Santa Fe, and Wahweap), the Navajo Nation Archives, Northern Arizona University, the Sharlot Hall Museum, Southern California Edison Company, the Southwest Museum, the Tulare County Historical Society, the Bureau of Land Management, the U.S. Geological Survey, the University of Arizona, the University of New Mexico, the University of Utah, the Utah State Archives, and the Utah State Historical Society.

Several very helpful individuals have done much more than provide answers, reply to letters, and grant interviews; they worked assiduously in recalling their parts in ferry history and suggested others who might have remained unknown except for their leads: Solena Emett Bennett, Edna Lee Brimhall, Clara Emett Davis, Ida and Sherman O. Decker, Ed Fisher, Eletha Jacobsen, Frank T. Johnson, Agnes and Joseph S. Johnson, A. H. Jones, J. E. and Christina Klohr, Marion B. Scott, George S. Tanner, Arthur C. Waller, and Hazel Weaver.

A special accolade is reserved for my wife, who not only supported me in my work but made herself invaluable in conducting research, editing, and making hundreds of valuable suggestions while keeping the home running smoothly and the writer well fed and maintained. Without my Susie, this work could never have been completed.

My heartfelt thanks are extended to artists Harper Goff for his sketches and T. J. Cardinale for his maps. Their skills have benefited the work in no small measure. I especially appreciate the work of Paul B. Terry, who spent hundreds of hours in his dark room developing and printing, copying old prints and documents, and working long hours overtime so that I could return borrowed items when promised.

A great number of knowledgeable people gave freely of their experience and views to make this work as comprehensive as it is. To each I express my thanks. Without their assistance, my knowledge would be less than it is. I would be happy to list the contributions of each person but there are more than two hundred, and space forbids.

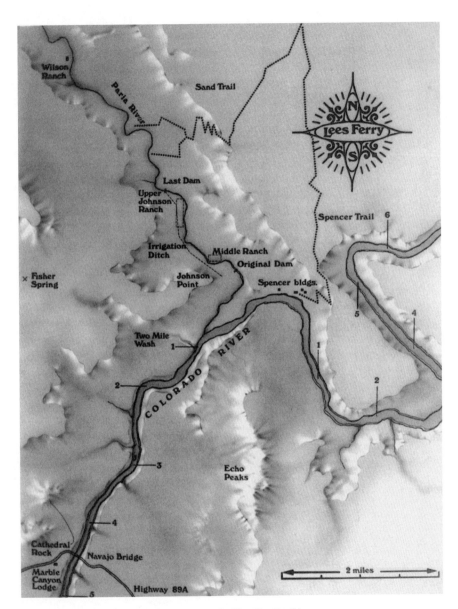

Lee's Ferry, Arizona, and vicinity (*map by Tim Cardinale*).

1

In the Beginning

*F*OR MOST OF ITS COURSE THROUGH THE CANYON COUNTRY, THE COLORADO River is entrenched between high walls that not only preclude a crossing but deny access to its banks. Even more of a natural barrier than the river are the rugged flanks of its drainage—nearly six hundred miles of sandy wasteland, incised gorges, sheer-walled mesas, and precipitous rimrock— that limited penetration as well as settlement. As in no other landscape, the eroded nature of the country added a third dimension to the obvious diffi- culties that restricted travel. Until the middle of the twentieth century, this severe topography constituted the least-known area of comparable size in the entire United States.

Routes traversing this inhospitable region and its nearly inaccessible river existed, but crossings depended on low-water fords or infrequent freez- ing of the stream in quiet places that were accessible. Even at the lowest flows, few places on the Colorado could be forded and sudden rises were common. The exacting conditions of access to both banks and to a place where the river was fordable limited the number of possible crossing sites, and most of these were merely seldom-trod tracks used annually by small parties of Indians on trading, hunting, or raiding forays. Near the center of the canyonlands, an ancient but not easily accessible pathway of migration and trade, known in historic times as the Ute Trail, crossed the Colorado at a low-water ford called the Ute Crossing. Both were misnomers, because cen- turies before Paiutes appeared on the scene, the route was used by Pueblo peoples and, before that, the Basket Makers. Forty miles downstream, how- ever, was a potential crossing place for wagons in northern Arizona less than ten airline miles from the Utah border. Here, at the very heart of the rough country, where one great river canyon ends and another begins, is the single place that offers access to the river at each bank and egress both north and south. In time, the crossing became known as Lee's Ferry.

Associated with this river crossing, so closely as to be identified with it, is a long tributary that heads on the eastern slopes of the Paunsaugunt Plateau called the Pahreah River. The tributary seldom flows enough to deserve the designation of "river"; Pahreah, appropriately enough, means "muddy water" in Paiute. This canyon drains more than fifteen hundred

1

square miles before emptying into the Colorado where the Vermilion and Echo Cliffs form an indented corner into the mouth of Glen Canyon. Most of the time the Pahreah appears as a small creek meandering between alluvium flats, but on occasion heavy floods pour down to fill the canyon with a stinking, viscid torrent nearly as much solid as fluid. The Pahreah periodically renews the topsoil of its lower reaches, yet it has been a constant threat to any man-made improvements. Its water is mineral-laden and chemically hard but has a perennial flow for irrigation of fields and orchards in the upper reaches and near the Colorado River. About twenty miles of the middle canyon is an entrenched gorge with few places for entry or exit. The mouth of the tributary offers some protection from the windy sweep of the main canyon, and it is this place that was to flourish as a green oasis in a desert of sand and rock. This was the hub of human activity connected with the crossing, and a radius of one mile would encompass most of the important sites and future developments.

It was only with the appearance of the wheeled vehicle that the Ute foot-and-horse trail was shown to be inadequate, while the downstream site offered advantages to more sophisticated forms of travel. With the advance of Anglo civilization the foot trail of antiquity fell into disuse and today has been obliterated and nearly forgotten. On the other hand, the ferry crossing has undergone one metamorphosis after another, and its latest revitalization suggests a long, future career.

The first known Caucasians to view the potential ferry site and the ancient ford were members of a little band of peregrinating Spanish friars and soldiers who were lost, disheartened, and doggedly hunting a reputed ford that would allow their return to New Mexico. Coming from what is now southwestern Utah, the Spaniards were seeking a crossing of the large river they called El Río Grande de los Cosninos. The Domínguez-Escalante Expedition arrived here on the afternoon of October 26, 1776, and opened the chronicle with a failure.[1]

The friars perceived that if successful in crossing the river, they would be forced to ascend a constantly rising ledge that terminated in a cliff in the direction they wanted to go. It was problematical if, once across, they could descend to the plain below. Accordingly, the two best swimmers removed their clothes to check the crossing and reconnoiter the left-bank (southern) exit. They immediately discovered that no ford existed at this point; not only was the water deep and swift but it was so wide they were barely able to reach the opposite bank. To make matters worse, they lost their small bundles of shoes and clothing in midstream and were not able to check the exit. They made the return swim with difficulty and now were naked and still astray in a savage place. That night gloom and frustration pervaded the camp. Appropriately they named it San Benito Salsipuedes— get out if you can!

Fathers Domínguez and Escalante camped here for six nights. Each day they sent men to hunt for the elusive ford and to probe for an escape route from their apparent cul-de-sac. Juan Pedro Cisneros rode up the small creek they had named Río de Santa Teresa and returned late that night without having found a way up the western cliffs, but he spotted an acclivity about a league from the "Rio Grande" that appeared passable though difficult. This was somewhat reassuring and the friars retired to rest if not to sleep.

In the morning, they built a raft out of driftwood, and Escalante with some of the men attempted to cross the river. Poles five veras long (approximately fifteen feet) failed to touch the bottom a short distance from shore and were useless to propel the raft out of the eddy. Three times the crude arrangement made the circuit and each time it returned to shore. Defeated, and convinced that the ford they sought must be located farther upstream, the leaders dispatched the Muñiz brothers, Andres and Lucrecio, to explore the possible exit reported by Don Cisneros. The scouts were gone three full days and returned on November 1 with the news that they had surmounted the cliff, crossed the mesa, and found the ford. Spirits rose immediately.

The men were eager to depart at once; they camped that night at the foot of the obvious track. Had they realized the significance of a petroglyph boulder near the foot of the trail, they would have known they were on an aboriginal route that was used by native people and reasoned it led directly to the ford they sought.[2] Ascending the difficult slope the next morning required more than three hours, prompting their application of the name Cuesta de las Animas. Later, pioneers were to call this the Sand Trail. Both names were fitting. Together with the exploratory passages of the Muñiz brothers, this very probably was the first mounted party to traverse the ancient foot-trail. On November 7, the doughty band achieved a crossing at the Ute Ford and brought yet another name—Crossing of the Fathers—to a place that already had several. This proved to be the most popular name and remained until the crossing was inundated by the rising water of Lake Powell reservoir.

Eighty-two years and two days later, Caucasians again viewed the setting. This time the men were twelve Mormons guided by a Southern Paiute named Naraguts. It was November 3, 1858, and the white men knew they were scheduled to use the ford where the Spaniards had crossed before them. Jacob Hamblin and his companions must have been surprised when Naraguts led them to the large river, then turned away from it to go up a wide tributary canyon that entered from the northwest. As in the case of the Spaniards, they went three miles and made camp. After ascending the Sand Trail over the Echo Cliffs, Naraguts led the party to the river a second time and the Ute Ford was crossed on the tenth day out of Santa Clara, which is near present-day St. George, Utah. They arrived at Third Mesa on November 10 and climbed to the ancient village of Oraibi, where they received a welcome somewhat warmer than that accorded the Spaniards before them.

This was the first of more than a dozen expeditions Hamblin led to the Hopi villages.[3] There were several reasons for the long trips, one of which was the Mormon practice of exploring adjacent lands for possible future settlement and the extension of Indian conversion. Paiute descriptions of Pueblo society and villages caused some Saints to think that these people could be Nephite remnants of Mormon tradition. If true, it was of utmost importance to convert them ahead of other Indians because they thus could reach the Lamanites through them. Up to now, they had found missionary work among the Paiute bands to be a very discouraging business. Moreover, the federally appointed Indian agent was deceived into thinking that one of the children who had survived the Mountain Meadows Massacre might be found living among the Indians near the Colorado River.[4] He approved the search, and thus the federal government, so despised by the Saints at this time, unwittingly underwrote the cost of this Mormon missionary effort. The Mormons spent eight nights among the Hopi and visited six other villages on Second and First Mesas.[5] Racial relations prospered for political reasons on both sides, although they were not fully understood by either.[6] Four men were left to serve as missionaries at Oraibi and the others departed for home on November 18.

Hamblin must have taken a good look in all directions from the crest of the Sand Trail because he readily saw that his party had looped many extra miles toward the north to reach the ford after first reaching the Colorado at the mouth of the Pahreah. It also was apparent that wagons never could be taken over the tortuous trail descending into Navajo Creek and climbing out of Chaol Canyon. There were no evident obstacles to hinder travel at the downstream place, however, if the river could be crossed. In his report to Brigham Young, Hamblin wrote, "we can Shorten the journey four or five days and shun the worst of the road by building a flat boat to cross the river, which I intend to do next fall."[7]

It is obvious that Jacob Hamblin knew little about the Hopi environment or pueblo economy. He assumed that food would be plentiful and easily available, but this was not the case. The Hopi were rudimentary farmers and ran a few goats, sheep, and burros. Their main crops were corn, beans, squash, peaches, and cotton, good harvests depending on the weather. The seven villages were located more than a thousand feet higher in elevation than Salt Lake City. Late frosts were common, and snow sometimes fell in April and May. Poor crops presaged winter famines; the people were accustomed to shortages.[8]

Agriculture was only one of their ongoing problems. They lived on the mesas for protection and farmed on the land below from necessity. The aggressive Navajos discouraged Hopi farming in areas removed from the mesas, resulting in a chronic shortage of irrigable land, although additional land was available if they dared use it. About thirty-five miles northwest of Oraibi, several clans held ancestral rights to farm the flats of Moenkopi Wash. During generations past, the people had lived here, built homes, and farmed, but the site was open, indefensible against their invasive neighbors. Absentee-farming was attempted, but the crops were harvested by others before their rightful owners could claim them. Cotton was the only crop from which they could expect a harvest; Paiutes didn't weave and Navajos preferred wool. As late as 1872 the Hopi still raised only cotton at Moenave, eight miles northwest of Moenkopi.[9]

The missionaries at Oraibi were victims of conditions beyond their control. That year (1858) had been one of poor crops and heavy Navajo depredations. The Hopi could barely feed themselves and had little for uninvited guests. Finding great difficulty in obtaining food for daily sustenance, the Mormons decided to return home by the end of November. Accumulating supplies for the journey was next to impossible, but by trading most of their guns and ammunition they managed to collect enough parched corn and goat meat to get them on their way. The meager supplies lasted until they reached the Colorado. There they gathered cactus apples, shot a crow, and finally killed their weakest horse to sustain them through the knee-deep snow. They were weak and nearly famished when they met a rescue party on December 27. The news they brought was bad; the Hopi, by tradition, would not cross the Colorado to resettle among the Mormons.[10]

Rough terrain defeated Hamblin's ambition to take a boat to the Colorado in the fall of 1859, but he repeated his initial journey with pack animals, although without benefit of a Paiute guide. The expedition is well-documented by the journal of Thales Haskell, one of two men left to live among the Hopi.[11] Hamblin's first expedition to Oraibi had opened the door to the Saints; the second resulted in lasting benefit because Haskell developed a friendship with a leading man of the village. The Hopi, whose name was Tuvi (anglicized to Tuba), had sensed that friendship with the Mormons might be the means of solving his people's most pressing problem—to bring the lands of Moenkopi and Moenave under cultivation and stabilize the area against their feared neighbors.[12] Tuba made his initial overture to achieve this objective on March 4, 1860, when he escorted Haskell and Marion Shelton to view the sites.[13] The Mormons were not impressed, but Tuba did not abandon his idea. He knew the presence of the Americans had neutralized Navajo intransigence east of them, also that the wild tribesmen respected Mormon arms. He would bide his time.

Hamblin readily saw that the Hopi were different from any Indians he had known, and wrote they "are of the blood of Israel."[14] Mormons in general were convinced that the pueblo dwellers were Nephites, would readily accept the gospel, and thus would become the means whereby the more primitive Lamanites would see the true meaning of Mormon Christianity. Thus each group had an interest in courting friendship with the other, and Hamblin was motivated to alleviate the rigors of the lengthy trips. This meant crossing the Colorado at the mouth of the Pahreah.

Jacob nearly achieved his objective in 1860. One of his crew, Isaac Riddle, constructed a small skiff at Santa Clara and carried it in his wagon

over the abrupt Hurricane hill. This wagon not only surmounted that topographic obstacle but became the first wheeled vehicle to cross Buckskin
Mountain. The descent of the steep slope was described by the leader in
these words, "went down the East side of the mt. the roufest road I ever saw
a wagon taken."[15] The deep sand near Jacob's Pools stopped the wagon and
the boat, forcing the brethren to proceed with pack animals. On October
26, the men constructed a crude raft at the Colorado. Three of them made
a partial crossing, but since the raft was not buoyant enough to carry much
load, they abandoned the attempt and went on to the Ute Ford.[16] A party of
disgruntled, dispossessed Navajos killed young George A. Smith, Jr., on
November 2, then plundered the supplies and trade goods as the Saints
beat a hasty retreat.

Hamblin led another party to Oraibi in 1862. In an effort to avoid
the hostile Navajos, they went south-southwest from recently-founded St.
George. Isaac Riddle again constructed a skiff and hauled it in his wagon
down Grand Wash to the Colorado. They reached Oraibi by this southern
route on December 18. Learning that the hostiles were drawing rations at
Fort Defiance, they decided to return home over the Ute Ford. Three of
Oraibi's leading citizens and another Hopi named Lye joined them en
route to the Colorado; one of them is thought to have been Tuba.[17] The
party arrived at St. George on January 10, 1863, having made the first
encirclement of the Grand Canyon.[18] The three influential Hopi were
taken to Salt Lake City, then returned to Oraibi in the spring of 1863, the
southern route being used on each trip. Riddle's boat made the crossing
easy and even made it possible to locate the ancient Paiute crossing at
Grapevine Wash.

Although Hamblin had visualized crossing the Colorado at the
mouth of the Pahreah River in 1858, it was more than five years before this
was accomplished. The achievement came about because some horses were
stolen from the outpost ranches along Kanab Creek. Paiute informants
indicated the stock had been taken by Navajos who previously had been
friendly. The Mormons undertook the trip with three objectives in mind:
possible recovery of the stock, to ascertain the present attitude of the suspected band, and to make another effort to induce the Hopi to settle in
southern Utah. But it was March and they knew it was too late to cross at the
Ute Ford.

Jacob Hamblin led the group of thirteen well-armed men. They
were guided by Lye, a loner, unmarried, and not particularly popular with
his tribesmen. He had lived among the Mormons at St. George and participated in their advanced agricultural techniques. Now he was returning to
his people, supposedly to relate the advantages of life in the Virgin River
basin. He also would be able to guide the white men over a new route to
Oraibi if the Colorado could be crossed at the Pahreah. The gifted James G.
Bleak was selected to record the mission. Bleak probably would have made a
good navigator because he usually recorded their course to the eighth point

and estimated the distance of each day's travel. This enables us to recon-
struct Hamblin's course with reasonable accuracy.

On arriving at the river, the brethren pulled logs off of the Pahreah
delta and dragged them upstream where the crossing was to be attempted.
That afternoon, they made a much better raft than the one thrown
together in 1860. On Sunday, March 20, 1864, the first full-fledged crossing of the Colorado at the mouth of the Pahreah was made by Jacob
Hamblin and Lysander Dayton. They landed on the left bank, then
recrossed to the right. The following two days saw all men, horses, and
packs crossed without accident. The journey was resumed by climbing the
rising ledge to the south. Descending, they followed a trail that happened
to lead to water, a brackish source they named "Navajo Spring." Here they
had lunch, and a few miles farther Lye took them up the Antelope Trail to
surmount the Echo Cliffs above Bitter Springs.[19]

None of the party's objectives was attained. The suspected band
and the stolen horses were not located, and the leaders of all seven Hopi villages were holding council with their Zuni counterparts in the Rio Grande
Valley, discussing the ramifications of the Navajo removal. The Mormons
started home March 30. They returned by the same trail, reaching the
Colorado on April 4, and crossed all of their effects and stock within five
hours.[20] Crossing here had proved to be feasible, even with so clumsy a con-
traption as a driftwood raft.

Native tensions had mounted steadily as the Anglo population
increased in Utah Territory. The Indians saw their choice encampment
sites preempted, their water appropriated, and their game killed by superior weapons or driven to less accessible areas. They saw Mormon livestock
given preference on open range to eat and trample the plants and grasses
that furnished seed and roots to native diets, yet they were forbidden to kill
the settlers' livestock that were replacing indigenous animals. Mormons
generally were aware of the unrest as displacement continued. The typical
white pioneer, Mormon and non-Mormon alike, believed that land use by
habitant peoples was an unfulfilled business, that it was morally right to dis-
possess those who were not using it as God intended. Indian resistance was
merely one of the problems of settlement that must be overcome. They
believed universally that it was the Manifest Destiny of the white man to
take over the land and its resources.

Local authorities knew the scattered ranches at Pipe Spring, Long
Valley, along Kanab Creek, and on the Pahreah River were exposed to raids.
In November 1865, Colonel D. D. McArthur appointed Lorenzo W.
Roundy Captain of Company O, Second Regiment of the Iron County
District, with orders to build a fort on Kanab Creek capable of housing all
residents of the general area in the event of an uprising. Roundy soon
ascertained that the Paiutes were rebelling at all places and many Navajos
were on the west side of the Colorado.[21] The dreaded outbreak took place
January 8, 1866, when James M. Whitmore and his helper, Robert

McIntyre, were murdered near Pipe Spring and Whitmore's stock was driven off. The violence marked the opening of the Black Hawk War during which many Utes of central Utah and Paiutes and Navajos in the south went on the warpath.[22]

Mormon retaliation was swift. Colonel McArthur had a well-armed force at the scene of the crime eight days after the murders occurred. A command of militia under James Andrus killed two Paiutes and captured five in a skirmish. Another captive led the Mormons to the bodies of the murdered men, and the brethren were so overcome by emotion that they turned the captives loose and shot them down.[23] Thus died seven Paiutes who probably had nothing to do with the actual killing of the white men. Jacob Hamblin later wrote to Erastus Snow, "We killed seven Piutes ... we killed the wrong Indians."[24] Before the end of March, the outpost ranches had been abandoned, the recently constructed fort was vacated, and Mormon expansion came to a halt. On April 2, Paiute rage was vented on brothers Joseph and Robert Berry and the latter's wife, Isabella. This settlement was on less than a one-for-one basis but apparently justice had been done according to the Paiute code.[25] From this time on, the tribesmen became more tractable.

Apostle Erastus Snow, in charge of southern Utah affairs, sent Captain James Andrus with a strong force into the field to explore the country and court better relations with the Paiutes. But as the Paiutes became more conciliatory, the Navajos remained alienated and continued raiding. Several skirmishes ensued and the Saints never felt secure. Navajos regarded Paiutes as being an inferior people; angered by increasing Paiute-Mormon amity, they turned on the weaker tribesmen and abused them. The Mormons exploited the situation by helping the Paiutes, who did their share by keeping track of the movements of their common enemy. Hamblin and a number of zesty young Paiutes spent the fall of 1867 and most of the succeeding winter protecting the eastern frontier. They knew of only two places where the Navajos could cross the Colorado: the Ute Ford, usable only at low water, and the frozen river near the Pahreah. Both were lonely, desolate places, far from the hum of society. It probably was at this time that Hamblin named the latter spot "Lonely Dell." With the prospect for peace bright, the Saints made plans to reoccupy the outlying ranches.

For some unexplained reason, Hamblin and his Paiute corps did not watch the Ute Crossing full time during the winter of 1868–69 and the Navajos took advantage of it. In February 1869, about twenty-five raiders hit Long Valley, escaping with fifty head of badly needed livestock. The Iron County Militia under Captain Willis Copeland was sent in pursuit on February 23 with orders to recover the stock if possible and to select a location for a fort to control the crossing. The forty-two Mormons never caught up with the raiders, but they followed their trail to the Ute Ford and made some valuable observations.[26] Adjutant Edwin G. Woolley provided the best descriptions to date of the country between Pipe Spring, Pahreah,

Wahweap, Warm Creek, and other tributaries as far as Cane Creek, as well as the right-bank approach to the ford itself. The troop covered the plateau above Glen Canyon, and on Sunday, March 7, found itself on the rim of the Echo Cliffs above the mouth of Pahreah Canyon. As luck would have it, they arrived at the head of an ancient trail which traversed the cliffs and ledges to the river below.[27] When the troop returned to St. George on March 12, the adjutant estimated they had covered 384 miles in sixteen days.

Although official confirmation has not been found, it is probable that Erastus Snow appointed Hamblin to head the Indian Mission in the east sometime in July 1869. A few days later, the apostle directed Hamblin's son Lyman to serve with him. The Mormons began active reoccupation of the ranches and villages they had abandoned in 1866. As head of the mission—and until a bishop was appointed—Jacob Hamblin was the most powerful person east of St. George, a majordomo answering only to southern authorities.

Kanab fort was refurbished before the end of August, and the village itself was occupied continuously after this time.[28] Some discussion ensued as to whether Pipe Spring or Kanab would make the better eastern base. The remnants of the Kaibab band were gathered at the latter, bringing the total number of Indians close to fifty.

An informant from the east side of the river brought news that the Hopi, using old guns given them previously by Hamblin, had killed eleven of sixteen Navajo raiders and captured their stolen livestock. The Hopi, having learned of the Mormon promise to help and protect the Kaibab band, wanted to receive the same benefits for themselves. Hamblin and John R. Young wrote to George A. Smith of the First Presidency, undoubtedly with Apostle Snow's blessing, detailing the above information as well as lobbying in favor of Kanab as a base because it was fifteen miles closer to the Colorado.[29] The letter stated that although Hamblin had received some material from the territorial superintendent of Indian affairs, more was needed. This appears to have been a little-disguised effort to have the federal government defray the cost of organizing the Indians.

The message evoked a quick response in the form of an order for another Hamblin expedition to Oraibi. A company of forty-seven men, twenty of them Paiutes, left the Kanab fort on October 3, 1869. They crossed the Colorado above the Pahreah, both ways on a driftwood raft, the second time Hamblin had accomplished the feat by this means.[30] Low water arrived early in the fall of 1869. By mid-October, bands of Navajo raiders began crossing at the Ute Ford, attacking the ranches as far north as Beaver and absconding with large numbers of livestock. Pursuing Mormons recovered about two hundred animals, but the Navajos with most of their spoils escaped. The militia was brought into the field, but there seemed no way to stop the depredations. The wily tribesmen slipped across the river at will. A. E. Dodge, grand jury foreman of Utah's Second Territorial District, appealed to Colonel Tourtellotte, superintendent of Indian affairs, for the federal government to indemnify the citizens for past losses and to prevent future ones. He also called for the Navajos to be retained on a reservation in New Mexico to keep the peace.[31]

Erastus Snow knew that Hamblin and his Paiutes were not sufficiently strong to guard the frontier. This opinion also was held by the military leaders, but Hamblin openly was jealous of their armed interference in his Indian Mission. The apostle, aware of Brigham Young's faith in Hamblin and his peaceful methods, hesitated to overrule the president's decision. On November 20, he avoided direct opposition by sending Young a lengthy telegram disclosing the disturbing information that the Navajos now had the latest Spencer rifles, apparently obtained in trade for stolen livestock.[32] Jacob Hamblin, his son Lyman, John Mangum, Hyrum Judd, Jehiel McConnell, and the Paiutes did what they could, but their defenses were ineffective. Some men thought the Navajos used crossings known only to them.[33] Knowing that his best efforts had failed, the depressed Hamblin searched for another solution. As he wrestled with his problem, the rising river accomplished what he could not: it confined the thieves to their side of the river and insured the safety of Mormon livestock until the next season of low water.

Sometime that summer, Jacob Hamblin conceived the idea of neutralizing the raiders by negotiating an agreement with their leaders. He expected the Indians to be controlled by a chief whose decision was final. If he could persuade the Navajo chief to clamp down on the western raiders, his problem would be solved. First, he thought it prudent to clear the idea with the church president. His opportunity came in early September, due to a number of events that were not of his making. Some of them originated three thousand miles to the east and were destined to exert considerable influence on the people living in the Great Basin and on the Colorado Plateau.

Since it became known to the general public, polygamy had been a major issue between the Saints and the non-Mormon world. Congress had passed anti-polygamy legislation in 1862, but it was weak and easily circumvented. Four years later, the Wade Bill was proposed in Congress but failed to pass. Rewritten as the Cullom Bill, it was passed by the House in March 1870 but failed in the Senate. During the same period, the Ashley Bill to dismember Utah Territory failed to pass. Nevertheless, these efforts continued to exert pressure on the Mormons and it was inevitable that their "enemies" would try again.

After Ulysses S. Grant assumed the presidency of the United States in 1869, the Mormons quickly ascertained they did not have a friend in the White House. Grant's federal appointees to Utah were men with a mission dedicated to the territory's reformation. At best, they were strict "law and order" advocates and foes of plural marriage. Shortly after his inauguration, Grant appointed Illinois Governor J. Wilson Shaffer to be the territorial governor. Shaffer was a Civil War veteran and friend of General J. A. Rawlins, Grant's first secretary of war. He did not leave immediately for his new post but tarried in Washington hoping the Senate would pass the

Cullom Bill. Had this taken place he would have come to Utah with greater power than any other governor and practically could have ignored local government. But the Senate failed to pass the bill. Shaffer arrived in Salt Lake City on March 20, 1870.[34] He succeeded in having the highly respected Chief Justice Charles C. Wilson removed and replaced by James B. McKean. Appointed June 5, 1870, the new justice arrived in Salt Lake City on August 30. Governor Shaffer died of tuberculosis on October 31, 1870; on November 9, he was succeeded by Territorial Secretary Vernon H. Vaughn, another anti-Mormon.

Chief Justice McKean did his best to enforce the intent of laws that were very unpopular in Utah. The next appointee, George L. Woods, a man of similar mind, was confirmed governor of Utah Territory on February 12, 1871. He took the oath of office on March 10 and arrived in Salt Lake City in mid-April. Both Woods and McKean became active in Liberal Party politics and used their positions to harass the Mormons for four long years. Their extreme views affected life in all Mormondom. The hostile appointees joined with other non-Mormons and several newspapers in exerting pressure on the Mormons and their leaders.

President Young protected his theocracy as best he could. In addition to plural marriage, a major criticism was the uncontested fact that no one had been brought to trial for the Mountain Meadows Massacre. The tragedy had taken place in 1857, yet the reputed participants were leading normal lives in various communities untainted by their past deeds.[35] Criticism was not confined to non-Mormons. Justly or unjustly, the tragedy was rationalized by the original settlers, but now the settlements were filling with newer converts, people who had not suffered persecutions in the east, and they viewed the matter differently. In fact, they exerted pressure from within the church, and the men most closely associated with the massacre felt it effects.

Among those living under the cloud of Mountain Meadows was John Doyle Lee, one of the reputed leaders of the massacre.[36] He had become a convert to the faith in mid-1838, had endured the agonies of Missouri, Far West, Nauvoo, and Winter Quarters. He had been one of the secretive Danite guards, held membership in Joseph Smith's guard and Council of Fifty, had crossed the plains to the Salt Lake Valley in 1848, built a large, comfortable home close to church headquarters, and owned a choice farm eight miles out of town. He was a favorite of the church president, who had exercised a short-lived Mormon practice of "adopting" him. This was a mark of esteem in which the adoptee was made a member of the leader's family so that he could serve in the same capacity in the celestial hereafter. Adoption created problems for the adoptee because some local leaders felt insecure around him and were afraid of his presidential connection; even more were jealous of him. Lee was a man who got things done. He had long been a leader in whatever activity he participated in but did not always handle contemporary relations gracefully. He was inclined to be domineering and passed his opinions

John D. Lee, no date (*Brimhall Collection, P. T. Reilly Collection, Cline Library, Northern Arizona University*).

to the brethren in a manner that many resented. Lee believed his dreams foretold the future if he interpreted them correctly, and often bored his companions by recounting them.[37]

Early in December 1850, Brigham Young requested firmly that Lee go south on George A. Smith's Iron Mission. Lee resented the call, but he went and became mission clerk. Lee's losses were heavy when he moved south from Salt Lake City, but he was no different from others who likewise suffered financial setbacks. He simply shrugged off the losses and prospered in his new location by hard work. He had taken thirteen wives and eventually would take five more; some had died, others had left him. In 1870, he still had five wives who lived in good homes in Harmony and Washington, some five miles east of St. George. By any criterion, he was a man of influence in his society.

At the time of the Mountain Meadows Massacre, Lee had held two official positions. According to the Rank Roll of the Iron County Militia for July 1857, he was major of the Fourth Battalion; he also was "Farmer to the Indians." He held no ecclesiastical position, having been asked to resign as presiding elder of Harmony Branch in 1864. Several men outranked him in both the military and ecclesiastic organization of the area, yet no one outranked him in devotion to the Mormon cause. Despite his lesser rank, he had been heavily involved in the treacherous ambush at Mountain Meadows.[38] In March 1869, President Young met with Lee during a trip south and advised Lee to sell his holdings at Harmony and Washington and move farther south, possibly out of the territory.[39] But Lee felt so optimistic about his present situation that he disregarded the advice or relegated it to the future.

Mormon expansion was reaffirmed when Kanab was resettled by Levi Stewart's and fourteen other families on June 6, 1870.[40] Stewart had left a fine home in Big Cottonwood to accept the call, yet he could not select a permanent location until President Young approved the townsite. Young intended to do this in September.

Meanwhile, non-Mormon explorers arrived on the scene. Major John Wesley Powell and his crew first landed on the right bank above the mouth of the Pahreah River on August 4, 1869.[41] They noted the remains of the brush beds and camp refuse left by Hamblin and the Paiutes when they guarded the crossing the two previous winters.[42] Jack Sumner commented on the desolation of the place, thus agreeing with Jacob Hamblin that it was indeed a lonely dell. They continued their difficult journey through Grand Canyon, exiting the canyon on August 30 with little food remaining. Three men—the Howland brothers and William Dunn—left the expedition at Separation Rapid. They headed for the southern Utah settlements but were murdered en route.[43]

Powell lobbied for additional funds for another expedition to the canyon country, ostensibly to do further topographical measurements and geological research. His quest paid off on July 12, 1870, when Congress approved an appropriation of ten thousand dollars for his continued explorations in the West. The money was to be expended during the fiscal year ending June 30, 1871, for a "Geographical and Topographical Survey of the Colorado River of the West."[44] This meant not only the Colorado River but also its tributaries and adjacent country. Powell convinced his talented brother-in-law, Almon H. Thompson, to become chief topographer and general scientific associate for the survey. Powell turned his 1869 notes over to Thompson and departed for Utah with Francis M. Bishop and Walter H. Graves, his topographical associates. Powell's objectives were to familiarize himself with the country, locate access trails to supply a more extensive river survey in the future, and learn more details regarding the deaths of Dunn and the Howlands.

The trio arrived in Salt Lake City August 19, and the Major wisely sought advice from those most familiar with the region. He called on President Young, explained his purpose and needs, and asked his recommendation for a suitable guide and interpreter. Young named Jacob Hamblin, thus setting up a relationship that was to prove beneficial to both men, but especially to Hamblin. Powell and the two topographers headed south on August 27, reaching Parowan on the thirty-first. Here Powell remained to rendezvous with Young, whose party was traveling south to explore the Sevier and Kanab country; Bishop and Graves continued on to Toquerville and the ranch of Ashton Nebeker. The presidential party arrived September 3, as did Jacob Hamblin, who went on the payroll at fifty dollars a month.[45] When the exploratory tour got underway on the fifth, John D. Lee was a participating member.

At this time no Mormon leaders, not even Erastus Snow, had observed the eastern country. Although it had been decided to resettle Kanab, the exact location of the townsite remained open. Young, remembering the situation at Harmony, wanted to cast his critical eye on any location before it was made permanent.[46] Too, his only description of the Pahreah River had come from Hamblin, and the president knew that the brethren sometimes became overly enthusiastic about pushing their own interests. If the Pahreah lived up to its reports, Kanab might become a way station and the main settlement would be shifted eastward. He also would have a better idea of the country's resources and the population it could support after seeing it for himself.

The Mountain Meadows Massacre and Lee's role in it had been on Young's mind for some time. He probably foresaw increased harassment from the federal appointees, recognized that his people were vulnerable, and sought to diffuse dangerous situations. Lee, despite his past contributions to the Kingdom, had changed from an asset to a liability—Lee had to become less visible. At the second camp, Young advised Lee that he should resettle at one of the locations scheduled for selection, but ultimately take his families to live near the San Francisco Peaks. Believing the advice was based on Divine Intelligence, Lee said he would follow it. Had he been as perceptive as the president, Lee would have followed the counsel literally, sold out, gone to an even farther distant land, and changed his name. But this was unthinkable.

Jacob Hamblin was impressed with the strategic location of the Pahreah site. It was on the northern fork of the Ute Trail and he had used it as a base when he guarded the river crossings. Young put his finger on the undesirable aspect as soon as he saw it: the danger from flooding, a fact substantiated in subsequent years.

Brigham Young selected the Kanab townsite on the morning of September 10, 1870, and church surveyor Jesse W. Fox began laying out blocks and parcels. While the survey was in progress, Young broached the subject to Lee and Stewart of operating a portable steam sawmill. It already was in transit, so sure was Young of acceptance. He offered it to them for $4,000 to be paid in lumber and improvements. Lee was uncommonly blunt in pointing out that the sawmill was badly worn, and Bishop Roundy had a new mill delivered for $3,000. After some haggling and presidential arm-twisting, they worked out a deal and signed an agreement.[47] Now Lee was obliged to move to the Kanab area.

The survey was completed the following day with the first parcels selected being around the public square. President Young then organized Kanab Ward of the St. George Stake and ordained Levi Stewart its first bishop. He also confirmed Hamblin's continuing as president of the Indian Mission. That afternoon, he and his party left for Pipe Spring, where he selected the site for the soon-to-be-constructed stone fort. Lee accompanied him to Toquerville on September 13 and ironed out all details relating to his move. Young apparently concurred with Hamblin regarding making an agreement with Navajo leaders.[48]

Young evidently had chosen Skutumpah, north of Kanab, as the sawmill site, and Lee headed there October 7. It was a difficult journey, made more so by the subtle opposition or outright resistance he encountered at every turn. Men had previously courted his good will and gone out of their way to help him; now there seemed to be a conspiracy to hinder him. On October 18, he arrived at Scutumpah to find the sawmill dumped among the rocks, a considerable distance from a possible mill yard and not close to timber. The president's visit touched off other activity as well. At the same time, Joseph W. Young left St. George with the stonemasons, twins Elisha and Elijah Averett, plus a crew of helpers, to start construction of a Pipe Spring fort.

Jacob Hamblin also had received orders to move. On October 1, he and one of his two families departed Santa Clara to make a new home in Kanab.[49] Hamblin's parley with the Navajo chiefs coincided with Major Powell's plans to return east. It was judged best to meet the chiefs when they gathered at Fort Defiance to receive their winter rations. Powell learned of this and turned it to his advantage, insuring a guided visit to the Hopi villages. He planned to accompany Hamblin to Fort Defiance, wangle passage to Santa Fe, and take the stage to the nearest railroad to return east. But it was too early to risk a traverse at the Ute Ford, so a means of crossing at the Pahreah would be needed.

Hamblin pressed Ashton Nebeker and Ammon M. Tenney into service at Toquerville to build a boat. Both were veterans of previous expeditions; Nebeker had been a member of last year's party, Tenney was on Hamblin's 1858 trek as an interpreter. Tenney spoke Spanish, having learned it as a boy when his parents lived in San Bernardino. None of the brethren spoke Navajo, but some of the Navajos spoke Spanish. Nebeker and Tenney hewed two cottonwood logs into three-inch thick planks twelve-feet long. They gathered a few boards from the Pine Valley sawmill, some nails, and departed for Kanab. Here, they picked up Bishop and Graves and started their pack animals for the mouth of the Pahreah. Powell remained in Kanab awaiting Hamblin's arrival and passed the time making short rides out of his base.

The scow was completed early in October. It was a crude affair, twelve feet long with a beam of nearly three feet. Cleats held the heavy cottonwood timbers together while the boards were nailed to their outboard edges. The bottom, of course, was flat, the ends angled up in horse-trough fashion. Graves painted *Cañon Maid* and his initials "WHG" on one side.[50] It was put in the water to swell the joints, then the men settled down to wait for Hamblin and Powell, who had not yet left Kanab. Hamblin housed his family in the already crowded Kanab fort about the time John D. Lee had pulled out of Harmony. Hamblin then set out for the Hopi mesas with Powell and two young missionaries who doubled at camp chores. The most important member of the party was the Paiute guide, Chuar, whom the Mormons called Frank or Captain Frank. He was taken along to point out additional trails to the Colorado River as possible supply routes for the Major's next river trip.

The quintet left Kanab on October 11 for the access canyon leading to the summit of Buckskin Mountain that Naraguts had shown them twelve years before. They camped at the large basin containing what was left of the winter's snowmelt that Powell mistakenly described as a large spring. Chuar then led them through the Kaibab meadows to Muav Saddle and the head of an ancient trans-canyon trail that W. W. Bass later improved, the south portion of which bears his name.[51] Chuar guided his charges off the mountain to Jacob's Pools where they were intercepted on October 17 by Tenney and Graves who, alarmed that Powell had not appeared, thought he had been killed by Indians and were carrying the news to Kanab.

A day later the entire party was together at the mouth of Pahreah Canyon. While others crossed the outfit in the *Cañon Maid* and swam the stock, Powell and Chuar rode a few miles up Pahreah Canyon. Powell observed enough to enable him later to write one of his better passages on erosion.[52] They crossed to the left bank and headed for the mesas on October 19. The helpers were left at Oraibi while the others visited the remaining six villages, then traveled on to Fort Defiance where they arrived November 1. Six thousand Navajos and their leading chiefs had gathered here to receive rations. The presence of Major Powell made it relatively easy for Jacob to set up a meeting with the chiefs through Captain Frank Tracy Bennett. The council took place on the fifth.[53]

Jacob went into this meeting with a very poor understanding of Navajo social structure or hegemony. He had been thoroughly steeped in the Mormon tradition of having an absolute leader who spoke for all of the membership, and assumed that the Navajos had a similar political situation. Brigham Young seldom delegated authority, preferring to involve himself in details from one end of Mormondom to the other. Access to the president was relatively easy, either directly or through bishops, stake presidents, or other officials. That a major chief could have command in one part of Navajo country and yet be independent of a more prestigious chief in another area was inconceivable to Mormon thought. Yet this was exactly the situation.

The Navajo Nation in 1870 did not exist as a political unit. After the treaty of 1868, less than nine thousand tribesmen, sharing a common language and culture, returned to an area of 3.5 million acres. The society was patriarchal, the economy pastoral. Political power rested with the leaders of local bands who were bound together by family or clan relationships. These headmen, called *naat'aanii*, held varying amounts of power based on personality and speaking ability.[54] They governed more by influence than delegated authority. The lack of formal political organization and responsible tribal leadership had posed a serious problem for Mexican and American military leaders and personnel charged with administrative functions. Now the Saints were about to experience the same frustrations.

The headmen who attended the council of November 5 were returnees from Fort Sumner. They had known the effect of Kit Carson's scorched-earth policy, had felt the strength of American military power. The misery and suffering they experienced at Bosque Redondo bound them together and at the same time set them apart from their blood brothers in the west who had escaped Carson's net. Those men who had returned from "the long walk" held a certain prestige that the western escapees would never know. Many resented that the suffering had not been equal.

Powell's presence was a considerable asset to Hamblin. The Major spoke first, extolling the friendly nature of the Mormons, their industry, and their desire for peace. He mentioned that they paid taxes which helped purchase the amenities now being dispensed. His remarks to the assembly were made entirely as Hamblin's friend and as a private citizen; he had no authority to speak for anyone or to promise anything. But it was clear whose side he was on, and the Navajos were impressed that Powell, the United States Army, and the Mormons held the same views. These eastern tribesmen had not been raiding the Mormon settlements; geographically it was impractical for them to do so, and they had no intention of raiding in the future. Therefore, it was easy for them to promise not to do that which they had not done. Besides, a year before the government had given them thirty thousand sheep and four thousand goats as breeding stock to rebuild their herds. Horses, however, remained in short supply. They hoped to obtain more stock by behaving themselves. It took no great persuasion for them to agree with Hamblin's request, but he failed to perceive this point.

The council ended as Jacob Hamblin had hoped. The eastern chiefs were friendly and desired peace, just as he did. He welcomed them to visit freely in Mormon country after procuring a pass from the Navajo Agent attesting to their intention of conducting peaceful trade. With such a pass Hamblin guaranteed their safety; he even invited them to visit his home and he would help them. Bennett's interpreter, Thomas V. Keam, recorded the gist of what had been said and the names of four of the most prominent *naat'aanii*, who were present: Barboncito, Zarcillos Largos, Ganado Mucho, and Delgadito. Keam identified these men by their Spanish and Navajo names. Next day, the emissaries separated. Powell, Bishop, and Graves were transported to Santa Fe in the Army ambulance; the Hamblin party took the extra horses and headed west. Hamblin met with several more headmen who had not attended the council at Fort Defiance, but word of the conclusions already had gone out and they were in agreement. He stopped at Oraibi to pick up the missionaries, then persuaded Tuba and his wife, Telesnimki, to accompany him to Utah.

The party returned, as it had come, over the Antelope Trail and thence to the mouth of the Pahreah River. It now had been eight years since Hamblin had crossed at the Ute Ford. Telesnimki became the first Hopi woman in several centuries to cross the Colorado, and certainly the first woman of any race to cross by boat at this location. The crude little *Cañon Maid* fulfilled her purpose when she landed the last load on the right bank and was cached above high water for possible future use. Hamblin was euphoric when he reached Kanab on November 21. He had his long-sought "treaty" and had induced Tuba and Telesnimki to live for a year among his people. That night he pressed one of his more educated brothers into service and dictated a letter to Erastus Snow.[55]

Meanwhile, the political pot bubbled in the north. Brigham Young had experienced considerable harassment from anti-Mormon Governor Shaffer for nearly seven months. Acting Governor Vaughn was no more friendly, and the next appointee was still more hostile. George L. Woods was confirmed February 12, 1871, and arrived in Salt Lake City in mid-April.[56] The Mormon president's reactions to their adversarial attitudes undoubtedly were responsible for his desire that Lee become less visible, as well as for subsequent actions concerning his adopted son. Young knew the pressure originated in Washington and that it was not likely to decrease until some kind of legal action resolved the Mountain Meadows Massacre. His first responsibility was to prevent the implication of the church in the final disposition. Brigham Young undoubtedly orchestrated the future of John D. Lee; Erastus Snow conducted the score.

Lee's immediate labors at Skutumpah were Herculean. He had to settle his families for the winter, set up the sawmill, fell the trees, and drag them to the mill. Obtaining dependable help was not as difficult as keeping the worn-out machinery running. Repeated breakdowns held production low, but he succeeded in sawing some lumber until the mandrel broke and had to be sent to Parowan for repair. It was not returned when promised, so he went to Kanab to learn why. There, on November 17, a fair-weather friend, Allen Frost, informed him that he, I. C. Haight, and George Wood had been excommunicated from the church. The following day, he received the notification from Apostle Albert Carrington, who doubled as editor of the *Deseret News* and secretary to President Young, that the action had been taken October 8, 1870.[57] No official record of Lee's excommunication has ever been found, and the question remains to this day whether the action really was taken or if the rumor was leaked to achieve the same purpose.

Lee became persona non grata in most Mormon circles, and many of his brethren now turned on him like a pack of dogs. It is very difficult for a non-Mormon to appreciate fully this sudden change in his social status. There was no anonymity in this commonalty; expulsion from the brotherhood was tantamount to a sentence of having been branded a traitor. Yet he continued to serve the mission to which he had been called; he paid his tithes, preached the gospel of Joseph Smith, and served his former brethren better than they served him. He even rationalized the act of expulsion by writing that the apostates and Godbeites were trying to implicate the church president in the Mountain Meadows Massacre, accusing him of harboring those reputed to have been involved. He thus justified the action taken against himself.[58] The mandrel finally was repaired and Lee got the decrepit mill running. He cut more than a thousand feet of lumber, which brought men from Kanab for his product, among them Jacob Hamblin who needed three hundred feet to build a cabin for Tuba and his wife.

Near the end of December, Lee visited President Young in St. George to request a hearing regarding his excommunication. Young and Snow appeared to accede before the president claimed to feel ill and excused himself. The apostle took some deposition, even set a date six days hence for the inquiry. The day before the hearing was to take place, Lee received an unsigned letter brought by Snow's son, advising him not to press his case and to keep out of sight.[59] On New Year's Day of 1871, Lee was at Harmony to visit some of his children and settle some debts owed him. Most of his erstwhile friends made excuses or simply refused to pay. He was chided by Lorenzo W. Roundy for being outside the fold, then learned that this former friend had attempted to poison the mind of President Young against him.[60]

After a major repair in mid-January, the sawmill at Skutumpah began a period of uninterrupted service during which considerable lumber was cut. The daily output rose to five thousand feet, but Lee held his breath, knowing this pace was not likely to continue. He sent a load of fifteen hundred feet to Bishop Winsor at Pipe Spring to finish the interior of the fort.

The steady production induced the bishop's son, John Stewart, to purchase Lee's interest and he subsequently moved the rig to Buckskin Mountain.

While Lee was carving out a new home at Skutumpah, Hamblin was busy with his Hopi guests. He escorted Tuba and Telesnimki to Dixie, where they toured the cotton factory and other Mormon enterprises. They saw large-scale agriculture beyond Hopi capability. Tuba realized his people had much to learn from the white man, but he knew that tradition would prevent the acceptance of change. Hamblin made two trips to Salt Lake City, meeting with Major Powell each time. On the second of these, in mid-July, he brought his Hopi visitors with him and their eyes were opened wider at what the white man had wrought.[61]

An incident in late November 1870 caused Hamblin's treaty to be re-examined. The raiding chieftains Patnish and Ketchene had appeared at Pipe Spring demanding tributes of stock as the price of peace.[62] Rebuffed, the Indians attempted to bully the Saints by hanging around for a few days before sulking back to their side of the river. Joseph W. Young and Jacob Hamblin counseled on the matter, then requested a reinforcement at Pipe Spring and a ten-man guard to be placed at the Ute Ford during the season of low water. Later that winter, Brigham Young, Counselor George A. Smith, and Erastus Snow analyzed the treaty that Hamblin had brought from Fort Defiance. They perceived it was not a normal treaty but rather a statement that a friendly meeting had been held between people who had never been in conflict. But none of the western chieftains was named. Those wise in the ways of the Navajos were questioned; obviously the peace had been arranged with the wrong people.

A clever plan was made. Many Mormons paid their tithing in live-stock because cash was scarce and food could not be spared. Livestock, however, became plentiful through natural increase; consequently, the church became so rich in this commodity that control was a problem. Several thousand horses were kept on open range on Antelope Island in the Great Salt Lake. Church leaders knew that Navajos had lost their stock before and after the internment at Bosque Redondo and that many were afoot. It was decided to hold another council and trade session at Kanab for the western chieftains and to secure their attendance by offering horses on very favorable terms. While Hamblin was making his second search for the elusive Dirty Devil River for Powell, Ira Hatch traveled among the western clans with the news that a big council and trade day was set for September 9, a date he described as so many days from when the news was told to each chieftain. Judging from those who attended, Hatch met with *naat'aanii* from the Moenkopi area to the Klethla Valley and Navajo Mountain. Since the river might not be low enough to cross at the Ute Ford, Hatch promised to ferry the Navajo at the mouth of the Pahreah.

There is no record of how many Indians the *Cañon Maid* ferried, but seventy-five Navajos, including thirteen headmen, gathered at Kanab on the appointed day. Some of them had walked the full distance. The

Mormon leader, Erastus Snow, opened the council with a speech in broad platitudes. Ketchene, also known as Muerto Deambro, responded for the tribesmen, followed by Hoskaninni, Peakon, and Komigezzi. Hamblin was present but did not participate; Hatch and Tuba did the interpreting. The council concluded with a feast, expressions of friendship, and Navajo embraces, whereupon Snow and his party left for St. George. The Indians retired to camp on a hill, but the council had not gone as they expected; no horses had been offered, and they were disgruntled.

Hamblin's efforts to withhold the horses temporarily—possibly to increase Navajo desire and raise the value of the stock—almost provoked a conflict, but he finally brought out the animals and trading was done on Navajo terms. Snow put the matter on record by telegraphing Governor Woods from Toquerville that seventy-five Navajos were demanding seventy horses, beef cattle, and trade items. He asked, "What shall I do?" The governor refused to be drawn into the affair.[63]

After the hectic council, Hamblin, seemingly indifferent to the near debacle, wrote a letter to Erastus Snow requesting ownership of land at the mouth of the Pahreah, although he veiled his personal interest by emphasizing that such control would bring greater safety to the people.[64] He also asked for another unnamed place, saying he would elaborate at the October conference. Then he prepared to carry out a multi-purpose plan, the details of which apparently were as familiar to the apostle as to the church president. On September 13, 1871, he pulled out of Kanab with supplies for the Powell men and to return Tuba and Telesnimki to Oraibi. That done, he intended to continue on to Fort Defiance to register a claim against the federal government for the stock he said had been traded under duress. Also in the party were I. C. Haight, George Adair, Joseph Mangum, Powell's packer Pardyn Dodds, and prospectors George Riley and John Bonnemort.

Hamblin crossed at the Ute Ford on September 22, leaving Dodds in charge of the supplies and the prospectors to their gold panning. He delivered his guests safely to Oraibi and departed at month's end for other villages, various Navajo camps, and Fort Defiance. At the same time, the Powell party landed at the mouth of the Dirty Devil. Here they cached the *Cañonita*, then began a dash for the Ute Ford and the expected provisions. The two overloaded boats landed at Cane Creek on October 6, where Dodds was waiting with the supplies.

Hamblin found disappointment at Fort Defiance. Barboncito, the prestigious Navajo chief who had embraced his peace overture most enthusiastically, had died on March 16. His passing left a political void in eastern Navajo society that no lesser chief was likely to fill. Even Barboncito had said he could not control some western leaders; now there was less chance than ever. Another blow was that Captain Bennett had been replaced by Agent James H. Miller, a sincere, conscientious man who considered his first duty was to take proper care of the Navajos. Miller reacted negatively to

Hamblin's claim for the horses but accorded him equal time with a Methodist minister for speaking to the Indians at Sunday meeting. After another day at the agency, Hamblin started a leisurely trip homeward, having no pressing objective except to be at conference on November 3.

Powell, Dodds, Jack Hillers, and the two prospectors set out overland for Kanab on November 10, leaving Thompson and the rest of the crew to run the boats to the Pahreah crossing. The river crew took its time, using nine days to cover the forty-one miles. When they landed on October 23, they found indications that the *Cañon Maid* recently had been used.[65] This, of course, was the result of the ferry service the Mormons had provided for the recent council and trade session at Kanab.

Almost as soon as Governor Woods had arrived in the territorial capital, he coordinated his efforts with those of Judge McKean to harass the Saints more intensely than had any previous administration. The struggle between federal appointees and the de facto government was joined in earnest, and Mormons—top to bottom—felt the pressure. Mormondom went into shock when President Young was arrested by U.S. marshals in Salt Lake City on October 2. Shock changed to trauma the following day when the marshals arrested Daniel H. Wells and George Q. Cannon. Warrants also were issued for lesser fry, some of whom were arrested while others went into hiding. The Woods-McKean coalition increased the pressure. The *Daily Tribune*, published by anti-polygamy liberals Godbe and Harrison, had come into being in the spring of 1871, and its editorials against Mormon theocracy added fuel to the fire.

On October 24, Brigham Young, out on bail, started for his winter sojourn in the south. Telegraph service, having reached St. George in February 1867, was extended from Toquerville to the Pipe Spring fort by November 25, 1871. It benefited the Powell Survey and the Saints, but not the U.S. marshals. President Young barely had settled for the winter when Judge McKean called his case to be tried in Salt Lake City December 14, necessitating his return north over icy roads. Zion's faithful were facing rough times.

Although John D. Lee now lived at one of the most remote places in the territory, he knew that warrants were issued for known polygamists, and he was lying low. He started for Kanab on November 2, hoping to consult with Bishop Stewart and Jacob Hamblin regarding the tense political situation in the north. Since both were attending conference in St. George, he decided to tarry until they returned, making himself useful in the meantime by doing chores for Sister Hamblin.

Stewart and Hamblin returned to Kanab on November 11, having remained several days after conference adjourned on the fifth. Undoubtedly Brigham Young had provided a master plan for the beleaguered Saints, part of which pertained to Lee and others implicated in the Mountain Meadows Massacre, and it fell to Snow, Hamblin, and Stewart to implement it. The way this was done is interesting. They gave Lee an exaggerated version of the entire situation. He was told that the president was only six hours ahead of arresting officers and had been warned to keep on the move or he would be caught.[66] Of course, Young was free on bail and federal officers knew his whereabouts; he had participated openly with George A. Smith, Erastus Snow, and Joseph W. Young in the ground-breaking ceremonies for the St. George Temple on November 9. Lee further was told that arrest warrants had been issued for himself, Haight, and others. This information sent him into hiding at a secluded cove near the village. Haight evidently joined him.

Lee was given his part in the plan piecemeal, as if a master psychologist had created anxiety and then offered the solution bit-by-bit to insure compliance. Jacob Hamblin was the "friendly informant" who brought him food and provided little tidbits affecting his future. The desperate fugitive eagerly grasped each morsel and savored it. During one such clandestine meeting, he was told to deed his various properties to his faithful wives to avoid seizure if he were arrested.[67] He did this promptly and legally before Justice Jehiel McConnell as effectively as if he were writing his will. His five loyal wives were Rachel A. Woolsey, Polly and Lavina Young, Sarah Caroline Williams, and Emma Batchelor.

On November 16, Hamblin gave Lee the key to his future by inviting him to settle at Lonely Dell as his partner.[68] Even as president of the Indian mission, Hamblin would not have allotted land without prior higher approval. Lee's identifying the place as "Lonely Dell" before he had seen it indicates he had obtained the name from Hamblin, and his wife Emma did not name the place as is generally supposed.[69] It is also clear that Lee accepted the proposition with Hamblin as a partner believing he expected only a half acre of cotton grown there for him and food when he should visit. Hamblin promised to provide seeds and fruit trees for a proportionate interest in the crops and said that John Mangum would reveal several mineral deposits to him. Hamblin had scheduled other Mountain Meadows Massacre participants—Haight, Higbee, and MacFarlane— to build a road to the Pahreah crossing, and Lee was advised to join them. Hamblin declared that the range along the creek could support two hundred head of cattle, a statement that reflected poor judgment.[70]

Lee undoubtedly recognized that Hamblin, as president of the Indian mission, was his ecclesiastical superior. Too, Hamblin had come directly from the church leadership in St. George, bringing their directions, and any thought of not following the instruction never entered his mind. Thus, his mission to saw lumber at Skutumpah ended and was replaced by another whose purpose he could only guess; but he was willing to do what he could to advance the Kingdom. He certainly had been out of the way at Skutumpah, a veritable end of the road on the Mormon frontier. His latest destination was even more remote for the time being, reachable only by horse trail, as no wagon had been there. It would be necessary to break a road. How long this place would remain isolated was anybody's guess because Powell's activity had drawn interest toward the Colorado

River. Even now, prospectors were pushing eastward out of Nevada. It is clear that Lee's latest move was not for his personal benefit but was made to advance the Mormon cause. He had been selected because of his ability to get things done, not out of increased concern for his safety.

Disappointment and impediments confronted him at every turn. Hamblin's promises were not kept, Mangum played him false, the road commission hindered him at each opportunity, and even two of his own sons were cruel and treacherous.[71] Despite the obstacles, Lee overcame the obstreperous road commission, Hamblin's questionable advice, and severe topography to attain his goal. He drove nearly sixty head of cattle down the unexplored Pahreah Canyon to the Colorado River, arriving in mid-December 1871. Great was his disappointment to find that Caroline, nearly eight-months pregnant and driving the lead of three wagons, had not arrived. Neither had the trouble-making road crew. Lee and his thirteen-year-old son took the back trail, such as it was, and finally reached Skutumpah. There, he learned that Caroline's wagon, containing about a thousand pounds of food, had broken an axle and been abandoned at the place of disaster. Caroline and the road commission had returned to Kanab.

Meanwhile, the Powell crew had cached the *Emma Dean* under a willow shelter on the left bank of the Colorado, then made a dugout in the mouth of the Pahreah River for the *Nellie Powell*, giving them a boat on each side of the river. They broke camp November 6 and two days later pitched another at House Rock Spring. They remained there until December 4, when they moved again, going by trail to their base camp eight miles east of Kanab. The slight difference in time and the somewhat larger difference in place prevented the Powell crew, the Mormon road commission, and Lee from contacting each other in December.

After he restored his vigor with food and a good night's rest, Lee began gathering his outfit for the next foray into the wilderness. This time, he took wives Rachel and Emma, their families, and five motherless children of other wives. Caroline was in Kanab awaiting the birth of her baby. Polly and Lavina had cabins at Skutumpah, so the number of Lee's relatives still was sizeable there, even after his departure. The entire company consisted of nineteen people, six of them adults or nearly so. The thirteen children claimed Aggatha, Rachel, Polly, Emma, and Ann Gordge as their mothers. The only non-Lees were Rachel's brother, William Woolsey, and his wife. Lee and Emma in the lead wagon apparently reached their destination late on Christmas Day, 1871; the hindmost wagon straggled in after dark on the twenty-seventh.[72]

2

John D. Lee and Lonely Dell

JOHN D. LEE BECAME A FERRYMAN ON JANUARY 29, 1872, WHEN SHORTLY
after daybreak a band of fifteen Navajos called from the left bank, asking to
be crossed. The old Powell-Hamblin flatboat, the *Cañon Maid,* had not
been in the water since September and required caulking. His sons
declined to risk themselves in so flimsy a craft, but the courageous Rachel
volunteered to steer while her husband rowed, thereby becoming the first
white woman to cross the Colorado River above Black Canyon.[1] The
Indians had brought a variety of trade goods they wanted to exchange for
additional horses. Lee accommodated them, thereby becoming the first
Indian trader at Lee's Ferry.

Barely three weeks after their arrival, Emma gave birth to a daughter on January 27, 1872. Named Frances Dell Lee, she was the first white
child to be born at this place. As usual in Mormon polygamous households,
one wife attended the confinement of another. Rachel had been in both
positions previously.

In late January, Lee evaluated his location more critically, then
decided to move into the mouth of Pahreah Canyon under the lee of the
chocolate-red slopes. He at once began building a dam behind his new site.
By creating a pond less than eight feet above the streambed, he could flood
a good-sized field and raise a garden—an indispensable necessity to the pioneer.[2] Through diligent labor, he plowed, planted, and brought water to his
field by the second day of March.

Next day, he and Rachel went up the trail, making their second visit
to the settlement of Pahreah. As luck would have it, Jacob Hamblin had preceded their arrival by an hour, having come for the organization of the
Pahreah branch of St. George Stake. He promised to send Lee some help as
well as vines, trees, seeds, and provisions without delay.

Instead of these things, a company of miners arrived at Lonely Dell
with a note of recommendation from Hamblin. They had been guided
there by a baptized Paiute, who slipped Lee a note from Nephi Johnson
that said there was nothing to fear from these men. The miners found and
began using the *Cañon Maid* to facilitate their prospecting. In a few days,
the boat was lost through carelessness; it apparently had not been secured

to the bank and had drifted away. The miners then began making unauthorized use of the two Powell boats that were cached nearby. An unsuccessful
member of the group, returning from the river, related the information to
F. M. Bishop in the Powell camp near Kanab.[3]

Several of the prospectors became indebted to Lee but left without
squaring up. Others built a raft, "borrowed" some of Lee's tools and utensils, and set off down the river. At an undetermined place, the raft was
wrecked and everything was lost. The men apparently walked out at either
Badger or Soap Creek, as the story was reported that they had traveled
some ten or fifteen miles before the accident occurred.[4] But the coin had a
reverse side, too. When the prospect of gold failed to live up to anticipa-
tions, many miners parted with the bulk of their tools and supplies rather
than pack them out. Lee was thus able to replenish the "borrowed" items at
minimum cost. Another, larger group of prospectors headed for the river,
preceded by a note of warning that asked Lee to claim the water at House
Rock Spring, Jacob's Pools, and Soap Creek before the outsiders got there.
He and two companions did this by April 7.[5]

While Lee was staking claims to hold the water, his dam washed
out. It had to be replaced immediately if the garden were to survive.
Pioneer dams were, of necessity, primitive affairs. Indigenous materials, a
team, wagon, and hard labor were required for their construction, and
engineering was patterned more after the art of the beaver than the craft
distinguished by degrees and calculators. The backbone of the structure
was a crooked cottonwood log as large as a team could snake into place
crosswise to the current. Innumerable wagonloads of earth, stones, brush,
and large tree limbs were piled against the base log. In this case, the earth
was the chocolate-red shale. It was abundant, but all of it had to be moved
by shovel. Willows were plentiful along the river, while the Pahreah delta,
which projected well into the Colorado, had plenty of driftwood, including
sizeable trees that had traveled from far upstream. The speed with which a
dam could be constructed depended on the number of men, teams, and
wagons employed; Lee had only himself and his young sons.[6]

At this time, cash was very scarce in Utah territory. Mormon society
lived on a barter system, translating whatever they had into dollar values.
Prospectors were treated as well as they were because they paid in hard
cash, gold, or goods. The Powell party's entry into the Kanab area was an
economic boon, bringing money and limited employment. Hamblin had a
rather dependable income from the Major, and small plums were dispensed on his recommendation as widely as possible. Blankets and other
Indian articles also brought ready cash from the crewmen, which increased
trade between Mormons and Indians.

When Powell had left the survey party in October to return to Salt
Lake City, he tarried a day or two in Kanab. Realizing his crew at the river
would need more supplies and Hamblin not having returned from Fort
Defiance, he hired John Mangum, who claimed to know the route to the

Colorado, and packers George Riley and Joe Hamblin, who had not yet made the trip. They left Kanab on October 23, electing to go via Pahreah and the Sand Trail because someone thought it provided more water than the trail over Buckskin Mountain. Mangum's party became lost and stumbled around in a strange country before finally finding the trailhead. He descended into the canyons and arrived in the Powell camp on the morning of November 2, not having eaten in twenty-four hours.[7] While the haggard old man ate and rested, Almon Thompson, Frederick Dellenbaugh, and Clem Powell struck out on foot to meet the packtrain and escort it to camp. The townspeople must have had misgivings about Mangum because they dispatched another load of supplies with I. C. Haight and Charlie Riggs, who took the track over Buckskin Mountain and arrived at the river only a day after the Mangum-guided outfit.

When Powell heard of the fiasco, he charged Mangum with incompetency and refused to pay him. Mangum learned of Powell's caches and evidently determined to be paid one way or another. He and his son Joseph allegedly robbed the caches, taking articles of value for what they felt Powell owed them. Moreover, Joseph was hired to guide some prospectors to the Moenkopi area. Perhaps to get attention, he talked about Lee's role in the Mountain Meadows Massacre, revealed the fact that Pahreah Canyon was passable for livestock, and revealed that Lee had a refuge in Cottonwood Canyon. Mangum's treachery not only neutralized Lee's hideout but embarrassed him with Powell.

Advised that he would be safer at Jacob's Pools than at the river, Lee decided to move Rachel, her family, and most of his cattle there. This was done early in May 1872, and the sixty-year-old fugitive erected the second of two ranches that were twenty-five miles apart. He referred to his first ranch as "Lonely Dell" and his ranch at Jacob's Pools as "Doyle's Retreat." At this relatively unspoiled stage, the range was good, although firewood was scarce. He had a cheese press, milk cattle, and plenty of water from several springs. Dairy products would be a welcome addition to their limited fare of beef and bread. But first, a shelter was needed and rocks must be gathered for corral walls. The shelter he built was a wattle shanty. While Lee was planting and building at the Pools, he received a meaningful message from Jacob Hamblin. He did not reveal the full wording in his diary, but, for the first time, a reference was made to a ferry.[8] Hamblin probably stressed the importance of the site and what it meant to future Mormon plans.

The Lees were working at the Pools on June 2, 1872, when E. O. Beaman, F. M. Bishop, and their wrangler guide, young Joseph Mangum, appeared. Beaman and the Major had parted ways on January 21, while Bishop had taken his departure from the mapping project in late May. They had joined forces for a proposed visit to the Hopi and Navajos before returning east, but the extremely high water of an early runoff canceled this part of their plan. Now they were heading back to Kanab and on to Salt Lake City. On the next day, despite a dark and forbidding sky, Beaman took a picture of Lee and three of his children standing on the north side of the wattle shanty before he moved on to House Rock Spring.[9]

A chronic problem resurfaced early in June. Sudden violent rains sent a flood down Pahreah Canyon, taking out Lee's dam. Along with this news came a letter, apparently from the president's office, commending him for being faithful to his mission and promising he would never be captured by his enemies if he remained so. His spirits were so buoyed by this significant message that he compared the importance of his mission with the "probable salvation of Israel."[10] On returning to Lonely Dell, Lee was forced to leave his wagon at the foot of the hill since the river was so high it covered the road running along the delta.[11]

Near the end of June, a white man and six Navajos appeared on the bluff over the left bank. They found the *Emma Dean* and used her to cross. The white man turned out to be John H. Beadle, a correspondent for the *Cincinnati Commercial.* He interviewed Lee about the Mountain Meadows tragedy, and the resulting story received wide publicity.[12]

Powell's second in command, A. H. Thompson, made an overland exploration to find the mouth of the Dirty Devil River. In so doing, he discovered the last major drainage in the continental United States: the Escalante River. He achieved what Jacob Hamblin had twice failed to do, and, on June 22, he found that the *Cañonita* left by the expedition at the mouth of the Dirty Devil, had barely survived the peak runoff. Thompson and two others took the horses back to Kanab while Jack Hillers, Dellenbaugh, W. D. Johnson, and James Fennemore ran the boat downstream to the mouth of the Pahreah River. They arrived July 13 to find Lee plowing his field. Made to feel welcome, they pooled their flour and coffee with his beef, vegetables, butter, and cheese, resulting in good meals for everyone.

Powell's crewmen even helped repair the dam. When the job was completed July 24, Lee was so grateful that he invited everybody to dinner to celebrate "the glorious twenty-fourth."[13] Although Major Powell and Almon Thompson were not present, cartographic assistant Dellenbaugh promised Lee that the name Lonely Dell would be put on the official map of the area. Not only was this not done, but the soft phonetics of the Paiute name "Pahreah" were replaced by the anglicized "Paria."[14]

Meanwhile, Powell was preparing for his second descent of the Colorado River through Marble and Grand Canyons. His party consisted of himself, his sister Nellie (now the wife of A. H. Thompson), Professor Harvey C. DeMotte, George Adair, and two Paiute guides, Chuar and Ben.[15] They left Kanab on August 6, stopped at Bishop Stewart's ranch at Big Spring, then took in the scenic grandeur of the Grand Canyon's North Rim. On August 11, Powell named the lovely meadow they were traversing "DeMotte Park" after his friend. They followed an old Paiute trail down one of the bald ridges to House Rock Valley, then cut northeastward toward the southernmost tip of the Vermilion Cliffs to strike the main trail, reaching the mouth of the Pahreah on the extremely hot afternoon of August 13.

Poor DeMotte had not filled his canteen at Soap Creek and was exceedingly dry. He had anticipated that the Colorado River would offer an inexhaustible supply of good drinking water but was dismayed when they rode down Two Mile Wash to find the river swollen from recent storms, turbid and uninviting. He was assured, however, that the waters of the Pahreah River would be pure as crystal, gurgling over a stony bed. Dismay turned to horror when he beheld the stream, also muddied from the rains. He described the water as "dirty soapsuds" and said he could more easily have sliced and eaten a portion. He walked back to the Colorado and wrote that the mouth of the Pahreah excelled as an "out of the way place," and he could not understand how anyone ever discovered it or why he made the sad tale known.

After the riders had rested, the first pleasure excursion occurred on this part of the Colorado. They put the *Cañonita* in the river, and with Hillers and Dellenbaugh at the oars, Jones on the sweep, and Nellie Powell Thompson, Lyman Hamblin, and Professor DeMotte as passengers, the craft was rowed a mile upstream. DeMotte recorded that they left their footprints on the opposite shore. Lee invited the entire party to supper and provided vegetables of the season. They feasted on green corn, squash, chicken, fresh bread, sweet butter, and coffee with fresh cream. Lee and Powell selected some watermelons for dessert. It was the last good meal the crew would have for many days. DeMotte appeared to be fascinated with his host and wrote that he was regarded as an outlaw by other Mormons. Besides describing Lee and the meal, he left historians a description of the fugitive's log cabin.[16]

Powell suddenly became impatient to begin the river trip, so the boats were loaded on the morning of August 14. Only the *Cañonita* and the *Emma Dean* were to be taken. The *Nellie Powell*, being least fit for the traverse, was left in the care of Lee to be used at his discretion. Its storage place was an excavated indentation in the right bank of the Pahreah. The hollow accommodated the full length and beam of the craft and then was covered with willows. The men apparently thought that by storing the boat in this niche it would be shielded from the force of the current. Possibly the site was selected because the soft alluvium was easy digging. At any rate, they misjudged the nature of the stream.

Hillers became the expedition's chief photographer when the sickly Fennemore decided the rigors of the trip would be too much for him. Clem Powell would assist Hillers while Fennemore would return with the pack train. For some unexplained reason, the boats shoved off at 5:30 P.M. and Nellie Powell Thompson became the first woman to run a rapid in either Marble or Grand Canyons when she rode as far as through the Pahreah Riffle on the cabin of the *Cañonita*. The party then pulled in at Two Mile Wash and pitched camp. The day's run had been little more than a mile.

Powell's eagerness to quit the previous camp possibly was to forestall any future criticism of his unduly associating with the fugitive Lee. The decision cost his crew extra work as the boats were removed from the water the next day for caulking and to fasten extra planks along the keels. Powell and Dellenbaugh returned to take a geological section on the east side of the Pahreah while Clem Powell and Hillers replaced the *Nellie Powell* in her cache and helped the Lee boys gather stock. All of this activity would have been done more conveniently at the upper camp, but Powell was not noted for being considerate of his crews. The party finally cast off from the river camp on the morning of August 17, and the drain on Lee's fresh vegetables decreased considerably.

Rachel accompanied her husband when he departed for the settlements on August 21. Three days later, they met Hamblin near Navajo Well and visited while the animals grazed. This was their first meeting since early March and they had much to discuss; Hamblin blamed Mangum for appropriating three hundred pounds of flour, seed corn, garden seeds, and tools that were intended for Lee. He bolstered Lee's ego, praising his faithfulness to the mission and conceded he had been imposed upon. Lee apparently failed to recognize that as Mangum's superior, Hamblin could have rectified the problem had he tried; Hamblin knew how to handle Lee.[17] Returning to the Pools again on October 5, Lee met James Heath, who had just delivered lumber at the Dell for a ferry boat. It is not known how closely Lee was advised of plans for the place, but it can be surmised that he was fed information by degrees. He couldn't plan ahead because the action was being called from afar.

Mormon interest in Arizona was twofold: first, a need for normal expansion to preempt the more choice locations before they were settled by non-Mormons, and, second, a possible regrouping where they would be free to practice their faith without interference. As the tempo of federal harassment increased in the early 1870s, Brigham Young sought the assistance of a long-trusted friend of the Saints, General Thomas L. Kane, who also was a respected intimate of President Grant. A lengthy correspondence, coupled with personal visits by Mormon lobbyists, resulted in Kane and his family coming west to accompany Young's party to St. George. They arrived December 23 and for seven weeks discussed political problems and the possibility of a Mormon regathering in Mexico.[18]

At this time, no church authority had been south of the Colorado. President Young's chief informant on the lands beyond was Jacob Hamblin, a man whose devotion to the Mormon cause was unquestioned but whose judgment was not always the best. His descriptions of forests, water, rich bottom lands, and plentiful range for stock raising caused the leadership to decide that the potential for expansion in this direction was high. Moreover, informants doing missionary work in the eastern states undoubtedly kept headquarters aware of publicity generated about western lands and of companies being organized to settle them. It was unthinkable that possible enemies of the church should be allowed to grab the choice locations.

Joseph Smith had conceived an ultimate Zion as the Mormon expression of Manifest Destiny. The Saints were driven from their first selection in Ohio and had made brief stops in Missouri and Illinois before coming to the Great Basin. Their enemies had followed them west and they might be forced to flee again, this time to Mexico. The Colorado River and its incised tributaries inhibited a large-scale exodus; a reliable ferry must be built near the mouth of the Pahreah because it was the most favorable place. A crossing here would neutralize the most difficult obstacle on the Mexican Corridor leading to a "City of Refuge" in Sonora or Chihuahua. Lee was impressed with the gravity of his mission and his response had pleased the leadership.

While alone at the Dell, Emma Lee and son Billy used the *Nellie Powell* to cross a band of Navajos who were mean enough to repay her kindness by strong-arming her of her flour. They later boasted of their exploit to a Kaibabits Paiute whom Lee had befriended, and he brought venison to the hungry family. Shortly thereafter the Pahreah flooded, washed out the dam, and buried the *Nellie Powell* in silt. Now there was no ferry until the boat could be excavated.[19]

For reasons still unknown, Major Powell concluded his river exploration at the mouth of Kanab Creek on September 7, 1872. This was only the mid-point of the Grand Canyon but he decided he could continue the rest of the survey overland. Hamblin, coming by trail from Pahreah settlement, intercepted Hillers, Hattan, and Clem Powell at Lonely Dell on October 12. The Powell men had driven a wagon carrying supplies and trade-bait for the Hopi. They would leave the wagon at Lonely Dell and make the remainder of the journey on horseback. Hamblin was guiding them to the Hopi mesas to take pictures and purchase Indian wares for display in the East. The men tried to dig out the *Nellie Powell* but concluded it would be easier to use some of Lee's lumber and build a new skiff. Assisted by Hamblin, Lee built the skiff in three days while the others stripped the fields and hauled corn to the corral. They crossed the river on the sixteenth.[20]

Hamblin's party spent eleven nights among the Hopi villages before leaving Oraibi on November 3. With them went the prominent Tuba and other tribesmen. It appears that Hamblin and Tuba had struck some kind of deal regarding future Mormon settlement, and Hamblin was going to examine the prospective area on his way home.[21] After a few miles on the usual route, Tuba turned them almost due west on another trail. They came to the Hopi farms at Moenkopi the following day, marking Hamblin's first visit to this place. There were a half-dozen homes here, including one belonging to their guide. Corn, melons, beans, squash, onions, and cotton were raised in many small garden plots that were irrigated by several springs. Next day, they visited Tuba's cotton field at Moenave, eight miles beyond Moenkopi. After breakfast Tuba sent them off with a lame Paiute named Shew, who guided them some fifteen miles to his ranch at a spring below a gap in the rising escarpment. Shew went no farther, but they had only to travel along the base of the cliffs for about thirty miles before striking the Antelope Trail at Bitter Springs. From there to the river Hamblin was on familiar ground.[22]

The four men reached the left bank of the Colorado on November 7, and a shout brought Emma and Billy over in the skiff. Two days later, they spent the night with Lee at Jacob's Pools. Farther on they met a detachment of George Wheeler's command under Gilbert Thompson, who imparted the news that Grant had been re-elected president of the United States, which visibly depressed Hamblin.[23] The re-election of Grant cast a pall of gloom over all Mormondom; most Saints thought it presaged a change from harassment by Woods and McKean to active persecution from Washington, and the "emergency" might mean evacuation to Mexico. The City of Refuge was the subject of much discussion between President Young and General Kane. From Young's standpoint, a ferry at the Colorado would not only be a safety valve if the need became urgent, but a necessary link in the migration.

Upon returning to Kanab with his report of the agreement with Tuba, Hamblin activated several projects. First, he made a round trip to Joseph W. Young's sawmill in Long Valley to accelerate the delivery of lumber for Lee and the new ferryboat. At almost midnight on December 18, Uncle Tommy Smith arrived at the Pools with the gunwales for the ferryboat and sixteen hundred feet of lumber for Lee.[24] A carpenter by trade, Smith was to have charge of the boat construction, but now he helped Lee finish the rooms of his new house in exchange for help on the boat. Young James Jackson rode in on the twenty-third with a bag of heavy spikes for nailing the cross-planks to the gunwales. He said Hamblin would be at the river by New Year's Day. Another note from Hamblin on December 26 advised that the ferryboat must be completed shortly and the egress road built for the "emergency." Jackson was assigned to labor at the Dell.[25]

Lee and Smith crossed the river on January 7, 1873, to select the most feasible route for a southern road. The ferry site was obvious, about a quarter-mile upstream from the creek mouth. On the left bank, they found a small wash in the corner of the southern flat where a little work would allow a wagon to be driven up to the tawny ledge that rose to the southwest. They walked the eroded, corrugated surface and judged that wagons might have to be double-teamed in places but could make the grade. There was no easy descent, but a strong work crew could build a switchback over the rocky slope and reach a long spur to descend to the relatively flat desert beyond. It would be necessary to climb and descend over six hundred feet. They estimated the road would cost the equivalent of two thousand dollars.

The alternative—Hamblin's preference—was to locate the crossing at the foot of the long rapid where the northern road came down another wash to the river. Here, a dugway must be cut into the side of the cliff that was at least one hundred fifty feet high. Building this quarter mile of road would cost more for labor than the first choice and would require a great amount of powder that was not available. It was doubtful, too, that the road could be used during periods of high water. As far as Lee and Smith were concerned, the choice was clear: they began building the ferryboat at the upper site.[26]

After three days of hard labor the boat was completed. She was crude and simple, really a scow whose strength was based on the two pine timbers used for the gunwales. They were eight inches by twenty-four inches by twenty-six feet long. The four ends were sawed at an angle on the bottom. Cross-planks two inches thick were spiked to the gunwales, the entire unit then turned over and similar planking used for the deck. The seams were stuffed with bits of rag and sealed with hot pitch. Hinged aprons at each end would allow wagons to roll on and off. As there were no rails, animals would have to be snubbed closely and held by hand. Two-by-fours amidship provided fulcrums for sweeps, themselves made from three inch saplings that had been stripped of bark, the side of one end flattened with an adze and a board nailed thereon for a blade. Once the decking was in place, the boxed cross-section was reasonably strong.[27] This particular ferry would hold only one wagon and team, its overall size being eight and one-half feet in beam and twenty-six feet in length.

The next day was Saturday, January 11, 1873. All twenty-two people celebrated the completion by having midday dinner on the deck of the new boat. Then a yoke of oxen dragged the craft into the river and she was launched. The boat was named *Colerado,* but in recording it in his diary, Lee added the euphonious phrase "and the skiff we named *Pahreah.*" The entire company twice crossed to the left bank, with Uncle Tommy Smith and his son rowing while Lee steered. They set a strong anchor-post well up on the beach and tethered the ferry to it with a stout rope. It was dusk when they returned to the cabins.[28]

Hamblin was very sensitive about others stepping into his field of authority and became upset if they contacted the leadership without him. Lee had written directly to Apostle Snow explaining why the location for the crossing and the exit road had been made. Hamblin and his son Benny arrived at the Dell on January 25 as the vanguard of a company under Lorenzo W. Roundy to explore the San Francisco Peaks area. Already piqued that Roundy had been named president of the exploring party, he was upset further that Lee and Smith had decided the location of the crossing without his participation. He asked Lee to recall the letter to Snow; Lee did so, then burned it before Hamblin's eyes.[29] A few days later, Lee walked Hamblin and Allen Smithson over his preferred southern road, and afterwards, they examined Hamblin's choice at the foot of the long rapid. Smithson agreed unequivocally that Lee's site was the better, and finally Hamblin reluctantly acquiesced—outwardly at least.[30]

Bishop Roundy, with eleven men, pack animals, and three wagons, arrived at the Dell on the first day of February 1873. They intended to leave the wagons at the ferry and proceed with pack outfits. Hamblin, still smarting at his minor role in the exploration, had decided to combine his job with a trading venture to the Hopi and had several pack animals loaded with cheap trinkets. Roundy first surveyed the land and water at Moenave. Hamblin left the group here, ostensibly to obtain a guide at Oraibi, but really to inform Tuba of the planned settlement and to pursue his trading. Wisely, Roundy sent Ira Hatch with him.

As his party followed up the Little Colorado Valley, Roundy observed the scrubby cottonwoods, the wide bottom, and the very alkaline water. Hamblin and Hatch, with a Hopi guide, joined them at Black Falls. The land, timber, and water improved beyond Grand Falls, but when Roundy decided to turn south into the high country, the guide demurred, saying the Apaches would kill them. Despite the offer of a horse if he would continue, the Hopi went back. The party then intercepted the Beale Road, followed it westward to the high, snowbound country south of the San Francisco Peaks. They fought the snow and cold for more than a week before starting back. Jacob Hamblin and Lehi Smithson left them at the Little Colorado River to complete Hamblin's business at Oraibi. Roundy reached the Colorado on February 25, and Lee wrote that he crossed twelve men and twenty-six animals. Then they loaded their wagons and started home, telling Lee that a company would be crossing at his ferry to settle the Little Colorado country before the next month was out.[31]

From his home in Kanarraville, Roundy sent President Young a summary of the trip.[32] The letter is noteworthy, not only for his description of the country and its resources, but for revealing the subtle infighting used by secondary leaders in their quest for recognition and advancement.[33] Roundy took pot shots at both Hamblin and Lee, with his heaviest criticism directed at Hamblin. Possibly he was jealous of both men, regarding them as rivals. He said Hamblin's handling of the Indian department was a failure and that the party would have been unable to secure a Hopi guide had it not been for Ira Hatch. However, he did not reveal Hamblin's personal trading activity that distracted from his duty to the party. He favored Hamblin's ferry site over Lee's, stating that the upper crossing had been selected because it was more convenient to Lee's houses in the mouth of the canyon. He said a dugway could be constructed at the lower site for about one-third or one-fourth the labor of putting a road over the hill. The difference of opinion developed into a running controversy that lasted nearly a decade and was not settled until the lower, or winter, crossing was established.

For reasons best known to himself, Brigham Young called Apostle Erastus Snow on a mission to Europe on January 11, 1873. The highest church authority permanently residing in southern Utah, and a man of unusually astute judgment, Snow was considered to be the backbone of the southern Mormon settlements. During his absence the leadership was handled by his second in command, Joseph W. Young, who had become first president of the St. George Stake when it was organized in November 1869. If Young could have envisioned events in the forthcoming months, he might have written a different scenario.

On March 4, Lee was alerted by the sound of gunshots to find Hamblin and Smithson with their packtrain of spoils signaling from the ledge across the river. Evidently Hamblin had completed arrangements with Tuba for the forthcoming settlement. It is not known whether all the trade goods were exchanged for Indian wares for Hamblin's benefit, or if some were given for land and water in a deal similar to that made by Peter Minuit for Manhattan Island in 1626. In any event, Tuba and other prominent Hopi agreed to let the Saints establish a farm at Moenave (which Hamblin still thought was Moenkopi) to demonstrate that the Mormon agricultural methods were superior to those of the Hopi, thus enabling the natives to increase their production. It is not known whether Hamblin was aware that Tuba's main purpose in settling Mormons on Hopi lands was to stabilize the area against marauding Navajos, thereby insuring that his people would harvest their crops at the actual Moenkopi.[34] Thus, Tuba traded the Hopi cotton farm that he didn't own for insurance he didn't get, while the Mormons obtained the foothold they desired.

On April 3, 1873, Lee ferried a young man named Juan Lorenzo Hubbell. The stranger, not yet twenty years of age, had ridden intermittently from Albuquerque. Hubbell and his horse were tired and he was looking for a job. Lee hired him for the summer, promising twenty-five dollars per month and his board. He never did get the man's name straight, usually referring to him as "John Spaniard." The young fellow worked wherever needed, from dam-building to ferrying or packing, as did James Jackson.

That same afternoon the local presiding church authority, Joseph W. Young, arrived accompanied by Bishop Edward Bunker, I. C. Haight, and a work corps of twenty-five men. President Young had instructed his nephew to examine both crossing sites, select the better, and build a road leading south from it. Hamblin had kept the crossing controversy alive, and the president noted Roundy's opinion in his exploring report.[35] The annual rise had started and the lower crossing site appeared to be anything but safe. The visitors estimated that a road blasted from the left-hand cliff would be more expensive and require more construction time than they now had. Had the site been examined during the low water of fall and winter, the conclusion might have been different. Hamblin had told Young that the southern dugway of his choice could be built for one hundred dollars, but the stake president estimated it would cost forty times that amount and he wondered aloud about Hamblin's lack of judgment; the bishop concurred.[36] Lee then walked the officials over the route he and Smith had selected and was elated, but not surprised, when they agreed it was preferable.

The crew hacked out a road from Lee's house to the upper crossing, blasting where it rounded the left cliff at the mouth of the canyon. Young then took road foreman Ephraim Wilson over the selected route, and the job was begun April 5. Wilson, a quarryman from St. George, was considered to be an expert in his work. The president's nephew blessed Lee for his devotion to the mission, then started homeward.[37] Unfortunately, the decision that had been made in Lee's favor put the issue to bed but not to rest. Future travelers said it was the worst road they had ever traversed.

They named it "Lee's Backbone" and "Lee Hill." The route was considered passable when work ended on April 16 and the crewmen departed. They had been gone for three weeks, twelve days of which were devoted to the road's last half mile.[38]

Brigham Young had not waited for Bishop Roundy's opinion of the Little Colorado country but had gathered a colonizing company while the exploration was under way. The Arizona Mission was placed under the leadership of Horton D. Haight, an experienced wagonmaster who had conducted several emigrant companies and freight trains across the plains. Late in March, he and some fellow missionaries started south for their gathering place at Pipe Spring.[39] Before the main company had assembled, an advance party of seventeen set out, led by Captain John R. Bennion and guided by Jacob Hamblin. Their objective was to locate a road from the end of Wilson's track, working out the rough spots as necessary. Hamblin was to get them to Moenave as soon as possible so a crop could be planted, then he was to take a companion with him to explore Walnut Canyon and the headwaters of the Verde River for additional settlement locations. Bennion was instructed to have his party locate a track up the Little Colorado toward its head. As they traveled toward the ferry, they camped at House Rock Spring on April 18 in company with Wilson's road builders.

Bennion's company arrived at the river on the afternoon of April 22. Lee and two hands were at work on the ferry adding three by four inch scantlings along the beams to keep the wagons from sliding off the deck when the boat lurched on hitting a change of current. By day's end, the ferryman had crossed thirty-three head of horses and two wagons. The job was completed the next day, and Lee recorded that he charged seventy-five cents per animal and three dollars for each wagon for a total of forty-six dollars.

Andrew Amundsen's journal preserves a vivid account of the first wagon train to cross the Colorado at this point. The writer was more adept in Norwegian than in English but his delightful phonetic renderings are pleasing and informative to read. He did not get all place-names correct, but Lee didn't get Amundsen's name correct either, recording him as "Bernisen." A portion of the journal entry follows:

> In the morning of the 22 we reachst the river, which is ten miles from creek [Badger], when we got there we found John Delee working at the boat and two others, after dinner we crossed over animals and one Wagon. Delee wass verry jocky and jovele, full of fun[.] The 23d the morning wass very calm no wind the Rivver still the wether pretty and clear, birds singing and all enjoyed a good spirrit. We then commenct crossing our Wagons, all over saf and sound, the ferrying wass one dollar a horse and two dollars a Wagon. We also left sum flour in his charge, on account of being too hevvy loaded. After dinner some went and worked the road that crosses the Mountain. no feed there, plenty of wood and water. The twnety-fourth in the morning we started up

the hill verry rocky and steep on both sides of the mountain after gitting down to the foot no track nor road ever made, for we wass the first ones that ever crossed the Cilordo with Wagons, so we had to break over road all the way, and in some places very rough so that we had to make it, after 8 mile driving we reachst Willow Springs [Navajo Spring] camped for the night.[40]

Bennion's company reached Moenave on May 1, and Hamblin, with two companions, went on eight miles to the Hopi farms at Moenkopi. They returned the next day with Tuba, another Hopi, and their wives. At this time it was decided which lands the Mormons were to farm. Plowing commenced on the fifth, the same day that Hamblin and Morell started on their exploration. Hamblin had achieved a quasi-legal right in Hopi eyes for a demonstration farm of about seven acres with undefined water rights.[41] Joseph W. Young gave final instructions to Horton Haight's main company at Pipe Spring on April 29. Because of limited feed and slow recovery at some of the watering places, the sixty-three men moved out in three groups to reassemble at House Rock Spring. Ira Hatch accompanied them as guide and translator.

Haight's first contingent arrived at Lee's Ferry on May 8. He and Lee argued about ferriage, with Haight claiming the rates were too high. Lee finally reduced the charge to fifty cents for each animal, but he got it back by raising the price for a wagon and single team to four dollars and five dollars for a wagon with a double team. He began crossing the company in the morning and completed the job the third day. Then twelve more wagons appeared and ferrying continued unabated. When the last was safely over, the missionaries prepared supper for Lee and his crew. Afterwards, they took a moonlight ride on the river.

Lee resumed his endless chores until May 19 when the last contingent of nineteen wagons, under Henry Day, arrived. By this time the river was rising fast, already having covered that part of the road that ran along the delta. It was necessary to relocate a half-mile of it and Lee's corps of eight was augmented by twenty of the missionaries to form a road crew. The relocation was accomplished in a day and a half, then Lee drove the first two wagons over it after dark. The men attempted to cross in the morning but the river was so high and the current so swift that they were obliged to tow the ferryboat a half-mile upstream. Even then it was touchy, and the current swept them dangerously close to the head of the rapid. The boat then had to be towed upstream along the left bank before the return trip could be made.

Captain Day was exasperated at the entire setup, calling it a "poor Shitten arrangement." He said that the mission should never have been called until a good road and ferry were available. This was indirect criticism of Brigham Young—intolerable to Lee, who replied that better men than Day had built roads, bridges, and ferries from Nauvoo to Salt Lake City with less whining than he did here. He noted that few of the men endorsed the captain's views.[42]

Meanwhile, the mission was not going well. After Tuba and Hamblin had agreed upon the site of the Mormon farm at Moenave, Haight drove his wagons as far as he considered practical, then continued up the Little Colorado with pack animals. The stream dried up as they advanced and soon they were forced to dig sump holes in the bed to water man and beast. The water thus obtained was very brackish and hardly fit to drink. Fierce winds and a blazing sun scorched them, and feed was poor. By May 29, they had penetrated above the present site of Winslow to find the country increasingly less inviting. Men and animals were becoming weak. Haight decided to withdraw and send a dispatch to Joseph W. Young asking if he really intended to settle such a barren country. On June 2, he sent the message by carriers Morell and Evans, while the main party began a retreat to Moenave. The messengers headed for Kanab, the nearest telegraph station.

Morell and Evans reached the Colorado on June 4, and a gunshot from the ledge brought Lee over with the boat. He was indignant at the way the Mission was going and chided the riders by comparing the Arizona thrust with the Battle of Bull Run and the settlement of St. George. He claimed the Devil had dried up the water to test the will of the immigrants and said President Young would not have sent the company to a country that could not support them. They spent the night with the ferryman, then pressed on towards Kanab. They met eighteen wagons at the Pools and turned them back to House Rock where better feed and more water were available. Two days later, seven of the missionaries rode in from House Rock to see the Colorado and take a bath in it. They reported the death of an infant who had been buried at the camp.[43] They also said their company would remain there pending further instructions, and if the mission were abandoned, there would be many provision bargains to be had. Lee sent his son Ralph back with them to size up the situation.

Unknown to those beyond the settlements served by the single-wire telegraph was the sad fact that the man responsible for decision-making in the Southland no longer existed. Joseph W. Young had died at Harrisburg on June 7, leaving the southern settlements without an ecclesiastical leader. He was only forty-four; he had been in poor health for some time but had pushed himself relentlessly. No one appeared willing to step into the breach unless directed to do so by Brigham Young, who remained silent. Morell and Evans had sent their telegram the same day Young died. Receiving no answer, they telegraphed lesser officials McDonald and Gardiner on the tenth. This time they drew a reply but it did not help much: "Your telegram has been sent to the President call for your answer." Then they learned that the wire from Rockville to Toquerville had been down for a week. It seemed more than weather was working against the success of the mission. Morell and Evans waited.

The river continued to rise and now was heavy with drift. Lee had not used the ferry since June 8, when he crossed two miners on their way to the San Juan River. There had been no signal shots from the ledge and no southbound traffic. The ferryman, busy planting and doing ranch chores, must not have realized that the ferry required extra checking during high and rising water. We can imagine his consternation on June 16 when the boat was discovered to be missing. This was a tragedy of no small proportion, as now the thirteen and one-half foot skiff with a four foot beam was all that remained and wagons were on both sides of the river. Lee rationalized the incident, blaming it on the heavy gale that roared in from the south in the early evening. He theorized that the wind blew a large tree up against the boat to break her loose and carry her downstream or sink her. But it is clear that he did not know the actual cause, only that the boat was gone.[44] It is likely that the craft had simply been grounded on the sand and the drift had piled up against her beam, creating enough added pressure to force her into the current. In any event, the first ferryboat had a short lifespan of 147 days.

News of the ferry's loss spread like wildfire in both directions. It brought Bishop Roundy, accompanied by Morell and Evans, to the ferry on June 23. It seems that the church president had requested Roundy to personally investigate the situation on the Little Colorado and report to him before he could make the decision to withdraw the mission or replace its members with more dedicated people. Obviously its failure irritated him. Roundy told Lee of Joseph Young's death and said that if the mission continued, another ferryboat would be built immediately. He added that a detachment of federal soldiers from Camp Douglas even now was en route to Lonely Dell to establish a post and was expected to arrive on the twenty-seventh. He promised to keep Lee informed, then left to report personally to Brigham Young in Salt Lake City.[45]

Thus it can be hypothesized that Roundy did not accept Lee's rationalization of the ferry's loss but privately charged it to his carelessness and resolved to punish him. He completed the deception on his way home. After passing the Pools, he probably was the one responsible for sending two men, supposedly from Kanab, to Lee's ranch with the news that six hundred soldiers and forty baggage wagons would indeed arrive at Lonely Dell on the twenty-seventh and had promised to hang Lee and all of his children. To add authenticity to the yarn, the messengers told Lee's family that the soldiers had turned their animals into the gardens at Kanab and ruined the crops. Two of Lee's children relayed the news when they reached the Dell after dark.[46]

The report was patently false but it galvanized Lee into action. He concluded to seek safety in the Indian country. The next day, he swam his horse behind the skiff and set off in company with three members of the Haight mission, leaving the ferry without a proprietor or a boat capable of crossing a wagon. Moreover, some fifty wagons and at least two hundred animals were on the south side of the still high river.

The mouth of the Pahreah River from Lee Hill, 1873 (*Timothy O'Sullivan photograph, courtesy of the National Archives and Records Administration*).

The Arizona Mission now was at an impasse. The man in charge of the effort was dead, and the colonists, accustomed to definitive leadership, were adrift without instruction. They couldn't believe the church president had sent them to claim such a barren, uninviting country. Brigham Young knew his nephew was dead but refrained from appointing a successor and elected not to reply to the pleas for further instruction. Bishop Roundy suggested the colonists fall back to Navajo Spring where there was better grazing. They did so, knowing their stay at this place also was limited.

As so often happens, unusually warm weather caused the river to crest in mid-June, but when snow in the high country had melted, the flow declined rapidly. It had fallen several feet from the peak. This was fortunate because Captain Day began crossing to the right bank on July 1; the only means of doing so was the skiff *Pahreah*. Wheels, axles, reaches, and tongues were disassembled and taken over by the rowboat, necessitating two or three trips to transport each wagon. All animals swam behind. To make the operation more efficient, Haight organized and directed ferry crews. It was necessary to move the wagons out quickly as there was no grazing at the river. They managed to cross twelve or fifteen outfits each day, finishing the entire job by noon of July 7. The total loss of stock was one horse, two oxen, and three cows; one hundred nine men, six women, one child, fifty-four wagons, and two hundred animals crossed the river.[47]

Meanwhile, Lee met Jacob and Benny Hamblin at Willow Springs as they were returning to Kanab, having left the new farm in the hands of an itinerant old man, Mr. Winburn, who was not a member of the church. Hamblin had borrowed Winburn's horse to pack some Indian wares for which he had traded, promising to return the animal within a month. Hamblin advised Lee to stay with Winburn and help take care of the crop while he would oversee Lee's interests at the Dell and Pools. Lee agreed, having had this in mind when he fled. Thus he was budged ever farther from the Mormon pale.

Hamblin did not return to Moenave until August 21. That night he and Lee sat up late, discussing his suggestion that Lee move his family from the Pools and settle here permanently. In the morning, Hamblin rode over to Moenkopi to examine with Tuba, Taltee, and other leading Hopi the matter of Lee taking over his responsibilities at Moenave. The tribesmen favored the change unequivocally, even convincing Hopi Agent DeFrees that Lee was a man of character and reliability. After obtaining the approval of both the Hopi and DeFrees on August 24, Hamblin traded his farm at Moenave for Lee's ranch at the Pools.[48]

The deal was rather peculiar. Tuba, with Taltee's consent, had given Hamblin permission to farm land that was communally owned; Hamblin traded the seven-acre farm he didn't own and the crop Bennion's men had planted for a ranch he had instructed the excommunicated Lee to claim in the name of the church. But it didn't matter because everyone was happy except possibly DeFrees, who was locked in a political struggle with the Navajo Agent William F. Arny at Fort Defiance and was shrewd enough not to become embroiled with the Mormons at the same time.[49]

Early in September, Lieutenant R. L. Hoxie and fourteen men of the Wheeler Survey crossed at the ferry. The gifted photographer Timothy O'Sullivan, a member of the party, took the first photograph of the mouth of Pahreah Canyon from a ledge where northbound travelers usually fired shots to bring the ferryman across.[50] The surveyors paused at Moenave on the twelfth and enjoyed some of Lee's melons before going on.

Lee returned to the Dell four months after his hurried departure. By traveling part of the way in moonlight, he arrived at the ferry about noon of November 6. Recognized from the ledge, Emma and Billy fairly made the skiff fly to the left bank. A number of changes had taken place during his absence. He had once again become a father; on October 25, Emma had given birth to a daughter whom she named Victoria Elizabeth in honor of the English queen and a girlhood companion on the difficult handcart trek west. She had been alone in her birthing travail but had come through admirably, although she was profoundly affected. Lee's eyes were opened at this turn of events because he had arranged with Jacob Hamblin to procure a midwife.

According to Lee's diary, Hamblin not only failed to inform Emma of this provision, which he did not fulfill, but chided her for bearing the child of a man who had been excommunicated. Husband and wife compared notes and Lee recorded enough detail in his diary to allow an educated guess regarding Hamblin's treachery.[51] Knowing that this crossing controlled migration into Arizona, Hamblin, in 1871, had asked Apostle Snow for the property rights here.[52] However, when the leadership decided that a man of Lee's drive and devotion was needed, Hamblin had accepted Lee as a working partner in a second-best situation. Guessing that the fugitive had no future in the church, he apparently hoped to obtain Lee's half of the venture if Emma could be turned against her husband. He already had worked the other end toward the middle by telling Lee that Emma was unworthy to be his wife. If he succeeded in splitting the marriage, Emma would retain her good standing in the church and Hamblin could control the entire operation, even if he were forced to take Emma as another of his wives. Hamblin might have rationalized his conduct as Emma's salvation and regarded any material gain accruing to himself as the Lord's will. But he gave no hint of his actions when he wrote to President Young from Kanab on September 19, nor did he speak of it in meeting two days later. In fact, he failed to mention Lee either time.[53] From this time on, Lee had no respect for his partner, knowing he could not be trusted.

Uncle Tommy Smith and John L. Blythe built the replacement ferryboat that fall.[54] It could accommodate two wagons and team at a time but was cumbersome and required a minimum of two strong men to handle the sweeps. The operation was beyond the strength of Emma and Billy, which was the reason they used the skiff to bring Lee across. Launched October 15, the boat had yet to cross a single wagon. Since he had not been a party to its construction, Lee characteristically gave no description of it.

Hubbell had moved on, deeper into Utah, but poor Jackson was still there, doing his best. Despite his efforts, the dam had washed out, leaving the trees, vines, and crops dead or dying, and Emma was out of food. Jackson was willing but not handy enough at the number of things needed to survive in that remote environment. Meanwhile, he would operate the unwieldy ferry as traffic warranted, assisted by the travelers he crossed.

After procuring the needed food, Lee salvaged what he could at the Pools and returned to Moenave on November 26, using the Blythe ferry to cross his outfit of one wagon, six horses, and five cows. The new boat, launched without aprons and barely usable, was fitted with them in December. Lee returned to the Dell again late in December, intending to move enough of his possessions to his newest ranch to make it livable. He met four prospectors from Pioche who had been advised to procure him as a guide. Lee agreed if they would wait until he took care of some personal business first. Lee was concerned about his future at the ferry and whether he was expected to continue as ferryman. In a sixteen-page letter to A. F. McDonald of St. George, he explained the situation and expressed his desire to support the next mission, then he applied to Territorial Governor Safford for a franchise to operate the ferry.[55] Lee began 1874 by crossing three prospectors and their six pack animals en route to the San Juan River, receiving eight dollars in gold for ferriage. Emma had accumulated twenty dollars for her ferry service.

Early in January 1874, a violent confrontation took place between four young Navajos and three Anglos. One of them, James Clinger, was a Mormon. The other two, Tom and Billy McCarty, were non-Mormons. The Indians were returning from a trading venture when they sought refuge from a bad storm in Grass Valley, in south-central Utah. Three of them were killed, but the fourth, badly wounded, managed to make his way through a strange country, ford the icy Ute Crossing, and reach his hogan in eight days. Since the fight had taken place in Mormon country, and all four men had carried the passes described by Hamblin at Fort Defiance, Navajos claimed treachery and held the Mormons responsible. A dangerous situation developed.

Tuba brought word of Navajo anger to Lee, saying they were about to take vengeance on all whites in the area. Lee rode part of the night to Lonely Dell and from there sent his sons with a letter to Levi Stewart containing the bad news. Hamblin was sent to meet with the angry Indians and settle the matter. Lee met him on January 23 as he was heading for the council. Hamblin spent the night at the Moenave ranch both before and after meeting with the Navajos. Winburn had gashed his foot with an axe and apparently the wound was infected. Lee arranged for Hamblin to take the old man to Fort Cameron in Utah, where he could obtain medical attention. Hamblin left Moenave on February 3, driving Winburn's wagon hitched to Lee's team with his own saddle horse tied behind. He vented some of his resentment of both John D. and Emma Lee when he dumped Winburn off at the Dell instead of taking him on as agreed. He simply parked the wagon near her cabin and continued toward Kanab on his horse.

Meanwhile, other events had taken place that would be affected by the Grass Valley affair. When witness Charles W. Baker recanted his false testimony that led to the indictment of John L. Blythe for the murder of Dr. Robinson in Salt Lake City, Judge McKean had no choice but to release Blythe. Mormon leadership thought it best that the man unjustly jailed be made less visible, and Blythe was sent south. After the Arizona Mission fiasco, President Young decided to put him in charge of a way-paving effort, which accounts for Blythe's availability to construct the replacement ferryboat in October. His final letter of instruction, dated December 28, 1873, was received in mid-January. He replied at once.[56]

Arizona had acquired the reputation of being "a hard country," and few Saints took joy in being sent there. Consequently, Blythe found it difficult to recruit members for his mission. He had the authority to be demanding but preferred persuasion to advance his part in "building the Kingdom." It was not until February 6, 1874, that he was able to get a small party started for the place of labor. He, his wife and son, William H. Solomon, and Oliver Anderson formed the nucleus of the company, while Orval Allen, John Averett, and Frank Gilesby came in as volunteers. Ira Hatch and John Mangum promised to join later. The eight people left Kanab with four wagons, three yoke of oxen, four horses, five cows, a calf, and two spans of mules. It was cold and snowing and the ground was frozen. Not until the ninth did they pull in at Navajo Well.[57]

Blythe had been instructed to build roads for a subsequent, larger migration. The initial improvements were made at Navajo Well, usually the first camp out of Kanab. The men dug a new well so that more animals could be watered and were building a nearby sixteen-foot stone house to serve as a way station when Hamblin came into Blythe's camp after dark on February 11. He was returning from meeting with the Navajos regarding the Grass Valley killings and mentioned that he was to meet with the Navajos again in twenty-seven days. In the morning, Hamblin continued on to Kanab. Ira Hatch and his four children joined them on the nineteenth. Hatch added talent and experience to the group, as he was adept with native languages and probably was the best frontiersman in the area. The stone building was nearly complete on the twenty-first, so Blythe started his son, Solomon, and Anderson toward the mountain with the slower ox teams. It was bitter cold when they stopped for lunch three miles out at the foot of the Buckskin.

While Blythe's company was laboring at Navajo Well, James Jackson left the ferry on a trip to the settlements. Ostensibly going for supplies, his real purpose was to propose marriage to one of the girls at Johnson settlement. Like many young, unmarried men, he had not found himself. He had been more or less in limbo until Jacob Hamblin assigned him a sandy, ten-acre claim adjoining Lee's in the mouth of Pahreah Canyon. He lived there alone in a small cabin, assisting Lee as he could. He was an awkward handyman, doing everything from farming and ferrying to teaching Lee's children the rudiments of reading and writing. Jackson worked cheerfully, practiced his religion faithfully, and accepted the rigors of his existence as the normal way of life. Now he wanted a wife and family, but he was not handsome or strong, or imposing, and the girls of his age were not attracted.

February's constant storms had left a heavy blanket of snow on Buckskin Mountain, and the near-zero temperatures made the area a bleak, inhospitable place. Jackson's light wagon became stuck just east of the crest, but he unhitched his horse and proceeded bareback to Johnson. He asked the girl to share his life, but she rejected him; despondent, he started back to the ferry. He spent the night of February 20 with the Blythe party in the new cabin, obtained some supplies from them, and went on in the morning. He passed the three advance members at their noon stop and continued up the mountain. But he lost the road in the deep snow, and he finally found his wagon after dark. His feet probably were frozen at this time, but he was so demoralized with cold and low in spirit that he didn't care.[58]

Jackson had been in his blankets for two days and nights when the main Blythe party left Navajo Well on the twenty-third; he had bread, cheese, wine, and a canvas shelter, but no source of heat.

The missionaries inched their way up the mountain. The icy track, when it could be identified, gave animals no footing; each wagon had to be double-teamed to a suitable place before bringing up the next wagon. It was five days before the party topped out and began to descend the eastern slopes. They had gone scarcely a half-mile when they met poor Jackson crawling on his hands and knees. He had heard them breaking track and, unable to walk on his rotting feet, had crawled through eighteen inches of snow to meet his rescuers.

They did what they could for him, which wasn't much. Blythe offered to convey him to his father's home in St. George, but the young man declined, preferring to be taken to his claim at the ferry where Sister Emma Lee would care for him. They started down the mountain, taking Jackson's wagon with them. John Mangum had joined the group the previous day. The enlarged party found downhill travel much faster than the laborious uphill portion, and that night's camp was made at the foot of the grade in Coyote Valley. March 1 was a Sunday, so a layover was called. Jackson's feet were washed and poulticed with sage and charcoal, a dubious remedy at best but all they could do along with their practice of laying on of hands.

The next morning, four of the brethren went back up the mountain to get the slow ox teams that had been left behind, while Mangum took Jackson and the ailing Allen ahead to House Rock Spring. The main party found the spring fenced off and a notice posted that the water was claimed by Jacob Hamblin. Snow fell continuously during the next four days, then the heavy sand replaced ice and snow as the major hindrance, forcing them to leave one wagon a mile short of the Pools. There, on March 5, they found Mangum and the sick men. Jackson underwent another treatment of washing, anointing, poulticing, and the laying on of hands. Unimpeded by oxen, Mangum went ahead with the ailing ones, hoping to get them under Emma's care as soon as possible.

The main party, slowed by fatigued animals, struggled on to Soap Creek, through the Badger sand, and finally reached the river about dusk on March 10. Allen had recovered and walked back a mile from Emma's place to meet them, bringing sad news. Mangum had reached Lonely Dell that morning. Jackson was happy to be at home and his spirits rose. They made him as comfortable as a man could possibly be whose feet were decaying and with blood poison spreading up his body. He professed great faith in the ordinances and sang "Hard Times Come No More." He had seen plenty of hard times and perhaps he realized his travail was almost over. When his song ended, he went to sleep and died peacefully about four hours after reaching his home.

The grave was dug in the afternoon as they intended to bury him that night. Allen's purpose in walking back was to bring Blythe to officiate at the service, but he decided the cold weather would give them a chance to make a coffin and burial would take place in the morning. Anderson used boards from the door of Jackson's cabin and his table to construct the coffin. Blythe conducted the service, and the first interment of the Lee's Ferry cemetery became history on the afternoon of March 11, 1874. The grave was just outside the former owner's cabin, less than ten feet from the trail to Pahreah and about seventy rods from Emma Lee's cabin.[59]

Meanwhile, Jacob Hamblin's January meeting with the Navajos had been a harrowing experience. Quite probably, only the presence of two "Mericats"—the Smith brothers—and four elderly Navajos, including Ketchene, who had known the consequences of American power, prevented the young firebrands from killing him. Hamblin came away convinced he had narrowly escaped torture and a hideous death. The tribesmen had demanded the Mormons indemnify them with four hundred head each of horses and cattle, a claim that Hamblin promised to relay to his leaders and return in twenty-seven days with their reply. He had no intention of exposing himself again to the uncertainties of Navajo justice, but he did plan to return to the Indian country on a slightly different timetable than the one agreed upon.

Leaving the Dell, Hamblin reached Moenave two days ahead of the promised time. Of course Ketchene was not there, and Lee was guiding the four miners on a prospecting trip. Hamblin left Lee's mail with Rachel and went on to the Hopi villages. John D. Lee returned March 9 and was overjoyed to find lengthy telegrams from Brigham Young and George A. Smith. They authorized him to use the new ferryboat and to charge travelers for his services. He was further advised to see that Emma obtained legal title to the ferry location. In effect, this nullified Hamblin's claim as half-owner. The telegrams tied Lee and his family to the ferry, at least for the present.[60]

Shortly after daybreak, the local Navajo headman, having heard that Hamblin was there but meant to return without meeting with them, arrived at Lee's ranch. Accompanied by one of Ketchene's sons and a Paiute interpreter, the headman had traveled all night to intercept him. Lee invited them in, showed marked hospitality, and allowed them to confront Hamblin, who had returned from the Hopi villages. Now the entire deception was revealed and it did not look good for Hamblin. The Navajos gave him a tongue-lashing and challenged him to meet Ketchene alone on neutral ground to settle the matter. Hamblin finally consented to meet Ketchene at Lee's house in ten days and to bring Ira Hatch, a good interpreter. The Indians agreed and departed.

Lee urged Hamblin not to treat the matter so frivolously, for the business was serious to the Navajos and they should be given a direct answer. Hamblin replied that he was the Apostle to the Lamanites and would run the affair to suit himself. A heated argument ensued during which Lee berated him for lying to the Indians and trying to tell them that twenty-seven days meant twenty-five (which revealed that Lee had picked up

the true figure when it was set). The acrimony stopped just short of violence. Lee's one-sided version is the only record of this quarrel but it
appears generally to be accurate.[61]

Hamblin and five others set out northwards for the river. Lee
remained to write President Young about the seriousness of the situation,
then left with his children Lehi and Amorah. Both parties crossed the
Colorado on March 14 to find Blythe's company encamped. Sunday, the fifteenth, witnessed a meeting in Emma's cabin. Everyone was impressed with
the fervent and pathetic prayer given by Lee.[62] Apparently he was a soul in
torment as he felt the hopelessness of his position.

After being assured by Hamblin that there was no danger, Blythe's
little party crossed the river on March 19. Ketchene, his two sons, and a
Spanish-speaking Navajo woman intercepted them near Limestone Tanks.
Convinced that Hamblin had no intention of keeping the appointment at
Moenave, Ketchene demanded that Blythe and Hatch meet with his people
in ten days. Then he became so threatening that Blythe agreed to the meeting and killed one of Lee's steers for a gift of beef. This appeared to mollify
them, but Blythe and Hatch now became as involved as Hamblin in the
Grass Valley affair.

The men kept the appointment that had been forced upon them.
The session began about noon on Saturday, April 4, and lasted until midnight. Both were subjected to even more stress than Hamblin had been, but
acquitted themselves admirably in adhering to the official line that the
shootings had been done by non-Mormons. In the end, the remuneration
in stock was reduced to two hundred eighty head and the return of the four
Navajos' property. The settlement was to be made in two and one-half
moons or they would be given a statement that payment would not be
made. Blythe figured the deadline as being June 13 to 15. Upon returning
to Moenkopi, he wrote an account of their experience to President
Young.[63] Besides noting the decreased Navajo demand, he pointed out that
Hamblin had neglected his duty to the mission and had lost face with the
Indians. Allen then became a letter-carrier, combining its delivery with a
visit to his family in Toquerville.

After he set the Blythe company and twenty-one of his own cattle
across the river, Lee started for the settlements to discuss his future with
Brigham Young. He was received warily at St. George by the man who had
told his wife Lavina that Lee would never be rebaptized by his consent.[64]
Lee learned during the post-supper presidential discourse that the
Mormons had no plans for the San Juan region. Instead, they intended to
settle as many as the country could support at Moenave and Moenkopi
before colonizing the Little Colorado, Verde, Salt, and Gila River Valleys.
Indian rights in the proposed settlement areas were not even considered,
and Tuba's agreement with Hamblin was ignored. Young started north
April 6, Lee riding with the party as far as Kanarraville. The morning of the
second day, just before the retinue took to the road, Young gave Lee a

fatherly talk that ended with his blessing but no specific instructions. This was the last known instance that the two held direct conversation.[65]

Jacob Hamblin and Levi Stewart had done what they could to ease the Grass Valley situation. On March 20 they had written one of the McCartys who had killed the Navajos at Grass Valley, asking for the return of the eleven seized horses and the personal articles belonging to the four young warriors. Blythe's list in his letter of April 8 was more explicit and evidently caused President Young to enlist the aid of his eldest son, Joseph A. Young, who was in charge of affairs in Richfield.[66] But Joseph had no more success with McCarty than had Hamblin and Stewart; in fact, McCarty claimed the property had been turned over to the commanding officer at Beaver who would not release it unless he was given an order by the Indian Agent. McCarty further said that he did not recognize the authority of Brigham Young, Joseph A. Young, or Jacob Hamblin. Part of his statement was false because Joseph A. Young reported that Clinger—the Mormon involved in the incident—had spent two days in Richfield recently and boasted that he had ridden one of the seized ponies to town.[67] Thus, a solution of the affair appeared to be held up because of a stalemate between the Mormons and the federal officials. McCarty was unwilling to cooperate, the Saints were unwilling to acknowledge Mormon involvement, and the Navajos demanded justice by their code. Something had to give; Mormon authorities decided to reinforce their brethren across the river.

The dependable Thales Haskell, Samuel Knight, and Ammon Tenney arrived at Moenkopi on April 26. Three days later John R. Young, Jacob Hamblin, and twenty-two well-armed men from Kanab and Long Valley appeared, and two days after that John D. Lee, David Bennett, and George Adair pulled into Moenave. The latter bore a telegram from President Young saying the Mormons would not comply with Navajo demands and the missionaries should return until the Indians learned to identify their friends from their enemies. When the president's instruction became known, there was considerable scurrying about as petitions and letters were written, delegates dispatched, and recall couriers sent after them. A letter was delivered to the Hopi agent to be read to the Navajo chiefs. It contained the declaration that anyone crossing above the ferry would be looked upon as an enemy, but Navajos of good will were invited to come to the ferry and verify that the Mormons had spoken the truth. Luckily, most of the Navajos were at Fort Defiance receiving their government annuities. At last, Hamblin was convinced that the Navajos were serious and the mission was in danger. The group concurred that it would be best to evacuate the missionaries swiftly to avoid a fight.

Blythe arranged with the Hopi to care for the crops, for which he promised them a half-share of the harvest. The men loaded everything into the wagons and began their withdrawal May 5, Tuba and his wife with them. Because the feed situation was so poor, Young and Gibbons commandeered the missionaries' seed grain for their animals. They went directly to

Moenave where they took such Lee property as could be distributed among the wagons and set out again with the Lee family. John D. and Rachel drove his two wagons.

They traveled after dark and by moonlight to lose no time before the Navajos learned of their departure. The wagons were double-teamed to get over the steep hill. Lee crossed the last one at dusk on May 9, finally putting the river between them and those who would have their blood. Emma, cooking continuously to feed all who crossed, was as tired as the ferryman when the long day was over. With the exception of the Blythes, Solomon, and Bennett, the missionaries all ate and traveled on. Unfortunately, several seized the opportunity to take advantage of the outcast; they neglected to unload his possessions that had been distributed among the wagons of the train. All that he had left was what he carried in his own two wagons. He lost corn, wheat, and beans that would have lasted until the next harvest, as well as his farm implements, numerous household articles, and forty-seven chickens. He charged no ferriage to any of the party either going or coming, and noted in a letter that he would have been better off to trust the Navajos than to have the protection of such men.[68] He concluded by recommending that several families be settled at the mouth of the Pahreah to obviate the need of a military detail.

On Sunday morning, Blythe officiated at the blessing of Lee's children, Frances Dell and Victoria Elizabeth. He baptized William Franklin Lee, John's son by Rachel. Blythe and the others started out late on May 11 and were welcomed in Kanab on the twenty-first; he telegraphed President Young at once with the news. John R. Young wrote his uncle on May 20 recounting the operation. He said the escort detail had evacuated the missionaries and the Lee family only one day ahead of a planned Navajo attack. He quoted Tuba as saying that no Hopi would incur Navajo enmity by aiding the Mormons in case of an attack. This letter contains the name "Lee's Ferry," apparently the first use of this newly-established place-name. The letter was read to and approved by the returning missionaries.[69] Thus the Arizona Mission ended in retreat because the Mormons and federal appointees had failed to apply equal justice in the country they controlled.

During the St. George Conference of June 5–7, 1874, it was decided to establish two trading posts on the Colorado: one near the mouth of the Pahreah and the other in the vicinity of the Ute Crossing. Robert Gardiner, Alex F. McDonald, and Daniel D. McArthur were to call sufficient men and means to construct the posts, with McArthur selecting the actual locations. Thirty men and five teams would be sent to do the work. After construction, a suitable force would man the outposts.[70] Men and teams were assembled at the river later in the month. McArthur chose the large flat behind the ferry landing for the post location. There was plenty of room for heavy wagons with several yoke of oxen to make the turn in boarding the ferryboat; best of all, the site commanded excellent views both upstream and downstream, taking in the entire left bank that could be approached on horseback.

McArthur's men did their work well. The stones were faced and closely fitted without mortar, and the chinks were filled with thinner slabs. The walls were straight; the corners were sharp. From a distance, the structure appeared to be a well-built stone cabin with windows on all sides, a chimney on the east end, and a front door facing south to the river and ferry landing. The outside dimensions, twenty by thirty feet, were considerably larger than an average cabin, with vertical stone slabs to form slot-shaped loopholes. A closer look revealed that the vertically placed slabs were easily removed from the inside and the windows could be made larger. The openings were placed higher than usual window position to make entry more difficult. The ridgepole was a conifer, as were the longitudinal rafters. Many armloads of willows abutted at the low ridge, held down by earth.

As soon as the work was well underway, Hamblin and McArthur went with a small party up the Sand Trail to decide on the location for the second trading post. Upon reaching the Ute Crossing, they found the river so high that it could not be forded for a long time. Usable rock supplies were distant; wagons and teams would be needed to collect them, but there were no roads. The conclusion was that it would be easier to maintain a guard camp in the open during low-water months, if needed, and it would not be necessary to build another guard post at this remote location. As they rode back, Hamblin gave McArthur his version of the Navajo trouble and said that some of the brethren had talked unwisely to cause the break-up of the mission.[71] This was a direct slap at Blythe and Hatch, whom he regarded as having intruded in his field. He ignored the fact that he had been present when the decision was made to withdraw the mission on the direct order of President Young, and there is no record of his having registered an opposing view at that time. McArthur listened to him but gave no evidence that he accepted Hamblin's story.

Meanwhile, the fort–trading post at the ferry had been completed in July and the fifteen remaining workmen were released. Haskell and Gibbons, assisted by others, remained to take care of the Indian trade, although there was none at this time, and would stay there until the Navajo matter was settled. The general plan was to confine the bartering to the river to prevent the Navajos from coming into the settlements where they disrupted life in general.

Hamblin told McArthur that the Grass Valley affair soon would be settled, and it turned out as he forecast. The investigative committee was waiting for him when he returned to Kanab. It included the Navajo Hastele, a representative of the Santa Fe Superintendency, and two translators, but not Ketchene, Ne chic se cla (another of the concerned headmen), Clinger, or the McCartys. They went to the scene of the fight, listened to what the Mormons told them, then started the long ride home. The affair finally was closed on Mormon terms at Fort Defiance on August 21, 1874, satisfying everyone except Ne chic se cla, Ketchene, and a few western Navajos who felt they had been sold out.

While sojourning in St. George during the winter of 1873–74, President Young had uncorked a plan for organizing his people into the utopian United Order. This was an idealistic concept in which Mormon communities were to pool their resources for the common good. A strong characteristic of the Saints was their willingness to unite their efforts in group endeavor. Young now proposed to do away with the system of private enterprise and hold all wealth communally. His objective was to isolate his people from the increasing number of Gentiles, whom he regarded as economic and moral threats to the Kingdom of God. The concept was not accepted for a number of reasons, but several months were spent in trying to make it work. During this period, the people were confused and disorganized; the residents of Kanab and Long Valley were particularly polarized as Mormon society was shaken to the core. The Order was favored by those who had little personal property and disfavored by those with more assets. The president ignored the fact that many church members had been born in Europe and had brought with them the common European's hunger for his own land. This leap into social idealism was too great for them to take.[72]

If the people of Kanab and Long Valley were unhappy and disturbed, it was because of overlapping command, personal ambition, and misunderstanding brought on by sudden, radical change. But their social and political distress was small compared to the adversity encountered by John D. Lee and his five faithful families. Discouraged by one calamity after another, he was against a wall with no place to go.

Mormondom in general was perturbed when the Poland Act was passed by Congress on June 23, 1874. It strengthened the hands of federal judges and other officials while weakening the authority of local jurisdiction. The bill would be appealed to the United States Supreme Court, but at the time the Saints felt that the Woods-McKean coalition was applying the laws of Babylon to an innocent people.[73]

If, to lessen the pressure, the church leadership devised a plan involving Lee, there is no official acknowledgment of it. Psychologically, he would have been receptive to any solution. A persuasive speaker could easily have convinced him that it was only a matter of time before he would be brought to trial, and that should a hearing result in his acquittal, he would be better off to face up to it now. Once this was done, he would be restored to church fellowship and the good will of his brethren. He then could participate in the building of the Kingdom, to him more important than his former wealth and prestige. An acquittal would restore everything. There is no record that Lee met with such a persuasive advisor, but if he did, only he and a few others knew of the proposed plan, the inducements, and the promises made or inferred.

Some historians ask us to believe an amazing coincidence regarding the "capture" of John D. Lee. According to them, the paths of Marshal William Stokes, who was based at Beaver, and Lee, whose main home was at Lonely Dell in northern Arizona, just "happened" to intersect at the village of

Panguitch at a certain time on November 7, 1874. It had to be an appointment of time and place that both men traveled to keep; yet these historians
call on anyone who doubts the theme of coincidence to furnish evidence of
the conspiracy, of which none is available. The two main adversaries were
astute politicians who realized that a simple solution of the Mountain
Meadows Massacre would benefit them both. If such a conspiracy occurred, it
most likely was oral; if documentation exists, it may never see the light of day.

Brigham Young was "unwell" when he left Salt Lake City on
October 29 for his usual winter visit to St. George. His party arrived in
Parowan the day Lee was arrested. It was common knowledge that Stokes
hoped to arrest Lee at Panguitch on this date, and Collins R. Hakes told
Joseph Fish that he went to President Young and volunteered to warn the
fugitive but was told to "let the law take its course."[74] Young was indisposed
the next day because of rheumatism, and First Counselor George A. Smith
conducted the meeting in his place.

Lee's diary covering the period from April 9, 1874, through August
8, 1875, has never surfaced. This accounts for sixteen months of a very critical period in his life, and it would have been inconsistent for him not to have
recorded it. His diary may not exist, possibly having been destroyed after his
arrest. Lee family tradition abounds with stories of armed men visiting his
various homes and reading his diary through intimidation. Some versions
say pages were ripped out; others describe seizure of an entire book. If the
volume was not destroyed, it may be in a vault in a church archive, but we are
unlikely ever to know. The period of his life when he bade his president
goodbye to the time of his transfer from Beaver to the penitentiary near Salt
Lake City must be evaluated from the words of others.

As he languished in jail at Beaver, the major item of general interest
was whether John D. Lee would turn state's evidence by naming individuals
and the church as being culpable in the Mountain Meadows Massacre.[75]
There were those who thought he might break down, but they did not
understand the situation Lee was in and certainly didn't know him very well.
Lee's hearing began in Beaver on July 23, 1875. The prosecution was weak,
the defense counsel divided, the defendant did not take the stand, and
Judge Boreman refused to throw the case out of court. The trial ended
August 5 with a hung jury, the panel dividing along the lines of faith.[76] The
judge remanded Lee to the territorial penitentiary until the date for a new
trial could be set. On May 11, 1876, Lee was released on bail of $15,000 for
a span of four months and was to surrender himself at Beaver in time for his
new trial date of September 14. The bondsman was William H. Hooper, said
by Lee's daughter Amorah to have been backed by Bishop James Murdock.[77]

How Lee came south is not known, but tradition has him spending
some time with each of his five families. He undoubtedly stopped first with
Caroline in Panguitch; Polly and Lavina were living with their families in
Skutumpah. Emma, of course, was at the ferry, and Rachel, who had been
with him at the prison, came south with him. Two of her sons had visited

Moenave to plant a crop and hold his claim. Moenave was Rachel's home, the only one she had, but the cabin had deteriorated while the owners were absent. In all probability, Lee spent only a day or two with the first four families as he would see them again on his return to Beaver. He and Rachel arrived in Moenave before June 11.[78]

It is not known how long Lee remained at Moenave, but he must have left for the last time during the second week of August. He was at the river when George Dabling and Joseph Wright crossed. Dabling wrote a letter to the editor of the *Deseret News* from Sunset on August 20; he was seething over Lee's ferriage of a dollar per wagon and seventy-five cents for each animal, with payment in provisions. They paid what was requested, then worked half a day to help him swim some stock that he was driving to Moenave for Rachel's benefit.[79] After an emotion-charged prayer meeting in Emma's cabin on his final night at the river, Lee rode off early in the morning for last visits with Polly, Lavina, and Caroline.[80] He arrived in Beaver on September 4 and surrendered himself on the eleventh. The week between his arrival and surrender is not explained, but presumably the time was spent with his counsel. He wrote Emma that Daniel H. Wells was in town coaching the witnesses, recommending jury selection, and in general acting as a liaison to both counsels.[81] Wells was a faithful servant to the president, still taking care of distasteful but necessary tasks.

The indictment against Lee was hyperbolic; he was charged with the sole responsibility of the murder of approximately one hundred twenty men, women, and children. The farcical trial began on September 14, and from the selection of jurors to the witnesses called it was apparent that rank collusion had taken place. Again Lee did not testify, several supposedly reputable brethren obviously perjured themselves, and six days later the all-Mormon jury deliberated a full three and one-half hours before returning a verdict of guilty. The sad affair can only stand as a black page in the administration of American justice.[82] That Lee was the only one convicted of the Mountain Meadows Massacre is preposterous. His lawyers' appeal of the conviction was denied by the Territorial Supreme Court. He was executed at Mountain Meadows on March 23, 1877. Three trusted representatives of the church—Solon Foster, Jr., Anthony W. Ivins, and Daniel Seegmiller—witnessed that Lee's last words gave no comfort to church enemies.[83]

Thus died one of the most dedicated Mormons of them all. He had said he loved his church more than life itself and would stand between it and the cannon's mouth, and he had done so.[84] Perhaps it was better that one man could serve as a sop to the ill-will built up over half a century. Fortunately for both sides, a man with the stature of John D. Lee was available to make the ultimate solution possible. Man's treatment of his fellows often results in questionable equity or tardy justice. John D. Lee supposedly had been excommunicated on October 8, 1870. He was reinstated by the Church of Jesus Christ of Latter-day Saints on May 8, 1961, a grandson standing in proxy for him.

3

The Ferryman

THE ST. GEORGE STAKE CONFERENCE OF NOVEMBER 1874 WAS NEAR ITS midpoint when the electrifying news of Lee's arrest crackled out over the telegraph. Jacob Hamblin is said to have left immediately, picked up his son Lyman at Kanab, and hurried to the river to control the crossing. This preemptive act was Hamblin's last effort to preserve his interest in the place, and it came close to working. There is no known record of a confrontation between Emma Lee and Jacob Hamblin over ferry fees, yet there appears to have been one. His name was not among those assigned to the post, although he admits he was there.[1] After the news got around, the Blythes laid the matter of the ferry seizure before Brigham Young at St. George.[2] Blythe's advocacy of Lee's interests motivated a presidential letter to Hamblin on December 28, 1874. Signed by Young and George A. Smith, the letter praised Hamblin for his past efforts and expressed hope that he would persevere. They closed by saying they wanted Emma Lee to maintain the place and have the "avails" of the transient travel. They expected her to take care of the ferry, and suggested Hamblin assist her by insuring the boat's safety, and that he select suitable families to settle there.[3]

Although Hamblin must have been disappointed by the edict, he accepted it as final. He and his son Lyman left the post to the assignees and returned to Kanab. Then he set about finding some families who were willing to settle at the remote ferry. This was a difficult task as the isolation, danger, and incessant labor attached to the place were well known. Never forceful in his requests, Jacob was turned down by the people of Kanab. He went to the new bishop of Long Valley, Howard O. Spencer, who was having trouble with the brethren at Mt. Carmel. Bishop Spencer searched for a volunteer, thinking that a prospect might be found among those opposed to the United Order. He finally found his man in the person of his first counselor, Warren M. Johnson.[4]

Johnson lived at Glendale where the people universally were opposed to the United Order, but since the church president was urging its acceptance, it probably would be adopted in degree sooner or later.[5] There is a strong probability that this slight New England school teacher volunteered to go on the unofficial mission to avoid being involved in the United

Order imbroglio. Apparently, Johnson took the job on a trial basis; if the work did not overtax him physically, he would dispose of his Glendale holdings and make a permanent move. He had two wives and a child by each. He would have little chance to use his formal training because there was not even a school house at the ferry; instead, Johnson would perform the hard physical labor associated with farming, stock-raising, dam building, ferryboat handling, and Indian trading. Outside of his propinquity to the agriculture of his day—from which few Mormons were far removed—Johnson had no experience for his new duties, but he was willing to try. In so doing, he spared his family the turmoil of the United Order.[6]

March was well along when he helped his first wife, Permelia, and baby, Mary, into his wagon and set out for the ferry, leaving his second wife, Samantha, and her daughter at Glendale. Jacob Hamblin accompanied them on horseback from Kanab to their destination; it was Johnson's first trip over Buckskin Mountain. He was assigned Jackson's sandy acres and he immediately went to work on the little cabin to make it livable for his family. Warren and Permelia hit it off well with Emma Lee, who willingly dispensed her knowledge and advice. Without her cooperation, he could not have done as well as he did.

Thales Haskell and Andrew Gibbons, whom Hamblin previously had left in charge of the post, were guarding the Ute Crossing, while John S. P. Adams and James Rawlings were taking care of business at the ferry. Hamblin remained long enough to define Jackson's claim and to leave notice that Haskell and Gibbons were released to return home to put in their crops. The guards decided the river had risen high enough so that fording would not be possible again until autumn. They returned to the ferry and stayed a few days more to help Johnson repair the dam and get water to the fields. After this was accomplished, they left Adams and Rawlings to tend the post until a higher authority would release them, too, and place the entire operation in Johnson's hands. Evidently this was done shortly after they reached the settlements, because Johnson took over the ferrying at the start of the month and subsequently reported that, during April, fifty-one Navajos and one Moki (Hopi) had crossed the river from the south side.[7] Blythe's large ferryboat required two men to operate, forcing Johnson to resort to the skiff. This insured that Johnson got a good feel for the river by making many crossings. He dealt mainly with Indians, because through traffic for Caucasians was almost nonexistent at this time.

How John D. Lee financed his defense is unknown, but evidently the trial exhausted his ready cash. Four lawyers represented him. Possibly the two attorneys who were content that the inquiry stop with Lee and not involve anyone else received external fees from an unknown party, but William K. Bishop and Wells Spicer, whose defense apparently would have involved anyone to save their client, seem to have been paid directly by Lee. It is known that Lee gave Bishop a manuscript of his life story in payment for his work, but Spicer—an equal creditor—was convinced that the defendant had a gold mine.[8] He might have arrived at this conclusion by seeing some of the free gold Lee had in his possession as ferriage from transient miners. Perhaps Lee even led him on and occasionally dropped Hamblin's name as being familiar with the mineral deposits of the country, knowing full well that the naive prospectors would pay well for guide service to find them. Lee had no love for Hamblin at this time but any cash brought in by outsiders benefited Mormondom, and he still was a loyal Saint. Spicer arrived at Kanab in mid-October, and for five dollars a day Hamblin agreed to guide and protect him from the Indians as he prospected for gold.

A previously unconnected episode had taken place several months earlier that was destined to have an impact on those concerned with the ferry. A Spanish convert, Mileton G. Trejo, had collaborated with Daniel W. Jones in translating selected passages of the Book of Mormon into a Spanish text of one hundred pages. Two thousand copies were printed with the idea of distributing them during a goodwill tour to Mexico that would combine exploring and spreading the faith. Jones headed the six-man party that left Toquerville on October 11, 1875, with books and outfits loaded on fourteen pack animals. They were in Kanab on the fourth day to pick up their last member, Spanish-speaking Ammon Tenney, who would guide them as far south as he had been.

Somehow, Jacob Hamblin dealt himself a hand in this game but said nothing about his contract with Spicer. Instead, Spicer, accompanied by an apostate named Tibbetts, went ahead to test the gravels at the ferry, pretending he was on his own. Evidently it was arranged for Spicer to join Hamblin and the Jones party somewhere south of the river. When the missionaries left Kanab on October 20, their numbers had increased by the addition of Hamblin and Thomas Chamberlain, the latter probably along to help wrangle. They now had thirty-two head of stock, twenty-two of which were pack animals. Very likely several, loaded with trade items, belonged to Hamblin. Since most Navajos went no farther than the post at the ferry, Hamblin's commerce at Kanab had greatly decreased, and he had to go to the customers. In three trips, Warren Johnson and Billy Lee ferried the outfit across the Colorado on October 26. This was one of the first times Johnson had used the big boat.

Jones, on Hamblin's advice, camped at Bitter Springs on the second night away from the river. In a short time, Spicer rode into camp, identified himself, and announced he was headed for the Indian territory to hunt for minerals. The Gentile's presence did not bring joy to the imperious Jones, but Hamblin adopted the attitude of the Good Samaritan, saying he intended to help a man traveling alone in a strange country full of unpredictable Navajos. The collusion was apparent. This led to a quarrel between Hamblin and Jones, and in the morning the missionaries left while Hamblin, Chamberlain, and Spicer declared they were going back.[9] Instead, they probably went up the Antelope Trail as soon as Jones was out of sight. It would appear that Hamblin's friendship with Spicer had developed remarkably fast and his pious altruism toward his new Gentile friend was much greater than it had been to Brothers Lee, Horton Haight, and John Blythe. None of the accounts even mentioned Tibbetts.

Spicer later sent five letters to the *Salt Lake Daily Herald*, a liberal newspaper, giving an account of his ramble.[10] He claimed his guide was James L. Tibbetts and did not mention Hamblin's presence. The letters indicate side trips were made to the Little Colorado, San Francisco Peaks, Grand Canyon, and points between. There was no mention of the Hopi villages, undoubtedly to conceal Hamblin's commerce. The dispatches were promotional in nature, such as could have been written by a future Coconino County Chamber of Commerce to benefit tourism. They did, however, emphasize mineral deposits, saying there was galena and plenty of gold, but it was too fine for profitable recovery by present methods. His last epistle, written from St. George, indicates he had abandoned prospecting in the Indian country to investigate the activity in the booming Harrisburg district.

What Spicer failed to reveal was that he had appeared at Lonely Dell and made a strong pitch for a grubstake to the unsophisticated Emma Lee. He persuaded her to advance him three horses and saddles and over a period of time to kill three cows. In prison, Lee received letters from Emma and Spicer on January 12, 1876, and five days later one from his daughter, Amorah, with more detail.[11] Spicer asked for Lee's help in locating his (nonexistent) gold mine, and stated that the Moenave ranch was vacant and in danger of being jumped. Lee's response to Emma was that she should have nothing to do with Spicer and should consult with Brother Johnson before making any move. He told her to have the boys put in a crop at Moenave to help hold the place. He made no mention of Hamblin, which indicates that Emma was unaware of Hamblin's involvement with the lawyer. Thus Lee's stock and beef supported Spicer's sight-seeing and Hamblin's trading, while Hamblin walked off with a three hundred dollar jackpot.

Johnson had his thirty-seventh birthday at the ferry in July but it, like most other days, was spent in working. Only the Sabbath was observed as a day of rest, and he never ferried Indians or traded if he could find a way around such action. However, groups of natives came regularly, asking to be crossed. He would row over in the skiff and persuade them to leave their horses on the left bank. This technique accomplished two things: it kept the Navajos from going into the settlements and he usually was able to complete the transactions sooner. Time meant little to Indians; they often took two or three days to make a minor exchange. If they had their horses on the right bank, their trading was extended or they threatened to go on to Kanab for a better deal. One such group arrived early in August, insisting that their stock be taken over. Even after they were crossed, they refused to trade and went on to Kanab. Allen Frost noted their arrival and indicated the case was not unusual.[12] Generally, however, Johnson was able to stop them at the river.

Johnson found that the best way to get along with the Navajos was to laugh and joke as he was trading, and before long he became known as

Ba Hazhoona, or "Happy Man."[13] He was honest in his trading, endeavoring to send every Indian away with a good taste in his mouth. He later reported to the authorities in St. George that between April 1 and November 1, 1875, he had crossed 522 Indians. Of these, 497 were Navajo, 24 were Moki (Hopi), and 1 was Paiute; 5 women were among the travelers—3 Navajo and 2 Hopi.[14]

Records have not been found to prove that Johnson agreed to take the job on a permanent basis but it is obvious that he assented. He was on duty when George Q. Cannon read his name in the Mormon General Conference at Salt Lake City October 10, 1875.[15] Brigham Young, Daniel H. Wells, and George A. Smith signed his official appointment the following day and specified that he be called to a life's mission to act as ferryman at Lee's Ferry. In recognition of the fact that he was already living there, Conference Clerk George Goddard listed his residence as Lee's Ferry, which had become an accepted place name.

Johnson's wife Permelia was expecting another child, and although Emma Lee was a capable midwife, they decided to go to Glendale for the birth. This would enable him to wind up his affairs before returning with both of his families. Accordingly, the Johnsons left early in November for Long Valley. The ferry once again was under the solitary care of Emma Lee and the trading post was closed.

The failures at colonization in northern Arizona and the dispatching of the Jones party to scout prospects for settlement farther south did not mean that President Brigham Young had abandoned his project on the Little Colorado. To reconcile the conflicting opinions of Hamblin, Roundy, Haight, and Blythe, he fell back on a faithful servant, James S. Brown. Informed that he had been selected to take charge of a mission to Arizona, Brown pointed out that he had just returned from a preaching tour, his family was needy, winter was coming on, his health was poor and he should have a rest. His objections were brushed aside. Reconciled to his duty, he gave the president a list of nine men he would like to have accompany him; among them was Seth Tanner. Young approved his choices and added six more, including Andrew Gibbons, Thales Haskell, Ira Hatch, and Warren Johnson.

The call was made official October 9, and Brown started on the thirtieth, preaching as he went. The brethren responded with liberal quantities of wheat, flour, potatoes, and a modicum of cash. Johnson would support the mission from the river, possibly having been named for that reason. They camped at Jacob's Pools on November 25, where Brown wrote in his journal that it was a desolate and forbidding place. Knowing the ferryman was in Glendale, he sent two men ahead to prepare the ferryboat. The main group arrived later on the twenty-seventh and were told that the day was too far gone to ferry everything over by nightfall. Brown took this as a challenge and ordered the operation to begin. Four large wagons were crossed after dark and it was late before supper was served. Brown noted that some of the brethren opposed him silently, and it was ten o'clock before the job was done. Food for the animals was no better here than it had been on the right bank. The next day was Sunday and nothing was done beyond ferrying the rest of the animals. Emma Lee came over in the skiff to tell Brown she was out of provisions. The company gave her some supplies, then took up a collection of ten dollars for her benefit, which they passed off for ferriage. In the morning, Emma sent Billy across with a Navajo blanket and handkerchief for Brown. Before they started up the hill, Wells Spicer and the apostate Tibbetts came into camp trying to curry favor. Brown treated him as coldly as Jones had a month before.

The party reached Moenave on December 2, and Brown thought it the most pleasant spot he had seen since leaving Johnson settlement. The main camp was set up next day at Moenkopi. After getting the fort construction under way, the leader and four companions left on a three-week exploration that penetrated one hundred ten miles up the Little Colorado, south to the Beale Road, and west to the San Francisco Peaks area. Back in Moenkopi on December 29, he called a meeting, more to improve relations with his brethren than to obtain their input because his mind probably already was made up. In any event, the party members concurred that he should hurry to Salt Lake City to report personally to President Young.

With Seth Tanner, Brown left early on January 1 using a light wagon. Traveling fast, they reached Young's office at 6 P.M. on January 14. After giving a preliminary report he was permitted to join his family and give a full account later.[16] Brown fully expected to be relieved at this time; he had been successful in his mission and knew he deserved a rest. But Brigham Young had no intention of releasing him; instead, he had Brown attend a meeting with Young and counselors, the twelve apostles, and other prominent brethren. Brown gave an account to the editor of the *Deseret News*, who printed "The Route to Arizona."[17] He was lionized as few Mormon leaders ever were.

In a very short time, Young gave the signal that unleashed an impressive colonization of Arizona. Two hundred men were called, to be led by four captains, each with a group of fifty colonists who had agreed to make new homes in Arizona, to live and labor under the United Order. The publicity given the mission was exceptional. Brown again broached the subject of his release, bringing up every reason why he should be permitted to remain at home with his family. Young turned these aside with the full presidential treatment, putting his arm around Brown and praising him highly.

Brown finally played what he considered a trump card. He said that his eighteen-year-old daughter was besieged by suitors and needed her father now more than ever. The president pricked up his ears, thought a moment, then told Brown to bring his daughter to the office at a given time tomorrow as he had a surprise for her. Young's request was Brown's command; father and daughter dutifully appeared at the specified time. Having ascertained the strong bond between Rachel and her father, Young immediately asked if she would like to accompany him on an important mission.

Her shining eyes gave the answer, but she timidly wondered if an unmarried girl would not be out of place with the missionaries. The president replied that she should be married, and furthermore he had just the man she deserved. He would marry them and send them both as missionaries to Arizona. He motioned to a clerk, who left the room and returned shortly with a stranger. Hannibal Octavius Fullmer was thirty-eight years old, had never seen Rachel before—nor she him—but Brigham Young married them on the spot on January 31, 1876.[18] Poor Brown's head was still spinning when he left Salt Lake City that same day to return to Moenkopi.

When he left the city, Brown believed the president had appointed him to head the Arizona Mission. His interpretation of the loosely written instructions undoubtedly led him to think that his exploration had made the project feasible, that the colonists would settle on the sites he had selected, and that he would direct the operation from his base at Moenkopi. But even before Young heard Brown's evaluation of the country, he had determined to colonize it. He had kept abreast of the Boston colonizing company's progress and did not intend for the Gentiles to appropriate the choice sites. Brown's favorable report had simply confirmed his decision and set the project in motion. Captains Lot Smith, William C. Allen, George Lake, and Jesse O. Ballenger were each to have fifty men to form separate, permanent settlements. Although all four captains theoretically were equal, Lot Smith was regarded generally as a major in charge of the entire operation. On February 3, Smith started from Farmington, firm in the belief that he had been named to head the Arizona Mission.

The president might have chosen to let Brown and Smith decide the matter between themselves, realizing that a power struggle would result in the stronger leader heading the colonies. The two men had much in common: both were strong, authoritative, quick to act, stubborn, and inconsiderate of others, especially those laboring under them. Tempers flared quickly and fiercely in them, yet on occasion each could be kind to the less fortunate, although the expression frequently lacked finesse.

At first, Smith traveled with the company, but he soon hurried ahead on horseback, leaving subordinates to bring his wagon through the mud and snow. Kanab was the gathering place; a number of wagons already were there while others had crossed Buckskin Mountain and were strung out along the road to the ferry. Among those who received an early call was Price W. Nelson, Sr., of Orderville. Knowing he could not get away until after spring, he outfitted his son, Price Nelson, Jr., with a wagon and a pair of oxen and started him out with sixty other wagons on New Year's Day of 1876. Nelson drove the only ox team in the company, was content to go slowly, made frequent layovers, and kept his animals in good condition.

Time was running out on Warren Johnson. He knew he should be at the ferry before the immigrants arrived, but Permelia's expected childbirth delayed him, and Melinda was born December 3, 1875. His wife Samantha also was pregnant but had not delivered her child and they couldn't travel until she did. That birth took place February 24, 1876, giving Warren his firstborn son, whom they named Jeremiah after his father and grandfather. Four days later, Johnson and both of his families left Glendale even though snow was in the air and the weather was ominous. Knowing that Buckskin Mountain with icy slopes and deep snow was no place for a newborn infant and mending mother, Johnson rented rooms for his families in the home of Zadok Knapp Judd in Kanab, then turned his team eastward with some Arizona-bound colonists who were trying to get over the mountain before being hit by the full fury of the storm. It was fortunate that he did. The teams started early and were driven late through ruts that were frozen solid. Double-teaming was necessary in many places as the wagons were inched along in relays. Once on the downgrade, Johnson went ahead, progressively widening the gap between his wagon and the others. He reached the ferry well ahead and was ready to cross them when they arrived.

Captains Smith and Allen departed Kanab in late February, leaving orders for the others to follow in groups of ten.[19] John Bushman left March 3, and his fast mule team caught up with the captains at Soap Creek on the seventh. Meanwhile, the leaders had overtaken Price Nelson near the ferry, where he witnessed an episode that was typical of Lot Smith. One of the missionaries, Joe Morris, lost a wagon wheel as he drove down the rough approach to the river. He had been a townsman all of his life and had no idea of how to contend with the mishap; he was so shaken and disheartened by the accident that he sat down and wept. Lot Smith ridiculed the poor fellow in front of the company, then, aided by others, pried the wagon up and had the wheel back in place ready to roll before Morris had dried his tears.[20]

If Johnson needed practice with the large ferryboat, he certainly received it during the days that followed. He worked from early morning until after dark, then tumbled dead tired into bed. The colonists willingly worked with him, usually paying their ferriage in provisions, although sometimes with spare stock, goods, tools, or occasionally cash. Billy Lee helped when he was free from farm chores. Johnson lived in the stone trading post since it was less than two hundred feet from the ferry landing. From there he could keep an eye on both the boat and the skiff—very necessary on a rising river—and could see travelers approaching from both directions.

The Adams company arrived on the morning of March 21. With them was John A. Blythe, who visited Emma and brought word from her husband while the wagons were being ferried over the river. John told her that he and his mother, Margaret, had visited Lee in prison on February 2 and told him how Hamblin had tried to seize the ferry and its revenues. They then informed Lee that James S. Brown had orders from Young to protect his interests at Moenave. Her son was starting to Arizona the next day and would be glad to carry a message to Emma. Lee seized the opportunity to send word by him and now Blythe had delivered it.[21] Emma was grateful and fed the youthful colonist both breakfast and dinner. When he finally took his leave, Johnson crossed him in the skiff.[22]

On the next day, the company of which Joseph H. Richards was a member crossed on the ferry. Richards noted in his diary: "no feed, a terrible, rough, rough country." It was no better the following day when they drove over Lee Hill. He wrote: "Came over a terrible rocky mountain. Double teamed 2 miles."[23] Depletion of water and grazing had modified Lot Smith's instruction for the immigrants to journey in groups of ten. Many now traveled in smaller aggregations of two to four wagons to mitigate the problem. Feed for the animals was quite scarce, especially around water sources; springs were slow to recover when the demand was so heavy. Most of the immigrants were aware of the country's poor reputation, but they seldom mentioned it. Some went out of their way to bolster morale. At a meeting in Kanab, Jacob Hamblin told the travelers they were going to a fine country with abundant grass, timber, and water, where the Indians were friendly and desired to live as white people did. Furthermore, if he had his choice, he would rather live in Arizona than any of the states in which he had resided.[24]

Despite John L. Blythe's development at Navajo Well, this source was very slow to recover. Frihoff G. Nielson recorded that the brethren dipped water all night to fill their water barrels.[25] Conditions were not much better at House Rock Spring, where Nielson noted ruefully that it took "a very long time to water 50 head of oxen."[26] Here they had to drive their stock a mile to water and two miles to feed; the close-in grazing had been exhausted. There was more water at Jacob's Pools, but feed was a problem and the road to it was three miles uphill through heavy sand. The next water was at Soap Creek, but few animals would drink there unless they were unusually dry. There was little feed on the gypsum-laden shale. Badger Creek had water in season and the grazing was better, but again there was heavy sand. Browse on both sides of the river near the ferry had been scarce for months. The road to the Little Colorado River certainly was not strewn with roses.

The J. R. Freeman company of ten men, eight wagons, four mules, thirty-five oxen, and seven cows arrived at the ferry on April 18. Frihoff Nielson was a member of this group, which was typical of those now pouring into the Little Colorado bottoms. He recorded that he slept in Emma Lee's alfalfa patch that night to keep the hungry oxen out. Warren Johnson crossed the entire outfit in a little over two hours, taking one wagon and six animals on a trip.[27] Ferriage was paid in flour and molasses. Interestingly, Nielson referred to "Mrs." Lee but "Bro" Johnson, indicating that he, like most Saints, considered the Lees to be outside the sphere of the church.

Smith, Allen, and Lake reached Sunset Crossing on March 22, and the following day Brown and Smith had their inevitable confrontation over leadership. Smith prevailed through sheer arrogance, and in the evening Brown "retired to ponder the situation if not to rest."[28] Before the month was out the three leaders had selected their locations and begun plowing and building. As he was returning to Moenkopi, Brown met Ballenger and his company on April 4. Ballenger was about three weeks behind the other captains. A small party consisting of Rachel and Hannibal Fullmer, Elvira and Benjamin Johnson, and Thomas G. Lowe arrived at Brown's Moenkopi camp on April 29, fulfilling President Young's promise that the devoted girl should labor in the missionary field with her father. Brown happily delivered his daughter's first child on March 25, 1877.

During a lull in the migrant stream, Johnson made a hurried trip to Kanab to pick up his families. Baby Jeremiah was blessed on March 23, 1876, and a few days later the ferryman moved his two wives and four children into the stone trading post at Lee's Ferry. Thus Johnson consolidated his families at his life's mission. For his work at Lee's Ferry, Johnson's name became a household word on the long trail to Arizona.

After the settlements were underway, the considerable traffic to and from Utah depended on Lee's Ferry as the key link in the transportation system. All mail between Utah and Arizona crossed on the ferry. The equipment for crossing the river at this time consisted of the Blythe-Smith ferry and a thirteen and one-half foot skiff, both of which were nearly two and one-half years old. The soft pine used in their construction was waterlogged and rotting, although the oars for the skiff and sweeps for the ferry were newer. The latter were four inch saplings from Buckskin Mountain, cut into twelve foot lengths. A slot was sawed in one end about eighteen to twenty inches deep to accommodate a board one inch thick. When nailed in place, the board extended about three feet to form the blade and provide purchase against the water.

After a severe winter and late spring, warm weather set in suddenly, triggering an early rise in the Colorado. At this time, one of Johnson's crossings scared him. The river was rising fast and he could feel its increased power. Strong cross-currents sometimes barely offered resistance to the river; at other times, they grabbed the sweep fiercely, almost tearing it from his hands. On this day, a sudden swirl had broken the blade at the end of the sapling but he managed to reach shore with the stub. He regarded the episode as a warning that the river now was too high to risk lives in the large boat, so he reverted exclusively to the skiff, making it necessary to take wagons apart before crossing.[29] The draft animals were made to swim, a difficult and time-consuming job but safer than venturing on the fast current with the clumsy, waterlogged ferryboat. Leeway for a left-bank landing had diminished and there was grave danger of being swept into the rapid and down the canyon.

Brigham Young realized that many of his gregarious Saints resented being uprooted from friends and relations. He didn't want them to think they had been sent to the hinterlands and forgotten by those who remained in Utah; consequently, he arranged a visit by high church leaders to bolster morale. He wrote Lot Smith that his own party would be leaving for St. George May 1, and his counselor, Daniel H. Wells, with some apostles and others, would go on to visit the settlements on the Little Colorado.

The presidential party arrived May 9 and immediately plunged into a series of meetings during which it was decided to have a small boat built so the brethren going to Arizona could carry it to the ferry. The skiff was completed in three days and loaded on a wagon. It was twelve feet long, had a bottom beam of four feet two inches, and was twenty inches deep. On the evening of May 16, Young told his son, Brigham, Jr., to take experienced men and examine both crossings of the river, especially the lower one. Hamblin still favored it despite Young's own nephew having selected the upper one as being less dangerous.[30] Brigham, Jr., promised to do so and left with Wells on the seventeenth to rendezvous with the others at Pipe Spring. The entourage was the most impressive array of churchmen to venture so far from the settlements up to this time. With Wells and Brigham, Jr. (who also was an apostle), it included Apostle Erastus Snow, Bishops L. John Nuttall, D. D. McArthur, Lorenzo H. Hatch, Lorenzo W. Roundy, a host of lesser dignitaries, Jacob Hamblin, and a large escort of horsemen from Dixie and Kanab. One member of the escort was a cowboy named Jim Emett.

The company rode into Lee's Ferry shortly after noon on May 24. Counselor Wells acted like he would rather have remained with the presidential party instead of being delegated to make the tiresome journey to the remote settlements. His subsequent actions indicate he wanted to get the distasteful duty over with and return to Salt Lake City. The river was high and still rising as ferryman Johnson explained that the height and increased speed of the current made use of the ferryboat unsafe. It would be necessary to take the wagons apart and cross everything in the skiff. In fact, Johnson said, they had been doing just that for almost a month, and with the newly-delivered craft the job could be performed much more quickly than usual. Although this was only Johnson's second high-water season here, he still had more experience on the Colorado than anyone else present.

Daniel Wells demurred, saying there was insufficient time; the schedule demanded that they cross the river by nightfall. This was Johnson's clue to abandon that which he knew to be right and to bend every effort toward carrying out the wishes of Brigham Young's counselor. To do otherwise would place him in the position of arguing with God, since Mormon society was structured on the premise that the First Presidency was the Oracle of the Lord. Everyone listening expected the ferryman to back down gracefully. But, to their consternation, he showed his mettle by reiterating that it was unsafe to use the large boat on such high water and he would not be responsible under those conditions. He would, however, cooperate fully if President Wells insisted on using the big boat and elected to appoint a temporary captain other than himself for the operation. The company was amazed at his effrontery. Adamant, Wells selected Bishop Lorenzo Roundy to supervise the crossing because he had done such work when the Saints had crossed the Missouri River. They caulked the seams of the dried-out ferryboat and put new blades on the sweeps.

Apostles Young and Snow saddled their horses to ride down to the place Hamblin had recommended for the crossing. In Young's words, "We found it wholly impracticable. It might be crossed from this side but nearly impossible and altogether unsafe to return because of the swift current and little Leaway [sic]. True there were many places where a landing could be made below and life saved but in most cases the boat could not be brought up the stream and would be lost."[31]

The repair work was completed and the ferrying began. It was obvious to all that starting from the usual landing would allow insufficient leeway to reach the left bank before the ferryboat would be swept around the point into the rapid and thence between the rising walls of the canyon. The ferry would have to be towed upstream along the right bank to allow more room for a landing on the left bank. It was three years to the day since John D. Lee had labored to tow the ferryboat upstream so the unappreciative Henry Day could be crossed. Roundy followed Lee's procedure roughly. Teams were hitched to the empty craft, and with two men on board to fend the boat from the bank, she was inched upstream about one-half mile to a shallow cove. Here, half of the animals were driven aboard, the sweeps were manned, and they successfully crossed. The boat was then towed back up the left bank and the return trip made. The operation was repeated for the remainder of the stock. It appeared that Johnson had been overly cautious as two round trips had been made without incident.

For the final crossing, the boat was brought to shore at the regular right-hand landing below the point. Here Hatch's wagon, Wells' carriage, the baggage wagon, the provisions, and bedrolls were loaded. The gross weight was less than either load of livestock, but the boat had been towed upstream empty and the animals driven aboard from the cove. By this time, it was close to sunset and the cooks had just called the brethren to supper. Wells told them to put the food on board and they would eat it on the other side. With the draft animals on the left bank, they fell back on man power and one of the cowboy escorts, Jim Emett, and his saddle horse. Emett took the lead, pulling with his lariat hitched around the saddlehorn. Eight men were aboard: Wells, Nuttall, Roundy, Hatch, Hamblin, Johnson, W. J. Carter, and E. W. Wiltbanks. Roundy and Carter used the sweeps turned end-for-end as poles to keep the boat away from the bank. All went well until they were just short of the cove upstream from a small rocky point that took the full strength of the current. Above this point, the banks curved toward the cliff and the tow rope pulled the boat into the point more than up the river. When the craft was empty the pole operators had been able to hold it offshore. It was necessary to take the boat outside of a large boulder just barely visible because there was insufficient room for passage between it and the shore.

Even if the men had been fresh, it is doubtful they could have bucked the strong current with the loaded ferryboat. Roundy and Carter worked the poles mightily as the boat inched abreast of the point. Then

The drowning of Bishop Roundy, May 24, 1876 (*Harper Goff drawing*).

they were spent; the inshore pull of the towline and the current shoved the craft against the boulder. Roundy shouted to release the tow but it was a few seconds before Emett's horse could back up to provide slack to shake off the hitch. By this time the rounded tip of the boulder had served as an inclined plane that raised the inshore beam of the boat and dipped the opposite gunwale below the surface.[32]

For an agonizing moment she hung there, the starboard gunwale awash. Then the craft careened, the cargo lurched into the river, and the ferry rolled over. Emett had loosened the hitch, but the knot on the end of his lariat became caught and prevented the boat from sliding downstream. The brethren on shore counted heads as they came to the surface, but the tally stopped at seven. Some of the men struggled to shore, but Carter, Hatch, and Johnson were in the grip of the current and were carried downstream. There was no sign of Bishop Roundy. In the confusion of the moment, Emett remained cool; he quickly wheeled his horse and galloped back to the landing where the new skiff was beached. Jacob Hamblin had reached shore almost as soon as Wells and he ran downstream, apparently with the same idea that Emett had. Hamblin arrived out of breath just as Emett and another were launching the skiff, and Hamblin jumped in behind them. They picked up Lorenzo Hatch first as he drifted in the quieter water. Carter and Johnson were hanging on to the baggage wagon near midstream, perilously close to the head of the rapid. Emett bent the oars and reached the wagon just in time and the ferryman was the last to be rescued.[33]

Men paced the bank and hunted among the willows, hoping Roundy had made shore without being seen. But the search was useless and they reluctantly concluded he had drowned. Hatch's wagon with most of its load had lodged on the Pahreah delta, which now was a submerged island, and was salvaged, but the baggage wagon and Wells' carriage went down the river with their supper and most of the provisions. One bit of luck resulted, however; as Emett and Hamblin probed waist-deep in the eddy below the point of the accident, Emett kicked a submerged bedroll that was brought to the surface. It was the one for which they were searching, as some important papers were inside.[34] But this was the only bright ray in the tragedy, and that night the camp was heavy with gloom.

Next day they followed the ferryman's advice, took the wagons apart and crossed what was left of the outfit in the new skiff, now dubbed *The Rescuer*.[35] On May 26, the abbreviated party—ten men instead of the original nineteen—continued the journey in four wagons, while Nuttall and the escort returned to Kanab. Emma Lee is said to have supplied the Wells company with beef from her meager rations. Although the ferry had been saved from going down the river, it was badly damaged with an entire section of cross planks torn from the gunwales. Pending its repair, there would be no question of how crossings were to be made, and no one was inclined to argue with the ferryman's recommendations. High water prevailed well into June, and for three months *The Rescuer* was the only means of providing service.

Daniel Wells and his prestigious company brought cheer to the colonists at Sunset on June 2. They also brought the mail and carried news of the Roundy drowning. At Sunday meeting the general instructions were dispensed, and apparently Erastus Snow kept a straight face when he reportedly said "all he was afraid of was the country was too good and we would not be able to keep it from our enemies."[36] How much stock the brethren placed in this incongruity is not known since nobody openly expressed a dissenting opinion. But when Frihoff G. Nielson was en route to the colony on May 5, he found some Gentiles from Boston camped on a bottom of the Little Colorado River, and he noted that they did not like the country.[37] These sentiments turned out to be true; the New Englanders traveled on to trim the sapling near Leroux Spring that eventually gave Flagstaff its name.[38]

Dan Jones and his three companions came into Allen's camp on June 6 as Wells was engaged in morale-boosting. Jones, irritated that Brown had released Tenney and Smith from the Zuni mission, thereupon released Stewart, Pratt, and Ivins. Although now free to travel as they pleased, the four chose to accompany Wells when he turned homeward the following day. Wells was not sorry to leave the constant wind and sand, the heat, and the alkali-laden water. After a brief stop at Sunset, they went across the river to Ballenger's camp to spend the night. In the evening meeting Wells reiterated Snow's sentiments about the country and their enemies.[39]

As the Wells party left Moenave, only two of the original members of the Jones mission remained: Jones and Ivins. Lot Smith's contentious nature had worn thin on his companions, probably the reason that Stewart and Pratt remained with Brown's men at Moenkopi.[40]

Brown was absent on a claim-staking trip for the Moenkopi mission on both the inbound and outbound appearances of the Wells party. On the latter, Wells, Snow, and Young left him a letter saying he had nothing to do with the four companies of colonists; he was to direct only the Indian Mission.

It would be interesting to know the counselor's thoughts on June 24 as the party came down to the Colorado River and found it higher than when Roundy was lost; even so, the stream had fallen four feet below the peak. He offered no dissent when the wagons were taken apart and crossed piecemeal in the skiff. He and Ivins waited until the animals had made the difficult swim and the brethren were reassembling the wagons before Johnson crossed them. Ivins wrote in his journals: "Bro. Wells took me where the accident to the ferry boat occurred and explained to me his own escape. When we reached a secluded spot on the river we knelt down and he offered thanks to the Lord for bringing us safely over. His prayer was a remarkable one and made a profound impression on me."[41] Apparently Elder Wells realized he had erred on May 24 but he was contrite and had not lost his humility.

The Mormon settlements in Arizona were not self-sufficient; they were supplied from Utah on a continuous basis with both food and equipment, leading to heavy traffic over Lee's Ferry. The universal complaints about ferriage and the rough road over Lee Hill had been more or less ignored until the Wells party joined in criticizing the difficult egress. The First Presidency notified the four captains that an exploring party would be sent to locate a better route and crossing in the eastern part of the territory.[42] Most colonists readily saw that the country to which they had come was not as desirable as that which they had left, and there was discreet grumbling. Some had migrated with marginal supplies; their very survival was threatened unless relief arrived from Utah. When word of the dissatisfaction got back to President Young, he wrote Lot Smith on July 16 to release those whose "hearts were full of murmurings or inclined to apostasy." Conditions in Ballenger's camp were particularly bad because the dam had been washed out, no crops were being raised, and supplies were dwindling. Some of the brethren returned to Utah to prevent starvation, saying they would return that winter, but Captain Ballenger doubted they would.

One of the returnees was Aaron Johnson, who started back with his wife and two children early in August of 1876. The family camped at Bitter Springs on the fifteenth. Aaron comforted them by saying that Utah was only seventy-five miles away and good water soon would replace the alkali-laden fluid they had been drinking for the past six months. He and two-year-old Winifred took the horses to graze. Possibly a sidewinder or a scorpion struck the child, leaving a puncture too small to readily be seen. At any rate, she suddenly became ill and died that evening. The grieving parents hurried to the ferry where Emma prepared the little body for burial two days later at Lee's Ferry.[43]

Since all the lumber had been cut for the St. George Temple, and other rigs could handle the demand in Dixie, Brigham Young decided to send the Mt. Trumbull steam sawmill to the Little Colorado colonists, who would bring teams to the ferry on September 1, hitch them to the same wagons without unloading, and proceed to the new location.[44] Each camp contributed three men, teams, and wagons to bring the sawmill from the ferry. They assembled at Sunset and left there August 19. Smith's contribution is recorded: three men, nine yoke of oxen, one wagon, one mule, and one cow.[45]

At about the same time, A. F. McDonald brought a crew from St. George to repair the ferryboat. They had cut some slender saplings on the mountain for new sweeps. Unfortunately the craft, having spent the summer out of the water on the beach, had dried out, resulting in many leaks. But the wagon train carrying the sawmill arrived on September 1 and the boat had to be used, leaks and all. The heavy wagons, which were pulled by oxen, carried the boilers and massive machinery. Lighter accessories and tools were transferred to the colonists' wagons. After the outfit was safely on the left bank, McDonald and his son hauled the ferryboat up on the beach to put it in proper condition for the low-water season now upon them. They were still caulking the boat on September 2 when Daniel McAllister arrived from Kanab with supplies for Allen's Camp.[46]

The emotional impact of Roundy's death, the physical hardships of the route to Arizona, and the nature of the country that awaited the immigrants continued to cause negative reactions to a call south. The Colorado crossing and the Lee Hill were the most dreaded places of the journey—facts that were appreciated by the hierarchy. But the search for another route had not been successful. Lot Smith and the other captains were notified to continue using the established road until directed otherwise because the eastern track was even worse.

At the St. George Stake Conference of November 4–5, Harrison Pearce and his son John were called to establish a ferry south of St. George where Jacob Hamblin had crossed in 1863. Setting up this ferry was more than finding an alternate route to Arizona; it was insurance in case Emma Lee turned hostile. Hamblin was instructed to guide Pearce to the river and then proceed south to the Beale Road, which he was to follow eastwardly as far as convenient before cutting over to Sunset Crossing. He was to map a new road to the Arizona settlements and, on his return to Kanab, assemble a party and take possession of Surprise Valley. This was the home of the Havasupai Tribe, and only its remote location, to which it was impractical to build a wagon road, prevented an Anglo takeover.[47]

Placing the awkward Blythe ferryboat back into service on September 1 disheartened Warren Johnson. Clearly, a boat accommodating a single wagon and team was more efficient than one capable of carrying a larger payload and was much easier for the ferryman. Once the mass migration was over, most travel was by single outfits, and if more traveled together, a little wait did no harm. By this time, Johnson had developed a good feel for the river in high and low stages with both the skiff and the larger boat. The main problem, however, was in getting the bureaucracy to listen to its expert.

4

The Widow and Her Mite

LEADERS OF THE MORMON CHURCH WERE FULLY AWARE THAT EVEN WITH the deficiencies of hazardous high-water crossings and the difficult hill, the ferry was the key link in the Mormon corridor to Arizona. They did not know how Emma Lee would assess blame for her husband's death or if she would remain faithful to the church. If she turned anti-Mormon, she could make the situation difficult for the Saints. It was logical to continue the search for another crossing and route and not leave all the church's eggs in one basket.

Part of the St. George Temple was dedicated on January 1, 1877—an event destined to increase travel from all directions. This was the only temple in Mormondom and the faithful converged on it as the spokes of a wheel join at the hub. The devoted Saints in the Arizona settlements now had another reason to return to Mother Utah. President Young undoubtedly had this in mind when he directed Jacob Hamblin to aid Harrison Pearce and his son in establishing a ferry south of St. George and to locate a new road to the settlements. Ironically, both Pearce and his son were present at the Mountain Meadows Massacre.

Hamblin led the way to the ancient Paiute crossing that he, Andrew S. Gibbons, and Lewis Greeley found in 1863. According to the Indians, the river was fordable here at its lowest flows; even when it was too deep to cross afoot or on horseback, the flow was quiet and admirably suited for a ferry. Hamblin remained two days and helped build a flat-bottomed skiff that would get the outfit to the other side. Pearce's ferryboat consisted of two planked skiffs lashed together with cross beams, with a double deck of one-inch boards and a railing on each side. As John W. Young described it in January 1878, it was tolerably safe for one wagon of not over three thousand pounds, or four animals.[1]

Hamblin returned to St. George on February 10, 1877, briefed Brigham Young, then described his trip in church on Sunday. This prompted a dispatch to the editor of the *Deseret News* from a metronymic "ARAM" in which the route was described as one of the best natural roads Hamblin ever saw. He is reported to have said "There is only one patch of grass, and that is all the way."[2] Such heavy-handed promotion of a route on

71

which Hamblin and his company had gone fifty-six hours without water in May 1863 can only be explained by the fact that the leadership was insensitive to the welfare of the rank and file and was willing to use Hamblin's name to promote its own projects.[3]

A wagon train was assembled that spring, and some official arm-twisting resulted in a decision to try the southern route. By the time the company met at Mokiac Spring on March 4, it included the John Hunt, John Bushman, and Edwin Westover families; Henry M. Tanner and his recent bride, Eliza Ellen Parkinson; and single men named Blackburn, Bentley, and Cunningham. They had ten wagons, Bentley's carriage, thirty-five head of horses, and thirty cattle.[4] When they reached the river some of the horned stock had been without water for fifty-three hours due to the small outflow of the springs. Pearce ferried them across the Colorado on the nineteenth and twentieth, then took them on a moonlight cruise that was enhanced by the singing of the Hunt sisters and the mellow tones of a guitar.

Wagons had never been taken south of the river, and they had not only to select the best route up Grapevine Wash but to build the road as they went. Before the month had ended, the party divided into three groups in an effort to solve the water problem: the slow recovery rate of the small springs simply could not accommodate both people and animals. This division was maintained until they were able to gather again as one company at the meadows below the San Francisco Peaks. They drove into Allen's camp on April 30; it had taken fifty-eight days from Washington, Utah.

When word of the difficult traverse filtered out to other potential travelers, Harrison Pearce became a ferryman without a business except from occasional prospectors. In 1878, he wrote church headquarters to say that despite his expenditure of $1,737.29 in establishing and maintaining the ferry, "there has not been much travel," and he now owed tithing amounting to $466.59. He asked that the church take over the road and ferry to relieve him of his burden, but the request was ignored.[5]

Although grumbling about the rough road over Lee Hill continued, it was acknowledged that even with this handicap the route over Lee's Ferry was the best. Emma Lee's hand was strengthened, and she continued to be friendly to all travelers with no outward sign of bitterness. Two-way travel was so heavy that Warren Johnson had little time to devote to farming and keeping water on the fields. He needed help and made the problem known to his ecclesiastic superiors, but no relief was forthcoming.

Especially acute was the shortage of feed for animals. Emma had a little patch of alfalfa but it barely sufficed for the milk cows. Travelers had to feed grain and move out quickly or their animals went hungry. Johnson considered it imperative that more alfalfa be raised but he was only one man and could not do everything. Frihoff G. Nielson and his wife were aware of the feed problem when they were returning to Sunset from Utah. He had wisely scheduled his camps so that he could spend a night at Badger Creek where there was grazing, drive the nine and one-half miles to the ferry, cross, and make Navajo Spring his next stop. At the river, he found several wagons ahead of his and did not get across until sundown. He camped on the left bank and was forced to empty their straw-filled bedticks to feed the animals; he was up until one o'clock to keep other livestock away from his feed.[6]

Brigham Young's health deteriorated rapidly in 1877. On August 28, Nuttall received a telegram from Salt Lake City saying the president was very low and urging prayer circles be maintained in all stakes. Young's death occurred at four o'clock in the afternoon of the following day, and the grieving Mormons knew that an era had closed. John H. Standifird recorded the sad news in his journal, undoubtedly expressing a thought common to most Saints when he wrote, "He has been a mighty son of Israel, Kind, Fatherly, and wise in his counsels.... May the God of heaven qualify another to take the lead who will have the work of the Lord at heart. When we had the news about half past four we quit work and felt as though we have lost a dear friend." Young had lived less than six months after Lee's execution, and the sacrifice of his faithful adopted son must have brought great anguish during his final months.

Many had doubts that the church would endure after the loss of its strong president. It not only survived but flourished under the capable leadership of John Taylor, who headed the Twelve Apostles. This quorum governed until Taylor was sustained as the third president of the church on October 6, 1880, at which time he selected George Q. Cannon and Joseph F. Smith as counselors. Wilford Woodruff headed the apostles. Other changes had taken place. When George A. Smith, Brigham's first counselor, died September 1, 1875, the president named his son John W. Young to take his place, and the action was sustained at the General Conference on October 7, 1876. Brigham's nepotism was neutralized in a gentle manner a year after his death when Young and Wells were named counselors to the Twelve Apostles—honorary positions with little real authority. Obviously, Young needed a prestigious position, and Arizona offered the best prospects for one.

John W. Young was a big-time operator, accustomed to good living and going from one important job to another. His father had placed him in charge of Utah's railroads and had bailed him out of his financial mistakes. Now Brigham was dead, and the conservative brethren viewed the flamboyant son as a liability who must not be allowed to manipulate the purse strings. He married his third and fourth wives about the time of his father's death and spent most of the following months dodging officers who sought to hold the women as material witnesses. On August 13, 1877, his property, including his famous museum and its contents, was seized for an indebtedness to the church of $16,673.50.[7]

On November 21, John Taylor notified the leaders in the Arizona settlements that John W. Young was about to visit them and would report their condition to the authorities in Salt Lake City. Young's interest was not entirely directed at the new settlements. His elder brother, Brigham, Jr., had been told by his father before leaving St. George with Daniel Wells in 1876 to examine the possibility of exchanging cloth for Indian wool, or even to set up a plant where Navajo wool could be made into cloth. Evidently, Jacob Hamblin's description of numerous sheep flocks and the cheap prices of the fleece gave him the idea in the first place. John Young also was interested in Hamblin's description of the meadows at the base of the San Francisco Peaks. He hoped to establish a ranch there; other ranches were possible at Hackberry and Truxton Springs. Young began his journey to Arizona from Salt Lake City on December 8, 1877. He was in Kanab two weeks later where Hamblin joined him. They went to St. George and gave Harrison Pearce's ferry a boost by taking the southern route, chiefly in order to have a look at the meadows below the peaks. His party of eight traveled in three vehicles and had thirteen animals.[8]

Shortly after Brigham Young's death, James Brown had been released from his Moenkopi mission. Andrew S. Gibbons was appointed to succeed him in December. Gibbons was an old lieutenant on several of Hamblin's expeditions to the Hopi and had served under Brown at Moenkopi. He assumed his responsibilities on New Year's Day of 1878. He and a companion were returning from a visit to Ballenger's and Smith's camps when they met John W. Young's party at the San Francisco Wash on January 23. Young was then twenty-five days out of St. George, having experienced a cold and disagreeable journey, and the animals were jaded. It was quite apparent to everyone now that the southern route to the Little Colorado was not as good as the eastern road.

Young and his party reached Ballenger's camp, then visited Lot Smith and his people. On January 28, 1878, Young organized the Little Colorado Stake of Zion, designating Lot Smith its president and Jacob Hamblin and Lorenzo Hatch as first and second counselors. The counselor positions were customary, and honorary in this case, because Lot Smith most probably never sought advice of any nature from either man. Smith's camp at that time was named Sunset, Ballenger's was changed to Brigham City, and Allen's location was called Saint Joseph. All were organized under the United Order, a concept that John W. Young promoted out of loyalty to his late father but one that was not particularly favored by John Taylor or George Q. Cannon and some of the apostles.

Starting back to Utah on January 29, Young stopped to size up the prospects at Moenkopi. He then examined Moenave and Willow Springs before moving on toward the ferry. At Moenave, he found the Joseph Foutz family, ex-bishop Farnsworth, and Hensen Walker, whom he placed under Gibbons and the Indian Mission temporarily and put to work improving Willow Springs. All of these brethren figured in Young's future plans. John D. Lee's thirty-four-year-old son, Joseph Hyrum Lee, had joined his "Aunt Rachel" and her family at Moenave and ultimately would take over the ranch. Warren Johnson crossed Young's party on February 6, and Young examined the situation minutely before going on the next day. With his arrival at Kanab, he became the first upper-echelon Mormon to have encircled the Grand Canyon, although it was the second time that Jacob Hamblin had accomplished the feat.

On the same day that John W. Young's party crossed at Pearce's Ferry, Anthony W. Ivins and Erastus Beaman Snow left St. George on a mission to New Mexico. The snow and cold encountered on the southern route also were experienced on the northern road, and probably were worse. They caught up with Lorenzo H. Hatch, C. P. Liston, and James Dean and reached Lee's Ferry on February 15 to find the Colorado River completely frozen—the first time since Mormons had lived there—and learned that Warren Johnson had been advising travelers for several days to cross on the ice. Just the previous day, the first accident since Roundy's drowning had occurred there. A party was crossing six oxen yoked and chained together when the ice gave away in midstream. Only one animal was lost, but they learned not to concentrate so much weight in one place, to separate the yokes and diffuse the load.

After sounding the ice, the Ivins party concluded to risk a crossing. By this time, the temperature was rising and the ice became more dangerous with each passing hour. They unhitched the teams, tied a rope to the wagon tongue, and pulled the wagon across by hand. The ice creaked every step of the way but did not break. They decided not to push their luck any farther but to cut a channel in the ice and cross the rest of the outfit on the ferryboat. The cutting required a full day, and the next heavy wagon was crossed by moonlight on February 18. Some of the loose stock were wild and could not be driven onto the boat; these were caught, thrown, tied, and dragged across the ice. The oxen, although more docile, were easily spooked. They were driven aboard but became frightened by the ice and jumped into the river when in midstream; despite being yoked together, they swam back to the right bank. The men then concluded that the boat was more dangerous than the ice, went a short distance upstream, and drove the animals over. Ivins recorded that he crossed the river thirty-two times during the entire operation.[9]

John W. Young returned to Utah with some grandiose ideas but with very little cash to carry them out. The Saints were wary about extending him credit; however, he managed to obtain the resources to get his Arizona venture started. On April 11 he wrote Lot Smith that his freighters would leave Salt Lake City in two weeks with goods for the wool business. The "goods" consisted of beads and other cheap items that were to be traded for Navajo wool.[10] Richard Blake, with the first load of trade-bait, crossed at Lee's Ferry and reached Moenkopi at the end of the first week in May. From this time on, a small building boom took place there.

Young did not pass up any bets. He called Thales Haskell to Moenkopi to be his clerk and interpreter. Thales, his wife, Margaret, and three children left their home at Pinto on May 12. At the ferry, they were crossed by Emma in the skiff; Johnson was foraging in Kanab and Long

Valley for flour and other essentials. They had three wagons, and their son, not yet eleven, was driving a number of loose cattle and horses. When they started up Lee Hill, Thales hitched all three spans to one wagon and took it to the top; sixteen-year-old Irene and her sister walked in order to block the wagon wheels when the horses stopped to rest. They all returned to the river and did the same thing with the other two wagons. They reached Moenkopi late in the month.[11] It was remarkable how individual Saints would abandon an established home and move to a new location on the whims of their leaders. When Thales reached his new home, he found Young and about twenty men constructing a stone building. Evidently this was to be a home and trading post for Young, as the woolen mill was not built until later.

In late March 1878, Lot Smith wrote John Taylor to tell how a Navajo headman, Pal chin clan na, had seized fifteen horses that had been stolen by Paiutes and renegade Navajos in southern Utah. The *naat'aanii* had accompanied James Brown to Salt Lake City in 1875 and wanted his Mormon friends to know that the animals would be returned to their rightful owners. Smith recommended that the ferryman screen the Indians passing into Utah and refuse passage to the thieves. He also noted that some Mormons stole their brethren's stock and sold them to Indians.[12] Taylor thought the recommendation a good one and ordered it carried out, but the screenings placed too much burden on Johnson and he did not do them for long.

The Kanab Stake Conference of March 9 and 10, 1878, sustained Warren Johnson as presiding priest at Lee's Ferry on the Colorado River.[13] This ranking was virtually the equivalent of bishop, except for the low number of people at Lonely Dell.[14] By this time, Johnson was reconciled to the fact that this isolated place was his permanent home; he tried to adjust accordingly and lead as normal a life as possible. He thought about his genealogy. On May 12, he wrote to a specialist, B. F. Cummings, regarding his ancestry, stating that he was the proprietor of Lee's Ferry, that he lived about eighty miles from the nearest post office and three or four months' time was normal for an exchange of letters. He gave his return address as "Lee's Ferry, Arizona via Kanab, Utah or via Sunset, Arizona."

The river rose early in 1878, and by mid-May Johnson stopped using the clumsy ferryboat and resorted to the reliable skiff. On the twenty-first, Ivins and Snow reached the left bank on their return to Utah from the New Mexico mission. The river was high and rising and the wind blowing a gale. A couple of shots brought Johnson across in the skiff, but he advised waiting for the wind to die down before crossing; while waiting, they disassembled the wagon. It was nearly sunset before they crossed, the last trip being made in the twilight. The wagon box, with both ends removed, was towed behind the skiff while the horses swam, one at a time. Unlike Daniel Wells, Ivins willingly accepted the ferryman's advice.[15]

The first white child who was not a Lee was born at Lee's Ferry on August 3, 1878. The parents were Warren and Samantha Nelson Johnson;

the boy was named Frank Tilton after his father's lineage. Frank claimed he was "born in a wagon box under a cottonwood, on the bank of Pahreah Creek," the same spot where Samantha's cabin was later built.

The settlements were continually being bolstered with a stream of immigrants, and morale was kept up by letting the first wave of settlers know they had not been forgotten. On August 10, Taylor notified Lot Smith that Apostle Erastus Snow and other high-ranking brethren would visit the settlements. They had already left Salt Lake City. A power struggle had existed at Parowan for at least two years between William H. Dame and the brothers Jesse and Silas Smith. Erastus Snow decided to call the Smiths to other pastures and requested Jesse N. accompany him on his forthcoming trip to Arizona. Smith joined Snow at Orderville on September 8.

By the time the party left the Johnson settlement on September 11, it consisted of Apostle Snow, Presidents Ira N. Hinckley, L. John Nuttall, G. H. Oliphant, Jesse N. Smith, E. A. Noble, D. H. Williams, and John Starley. They traveled in one carriage and two wagons that were drawn by twelve mules; a bell mare rounded out the animals. The group reached Lee's Ferry on the fourteenth and was given dinner by Sisters Lee and Johnson. Warren Johnson had the outfit crossed over by 5 P.M., in three round trips. As they climbed Lee Hill, the officials determined to look for another crossing and road on their way home. Smith joined many others in describing the hill in this general opinion: "The ascent was bad and the descent difficult and dangerous, the worst road I ever saw traveled with vehicles."[16]

Apostle Snow had now seen the Colorado at both stages: that of a raging lion, as in 1876, and in its present quiet state. Now, when it was docile, it appeared more favorable for Jacob Hamblin's choice of crossing sites. He thought that they could establish a lower crossing that would be usable with reasonable safety during nine months of the year. Relatively little traffic occurred during the period of high water in the early summer, and that could be handled as it had been—by skiff. The main problems would be the small left-bank landing area and building a dugway up the cliff. Snow's party returned on its northbound leg on October 30. While the wagons were being inched up the steep west spur of the Lee Hill, Snow, Nuttall, and Hinckley looked over the prospective lower site and liked what they saw. The dugway route from the river to the rim did not appear as formidable as it had from the right bank.

The ferryboat, however, was old and leaked badly. They thought it should be replaced as soon as possible. Johnson crossed Snow's party in two trips and they went into camp near Emma Lee's cabin. To overcome his apprehensions about the left-bank landing, they suggested attaching the boat to an overhead steel cable. When they moved out in the morning, the ferryman knew that change was forthcoming; the only question was how soon it would arrive. On December 5, Erastus Snow wrote to L. John Nuttall regarding a new ferryboat and road for Lee's Ferry, suggesting he consult with Johnson on the details.

On September 20, Snow had informed Jesse Smith of his plan to split the Arizona settlements into two stakes, but it was several weeks before the plan became known.[17] On November 27, John Taylor wrote Lot Smith that the Arizona settlements would be split into eastern and western stakes, the dividing point being Berardo's ranch at Puerco Crossing. The Eastern Arizona Stake of Zion would be under the presidency of Jesse N. Smith; the Western Stake, including Moenkopi, Moenave, and Lee's Ferry, would be under Lot Smith.[18]

Mormon migration continued at a constant pace, but it didn't all come from Utah. Hyrum Smith Phelps led a company from Montpelier, Idaho, late in 1878. They paused at the ferry on December 1, and on the following day the fourth white child was born there to Phelps and his second wife, Elizabeth. On the third day after the birth, they ascended the Lee Hill—making Gove Phelps the youngest person to traverse the difficult track. The Phelps party was the second Mormon pioneer company to settle in Mesa and the Salt River Valley.[19]

Meanwhile, Jesse N. Smith had gathered a constituency of ten men, six women, and fourteen children to make new homes in eastern Arizona. The party included the reliable Joseph Fish and his family. On December 3, they left Paragonah in ten wagons, each loaded with about two thousand pounds. Besides the teams, they had a number of loose cattle and horses. It was a typical group of pioneers. They reached the Colorado River on the eighteenth, and Warren Johnson spent all of the following day ferrying the outfit to the other side, taking one wagon and four animals at a load. The charges were a dollar for each wagon and seventy-five cents for each animal.

Among other newcomers to Arizona was a New Englander, Franklin Marquis French, who drifted in from Silver Reef that winter and paused at the ferry to placer-mine the sands along the river.[20] He and Warren Johnson soon became acquainted and found they had several things in common; both had lived in Boston and had been better educated than most people in the West at that time. French helped Johnson at the ferry and was invited to dinner; a friendship developed. He learned Emma's story from the ferryman and through him met the widow. Another friendship developed that proved beneficial to them both.

John W. Young and three companions left Moenkopi on November 8 for Salt Lake City. They crossed the Colorado two days later, noting that the proposed improvements would be of great benefit to the traveling public. The place must remain in Mormon hands. Young had determined to start construction of his woolen mill at Moenkopi immediately and to buy all the Navajo wool that could be gathered. Several freight wagons carrying machinery for the mill crossed the river that winter, and the brethren at the Indian Mission labored more for Young than to spread the faith among the natives. In fact, the mission now could more accurately be described as the John W. Young enterprise. He remained in the capital until February before starting south again. He paused in Kanab on the twenty-fifth and

Emma Batchelor Lee
French, ca. 1890
(*P. T. Reilly Collection,
Cline Library, Northern
Arizona University*).

Franklin M. French
seated between two of
his sons (*Gladwell
Richardson Collection,
Arizona Historical
Society-Pioneer
Museum*).

agreed to give L. John Nuttall a contract to freight Navajo wool to Salt Lake City for two and one quarter cents per pound.

In the meantime, a constant exchange of letters had taken place between Warren Johnson, Nuttall, Snow, and various bishops who would contribute labor and material for the new ferryboat and road. The only part of Johnson's recommendations they accepted was that the old Blythe ferry, now waterlogged and rotting, was not worth running down to the new crossing. They rejected his proposal to reduce the boat to the size that would accommodate only one wagon and team, preferring instead to retain the two wagons and teams concept. Clearly the men making the decisions had never propelled a forty-five foot flat-bottomed scow across the Colorado with crude sweeps. Young, fully aware of the intended ferry improvements, evidently had been authorized by John Taylor to determine Emma Lee's attitude about selling her interest to the church before the changes were made. When he arrived at the river on March 1, he was shocked to find that an outsider had expressed interest in purchasing Emma's holdings. Although she showed no intention of disposing of her claim, Young was uneasy as he started for Moenkopi.

After French arrived at the ferry, the inevitable change came swiftly. Apostle Wilford Woodruff had gone into exile to escape arrest by U.S. marshals over the polygamy issue; according to L. John Nuttall, Woodruff's sixth wife had informed on him even though they had been divorced. The apostle hid in St. George for some time, then went surreptitiously to Kanab before losing himself in the emptiness of Arizona. Using the pseudonym of Lewis Allen, he left Johnson on March 10, hidden in the wagon of William Johnson and Brigham Y. Duffin. They arrived at Lee's Ferry on the fourteenth and were crossed by Warren Johnson, who spoke privately to the apostle and informed him that a Gentile merchant now living there was interested in both Emma and the ferry. He called Lee Hill "The Hogback," recording in his diary that "it was the worst hill, ridge, or mountain that I ever attempted to cross with a team and wagon on Earth. We had four horses on a wagon of 1,500 pound weight and for two rods we could only gain from four to twenty-four inches with all the power of the horses and two men rolling the hind wheels. Going down the other side was still more steep, rocky and sandy which would make it much worse than going up on the north side."[21]

Erastus Snow had expressed the desire to superintend the building of the new dugway, but this appears to have been wishful thinking because his many duties would not allow it. Various wards responded with the manpower they could furnish, and Bishop Leithead drew up a list of lumber that would be needed for the new boat. Nuttall did his share by asking all the Saints to respond favorably to the apostle's request for work on the road.

While plans to improve the ferry were proceeding under the local authorities, other plans were being hatched at the ranch by Emma Lee, Franklin French, and Warren Johnson. Possibly there was collusion between the three, motivated by the men's desire that the widow receive simple justice. It also is possible that Johnson, anxious to preserve his own interest, perceived the deepening relationship between Emma and French and knew it would be unfortunate if the ferry passed out of Mormon hands. He had little money and only a squatter's rights to ten sandy acres above Emma's claim, but he was willing to go into debt to purchase her equity. His interests would be served best if the church bought her out and left him in charge, as there was little chance of his being able to make the deal himself.

On April 21, Nuttall received a letter from Warren Johnson telling him that Emma Lee had tendered a written offer to sell the ferry for three thousand dollars to John W. Young. Nuttall immediately telegraphed the news to Erastus Snow.[22] Apostle Woodruff wrote to John Taylor and the Twelve Apostles of the importance of Lee's Ferry and of the Gentile's interest in both Emma Lee and the ferry.[23] He did not mention her offer to John W. Young. On the afternoon of the twenty-fourth, Nuttall received a direct telegram from Taylor instructing him to "Send a judicious man to John W. Young, request him to arrange for Lee's Ferry for the church. Let the messenger inform Sister Lee on his way that he comes for that purpose and that the church as before stated will make all satisfactory with her. If agreeable to herself we would like Sister Lee to remain in charge. Send this along."[24]

Zadok Knapp Judd, Jr., was selected to carry the message, and he left on horseback for the ferry on the morning of April 25. Nuttall was exceptionally busy writing instructions for Bishop Leithead regarding the new ferryboat and to John Seamon for cutting the lumber from which it would be built. He was leaving shortly to become clerk to his father-in-law, John Taylor, who was immersed in settling the Brigham Young estate. Nuttall was badly needed in both places because of his knowledge and ability, and affairs at Kanab slowed perceptibly after he left.

Emma Lee's negotiations benefited from the slow communications of the time, miscommunication among the Saints, and a bit of clever negotiation. John W. Young was pushing the construction of his home-trading post and the woolen mill, but he took twelve days to show Apostle Woodruff the ranch below the San Francisco Peaks that he had claimed in January 1878. Before leaving on this jaunt, he sent Joseph L. Foutz to the ferry to accept Emma Lee's offer and to bind her to the deal with a rough-draft contract but without actually doing anything to seal the bargain on his part. He expected her to be pliable. Young Judd brought Nuttall's message shortly after their return, but Foutz had already been sent back to the river to close the deal.

Foutz was the victim of some clever bargaining. He unwittingly carried a false idea of the situation at the ferry back to Moenkopi, which resulted in making the brethren eager to close the deal on Emma's terms. Billy Lee appears to have been coached in the key role and he carried it off as a veteran performer; he "managed" to be talking to someone when Foutz was within hearing, saying that Emma had received two offers from Gentiles of $5,000 and $4,000 besides the one from Foutz of $3,000 and that she was going to accept the higher, whether it came from Mormon or Gentile.[25] The inference was that French was behind the $5,000 offer, and perhaps Johnson lent his name to the other, although the bidders were not identified. At any rate, Foutz could not make the deal because of the demand for cash. He returned to Moenkopi with the refusal.

The main point of disagreement was whether Emma should receive cash or would accept a note. Aware that Young was away on a trip, they waited until he had returned, then Emma and Warren Johnson went to Moenkopi and rejected his offer of stock and a note. Young was not accustomed to opposition from the brethren. He wrote a vague summary for President John Taylor, justifying the actions he had taken, enclosed a copy of the agreement for the sale, and sent both by Judd, who was ready to take the trail back to Kanab.[26]

In the negotiations with Foutz at Lee's Ferry, Emma was represented by Franklin French and her eighteen-year-old son, Billy, while Warren Johnson participated when he was not busy with the ferry. Again Foutz had very limited bargaining latitude and could not accede to all of French's requirements, but the deal was closed orally for $500 in cash and $2,500 in stock, wagons, and accessories. Foutz handed over a draft signed by John W. Young for $500. Warren Johnson then wrote a letter for Emma Lee to L. John Nuttall, asking him to cash the draft on John Taylor and to forward the money to her by some reliable person. Her advisors saw to it that she would not be stuck with a worthless piece of paper.[27] Then French and Billy rode to Moenkopi to examine the livestock to be provided by that group. Warren Johnson now was out of the bidding, if indeed he had ever been in it.

After Foutz returned to Moenkopi with Emma's oral commitment to the sale, John W. Young, his nephew Howard O. Young, and Foutz went to the ferry to work out the final details and, hopefully, to sign the papers. This was completed on May 16, 1879, but not without argument and aggravation from both sides.[28] French and Johnson opposed Young and Foutz, and again the ferryman encountered the maneuvering of his ecclesiastical superior with the simple logic and sense of justice that could have been derived from the Ten Commandments. In fact, it was clear that Johnson and Young had different interpretations of the eighth and tenth laws of Moses. In the end, agreement was reached and Young gave Emma an order on Lot Smith for $1,432 worth of horned stock.

When Emma finally signed the papers, Young revealed his resentment of Johnson's opposition by placing Foutz in charge of the ferry with Johnson as his assistant. This brought a strong reaction: Warren accused the counselor of crowding him out after he had been called to the ferry on a lifetime mission. In time, Johnson cooled down and agreed to remain as assistant, at least for the moment. Ironically, Foutz had no knowledge of the river or the ferry and no interest in taking it over, but he knew better than to express his sentiments. Young, Foutz, and Johnson then examined the lower crossing site favored by Hamblin and Snow. It was mid-May, the river was high and rising fast and the crossing did not appear at all safe. Young later wrote that if the rope should break or the boat miss the landing he would want a month's supply of food on board, would steer for mid-river, and not expect to land until he came to the mouth of the Virgin. He didn't know it but he would have been unlikely to have gotten that far.

Young then evaluated the over-all situation and came up with the best solution yet devised. He drew a map showing the present ferry located at the fort, the lower site and proposed dugway, the point where Roundy drowned, where they must tow the boat to cross in high water, and the road over Lee Hill. He proposed to move the crossing one-quarter mile above the present ferry site and to build a new road along the red shale under Lee Hill. He thought the old ferry could be used for the rest of the season by reinforcing the decomposing gunwales. However, he suggested a new ferry-boat be constructed similar to the one in use at Harrison Pearce's crossing: two flat-bottomed craft, each with four water-tight compartments and secured at a proper spacing with cross timbers, covered with a safe floor, and a railing installed along each beam. He advocated that four good hard-wood oars and ten life preservers be kept on board, and the boat be swung from a rope in midstream to let the current do the work.[29]

The description of Emma's land claim is interesting. The starting point was where the road from the north came down Two Mile Wash to follow along the river. From there, the boundary ran along the dugway road northeasterly to the cliff on the right mouth of Pahreah Canyon, then northerly along the bluffs west of the yard and sheds to the fence between Emma's land and Johnson's ten acres. From there, the boundary was easterly across the canyon and creek to the east cliff, then southerly along the cliff to its junction with the northern cliff of the Colorado Canyon and easterly along it to where the cliff comes to the river's edge. The right bank of the river was the southern boundary.

The contract stated that Emma was to have possession of her house and alfalfa until September, but she didn't wait that long. With her younger children and French, she pulled out at the end of June, intending to travel in easy stages, collect her stock at Moenkopi and the other settlements, and ultimately settle near the head of the Little Colorado River. Billy Lee, now nearly nineteen, was left at the ferry to receive the five hundred dollars and then catch up with the wagons.

Cashing Young's draft was no easy matter. Church authorities in southern Utah could not raise $500 in cash, so the money had to come from Salt Lake City. Nuttall, now in the north, entrusted the money to his son, Leonard, who left the city on July 11 with a load of freight for the ferry that included two hundred feet of one inch rope for a towline.[30] Young Nuttall reached Kanab on August 6, and the ferry a few days later, but Billy Lee did not get the money until after his mother had changed her name from Lee to French.[31] When Billy departed for good, Warren Johnson moved his first family—Permelia and her three children—into the Lee cabin. It wasn't much of an improvement but at least three graves were not just outside the door.[32] It was here, on November 8, that Permelia gave birth to her fourth child, a girl whom they named Nancy.

Earlier in the year Warren Johnson had been directed to apply for a post office at Lee's Ferry. The application was granted April 23, 1879, but it was several weeks before the news reached him.[33] Shortly after, he went to Sunset where Frihoff G. Neilson, as Justice of the Peace, signed his bond and administered the oath of postmaster.[34]

Migration to Arizona continued unabated; many new families were sent to replace the recalcitrants and grumblers at the Little Colorado. Among those newly called were Newman Brown and his wife, Lora Ann. The couple made it to Arizona, but just barely. Two days short of the Colorado River, Newman died—some of his family think it was from scurvy—and he was buried in the little cemetery on Johnson's land claim.[35] He was less than three months from his fiftieth birthday.

Although Joseph Foutz technically was in charge of the ferry, Warren Johnson made all the decisions, collected the ferriage, and farmed as he could while doing the chores. It was apparent that he was being punished by Young, and the matter was discussed at high levels. Erastus Snow broached the subject to John Taylor, and the acting head of the church had Nuttall send the following telegram to the apostle: "In regard to the ferry and Bro Johnson use your best Judgement. Elder Nuttall cannot be spared to return to his stake at present. John Taylor."[36] With this blessing from his chief, Erastus Snow, on November 30, 1879, gave Warren Johnson sole jurisdiction of the church operation at Lee's Ferry.[37] Foutz quietly faded from the ferry scene and Johnson began the period that was to make him known as the kindly ferryman to many travelers passing between Utah and Arizona.

5

Building the Oasis

Warren Johnson was under no illusion that his mission at Lee's Ferry would be a bed of roses. There was much work to be done and he had no help; church officials had not responded to his request for an assistant. In operating the big boat, those he ferried had to work one of the sweeps, then help get the boat back to the right bank, after which they would be returned to the left bank in the skiff—repetitious labor that was necessary under the circumstances. Occasionally, he crossed a southbound party and picked up a northbound wagon for the return trip, but this was not often. Keeping the dam in repair and the fields planted, watered, and harvested was a full-time job in itself, but he also had to gather wood, feed and milk the cows, and take care of a hundred other chores. His oldest girl was not quite eight and his oldest son had yet to see four years. Johnson actually was doing the work of three men and doing it well by concentrating on what was necessary to survive. It was impossible to get everything done and few improvements were made even though he started early and finished late.

The capable Bishop James Leithead of Long Valley was chosen to design the new ferryboat, get the lumber cut at John Seamon's sawmill, and build it. Unfortunately, the size of the craft had been determined by high-level officials who were not inclined to take advice from the man who knew the river crossing best. Johnson had recommended building a small boat that would cross one wagon and team at a time, but his advice was disregarded in favor of a clumsy monster so ungainly as to be practically worthless except in low water. It was better suited to serve as a scow on a small lake than to carry several tons across a fast-flowing river with troublesome, changing currents, propelled only by two men with crude sweeps. Johnson knew, when he saw the plan, that God had not inspired the brethren who designed it, but he said nothing and resolved to do his best.

John Seamon's sawmill cut 8,195 board-feet of lumber for the job at sixteen dollars per thousand. Seven different freighters hauled varying amounts of lumber to Johnson settlement during the summer of 1879, but there it sat. It was only by chance that Erastus Snow put the facts together and got the project moving by telegraphing James Leithead. After this, things moved rapidly. Freight cost twelve dollars per thousand from

Warren M. Johnson, September 1882 (*P. T. Reilly Collection, Cline Library, Northern Arizona University*).

Seamon's to Johnson, but from there to Lee's Ferry the cost went up to forty-eight dollars per thousand. The two gunwales were the most difficult to transport because they were one by three by forty-seven feet in length; they were the key structural members of the boat and each had to be in one piece. Each gunwale was strapped between front and rear wagon axles. Pulled by oxen, it was difficult to negotiate some mountain curves as well as rises and dips in the road with this extended wheel base, but eventually the timbers reached the river. A coil of one inch Manila rope, nine hundred seventy-five feet long, had been hauled from Zion's Cooperative Institution to the river in early summer. The hinges for the aprons and the sheave-brackets to control the boat from the overhead rope were being made by a blacksmith at Orderville, but this phase lagged because no one had a clear idea as to how the boat should be suspended.

James Leithead, Reuben Broadbent, Lorenzo Watson, and Charles S. Cram began construction early in December 1879. Since there was no feed for their animals at the ferry, the men sent their team back and depended on some passing traveler to come along and transport them to the settlements. The ferryboat was completed in January except for the hinged aprons that would allow wagons to be driven on and off the deck. To Johnson's consternation the boat turned out to be forty-seven feet long, with a beam of thirteen and one-half feet, and when empty drew six inches of water. Of the lumber freighted to the river, six thousand board feet were used. The Manila rope was not hung because the suspension problem was not settled. The operation ended on a low note when no northbound wagons appeared and the four men had to walk home in the dead of winter, hiring a pair of scrawny ponies from the ferryman to carry their bedding, tools, and provisions. Allowing Warren Johnson $30 for the use of his span, the total bill for the ferryboat came to $1,158.51.[1]

The First Presidency and Twelve Apostles met February 23 and made official Warren Johnson's appointment as proprietor of the ferry. At the same time, they established a double set of ferry fees, one for the missionaries and one for "other travel." The missionary rates were: wagon and single team, $2.00; wagon and double team, $2.50; loose stock per head, $0.25; and horseman and horse, $1.00. The rates for other travelers were: wagon and single team, $3.00; wagon and double team, $4.00; loose stock per head, $0.35; and horseman and horse, $1.50.[2] The crossing was referred to as "Pahreah Ferry" in an effort to disassociate it with the unsavory name of its founder. Although usually employed in official correspondence, the new name did not catch on with the public.

Wilford Woodruff and Lot Smith and his son set out from Sunset on March 3, headed for St. George. Five days later they reached the ferry and were crossed by Johnson, who extended his hospitality to the trio. The river was rising and Woodruff saw for himself the difficulty inherent in using too large a boat on the river. Before leaving in the morning, he looked over Johnson's ferry accounts and liked what he saw. He instructed the ferryman to keep half of the ferriage and all he could make from the farm.[3] Woodruff's two visits with Johnson were the beginning of a good relationship that lasted through their lifetimes. Both Smith and Woodruff promised to carry the problems to headquarters and try to have them resolved, principally the matters of ferry fees, use of the awkward new ferryboat, the need to raise more alfalfa, and to obtain auxiliary help.

When Jesse N. Smith was in St. George preparing to return to Snowflake, he thought he might try the southern route. However, Harrison Pearce, who was in town, told him that no one was tending his ferry nor was a boat there now.[4] Smith and his two wives then returned the way they had come and camped near Johnson's house—near Emma Lee's old cabin—on the night of April 28. They found that feed for the animals was exhausted between Badger Creek and Navajo Spring.

Food for humans also was scarce, not only in the Arizona settlements but in southern Utah as well. On May 12, Johnson wrote Stake President Nuttall that conditions were deplorable. Many travelers paid their ferriage in livestock, but the poor animals found no feed on the range and about half of them died of starvation. Some travelers had to be trusted for their ferriage because they had no spare stock. The river, now rising fast, was within two feet of the flow when Roundy drowned. The rope still was not hung and the new boat was too clumsy to be used, so crossings were made by skiff. When a wagon was taken apart, four or five trips were needed to get the outfit to the other side.[5]

Later in the month, Nuttall, still in Salt Lake City, notified Johnson that some ferry rates had been revised downward and a new, single fee would apply to all travelers. The previous missionary rates would be used. He asked the ferryman to submit reports of the business done, noting the number of people, wagons, and animals crossing, the kind and amount of payment received, and the farm income.[6] Johnson sent his first accounting to President Taylor on July 1, stating that he now had $88.76 on hand belonging to the trustee-in-trust. His full account covering the period from May 1 to June 30, 1880, was: cash received, $97.00; flour, $8.60; dried peaches, $9.55; order from J. W. Young, $8.00; one axe, $1.50; cold chisel, $.25; Indian goods, $5.20; W. M. Johnson assumes $9.50; due, $24.00; for a total of $163.70.[7]

Newly appointed Apostle Francis W. Lyman was not present at the conference that sustained him but was returning from visits to the eastern Utah and Arizona settlements with Erastus Snow, William H. Dame, and some others. On October 3 they climbed the infamous Lee Hill to be met at its foot by Warren Johnson. Lyman recorded that during the crossing the passengers were forced to bail to keep the old boat from sinking, thus inferring that Johnson was using the Blythe ferry in preference to the newer but clumsier craft. He did not record whether Apostle Snow commented on this state of affairs. Johnson invited the ecclesiastics to camp in his yard and provided plenty of good alfalfa for the hungry teams. Before leaving in the morning, Snow and Lyman examined the proposed lower crossing. The river was low this time of year, displaying no signs of danger, and the men concluded that the crossing should be moved downstream. For the first time, another element was introduced when it was proposed that the Arizona legislature be petitioned to appropriate five thousand dollars to construct a four-hundred-yard dugway to the first bench.[8]

On December 7, 1880, William J. Palmer organized a Utah branch of the Denver & Rio Grande Railway—named the Sevier Valley Railway—to build a track from Ogden south to Arizona. Another Palmer subsidiary, the Northern Arizona Railway, was incorporated in Arizona and slated to cross at or near Lee's Ferry, then connect with the Utah track at the state line. The Sevier Valley Railway planned a second route to extend east from Salina through Salina Pass, cross the Green and Grand Rivers and tie in with the Denver & Rio Grande Railway west of Grand Junction. Two survey parties left Salt Lake City on December 16 to mark preliminary routes; one group headed for Salina Pass and the other to Lee's Ferry. The critical areas for each track were Salina Pass and a crossing of the Colorado River at or near Lee's Ferry. Late in the year, the chief engineer, M. T. Burgess, learned that the Utah Southern, a one-time Mormon line now controlled by Jay Gould's Union Pacific, planned to dispute the occupation of Salina Pass. As the history of railroading appears to point out, those who occupy strategic areas with superior forces seem to wind up with the legal title. Burgess sent an urgent message to the Lee's Ferry crew diverting it to the Salina Pass area in an effort to get the necessary surveys made before the Utah Southern could swing into effective action.[9]

In the spring of 1880, David K. Udall was called to Arizona to serve as bishop of St. Johns. Udall and his family left Kanab in late August and crossed the Colorado on the big boat December 7; three weeks later they reached St. Johns. Erastus Snow had selected a new townsite only a few days earlier; the urgency was based on getting the land before some outsider beat them to it. Udall arranged a good deal, then headed back to Utah six weeks after their arrival. At a meeting on December 9, the church leadership approved the steps he had taken and issued a tithing order to release 450 cows to Udall from the Canaan herd. Another telegram was sent to Warren Johnson to provide the bishop with 600 pounds of hay and to charge the trustee for the ferriage of the teams and loose stock.[10] The gathering of the stock was the last service performed by Jim Emett—the young cowboy who was towing the ferry when Roundy drowned—as his superintendency of the Pipe Spring Ranch was nearing an end. The Canaan management could furnish only 275 head, however, resulting in the settlements providing the remainder. Lot Smith contributed 100 cows. Udall, A. S. Gibbons, and James Ramsey, aided by some of the Canaan cowboys, drove the herd to the river and found it frozen, only the second time since the place had been settled. As when Ivins had crossed on the ice two years before, the Johnson children sprinkled buckets of sand on the frozen surface to give the animals better footing.

The fall of 1880 and spring of 1881 saw heavy migration into Arizona. When en route to Salt Lake City, Udall met nearly one hundred wagons going to the southern territory. Having no knowledge that families had been called to build up the stake, he concluded that contrary to Mormon practice, many were starting out on their own volition. Lot Smith was instructed by the presidency and apostles to divert the travelers to the St. Johns area and to continue the practice until Udall had at least one hundred families or said he had enough people to control the politics of Apache County.[11]

One such family heading for Arizona was that of Sam Stowe, his wife, Mary Ellenor Avery Stowe, and some of their ten children ranging in age from three to twenty-three years. They probably should not have been on the road because Mary Ellenor was quite advanced in pregnancy. A pioneer tragedy unfolded at Lee's Ferry on December 18, 1880, when the mother went into labor and, although this was her eleventh birthing experience, complications set in that Permelia Johnson could not control. Neither mother nor child survived. They were buried in a single coffin between the graves of little Winifred Johnson and Newman Brown.[12] In a few days, the grieving family headed south.

Warren Johnson wrote to Wilford Woodruff on Christmas Eve to give a general account of affairs at the ferry. He provided a statement of the business conducted while Foutz was in charge and noted that Emma Lee's ferriage, until she moved, was included in the price paid for the ferry. He said that the Leithead-Broadbent boat was completed, in use, and was just what they wanted for low-water crossings. However, it was not safe in high water because it was so cumbersome, and the Manila rope had never been installed. Then Johnson made a pitch for his most urgent need: a smaller ferryboat to accommodate one wagon and team at a time, and a new skiff. The old skiff was rotten and so unsafe that he had taken the unauthorized initiative to have Leithead build a new, larger, twenty-foot rowboat. In conclusion, he said he had ferried three hundred ninety-three wagons since August 1, 1880.[13]

Meanwhile, with Salina Pass secured for the Sevier Valley Railway, the survey crew once again headed for Lee's Ferry. They arrived in early spring and by mid-April found the best place to build a bridge across Marble Canyon—about five miles downstream from the ferry—and had staked a rail course south to Willow Spring. They were preparing to survey for a track through House Rock Valley to Johnson, but a change in orders diverted them elsewhere.[14]

When Warren Johnson wrote of this to the church president, he again castigated the big boat for high-water use and noted that since he had received no reply to his letter of four months ago, they apparently did not sanction his ordering the new skiff. He said the old one was so rotten he could put his fingers through the hull, and rather than use it he would prefer to pay for the new one with his own funds. This letter probably caused the authorities to approve the building of the new skiff and legalize Leithead's construction of it.[15]

Several years had gone by during which neither the local nor general authorities had done anything to solve Johnson's chronic need of auxiliary labor. Finally, in the spring of 1881 the ferryman took matters into his own hands and persuaded his brother-in-law, David Brinkerhoff, to become his partner in operating the ranch. Warren and David had married sisters, the daughters of Price William Nelson; Samantha became Warren's second wife, and her younger sister, Lydia, became David's first. Both the Nelsons and Brinkerhoffs lived in Glendale, which had been Johnson's home before he came to the ferry. David was capable, energetic, ambitious, and an excellent farmer—the ideal partner for Johnson because he possessed many varied skills that were needed to thrive in this remote spot.

Almost immediately, Lee's Ferry began to change. First on the agenda was additional housing. The men pulled logs out of the Pahreah delta and raised two cabins a short distance south of Emma's old house, now occupied by Permelia and her family. The larger cabin was for Samantha and her brood; David, Lydia Ann, and their children moved into the second. Johnson added to the ferry's vital statistics on April 3, 1880, when his second wife, Samantha, gave birth to her fourth child and his eighth. The little girl was named Lydia Ann. Of his eight living children, only two were boys. The fourth child of David and Lydia Ann was born at Lee's Ferry on March 23, 1882. The boy, named William, interrupted the string of Johnson births there after the Lees. As usual, Permelia and Samantha acted as midwives.

Although David Brinkerhoff helped operate the ferry as needed, his main forte was farming. Johnson and Brinkerhoff soon made plans to bring more land under cultivation, raise more alfalfa, and plant more orchards and a vineyard. Alfalfa promised greater benefit than any other crop, as the natural range for ten miles on both sides of the ferry was exhausted from overuse. Most travelers were aware there was no feed close to the ferry; they planned their camps so they could cross quickly near mid-day and get far enough away to where there was some grazing. As this practice became standard, the range became bare from Soap Creek to past Navajo Spring. Until more alfalfa could be grown, Johnson was in desperate need of sufficient feed for his cows. He had explored for additional range after the Pahreah flats had been stripped, and he found surprisingly good range on the sandy plateau just west of his house. Getting the cows to this range was more difficult, necessitating driving them a mile and one-half on the road back to Kanab, then up a gulch to the low bench. The animals had to be taken out in the morning and then brought back in time for the evening milking. His oldest children—Mary, not yet eight, and Lizzie, less than six—performed the job faithfully, and the cows fed on virgin range that had not been overgrazed by migrant stock, thus keeping the family in milk.

Johnson discovered a spring higher up the slope, almost under the great red cliff. It was in the head of a ravine, and since it appeared so suddenly and sank quickly into the sandy wash, he named it "Phantom Spring."[16] He had climbed a sandy slope hunting for a strayed animal when he spotted several cottonwoods that led him to the water. He then realized that if he built a trail in the soft red shale directly west of his house, the long drives could be shortened to a matter of minutes. He appears to have constructed the trail during the winter of 1880–81.[17]

Apostles Snow and Brigham Young, Jr., met with quite a surprise when they arrived at the ferry on August 28. The area was a beehive of activity, although not quite as busy as it had been.[18] A large company of surveyors and engineers for the Denver & Rio Grande Railway was encamped, picking up the work of the group that had left in April. Some minor excavation had been done to test the base for a bridge over the Marble Gorge, and lines were being surveyed north toward Johnson and south toward the Little Colorado. Naturally there was much crossing of the river, and the engineers immediately saw that the problem of Lee Hill and lack of a lower ferry had to be overcome. When they spoke of putting in their own ferry and building a dugway up the cliff to the bench, Warren Johnson realized that something had to be done quickly or this valuable crossing would slip from Mormon control. He stalled the engineers by telling them that a ferry was already planned for the lower site and a Mormon crew would arrive any day to begin dugway construction.

Whether or not Johnson knew it, a company under Daniel Seegmiller and Archibald McNeil was headed for Arizona to repair the Sunset dam that had washed out July 21. When they arrived at the ferry, Johnson wisely requisitioned their services to begin work on the dugway. He unquestionably exceeded his authority, but his bold action was for the good of Zion and so obviously the correct thing to do that he willingly went out on a limb. The construction men had no difficulty in seeing the logic of his action. They managed to get the lower quarter of the dugway completed before exhausting Johnson's meager supply of powder, and they traveled on to the Little Colorado in mid-August.

Apostles Snow and Young realized that the ferryman had overstepped his authority, but they approved the action and hoped President Taylor and the other apostles would concur. They proceeded on their way and reached Sunset on September 9. Two days later, they wrote a letter to the president explaining the situation and asking for his approval to send Johnson enough powder to complete the job.[19] Then, assuming approval would be forthcoming, they obtained the powder through John W. Young, who was doing contract work on the Atlantic and Pacific Railway roadbed, and when Seegmiller and McNeil completed the dam, Snow scheduled them to stop at the ferry on their return to finish the dugway. The work crew, augmented by a contingent from Moenkopi, completed the dugway late in November 1881. F. G. Nielson, traveling from Utah to Sunset, arrived at the ferry on November 23 and was crossed on the big boat the following day. He was one of the last to use the original ferry in low water and to double-team up Lee Hill. Had he come two weeks later, he could have used the lower crossing and the new dugway.[20]

It was an eventful day when the large ferryboat was run down to the new crossing. The Leithead skiff was already there, having been used to ferry alfalfa and food to the work crew who were camped on the left rim. Three men were in the boat circling in the eddy. Women and children gathered on the boulder bar at the foot of Pahreah Riffle. Warren Johnson and David Brinkerhoff manned the power-sweeps while another man manipulated a third sweep rigged as a steering rudder. Two others stood in the bow and stern, coils of rope in hand, ready to throw a line to the men in the skiff in case they missed the eddy.

Excitement was high when the cumbersome craft rounded the point and headed down the channel. The main concern was to avoid a large rock about two-thirds of the way down, yet not get so close to the left bank as to neutralize use of the port sweep. They shot the gap beautifully and the watchers could see spray outlined against the red cliffs as they crashed through the waves. The boat was steered into the quiet water below the mouth of the tributary down which the road came, and was easily rowed to the right landing. Then they made several crossings with those who had watched the operation.[21]

Although the lower crossing eliminated climbing Lee Hill, it presented new problems for both travelers and ferryman. The site was a good mile below the mouth of Pahreah Canyon, and those wanting to cross no longer could fire a gun from the ledge to alert the ferryman that business was waiting. Johnson solved this by having his children scan the approach when they drove the cows to the bench after the morning milking, as white canvas tops could be seen for a long distance. Horsemen were more difficult to pick out but most travelers were accommodated with no more than a short wait. The new road joined the old one at a Y at the foot of the Lee Hill. Some rocks were placed in a line across the one not in use at the time. Young Jeremiah and Frank Johnson fell heir to the job of changing the rocks from one fork to the other twice a year.

Warren Johnson received an unpleasant surprise five days before Christmas. A letter from L. John Nuttall of Salt Lake City arrived, acknowledging receipt of his third-quarter report, but questioning the charge of hay and supplies to the McNeil Company. President Taylor, he said, disclaimed knowing these brethren and emphasized that he had not authorized anyone to draw supplies against the ferry account; if Johnson elected to honor such orders without the approval of the trustee-in-trust, he did so at his own responsibility.[22] The ferryman was flabbergasted, as he naturally assumed that the leadership was coordinated in all activities and that Erastus Snow handled affairs under Taylor's direction. It is inconceivable that the letter written by Apostles Snow and Young from Sunset on September 11 had not been read and discussed by the authorities by December 10, and that they were not aware of the situation. Now, instead of being congratulated for his enterprise in performing a valuable service to Mormondom, Johnson was threatened with having to pay the cost of the improvement out of his own pocket. It would appear that Nuttall's letter expressed executive pique that the ferryman had acted without going through official channels, but had he not acted, the lower ferry would be in the hands of the railroad company.

Johnson was so disgusted that he immediately wrote to President Taylor. He was respectful in explaining the entire affair but noted that Apostle Snow not only had approved the action but directed phases of it, and traffic now was crossing at the lower ferry and over the new dugway. He concluded the letter by saying that since the road work would be charged to him, the question arises: "If I pay for making the new road, who will own the lower ferry?" Finally he said that a release from his having anything to do with the ferry would be acceptable any time it was granted.[23] John Taylor thus learned what Daniel H. Wells and John W. Young could have told him—that this quiet man at the isolated ferry would not compromise his principles or stand for being pushed around. Johnson's letter arrived in Salt Lake City on the morning of January 7, 1882, and it evoked a reply that afternoon. Taylor was conciliatory, made no mention of lower ferry ownership, and assured the ferryman that he was in no danger of having to pay for the new road. He acknowledged receipt of the ferry reports and $578.75 in cash which was credited to the ferry account. He concluded by advising him to follow Brother Snow's instructions.[24]

With the matter of payment for the lower dugway put to rest, the ferryman bent his energies toward learning the intricacies of the lower crossing. The height of the river caused considerable variation in the right-to-left crossing technique. When the river was extremely low, they could row upstream in the slack water—nose into current—and a few hard strokes would land them on the small beach; when the river was higher, the current and eddy were more intense and it was difficult to make the landing. In general, the higher the water, the more difficult it was to cross below the riffle. In addition, another person had to be ready to leap ashore with the line because the offshore end of the unwieldy craft was still in the current when the bow was grounded. The seasonal rise set in early in 1882 and the river was unusually high in March. Johnson was still learning the peculiarities of this site in rising water when the current tore the sweep from his grasp, breaking his left arm just above the wrist. The crossing was touch and go and they barely made the landing. Now the full load of the entire ferry and farming operation fell on David Brinkerhoff.

For some time, Warren Johnson had hoped to convert his paternal family to the Mormon faith. Since he had become a one-armed man on a job requiring two good arms, he felt this was an ideal time to make the attempt if the authorities would agree. He asked permission of President Taylor to go on a mission to New England and the east coast. The letter was passed to Erastus Snow, who agreed to approve the trip if the ferry were left in the hands of David Brinkerhoff. David was willing, and Johnson departed on April 12. The trip was mostly in vain. He enjoyed seeing old friends in Iowa where he had taught school twenty years before, but noted ruefully that they almost hooted him out of the hall when he preached Mormonism. He wrote: "Polygamy is all they talk about." He visited his brother Levi in Vineland, New Jersey, and his mother in Bridgewater, New Hampshire, and stopped in Philadelphia, New York, and Boston. He failed to convert any of his family and wrote mournfully on September 20 as he departed for Utah: "The tears ran down my bro. Levi's cheeks as we took breakfast this morning. I leave my people with the feeling that all of them have rejected the gospel. May God grant to bring them to knowledge of the truth. It was a sorrowful parting, as in all probability I shall not see them all in this life again. Oh, may I be faithful, that I may do them good in this life or in the life to come."[25]

He was back in Salt Lake City on October 6 and attended General Conference that afternoon and the following two days. For more than a week he discussed the ferry and his needs with the authorities, but he failed to convince them that a smaller ferryboat was preferable to the ungainly scow they had forced upon him. They finally compromised by giving him two craft in the temple yard that were too small to carry a wagon and more or less useless for his purpose. They did agree to have the boats rebuilt for his need at Seamon's sawmill. Johnson met Howard O. Spencer, who was in the city for conference, and arranged to travel south with him. When they started homeward on the twenty-first, one of the flatboats overhung the tailgate. At Orderville, he purchased a load of flour, bacon, and apples, and contracted for other loads of flour, potatoes, lumber, oats, and corn to come later. He obtained a saddle horse at Johnson and arrived at his home November 7, 1882.[26]

Spencer had previously urged Brinkerhoff to bring more land under cultivation. David wrote to Stake President Nuttall, noting that they had raised three times the normal amount of alfalfa this year and now had five tons of tithing hay on hand, with a final cutting still to be done. He suggested leveling about eight acres on the flat across the creek, and claimed it would be easy to run water through a flume from the present reservoir. He already had rooted a large number of grape cuttings, and fruit trees were cheap and easy to obtain. Mainly, Brinkerhoff was angling to get paid for improving the farm that he and Johnson now shared in full, and he also desired the loan of three hundred dollars that was the accumulated ferriage belonging to the trustee.[27] His proposition was rejected but church authorities approved their bringing more land under cultivation for their own benefit. The two went to work on the project and made considerable progress that winter in clearing and leveling the plot.

Someone must have thought Warren Johnson didn't have enough to do because he was called on a mission in February. He and seven others joined Apostles Brigham Young, Jr., and Heber J. Grant in visiting several Navajo camps and the Hopi in Third Mesa. They concluded the jaunt at

Sunset when the quarterly conference opened on March 17. The group disbanded and Johnson returned home. He had been away for more than three weeks and progress in breaking the new farmland had suffered.[28]

On March 30, the Denver & Rio Grande completed the track between Grand Junction and Salt Lake City, which in effect connected Denver and the Mormon capital. Regular narrow-gage passenger service between the two cities was established on April 7, 1883.[29] This advance in transportation reduced some travel over Lee's Ferry, and ferry travel decreased more as the years went on. Traveling apostles—and they were always on the go—went by rail wherever possible, yet most rank and file Saints, too poor to travel by rail, relied on wagons and buggies. In his first-quarter report to President Taylor, Johnson noted that there had been less than the usual amount of travel although a few outfits were crossed every week. He further noted that the river was lower than normal but still too high to allow use of the big boat at the lower crossing; consequently, all wagons had to be disassembled and everything crossed in the skiff. He did not mention his need for a smaller, one-wagon ferry at the upper crossing, but the inference was plain. He said his arm was improving slowly and he hoped to have normal use of it eventually.[30]

Although Johnson and Brinkerhoff failed to bring the new plot across the creek into cultivation in time for a spring planting, they did get the land cleared and leveled. After much discussion, they abandoned the plan to use water from the existing dam; instead, they would build another dam a half mile up the canyon and bring water to the new plot in a ditch, running laterals to the various fields as needed, by the use of headgates. At this time, the cultivated land southeast of the houses—almost seven acres—was devoted to alfalfa. The orchard was on four acres northwest of the hayfield, between the houses and the creek. The large garden lay between the orchard and the road that crossed the creek just below the dam. On the upper side of the road, they raised cane and melons, and beyond that was the vineyard, which was the most difficult to water. Some twenty-five acres were being cultivated, and the men calculated that the upper site would give them possibly ten more.

Pahreah River emptied into the Colorado just east of the alfalfa field, and at times of high-water, the fishing was very good in the mouth of the Pahreah. The largest fish, known as "Colorado River salmon," sometimes weighed over thirty-five pounds. The women and children did most of the angling because the men could not spare the time. One day in early June, Samantha, Lydia, and the older girls went to the mouth of the creek hoping to make a good catch. The younger children were playing together in one of the cabins, and the Brinkerhoff baby was asleep in the other. Fourteen-month-old William awoke and wandered outside in his bare feet. They found him standing in the sun, crying; something obviously was wrong. No mark was found, yet the child rapidly grew worse; he died June 5 and was buried beside Winifred Johnson. David and Lydia Brinkerhoff now had three living children; Warren had ten, five each by his two wives.

The concept of trading with Indians at the ferry to keep them from going into the settlements had long been abandoned. Some still bartered there, but most preferred going the extra distance into Kanab where goods and food were available in greater variety. After he had been denied payment after a crossing, Johnson learned to exact his fee before he performed the service. This often led to lengthy bargaining because Navajos thought of each transaction as an individual matter and did not comprehend a set fee for a given service. Johnson knew they were poor and that bargaining for the fee was a serious business with them, so he always conducted each transaction carefully and concluded by taking what the tribesman could afford. The ferriage might be a buckskin, a quarter of venison, a sack of pinyon nuts, or a live sheep. Sometimes they paid in wool that the Johnson girls washed, carded, dyed, and spun just as their Navajo sisters did, then knitted the yarn into stockings for the entire family.

One afternoon, two Navajos arrived and argued about the fee for the rest of the day. When no agreement was reached, Johnson returned to the ranch, leaving the Indians camped on the river bank. He went down to the crossing early in the morning to check the ferry and was exasperated to see the two men aboard the big boat in mid-river being carried into the canyon. He jumped into the skiff, overtook them, and managed to get the ferry into slack water and then back to the landing. The Indians were rather shaken by this time and he had no trouble in obtaining a fee.

Another time, two Navajo men and a woman came to the upper crossing during high water and, not seeing any evidence of the ferryman, decided to use the skiff and swim their horses behind. An animal gave them trouble in midstream and the skiff capsized. One of the men drowned, and as he was being carried downstream the woman ran wailing along the river's edge, throwing half her possessions into the water—flour, cornmeal, dried fruit and meat.[31] Indian travel was heaviest in the fall when the natives customarily headed for Buckskin Mountain to hunt and gather pinyon nuts.

Life at the ferry had slipped into a routine that saw little change. Wash day was followed by one devoted to ironing so that all could have clean clothes for Sunday School. They made their own soap, a mixture of animal fat, lye, and cottonwood ashes. Thursday was "fast day," and the practice was adhered to faithfully.[32] Mary and Lizzie took over the milking, an event that was anything but predictable. The two girls would climb up on the roof of the milk shed, throw a little hay down to the wild cows, then drop a loop over their heads; after tying them up, they got down to the milking. All of the children, as soon as they were old enough, helped in the garden. Dinner was taken in midday; suppers were light, always consisting of bread and milk or cornmeal mush and milk. Chickens and turkeys provided plenty of eggs and meat, and Warren killed a beef often enough to keep the families in red meat. He had a sorghum mill; when the cane was ready they would strip the leaves while it was still growing, cut the stalks, and run them through the mill to extract the juice. The juice was boiled in kettles over an open fire until it reached the consistency of syrup.

When John Standifird moved to Arizona in 1878, he carried four colonies of bees in his wagon. He left one hive with Warren Johnson because the protracted confinement was causing the condition of the insects to deteriorate. The bees had multiplied and Johnson subsequently bought additional colonies in Kanab. He now had more than thirty hives, from which he collected several hundred pounds of honey each year. The garden produced well and in time the trees would bear fruit. Except for flour and cornmeal, the ranch was well on the way to being self-sustaining.

When the lower ferry was made usable in December 1881, Apostle Snow had instructed the ferryman to increase the fare by fifty percent to pay for the dugway. This increase was intended to reimburse the trustee for building the road. In his first-quarter report for 1884, Johnson wrote that the new road now was paid for and he had an excess that could be applied to future improvements. He asked if he should continue to charge the higher price or lower the fee.[33] "Pahreah Ferry" was one of the few enterprises that brought a steady, dependable flow of cash to the church coffers, and Johnson's reliability and honesty began to be more fully appreciated.

The winter of 1883–84 was very severe. It was unusually cold and repeated storms piled up the snow. There was much suffering and many cattle perished.[34] Travel was restricted, and people huddled in their homes on light rations, waiting for better weather. Life at the ferry was less severe than in town, however, as a nearly inexhaustible wood supply was available on the Pahreah delta. In another letter to President Taylor, Johnson noted that the river was rising very fast and was already higher than when Bishop Roundy drowned; it was about fourteen feet above the low-water mark at the lower ferry.[35] The record winter snowfall was beginning to make its presence felt. The spring runoff in 1882 had provided a good guide as to when they would stop using the lower crossing, and the runoff of 1883 had verified their experience. When the river poured over a large rock in midstream about two-thirds of the way down from the upper crossing, it was time to change to the upper crossing.[36] This became known as the "Gage Rock."

Both of Johnson's letters brought responses. On May 9 he was told to continue the higher ferriage until directed otherwise, and to accumulate the excess in a fund for future improvements on which he would be instructed. He was not to make any appropriations on his own volition. Then, as an indication of how closely the authorities followed local conditions, he was informed that an order in favor of C. L. Christensen had been issued for one thousand pounds of flour. He was asked to submit monthly reports on the condition of the river so they could notify those traveling to Arizona.[37] Two weeks later, he received word from L. John Nuttall to expect quite a number of wagons to cross into Arizona at an early date. He could just as easily have been told that thirty-five families had been called to bolster the St. Johns Stake. He received Nuttall's letter on June 1 and dispatched a reply the next day, saying the river was four feet higher than it had ever been since he came there nine years before. No white man had seen the river higher. It now was almost impossible to reach the ferry due to the inundated roads. He said he was glad to issue the flour to Bro. Christensen and could provide more if needed.[38]

Up to this time, mail to Lee's Ferry had been carried by whoever happened to be traveling there. Services were unreliable at best, nonexistent when there were no travelers. Postmaster Johnson complained for a long time before the Post Office Department agreed to establish carrier service between Johnson settlement and Lee's Ferry. Early that summer, Lawrence C. Mariger of Kanab obtained a subcontract from W. R. Judd of Grantsville to carry the mail twice a week from Johnson to the ferry. Nuttall had to endorse Mariger before he was given the contract.[39]

C. L. Christensen and his wife, Ann, left Moenkopi on June 10 and reached the ferry on the twelfth, where he intended to meet his brother who was bringing his family for a visit. The Colorado was a raging torrent, roily and heavy with drift. Johnson used the skiff to bring the Christensens over, but the river was too high to risk swimming the animals. The water level was now seven feet higher than the ferryman had ever seen it, and it was still rising. Half of the road between the house and lower ferry was inundated, and it was impossible to reach the house with a wagon.[40] Christensen helped cross a Paiute on horseback and a man with three horses. They embarked from the skiff a short distance from the ranch house, and because of the swift current, they towed the boat upstream before heading back across. The line broke and the skiff was swept downstream. Both men knelt and prayed that the boat would come ashore and it did, just below the mouth of the Pahreah.

The river peaked on Wednesday, June 18, 1884.[41] It flowed over both dugways and almost reached the houses. The alfalfa field was completely covered, the orchard was nearly so. A few days previously, the children had watched large fish come in from the creek mouth to nibble alfalfa as the field was being inundated. On the day of the peak, Jeremiah saw a rabbit, encircled by the incoming water, forced to hop into the fork of a tree to keep dry. He rescued the rabbit and later cut a notch to record the high-water mark on this tree.[42]

Christensen's brother and family could not get their wagon past the wash above the lower crossing, so they left it and began walking over the boulder bars and ravines toward Pahreah Canyon. They reached the houses about ten o'clock in the evening where a joyous reunion took place. The river was perceptibly lower on Thursday, and near sundown Johnson crossed the two families. In the words of the diarist, "We had to toe and Row the Boat from near the house clear to the crossing. With Joy and fears we left the Shore and Comendid our Selves to God and the angry Deep Waters and in a few minutes We Landed Safe on the South Shore full of Joy."[43]

The river continued to fall slowly but it was several days before the alfalfa was exposed, little the worse for its lengthy irrigation. The river remained high, and Johnson wrote Nuttall on July 7 that the water had receded only two and one-half feet from its peak. On the thirtieth, Johnson sent in the second-quarter report, noting that the water now was falling fast and he was crossing travelers at the upper ferry. He expected it would be five or six weeks before the lower site could be used. The St. Johns missionaries were complaining bitterly to him about the ferry rates, claiming they should have reduced fares because of having been called to that country.[44]

When the W. C. Allen family, returning to Utah for good, came to the turnoff to the lower crossing, the rocks across it directed them to climb the Lee Hill. The mother and children were so frightened of the precipitous road that they refused to ride in the wagon and got out and walked. To make their distaste for the place complete, a strong wind, heralding another storm, blew in as they crossed the river. They did not feel safe until they landed on the right bank. Allen had been one of the original four captains of the 1876 migration and this was a representative climax to his trying Arizona adventure.[45]

C. L. Christensen came from Tuba City on October 30 to perform six weeks of Mormon labor for Warren Johnson. He put in the last two days of October to settle the ferry bill for himself and his brother, then started the tithing labor on November 1. Chris Lingo was large and powerful, a welcome addition to the labor force. Johnson used him wherever needed, but especially on the ferry and digging the ditch.[46]

Meanwhile, things were not going well for the Saints. After the Edmunds Act was passed in March 1882, a clamor was raised against polygamy, and the acrimony was reflected against the brethren in Utah and Arizona. The situation in Arizona territory was complicated by a political power struggle in Apache County. D. K. Udall, C. I. Kempe, P. J. Christopherson, A. M. Tenney, W. J. Flake, and J. N. Skousen had been indicted for polygamy; the latter five were convicted in Prescott. Sumner Howard, who had prosecuted the John D. Lee case, sentenced Tenney, Christopherson, and Kempe to three and one-half years in the Detroit House of Correction. After seeing their companions convicted under an Arizona bigamy law, Skousen and Flake pleaded guilty and received six months in the territorial prison at Yuma. All were given fines of five hundred dollars.

The proceedings shook the Arizona brethren to the core. Several prominent polygamists decided to let things cool off by going to Utah to consult President Taylor about their best course of action. Jesse N. Smith, John Standifird, Joseph Fish, and Lorenzo H. Hatch left Snowflake at 6 A.M. on December 6. They drove all night through bitter cold and reached St. Joseph at daybreak. John Bushman joined them there and used his fresh team to get them to Sunset where Lot Smith was waiting with yet another rested span. Near Willow Spring they encountered snow, which became a foot deep by the time they reached Cedar Ridge. They arrived at the ferry just before dark on December 14.

Brinkerhoff and Christensen rowed over in the skiff to get help to bail out the ferryboat. That done, they crossed teams and wagons. Informed that some ten non-Mormons were there, the brethren kept out of sight until the outsiders left in the morning, hurried over by the ferryman. The party remained at the ranch all day and, after Mormon fashion, held a meeting in which all spoke. Lot Smith, noticing that Chris Lingo's shoes were so worn they virtually were sandals, gave him a pair of shoes. In the recipient's own words, "Until this time I had suffered very much with Cold wet feet, my Shoes being very old. Them shoes was thankfully Received."[47] Ice was in the river and Chris Lingo's feet were nearly frozen. Henry M. Tanner, one of Bushman's neighbors in St. Joseph, had started for Utah ahead of the others but encountered snow too deep to get through on Buckskin Mountain. He turned back to the ferry, joined the group there, and left with it on December 16.

The Smith party arrived in Salt Lake City on New Years Day to begin a series of meetings. The main items discussed were Gentile persecution of Mormons for polygamy and the prospect of purchasing land in Mexico where a city of refuge would be built. Smith left on the train with the presidential party January 3. He got off at St. Joseph on the seventh—a far cry from the twenty-five days expended on the trip north by wagon.

Christensen, his tithing labor apparently worked out, departed for home on January 19. One more tribulation came his way when his draft animal broke its hobbles and went fourteen miles back to the river. Poor Chris had to walk this distance with the skin peeling from his frostbitten heels, but such was the life of a pioneer. He merely said the experience caused him "a little vexation of Spirit and pain of Boddy."[48]

In a letter sent December 16, President Taylor allowed Warren Johnson to use up to eight hundred dollars from ferriage due the trustee to build a new home for his family. In addition, Johnson was given free rein to make other such improvements as he deemed necessary. Evidently this was in appreciation of the steady cash flow he had sent to headquarters. Taylor also made a slight change in ferry fees for persons with more than fifty head of loose stock; other charges were to remain the same. Of the total ferry income, one-third was paid to the trustee-in-trust, one-third was kept by Johnson, and one-third was used for improvements.[49] When Johnson sent in his fourth-quarter report, he included sixty dollars and noted that he had not yet been troubled with visits from their "friends," the federal officials hunting for polygamists.

On January 18, 1885, President Taylor appointed a committee of four—Moses Thatcher, A. F. McDonald, Lot Smith, and Christopher Layton—to purchase a land tract in Chihuahua where the city of refuge was to be built.[50] These men were scheduled to meet at St. Joseph, Arizona, and from there proceed with animals into Mexico. Near the end of the month, the president advised all who were exposed to persecution under the Edmunds Act to go to the Rio Casas Grandes in Chihuahua.[51] This accelerated traffic over Lee's Ferry.

To circumvent Utah marshals, the Saints built a new settlement in Arizona just south of the territorial border. Some of Utah's polygamists established second homes here for their other families. Erastus Snow suggested the name "Fredonia"—standing for "Free Women"—but during the hard early years it was popularly known as "Hardscrabble" or "Lickskillet." Similar border-hopping villages also were established, allowing polygamists to evade Arizona officials by crossing northwards and Utah officials by crossing southwards.

Rudger Clawson had been convicted of polygamy under the Edmunds Act in October 1884; his appeal was denied on March 3, 1885. The ruling upheld the constitutionality of the law and, in effect, opened the hunting season on polygamists. At this time, many polygamists were fleeing into Mexico. It was rumored that Warren Johnson would have been easy to apprehend, but officers recognized his service to all travelers and elected not to bother him. Johnson attended the Kanab Stake Conference on March 7 and 8, and in speaking to the gathering noted that the name had been changed from Lee's Ferry Branch to Pahreah Ferry Branch of the stake. There still were only two families living at the ferry. Life was rough but he said it might soon become better known if a number of the brethren found it necessary to go into hiding.[52]

He did not report the first-quarter business until May, yet he sent eighty dollars to John Taylor on April 21. His letter elaborated on ferry practice and made an indirect pitch for the small ferryboat he had so long advocated for the upper crossing. He noted that in high water, when the large boat could not be used, they still had to charge two-fifty for each wagon and fifty cents for towing each animal. The charge roughly represented the number of trips that had to be made; only one animal could be crossed at a time, and without a small, one-wagon boat to be used in high water, such crossings resulted in more work than was necessary.[53]

Knowing that high-water crossings and use of Lee Hill must continue during the summers, Johnson and Brinkerhoff decided to lay out a bypass that would eliminate the steepest and roughest section during the winter of 1884–85. They began moving earth the following March. The bypass forked from the Lee Hill road at the edge of the flat just above the willows. It followed the contours of the low hills in easy grades and joined the old road in less than a mile and one-quarter from the river. It was a vast improvement for south-bound travelers but had little effect for those heading north. The pick and shovel work would not be completed for a long time. Johnson used Indian labor when available. Indians generally were good workers but few would remain for more than two or three weeks. Johnson boarded them, fed them the same food he and his family ate, and paid a small wage. There was always more work than hands to do it, as the ditch was being dug from the proposed new damsite farther up the canyon. The new ditch was to be about one-half mile in length and although the digging was easy, there was much earth to move. The ditch ran down the northeast side of the creek and brought water only to the upper field; the old dam still brought water to the lower field.

Since many of the leading brethren were polygamists and were in or en route to Mexico, the Mormon settlements along the Little Colorado took on a deserted appearance. Sunset, especially, looked like a ghost village. Lot Smith's tyranny had driven many good men to other settlements, and when he went to Mexico there was not much left. Samantha's brother, Price W. Nelson, was named acting bishop there in February 1884, but a year later he was a bishop without a flock, serving more as a caretaker to the once-bustling settlement. He appears to have gone to Glendale where some of his family lived, then returned to work at the ferry. On August 12, he and his wife Louise again crossed the river, undoubtedly southbound.[54] In his autobiography, Nelson claimed that he worked for Warren Johnson in the summer of 1885 and remained there for one year. Possibly his crossing on August 12 was a trip to Sunset to pick up some personal property.[55]

Nelson's presence meant that both Warren Johnson and David Brinkerhoff could make occasional trips to the settlements. In September, David attended the quarterly conference at Kanab to represent the Pahreah Ferry Branch. He reported that their irrigation ditches had been washed away, referring undoubtedly to the new system for the upper ranch. In December, he reciprocated by tending the ferry so that Warren could attend the conference held in Orderville on the fifth and sixth. In all of these meetings the old Lee's Ferry name was used. Renaming the place had never caught on and the only time "Pahreah Ferry" was employed was in correspondence between Johnson and church headquarters.

The Nelsons added to the ferry's birth record on September 26, 1885, when their son Mark James was born. Slightly over a month later, on October 30, Permelia broke her string of girls by giving birth to a boy whom they named Jonathan Smith after her father. Samantha echoed Permelia's performance when she gave birth to a boy on February 2, 1886. The child was named Price William in honor of her brother. Exactly two weeks later, Lydia Ann duplicated the event when her boy was born. Again their brother was honored by bestowing his name on his sister's child. Two days after the birth, David Brinkerhoff took his family over Lee Hill and headed for a new home at Tuba City.

Price Nelson was a stubborn man, for even after witnessing the trouble polygamy had wrought, he began thinking about taking a second wife. The girl who so stirred him was Charlotte Annie, the fifteen-year-old daughter of Seth Benjamin Tanner, a stalwart of Moenkopi from the days of James Brown. Price first obtained the consent of his wife and Seth, then courted her during the fall. Finally, after he had pursued her to Mormon Dairy, she accepted his proposal. He picked her up at Moenkopi late in December, brought her to the ferry for a few days, then went to St. George where they were married in the temple on January 23, 1886. It was from events such as this that the road between the Little Colorado settlements and St. George acquired the name "Honeymoon Trail."[56]

November brought word that David Brinkerhoff had been appointed the new bishop of Tuba City. His departure would slow the rate of improvements at the ferry but the Johnsons were glad that his ability had been recognized, and thought he was just the man for the job. Friction had developed in Tuba City between the local leaders and a pair of independent souls who sought to obtain land and water rights that were controlled by local authorities. Apostle Snow borrowed a page from Brigham Young's method of handling disputes by appointing a new bishop. Besides, Bishop Farnsworth planned to leave for Mexico to escape the consequences of the law regarding bigamy. David Brinkerhoff was ordained bishop of Moenkopi Ward on January 31, 1886.

An old customer, F. G. Nielson, stayed with Johnson on March 1. He had left St. George on February 22 en route to his latest home at Ramah, New Mexico. As with most of the rank and file elders, he still traveled by wagon instead of the train. He was ferried over the Colorado at 10 A.M. and noted that he made it to the top of Lee Hill by 11:00 A.M.[57] If anyone ever made better time, it is not recorded. The Johnson cutoff was not yet usable, and for some reason the lower ferry was not operating.

Samuel Clevenger and his wife were getting on in years, which was the reason they decided to sell their small ranch in Gila County and return to Utah. They were childless but had a fifteen-year-old adopted daughter, Jessie. Their outfit consisted of two sturdy wagons, a good team of six horses, and some loose stock. They had hired a man named Frank Wilson as teamster and camp roustabout, and a black man, John A. Johnson, as wrangler. The party reached the ferry early in May and decided to recruit the animals, purchasing alfalfa from the ferryman. This was the first time the Johnson children had ever seen a Negro, but their father assured them there were many more like him living in the eastern states. A few days later, the outfit pulled out and started north.

They camped at the top of Buckskin Mountain on May 20. The following morning Clevenger and Wilson became embroiled in a heated argument over the latter's attention to Jessie. John Johnson was out rounding up the horses, and Jessie was the only witness to what took place. The argument turned violent; Wilson grabbed a camp axe and murdered first Samuel and then his wife. He buried the bodies in a shallow grave, broke camp, then headed out with the girl. Catching up with the wrangler, he said the old couple had met friends and would join them soon. Wilson later gave John Johnson two hundred dollars and a good team of horses, told him of the murders, and warned him to keep quiet or he would be charged. Eventually, animals exposed the bodies and the crime was revealed.

Wilson, Jessie, and Johnson were apprehended and taken to Prescott for trial.[58] Sheriff W. J. Mulverson of Prescott captured one of the suspects in Eureka, Nevada.[59] The ferry had been a key point at which he hoped to apprehend the fugitives, and as part of the search, Warren Johnson loaned a horse to deputy Young, who made a fast ride to and from Kanab. Young claimed he returned the animal in good condition, the fee for its use had been paid, and the case was considered closed. Johnson contended otherwise, saying the horse was so severely used that it was ruined, and he put in a claim for remuneration. Mulverson rejected the ferryman's case and Johnson dropped the matter, believing he could not win in a Gentile court.[60]

By the summer of 1886, Warren Johnson had enough money to begin construction of a house that would shelter both of his families. He hired William James Frazier McAllister, a carpenter of note who drew up a plan from the ferryman's description of his needs, and provided a list of lumber that could be ordered in installments without slowing construction. Several loads of lumber were freighted to the ferry that summer. McAllister promised to start work as soon as he had made some water troughs for Dan Seegmiller, who was running the cattle ranch at Cane for the Orderville United Order, controlled at the time by proxy owners for John W. Young. It was a momentous day for the Johnsons when work was begun on their new home. The first step was to pull down Emma Lee's old cabin where Permelia had lived. It was cleared and everything was moved into the cabin vacated by the Brinkerhoffs. A few of the sounder logs were added to the woodpile, and the remainder was burnt. This was the last vestige of John D. and Emma Lee's presence. When the ashes were cool and the ground had been worked over with a drag, they began gathering and hauling foundation stones.[61]

Shortly after David Brinkerhoff was ordained bishop at Tuba City, C. L. Christensen, his first wife, Severina, and her children fled to Utah to escape the officers of Flagstaff. His second wife, Ann, remained behind. He visited his brother in Sanpete County, then worked his way south to St. George where he did temple work. On June 20, Chris and his family, along with some others, started for Tuba City. They arrived at Lee's Ferry late in the month and stayed about two days helping Warren Johnson lay the foundation for his home to pay for their ferry bill.[62]

Warren extracted 1,113 pounds of honey between July and October 30, storing it in barrels. It was a welcome change from the usual pioneer sorghum, and both were the major attractions for Indian labor, as sweets were lacking in native diets. Will McAllister, the foremost apiarist in Kanab, and the one from whom Johnson had obtained most of his bees, came early in the fall to help gather the honey. However, McAllister's main job was building the house, a slow job because he worked alone most of the time.

Christensen was tired of dodging marshals. He decided to return to Utah where the proportion of his brethren to Gentiles was in his favor. He and his family left Tuba City for good late in September and reached the Colorado on October 1.[63] Johnson crossed them in the skiff after disassembling the wagon; the animals were towed one at a time. Chris paid the ferryman a mare on a sixty dollar flour debt and gave him his saddle for the ferriage. Johnson used the skiff at this time of low water because no one was available to help row the large boat over at the lower crossing, and Chris did not elect to cross Lee Hill both on foot and with his wagon.

Johnson sent his third-quarter report and $25 cash to Salt Lake City on November 1, noting that no accidents had occurred this season. Travel had been light compared to other years. When the final report was compiled and sent to headquarters, John Taylor—in his last letter to the ferryman—acknowledged that the church's share of the ferriage for 1886 had come to $118.[64] Although the total ferry income seemingly had amounted to a mere $354 for the year, this sum represented only the cash received. Many payments were made in perishables that had to be used quickly by the ferryman, resulting in an ever-increasing debt that he owed to the church. With this report, Johnson provided a detailed explanation of how the large boat could not be used in high water, and the constant necessity of swimming stock. Taking wagons apart and reassembling required far more labor than would use of a smaller boat if one were available. Whether his message got through or he simply took it upon himself to make the improvements he deemed necessary is not known, but he built the desired one-wagon ferryboat during the winter of 1886–87.

Passage of the Edmunds-Tucker Act by Congress on February 19, 1887, was a severe blow to the Saints, bringing the polygamy issue to a head. Enacted into law without the signature of President Grover Cleveland, it was more harsh than previous measures and the Mormons were unable to find loopholes as they had under former statutes. In short, the act dissolved the Corporation of the Church of Jesus Christ of Latter-day Saints, the Perpetual Emigrating Company, and the Nauvoo Legion. It escheated all church property and provided that the realized proceeds be applied to Utah schools. Church leaders took the position that the law of God transcended the laws of men. Only God could revoke the principle of plural marriage, and if He chose to do so, He would make it known to the church president by revelation. They countered the escheatment of church property by placing their most valuable real property in the names of trusted individuals. Lee's Ferry, Arizona, was held in the name of John Taylor, trustee-in-trust, but his untimely death complicated this phase of the ownership.

The independent townsmen of Kanab began to resent what they considered an abuse of power on the part of Stake President E. D. Woolley. They made threats against him.[65] Allen Frost, growing weary of the developing cliques and endless infighting, decided to move from Kanab to Arizona. He resigned his offices, sold his property, and set out with his family on March 21, 1887. He arrived at the Colorado on the twenty-sixth to find the ferryman busy crossing sheep at the upper site. He noted that the small ferryboat was safe only for light wagons, and since his was heavily laden they thought it best to lay over and hope that the falling river would allow use of the lower crossing. They gave it a try two days later, putting the heavy wagon and a double team on the large boat. The current was too strong, however, and they were obliged to turn back. The men unloaded the wagon and took the cargo over in the skiff to be deposited on the left-bank landing. Then they went to the upper crossing and took the horses and one wagon over; the other wagons were crossed by noon of the twenty-ninth. Even with reduced loads they had a difficult time getting up Lee Hill, but they were able to camp at its foot on the south side.[66]

Johnson and Brinkerhoff had constructed several small shacks close to their own cabins for the convenience of travelers who desired to lay over a few days to recruit their animals on the ferryman's alfalfa. This increased his hay sales and the families were glad to visit with people from the settlements. The cabins also provided shelter for any who might pause here for temporary work. John Adams and his two families were returning to Utah in the spring of 1887 when he decided to work for Brother Johnson rather than continue their journey. He took over two of the shacks, settling a family in each. This decision was opportune for the ferryman because he was summoned to Prescott as a witness in the Wilson-Johnson murder trial; Adams could operate the ferry in his absence. He made the long trip to testify that the Clevengers were alive when they left the ferry. Both of the accused were found guilty and sentenced to hang, but on August 9, Wilson confessed that he alone had committed the murders. Thus, John Johnson was exonerated and Wilson was hanged at noon on August 12.[67]

President Taylor died August 25, 1887. He was succeeded by Wilford Woodruff, who headed the Twelve Apostles. The new leader was the first president who had crossed on the ferry and knew by experience the inhospitable approaches to it. The leadership of John Taylor had ushered in the greatest change the remote ferry had known. The ranch at the mouth of the Pahreah was beginning to bloom and now was showing the potential for becoming a green oasis in a veritable wilderness of rock and sand.

6

Brother Johnson's Green Acres

*E*IGHTEEN EIGHTY-SIX PROVED TO BE THE TURNING POINT FOR THE RANCH IN the mouth of Pahreah Canyon. The young fruit trees and grapevines had nearly mature production. The garden continued to yield a bumper crop of vegetables as it had for several seasons, and melons were plentiful. Alfalfa from the upper ranch enabled Warren Johnson to get through the winter without driving his cows to the open range; now, several tons were available for winter use. The range for a number of miles on both sides of the ferry had been so overgrazed before 1880 that few travelers depended on it, knowing they could purchase what alfalfa they needed from the ferryman. In 1887, the ranch's production was even higher. Animal feed was the key to the nineteenth century transportation system.

Will McAllister worked all winter on Johnson's house but was delayed when additional lumber was not delivered as promised. When he finally returned home in early June 1887, the siding and roof of the two-story structure were on and the windows and doors were installed, but the interior rooms were only partially partitioned. The porch and steps, along with some interior cabinets, were never built. The house was livable, however, and Permelia's family moved in. Samantha remained in her little cabin with the dirt floor and roof. The ferryman was buoyed personally when, on Christmas Day, Samantha presented him with another child, her eighth, a girl whom they named Estella. Permelia was pregnant, too, expecting her ninth child in about six months. The boy, LeRoy Sunderland, was born June 12, 1888.[1]

Everything considered, the people at Lee's Ferry were thriving and probably had a better life in their remote oasis than did most of the people in the settlements. Outside of having to import flour and cornmeal, Johnson had only two worries: schooling for his children and his mounting debt from use of the church's share of perishable items taken as ferriage. He attempted to solve the first problem by teaching his oldest daughter reading, writing, and arithmetic at night by the light of a kerosene lamp. Mary was an apt pupil and applied herself so that she was able to impart what she learned to the younger children. Melinda, Permelia's second daughter, was learning to read and write and began keeping a diary on January 1, 1889.[2] Her older

108

Warren M. and Permelia Johnson and family, ca. 1890 (*Frank Johnson photograph, P. T. Reilly Collection, Cline Library, Northern Arizona University*).

sister, Mary Evelette, also kept a diary. As a former teacher, Johnson was aware that his offspring were not getting the education he would have preferred; eventually, he would have to find a better solution. As for the mounting debt, he thought he would be ruined financially should the authorities call for full payment of their share of the ferriage.

The territorial Supreme Court of Utah granted a receiver for the escheatment of church property in November 1887. Ten days later Frank H. Dyer was appointed despite the disapproval of Judge Zane. Of course this made the headlines of the *Deseret News*, to which Johnson subscribed. Wild rumors accompanied news of the church's receivership, and the ferryman envisioned his pleasant home life being disrupted by Gentile interference. He wrote Wilford Woodruff that the ferry was in danger of being jumped as the title was tenuous and he had never been granted a license to operate it. Too, if Marshal Dyer took over the ferry and got his hands on Johnson's statements of past ferry income, he might be held liable for the old account and thus be forced into bankruptcy. In mid-December, he received a reassuring reply from the church president saying that his fears were groundless but urging him to learn the Arizona law on ferry operation.[3]

After the receivership was granted, considerable property was transferred from trustee ownership to certain trusted individuals. Some livestock was hustled into Arizona, even to Mexico. An example was the case of Lucius "Luke" Fuller, who trailed a large band of church tithing sheep from the Kanab range over Lee's Ferry to St. Johns, arriving late in the year. From there they were to be taken to the Mormon settlements in Mexico.[4]

In the spring of 1888, President Woodruff dropped the name Pahreah Ferry in favor of the original, more popular usage. When the aging frontiersman, Ira Hatch, decided to move from Kanab to Ramah, New Mexico, Woodruff told Johnson to give Hatch free passage over the ferry. He crossed July 25, the last time Hatch passed through the area he had helped tame.[5] The Johnson cutoff, pushed toward completion by expending thirty-two construction days in 1887, was finished the following spring and ready for use before the high-water period. It was an effective bypass of the dreaded lower third of the Lee Hill road, eliminating sections that always were double-teamed. In his road account, Johnson recorded that he had spent twenty man-days on the project in 1885.[6]

Stake President E. D. Woolley; Dan Seegmiller, field superintendent of the VT Cattle Company; and Bishop Lawrence C. Mariger decided to seek a market for cattle and sheep in the burgeoning Flagstaff area. The trio had a buckboard, a good team, and a saddle horse when they left Pipe Spring; they arrived at Lee's Ferry on July 31, 1888. On the morning of August 1, they met with Warren Johnson and family, after which they ordained Jerry and Frank Johnson as deacons.[7] The visitors crossed the river that afternoon and five days later were at the headquarters of the Arizona Cattle Company.

When Johnson learned that John Adams intended to move on, he decided to take care of some business while it was possible to be away. He left for Kanab on the morning of October 9. Although he had yet to make a final settlement for the lumber that went into his house, he had another project in mind—building a new ferryboat—as well as finding a replacement for Adams. He alone was making the decisions for improvements at the ferry and determining the size for ferry boats. He showed he was a far cry from the well-meaning but incompetent fool that John W. Young had attempted to make him out to be. Johnson returned to the ferry, spent the night, then crossed the river to discuss the next step with his brother-in-law, Bishop Brinkerhoff, at Tuba City. Brinkerhoff agreed to help with the boat construction, and Johnson was back at the ferry on October 30. Next morning he crossed Adams and his families in two wagons with six animals. Once again he was without adult help.[8]

Fortunately, a family soon arrived en route to Utah carrying a hitch-hiking neighbor named Frank Ivie. The young man wanted to attend school and, upon hearing that the ferryman once had been a school teacher, made a deal to work for him in exchange for being taught. Later in the winter, another young man went to work for Johnson. Will Clayton was the son of W. H. Clayton, one of the trustees when Kanab was incorporated in 1884. Both men proved to be good workers who could handle the variety of jobs at the ferry.

On December 8, a Brother Cox, headed south, paused at the ferry. He appeared to be sincere and convinced Johnson that the church was about to make sweeping changes in the ferry operation. He turned out to be a rumor-monger, but the ferryman was not aware of impending changes and immediately wrote President Woodruff to learn his status. Receiving the letter on New Year's Eve, the president branded the rumors untrue and raised the ferryman's share of the total ferry proceeds from one-third to one-half. Of course this also increased the church's share and the over-all effect was to eliminate the improvement fund that had amounted to one-third. The new division was to start January 1, 1889, although Johnson could have half of any 1888 fees that remained uncollected.[9] But Woodruff did not answer the problem that troubled Johnson most—his rising indebtedness to the church for the use of perishable items taken in lieu of cash. He calculated this as now amounting to between two and three thousand dollars.

As soon as the letter arrived, Johnson wrote again to address the omission. His sole subject was his indebtedness, and he suggested that he could reduce the sum by turning some stock in to the herd at House Rock that now was controlled by John W. Young. As an afterthought, he enclosed forty dollars on the ferry account.[10] His use of the word "perishables" did not get the idea across. Not understanding, the president sent a return letter telling him to ship the perishables to Salt Lake City whenever convenient and asked for a list of the perishable property on hand. Woodruff stated there was no existing arrangement for John W. Young to receive cattle for the church, but they could be turned in to the church herd at Pipe Spring through E. D. Woolley. The letter closed with an enigmatic blessing "in all your lawful undertakings."[11] Johnson temporarily dropped the subject.

On February 24, two brethren, Joe Stewart and George Beebe, came down from Pahreah settlement to start work on the new ferryboat. The lumber ordered in October had just been delivered but construction had been delayed until a more convenient time and better weather. Evidently the work on this project was tithing labor because some of the men did a certain amount of work and then went home. Stewart returned to Pahreah on March 12. Two days later, David Brinkerhoff came from Tuba City with Robert Sainsbury, Will Baird, and his wife and three children, which delighted the Johnson families. Although the main purpose of the visit was to work on the ferryboat, Will Baird had promised Bishop Brinkerhoff to do a special job. On the twentieth, when the boat was well along and he could be spared, he hunted a likely slab of sandstone and made a grave marker for Brinkerhoff's son William, who had died and been buried there five years before. In her diary, Melinda noted this simple act of remembrance, which was as important to her as the new boat.[12]

Bill Lee arrived early on the morning of March 13 and went up the old trail a half mile above the ferry. He said he intended to turn some stock loose on the plateau and wanted to check out the water situation. Apparently satisfied, he returned by the same route, crossed, and continued south. As it turned out, he was camping with his half-brother, Jim Lee, at Navajo Spring. On Wednesday evening, March 20, 1889, four men stopped and robbed the *Los Angeles Limited* on the high trestle over Canyon Diablo. The thieves got away under cover of night although it was ascertained that they rode north on horseback. The train continued the thirty-one miles to Flagstaff where the crime was reported. Yavapai County Sheriff William O. "Bucky" O'Neill and three deputies immediately saddled up and set out to pick up the trail. After finding the tracks and following them, they concluded that the outlaws were heading for Lee's Ferry.

The new ferryboat was completed on March 25, and the next day Bishop Brinkerhoff and his companions started back to Tuba City. On the second afternoon, they stopped for water at Willow Spring and met Sheriff O'Neill and his deputies, who were camped and watching for four men riding north. When told that the bishop had seen no northbound horsemen and none had crossed at the ferry while he was there and the Lee boys were at Navajo Spring, O'Neill sent Sainsbury back to the ferry to see if their quarry had avoided the southbound men and crossed after they left. He told Sainsbury to say nothing of the train robbery and to avoid the Lees if possible.

Late in the afternoon of March 26, Jim Lee came to the left bank and was crossed. He told Johnson he was checking for water on the bench, that Bill Lee would be along shortly for some grain. Jim headed up the trail just before dark, and Johnson took the grain across the river and left it where Bill couldn't miss it. Jim Lee came back down the trail in the morning and said he had been riding all night. He crossed and continued south to the camp. Then some wagons appeared and Warren Johnson, Will Clayton, and Frank Ivie labored until after dark getting the outfit across.

On March 28, Johnson, George Beebe, and the boys worked until noon putting some finishing touches on the new ferryboat when Robert Sainsbury reined in a lathered horse at the left-bank landing. Johnson went over in the skiff to see what he had forgotten and was told about the train robbery. No one had seen the highwaymen, but they were headed toward the Colorado River and the ferry was the only place where they could cross. Then the men began to put the story together and a closer look at the landing revealed that, unknown to the ferryman, the boat had been used surreptitiously on the night of March 27 when Jim Lee went up the trail. They concluded that Jim had only pretended to take the trail until it was dark and Johnson had returned home; then he came back to the river, brought Bill over in the skiff, and the two ferried the thieves and their horses. Jim then returned Bill in the skiff and guided their friends up the trail. After getting them headed into Utah, he returned to the ferry and lied to Johnson about his activities.

O'Neill and his men came into the Lee camp at Navajo Spring. To avert suspicion in case they were in league with the bandits, the sheriff told them he was after Lot Smith, who he had heard was fleeing to avoid arrest as a polygamist. The story sounded plausible to the Lees, so each group maintained its deception and the train robbery was not mentioned. The O'Neill party arrived at the ferry on March 29, obtained a couple of fresh horses from Johnson and, guided by George Beebe, went up the trail after their quarry. Deputy Wilcox was left at the river should the fugitives show up there unexpectedly.

The train robbers rode forty-five miles to Pahreah settlement, where they obtained food for themselves and their horses, then rode another twenty-five miles to Cannonville and spent the night with a rancher. At Pahreah, O'Neill and his deputies learned that the desperados were just ahead of them. He sent Joe Stewart and a companion to learn their exact location and report back. The scouts located the bandits while Stewart tried to round up enough men and guns for their capture. Most of the impromptu posse had not held a working gun in forty years, but capture them they did. Unfortunately, one of the bandits pulled a hidden gun, took a hostage, and turned the tables on the townsmen. They rode off southeasterly toward the benches of the desolate Glen Canyon country.

The O'Neill posse came to Cannonville, learned the details, and departed on the now hot trail. They caught up with the fugitives at their first camp and captured one man and two horses after an exchange of gunfire. The remaining bandits went toward Lee's Ferry, but now two were afoot. The final confrontation took place the next afternoon among the rocks at Wahweap Creek, about ten miles northeast of the ferry. Considerable lead was thrown and the battle ended only when the outlaws' ammunition was exhausted. O'Neill took his prisoners back to Cannonville, picked up a buckboard, then continued to Panguitch where a blacksmith shackled the captives. They drove to Milford, took the train back to Flagstaff and Prescott. Deputy Willcox remained at the ferry until March 31, then went back to Flagstaff.[13]

Criminal justice was relatively swift in 1889, but transportation wasn't. Warren Johnson was called as a witness in the Canyon Diablo robbery case to be heard in Prescott. He left home on April 29, swam his saddle horse behind the skiff, then cached the boat among the willows so he could come back the same way. He returned May 10 because the trial had been postponed and there was no practical means of notifying the isolated witness; the shortest round trip would be about four hundred fifty miles had there been a direct way of making it. Johnson could have taken the train from Flagstaff to Ashfork, a distance of fifty miles, but that would have left him without a horse; the railroad between Ashfork and Prescott was not completed until 1893. What he did was to put his horse in a livery stable at Flagstaff, catch the train west to Prescott Junction (now called Seligman), and there transfer to the Arizona Central which took him to Prescott. But he still had to make the long horseback ride between the ferry and Flagstaff.

The Canyon Diablo train robbery served as a base for two far-fetched bits of fiction that were accepted as fact in some quarters. In 1940, Matt Warner published an exaggerated story of his life as a "bandit rider," with two chapters devoted to an episode in which Warner, Josh Sweat [Swett], and Tom McCarty supposedly tried to rustle some cattle south of the Mexican border and got into a gunfight with U.S. officers. After Josh was wounded, the three set out across Arizona heading for Lee's Ferry with the officers close behind. They supposedly reached the ferry twenty minutes ahead of the officers, commandeered the ferryboat, and put the river between themselves and the law. After resting, they took the ferryman as a hostage and turned him loose afoot, ten miles from the ferry.[14] Warner's description of the ferry and Johnson make it clear that he had never laid eyes on either. He described the southerly approach as a long, two-mile canyon and described Johnson as a "big powerful Swede" who just happened to be alone on the right bank of the river. Far from being a big, powerful man, Warren Johnson was a small, slightly-built man who weighed about 130 pounds.

In 1964, an enterprising hack named Hardy read Warner's fiction and wrote the same episode from the standpoint of "Sweat," whom Hardy met at a mine in the vicinity of Mountain Springs, Nevada, in 1930. After reading Warner's book, he "realized" that Sweat had told him the "truth" about the incident at Lee's Ferry. He wrote a nearly identical yarn but added an embellishment or two, such as taking Johnson out about five miles and turning him loose with his hands tied and ankles hobbled.[15]

The ferryman again set out for Prescott on May 29 to give his testimony. While he was away, an oddity of the times—Mormon prospectors—arrived. C. A. Huntington and C. E. Holladay knew the ferryman and apparently had been invited to come to the isolated location to "look around." Clark Allen—usually called Al—was nearing fifty-eight years of age and was not as active as he once had been, but he liked to putter at prospecting and to spin tall tales to anyone who would listen. The two men rode up as the children were playing beside the willows and immediately began asking questions about the ferryman and his wives. Fearing that the strangers were officers who had come to arrest their father, they gave evasive answers and refused even to tell their names. They were relieved to learn that the newcomers were good Mormons who knew their father well, and in time Al became the grandfather they had never known.[16] But for now, the two men settled in one of the guest cabins and used the ferry as a base for their short prospecting trips.

Glen Canyon was a desolate world of trappers and prospectors. John R. Nielson, an imaginative blacksmith, dreamed of building a floating placer outfit on the river, using the water of the Colorado to process the sands of the high bars along the river. In the fall of 1888, he hired Thomas Fotheringham and two other men from Beaver to help haul wagonloads of equipment and lumber down the pioneer track at Hole-in-the-Rock. It took a month to get everything from the rim to the river, where the four men built a craft that was unlike anything ever seen on the river. She was as large as the ferryboat, about thirty-eight feet long with a beam of thirteen to sixteen feet. A twelve-foot diameter waterwheel on the side generated power in the manner of a gristmill. The boat was a double-decker; the upper deck contained the carpenter-blacksmith shop and the galley, and the lower deck was where the men slept and stored the provisions and chemicals. Alluvium was brought on board with wheelbarrows, where it was screened, put in a large open tub, mixed with water pumped from the river, and stirred by rotating paddles. The dross was discarded into the river through a trough, while the residual fines were washed through two boxes, each of which contained seven amalgamating plates. The entire load amounted to two or three tons. The boat was steered by two large sweeps, one at each end, which were mounted in clevises so they could not be lost. There was an auxiliary skiff that proved to be extremely useful.

The boat completed, the men started down river in December, pulling in about eight miles below Hole-in-the-Rock. The equipment worked but the diggings were not rich enough to turn a profit. Nielson obtained some gold but scarcely enough to pay the wages of his three employees, so they moved ten miles downstream, possibly to Klondike Bar. By this time the spring rise had set in, making it difficult to maneuver the cumbersome craft. They worked here all of May before Nielson felt the urge to hunt for richer ground. His crew disapproved of moving the boat in high water, but Nielson convinced them it could be done and they cast off. The crew were right—the strong current rendered the boat almost unmanageable and she did not stop her downstream plunge until she was grounded on a sandbar in a strong eddy in the mouth of Glen Canyon on June 4.[17]

Figuring they were near Lee's Ferry, Nielson took the skiff and went down to get help. Will Clayton was sick, but Permelia, Samantha, and the older children walked up along the shore. Although the craft still could not be budged, they got a line to shore in case the river continued to rise and floated her free.[18] The next morning, they found the boat floating on a rising river. They lined the boat downstream where she was tied securely about a quarter-mile above the ferry landing. The miners then hitched a ride to the settlements; of the four, only Nielson returned after a few months. The river peaked early in 1889, probably on June 5, as the boat was stranded at her new tie-up on the sixth.

The Johnsons worked hard to keep the ferries afloat on the fluctuating river, and they also managed to get the Nielson boat floating on June 8. Confusion in later years was generated because the Nielson boat was named the *Nellie*, and when the Johnson boys were grown men and had occasion to refer to the *Nellie*, others who had never heard of Nielson or his boat thought they spoke of the *Nellie Powell*, which Major Powell had cached in a dugout in the banks of the Pahreah River in 1872.

Meanwhile, some entrepreneurs headed by Frank Mason Brown organized the Denver, Colorado Canyon & Pacific Railroad for the avowed purpose of transporting coal from southwestern Colorado to San Diego by way of a water-level rail line down the Grand and Colorado Rivers.[19] Frank C. Kendrick started the railroad survey from Grand Junction, Colorado, on March 28, 1889, and ran the line down to the confluence of the Grand and Green Rivers (the head of Cataract Canyon). Brown, the company president, hired Robert B. Stanton as chief engineer. With sixteen men in six boats, the group floated down the Green River on May 25, reaching the end of Kendrick's line on May 30. Cataract Canyon treated them roughly by slowing their progress and taking two of their boats. Running out of food in the lower end of Cataract Canyon, eleven men abandoned the survey and made a dash for Dandy Crossing in three boats, leaving Stanton and four others to at least get the line past the last rapids.

On June 20, crew members Hansbrough, Coe, and Howard brought a boatload of fresh supplies upstream to the hungry surveyors. By adding their help and another boat, the surveyors reached Dandy Crossing four days later. On June 29, the railroad survey split again. The Brown-Stanton group of eight men left Dandy Crossing headed for Needles, California, while William H. Bush and four others continued the instrumental railroad survey down to Lee's Ferry.

The Brown-Stanton expedition pulled into the ferry landing at 5 P.M. on July 2 and housed themselves in the old fort. Johnson had returned from Prescott but was in Kanab; Al Huntington spoke for him. Since the supplies that Brown had ordered from Dandy Crossing had not been delivered, he borrowed a horse in the morning and set out for Kanab. The rest of the crew gorged themselves on the ferryman's fresh vegetables, fruit, eggs, milk, butter, and beef—feasting in the land of Canaan after their reduced rations on the river. Upstream, when they had so desperately sought to augment their vanishing supplies with fresh fish, they could not catch any; now, when they didn't need them, they found more in the mouth of the Pahreah River than they could use. Stanton related that Huntington amused the newcomers with an unending supply of wild yarns.

According to Frank Johnson, Stanton spent considerable time examining the *Nellie* but made no mention of it in his notes. In all probability, the *Nellie* may have influenced his decision to devote most of the next decade of his life to recovering gold from the sands of Glen Canyon. His desire to prevent Brown and the rest of the crew from becoming interested in the odd boat may have prompted him to move camp to the lower ferry site on July 6. The road from Kanab came down the wash here and there would be no reason for Brown to see the *Nellie* again. The Johnsons turned out en masse to watch the boats run the Pahreah riffle.[20] Brown arrived with the supplies two days later.

The next morning, the entire expedition started down the canyon, with Johnson and his families watching from the landing. The Brown-Stanton group intended to continue downstream to Needles to visually evaluate the feasibility of putting a railroad through the canyon.[21] Unfortunately, the round-bottom, narrow-beam boats were ill-suited for the job. Frank Brown drowned in a capsize at Mile 12 on July 12; five days later, Peter M. Hansbrough and Henry Richards drowned at Mile 25.[22] Stanton took the remaining crew down to South Canyon where they found a well-worn trail behind some aboriginal ruins. They followed this to top out, and next day stumbled into a line camp of the VT Cattle Company. They were driven fourteen miles to House Rock, and from there Stephen W. Taylor took them to Johnson settlement. They went on to Salt Lake City and Denver where Stanton regrouped the survey for another try.

The deaths of Brown, Hansbrough, and Richards, coming thirteen years after that of Roundy, established the popular concept that the Colorado was the most dangerous river on the continent. Major Powell had played up the heroic phases of his struggle with the river, and his many speaking engagements magnified his feat in prevailing over "the beast." The boxed entry into the Marble Canyon was viewed as the gateway to a watery Hell from which a traveler was not likely to return. Warren Johnson, who knew the power of the river as few men did, was extremely careful about using the lower crossing when the current was strong. He implanted a fear of being swept into the box in the minds of his sons that lasted for many years after they were adults, and they questioned the sanity of those who ventured down the river except through dire necessity.

Bush and his four-man crew ran out of food at Labyrinth Canyon, 35.5 miles above Lee's Ferry. They marked the end of the line where high water would not take it out, then made a dash for the ferry, arriving on July 21. Apparently neither Brown nor Stanton had made any arrangement with the ferryman to care for the surveyors, but Johnson and Bush worked out a deal between themselves. The following day Bush and his men made a survey of the Johnson ranch; as payment, the ferryman killed a beef for them and jerked most of the meat.[23] The surveyors hitched a ride to the settlements, and on the twenty-fourth, Johnson started for Flagstaff and Prescott to record his claim.[24]

Lee's Ferry was much more than a highway to Arizona. It was identified over a wide area as a gathering place where families either met or often parted. When the Saints' problem with polygamy began to fester, some of the men kept one wife in Arizona and the other in Utah; reunions were made as frequently as possible and the ferry was the natural place where they felt relatively safe. This was the reason Johnson had built the guest cabins. One such instance was that of Henry Lunt, resident of Apache County, and his wife Ellen, temporarily living in Utah, who were to meet there at the end of July. Lunt planned to travel to the ferry with the Elam Cheney family.

Stake President Jesse N. Smith decided to accompany his friends as far as Tuba City, where they arrived on July 22. Even in Arizona, the twenty-fourth of July was a greater holiday in Mormon communities than Independence Day, and Tuba City was no exception. Smith remained for the celebration, then started home. Before leaving, he learned that Bishop Brinkerhoff intended to accompany Lunt and Cheney to the ferry, so Smith gave him fourteen dollars to pass to Warren Johnson to settle an old ferry debt.[25] Johnson met the three wagons near Willow Spring, received the money, and continued on to Flagstaff. Smith's debt dated from December 1884 when Lot Smith had given Chris Lingo the shoes. Johnson knew that he would get the money sometime and never would have asked the president of the Eastern Arizona Stake to pay. He was aware that his function was to serve the traveling public—even non-Mormons.

The Johnsons kept busy at Lee's Ferry. Mary Evelette, Johnson's oldest daughter, now seventeen, began to keep ferry records for her father in 1889. The entries that year were made by both father and daughter but Mary's can be distinguished by her habit of reversing the vowels in the word "Indian," always spelling it "Indain." Her handwriting closely resembled her father's. Warren Johnson had a project in mind that involved the use of adobe bricks. What it was and how far it progressed has never been determined, but his records carry the notation that between September 5 and October 8, 1889, he and his helper made 6,480 adobes. On the days they worked they produced about three hundred bricks.[26] John Swapp went to work for the ferryman early in November, settling his family in one of the guest cabins. His wife, Martha Ann, gave birth on November 12, 1889, to Stephen Addison Swapp, with Johnson's wives in attendance.

Evidently John R. Nielson had done some deep thinking about his floating placer rig and the possibility of recovering gold from the Glen Canyon bars. He couldn't get the *Nellie* back upstream, and the highly publicized deaths of the Brown-Stanton expedition deterred him from going downstream. He returned to Lee's Ferry in a wagon that fall to salvage what he could and write off the rest of his project as a loss. He boarded with the Johnsons and gave the ferryman a large blacksmith bellows that had been on the boat. He even set it up in one of the cabins and taught Jerry Johnson, Warren's son, the rudiments of the craft. Jerry was an apt pupil, although he was not yet fourteen, and from this time on he did all the blacksmith work. When Nielson departed this time, he never came back.

Meanwhile, Stanton regrouped the railroad survey in Denver, built three new boats of his own design, and started off from the mouth of Crescent Wash on December 10. The expedition reached Labyrinth Canyon eleven days later to pick up the measurement where Bush had ended it in July. On the twenty-third, they arrived at Lee's Ferry and settled in the old fort. Stanton went to the ranch for the mail and picked up fifty-six letters, ten of which were for him.[27] He and his crew became so engrossed that they neglected to cook supper.

They made up for the missed meal on Christmas Day. A table was set up on the east side of the fort for dinner. Johnson and Stanton both contributed food; Permelia made cook James Hogue's task easier by preparing several dishes in her own kitchen. She, her husband, and Al

Christmas dinner at Lee's Ferry, December 25, 1889. From left to right, Robert Brewster Stanton, Franklin A. Nims, William Hyram Edwards, Reginald Travers, H. G. Ballard, Langdon Gibson, Elmer Kane, L. G. Brown, Arthur B. Twining, James S. Hogue, Harry McDonald, and John Hislop (*Al Huntington clicked the shutter; Franklin A. Nims photograph, courtesy of the National Archives and Records Administration; identifications are from Dwight L. Smith and C. Gregory Crampton, eds.,* The Colorado River Survey: Robert B. Stanton and the Denver, Colorado Canyon & Pacific Railroad [*Salt Lake City: Howe Brothers, 1987*]).

Huntington joined the crew for dinner, and at its conclusion tried to convert Leo G. Brown to their faith.[28] The menu included three kinds of soup, fish, beef, turkey, and chicken; it lacked nothing except salad; later one of the men wrote that the three soups appeared to have come from the same pot. Nevertheless, it was the best meal the men had eaten in weeks and it would be a long time before they had another that came close to it—especially one on Christmas Day with fresh wildflowers on the table. Franklin Nims posed Warren, Permelia, and ten of of the Johnson children in the now barren plot behind the house and took their picture. All of the children were Permelia's except Jerry and Frank.[29] Since Stanton and his men were fully aware that Johnson had two wives and families, it is regrettable that Samantha and her other children were not included.

The crewmen got the Johnson girls to wash and iron their dirty clothes. It was two days before the laundry was completed, but everything was ready for a launch into Marble Canyon on December 28. Stanton augmented his supplies from Johnson's larder, including five quarters of fresh beef. Seventeen Johnsons lined up along the river to see the expedition run the splashy Pahreah Riffle. Stanton said there were thirty-two Johnsons on shore, not realizing that fifteen of the spectators carried other surnames. Then the boats rounded the bend below the lower crossing and were gone.

New Year's Day of 1890 was a disastrous beginning for Franklin Nims, the expedition's photographer. While climbing among some ledges along the left bank about fifteen miles downstream from Lee's Ferry, Nims lost his footing and fell twenty-two feet. At the time, they ascertained that he had broken his right leg and apparently fractured his skull. Nims was unconscious and bleeding from the mouth and ears. Stanton had hard decisions to make: the injured man must be removed from the canyon, a new photographer must be obtained, and the survey must be continued. They camped on the spot while Stanton sought answers, rationalizing that Nims should not be moved that day. Despite having his notes from July, which carried him much farther downstream to South Canyon, the leader did not know exactly where he was. He thought there was a tributary about ten miles downstream coming in from the north that might be accessible to the plateau. The next day, the men improvised a stretcher from two oars and a piece of canvas, put the unconscious man aboard and strapped him in. They ran what seemed like ten miles to Stanton (but actually about two), landed at the mouth of House Rock Canyon, and made camp, placing Nims in a dry bed under an overhanging ledge.

On January 3, Stanton, Hislop, and McDonald started up the tributary to find a way to the rim. In two and one-half miles, they spotted a crevice above the red talus and topped out before noon.[30] After lunch, Hislop and McDonald started back to the river while Stanton began the long trek to Lee's Ferry. Since they had emerged on the south rim of the tributary, the canyon's walls now were between him and his objective, so he was compelled to walk about two miles southwesterly away from the ferry in order to cross the wash before it became entrenched. Another three and one-half miles due north took him to the Mormon road about five miles from Soap Creek. It was thirteen miles more to Johnson's ranch where he arrived on sore, blistered feet shortly after midnight. Although the distance was not the thirty-five miles Stanton estimated, it was at least twenty-five and a worthy feat for the forty-three-year-old engineer. Johnson made him welcome and bedded him down in the kitchen among some Navajo blankets.

In the morning, Johnson hitched his team of Moose and Kelly to his weathered wagon and, with eleven-year-old Frank driving, they set out toward the Pools. Stanton did not know the country well enough to describe the route from where he topped out, but he guided them visually. However, they had not made an early start and failed to reach the place where he thought they should cut across country to the exit crevice before night overtook them. Their team was exhausted and they made camp on

Warren Johnson, Robert Stanton, and young Frank Johnson praying during a light snowstorm on the night of January 4, 1890, before the rescue of Franklin Nims (*Harper Goff drawing*).

the desert about four miles past Soap Creek. A light snow was falling as Warren knelt beside the campfire and offered a fervent prayer for the success of the rescue effort.

The same day the rescue wagon was heading west, eight of the crewmen started up House Rock with the unconscious Nims on a makeshift stretcher. They left the river at 8:30 A.M., and by alternating stretcher-carriers, topped out about 3:30 P.M. It was a Herculean job in which ropes were used on several occasions to hoist the stretcher past ledges. Once, they had to work their burden through a hole under a chockstone. Langdon Gibson noted that the difficult task was alleviated by Harry McDonald "who at critical moments had the most original and unconventional ways of expressing his thoughts."[31] They hoped to meet Stanton and Johnson, transfer Nims to the wagon, and then return to the river, so they had not brought food or bedding. Gibson, Travers, and Brown returned to camp for food and were fortunate in getting past the precipitous places while there still was light. The rest remained with Nims and kept the fire going. All of them would carry Nims to Lee's Ferry if the wagon did not appear.

On the morning of January 5, when it was apparent that the wagon would have to head several washes which a man on foot could cross, Stanton became impatient, loaded a rucksack with bread and a can of milk for Nims, and started out on foot while the wagon went around the easier course. He reached the bedraggled crewmen in less than two hours; fifteen minutes later, food and water arrived from the river camp. The wagon, however, did not arrive until mid-afternoon. Nims was lifted onto a mattress in the wagon and tied into place—he still was unconscious and the going was rough. One-half hour after arriving, Johnson started back, while Stanton and his men returned to the river through the crevice. Young Frank drove all the way and reached the road before dark, but it was long after midnight when they pulled into the ranch at Pahreah Canyon.[32]

It is not known whether Stanton made any financial arrangement with Johnson to care for Nims, but it appears that he simply slid out of any responsibility in the case. Nims stated that he was cut from the payroll on the day of the accident, and Stanton did not provide any remuneration for his care. The only times Nims was mentioned again were when Stanton commented on the extra work thrust upon him in taking over the photographic duties and in a false report printed in the *Denver Times* that the entire expedition except Nims had been lost in the canyon.

Franklin Nims regained consciousness on January 12 as the Johnsons were eating dinner. He was lying on a mattress on the kitchen floor, having no knowledge of his location or why he was there. After explaining his predicament, Johnson told him the nearest doctor was ninety miles away at Kanab and it would not be possible to send for him until spring. Permelia offered him food but he was unable to eat as the right side of his face was partially paralyzed. The patient must have lapsed into unconsciousness; he lost two days when he resumed his diary on the sixteenth, writing it as the fourteenth. He heard wagons outside and asked the girl watching him the reason. Johnson soon came in with word that two of his brethren had arrived en route to their homes in New Mexico. Nims asked if they would take him to the railroad. Johnson returned saying they would cross the railroad at Winslow, 185 miles away, and would transport him there for $85. The true distance was closer to 150 miles but the means of travel could have made it seem like more, and Nims didn't know the difference. He accepted the proposal, saying he would pay when he reached Winslow.

The group Nims joined was led by Frihoff G. Nielson, who with J. E. Garn had left St. George on January 7. The two wagons had encountered heavy going over Buckskin Mountain, where there was a foot and one-half of snow on the ground with more coming down. They pulled into Johnson's ranch on the sixteenth, laid over a day, crossed the river on the eighteenth amid floating ice and against strong winds, and reached Winslow on the twenty-sixth. Nielson did not mention Nims in his journal although he dated his arrival and departure at the ferry, Tuba City, and Winslow, where they remained for three days. Nims tells why in his diary. It took that long to get his money from Denver.[33] An Oddfellows lodge brother finally came to his rescue, paid his Mormon benefactor the $85 and Dr. Sullivan of the Santa Fe Railroad $50 for the train. Nims arrived in Denver on January 31. He remained incapacitated until mid-June.

Al Huntington made many short prospecting trips out of Johnson's ranch. It probably was in the fall of 1889 that he went up the ferryman's old stock trail to the bench and continued on to the sandy hollow at Phantom Spring, where he pitched camp. He had the shade of cottonwoods, plenty of good water, and food as long as his supply lasted. According to Frank Johnson, this was one of Al's favorite hideouts. It must have been on one of his trips here that he cut the inscription:

C E HOLLADAY 1855
C A HUNTINGTON

Huntington undoubtedly equated his presence at Lee's Ferry with his having been a member of the Elk Mountain Mission in 1855. He knew that both places were on the Colorado River but he had little knowledge of the intervening land and would have been surprised to learn that two hundred eighty-two miles separated the two places. Therefore, when he chipped his glyph at Phantom Spring, he merely proclaimed his entry into a general region that was unlike any other he had ever known and whose extent he only superficially realized.

Next spring, Huntington joined Harry McDonald, C. E. Holladay, Nels Johnson, and Al Peterson in a prospecting jaunt into the Nankoweap basin in Grand Canyon.[34] Several claims eventually were filed and Warren Johnson's name was included on most of them. In fact, Johnson might have backed the group, because this wasn't the last time his name was connected with mining. When the weather became too warm for prospecting in Nankoweap, Al Huntington returned to the ferry to help out.

A Mexican and his burro crossed the ferry on February 7. The fee was a dollar but he only had fifty cents and cheerfully gave it to the ferry-man, who did not ask for more. Seeing that the man had practically nothing to eat, Johnson gave him some food and he continued on toward Utah. It was a poor time of year to be looking for a job and in about a month the Mexican was back at the ferry, where he went to work for the kind-hearted proprietor. He said his name was Jesús, but the Johnsons knew nothing of Spanish phonetics and recorded the name as "Haysuce," which was close to the way he pronounced it. Jesús spoke English, proved to be a good worker, did a little of everything, and dependably carried the mail on to Tuba City. His shelter was the smallest guest cabin as he didn't need much. He now was eating better than he had in months.

Samantha's ninth child was born that spring, a boy who was named Warren Elmer. As usual, Permelia attended, this time assisted by Martha Ann Swapp. While the youngsters had certain specified tasks, they also had time to play. Frank Johnson and Ben Swapp developed a unique pastime that probably was not duplicated in any other part of the country. They carried turkeys up the trail to the point west of the barn and flung them into space to see whose bird could glide the farthest. On more than one occasion the birds landed on the Pahreah delta.[35] Frank lost his playmate when John Swapp moved his family to Johnson Canyon later that spring.

Fishing was unparalleled during the late 1880s and early 1890s; many large catches were hauled in. Warren Johnson once trudged up to the house with his shovel over his shoulder and the handle thrust through the gills of a monster fish that hung down his back and whose tail dragged the ground. Another time, Al Huntington caught one and tied it behind his saddle; the head and tail hung down to the stirrups.[36]

Mormon leaders now traveled by rail whenever they could. On August 1, 1890, President Woodruff and his counselors went by rail from Salt Lake City via the Colorado stakes to Arizona, bypassing Lee's Ferry completely.[37] In the fall, Woodruff sent Apostles F. M. Lyman, J. H. Smith, J. W. Taylor, and A. H. Cannon to adjudicate a matter between Stake President E. D. Woolley and Bishop Lawrence Mariger. This coincided with the Kanab Quarterly Conference, which Warren Johnson attended. The ferryman managed to corral the apostles and explain the problem of his indebtedness to the church by having to accept and use perishable items as ferry fees. He also pointed out how long he had been on this mission and that he had his two families and seventeen children; ten of them should be in school and among the society of their peers. The apostles praised his faithfulness in performing the duties of his mission, said they would recommend his indebtedness be canceled, and advised him to move one family into town.[38]

The seizure of church property had backed the ecclesiastical corporation into an untenable position. Finally, President Woodruff wrote his manifesto denying church sanction of plural marriage, then presented it to his counselors and some apostles on September 24. They concurred, and it was sustained unanimously at the General Church Conference on October 6. This was the first reversal of church policy; not all agreed with it, and the reverberations would be heard for many years to come, particularly at Lee's Ferry. Johnson read and reread the manifesto in the *Deseret News*, fasted and prayed, but still did not understand the meaning. He knew he could not abandon Samantha and his children by her, yet the words were there: the president and his associates did not inculcate or encourage polygamy and they advised other Saints to submit to the laws of the land.

Johnson finally accepted the view that since the manifesto was directed "to whom it may concern," it did not concern him; therefore, he was not required to take action. He regarded it as a test by the Devil to try the will of the people. He believed that the Lord had given the law of plural marriage to this generation and it was never taken away or given to other people, that the principle of plurality of wives never would be done away with, and if the Saints did not keep it they could not enter the Kingdom of Heaven. This was the basic creed of the fundamentalists; Warren Johnson believed it, and some of his fourth-generation descendants still do.

Later in October, Johnson received a letter from President Woodruff saying that his indebtedness arising from the use of perishables—now amounting to some twenty-five hundred dollars—had been liquidated. He also stated that the presidency and apostles unanimously concurred with the advice given him to divide his families and get his children in school. He expressed his appreciation for Johnson's fifteen years of faithful service, blessed him, and asked God to preserve him from harm and accident as well as to help him prosper and educate his children.[39] To the devout ferryman, this blessing was an assurance that he had God's favor.

Almon Draper had left his home in Springdale to sample life in Arizona. He did general labor and had no special skills, but he was a good horse-trader. He settled in Silver Creek near Snowflake but did not like the country and started back to Utah in the fall of 1890. When he reached Lee's Ferry he saw that the proprietor needed help, so he went to work for Johnson. With Draper were his three children by his first wife, who had died in 1889, and his second and third wives, who were hoping to start their families. The six people settled in the largest guest cabin, a one-room affair.[40]

With the three Draper children added to his own, Johnson set up a schoolroom in the upper story of his house, built benches, and gathered what books were available. Mary and Lizzie acted as teachers. The school lasted through the winter but was abandoned when one teacher and half of the class caught chicken pox from a passing family and the course of events dictated its permanent demise.

The Pahreah River had washed out several of Johnson's dams, but the structures were rebuilt each time in the same place or moved upstream if the scouring had been severe. Now he was using his third damsite, and with each move upstream the ditch became longer. The normal time to clean the ditch, remove the intruding cottonwood shoots, and prepare for the spring flooding of the fields was in January and February. This was hard work with a shovel, and Johnson never delegated it completely to his hired help. The ditch now was about one mile and one-half long and it provided water to raise up to a hundred tons of hay each year, which was well worth the effort.

Winslow was a railroad town divided roughly into two factions—the railroaders and the cowboys. Rivalry was intense and fights between individuals or groups of the two sides were common. Saturday nights were especially boisterous, often ending violently. Bill Lee was unmarried and nearing thirty years of age; he wore two guns and despised the railroaders as much as they did any working cowman. In the spring of 1890, he became involved in a disputed horse race in which the railroaders claimed a foul. They were about to pocket the bets when Bill swooped in from the finish line, scooped up the money, and spurred his horse out of town. The railroad men, who controlled the sheriff, got a warrant for his arrest. Bill considered himself to be outside the law and went into hiding. Whether out of sympathy to his cause or loyalty to his mother, Franklin French joined him and the pair headed for the ferry and the safety of Utah.

They followed French's love of prospecting in the Mormon hinterlands but failed to find anything worth developing. Bill met a vivacious girl, Clara B. Workman, and married her at the little hamlet of Georgetown on October 6. He would have preferred to return to Winslow but decided it wasn't safe. He eventually took over an abandoned cabin and homesite at Pahreah settlement and, with French's help, he expanded it into a livable home. In January 1891, they came to the ferry to obtain some grape cuttings and bare-root trees from Warren Johnson.[41] Apparently at this time the Johnsons no longer regarded Bill as a Saint because in her diary Mary referred to him as "Mr. Lee."

On January 16, 1891, an event took place that had never happened before at Lee's Ferry. A group consisting of Kanab Stake President E. D. Woolley, his counselors Thomas Chamberlain and Dan Seegmiller, Bishop H. M. Cutler and his son Scott, Jim Emett, Thomas Robertson, and A. D. Young arrived at the ferry after dark. Why the local authorities suddenly developed an interest there was not explained, but the following day they held meetings in both the morning and afternoon. It was a known fact that Johnson had created an oasis of plenty in the desolate place and possibly the shrewd brethren saw the beckoning finger of opportunity in the event his mission should come to an end. The Johnsons treated their eight visitors royally, feeding them the best their larder afforded. The townsmen started home on the eighteenth.

Life again settled into the routine sequence of necessary chores. Draper went to the settlements for supplies, Warren Johnson and the hired Indian worked on the ditch, the wives sewed, and Mary conducted her school. In her diary, she noted ruefully that on January 19: "The children say we have a school but we can hardly call it that." Johnson, of course, was painfully aware that his children were being short-changed in education. Permelia's last child, a boy whom they named Joseph Smith after the prophet and her father, was born March 28, 1891. Of her ten children, nine had lived.

Al Huntington and his partner Gene Holladay again became active in prospecting as soon as the coldest weather was past. They filed the "Polly" claim adjoining the ones previously staked at the head of Nankoweap Creek and then wandered over to the east Kaibab monocline. They located several claims in the Cockscomb section and recorded them at Kanab in February. No doubt Warren Johnson grubstaked them since he was listed as a full partner.[42]

Having obtained the approval of President Woodruff and the apostles, Johnson offered L. John Nuttall three hundred fifty dollars for his house in Kanab. Nuttall accepted on January 16, 1891.[43] In late April, and needing cash to pay for the Nuttall place, Johnson and Frank went up Pahreah Canyon and drove down twenty-three steers. Two days later, helped by Alex Swapp who had carried the mail that day, they drove the steers to a holding corral at Soap Creek. While they worked with the cattle, Mary and Melinda checked the boats—now on a rising river—and took up the slack in the lines.

Now that he had a house in Kanab, Johnson lost no time in following the rest of the apostles' instructions. On April 27, Draper and Jerry Johnson moved Samantha and her family into town. The younger children had never been far from the ferry and the shock of suddenly living among neighbors was acute. Frank did not stay long; young Ami Judd, who with his brother, Eli, and Alex Swapp carried the mail to the ferry, brought word that he was needed at the ranch, and within ten days he was back working with his father. Jerry remained with his mother, at least for the present. Change had set in, but the Johnsons did not realize its extent. The old carefree days of the two families living in their isolated oasis had ended forever, but so gradually did the transition take place that it would have been difficult for any member to pinpoint a date. Now, each family was diminished without the other, forced to function normally with only a part of the human resources. The new order was to prove more drastic than any of them could have imagined.

May 12, 1891, was a fateful day for the Johnsons. Two families, those of Alonzo Foutz and A. M. Farnsworth, arrived from Tuba City after visiting relatives in the Richfield area. An unrecognized disease was epidemic there, and evidently some of their children had picked up the malady without its seriousness being realized. Foutz had buried a child in Panguitch, never perceiving that he had died from the highly contagious diphtheria. Sanitation in those days was not what it is now; they put the dead child's clothing in the wagon with other soiled garments and continued the journey. Apparently more of the children also had the disease but no effort was made to isolate them. The Johnsons took both families into their home, fed them, and allowed them to mingle freely with their own youngsters. The children played together all of the following day, as the wind was so strong that crossing was hazardous. When it subsided on the fourteenth, Johnson ferried the wagons across the river, but it was too late—his family already had been exposed to the deadly disease.

The next day, Jonathan, who would have been six in five months, came down with a fever and sore throat. Two days later, eleven-year-old Laura showed the same symptoms. Jonathan died at 1 P.M. on May 19. The desperate family did not understand the concept of disease and thought God must be punishing them for sins they had unknowingly committed. They fasted and prayed but to no avail; Millie was stricken on the thirtieth. Laura died the morning of June 11 and was buried the following day, which was LeRoy's third birthday. Travelers arrived and departed, leaving sure-fire remedies of turpentine, coal oil, sulphur, or soda water to treat the sick children. Nothing worked; Millie died at 1:45 P.M. on June 15 and was buried after dark on the same day. Young E. A. Draper described a pathetic scene with the remaining children tearfully singing hymns after being told by their father to "stand up there, sing, and make the best of it."[44]

Melinda came down with the dreaded, now familiar symptoms the evening of June 19. Her parents were completely helpless and could only pray that she would be able to overcome the insidious malady. Austin Farnsworth rode horseback seventy miles one way to bring a sure cure of one teaspoon each of turpentine and saltpeter-water every three hours. Jesús arrived with the mail and some medicine—mercurate of iron—to be used to swab the sore throats and to be gargled in diluted form.

Help came from several quarters. A relief party from Kanab, composed of James Bunting, Asa W. Judd, Emma B. Woolley, and Mary E. Broadbent, arrived on the evening of June 29. Their aid was mostly spiritual, in the Mormon tradition. Twenty-three-year-old Asa Judd had a romantic interest in Melinda and there was some discussion as to whether they should marry while she was afflicted. He maintained a vigil at her bedside. A Cherokee Indian, Doctor King of Nephi, arrived on July 3. He diagnosed the disease as "diphtherial tonsilitis" and said the patient had not been given enough physic. On the afternoon of Independence Day, as Melinda began to sink, King administered liquor and sweet niter every seven minutes. It did no good, and he told the family to bid her goodbye.

They placed cold compresses to her throat, back, and wrists, and put heated bricks at her feet. She alternated between periods of calm and violence, but toward morning became quiet. Melinda died peacefully at 5 A.M. on July 5. Warren Johnson later told Asa Judd that sometime in the early morning—about 2 or 3 A.M.—he heard some unseen and unknown power making a commotion out near the old shop. He heard chains being rattled and the banging of objects.[45] Possibly the ferryman revealed that the

LEE'S FERRY CEMETERY

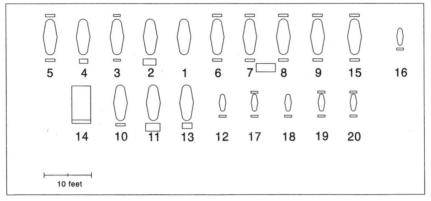

Map of the cemetery at Lee's Ferry.

1. James Jackson, March 10, 1874
2. Winifred Johnson, August 15, 1876
3. Neuman Brown, April 6, 1879
4. Mary Elinor Stowe & baby, December 18, 1880
5. William Brinkerhoff, June 5, 1883
6. Jonathan Smith Johnson, May 19, 1891
7. Laura Alice Johnson, June 11, 1891
8. Permelia Johnson, June 15, 1891
9. Melinda Johnson, July 5, 1891
10. Archimedes McClurg, shot a day or two prior to discovery of his body on November 24, 1894

11. John Green Kitchen, July 13, 1898
12. Lucy Emett, June 11, 1902
13. John Taylor Emett, January 27, 1909 [1910]
14. Waddy Thompson Ligon, October 28, 1925
15. Calvin Marshall Johnson, December 14, 1928
16. Lucius Henry Spencer, March 10, 1931
17–19. Stillborn infants of the polygamous period, 1923–1933
20. Premature infant of A. Shumway–W. E. Johnson, ca.1933

America of 1891 was not very far removed from the Salem of two centuries earlier. Warren and Asa dug the grave while Permelia, Mary, and Polly, with the assistance of Draper's wives, made the clothes. Melinda was buried in mid-afternoon beside the three who had preceded her. Outside of a dedicatory prayer by Asa Judd, there was no service. It was the saddest Sunday any of those in attendance had ever experienced.

King pointed out one fact that made his long call worthwhile—the need for sanitation. They took all the soiled clothes and linen and boiled them thoroughly. Permelia and Nancy recovered, and soon "diphtherial tonsilitis" was a painful page from the past. Asa Judd remained at the ranch for about three weeks to help Johnson mow his alfalfa. The old mower was broken and the cutting had to be done by hand. Asa's presence was beneficial to the depressed family, as well as great physical help since Draper had decided to move on and the ferryman would now be without assistance except when Al Huntington was present. Al did most of his prospecting in the fall and spring; he wintered at the ferry, and when it was warm he retired to the cooler mountains.

The deaths of the four children demoralized Johnson. He told Draper just before the handyman departed that the Lord had promised to take care of his family if he went to the ferry; that promise was broken when his children died.[46] His anguish culminated on July 19 when he poured out his heart to President Woodruff, finishing with the plaintive question: "What have we done that the Lord has left us, and what can we do to regain his favor again?"[47] Johnson gave no indication that his faith had completely failed because he signed off with "Yours in the gospel." Johnson's letter touched the hearts of the brethren in Salt Lake City. On August 3, the president and his two counselors replied that he had done no wrong, that the Lord loved him, and they likened his troubles to the trials of Job.[48] The reassurance must have been a great comfort to the ferryman, giving him the strength to persevere.

News of the family's bereavement spread far and wide. Many murmured sympathy when they heard the story. Warren Foote of Long Valley wrote Johnson a letter of condolence. Both men had been on the Muddy Mission and had followed Bishop Leithead to Glendale. They had been friends for almost a quarter-century. Foote's letter meant much to Johnson and in his reply he unburdened himself even more than he had to the church president. He repeated his statement that God had promised him protection if they all remained faithful to their religion, but that unseen influences were working to destroy that faith.[49] To Johnson, diphtheria represented a struggle between good and evil, God and the Devil, and part of the persecution of the church by the federal government. It never occurred to him that contagious disease was spread by poor sanitation, affecting the good along with the sinners.

Few polygamous families were as close as Warren Johnson's. Samantha and her children agonized in Kanab as much as those at the ferry; misfortune to any one of them was lamented by all. The children of one family regarded their counterparts in the other as full brothers and sisters, and they didn't know the meaning of a half-relationship. Although not experiencing the actual demise of their kindred at the ferry, the Kanab family was just as devastated by the deaths. Draper never learned which children belonged to each wife although he had lived among them for months.[50]

Despite his grief, the ferryman did not ignore the needs of others. On August 2, he recorded crossing a destitute tramp named Peter Baume and charged him nothing. When the Colorado, Grand Canyon Mining and Improvement Company terminated its fruitless trip at Lee's Ferry in mid-August 1891, several members—Best, McDonald, Kane, and Ballard— attempted to reach Lava Canyon overland. These men crossed the ferry regularly. The Best party helped Johnson realize that regardless of personal grief, life still goes on. He was impressed that mining had a future in the immediate vicinity.

Coconino County had been carved out of Yavapai County on February 19, 1891, with the county seat at Flagstaff, making the recording of claims much easier than going all the way to Prescott. That helped the prospectors, who were busy staking claims. Al Huntington located the Copperopolist and Kailabits lode claims near Lamb and Jacob Lakes on August 29, which Warren Johnson recorded at Flagstaff September 28, 1891; he was listed as having one-third interest.[51] In mid-November, Best, McDonald, and Kane located two claims near the Copperopolist at Lamb Lake.[52]

The Judd boys had more than mail contracts on their minds when they carried the pouch between Kanab and Lee's Ferry—Asa, Eli, and Ami Judd were attracted to the Johnson girls. Asa's hopes were dashed when Melinda died, but Eli never slacked off in courting Mary Evelette. On November 26, Warren and Permelia wrote a consent note for their marriage. The young couple put their bedrolls in Eli's buggy and headed for Kanab to spend a few days in the Judd home. They were married in the St. George Temple on December 6, 1891. The Johnson family at Lee's Ferry now had dwindled to the parents, fourteen-year-old Polly, twelve-year-old Nancy, three-year-old LeRoy, and Jody, a babe in arms.

Samantha's older children entered school in Kanab, but Frank soon withdrew to help his father at the ranch. Jerry, two years his senior, stayed in school on a more or less regular basis and became his mother's mainstay at the new home. He hauled wood, made fence, and did the chores of a village youth. Even though Mary's home now was in Kanab, the close family bond was maintained by mail, and a number of letters still exist. At this time, Assistant Church Historian Andrew Jensen noted that the Kanab Ward was the largest in the stake, consisting of the town of Kanab; the villages of Fredonia, Johnson, Pahreah; and two families at Lee's Ferry.[53]

Summers were busier times for the people of Lee's Ferry. The first crop of alfalfa usually was cut in late May or early June, water had to be kept in the ditch, and the fruit ripened—apricots first and peaches second. In the week of July 11–16, the Johnsons extracted 1,338 pounds of honey.[54] August was fruit-drying time; thankfully, the apricots and peaches were out of the way when apples and plums were ready. Grapes ripened in September and most of the crop was dried into raisins. Drying the fruit was more practical than canning because of the expense and difficulty in obtaining jars.

David Brinkerhoff had taken a second wife in November 1888— Lovina Lee, a granddaughter of John D. Lee. He often brought "Aunt Vina" and some of the children of his first wife to the ferry. This was a treat for the youngsters and eased the burden on Lydia, who was not in the best of health. Jerry Johnson, having spent the summer at the river, returned to Kanab before school started, leaving Frank Johnson at the ferry. He had to get in the winter wood supply for Samantha's family and he also was scheduled to cut and haul the Johnson share of fence posts for the Kanab property. Warren

Johnson indicated that he knew his son rather well when he wrote he was not afraid of Jerry's hauling too much wood.[55]

Meanwhile, the dreams of the Arizona Strip's first promoter generated an interest in far-off England that would in time affect the people of northern Arizona. John W. Young had jumped from one promotion to another, going from railroad-building in northern Utah to wool-trading and cloth-manufacturing at Moenkopi. He turned again to railroading and took bed-grading contracts for the Atlantic and Pacific from near the Continental Divide in New Mexico to mid-Arizona. Poor management and failure to follow instructions brought him the mistrust of church leaders and cost him the respect of his loyal Mormon workforce. He shifted to a large-scale operation in the cattle business, somehow acquiring the United Order range rights on Buckskin Mountain and in House Rock Valley. He involved himself in party politics in New York and carried on an effective lobbying campaign on behalf of Mormon interests. He formed corporations, using his ranch holdings as collateral, and dealt in high finance in Europe as well as the United States. Young lived on a high scale and always needed money.[56]

Young conceived the grandiose scheme of building a hunting lodge on the Kaibab where wealthy sportsmen could experience a taste of the Old West. Evidently William F. Cody's Wild West Show, then playing in England, provided the motivation. Young got Cody's interest by emphasizing the number of horses in his herds and the opportunity whereby Buffalo Bill could replenish his stock. He painted such a glowing picture of the area that two well-heeled Englishmen, with Cody and his key personnel, decided to take a look.

The prestigious party, which detrained at Flagstaff on November 3, 1892, was representative of the circles in which Cody traveled. The Englishmen were Major St. John Mildmay, Baronet, and Colonel W. H. McKinnon of the Grenadier Guards of London. Both had participated in Britain's wars of the times and had helped put down the Sepoy rebellion. They were typical tweed-wearing members of the sporting set who sipped fine whisky between shots at grouse that were flushed by the beaters. They had brought a goodly supply of choice Scotch from the homeland, liquor that simply was not available in the hinterlands. The one who arranged the details and saw that they were well publicized was Cody's public relations man, Major John M. Burke. Colonel Prentiss Ingraham, the well-known dime novelist; Johnny Baker, the crack shot in the Wild West Show; Horton S. Boal, Cody's son-in-law and present manager of his old ranch; R. H. "Pony Bob" Haslam, Cody's old friend and noted Pony Express rider; and Captain W. H. Broach of North Platte, Nebraska, constituted the Cody faction. Broach had lost an arm in the Civil War and had taken up photography and he recorded the trip for posterity.

John W. Young was not present, having remained in London, but with the famous Buffalo Bill acting as guide and being the center of attention,

Young didn't need to be present. Meeting the party were the astute Julius F. Wells, who represented both Young and the church interests, along with E. D. Woolley and Dan Seegmiller, who headed the Mormon teamsters and would serve as local guides. A French chef handled the culinary department. Several businessmen, attracted by the general glamour of the group, probably footed some of the bills and hung around the fringes as far as Flagstaff and Grand Canyon. The industrialists were George P. Everhardt and R. H. Hoslin of Chicago; Clarence Chandler, Arthur Patterson, and W. P. Dowd of New York; and Edward C. Bradford of Denver, who most likely procured the passes from the Union Pacific at John W. Young's request. Colonel Allison Naylor represented Washington, D.C. Although the visitors could have taken in all the sights of 1892 Flagstaff from their windows in the Del Monte Hotel, they strolled around town to sample the local color firsthand. Next day, they chartered teams and headed for Grand Canyon. They were back in Flagstaff on November 10, where the city men caught the train for their respective homes.

On November 12, the Mormons loaded the Englishmen and Cody's people in their wagons and started out for Lee's Ferry, arriving late in the afternoon of the fifteenth. They crossed at the lower ferry, then drove to the ranch and pitched camp in Johnson's field. The garden bounty, grapes, melons, fresh beef, milk, and butter were welcome treats, and the group remained several days. During this period, Broach took some pictures of the ranch, including one of Warren and Permelia Johnson, Lovina Lee Brinkerhoff, and their children sitting at the front of the house where the porch was to have been.

When they moved on later in the week, Al Huntington became a member of the party to help guide the visitors to the best hunting. They went first to Cane Ranch, which at that time was the headquarters of John W. Young's operation. Anthony W. Ivins had just replaced Woolley and Seegmiller as manager of the spread, and he appeared in some of the pictures when Broach again unlimbered his camera. The stay at Cane was brief; the party soon moved into the forests and meadows of the mountaintop as it was getting too late in the season for dallying in the high country. On November 26, Broach took a picture of the party on the north rim of Grand Canyon and Cody named the place "MacKinnon Point" in honor of the visiting Englishman who had just killed his first buck of the trip. Seven of the group signed a paper which was put in a can and placed in a cairn.

The party went on to Kanab at the end of the month where those not accustomed to a steady, vigorous life rested at President Woolley's home for three days. The imported chef attempted to prepare gourmet meals but failed to master the technique of getting performance from the wood-burning stove. Sister Woolley then took over the cooking and put on a Mormon-style feast. When the company gathered at the heavily-laden table, Dee Woolley asked Cody to give the blessing. Ordinarily this would have been a risky request, but Buffalo Bill rose to the occasion just as he had in the duel with Yellow Hand. As the evidence of Woolley bounty stimulated his taste

Buffalo Bill Cody and his entourage on the ferryboat, November 15, 1892 (*W. H. Broach photograph, P. T. Reilly Collection, Cline Library, Northern Arizona University*).

buds, nose, and eyes, he said, "God bless the hands that made them custard pies."[57] They traveled on to Skutumpah to enjoy more hunting at Seegmiller's ranch before going north to the railroad. Despite the good hunting and spectacular scenery, the Englishmen did not invest in Young's scheme; the promoter was left high and dry, still needing money for the hunting lodge.

Extensive publicity from the Stanton and Best adventures had renewed interest in Glen Canyon gold recovery. Several veteran trappers and promoters had been working the canyon and its drainage in recent years, among them Jack Sumner of the Powell party and Ed Mesken, a loner. Stanton talked to both men in December 1889.[58] Now others entered the game, coming in by trail or down the river in rowboats.

Two men who had the same idea at almost the same time were Friend Grant Faatz and George M. Wright. Faatz and an unnamed partner built a boat and embarked at Green River, Utah, in August 1892. When they came to the rough water in Cataract Canyon, they had the good judgment to stop and examine the rapids before plunging in. Thus it was that they were led to the boulder at Rapid 15, where the Best party had lost their number one boat on July 22, 1891. Faatz cut his own name close by and the date

The Johnson house at Lee's Ferry, November 1892. From left to right, foreground, LeRoy and Frank Johnson and, background, Johnny Baker, Colonel Prentiss Imgraham, Lovina Lee Brinkerhoff, and Permelia S. Johnson (*W. H. Broach photograph, P. T. Reilly Collection, Cline Library, Northern Arizona University*).

"Aug. 27, 1892." They made it safely through Cataract Canyon and worked their way down Glen Canyon. They ran into Billy Wright's camp at Gretchen Bar and helped themselves to his supplies. When they heard voices and the sounds of approaching horses, they thought it best to get in their boats and wait offshore in case the campers turned out to be unfriendly. This was a wise precaution because as soon as the men saw they had been hosts to uninvited guests, they let loose with curses and pistol shots that forced Faatz and his partner to pull into the current and run the minor rapid in the dark. Somewhere downstream, the partner died and Faatz continued on alone, working whatever unoccupied bar caught his fancy.

George Wright was grubstaked by two groups in Salt Lake City that were headed by Abraham Hanauer, president of the Alliance Mining Company and manager of the Hanauer Smelting Works, and Charles B. Markland, co-proprietor of the Conklin Sampling Works. Wright started from Green River about three weeks after Faatz and, like him, cut his name in the boulder at Rapid 15 on September 18, 1892. He documented his progress downstream by cutting his name at Sheep Canyon on October 11, and at the mouth of Aztec Creek early in December.

Wright continued downstream and late in the day spotted a shallow cave at the head of a right-hand bar. It was getting cold, the weather was threatening, so he made camp. In the morning he did some panning with no appreciable return. Purely on impulse, he used a spoon to scoop out the material between two bedding-plane cracks. He picked out some pea-size nuggets and coarse gold with his fingers without panning, but use of the pan resulted in the recovery of a considerable amount of finer gold. He worked steadily until the elongated pockets along the surface exposures were exhausted, then staked a claim called the "Pure Gold" on November 14. Later, he recorded his claim in the names of himself, his wife L. C. Wright, five members of the Markland family, and A. Hanauer, Jr.[59] He described his claim as being on the right bank, three miles below Warm Creek and about fifteen miles upstream from Lee's Ferry.

In the afternoon, Faatz pulled in at the camp and learned of Wright's good fortune. The next day, they departed together as their supplies were getting low and they thought they were close to Lee's Ferry. They camped that night on a small bar on the right side; unwittingly, they had stopped at an old Indian winter camp that offered access to the rim. Both men cut their names in the sandstone, along with the date—November 16, 1892. In the morning, they moved on toward the ferry and made camp on the bank above the *Nellie*. On a sandstone ledge above the mooring, Wright cut his name and the date—November 17, 1892. The men purchased fresh supplies from the ferryman and, as had so many before them, began panning along the shore. Wright made friends with Warren Johnson and roused his interest in placer mining by showing him the gold he had gleaned from the Pure Gold claim. The ferryman had never seen so much gold and was as impressed as Faatz.

From this time forward, Johnson's opinions about gold mining changed. He no longer held it in disdain as did most Mormons, and he grasped how mining laws could benefit him and his church. At the Kanab Quarterly Conference in May, he donated fifty-four dollars in the name of each member of his families toward the building of the Salt Lake Temple. He also discussed his interest in gold mining and the ease with which claims could hold land legally with the local authorities. He received their approval not only to stake some likely ground for himself but to secure strategic locations for the ferry and access roads through the filing of such claims. He was quick to see that the ferry locations could best be controlled by mining claims because land titles in the area at this time were not obtainable until legal descriptions could be furnished, and the region had not been subdivided.

On June 4, 1893, he located the Johnson Placer, eighty by three hundred rods, which took in the right bank of the Colorado River to one-quarter mile inland, and from the mouth of Pahreah River one mile west to the wash down which the road approached the river. The co-locators were his two wives, H. E. Judd, C. A. Huntington, Jeremiah Johnson, J. B. Francis, and Joseph Meeks. Three days later, he located a lode claim, six hundred by fifteen hundred feet, at Five Mile Point. Appropriately, he named this one "Wayside" and listed F. G. Faatz as his witness. These two claims controlled the approach to the ferry and the ranch. Both were recorded at Flagstaff on June 19, 1893.[60]

George Wright, his wife, and two employees returned to the ferry in mid-September. He erected a tent in Johnson's field near Samantha's old cabin and settled down to spend the winter. They had a skiff, and with Ervin and Faatz as his assistants, Wright went upriver to work the Pure Gold claim.[61] He took gold out and enough people saw it so that the site between twenty-four and twenty-five miles upstream of Lee's Ferry became known as "Wright Bar." It proved to be a magnet to gold hunters for almost two decades.

Further evidence that Johnson's plans for the future had wandered away from the ferry is indicated by the fact that he, Al Huntington, Joseph Meeks, and Jarod Taylor had planted five hundred fingerling trout in Duck Lake (now called Navajo Lake) in the northwest corner of Kane County. They filed their intention to appropriate the lake for the purpose of raising fish and stated they intended to plant five thousand more in the summer of 1894.[62]

Jesse N. Smith was one Mormon leader who still depended on draft animals instead of the train exclusively. He and his family set out from Snowflake August 31, 1893, crossed at Lee's Ferry September 11, and reached Salina on October 4. He took the railway to Salt Lake City, attended conference, and started home four days later.[63] Early in November, Bill and Clara Lee stopped at the ferry as they traveled south. They had given up the Pahreah place and hoped that Bill's brush with the law had blown over in Winslow. Permelia showed Clara a grapevine that Bill's mother had planted and nourished while her husband was in prison. Clara was eight months pregnant, so they settled for the time being in Tuba City where Bill Lee, Jr., was born on December 8.[64]

The county seat at Flagstaff slowly was becoming important to the residents of the strip for matters that once had been taken to Kanab. On November 27, 1893, Warren Johnson registered his brand there— ⋉ . His cattle and horses were branded on the right sides and right thighs, respectively.[65]

Wright and his men worked the Pure Gold claim all winter, returning to the ferry only when they needed supplies. He paid cash for everything, and the money augmented Johnson's ferry income. Coming down river was easy but going upstream with a loaded boat was slower, requiring most of two days. On one such trip, Wright cut his name and the date "Dec. 23, 1893" in a large, arch-like cave seven and one-half miles below his claim.[66] On January 6, 1894, Nathaniel Galloway, trapping his way down Glen Canyon on his first trip to Lee's Ferry, camped there and wrote his name and the date on the back of the cave using a piece of charcoal from his campfire.[67]

Digging paydirt on the Pure Gold claim was different from the method used on other Glen Canyon bars. The overburden was thin, and in places the cross-bedded sandstone was exposed. Wright found that the thin-bedded strata had acted as riffles in a sluice box; the gold had collected in the cracks that formed naturally along the bedding planes. Therefore, instead of moving vast amounts of sand and gravel and sluicing it, the job consisted of patiently scooping out the material in the cracks with a spoon and working with a goldpan. Some nuggets and stringers were large enough to be picked out dry. His helpers received wages for removing thin overburden and exposing more fissures.

Evidently exhausting the workable crevices by early spring, Wright decided to search the higher ground for the source of the gold. He and Faatz probably used the same route that Juan Domingo and Lucrecio Muñiz had taken in 1776 to reconnoiter Navajo Canyon. They covered the plateau extensively without finding a likely outcropping where the gold could have originated. They even reached the rim of the Echo monocline and looked down on the ranch in the mouth of Pahreah Canyon.[68] Figuring that further working of the Pure Gold claim was fruitless, they returned to the ferry but kept their opinions to themselves. On April 13, 1894, Wright sold one-eighth interest in the Pure Gold claim to Warren Johnson for six hundred dollars It is not known that Johnson ever visited the claim, but he bought his interest on the basis of the gold poke that Wright had exhibited. He recorded the purchase on his next trip to Flagstaff on May 28.[69]

The Wright-Johnson practice of holding strategic areas by filing mineral claims had not gone unnoticed. Anthony W. Ivins, endeavoring to pull John W. Young's cattle operation out of the red, filed lode claims on November 19 and 20 to hold springs at Two Mile, House Rock, and the Pools; George Wright signed as witness.[70] Wright maintained his camp at the ferry and began prospecting along the Vermilion Cliffs. On April 30, he cut his name in a panel of petroglyphs near the top of an old Indian trail above Jacob's Pools. He did not remain out very long at a time and his frequent visits to the ferry enabled him and the ferryman to maintain a friendly relationship.

At the same time, Johnson appears to have developed some long range plans that would affect his family and the ferry. He had been negotiating with the Beebe family for more Kanab property and concluded an agreement early in the summer. Customarily getting double duty from any trip he made, he spoke at the assemblage. Six days later he finalized the purchase of Lots 1 and 4 in Block 26 from Gilbert R., Emma A., and Sarah E. Beebe.[71] He returned to the ferry, and June 27 he and Wright notified their six co-owners of the Pure Gold claim that they had done the assessment work on the claim for the previous year and for them to remit their share of the cost within ninety days or lose their interest in the claim. Johnson recorded the notification at Flagstaff on July 27, 1894.[72] It is not known what plans he and Wright had for the claim they now owned jointly.

In September, Lorenzo Hill Hatch, Jesse N. Smith, Z. B. Decker, Jr., and Henry Copland formed a party to travel together to Utah. They reached the left bank at 11:30 A.M. on the eighteenth and fired their pistols until 4 P.M. before rousing anyone at the ranch. Finally, Al Huntington and Jeremiah Johnson arrived to cross them; Warren Johnson was away and Al Huntington was in charge.[73] This is the first recorded instance of Jerry Johnson ferrying travelers, although he had probably helped his father previously. He would make many more trips across the river in ferryboats. As it turned out, Johnson was in Kanab where he spoke in church meeting on the twenty-third. With a second home in town, he spent more time away from the ferry. He added to his town holdings on November 12 when he purchased Lots 2 and 3 in Block 25 from Sarah Beebe.[74] He now owned the equivalent of an entire block and obviously had plans for using the property.

Some time that fall of 1894, a lone man named Archimedes McClurg appeared at the ferry. His wife had last seen him in August of 1891 at Denver and had no idea of his where-abouts. Passing himself off as a Mormon missionary, he remained in one of the guest cabins for a week or so, then continued south. His body was found at Navajo Spring on November 24 by Seth B. Tanner and two teamsters who were freighting between Utah and Tuba City. They went back to the ferry and brought Warren Johnson, Al Huntington, and George Wright to join Tanner, his son Joseph, and Reuben E. Powell in holding an impromptu inquest. McClurg had been shot at close range, the bullet entering the left breast and exiting under the right shoulder. Both of his pockets were partially pulled out and his watch and glasses were missing. Those from the ferry identified him by his appearance, clothes, and two missing fingers on his left hand. They pronounced him killed by persons unknown, although they suspected the murderers were Navajos who had killed him for whatever he had. They took the body to Lee's Ferry for burial in as Christian-like manner as possible on November 25.[75]

Travelers now were just as likely to be crossed by Al Huntington or Jerry or Frank Johnson as by the assigned ferryman. Warren Johnson managed to visit Samantha more often than at the quarterly conferences, and he frequently attended Sabbath meetings in town, which he had never done in the earlier days. He was among the speakers whenever present and was obviously one of the leading men in the stake. His last child, Elnora, was born to Samantha in Kanab on September 9, 1895; she was Johnson's first child not born at the ferry since 1877.

Warren Johnson's plans for the next phase of his life culminated when he attended the stake conference held December 7–8, 1895, at Orderville.[76] As usual, he was one of the speakers, but it was between and after sessions that the significant meetings took place. Previous discussions between President E. D. Woolley and himself had established the fact that his mission could end when suitable replacements were found for him and the property in the mouth of Pahreah Canyon, including the upper and lower ferry sites. Woolley discovered both in the person of James Simpson Emett, who operated the Cottonwood Ranch. The place was located about five miles west by north of Kanab. To reach it one had to travel to Fredonia, go west a couple of miles, then go northward up a wash that became a canyon—a roundabout way of over twenty miles. Although isolated, it was well watered, had about twenty acres of meadow and was surrounded by a good range. A deal was worked out whereby Warren Johnson would trade the Pahreah Canyon ranch and ferry proprietorship to Emett for the Cottonwood property. Woolley favored the proposition and assured him that he could obtain church approval. Instead of returning home after the conference, Johnson remained in Kanab to examine the proposal.

On December 12, 1895, Johnson and Woolley were returning from Cottonwood Ranch after picking up a load of hay for the president. As they approached the state line, about three miles from town, the wagon lurched and both men were thrown out. Cat-like, Woolley landed on his feet, but Johnson came down heavily on the base of his spine.[77] Paralyzed from the waist down and in great pain, he was taken to Samantha's home, was made as comfortable is possible, and was prayed over. The ferryman was about to fall victim to the same medical deficiencies that had plagued Franklin Nims and the four dead children.

Frank Johnson had been sent to Glendale for a load of flour and potatoes, and did not learn of the accident until his return. Early the next morning he set out for the ferry to break the news to Permelia and to bring her, Nancy, LeRoy, and Jody to Kanab. The team of Moose and Kelly was getting old but he drove there in three days' time and returned just as fast. The once-busy ferry was a silent place occupied only by Jerry Johnson and Al Huntington. Luckily, at this time of year only the livestock and ferry required attention, while both wives were needed in Kanab to attend the invalid. In addition to rustling firewood and attending to other chores, Frank sat with his father and saw to his needs at night.

Several days passed before it was realized that Johnson's spine actually was broken. The sad information was relayed to Salt Lake City and printed in the *Deseret Evening News* on December 20, 1895. The ferryman had many friends throughout Zion, and numerous prayers were said for him. In a Kanab fast on January 2, 1896, with Bishop J. H. Johnson presiding, James L. Bunting offered a lengthy prayer for the injured man. Twelve days later, President Woolley, his counselor Thomas Chamberlain, and a number of the leading brethren, after fasting for twenty-four hours, met at Johnson's home where they prayed and administered to him. Before leaving, they announced that he was blessed and improved.[78] While he might have been soothed spiritually, his physical condition was no better, and his pain was just as great.

The stake leader left for Salt Lake City late in January and called at the church office on February 5. He discussed Johnson's case, suggested terms of the property exchange, and endorsed James Emett as the next ferryman.[79] It appears that the recommendations were taken under consideration and no immediate answer was given, at least until hearing from the paralyzed ferryman. The First Presidency responded with a tithing order of one hundred dollars on Kanab Stake for Johnson, and a letter, which boosted his spirits, that told him they understood he was recovering.[80] Under the circumstances, no one broached the subject of the property transfer. Johnson wanted a firm idea of his possible recovery before he came to a decision.

Henry Eli Judd (Mary Johnson's husband) carried the mail to and from the ferry during the entire month of February. The Mail Trail was developed from an old Indian route between House Rock Spring and Navajo Well. It went across the valley, descended a mile north of Rock Canyon, and cut across the flats to Eight Mile Spring. Powell's packers had learned about it from local Paiutes and used it in December 1871. It had been in use for more than fifteen years, and although it was considerably shorter than the wagon road, it still required a good horse and a hard ride that began before daylight and usually ended after dark. The all-time record for this leg probably was held by Warren Johnson as he once rode to Kanab in nine hours during an emergency; his horse was a pacer named Billy whose stride ate up the miles.[81]

Al Huntington no longer could take the summer heat at the ferry. When warm weather approached, he retired to the cool elevation of Hatchtown. Jerry Johnson could not operate the ferry alone, so his father hired Alex Swapp of Kanab for twenty-five dollars a month plus board. Both lads were the same age and more inclined to play than work. They spent their time swimming, diving off the old Nielson boat, and riding trees at flood time down to the lower crossing. Little farming was done and the ditch wasn't cleaned. Although Warren Johnson had put up almost one hundred tons of hay a year, Jerry and Alex barely cut enough to feed a team and one cow over the winter.

That summer Frank Johnson took Permelia to the ferry to collect the remainder of her things that had not been taken in the hasty trip of December 1895.[82] She and Frank were not impressed with Jerry's assiduity. Her report of the lackadaisical work ethic exhibited by his son probably helped her husband decide to relinquish his interest in the ferry. Johnson must have realized that his eldest son lacked the sense of responsibility needed to operate both the farm and the ferry and was better suited to be a small-time rancher. He finally concluded it was best to give up the larger operation.

September frequently brought intense storms to the country. One such storm struck east-central Utah during a visit Frank Johnson made to the ferry.[83] The initial inkling of heavy rainfall upstream came when he went down to the river to get a barrel of water. The first channel, which should have been dry, was filled with a muddy torrent and high amount of trash, indicating heavy runoff from upstream. Obtaining the water became a matter of minor importance; he ran back to the ranch for Jerry to help save the ferryboat. When they reached the crossing, the two anchor posts were submerged and the boat was sixty to seventy feet offshore and plunging crazily in the eddy, which was changing by the minute. The boys fastened two lariats together and Jerry tied the end of one around his waist. He swam out, climbed aboard, and Frank pulled them both to shore.

The river rose at the rate of one foot per hour. Knowing from experience that it would fall just as quickly, they remained there to keep the boat snubbed to shore because, when the flow receded, she must be pushed out to prevent being stranded. It was twenty-four hours before the river approached its normal flow. The boys worked through the night and took turns napping when they could. The silt content had increased so extensively that thousands of fish were killed, some of them five to six feet long. During the height of the flood, Frank saw the old *Nellie* come into view, heading downstream. After tying the ferryboat securely, they took ropes and walked upstream, hoping the runaway would come close enough to shore for them to get a line on her. Nielson's boat had grounded in the first channel, so close that they splashed out and tied her up with little trouble. The peak runoff in 1897 did not reach the flow of this September flood and the *Nellie* sat there in the rocks, a monument to her free-thinking builder.[84]

While the details of Warren Johnson's property exchange were being ironed out, George F. Flavell and his companion, Ramón Montéz, arrived at the ferry on October 12. They had come downstream from Green River, Wyoming, the first since Powell to have boated this far on a continuous trip. In his own delightful style, Flavell described their debarkation in his journal entry of the thirteenth: "We arrived here yesterday; went up to the house, which is some distance from the river. We were received by a B. Goat, 3 pups, and 2 hogs but nothing that could talk. I skirmished around and my gentle voice echoed among the hills til it roused 4 Navajo squaws up on a spur of the mountain, and they pointed down the river. I finally found out that the Ferry Man, Post master, and sole occupant of the country was down below getting off a boat the high water had deposited upon the side of the mountain. We built a log fire on the beach which brought him up."[85] The lone occupant, of course, was Jerry Johnson—Alex Swapp had returned to Kanab after the summer. The September flood had receded even more after Frank Johnson's departure, leaving the ferryboat stranded. Jerry had neglected to check and he was trying to refloat her, extending more labor than if he had paid proper attention to the situation in the first place; now, he was forced to dig and pry to be ready for the fall season. He accomplished the job by the fifteenth in time to cross forty Navajos who were going hunting on Buckskin Mountain.

That night, Flavell and Montéz slept with their guns handy in case anyone snooped around their camp. The voyagers spent the next four days overhauling their boat. The slow water of Glen Canyon caused them to add another pair of oarlocks so that two men could row at the same time. They departed on October 17 but soon learned that the water in Marble and Grand Canyons was quite different from that of Glen, and the extra oarlocks were unnecessary.

Clark Allen (Al) Huntington died at the Johnson home in Kanab on November 16, only twenty days after his sixty-fifth birthday. He had lived a hard but adventurous life. Along with the Johnson family, most of the early residents turned out for his funeral.

President E. D. Woolley acted for the church in the sale of the ferry. He selected one appraiser, Warren Johnson selected another, and both selected a third. The present value was to be determined, the purchase price of three thousand dollars paid to Emma Lee was deducted, and the remainder was given to Johnson for the improvements he had made. The ferry was appraised at sixty-five hundred dollars. Warren M. and Permelia J. Johnson quit-claimed the property to Wilford Woodruff, trustee-in-trust for the Church of Jesus Christ of Latter-day Saints, on November 28, 1896. Although Johnson claimed one-third interest—the other thirds belonging to Permelia and Samantha—the second wife was not mentioned and neither was the Cottonwood Ranch.

In this deed, Lee's Ferry consisted of the upper and lower ferries on the Colorado River; ferryboats and all the apparatus; all lands and improvements; thirty-two acres of alfalfa and six acres of orchards, vineyards, and garden; and one and one-half miles of ditch.[86] At the same time, Wilford Woodruff, through his agent E. D. Woolley, signed a lease to James S. Emett of Orderville for the same property to cover a period of five years. This document is more specific, listing upper and lower ferries, two ferryboats, three skiffs, farm, orchard, one and one-half miles of ditch, one frame house of six rooms all unfurnished, outhouses, and corrals, for an annual rental of a hundred dollars, to be made in improvements.[87]

The Johnson family fortunes went from bad to worse. Warren, permanently bedridden, was determined to keep his two families together despite the ban on plural marriage. Mormon thinking in general was that this way of life could be maintained better in Canada than the United States. Succumbing to pressure from Jeremiah and his new son-in-law, Jim Smith, Warren decided to move there.[88] Jerry had married Annie Young in the St. George Temple on September 1, 1898, and their first child was born in Kanab on May 24, 1900. Early that summer, Warren Johnson was placed on a mattress in a wagon headed north, driven by Permelia, and carrying their remaining two young children, LeRoy and Jody. Another wagon driven by Jerry conveyed his wife, their child, Alice, and Samantha's two daughters, Mattie and Lucy. At Leamington, they picked up a third wagon driven by Jim Smith with Nancy and their child. In Salt Lake City, their destination was changed to the Big Horn Basin, Wyoming, where they arrived in August. Two companies of migrants had preceded them that spring.[89]

Frank Johnson was left in Kanab to sell the town lots and the Cottonwood Ranch. At age twenty-two, he married Rhoda Young, Annie's cousin, at St. George on December 19, 1900. The unsophisticated young man had trouble finding buyers for his father's property, but he had orders from him to take whatever prices he could get. There was no money in the country and the potential purchasers beat him down unmercifully. He finally sold the town properties for some poor teams and wagons. Jake Crosby offered him sixty head of cattle, a team and a wagon for the ranch, and Frank took it. The responsibility was awesome for a young man with less than three months of schooling.

Dan Judd agreed to help drive the cattle and Frank assembled his outfit. Just then Jerry Johnson appeared on the scene, having been sent by his father to aid the move. On June 17, 1901, Frank and his pregnant wife Rhoda; Jerry; Samantha and her four youngest children, Price, Estella, Elmer, and Elnora; and the widowed Lizzie Johnson Carling and her two children pulled out of Kanab with three wagons and six work horses, some riding stock, and one hundred cattle. Judd went as far as Marysvale before returning home. Warren Johnson recorded the party's arrival at Byron, Wyoming, on September 7 and noted that eighty-six cattle survived the long trek. The people arrived broke.

The winter of 1901–02 was very severe, even for Wyoming, and most of the Johnson cattle perished. The northern growing season was brief, little crop was raised, and food was short. The adults reduced their consumption to a bare minimum, often going hungry to provide meals for the youngsters. After a month of intense suffering, Warren Johnson died just before dusk on March 10, 1902. Permelia wrote the sad news to Mary Judd two days later, noting that "he was the poorest person I ever saw."[90] Frank estimated that his father's weight was under one hundred pounds at his death. Warren Johnson had control of the ferry for more than twenty years and created an oasis of productivity in a barren wilderness. He is remembered best as the helpful Saint on the Arizona Road who extended a hand to anyone who needed it, regardless of creed.

7

The Controversial Emetts

JIM EMETT'S ROOTS WENT BACK TO THE EARLY DAYS OF THE CHURCH OF Jesus Christ of Latter-day Saints and a different spelling of the family name. Jim's grandfather, James Emmett, was said to have been born February 22, 1803, in Boone County, Kentucky, where he married Phoebe Simpson in 1823. The couple's son, Moses Simpson Emmett, was born on May 14, 1824. The family joined the church in September 1832, and James Emmett became a devout follower of Joseph Smith. He was active in the church in Kirtland, Ohio, and then in Missouri in 1836. As a result of a family disagreement in 1849, Emmett started for California with his seventeen-year-old daughter, Lucinda; his wife and their other children remained in Iowa with their son.

Moses Simpson Emmett started for the gathering place in the Salt Lake Valley in the summer of 1850, accompanied by his wife, Catherine, their two children, his mother Phoebe, and two of her children. On July 28, beside the bank of the Platte River in what is now Nebraska, Moses and Catherine's third child and first son was born. They named him James Simpson Emmett after his grandfather and father. On reaching their destination, the family was assigned a ranch on the Weber River in what is now North Ogden. Here, four more children were born, including Thomas Carlos in May 1854.

The Emmetts were called south to support the Cotton Mission in 1863. They settled at Fort Hamblin, on the edge of Mountain Meadows, where their last child, Moses Mosia, was born on the final day of the year. Moses Simpson took a second wife, Electa Jane Westover, on October 24, 1870, but the diminutive seventeen-year-old girl was not received well by his first wife or her children. It is said that her family position was closer to that of a servant than a wife. She never bore children and was turned out of the house on her husband's death in 1907.[1]

Jim and Tom Emmett grew to maturity at Mountain Meadows, learning to ride, rope, and shoot. Jim often packed two guns, was adept with either hand, and gave exhibitions at social gatherings; he was even better with a rifle. He could ride almost anything, appreciated blooded stock, and was a good handler of animals. He married Emma Jane Lay of Santa

145

James S. Emett, ca.1875 (*P. T. Reilly Collection, Cline Library, Northern Arizona University*).

Clara on April 2, 1872, then returned to live at Fort Hamblin. Early attempts to raise a family were only partly successful. The first child and third child lived only a few months; the second, named Emma Jane, and fourth, named William, made it to maturity to become important members of the family. On June 12, 1880, Jim and Emma Jane became parents of the first of four children to be born at Kanab. The boy was named John Taylor Emmett, but he grew to maturity as "Jack."

Shrewd and ambitious, Jim Emmett went after his objectives aggressively and began accumulating land and stock. In 1874, he paid taxes on three and one-half irrigated acres at Glendale.[2] The entire Emmett clan moved east in 1878 when Moses Simpson Emmett and his two sons leased the Cottonwood and Cave Lakes ranches from the Winsor Castle Stock Growing Company. Apparently, they had options to buy and Tom Emmett exercised the right to acquire Cottonwood at the beginning of 1879, while Jim took Cave Lakes.[3] The following day, January 3, the Winsor property was transferred to the Canaan Cooperative Stock Company.[4] A month later, Tom Emmett purchased seventy-one head of livestock for the place, and both Emmett boys were in business.

James Andrus resigned as superintendent of the Canaan operation on July 21, 1879, but agreed to stay on until a replacement could be found. On November 4, Erastus Snow offered the position to Jim—who by now had shortened his last name to Emett—and he immediately went to work without discussing his compensation.[5] When Jim attended the board meetings at St. George in mid-December, he demanded an annual salary of fifteen hundred dollars plus board for himself and family. Snow and Andrus considered the demand unreasonable but agreed for the time being as there was no one else to whom they could turn. At that time, Emett had charge of company operations at Andrus Spring, Short Creek, and Pipe Spring Ranches, but all sales of stock were to be made through the board.

In June, Snow made a tour of the company ranches and noted that Emett and his hands were "having trouble distinguishing the company's unbranded calves." The apostle's terminology may or may not have been a euphemism.[6] During the board meeting of December 8, 1880, Emett insisted that his salary be $1,200 in cash or $600 in cash and $1,000 in capital stock, plus board for himself and family. The offer was rejected; at the meeting a week later, D. D. McArthur and James Andrus were instructed to appraise the stock, take inventory of the property, and release Emett.[7] His superintendency had run from November 1, 1879, to December 31, 1880.

Jim Emett was not above working as a cowhand for the outfit he had once bossed, as the Canaan Minute Books record that he gathered stock for them in November 1881. He maintained the good will of the Canaan board by tipping them off when independent cattlemen jumped their springs. Evidently he based his operations in Kanab and on April 7, 1882, was awarded two shares of water by the Kanab Irrigation Company for Lot 3, Block 13.

A widespread rustling operation came to a head in the summer of 1882 when a number of motherless, long-eared calves were found in the tributaries of Cottonwood Canyon. Gentile cattlemen such as John G. Kitchen and the Webber brothers had experienced losses for several years, but when it was ascertained that some of the calves had come from the Canaan Co-op herd, the matter became a full-fledged crime. Secular law in Kanab at this time was only nominal, but ecclesiastical justice touched three Emett boys, Wilford Holladay, and Gentile Arthur Sawyer. On Sunday, August 13, 1882, the hand of fellowship was withdrawn from Thomas C. Emett and Wilford Holladay. The same action was taken against Moses M. Emett the following Sunday. Sawyer was charged with grand larceny and placed under bond. Tom Emett fled, leaving his wife and six children at Cottonwood Ranch. John M. MacFarlane and Richard Bentley came from St. George to help Bishop William D. Johnson with the interrogations. Moses M. Emett, not yet nineteen, turned state's evidence and confessed; Holladay and Sawyer confessed in part. According to the bishop, they all implicated Jim Emett.[8]

The affair touched off a political battle between Erastus Snow and Bishop Johnson. MacFarlane exposed the accusations against Jim Emett, which started a life-long feud between him and the bishop. Tom Emett's wife then tried to sell Cottonwood to Mr. Webber, and when Bishop Johnson heard about it he forbade her to sell to any Gentile. This provoked a quarrel in which Sister Emett said she would sell to the man despite the bishop's objections. However, Webber was more interested in the Pipe Spring Ranch and attempted to purchase it. Again he encountered ecclesiastical roadblocks. The bishop wrote to Nuttall saying that if a reputable Mormon could not be induced to lease the place, Kanab Ward or the co-op would take it over in preference to selling it to an outsider.[9] Jim Emett solved his sister-in-law's problem by assuming control of the ranch on a sub rosa arrangement, and Sister Emett joined her husband in 1883 to make a fresh start in the Pine Valley Mountains.

The entire case might have been blown out of proportion by a power struggle between the L. John Nuttall–W. D. Johnson faction on one side and their detractors on the other. Jim Emett and the bishop never buried the hatchet, and early in 1884, Johnson wrote Nuttall that Emett was about to jump some of his son's land.[10] E. D. Woolley replaced Nuttall as stake president on June 8, 1884. The bishop's last years were not happy ones and with this change Jim Emett became a minor part of the new power structure.

Emett sparked controversy wherever he went. Many men attributed his ethics to those of a wolf, but he also possessed some of that animal's admirable qualities—loyalty and perseverance. He was a hard bargainer in an acquisitive society, had a strong sense of self-preservation, and was quick to see the nature of a problem. He was unconventional in his use of new methods to attack old problems and rarely used traditional techniques when it was obvious to him that something new would result in improvement. His judgment in practical matters usually was exceptional save where his children were concerned, and there he was indulgent. He was driven to improve and mixed a nimble sense of humor with his work. He loved animals almost as much as children and had a profusion of pets around his home. Politically aware, he cultivated and maintained friends among the leaders of any group with which he was associated, be it Mormon or Gentile.

Sixty years after his death old-timers still spin yarns about him and his exploits. Some of the stories might be exaggerated or inexact in detail but probably are based in fact. It seems that Nephi Johnson had a cutting horse that was far superior to any other in the country and Jim Emett decided he had to own the animal. Nephi, however, turned down every offer Jim made; the horse simply was not for sale at any price. One day Emett found the animal unattended and could not resist the temptation. He roped and threw it, then skinned Nephi's brand off with a sharp knife and seared the wound with the bottom of a heated frying pan. Nephi and everyone else knew what had taken place but without his brand Johnson could not prove the horse was his. A deadly enmity grew between the two men. Each uttered some harsh words against the other.

A year or so passed. Jim Emett was on the range when he came upon one of Johnson's cows mired past her belly in quicksand. He tied his horse and began digging on one side of the animal, having no tool but his hands. He had been at work for almost two hours when Nephi happened by, took in the situation, and without saying a word began digging on the other side. He, too, had nothing but his hands. The men worked in silence for more than an hour, then just as the cow was about to be freed, their eyes locked over the animal's back. Each stuck out a hand and the interrupted friendship was resumed.[11] This time it lasted.

An example of Jim Emett's appraisal of needs was his reaction after Samuel Brinkerhoff had lost a leg in a threshing machine accident at Glendale. Everybody expressed sympathy except Emett, who said he needed something more, and he gave him a $20 gold piece.[12]

Records indicate that Jim Emett gave strong support to the ecclesiastic side of life, frequently speaking in Sunday meetings and offering prayers that opened and closed quarterly conferences. Often he administered the sacrament. He was one of the signing founders of the Church Association of the Kanab Stake of Zion on December 9, 1886. In 1887, he went on a mission to northern Mexico and met the girl who would become his second wife. He returned to Kanab in July 1888 and related his travels in the sacrament meeting of August 5. At the quarterly conference held December 9 and 10 he was named an alternate to the High Council of Kanab Stake. He was appointed town marshal in 1889, and late in December was made a selectman.

Emett spoke in Sunday meeting on August 3, 1890, and shortly thereafter he left for Mexico. He returned in mid-October with a second wife, the former Electa Jane Gruell, not yet nineteen, whom he married September 12, shortly before the Woodruff Manifesto was sustained. The pretty new wife was in sharp contrast to the thirty-eight-year-old first wife, a woman of plain appearance. Emma Jane bore nine children, seven of whom were alive in 1890, and she felt that this addition to the household was an unnecessary intrusion. Neither she nor her children made the newcomer welcome and Jim eventually was forced to keep the two women in separate homes. He settled Electa Jane at Cave Lakes while Emma held sway in Kanab.

Meanwhile, the local ecclesiastical leaders, E. D. Woolley, Dan Seegmiller, and Tom Chamberlain, worked on Emett to make him see the position in which he had placed himself by an angry outburst against a severe critic, Brother R. Shumway, whom he threatened to kill. Jim finally agreed to square himself. During the Sunday meeting of November 16 he was called to speak of his recent trip to Mexico, but prudently declined until he had atoned for his misdeed and been cleared by the High Council.[13] He admitted his guilt, apologized to Shumway, and agreed to make a public confession of apology at the Kanab quarterly conference to be held at Orderville on December 7. He did this and was forgiven by unanimous vote.[14] The following Sunday he repeated his performance at Kanab and again was forgiven.[15] The forty-year-old Emett had matured considerably during the past six months.

Jim and Electa Jane Emett bore their testimonies at a fast meeting on April 2 and it seemed that he appeared in public more often with her than with Emma. A bitter enmity festered between the two women. Electa Jane gave birth to her first child, Rose Nell, on March 8, 1893. On September 19 of the same year, Emma Jane had her eleventh child at Cottonwood Ranch, a girl whom she named Ellen Elizabeth. Jim's eldest child, Emma Jane, or Janey as she was called, married Tom Chamberlain, Jr., on October 24, and the Emetts became more firmly entrenched than ever in the local power structure. Tom Chamberlain, Sr., already was related to President Woolley when he took his daughter Mary as his sixth wife.

John Green Kitchen was a Canadian-born non-Mormon cattleman who had built his herd by channeling the money earned in the mines of California and Silver Reef into Utah livestock. He arrived at Johnson, Utah, in 1873 with a small herd of heifer calves that he had purchased at St. George. He struck a deal whereby Sixtus Johnson was to manage the cattle on shares while he returned to earn more money. In June 1874, he had 60 head valued at $1,200 on which he paid a territorial tax of $3. The next year he had 85 head valued at $2,145; his territorial tax was $5.30, his county tax $15.95. The herd increased rapidly and he acquired his own range about 28 miles northeast of Kanab which he named the "Nipple Ranch" from a well-shaped butte of red and white sandstone that he had called "Molly's Nipple."

Kitchen drove some cattle to Nephi in 1878 and met twenty-one-year-old, English-born Martha Grice. The forty-eight-year-old bachelor married her and brought her to live at the Nipple Ranch. Between December 1879 and August 1894, the couple had five children. Neither belonged to the church but whenever they visited or had company, the Mormon women called her "Sister Kitchen." Her husband picked this up but shortened it to "Sis" and that was her name for the rest of her life. She always referred to him as "Mr. Kitchen." She could ride and rope as well as the average cowboy and was his chief hand in caring for the stock.

John Kitchen lived by the Golden Rule and was exceptionally considerate to animals. He rode with only one spur which always was on his left foot; he never used a quirt, preferring a willow switch. He raised quality vegetables and was generous in dispensing them and beef to his less competent neighbors in Pahreah. He treated Indians well, always buying some of what they had to sell, which usually was buckskin, baskets, and venison. He never wore a buckled belt or suspenders, but cut a strip of deerskin that he slipped through the belt loops and tied a bow in front. He was a unique, colorful character, generous, trusting, and hard-working.

Kitchen's weakness was a liking for whiskey, and he usually brought a barrel back with him when he drove cattle to the railroad. It is not known what sparked his reliance on alcohol, but he drank to such excess that eventually he alienated his wife, children, and many of his non-drinking associates. Martha's Mormon sisters urged her to divorce him and to join the church. His drunkenness later was perpetuated in doggerel verse based on using each letter of the alphabet to commemorate a pioneer: "K is for Kitchen, who was full all the time; L is for Jim Little, who named him the swine."[16] Undoubtedly the depiction was relished sixty years after his death, not for his weakness alone but because he was flawed and did not join the church.

John Kitchen had a number of good Mormon friends, mostly cattlemen. More than a few enjoyed drinking with him, and some were given to excessive guzzling in the same manner. Jim Emett was known to drink at Kitchen's place, and the two became more friendly than merely two cowmen enjoying an occasional drink together. On April 19, 1895, Emett was called before the high priests to answer a charge of getting drunk at Kitchen's. He acknowledged drinking whiskey there on several occasions but said he was sick, not drunk. He promised not to do so again and was forgiven. The same thing happened a month later with the identical result.[17]

Although alcohol abuse was widespread and not confined to Mormons, it was not the main thing that troubled the brethren. Of more concern was the fact that Gentile cattlemen were replacing Mormon operators. Vast church herds under the aegis of the Winsor Castle and Canaan Cooperative Stock companies, in which the church and the ecclesiastical leaders were the chief stockholders, had overgrazed the once lush range and the directors considered it worthless enough to sell. Knowledgeable outsiders realized that the range still could support sizable herds. One such operator was Benjamin Franklin Saunders of Salt Lake City. He had bought the Parashont Ranch from Canaan in 1883 and now was moving into the eastern range. The Canaan Cooperative had given Pipe Spring Ranch back to the trustee-in-trust in 1879 and thereafter paid rent. Joseph G. Brown leased the ranch from the trustee, while brothers-in-law E. D. Woolley and Dan Seegmiller maintained a vital interest in the place. Since the property was in Arizona Territory, Woolley found it convenient to keep one of his families there; it was even called the "Woolley lambing ground." Other plural families also made use of the facility.

Rumors that the church was on the verge of selling the Pipe Spring Ranch to B. F. Saunders prompted Woolley, on June 7, 1895, to send a frantic telegram to President Wilford Woodruff. Originally from Missouri, Saunders was a large operator having herds and ranches all over the west. He appears to have been a trusted friend of the church, possibly having been of service during the 1880s when Gentile friends were few and far between. Woolley and the local cattlemen were not privy to the facts of the Saunders-church relationship, and the telegram went unheeded. Church Bishop Preston, with the consent of Presidents Woodruff and Smith, agreed to sell the Pipe Spring Ranch to Saunders on May 8 and made it official August 16, 1895. Then the new owner enhanced his holding by purchasing Canaan on October 1 and two weeks later located three placer mining claims on the Harris Ranch to sew up the water rights.[18]

The reasons for the decision to sell were not explained to the local people, who resented the apparent intrusion and decided to oppose it covertly. Dan Seegmiller was the most effective roadblock to the sale by his claim of an interest, and was not quieted until Saunders paid him $2,500 on July 23.[19] This was in addition to the $2,300 paid for the ranch itself. Seegmiller could not prove a legitimate claim to the property but the payment effectively removed a nuisance. For reasons best known to himself, Saunders sold Pipe Spring to Bullock and Jones—a pair of respected Mormon cattlemen—on December 2. Ten days later, Warren Johnson became an invalid and Woolley saw Emett as the best means of countering Saunders' march to the eastern ranges. Already rumors were circulating that the Gentile's ultimate target was the VT Ranch and its resources.[20]

Emett was more or less in limbo in 1896 until Warren Johnson became convinced that he was paralyzed permanently and that his youthful sons could not assume the responsibility of both ferry and ranch. When the papers finally were in order, winter had set in making a move impractical. Emett hired Jerry Johnson to operate the ferry and prepared to move there as soon as snow was gone from Buckskin Mountain. He arranged with Johnson to have young Frank freight loads of Emett household goods while removing theirs on return trips. Frank did this all through the winter and spring.

Nathaniel Galloway and William Richmond had embarked at Henry's Fork on the Green River in September 1896. They prospected, panned, and trapped down to lower Glen Canyon where they located the Glenn Placer on a right-hand bar six miles above Lee's Ferry on January 4,

1897.[21] Somewhere in the lower canyon they met Ed Mesken and traveled together to Lee's Ferry. Mesken kept company with Jerry Johnson for a few days, then caught a ride with a passing wagon to Kanab where he recorded the Glenn Placer for his friends, along with a claim for himself. Galloway and Richmond obtained supplies from Johnson before entering Marble Canyon. Galloway left his name in a cave one hundred sixteen miles downstream on January 24, and the pair reached Needles on February 17.

Meanwhile, Kitchen family affairs had come to a head in late 1896. The sixty-five-year-old cattleman, allegedly while intoxicated, sold one-half interest in his two ranches, their improvements, and all of his livestock to Henry E. Bowman for $25,000. The money was to be paid in five installments of $5,000 each spaced over five years.[22] Martha considered this the last straw. She filed for divorce, asking custody of the five children and a fair amount for support. She listed his assets as the Nipple and Meadow Ranches, 4,100 head of cattle, 50 head of horses, and a bank account of $2,000 for a total of $58,500. The judge issued a restraining order to Kitchen on December 7, 1896, and two days later he and Emett were ordered to appear in court to answer a charge of contempt for having transferred $1,655.60 into Emett's name. The divorce was granted March 18, 1897, with Taylor Crosby authorized to dispose of Kitchen's property as necessary to pay Martha $50 per month until the sum of $15,000 had been expended. Some covert arm-twisting terminated the Bowman-Kitchen partnership, and the cattleman paid any accrued costs.[23]

John Kitchen needed money before the divorce was granted, and he decided to sell some livestock. Frank Farnsworth, who was involved in gathering the cattle, related this phase of the story to Kitchen's grandson, LeRoy Harris. Scott Cutler and Hack Jolley took part of the herd for $31,000 while John Findlay bought the remainder. Kitchen didn't trust banks and kept large sums of money at his ranch or on his person. He was very distressed over the divorce, believing that his family had turned against him when he needed them most. Jim Emett was the only friend who offered support, even promising him that he could live with the family at Lee's Ferry.

It was early March of 1897 when young Frank Johnson hauled Jim Emett, his second wife Electa Jane, and their two children, Rose Nell and Pearl, to their new home. Jim then returned with Frank to get his first family and his own wagons. According to Jim's daughter Clara, Emma Jane and her children arrived on March 25. There was still some snow on Buckskin Mountain, but the apricot trees were in bloom at the more temperate ranch elevation. Jerry Johnson remained to operate the ferry. After the families were settled, John Kitchen piled his few possessions into a wagon and drove to the ferry. He is said to have carried a large sum of money—several thousand dollars—but his children never learned what became of it. Jim built a tenthouse with wooden floor and sides under a cottonwood for him and the Emett girls brought him his meals.[24] A jug of whiskey was close by, his means of deadening the pain of his family failure.

The Emett family at the Johnson ranchhouse, no date (*P. T. Reilly Collection, Cline Library, Northern Arizona University*).

With high hopes for the Glenn Placer that he and Richmond had located in January, Galloway found his way back there alone later in the spring. He puttered around doing assessment work until the high water in June made work on the low bar impractical, then he ran down to Lee's Ferry. He became acquainted with the Emetts and developed a casual interest in Jim's fifteen-year-old daughter, Clara. His wife was dead but he had children in Vernal.

Although Ed Mesken had been working the bars of Glen Canyon since 1885, he finally selected one on the inner side of a bend centered five miles above the Ute Ford as having the highest potential. He named this "Diamond Placer" and located it October 7, 1895.[25] He relocated the claim slightly downstream on August 13, 1896, and worked the new location for nearly a year before recording it. Mesken traveled by boat on the river and on foot when he went overland. He frequently went to Escalante or Hanksville for supplies, which he packed out on his back. While in Escalante, he stayed with Llewellyn Harris, another loner who sought the remote areas; in Hanksville, he put up with the Hanks family. He ran out of beans in the summer of 1897 and was forced to visit civilization not only for supplies but for the wherewithal to purchase them. He ran his skiff down to Lee's Ferry, met Jim Emett, and agreed to work for him after he had recorded his amended claim in Kanab.

During the first half of his life in Glen Canyon, Mesken had a large Newfoundland dog named Sport. The two were inseparable, shared equally in everything they acquired, and were faithful to each other. Sport was unusually intelligent, and Mesken had trained him to perform a variety of tricks that amazed people from Escalante, Hanksville, and Hite to Lee's Ferry. Sport balanced Mesken's boat by moving from port to starboard as the occasion warranted. He would jump over, through, and under a hoop on command. Mesken often placed a piece of meat on the dog's nose and told him he could have it on a certain number. He then called digits out of order and when the right one was named, the dog flipped the meat in the air and caught it on the fly. Unfortunately, Sport ate some poison that the sheepmen had put out for coyotes. He died in camp that night near the Navajo Slide, under 60 Mile Point. Mesken wrapped him in his coat, buried him in a cave-like alcove, and erected a chiseled headstone. Life for the grieving prospector was never the same after this.

Frank Johnson made one of his last trips to the ferry in July, and on his return hauled both Galloway and Mesken to Kanab where they filed their claims.[26] They caught another ride and returned to the ferry. Mesken went to work for Emett to build up his grubstake, and Galloway used the ferry as a base to develop his Glenn Placer. But first, Galloway decided to build a new boat as his old one was waterlogged and leaking badly. He bought some boards and nails in Kanab and obtained pitch from the pinyon trees of Buckskin Mountain. Building a skiff to travel up and down Glen Canyon was no big job for the old trapper.

Meanwhile, an English-born tourist, George Wharton James, had visited the Grand Canyon in the 1890s. He was so impressed that he determined to make a career out of its exploitation. He collected some glass slides to give lantern shows and lecture on the scenic beauties. He learned some regional history to add interest to his presentation but never got deeply into anything or allowed fact to interfere with his viewpoint. He ascertained that the country surrounding the canyon was worthy of his talents, and during a stereopticon show in Winslow on March 25, 1897, decided to procure a guide to show him the old Mormon road, the adjacent country, and Lee's Ferry.[27]

He scheduled another lantern show for August 3, spent an additional week in town, and obtained the services of Franklin French.[28] This was a fortunate piece of business because through his guide and teamster he was able to add five chapters to a book he had in mind. Morever, he met French's wife, the former Emma B. Lee.[29] She allowed him to read the letter that John D. Lee had written right after his conviction.[30] James not only printed this letter in his book but included the fiction of Lee's living three years among the Havasupai, participating in cannibalism, and having a secret gold mine. James couldn't have timed his visit better because Emma died of a heart attack less than four months later on November 16, 1897.[31]

The outfit of a four-up covered wagon and a light buggy pulled out of Winslow on August 9 bound for Indian country, the Little Colorado gorge, and Lee's Ferry. They stopped at Tuba City to visit Joseph Hyrum Lee and obtained some more material on his notorious father. The outfit arrived at the lower-crossing dugway early in September and experienced considerable trouble in gaining the attention of someone at the ranch. Finally, Ed Mesken and John Taylor Emett came to ferry the travelers across the river. As they pitched camp at the ranch, James was astounded to find such a lush oasis in the midst of this barren desert. No doubt the animals were no less happy to feed on alfalfa after the scant forage along the over-grazed trail.

James had unlimbered his camera at the head of the dugway to take views of the river, the mouth of the Pahreah from the ledge, and the wagon driven onto the ferry and being crossed. Later, Mesken took the pair to the river where they met Galloway, who was just finishing his new boat. Here, James took more pictures of panning and of men on the beach. One picture of Ed Mesken using his goldpan has been reprinted as late as the 1970s with the inference that the scene pertained to the gold fields of California.[32] After some hard persuasion, James got Galloway to take him to his claim in Glen Canyon, and on the following day, down Marble Canyon to Badger Creek Rapid. It was the adventure of a lifetime for the photographer but he failed to keep notes, confused a picture taken at the claim in Glen Canyon with Marble Canyon, and thought Badger Creek Rapid was Soap Creek Rapid.[33] Possibly Galloway told him too much in a brief period.

Shortly after the James visit, Mesken quit Emett's employ. He and Galloway departed upriver in their boats now loaded with supplies. Travel upstream was not difficult in Glen Canyon; experienced rivermen avoided the current by using the slack water along the sides and inner parts of the curves. Mesken had a longer distance to go (about forty-five miles), and Galloway only had to go six miles. Galloway worked the Glenn Placer until mid-October, then decided that he, too, would travel upstream. His destination is not known but he probably switched from mining to trapping, as beaver pelts were becoming prime with the advent of cold weather. Galloway and Will S. Rust purchased Mesken's Diamond Placer on March 3, 1898. The price of four hundred dollars enabled Mesken to quit the country and head for the Klondike. The last word about him comes from Dave Rust who, while in Seattle, saw him as a member of a Salvation Army group soliciting donations on a rainy street corner on the waterfront.

In the meantime, Robert Brewster Stanton had not been idle. Stimulated by the derelict dredge *Nellie,* he had developed large-scale plans to dredge Glen Canyon. While James and French were heading for the ferry, he was working with officials of the Bucyrus Dredge Company of Milwaukee, ordering boats and gathering supplies. One of his major investors, John Ginty of San Diego, and his young son, Eugene, accompanied Stanton when he left Salt Lake City on September 11, 1897. Two

From left to right, Nathaniel Galloway, Ed Mesken, George Wharton James, Franklin French, and a man named Fluke, in Glen Canyon, September 1897 (*George Wharton James photograph, courtesy of the Southwest Museum, Los Angeles, photograph #N.2677*).

dependable employees, George Platte and George Uden, also were with him; J. W. "Jack" Wilson joined him at Hite. Heavy storms and washouts delayed their arrival at Green River until 2:30 A.M. the following morning. From Green River, they went by wagon to the Colorado River and established their first camp at the mouth of North Wash on September 23.[34] From this base, named Camp Brooks in honor of a principal backer, they built two boats, selected two damsites on the Dirty Devil, surveyed for a flume, and began locating claims in the area. His plan was to locate a series of contiguous claims from the Dirty Devil to Lee's Ferry and dredge the entire length of Glen Canyon.

They began working downstream on October 13. At noon of the next day, at White Canyon, a heavy rain began falling. The rather massive storm continued until nightfall of the sixteenth.[35] The result was like opening a floodgate; water poured down the bare sandstone and into the Colorado, raising its level at an unbelievable rate. Galloway caught the rise about twelve miles above his claim as he was camped in the large cave-like alcove at Glen Mile 17.4 that came to be named after him. The water rose into the cave itself, causing him to take the bowline of his boat in hand and

Nathaniel Galloway in Glen Canyon, September 1897 (*George Wharton James photograph, courtesy of the Southwest Museum, Los Angeles, photograph #N.2848*).

Ferryboat at the lower crossing at Lee's Ferry, September 1897 (*George Wharton James photograph, courtesy of the Southwest Museum, Los Angeles, photograph #N.7351*).

retreat up the talus at the end of his failed shelter. The river began to recede on Sunday October 17, and he re-entered the cave. In the morning he took a piece of charcoal from the campfire and under his name written on a previous visit, wrote "Oc 18th 1897."[36] He then started upstream with no particular destination in mind, probably trapping beaver as he went.

Stanton continued his work downstream, but near the end of the year had reached only to California Bar, a distance of forty-eight miles. Unusually cold weather and increasing slush ice induced him to discontinue the job for the winter, and the party started downstream for Lee's Ferry on December 30. Their destination was one hundred thirty-one miles away and in places the river was packed solid with ice. After being confined to "Camp Hardscrabble" for two nights and a day due to steady snowfall and a hard wind, they started downstream again on January 12. A run of less than two hours brought them to the camp of the three Rust brothers, about twenty-two miles below the mouth of the San Juan. Dave Rust came aboard and ran with them down to Rothschild Bar where Galloway and Mesken were working. They held a short visit, then pushed on to make camp at the Ute Ford. The cold was intense and steady rowing was their only means of keeping warm. Even so, they were forced to stop and build fires. In places it was necessary to open channels through the ice with axes; in others, they skidded the boats over solid ice floes. They finally landed at Lee's Ferry at dusk on the thirteenth and went into the old fort for protection from the bitter weather.[37]

Jim Emett had gone to Tuba City but was expected back shortly. Stanton, always eager to discuss mining with local prospectors, talked with George Ayers, who generously passed on his views regarding the low and high river bars. The engineer noted somewhat smugly that Ayers had prospected only to water level and quoted him as saying that the rest could not be mined.[38] This, of course, was in contrast to his own plan to dredge the entire river channel down to bedrock, but he said nothing. Ginty roamed about taking pictures, including one of John Emett on his horse in the snow-covered field.

Stanton turned his two boats, the *Little Jean* and *Nancy Lee*, bottoms-up behind the fort, stored his tools and supplies inside the structure, and on January 15 he disbanded his crew for the season. Ginty and his son set out for Flagstaff; Stanton, Wilson, Uden, and Platts began walking north along the Mormon road, carrying what blankets and food they could. The ground was covered with snow and temperatures were from ten to thirty degrees below zero. The group reached Marysvale in nine days; it is not known how the Gintys fared.

John Kitchen's failure to retain the loyalty of his family bothered him excessively, and he continued to drink and pity himself. He now believed that Jim Emett was his only friend on earth, the sole person who cared about his welfare. Kitchen felt that his former wife was intent upon ruining him financially. It is probable that Emett advised him how to counter her action, but no direct evidence exists. At any rate, he decided to liquidate his holdings in Utah, where they were more vulnerable to Martha's claims, and to reinvest the funds in Arizona. Emett agreed to buy the Nipple Ranch, and in the fall of 1897 Kitchen turned his team southward to hunt for a suitable place. He bought a ranch that was stocked with some two hundred fifty cattle in the vicinity of Signal, Arizona. On his way back to the ferry from Kingman, he wrote his attorney, John F. Brown in Kanab, that he had sold the Nipple Ranch to Emett and requested him to draw up the deed. He stated that Emett was his agent and had power of attorney.[39] Kitchen then hurried back to the ferry and began drinking himself into oblivion.

Emett had five children who should have been receiving instruction. In keeping with his typical behavior, he put his plans into action as soon as possible. He and his son John hitched a team to John R. Nielson's old *Nellie* and dragged her to the ranch. There they dismantled the boat to use what they could of it to rebuild the largest Johnson cabin into a schoolhouse. This work, begun in the fall of 1897, was finished that winter. They used the heaviest timbers for the outer walls, added a window in the south wall, and installed a floor. Most of the lumber was used for one thing or another and the rest went into the woodpile. They built benches for the children and a table for the teacher, who was the only part of the operation for which there was no ready answer.[40] Emett's trip to Tuba City had been an attempt to solve this need, but it was not successful. He wasn't discouraged, however. He planned a trip to Salt Lake City, and every town held a potential school teacher.

Warren M. Johnson had been postmaster at Lee's Ferry since the post office was established there in 1879. His incapacitation had never been communicated to Washington. After application, James S. Emett, on January 8, 1898, was appointed to replace him.[41] When notice of the appointment came through, Jim was obliged to find a Justice of the Peace and take the oath of office. This would not be a problem as it could be taken care of on his way north.

Emett's main reason for traveling to church headquarters was to present his plan for improving the ferry and to obtain financial backing for the entire project. His argument was sound: it demonstrated that one ferry could replace two, improve the safety factor, and reduce the number of ferrymen. By making a new crossing about one-half mile upstream from the present upper ferry, installing a steel cable, extending the road along the right bank, and making a new dugway along the red talus below the ledge, both old crossings could be replaced by one. The proposed crossing would be farther upstream from the head of the Pahreah Riffle and therefore was safer, as it was to be located where they had towed the oar-driven boat during the high water of earlier days. Emett's proposed site was close to where John W. Young had suggested moving the crossing in 1879. Both of the old ferryboats were water-logged and too rotten to stand being fastened to a cable, hence a new boat should be built. This, the road construction, and the new dugway would be the chief expenses, and he hoped the authorities would allow the use of tithing labor and provide funds as needed.

Jim made his presentation in Salt Lake City on February 1, 1898, and the authorities liked it. The secretary took a list of the data he provided, noting that the approximate width of the river at low water was three hundred feet and it increased to four hundred feet in high water. Emett told them that the vertical extremes amounted to a range of eighteen feet, and they concluded that a steel cable $1^1/_4$ inches in diameter by five hundred feet in length would suffice. It was to be shipped to Flagstaff no later than mid-March. The San Francisco vendor was to furnish plans for anchoring and buttressing, as well as provide the weight of the cable so the ferryman would have sufficient teams to pick up the freight at the delivery point.[42] A new ferryboat would require five thousand feet of lumber, and Emett said he would investigate the possibility of procuring it on a tithing order on his way south.

The trip was very successful. On February 4, he stopped in Junction where one of Emma Jane's distant cousins, Sadie Staker, was teaching school. He sought her services at the ferry, and because he offered her more money than she was making, she promised to teach his children when

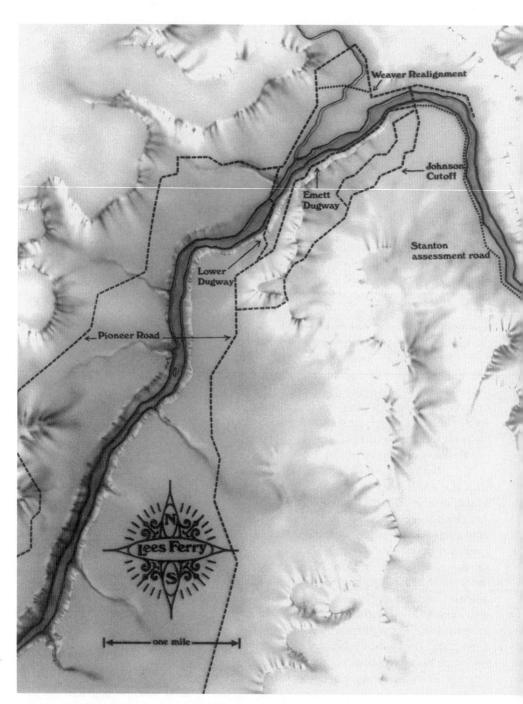

Historical roads in Lee's Ferry vicinity (*map by Tim Cardinale*).

the present school term ended.[43] It appears that another inducement was the anticipated construction work that offered a job for her father, Joseph S. Staker of Annabella. Emett's next stop was in Panguitch, where the stake tithing clerk agreed to furnish the necessary lumber if the church would issue a covering order. Jim had a letter on its way to Salt Lake City before he left town. Secretary George F. Gibbs authorized the withdrawal on the seventeenth, merely asking the cost so it would be credited to the Panguitch tithing office. The clerk, Mahonri M. Steele, was sent an order for $57.20 on March 8, and on the same day Emett was notified that the lumber would be ready by May 1.[44]

Meanwhile, John Kitchen's physical and mental condition had deteriorated steadily. He had been confined to his bed since mid-January and was usually too intoxicated to care for himself. According to Jerry Johnson, Emett kept a jug of whiskey at his side and the girls brought food when he asked for it. On March 8, Emett wrote a last will and testament for the old man, naming himself as executor without bond, listing his assets and outstanding debts owed him amounting to $1,239, and nothing owed by him. It was ten days before Kitchen was able to sign the document, and even then the signature was a far cry from his former one. George S. Ayers and a teen-age lad named Roy Peterson, then working for Emett, signed as witnesses.[45]

Emett was planning a trip to Signal to gather and dispose of Kitchen's cattle when a telegram from Secretary Gibbs arrived at Kanab on the morning of April 2 saying that the cable and accompanying fittings had just reached Flagstaff. The entire freight weighed five thousand pounds.[46] A special messenger brought the news to the ferry and Jim and his son Jack (John T.) departed April 5 on a multiple mission, leaving the oldest son, Bill, in charge of the ferry.

Emett made a stopover in Tuba City, during which a strategy meeting with Bishop Brinkerhoff was held. The people in Tuba City had been through the wars and obtained county recognition only after fighting to attain what less remote communities received as a matter of course. At this time, the Tuba City School District was the most remote in Coconino County. John D. Lee's son, Joseph, became the first Tuba City Justice of the Peace in 1892, and finally a mail route from Flagstaff replaced the much longer one from Holbrook. Usually nothing was granted on the first request; a service had to be petitioned, appearances made before the various boards, and political influence used before improvements were granted. Brinkerhoff had succeeded in getting the Moenave School District established in mid-April 1894 and was familiar with the procedure.

Jim Emett knew how to make friends, and now he cultivated some in county government. His Flagstaff stay amounted to several days. He appeared before the Board of Supervisors on April 12 requesting that one thousand dollars be expended on a dugway road to his new ferry crossing, and he also asked that a school district be established so his children could be educated at home since it was seventy-five miles to Tuba City and ninety miles to Kanab. Both requests were rejected for the simple reason that the county treasury had no funds.[47] He remained in town until the cable and accessories were loaded and headed for the ferry on the fifteenth, then he and Jack went to Signal. He took count of the livestock and struck a deal with William Knoshland, a leading merchant, saying he would consult with Kitchen and let him know his reaction.

While Emett was in Flagstaff, Stanton also was there, arranging for two boats to be shipped to the ferry. One boat was a twenty-foot steam launch, the other was a rowboat. Stanton then hired a team and drove to the ferry where he sized up the situation and staked nine placer claims from White Canyon to Bullfrog. This was the first phase of a large-scale operation involving all of Glen Canyon, and Lee's Ferry was one of the bases. Back in Flagstaff on May 22, Stanton filed his claims the following morning, then boarded the train for the east.

The Emetts returned from their lengthy trip on May 18, but next day Jim turned around and headed back to Flagstaff. On May 23, he filed his intention to locate and maintain the Lee's Ferry Toll Road. He proposed a north gate located in the wash down which the road from Kanab first approached the river, extending up the right bank to the original crossing at the fort, then down the left bank to the head of the lower crossing dugway where the South Gate would be located.[48] No mention was made of establishing a third crossing one-half mile upstream, but there was no need to do so since the two gates controlled access in both directions, thus encompassing the two old crossings and the potential new one.

Jim took the train to Kingman where he set up the stock sale with Knoshland. He returned home on June 5 to complete a seventeen-day round trip.[49] Almost immediately, he took to the road again, going to Kanab on an errand for Kitchen. The old cattleman, while firmly believing that his family had rejected him without reason, still was concerned about their welfare. On June 13, Emett and Martha G. Kitchen appeared before Notary Public John F. Brown, where he executed a lease of the Meadows Ranch to her for a dollar a year. The lease ran for her lifetime and would guarantee a roof over her head.[50] When they were alone, Brown gave Emett some legal advice that insured more travel.

Meanwhile, Sadie Staker had left her home in Annabella on June 1, traveling with four local boys who were going on missions in Arizona. All five had bedrolls, although Sadie stayed with friends whenever she could. They all became dejected after leaving Panguitch. None had been so far south and the desert was strange to them. They reached Lee's Ferry on the thirteenth and although she was glad that her long journey was over, she was sorry when her traveling companions went on. Here she was two hundred fifty miles from home, living with strangers, and the ferry disappointed her by being more isolated than she had imagined. She started her school immediately with five pupils in the refurbished cabin.[51] Two days later, a five-wagon company arrived from the south, crossed the river, and went into camp at the ranch. The Prouse family had an organ, a violin, and a cornet with them and they provided a happy evening of music. Sadie taught school during the day and danced at night while they were there. After they left, her only entertainment was boating on the Colorado with one of the Emett boys or Jerry Johnson—a major change for the pretty young school teacher.

Fearing that the sale of the Nipple Ranch in December might not be legal because his power of attorney was open to question, Emett took Kitchen to Kanab on June 20 to have a quit-claim deed signed before Cass Lewis, a justice of the peace. Roy Peterson and Jerry Johnson were witnesses.[52] This time the purchase price was quoted as being five hundred dollars instead of the four hundred recorded previously. It really didn't make any difference as the money probably never reached the befuddled old man anyway. They immediately returned to the ferry where Kitchen betook himself to bed and jug.

Hearsay, possibly based on fact, tells us that a case of euthanasia took place at the ferry in July. According to Jerry Johnson, Kitchen never came out of his tent after returning from Kanab. Emett kept the whiskey jug full, and the besotted cattleman came to his senses only long enough to take another drink. Blow flies got in his ears and laid their eggs. Unable to care for himself, he was a passive victim and the Emetts did not discover his state of affairs until the larvae had become pupae and the irritation brought him out of his stupor. By this time, Emett judged he was beyond help and gave him an overdose of laudanum. John Kitchen died, insensible to anything, on Wednesday, July 13, 1898. He was buried immediately, and even as the grave was being dug, Emett dispatched his son George to Kanab to notify the family. Young Emett made a fast ride; he reached town in fourteen hours by riding all night and arrived at sunrise.[53] John Grice Kitchen, not yet eighteen, hurried to the ferry but lamented he was not in time for the service. Actually, there was no service regardless of what young Kitchen was told.

According to Sadie Staker's diary, Jerry Johnson took her boating on July 17. It was one of the last things he did at the ferry for some time, because a few days later Emett took him and George Ayers to Kanab where he recorded Kitchen's quit-claim deed to the Nipple Ranch on July 28. He paid Ayres twenty-seven dollars for making the trip and for being present when Kitchen's will was admitted for probate on August 8. Jerry was separated from his job at least until fall, the reason being given that he was not needed during the slack summer season. He attributed his discharge to the fact that he knew the details of Kitchen's death, but he said nothing and joined his brother Frank at Cottonwood.[54]

While his father was in Kanab, John Emett got into Kitchen's whiskey supply and became so intoxicated that he frightened Sadie Staker. She recorded that she got no sleep that night for fear she would be attacked.[55] She had never before been this close to a drinking person and developed a negative attitude toward alcohol and those who used it. She described the eighteen-year-old youth as if he had undergone a seizure.

Staker taught school all summer, her only diversions being rides or short trips on horseback with Bill Emett. She donned what she called "blummers" when she went riding. On August 27 she crossed the river and walked over Lee Hill. Having read a book on the Mountain Meadows Massacre during her first days at the ferry, she had some knowledge of Lee's role at this place. Characteristically, she made no comment of her thoughts or impressions in her diary. The young school teacher came from a monogamous home and appears to have had as great an aversion to polygamy as to alcohol. On September 1, she witnessed the culmination of the animosity between Jim's two wives. The quarrel was lengthy and extremely bitter but Sadie summed it up with one terse statement: "I saw the spirit of the devil manifested through polygamous women."[56] Evidently Emma Jane gave her husband an ultimatum either to get rid of his second wife or he would lose his first. The atmosphere was so unpleasant that when Sunday came, Sadie put on her "blummers" and rode alone to the rim overlooking the mouth of Badger Creek, which she estimated was a twenty-mile round trip.

Monday brought the Durfee family en route from Utah to Mexico. Emett seized the opportunity to solve his family problem by inducing them to take Electa Jane as a passenger to her parents' home in Chihuahua; tradition says he gave Durfee a horse for the service. Electa took her youngest daughter, Pearl, with her. Her half-sisters said Pearl died young of typhoid but they were vague about the location and date.[57] Electa's other child, Rose Nell, then five years of age, remained with her father.

Kitchen's death and Emett's solution of his marital problem did not allow life at the ferry to settle into a humdrum pattern. They merely solved abnormal situations that did not ordinarily exist at the remote crossing. The church still controlled the property but the operation and income now reverted to the proprietor. The bustle of migration was a thing of the past. Wagons were apt to appear singly or in pairs, less often in groups. The place was just as isolated, the Colorado a barrier that made travel more difficult and expensive. Commercial freighting on an individual basis was beginning to come into its own. The farm—that green oasis in the desert that Warren Johnson had labored to build—metamorphosed into a ranch, the two-man ferry operation was about to become a single-man function, and influence from Gentile Flagstaff began to supercede that of Mormon Kanab. The upper ranch, which had provided hay for travelers and residents alike and brought income to Johnson and the church, was allowed to revert to the environment. Travel had fallen off to the extent that Emett could raise all the alfalfa he needed in the lower field. Besides, Jim Emett never pretended to be a farmer—he was a cattleman.

Incorporation of the Hoskaninni Company under the laws of West Virginia in March 1898 ushered in the greatest large-scale mining activity that Glen Canyon had ever seen. Stanton unquestionably was the instigator, and he succeeded in being named its vice-president, chief engineer, and superintendent on a salary basis. Five of its largest financial backers were the incorporators, with Julius F. Stone as president and Frank S. Brooks as secretary; other backers were E. C. Morton, W. A. Mills, and R. K. Ramsey. The head office was located in Columbus, Ohio, seat of Stone's manufacturing enterprise. The rest of the canyon was staked in the first half of 1898, giving the company over one hundred sixty-five miles of contiguous mining claims. Holding these claims meant that assessment work had to be done, and the engineer wisely decided to expend this labor in testing equipment and building access roads to facilitate the eventual installation of dredges.

Stanton arrived at Hite on October 1, bringing with him a Keystone driller. His plan was to sink test holes at selected places, pan the material brought up, and check it for values before deciding on the location for the first dredge. He had hired some experienced Glen Canyon miners, including Nathaniel Galloway, Walter S. Russell, Bert Seabolt, and Frank Gilham. He made several test holes in various locations and apparently recovered sufficient colors to justify continuation, but this is not clear. Two of the major backers, Julius F. Stone and J. S. Knox, arrived late in October. They were prepared to devote nearly a month to evaluate the situation but wanted to be home by December 1.

Meanwhile, a knowledgeable mining friend and associate of John Ginty, W. S. King, came to the ferry from San Diego on October 16. Evidently King was on a fact-finding trip for Ginty and had been briefed on the Lee's Ferry phase of development. Clara Emett and Sadie Staker escorted him to the river to show him the planned improvements.[58] The cable had not been hung but it was on site; work on the new dugway had not begun and therefore the new ferryboat would have been useless, so it wasn't built yet either. A week later, Samuel Alvarus Mecham arrived with the Hanchett family. He, along with Joseph Staker and Nephi Foreman, had agreed to take the contract to build the new dugway, and he undoubtedly wanted to check out the job.

On October 23, William S. Lamb and his wife Charlotte; her two brothers, Ben and George Grainger; and the four Lamb children, traveling back to Utah, stopped at the ferry. Lamb was a large man whose feats of strength were legendary along the Little Colorado. Lot Smith, in a letter to President Woodruff in 1889, related how Lamb caught up with a trouble-causing Mormon who had induced a Gentile to jump the ranch at Mormon Dairy and told him he would "stick him under the ice in the lake or pull his ears out as long as a mule's" if he caught him up there again.[59] Lot considered him to be even stronger than Seth B. Tanner, and he knew them both. Jim offered Lamb a job because he would be a great asset at the ferry. Lamb accepted. Too, he had three children of school age whose entry would strengthen Emett's request for a county school. The Lamb children entered Sadie's class on the last day of the month, bringing the pupil count to eight.

Sadie Staker had learned the procedures of the post office and she also did household chores as required, besides teaching. Emett paid her thirty dollars a month in addition to providing her board, while Emma Jane saw that she seldom had an idle moment. When the Emetts were away, she acted as head of the family in caring for the house and children. Mecham, Foreman, and the road crew arrived October 26, but Joseph Staker was not with them, which disappointed and depressed her. Cousin Emma caught her moping and expressed the opinion that hired help should devote every minute of their time to the master. Sadie took issue with this viewpoint, calling it slavery.[60] The argument did not help her, for besides being homesick she had another matter to worry about—an impending examination for teaching school in Arizona. Emett had made good use of his contacts in Flagstaff. By building his own schoolhouse and hiring his own teacher, he established a sympathetic attitude among county officials. He finally was told that if his schoolmarm could pass the Arizona teachers' examination, the county would pay her salary.

Jim Emett had the relatively uneducated, active man's disdain for clerical matters and no clear understanding of paperwork or its importance in society. To him, an oral agreement and a handshake meant more than a written document that had been witnessed and notarized. In particular, he did not understand the system of tithing credits and collections by which the church did business. Undoubtedly he returned from Salt Lake City in February with the idea that he had opened a line of credit and cash that he could draw upon at will and dispense as he saw fit. It did not turn out that way. Except for the cutting of the lumber, which remained stacked at the Panguitch mill, the improvement project was on dead center.

Emett sent a letter to President Woodruff saying that the bottom had rotted out of the old ferryboat, the cable was at the ferry waiting to be installed, and he needed $300 in cash and $1,200 in produce tithing orders. Panguitch and Kanab stakes were to contribute $600 each, but by August 8 nothing had been forthcoming.[61] The letter was typed, indicating President E. D. Woolley's advice and use of his equipment. There was an immediate response from Secretary Gibbs, who enclosed two tithing orders for $750 on each stake, $600 of which was for produce and $150 for merchandise. Gibbs left it to Emett to raise the cash.[62]

Unbeknown to the brethren in the south, the church had become involved in many speculative business ventures during the 1890s, was now heavily in debt, and had little money available. It was the same with Utah and the entire nation; all were affected by the panic of 1893, which lasted throughout the Cleveland administration. The conservative authorities realized the enormity of the problem and were working to reverse the tide. Aged Wilford Woodruff, the fourth church president, died on September 2, 1898; Lorenzo Snow, a fiscal conservative, succeeded him on the thirteenth. In keeping with the change in church leadership, the ferry had moved from being a major link in the colonization phase to one of maintaining a flow of decreased traffic. Nevertheless, the facilities would be improved.

It was getting late in the season when mining investors Stone and Knox had to return to civilization. On November 21, Stanton placed the two easterners in the care of Galloway, and the trio departed Illinois Bar for Lee's Ferry and Flagstaff. Their first destination was slightly more than one hundred fifty-eight miles downstream, a distance they covered in five days. This trip did more than interest Stone in the river; it formed a bond between him and Galloway that was destined to last the rest of their lives. Their arrival at Lee's Ferry was opportune for more than themselves, as Emett was ready to take Sadie Staker to Flagstaff for her examination and the timing solved their problem of transportation to the railroad. They all left in Emett's wagon on Monday, November 28, reached Flagstaff at noon on Friday, December 2, and found accommodations at the Bank Hotel. The investors caught the eastbound train on Sunday. Before leaving, Stone gave Galloway his camera and the film he had left. Applying the same intelligence to photography that he had to trapping and boating, the riverman mastered the instrument before he returned to the ferry.

While the others rested from their arduous journey, Emett—always alert to use time to his best advantage—visited attorney E. S. Clark and engaged him to handle the legal side of his appointment as administrator of the Kitchen estate. Clark petitioned the court to name his client executor on December 7; Judge Layton approved the appointment on Christmas Eve. Emett made the arrangements on Monday, and Staker took her examination on Tuesday. Her pleasing personality and excellent handwriting probably had as much to do with her passing as her proficiency in academic matters. Emett agreed to pay her salary until the county budget could accommodate it.[63]

All objectives accomplished, Emett started back with Sadie Staker and Galloway on Wednesday, December 7. A storm front moved in bringing snow deep enough to impede travel; they barely reached Willow Spring by the ninth. Making a one-day layover here, they socialized with trader Sam Preston and old-time residents, the Allens and Sainsberrys. Galloway brought out his camera and took a picture of the company. Resuming their northward journey, travel remained difficult and they suffered from snow and cold. Jim killed an antelope and a large wildcat during the day, then they pitched camp in the snow at Cedar Ridge. Sadie enjoyed her supper of broiled antelope meat but said it didn't raise the temperature. Galloway skinned the wildcat, later making it into a rug for Sadie which, combined with the wares that she bought from Sam Preston, provided mementos of her trip. Reaching the ferry on Monday afternoon, they found Al Mecham and his son Sam there. Such was one two-week span in the life of a Lee's Ferry school teacher in 1898.

Ordinarily Nathaniel Galloway would have spent the winter trapping in Glen Canyon, but he was smitten with the pretty young schoolmarm. He holed up in the old fort, going upriver from time to time to work his claim. He managed to see Sadie nearly every day, and on several occasions used Stone's gift camera to take her picture. On Sunday, December 18, he posed her on the ferryboat at the lower crossing, then accompanied her as she skated on the frozen eddy. She had celebrated her twenty-second birthday November 6; he would be forty-five on January 11. She respected him as her elder and was flattered by his attention, but attached no significance to the relationship.[64]

That evening Sadie went through a very trying experience when she and Emma Jane Emett helped Charlotte Lamb deliver a baby daughter.[65] Although this was her fifth child, the thirty-one-year-old mother had a difficult time and did not fully recover for several weeks. Emett would have been a strong support during this crisis but he was undertaking a pack trip to the Nipple Ranch. The real objective is not known as he held legal title to the property, but he ultimately charged the trip to the Kitchen estate.[66]

Sadie Staker turned her attention to a Christmas program to be put on by her pupils—undoubtedly the first ever given at Lee's Ferry, although the earlier proprietors had observed the significance of the day in their own spiritual manner. The audience consisted of two: brothers Richard of Panguitch and Mecham of Annabella. Christmas came on Sunday and it was the most unusual one the devout school teacher had ever experienced. There was no holiday spirit and no services were held. It was a very lonely day for her until the mail came with word that her father would be there shortly. Her gloom turned to joy. Joseph Staker arrived a little after noon on Monday and departed Wednesday morning. His visit was very brief, evidently a final survey of the dugway route and the needs for construction, but his visit lifted Sadie's spirits, leaving her feeling less isolated than before.

The winter was colder than usual and the river, in the quiet stretches, froze solidly from shore to shore. Under the circumstances, the ferry was not used and wagons crossed on the ice. On two occasions, the Emetts and Bill Lamb learned what Anthony W. Ivins and Warren Johnson already knew—not to let wagons or livestock cross too closely together. On the first occasion, three wagons were crossing one after the other, and the last was heavily laden. Just as it was over mid-river the ice started to crack. Quick as a flash Lamb yelled to the drivers to apply their whips while he darted to the tailgate and used his tremendous strength to literally push the wagon into the draft animals. They made it across safely. After that all wagons crossed singly.

The weather had warmed somewhat a few days later when Bill Lamb was helping a herder drive a band of sheep across. The animals were allowed to bunch too closely instead of being strung out. The ice creaked as the terrified creatures huddled together and began bleating. Bill grabbed an animal, dashed to shore and used his bandana to tie it to a bush. It stood there bleating as the others came to it, at first in twos and threes, then as a group. The ice held firmly and not an animal was lost. The herder was so grateful for Bill's action that he gave him a sheep.

Sadie Staker at the Lee's Ferry schoolhouse, January 8, 1899 (*Nathaniel Galloway photograph, Cornelia Staker Peterson Collection, P. T. Reilly Collection, Cline Library, Northern Arizona University*).

Jim's oldest daughter Janey, who had married Tom Chamberlain, Jr., found that she had espoused an irresponsible man of questionable morals. The couple separated in 1897. Janey moved into one of her father-in-law's homes after her husband went on a two-year mission, leaving her with no means of support. She remained there for more than a year, then decided to rejoin her paternal family. When Emett made his second trip to the Nipple Ranch in late December, he went to Orderville to bring Janey and her two children, Eva and Cora, to the ferry.[67] At Kanab, he rehired Jerry Johnson to help in the heavy construction program.

Galloway was pushing his wooing of Sadie Staker vigorously. On January 8 he took a picture of Sadie's beautiful long hair streaming down her back as she sat out by the schoolhouse. The following Sunday, she and Clara, now sixteen, went over to the fort to cook dinner for him, Clara being taken along to keep the event more impersonal—much to the trapper's disappointment.

The next week the dugway workers gathered at the ferry. The roster was complete on January 27 when Joseph Staker arrived with young Rollo Gauchat and Joshua Carpenter. The workers consisted of thirteen men, many of them Sadie's friends from the Annabella area, and Jerry Johnson, who was to help build the ferryboat, operate the old one, and lend a hand on the cable installation. The entire company visited Sadie on Saturday evening, January 23, and she had a glorious time—one such as she had not enjoyed in months. She even went down to the lower crossing on Sunday morning to see the boys cross the river and set up camp at the head of the dugway.[68]

Work on the road began in earnest on Monday, January 30. In laying it out, Al Mecham had followed Emett's general route but refined it to minimize labor. There was no problem for the first quarter mile above the head of the lower-crossing dugway; they merely followed the contours until they reached the foot of the shale slope. Here, Mecham saw that it would be advantageous for the road to gain elevation to a rather prominent ledge about halfway to the immediate rim.[69] They followed along the top of the more durable ledge for about five hundred feet, then descended to a level fairly constant with the river. Loose rock walls were constructed on the outer side and the shale was shoveled in to level off the roadbed, which was easier than digging deeper into the slopes. It was a tedious job, and the work was by hand because the slopes were too severe for teams.

Judge N. G. Layton, on January 3, 1899, had followed Emett's recommendation and signed an order appointing William Lamb, Joseph B. Tanner, and Nathaniel Galloway to be appraisers of the Kitchen estate. They evidently accepted Emett's opinion of its value as they turned in a figure of $2,147.75 on January 15. Most of the value was attributed to the cattle and ranch on the Sandy. Only Lamb and Tanner signed the appraisal; for some reason, Galloway abstained.[70]

Emett arrived in Flagstaff on January 8 and left on the twelfth, very likely in connection with his duties as executor. While there, he was interviewed by the editor of the *Coconino Sun* to whom he gave a good promotional report of his improvements under construction, as well as the role of the ferry in Stanton's plans.[71] No doubt he received some legal advice from attorney Clark because he hurried north, stopping at Tuba City, where Justice of the Peace Joseph L. Foutz witnessed his signature on a quit claim deed whereby he and Emma Jane transferred title of the Nipple Ranch to his brother, Moses M. Emett. The document was not recorded in Kanab until February 5, 1900.[72]

Saturday night, February 4, was probably the happiest that Sadie Staker spent at the ferry. Galloway took her to the camp of the road crew and someone broke out a fiddle. She danced until midnight, rotating her partners among Galloway, Duffin, Grange, Tanner, Spilsbury, and Jerry Johnson. The red dust was raised and the rocks echoed the merriment, a departure from the usual human sounds heard in the area. Sadie now spent Saturdays with her father and the road crew, which made life at the ferry more enjoyable. The class enrollment had grown to ten with the addition of Janey's two children; girls now outnumbered boys seven to three. The difficult part was that most of the pupils were of different ages, ranging from Archie Lamb, who was not yet five, to George Emett, who was fourteen. When Clara attended, the spread rose to sixteen. Teaching was no easy task in the one-room log schoolhouse with outside dimensions of fourteen by nineteen feet.

Sunday, February 12, 1899, was a banner day in the life of Sadie Staker, and the description of it was the sole entry in her diary. That day Galloway had promised her a ride through the Pahreah Riffle, and the Emetts, the road crew, and visitors all turned out to watch. The riverman even offered to take another passenger but there were no takers. The three drownings in 1889 were still discussed, and anyone entering between the rising walls of Marble Canyon was considered foolhardy at best. The question was: what if Galloway should miss his landing and be swept down the canyon? The combination of danger and romance added spice to an operation that, to the trapper, couldn't have been more routine. But he kept a straight face and assured Sadie that he would land her safely.

Everyone selected a vantage point, most of the onlookers congregating on the right bank near the foot of the rapid. Soon the cry went out, "Here they come!" Galloway took the open boat down the center of the best water the rapid afforded and managed to give the young schoolteacher a splash or two. He ran the riffle at Two Mile, pulled into the eddy, and landed on the beach above the lower ferry. Sadie was so overcome by excitement that she swooned—or appeared to—and had to be lifted out of the boat.[73] Sadie was so proud of her feat that she noted the rapids were a mile long, fell twenty feet (the true fall is seven feet), and that not one of the men would attempt the ride. Galloway said nothing, but he might have had second thoughts about taking her for a honeymoon trip through the Grand Canyon.

When Joe Robinson went to Flagstaff earlier in the month, he was accompanied by another member of the Kanab City Council and a civic leader in his own right, William T. Stewart. The latter's business, however, differed from Robinson's, although each supported the other. Stewart retained J. E. Jones as attorney for the Kitchen heirs to fight the appointment of James Emett as executor of the estate. Jones soon found that Emett had not followed the letter of the law by failing to give notice of the sale of the Kitchen property in the newspapers within the proper time allotted. He therefore petitioned the court to discharge Emett and appoint another executor. A message to the ferry brought Emett to Flagstaff to show cause why his letters of testamentary should not be revoked. He failed to satisfy the court and was discharged on February 15.[74] The revocation nullified the appraisement that Galloway did not sign. On March 4, Judge Layton issued letters of administration for the Kitchen estate to Undersheriff John W. Francis. The new administrator had just completed a term as mayor, was judged to be impeccably honest, and was part of the Flagstaff power structure. He also was one of Emett's friends, as were several others high in local politics.

Meanwhile, Dee Woolley's fears came to pass. The Kaibab Land and Cattle Company—the dummy corporation controlled by John W. Young—had sold the VT spread to John M. Murdock and A. L. Fotheringham in November 1897. Murdock quit claimed his share to Ebenezer Gillies. On February 24, 1899, Fotheringham and Gillies sold the property to Thomas S. Kingsberg, agent for B. F. Saunders. It was a mere formality when Kingsberg quit claimed to the real owners, Saunders and his silent partner, Ora Haley of Wyoming and Colorado.[75] This brought Bar Z to the Kaibab and House Rock ranges to set up a future confrontation with Jim Emett.

While the road crew was hacking out the new dugway, other workmen, including John F. Brown and Jerry Johnson, had erected the cable. The left bank presented no problem, as a hole was single-jacked into the solid rock of a ledge behind the landing, sufficiently elevated to allow for cable-sag even in high water. The right bank, however, required a different solution since the cable was not long enough to reach bedrock behind the bar at the right landing. Emett was equal to the task. He had logs collected, and built a truncated pyramid whose top was level with the left-bank anchorage. Then a smaller log crib was built behind the first, slanted to oppose the thrust of the cable that was anchored to a deadman. A handline of three-quarter inch manila was set lower so that it would be within reach of the boat. It was adjustable at one end to allow for variations in the water level.

The boat itself was similar to previous ferries, but there were no oarlocks. Instead, there were two long eyebolts fore and aft in one of the gunwale beam-timbers. It was longer than Johnson's last ferries and would hold two wagons and teams in tandem loading. The attaching hardware consisted of a pair of brackets, each with tandem sheaves in a closed "Y" clevis, which prevented disengagement from the cable. There was a ring at the base of each clevis with an ordinary block and tackle connecting each pair of sheave-brackets to eyebolts anchored in the gunwale beams. This allowed individual adjustment according to the direction the boat was headed. By close hauling the forward block and letting the aft one out, the boat was held at an angle to the flow of the stream. The current struck the angled side of the boat and pushed it across the river. The overhead handline was used to get the boat into the current and the river did the rest. It was an old method but new in actual practice to these operators, and they had to learn from experience. The cable-driven boat was completed in March, a few days before the road rounded the ledge. After it was given several test runs, Sadie Staker took one of the first rides on Sunday, March 5.[76]

Nate Galloway normally trapped all winter and sold his beaver pelts in Flagstaff when the fur became less than prime. Without saying anything to those at the ferry, he diverted some of the best skins and had a cape made for Sadie, the object of his affections. He knew that she was due to return home after the school term and there was some anxiety as to whether the cape would be finished and brought to the ferry in time to present it, but everything worked out satisfactorily—except that it did not advance the trapper's suit. Staker was grateful for such a fine garment, and it still was being displayed by her grandchildren sixty years after her death.

Sadie Staker and her students, 1899 (*Nathaniel Galloway photograph, Cornelia Staker Peterson Collection, P. T. Reilly Collection, Cline Library, Northern Arizona University*).

The new road was completed a few days later, and Staker walked its length on March 15. Galloway, still pressing his suit, picked her up and gave her a boat ride up river. She kept him at a distance when she went fishing with Ernest Duffin, one of the boys working on the road. After her father and most of the crew started home on March 21, she was lonesome again and lamented that she had to teach for another six weeks. As the term neared its end, the children were aware that they would have a new teacher next year and they became troublesome. On April 7, she noted that she "had to conquer the children for lieing."

Believing that April 21 would be her last day of school, Staker ended the term with a program put on by the class. But it was not to be; Emett told her firmly that he expected the term to last until the end of the month. She was so upset that she nearly had her trunk put on the wagon of a passing traveler, but she thought about the possible loss of her salary and decided to stick it out, consoling herself by reading the Book of Mormon. She taught for another week, had a last boat ride with Galloway on Sunday the thirtieth, and prepared to depart on Tuesday. Again she was disappointed and wrote that she "was made to feel very bad." She finally left on Wednesday, May 3, in company with Mrs. Emett, Janey Chamberlain, and Pete Granger, the last member of the road crew. They reached Kanab on Friday where Sadie visited friends and relatives, attending parties and church through the twenty-first. She left Kanab on June 2 to arrive at Annabella on the twenty-sixth, her Lee's Ferry experience at an end.

The contractors had returned home without a settlement, having Emett's assurance that tithing orders would be sent to them from church headquarters in Salt Lake City. On April 17, he notified George Gibbs that the entire job had been completed. Back came a telegram asking for a full report detailing the improvements. Emett apparently ignored the request because it involved detested paperwork, and the contractors now demanded payment and said they would force a settlement. Buck-passing letters and telegrams went back and forth for three months until on August 3, Emett finally telegraphed Gibbs to ask why his report had not been considered. Gibbs again wrote that no report had been received, and asked him to send a duplicate.[77] This was done in a semi-satisfactory way and partial payments were made to Staker, Foreman, and Mecham in September, although the full settlement was not made until December when Emett was told bluntly that he first had to obtain an order from the church office, then draw against it.[78] The contractors found, as had Sadie Staker, that dealing with James Emett could be a difficult business.

If Emett had trouble learning to cope with the accounting procedures of the church, he also had something to learn about building and operating a cable ferry on the Colorado River. The spring runoff had set in early and by May 18 was already at a higher stage than when Roundy drowned. Jim was crossing four south-bound travelers with a like number of saddle horses and pack animals. He pulled the boat into the current with the hand line but failed to let the aft tackle out quickly enough to put the boat at an angle. The strong current hit full force against the beam and the ferry began to bounce. The animals crowded to the low, upstream side, which intensified the problem. The full force of the river now poured into the boat. Men and animals were in the river, and Jim shouted for Clara to bring the skiff. The right-hand deadman pulled out as one of the passengers scrambled to shore. The boat now swung on the cable toward mid-river when the left anchor held fast. As the others reached shore, the ferry broke completely loose and disappeared. The cable, trailed into the river from the left anchorage, was covered with silt and could not be salvaged.

Emett did not want to ask the church for additional credits for lumber or to procure a new cable. He ordered his first need from John Brown's recently-established sawmill at Jacob Lake and paid for it himself. He decided to replace the steel cable with a two-inch manila line which he obtained wholesale in Salt Lake City through Dee Woolley's merchandising connections. The rope was freighted to Kanab, and Dee Woolley had his son Roy pack it to the ferry. Roy claimed that the heavy coil, placed on two pack saddles, ruined his horse by breaking its withers.[79] The hardware had been lost with the cable, so Jim obtained larger sheaves and made new fittings to accommodate the increased diameter of the suspension line.

The old waterlogged boat at the lower ferry was still usable but the river was too high to risk crossing there. The oar-driven upper ferryboat was too rotten to use. Therefore, until the river went down, all crossings were made by skiff. This meant that wagons were taken apart and ferried in pieces, and the livestock swam. Things really hadn't changed much from Johnson's early days, at least until a new ferryboat could be built. The most recent one had lasted only seventy-four days.

The river still was high when a rider arrived with a band of horses he was trailing to Arizona. There was no choice but to swim the stock—frequently a difficult and hazardous operation. Jim Emett was away but John agreed, for a price, to use the skiff and herd them to the left bank. It usually was no easy matter to induce animals to swim a river, especially when it was high. The technique was to get the leader into the water and started across, keeping the others strung out behind in single file. Someone in a rowboat had to keep the animals headed across the river and not allow them to turn with the current. The oarsman would stay on the downstream side of the stock, close enough to influence them without losing oarspace to maintain his own heading.

All went well for almost a third of the way across, but when the leader felt the full force of the main current he started to veer downstream. Young Emett rowed directly at the animal, but it did not give way; he came too close, was unable to use his right oar, and the horse got a leg over the gunwale. John lashed out with an oar, the animal lunged, and the boat tipped, allowing water to pour inside. In a flash, it was capsized and John was trying to swim. Fully clothed and wearing boots, he was not making much headway and was getting tired when he called to Ring, the large Newfoundland on shore. Ring plunged in and reached him; John grabbed the dog's tail and they struck out for shore, making the bank through Ring's swimming ability. The rowboat grounded on the island delta and was recovered when the river went down.[80]

Jim Emett's powers of persuasion appeared to have failed him when September came and he still had not found a replacement for Sadie Staker; consequently, there was no school that fall. He persevered, however, and with President Woolley's help obtained a teacher for the second half of the term. Miss Tamar Stewart, a nineteen-year-old girl in Kanab, was persuaded to teach the spring term and Coconino County paid her salary. This was accomplished by a little white deception in Flagstaff whereby Lee's Ferry was declared to be a branch of Fredonia's District 6, thus officially putting Tamar on Fredonia's payroll. She started teaching in mid-January and completed the term in April. She did not like the situation any better than had her predecessor and refused to return in the fall.

Meanwhile, Stanton had decided on a plan for the placer mining of Glen Canyon, and Lee's Ferry—being most accessible—was a key part of it. First, he had to perform assessment work to hold the claims; for this phase, he selected three reliable men, each to head a crew in a different part of the canyon. He met with his foremen in Salt Lake City late in October 1899. J. W. Wilson was placed in charge of work near Bullfrog Creek, Nathaniel Galloway supervised at Hole in the Rock, and Will S. King worked at Lee's Ferry.[81] George Uden assembled a fourth crew a couple of miles below Hite. Each foreman hired enough men locally to perform his part of the project. The prospect of wages and board solved the labor problem as men scrambled to get jobs. All crews were at work in November.

King hired Mrs. Emett and her daughter Clara to cook for his crew. He obtained a number of men from Kanab, including Jerry Johnson, Roy B. Woolley, Bert Riggs, and Walter McAllister; even Bill Emett went to work on the project. They set up a tent camp at the fort and later moved across the river and made two more camps as the work progressed upstream.[82] The immediate task was to extend the road up the left bank from the ferry crossing, because Stanton planned to install a dredge in this quiet section of the river. At the start, the foreman made a little speech to the crew, admonishing everyone to be considerate and respectful to the two women.

Stanton came to Glen Canyon later in November to examine the work performed by the four crews and to post work assessment notices as required by law. He spent about a week at Uden's camp, then proceeded down river to the others. On December 13, he came to Galloway's camp, now located near the end of the road a mile and one-half above the ferry crossing. He picked up King, Mrs. Emett, and Clara, then ran down to the fort to spend Sunday and Christmas Day. They had tents set up for a base camp, but Stanton continued on to the ranch as a guest of the Emetts. Proud of his cooking ability, he invited himself into the kitchen where he prepared a French rarebit, furnishing the cheese from his own supply.

During the last week of December, Stanton shifted King's crew to another phase of assessment work. He had walked over the new road and thought that a couple of curves were too sharp for the heavy loads he envisioned passing over it. Consequently, he ordered some retaining walls built and reduced the severity of the curves. He claimed to have posted one hundred ninety-seven notices of performed assessment work during the last five weeks, thus holding the company's claims for another year. Included in his proof of labor for 1899 was a credit for "betterment of the Hoskaninni Company's rock house at Lee's Ferry." This, of course, was the old fort trading post, and the improvement consisted of removing the flagstones that transformed the windows into loopholes. In all, he listed an expenditure of over fourteen thousand dollars.[83]

The end of the nineteenth century brought the assessment work to a close. The men were paid off and most of them started for home on New Year's Day. Ten remained who were scheduled to take the twenty-foot launch, *Little Jean,* and two row boats to Hall's Crossing. These men under M. J. Ryan included Jerry Johnson and Bill Emett.[84] Only bedrolls and provisions were taken on the difficult, cold trip. Ice was in the river and the boats were muscled upstream by manpower. The *Little Jean* had a steam engine but it had stopped working. The engine was removed and she was towed with the others and rowed where possible. The destination was one hundred twenty miles away and the trip required three weeks. They came down river in two days, using two homemade skiffs.

Stanton settled up with Emett on January 2, 1900, whereupon he departed for Salt Lake City and caught the train for his home in Pennsylvania. The Emetts were convinced that Lee's Ferry was about to experience a boom of unprecedented proportions and they held the key to a gold mine. However, January 2 was the last they ever saw Robert Brewster Stanton.

8

The Antagonists

THE ECONOMIC BOOM EXPECTED FROM MINING AND TOURISM ON THE Arizona Strip did not turn out to be what everyone envisioned. On January 5, 1900, Secretary of the Interior E. A. Hitchcock recommended to President McKinley that the Navajo Reservation be enlarged, and three days later the president signed an executive order extending the boundary south to the Little Colorado River and west to the Colorado River.[1] This placed land claims in the Tuba City area in jeopardy and halted plans for development along the left bank of the Colorado. Robert B. Stanton's new road was now on Indian land. Political leaders had protested reservation enlargement directly to Washington.[2] Nevertheless, the enlargement was made; left-bank development plans came to a halt, and a quarter century of Mormon improvements faced a bleak future. For the Hopi, things looked even bleaker.

That winter two prospectors found some copper-stained ore near the mouth of Warm Springs Canyon at the western slope of Buckskin Mountain. In the ensuing rush, many claims were filed. The main camp was called "Coconino." One of the discoverers, Aquilla Nebeker, sold out to his partner, Ryan, who was said to have been the father of professional boxer Paddy Ryan. He renamed the camp after himself. Jim Emett carried news of the so-called "strike" into Flagstaff. The *Coconino Sun* gave the story its usual treatment in the issue of March 3, 1900, which had the effect of increasing ferry business as Arizonans rushed to the area.

John Emett was visiting maternal relatives in Escalante when he made the acquaintance of pretty eighteen-year-old Sarah Ellen Wooley. He was relatively unknown here but the young people were attracted to each other and the interest was encouraged. His courtship was aggressive and the couple obtained a marriage license from Mahonri Steele, Garfield County clerk, in Panguitch on April 28, 1900. They were married in Escalante May 2 by Bishop Andrew I. Schow and started married life at the ferry a few days later.[3] At first they lived in the fort, but later every able-bodied person at the ferry pitched in and raised a cabin for them by a cottonwood next to the Pahreah River, just above Lee's original damsite and beside the road leading to the upper crossing.

In mid-April, a rather remarkable expedition departed from Provo en route to South America. A double column of horsemen was sandwiched around two covered wagons; the men were uniformed, carried rifles, and were headed by a member bearing a large American flag. A bugler sounded all commands of the leader, Benjamin Cluff, Jr., who was the president of Brigham Young Academy. He was one of the best educated men in Mormondom, having received a master's degree from the University of Michigan. He had been a member of the BYA faculty for over nineteen years and was president for eight. Officially known as "the Brigham Young Academy South American Exploring Expedition," Cluff's party hoped to discover archaeological evidence sustaining the claims of the Book of Mormon, gather scientific specimens for the school's museum, and assemble detail for future proselyting and colonizing efforts.[4]

The seriousness with which the Saints regarded the venture is emphasized by the fact that all members went through the temple, were set apart, and the trip was officially blessed. As it was a mission, the First Presidency advised Cluff to obtain the consent of the students' parents or release them from service.[5] Every man carried a Bible and a copy of the Book of Mormon, and each day started and ended with prayers. Two of Cluff's more logical additions to the party were John B. Fairbanks and Roy B. Woolley. Fairbanks was Utah's version of artist Thomas Moran; he painted in the same style and almost as skillfully. On this occasion, however, he left his canvasses and paint tubes at home to rely on a camera, an instrument he had not fully mastered at this time. Roy was the son of Uncle Dee Woolley, Kanab stake president. Apparently Roy was included because of his competence with horses and his knowledge of the local area. He joined the company at Kanab, riding out from there with the others on May 5.

Up to this point the company had spent each night dispersed in various Mormon homes, with meals and beds provided by supporting brethren. Now they were forced to camp, and Woolley immediately saw that Cluff's logistics were nonexistent except for himself. He also saw that most of the members knew little or nothing about livestock and could scarcely handle a horse. He guided them to House Rock, South, and Wildcat Canyons. They descended into Wildcat Cave, rang the stalactites, explored pueblo-type ruins, and gathered potsherds. They ran out of food, hunted deer, and nearly drilled eight Bar Z cows before realizing they weren't game. Woolley considered himself to be as much a shepherd as if he were driving a band of sheep.

On May 17, exactly one month after leaving Provo, the company reached Lee's Ferry. The oasis appeared as a gem in a gravel bed, and the travel-weary members looked longingly at the ripe cherries, almonds, green fruit, and lush garden. While Cluff refreshed himself in the Emett home, he sent word to the company to proceed to the crossing and he would follow shortly. They did as told but went by way of Sister Emett's henhouse and, according to Woolley, surreptitiously gathered what eggs were available.

Fairbanks took pictures from both sides of the river as the wagons and horses went over in the ferryboat. The men and their packs were crossed in the skiff. Woolley looked critically at the overhead Manila line that had ruined his horse's withers and hoped that the animals' sacrifice had been in a good cause. The ferryman forgave them their ferriage of thirty dollars. They all took baths in the river along the left bank, then went on to camp at Navajo Spring.

The start of the new century saw another notable party use the historic crossing, and the ferriage of their thirteen horses earned Emett seventeen dollars. On June 13, five renowned geologists headed by Dr. Herbert E. Gregory camped in Emett's yard and enjoyed his fruit as they were en route from Flagstaff to Toquerville. Their field trip was the first geologic study of the region bordering Glen Canyon since the Powell and Wheeler surveys; eventually it resulted in a worthy contribution to that field.[6]

Strangers frequently got into trouble when they ventured into the inhospitable region, but sometimes they performed more capably in extricating themselves than people who were experienced. Such an example occurred in September 1900. There had been talk of creating Grand Canyon National Park for more than a decade; mining, timber, and grazing factions were opposed, while tourist promoters and conservationists approved the concept. Progress in advancing the idea was slow, and political nudges in various directions were frequent. President Benjamin Harrison proclaimed the Grand Canyon Forest Reserve in 1893. Administration was given to the General Land Office four years later, but this failed to satisfy anyone, so the Division of Forestry of the Department of Agriculture was created in 1898 with Gifford Pinchot in charge. He was a distinguished forester, a conservationist, a friend of Theodore Roosevelt, and later became known as the father of the Forest Service, but for the present he worked assiduously to strengthen his position and advance his ideas. Two of his appointees were I. B. Hanna, superintendent of all forest reserves, and A. E. Herman, superintendent of the Grand Canyon Forest Reserve.

These two men hired a guide, W. H. Pierce, and a team to tour the northern part of the reserve. They were returning south, had crossed the Colorado River and pitched camp at Cedar Ridge, where Pierce turned the horses out to graze. Unfortunately, the animals had been without water since leaving the ferry, and during the night they started back to the river. Pierce discovered the horses were gone in the morning and went in pursuit, but he failed to catch sight of his quarry and barely managed to stagger back to camp. Hanna and Herman started walking the next day as the elderly guide recuperated. Hanna became exhausted five miles short of the ferry and stopped to rest. Herman plodded on, reached the ferry at 9 P.M., and when his shouts could not raise anyone at the ranch, he filled a canteen and went back to help Hanna, who had managed to struggle to within three miles of the ferry. Together they returned to the ferry and soon got Jim Emett's attention. They rested at the ranch from their ordeal as Emett sent a team and water to Pierce. After a three-day layover, the travelers rented another team and resumed their interrupted journey to Flagstaff.[7] Herman, Hanna, and Emett had saved an important element of Pinchot's organization.

When the 1900 fall school term opened at Lee's Ferry, Miss Mae Rogers, a member of the Mormon Tabernacle Choir in Salt Lake City, was the teacher. Her salary of fifty dollars a month was charged to District 6 of Fredonia, but she had to arrange for her own board. According to his daughter, Emett charged her nothing and she ate with the family. Mae didn't mind the isolation as much as had her predecessors and she remained for a full year, but no record of her life at the ferry is available beyond Emett family recollections.

Jim Emett's family continued to increase. Sarah Emett elected to return to Escalante for the birth of her first child because she had confidence in the midwives there. John did not think this was necessary and delayed taking her until the pregnancy was so far advanced that the rough trip endangered both mother and child. The result was the premature birth of twins at Escalante on January 5, 1901. The first child was named Julia Mae; the second, Bessie, obviously the weaker of the two, died the following day. John Emett knew he was responsible for her failure to survive. Bill Emett had married Mary Church the previous year and, as in the case of his brother John, had brought his bride to the ferry. The couple's first child, born on April 11, 1901, was a boy they named William Glenn. There now were three Emett families living at Lee's Ferry.

John Kitchen's family decided to erect a monument at his grave, and since Flagstaff was the closest railroad delivery point, Emett was given the job. M. H. Rice of Kansas City made the monument for $80. It was delivered at Flagstaff on March 30, 1901, the rail freight amounting to $42.10. An impressive headstone in polished grey granite, the upright portion was twelve by twenty-four by thirty inches, set in a similar base with dimensions of eighteen by twenty-four by thirty inches. Graven on two sides, the entire unit weighed 1,650 pounds. John Tanner of Tuba City freighted it in mid-April from Flagstaff to Willow Springs—approximately seventy-seven miles—for $16.50. It remained there for three and one-half months until Emett freighted it to the ferry. He charged $215 for taking it sixty miles and setting it in place.[8] Emett never worked cheaply.

Jim Emett's delay in picking up the monument was due in part to the fact that on May 16, 1901, he was indicted by a Kane County grand jury for embezzling from the Kitchen estate.[9] The action appeared to have resulted more from old enmities and present Kane County politics than solid evidence. Four witnesses were questioned before the indictment was handed down—John F. Brown and James S. Emett on one side, William T. Stewart and Abraham Fotheringham on the other. As usual, legal actions dragged the case out and Jim spent as much time on the road between Kanab and Flagstaff as he did at home tending the ranch and ferry.

Robert Brewster Stanton left no indication that the extension of the Navajo Reservation to the Colorado River influenced his decision not to install the first dredge at Lee's Ferry, but neither did he have any figures to suggest that the test runs induced him to put it where he did. The preliminary tests did not justify the expenditures of 1900, but he went ahead anyway. A floating dredge had been ordered from the Bacyrus-Erie Company. It exceeded 105 feet in length with a 36-foot beam—the largest craft ever to float above the lower Colorado and the seventh largest to work the river. He set up a base office at Green River, Utah, in June 1900.

The disassembled dredge was shipped in by rail and loaded on freight wagons. A road of sorts already ran to Hanksville, and a track had been hacked through the Henry Mountains to Glen Canyon by sheepherders and prospectors. Stanton had this extended to Wilson Canyon, then blasted a precipitous dugway to its bed. The wagons went down the wash to the Colorado River where the material was loaded on barges and smaller boats to be floated upstream one and one-half miles to the place of assembly, soon called "Camp Stone." This was on a river flat one hundred twenty-three miles upstream from Lee's Ferry. In time, Wilson Canyon became known as Stanton Canyon. Its mouth was more than one hundred miles from Green River, half of them very rough miles. The railroad at Flagstaff was slightly farther from Lee's Ferry, but the road was much better and the heavy loads would have traveled mostly downhill. The only negative factor between Lee's Ferry and Flagstaff was the crossing at the Little Colorado River.

The summer of 1900 was devoted to transporting material and equipment to Camp Stone. The dredge was assembled during the fall and winter and apparently was completed in February 1901. Most of the spring was given to testing and working out the bugs. A major source of trouble was fluctuation in the river level, as sudden drops led to the craft being grounded. The few dollars realized from the little gold that was recovered did not begin to pay the grub bill for one day, and the rig ceased to operate beyond midsummer. The company went into receivership in the fall of 1901. Although Green River reaped the economic boom that Emett had hoped would come to his ferry, it lasted only a few months and the aftermath was depressing. This episode ended Stanton's dream of promotion on the Colorado River.

Emett now had many friends in Flagstaff including civic, political, and judicial leaders. He generated sympathy in most quarters for not having the benefit of a county school. He evidently discussed the matter at length with these people because he came up with a plan for achieving his ends. On July 1, 1901, he petitioned the Coconino County Board of Supervisors to form a new school district. The proposed size of the district was as grandiose in proportion as Brigham Young's claim for the State of Deseret had been in 1850. It probably was the largest such politically defined area in the United States, running from the Ute Crossing—then thought to be the point where the Utah-Arizona line crossed on the Colorado River—westerly to the summit of Buckskin Mountain and south to the Colorado River, then along the river to the beginning. It was nearly one-fourth of the entire Arizona Strip. Even Emett's critics were forced to admit that he thought in large terms.

If Jim inflated the size of the proposed district, he did the same with his enrollment, claiming that a total of twelve pupils would attend. Seven were his own, ranging from five-year-old Bessie to nineteen-year-old Clara. Janey Chamberlain had two children of school age; Joe Hamblin, who visited occasionally, had one. John Emett was listed as a head of family and his school-age "children" were his twenty-year-old wife, Sarah, and her younger sister, Mary. If the latter ever visited at the ferry, none of the Emetts remembered it in later years. Nevertheless the petition was approved on November 7, 1901, and School District Number 11 was created.[10]

This extension of county government brought drawbacks as well as advantages. On July 9, the Board of Equalization sent notices to Jim Emett and B. F. Saunders that their properties would be reassessed. They could appear at the next board meeting on July 20 if they wanted to protest. Neither did. The value of Emett's taxable property was raised from seventy to a hundred dollars, while the head count for the Bar Z was raised from fourteen hundred to five thousand, still well under the actual numbers.[11]

Utah's interest in acquiring the Arizona Strip continued unabated, and in no one did it burn more intensely than Dee Woolley. He firmly believed that Utah eventually would get the land and in due time God would reveal the process of its acquisition. He prayed repeatedly in meetings for this to happen; meanwhile, the people of southern Utah continued to lobby and prepare for that time. The axiomatic theme in Kanab circles held that it was Utah's manifest destiny to own the strip. Emett kept Woolley abreast of the changing times in Coconino County, and the two were as up to date as anyone in Flagstaff. The action wherein the Atchison, Topeka, and Santa Fe had acquired the Anita holdings and planned to extend the railroad to Grand Canyon did not go unnoticed. With the railroad bringing thousands of visitors to the canyon's rim, there had to be a way to move some of these people on to Buckskin Mountain and the scenic grandeur of southern Utah. It is not clear who came up with the original concept, but Woolley and Emett envisioned roads from Kanab to the North Rim and a good trail traversing the canyon to the railhead.

Besides the rise of tourism to Grand Canyon, B. F. Saunders was expanding the Kaibab–House Rock range at a rapid rate. Already several thousand Herefords had been brought in with the Bar Z brand, much to the dismay of Woolley and Emett. To counter the expansion of the new outfit, Emett decided to use Greenland Point (Walhalla plateau) as a summer range for his horses. Woolley helped him drive the animals there in the summer of 1901. The pair camped at Greenland Spring and made a visual survey of possible cross-canyon routes. Before breaking camp, they had settled on the general location for their trail down the long fault tributary named Bright Angel Canyon. They even descended through the faulted areas on foot and walked to the river to prove the route passable, then returned home to generate support. By this time, Emett realized that the extension of the reservation to the Colorado, the railroad to Grand Canyon, and the failure of the Stanton mining promotion had bypassed the ferry, and any success he would enjoy by living at the remote location must come from other means. Too, the entire range must not be left to Saunders.

Although Emett was fairly certain that his petition would be assented, notification that it had been approved brought him to Flagstaff. Much remained to be settled, including obtaining a teacher, setting up a board of trustees for the new district, and gathering school equipment. District 11 was starting from scratch. Emett, his wife, and his son Bill agreed to act as trustees and to board the teacher, but the other problems were more difficult and it did not seem possible to start school on time. Teachers were not readily available and the county treasury was in such poor condition that the school administrators had to be magicians to procure minimum equipment. But Judge Layton was up to the task.

On November 9, 1901, a three-man party left Flagstaff bound for the outlying school districts. The trip was instigated by Probate Judge and School Superintendent N. G. Layton, who had as his guest the eminent astronomer Dr. Andrew Ellicott Douglass, recently terminated from the Lowell Observatory. Ashton Nebeker, a prominent Mormon of Tuba City, served as guide and teamster. Ash was a genuine pioneer, having been on the Mormon migration to the west, was an early settler of Utah's Dixie, and had made trips to Oraibi with Jacob Hamblin in 1869 and 1870. Now his services, buggy, and team earned him four dollars a day; but had employer or guest been able to interview him, history would have been far richer. The party was self-contained, carrying copious supplies, water, and an unidentified liquid to ward off the November chill. The men had bedrolls and were prepared to camp wherever a day's travel ended.

With his camera, Douglass made a pictorial record of the Layton odyssey as they went along. Being more or less in limbo after his abrupt discharge by Percival Lowell in August, Douglass was groping for some phase of scientific activity to take the place of his beloved astronomy.[12] Layton had recognized his friend's need and invited him not only for his good company but to fill his void of activity. Douglass had a reserved way of putting things; on one occasion, he recorded how they stopped in the middle of the dry Little Colorado River to have lunch. This was the ancient Hopi ford that the Mormons had renamed "Tanner Crossing." When Nebeker was offered a drink he replied as he always did, "I very seldom take a drink of anything stronger than water, but when I do it is just about this time of day."[13]

Layton had persuaded Alex J. MacKay to leave his teaching post at Tuba City and move deeper into the hinterlands to handle the same position at Lee's Ferry. The salary now was sixty dollars a month, at least for a male teacher—a fact that might have annoyed Sadie Staker, Tamar Stewart, and May Rogers. In any event, the Layton party picked up MacKay, inspected the schools at Tuba and Moenave, and traveled on to the ferry. En route, the judge kept his eyes open for anything that could be used in District 11. Unfortunately, years of frugality had not led to surplus, and both Tuba and Moenave were in need of additional books and equipment. When they reached the ferry and had inspected the setup, Layton saw that outside of an acceptable one-room building and home-made benches, he really was starting from scratch; he still had hopes of obtaining some items from Fredonia. Meanwhile, they partook of Emett's hospitality, Layton and MacKay conferred, and Dr. Douglass took a picture of them with the family, for which Jim donned a frock coat.

They moved on to Fredonia and even went to Kanab, where Douglass again unlimbered his camera to record some of the town's leading citizens and small boys.[14] Layton found that the teachers in Fredonia's District 6 were doing good work, but the school trustees were quite extravagant and he refused to pay some of the bills unless they were reduced radically.[15] When the party started back to Flagstaff, it was decided to bypass the old pioneer route via Navajo Well in favor of the steeper but more direct road to Jacob Lake. The even newer track that Bar Z had hacked out the previous year would take them directly to House Rock Valley and would save many miles. It had been a dry year; Jacob Lake was a mere puddle, although it still provided plenty of drinking water and the forest was as lush as ever.

Of the next days' travel, Douglass wrote:

> We went down the precipitous east side of the Kaibab, passing from the well-timbered top to the barren and desolate House Rock Valley over 3000 feet below.... Sitting beside the driver I realized the possible inference from that remarkably sudden change from the moist forest down to the dry desert, and that this change was analogous to the changes in rain fall from year to year in the seven years which I had spent in Arizona. So it would be possible to find in the rings of the trees growing in that forest a history of those annual changes in rainfall. Such a history I thought could perhaps be connected with changes in the sun by which an astronomer without a big telescope could develop a solar history that would have scientific value.[16]

They camped that night at Jacob's Pools, which Douglass mistakenly thought was Emett Spring, and he mulled over his new hypothesis as he photographed the setting. The country intrigued him. When they reached the ferry and he learned that Emett would be going to Flagstaff in a few days, he remained there while Layton and Nebeker went on without him.

Douglass made good use of his time while he was Emett's guest. He was curious about the life-zone changes in the flora as the elevation increased, and when he questioned his host about the vegetation above the

Echo Cliffs and was told of the old Indian trail that E. D. Woolley had recorded more than thirty-two years previously, he ascended to the rim to see for himself. He estimated that he was two thousand feet above Emett's ranch (an estimate four hundred feet too high) and thought his vantage point was about midway between Jacob Lake and House Rock Valley. That estimate was fairly accurate. He noted that the view before him showed a "startlingly bleak and barren, rocky plateau, apparently with little or no vegetation or soil on it, through which the Colorado River had cut its canyon."[17] He emulated George Wharton James on the next day and induced an unnamed prospector to take him boating a few miles upriver into Glen Canyon where he observed vegetation along its banks.

Emett took Douglass to Flagstaff during the first week of December. The scientist was elated over his month-long trip and his new hypothesis. Deprived of working with telescopes, he turned to correlating the relevance between the eleven-year cycle of sunspots to weather as interpreted by tree rings. He thus founded the science of dendrochronology, but it was several years before the full-blown idea emerged from its cocoon.

An immediate result of the Layton trip came to light during the board meeting of the county supervisors when Gus McClure was awarded a contract for $65 to erect road and mileage signs between Flagstaff and Lee's Ferry.[18] Another result, undoubtedly at the direction of Superintendent Layton—and the motivation for Emett's trip to Flagstaff—was that Jim returned to the ferry with five double school desks procured from District 1. Layton also obtained seven text books, a dictionary, pens, pencils, blackboard erasers, a box of crayons, and twelve copy books. These supplies were bought on credit from the D. J. Brannen drug store at a cost to the county of $9.90. Although MacKay commenced the school term officially on November 20, he was forced to devote the first three weeks to verbal basics because there were no books or other equipment.[19] He ended the school term on April 4, having taught one hundred days at the ferry for a salary of $180. The class more often numbered eleven than ten, nine of whom were girls.

On June 11 Emett dated his final claim against the Kitchen estate for a sum of $83.26. The figure was derived from subtracting his credit of $1,386.50 from his total expenditures of $1,469.76. No one challenged the costs of dying, even approving the payment for a pair of boots and three bottles of whiskey for John Emett. Other sundries besides food, tea, and coffee were overalls, horseshoe nails and horseshoes, cooking utensils, a coffee mill, tobacco, a hat, towels, and soap. The final settlement of the Kitchen estate was made on September 9, 1902. The grand sum of $2.32 remained to be dispersed among the five heirs, and executor John W. Francis was honorably discharged.[20] If the ghost of the cattle king of southern Utah could have smiled, it likely would have been a wry one. Emett's embezzlement case came up in Kanab on September 19, but it did not last long. He produced receipts showing that he had expended $1,196.50 in behalf of the Kitchen estate, and the indictment was quashed.[21] Once again Emett's enemies were confounded.

N. G. Layton resigned his positions of probate judge, ex-officio clerk of the probate court, and superintendent of public county schools at the supervisors' meeting of July 24, 1902. On September 19, Harrison Conrard was appointed school superintendent for the balance of the year. He liked the job and campaigned for it in the fall election. At the same time, A. E. Douglass decided to run for the position of probate judge. Both men were elected handily on November 4.[22] When the Lee's Ferry school opened in the fall, Thomas W. Brookbank of Tuba City and Moenave was the teacher. He was one of the older Mormon settlers, had been heavily involved in Lot Smith's machinations of the Sunset United Order, was authoritarian, and was inclined to be too strict to secure the friendship of the pupils.

That winter, Sarah's younger brother, Ed Wooley, and a friend named Potter rode down from Escalante. Fifteen-year old Ed was going to work for Emett and his companion was along to keep him company on the ride. They intended to take the road to Cannonville, follow down the Pahreah to the Clark Bench, then cut over the Wahweap flats to the head of the Sand Trail. All went well up to the trailhead, which they missed. They finally realized their mistake, but continued on to the old Indian trail that descended to the Colorado at the ferry crossing. Ed Wooley moved in with Sarah and John and Emett employed him at fifteen dollars a month plus board.[23] His main job was to carry the mail twice a week between Lee's Ferry and Kanab.

November brought the news that Congress had appropriated the forty-eight thousand dollars needed to buy out the whites living at Tuba City and Moenave. U.S. Indian Inspector James McLaughlin had appraised the holdings in May 1899, noting that the settlers were squatters on unsurveyed land, had no property rights, but should be paid for their improvements. Of the twenty-one claimants, only trader Charles H. Algert was not a Mormon.[24] Now the money was available for payment, and the settlers were given six months to vacate. Emett expected travel to fall off considerably; an era was coming to an end. Most of the Tuba City people stayed in Arizona and moved farther up the drainage of the Little Colorado. A few returned to Utah, but all relocated early in order to get their spring crops planted. Only the trader remained to carry on his business at the pleasure of the Bureau of Indian Affairs.

Clara Emett was appointed postmaster at Lee's Ferry on January 2, 1902, but she did not arrive until mid-month.[25] She had reached her twentieth birthday in September, having spent her entire girlhood at the isolated ferry. She and her sisters had little contact with anyone except travelers, the school teacher, and occasional visitors from town. Jim and his three sons were away frequently, but his daughters passed their teen years there and grew up more as tomboys than young girls enjoying a social life.

All could ride, rope, and hook up teams, as well as do everything from household duties to planting, harvesting, and caring for livestock. They even helped out on the ferry occasionally.

When the mail carrier was observed on the dugway, Clara often used the rowboat to cross the river and receive the pouch on the left bank. She became rather adept at the oars and twice managed to extricate herself from predicaments that could have become serious. She and her sisters wore divided skirts when they rode and worked with livestock as required; about the only thing they didn't do was use firearms or break horses. Father and sons were good riders and always packed guns. Jim rarely was without his rifle; the boys favored six-shooters. Ring, the large Newfoundland, was a good "cowboy" and could bring the cows home on command. All family members milked as the occasion warranted.

Bill Emett was not the rider his brothers were, and there was one horse he still could not handle. Jim became so exasperated at repeated throwings that he finally got Bill on the animal and tied him in the saddle. When the rider could not be dislodged, the horse sunfished, then fell backward, breaking Bill's leg at the thigh. Jim set it as well as he could, but it was not a perfect fit. Since there was nothing to use for a cast, the leg did not heal as it should have, and Bill walked with a limp for the rest of his life. Most of Jim's efforts at bone-setting turned out better, however, and there were several. In 1901, Clara's horse stepped on a stick that flew up and hit him. The animal shied and threw his rider, breaking her arm. Jim set it with splints and bandages and it healed perfectly. He never backed away from a strange or difficult task but studied how it could be surmounted.

The dams Emett built were different from Lee's and Johnson's, but he lost just as many. He used logs and sandbags exclusively, departing from the loose dirt and brush used by his predecessors. Filling the bags was a constant job for the girls; any spare time they had was devoted to this work because the dams were always washing out.

School Superintendent Harrison Conrard toured his northern districts in January 1903 with Emett as guide and teamster. The pair left Flagstaff on the third to inventory school furniture in the Tuba District, which was due to lapse when the students moved elsewhere. Lee's Ferry could use some of the equipment and Emett agreed to store the remainder. Back in Flagstaff on the twenty-third, he was paid ninety-two dollars for the round trip.[26] His son John and Ed Wooley later picked up twenty-two hundred seventy pounds of school furniture and brought it to the ferry. Jim charged twelve cents per pound, or $35.05, which was considerably less than his bill for freighting the Kitchen monument.[27] When Brookbank's term ended April 17, he apparently had no desire to return to the isolated District 11. But because of closures at Tuba City and Moenave, there wasn't a shortage of teachers.

Theodore Roosevelt was making a well-publicized western tour, and Jim decided to take several of his children to Flagstaff to see a living president, even though it was a three-day trip each way. When the presidential train stopped in the town to take on water at 4:03 A.M., the Emetts were among the crowd expecting Roosevelt to make an appearance on the observation car. But the people waited in vain as the president slept through the stop. His car went on to the Grand Canyon where, at 9 A.M. on May 6, he made his famous speech to "keep it as it is."[28]

Despite his disappointment, Emett was impressed with the near-visit to Flagstaff and the stop at Grand Canyon by so important a person. He anticipated increased tourist business in the future. After taking his family home, he drove on to Kanab to impart his enthusiasm to Dee Woolley. There were several days of intense meetings wherein the pros and cons of their planned venture were discussed. The Grand Canyon Transportation Company was formed, based on the premise that if the Santa Fe Railroad brought tourists to the Grand Canyon's South Rim, the Mormon businessmen could build a trail and transport them a step farther to the North Rim. This would regenerate the cash-scarce local economy and benefit local business. The articles of incorporation were signed by E. D. Woolley, Thomas Chamberlain, Thomas G. Hoyt, James S. Emett, and Flagstaff attorney E. S. Clark on May 25, 1903; notarized by attorney John F. Brown at Kanab on June 15; and recorded by Clark at Flagstaff on June 27.[29]

On August 23, three strangers from Los Angeles came to the ferry, driven there by a Navajo in his wagon drawn by a team of wild ponies. Unable to get the attention of anyone at the ranch, they camped that night on the left bank. The men were Elias Benjamin "Hum" Woolley, John King, and youthful Arthur Sanger. In the morning, they were crossed to the right bank where they assembled a boat that was intended to take them down the Colorado to salt water. Naturally the residents regarded the trio as brash fellows who didn't know what they were doing, while the newcomers had the non-Mormon's curiosity about polygamy and regarded every woman they saw as a wife of the proprietor. Emma Jane thought the men were going to their doom and was especially sorry for young Sanger. That night she cried herself to sleep wondering if his mother knew where he was and what he was planning to do. The men assembled the boat, disregarded the warnings, and departed downstream on September 1.[30] The Emetts never saw nor heard of them again.

Jim Emett was absent from the ferry most of the summer, leaving his sons in charge. He did, however, make several trips home as the group members alternated duty on the North Rim trail construction. It was on one of these trips back to the ferry that friction with the Bar Z was generated. Emett shared the average Mormon's resentment of the big outside outfit taking over the range; he favored its use by the families who had settled the region. Although some of the Bar Z cowboys were local men, there were a number of imports from the villages to the north who were resented as much as if they had come from Texas. Moreover, the range-and-trail bosses were strangers, as were the owners.

The first dispute resulted from the trail crew and the cowboys having to share the water of Greenland and Neal Springs. Bar Z had several thousand cattle dispersed over the summer range on Buckskin Mountain, and the animals consumed large amounts of water. The trail builders had to have water and wanted it undefiled by cattle. They built fences around the springs which were promptly torn down by the cowboys, who regarded Emett as an interloper on Greenland Point. No shots were fired by either side but intimidation was practiced by both, and everybody packed guns. Meanwhile, the trail construction proved to be slow work but a route had been hacked out from the nearest stock road to the proposed trailhead at the rim. The project stopped for the winter in November.

Of all the divisions in the Coconino County school system, Lee's Ferry District was the least desirable. When word got around about the primitive nature of the facilities and its isolation, few teachers were willing to go there. Superintendent Conrard finally sent J. W. Tonnies to open the fall term on November 16, but he only taught until January 18, 1904, when he was relieved by William C. Jones.[31] Tonnies earned $149.50 for teaching forty-three days, and his abrupt departure suggests friction with the Emett families. Teachers at this time were paid $70 per month. Jim and his sons shared a little supplemental income from the county school in the form of fees for janitor service, freighting of supplies, and fuel. They collected driftwood from the Pahreah delta, sawed it into stove-lengths, and stacked it outside the schoolhouse for $3 per cord—probably the best bargain the county received. Between April 25, 1902, and September 29, 1909, the Emetts collected $481.95 for these services.[32]

Willie Jones, a member of a prominent Flagstaff family, was not the disciplinarian Tonnies had been. He got along with his students in a happy-go-lucky camaraderie. Jones was young, just embarking on a teaching career, and was not too far removed from school life himself. Between classes he played with the children, and even helped gather the asparagus that grew along the ditches. His salary was seventy dollars a month and his board was a pittance.

Shortly before the spring term ended on April 29, 1904, Jones wrote his mother in Flagstaff that he would return home either by wagon or by boat down the Colorado. She lost no time in sending him a telegram. It went to Barstow, California, and thence back to Kanab where a special rider took it on horseback and rode straight through to Lee's Ferry, arriving just before Willie was due to depart. The telegram was delivered collect and cost fifteen dollars; Jim Emett said the rider should have charged twice that sum. Fearing the worst, Willie opened the envelope and read "Don't go down the river."[33] He climbed into the wagon with a wry smile; his joke had backfired and cost him nearly a quarter of a month's pay.

John Neal, a trusted old cattleman and long-time employee of B. F. Saunders, managed the Bar Z operation. Neal had succeeded Tom Kingsburg, Will Crosby, and Hammy Kearns in 1902, but he was getting too old to handle the scope of work that Saunders had in mind. The outfit already had several thousand head of cattle on the range and planned to bring in more. Saunders ran Herefords, used blooded bulls, and had been weeding out the scrubs for beef. Range improvement and water development had high priority, and this demanded that water rights be acquired to all sources within the Bar Z range.

Several sheepmen in the Flagstaff area began enlarging their flocks by purchasing bands in Utah and driving them over the ferry to the Arizona range. This business, which began in the spring of 1904, took up some of the slack caused by the decrease in transient travel at Lee's Ferry. However, it tied up the ferry for extended periods in the spring and fall. The drives were difficult because of inadequate watering places. The animals suffered, often going two days without water. In February 1904, Saunders located lode claims and mill sites to take in important water sources. He named these the Frank, Crane, Snipe, Kane, Sunset, and Alaska Lodes, and recorded them at Flagstaff on March 1.[34]

Emett trailed his horses to Greenland Point every spring and brought them back to the valley before they could be snowed in. He attempted each time to water them at Bar Z outlets but succeeded only when the Saunders men were absent. He kept cattle at Soap Creek, and in the spring of 1901, he built a water trough at a seep about two miles southeast of Jacob's Pools as part of his ongoing effort to limit the Bar Z takeover. He named this seep Emett Spring, but he never developed it enough to obtain a constant flow. Nevertheless, its proximity to Jacob's Pools, which was the secondary headquarters for Bar Z, created a potentiality for conflict. As he and his sons worked their cattle between the ferry and their outlying range, the Bar Z men began to circulate rumors that they were missing livestock and the Emetts were suspected of rustling. Various cows that were known to have calved were seen alone, but there was no trace of the calves.

Emett employed Navajos from time to time, and early in the spring of 1903 had settled two brothers on the unused upper ranch. He helped them run a ditch to a corn and melon patch where they did small-scale gardening, but they mainly worked with the stock. According to Ed Wooley, the brothers spent much time at Emett Spring where Jim had a water trough and gate. Their principal job was to keep track of Bar Z movements with field glasses, and when no riders were present, they were alleged to have swooped down and collected a few long-eared calves which were taken to the ferry, hustled over the river, and hidden on the reservation.[35] Bar Z riders searched the area around Emett Spring but found it clean.

The relatively mild winter of 1903–1904 made it possible to start work on the trans-canyon trail earlier than usual. Woolley's son-in-law, David D. Rust, now unofficially became part of the project and began helping in March. Rust obtained the services of surveyor Hyrum D. Roundy and his Heller & Brightly transit. Roundy's job was to run the traverse of the trail so they could claim legal title and to maintain a constant trail grade below the rim. The work was started March 18 and the trail was surveyed and staked by the twenty-seventh, allowing the actual construction from the trailhead to begin.[36] Roundy's map indicated that it was seventeen miles from Woolley's station on the rim to Clark's station on the Colorado.

For several years, Jim had pondered the problem of improving the irrigation system at the ferry. As with Lee and Johnson, his dams had washed out repeatedly, the initial breaks usually appearing at the headgate. Sometimes a heavy flood down the creek would overflow the dam only to take out the ditch or fill it with viscid mud and leave the dam intact. In such cases, the ditch had to be shoveled clean before the next irrigation. It was useless to extend the dam farther upstream from Johnson's final location because the creek had cut deeply into a shale slope and sloughing had turned it into a cliff. At the same time, the latitude for water removal was reduced. The remedy was in moving the ditch above the floodline, but this was impractical due to the presence of lateral washes and a shale point that projected into the flat. If the ditch were to go around the point, it would be forced back into the flood plain. The washes could be bridged with small flumes and a tunnel through the point would keep the conduit above floodwater, but neither Jim nor his boys relished underground work, so the project languished.

The problem was solved that fall when the Irving C. Pierce family headed from Arizona toward the Utah mines. They came over the ferry and spent the night with its proprietor. Learning that Pierce was experienced in handling powder and sinking shafts, Emett offered him the job of making the tunnel. Pierce looked the job over the next morning and accepted. He and his wife Berti were surprised to learn that school would begin and their teenage son Francis could attend when he wasn't needed on the tunnel.[37] Emett settled the family in a cabin and the work got underway.

The new school teacher, L. L. Steward, arrived in mid-October and opened the fall term on the seventeenth. He averaged 9 students for the first three months and 8 for the second three months, but nobody questioned the size of the class or what it cost the county. Coconino County had a total of 522 students spread among six districts, with Lee's Ferry the smallest. The November election brought a change in school administration; J. S. Amundsen defeated Harrison Conrard for the superintendency by 83 votes. At the same time, the popular A. E. Douglass won re-election as probate judge.

Weather permitting, Emett made it a practice to take a load of turkeys to Flagstaff for Thanksgiving and had established a reputation for reliability. He arrived this year on November 22, as noted in the *Flagstaff Gem.* He dispensed gift birds to his choice friends and sold the rest. Demand exceeded supply and he sold out early and returned home quickly.

B. F. Saunders and Preston Nutter, for all practical purposes, controlled the livestock business on the strip in 1904. Saunders sold his holdings west of Cane Beds and now concentrated his operation in the east area, which took in the Kaibab and House Rock ranges to an undefined point east of Jacob's Pools. Some small operators were scattered about but their water resources were too limited to allow running many head. Emett Spring could not furnish a dependable supply to maintain even a small herd, and Jim's water trough was more for looks than utility, although he insisted it was enough for his purpose. No doubt it was, so long as he didn't define the reason for its existence, and while it was a convenience for him, it was a thorn in the side of Bar Z.

John Neal knew that age was catching up with him and the magnitude of the growing operation at the Bar Z was more than he wanted to assume. He made known his wish to retire and was asked to remain until a capable replacement could be found. Saunders had Neal's replacement in mind but did not identify him immediately. He had met a mature young man in Salt Lake City through mutual friends, the Keuhner family. Charles Dimmick was thirty-one years old, open, honest, and decisive in action. Saunders liked his potential, hired him, and sent him to the historic Canaan Ranch that he had purchased in 1895. When he sold his ranch in 1904, he sent Dimmick to work for John Neal. Thus, Charlie Dimmick was well-acquainted with the Bar Z–Emett controversy when Saunders made him his ranch foreman at the end of the year.

The Bar Z was expanding at a rapid rate. The headquarters was the old stone ranch house from VT days, at the mouth of Cane Canyon. Frank Rider, an expert mason, had built another stone house one-half mile south of Jacob's Pools in the winter of 1902–1903, and the cowpunchers had piped water down to a long water trough near the building. The overflow eventually filled a shallow basin about one hundred feet in diameter. This site became known as the "Lower Pools" and was the operation that Emett's Navajos allegedly watched and from which they ran off calves. In December Rider, with the help of brothers Bill and Willard Ford, began building a third stone house about three miles south of House Rock Spring, close to where the recently built road came off Buckskin Mountain. Prior to this, the Bar Z men had started a pipeline from the spring to the new location. This work was begun under Neal and finished under Dimmick in February 1905.

Pierce and his son completed Emett's tunnel that winter, blasted off some rocky ledges projecting into the elevation of the proposed flume, and dug some of the ditch. However, disagreement regarding payment resulted in a prolonged argument; bitter words were said on both sides and the Pierces departed in a huff. During the school term, Francis Pierce had recorded only forty-five days of attendance out of a possible one hundred fifteen.[38] Pierce still was seething when he stopped at the Bar Z house at the foot of the Buckskin grade and asked Charlie Dimmick for a job. It happened that the foreman could use the miner's services in spring development and put him to work. During the ensuing days, Pierce related his grievance against Emett and found sympathetic listeners. Then he related something else that caused Dimmick to blink; surely Providence had directed this man to Bar Z.

According to Pierce, he and his family had seen Jim and Bill Emett drive a Bar Z cow to the ranch on Sunday morning, October 23, 1904, where the animal was butchered for beef. Pierce was so angry with Emett that he would welcome the opportunity to testify against him. Dimmick immediately wrote Saunders about the matter. At last, it seemed, they had Emett where they wanted him. By the time Pierce had done some spring development work, Dimmick received instructions from Saunders to send the man on to Salt Lake City, where he would see that he got a job and was taken care of while a case against Emett was prepared. Saunders retained Henry F. Ashurst, prestigious attorney and rising Arizona politician, for the prosecution of a grand larceny case.

They dropped the bombshell on Emett in April 1905. He retained the highly respected E. M. Doe and J. E. Jones as defense attorneys. The trials were set for the April court term, but it was apparent that legal maneuvers and ordinary delays would set the cases back farther. Bill Emett was hailed into court on June 28 to face his charge and register his plea before he was released under a thousand dollar bond. A few days later, on July 10, George Emett was brought in by Sheriff Campbell, also was charged with grand larceny, and was released on a five hundred dollar bond.[39]

Attorney Ashurst searched the records and found that Jim Emett had not bothered to file a claim on the damp spot he called Emett Spring. Dimmick regarded this location as a cancer on the Bar Z operation, and he knew that if he could deprive Emett of this outpost for his Navajo spies he could cripple his efficiency. He filed a lode claim there in Saunder's name on June 27, 1905.[40] The claim was only fifteen hundred feet long by six hundred feet wide, but it took in the so-called spring, water trough, and gate. Appropriately, he named it "Emett Lode," and the claim was recorded on July 18. Jim was chagrined when his Navajo hand was run off as a trespasser by a rider with a .30–.30, but he acknowledged that although he had lost a round he had not lost the fight.

Now everything seemed to hit Emett at once. The runoff of the Colorado River began early and was judged, even before the peak, to be the highest since 1884. The Little Colorado also flooded early, isolating Tuba City and points north from Flagstaff.[41] This flow lasted only a few days but it effectively closed the old Tanner Crossing. However, in the lower river basin it was a different matter; although upper-basin damage was minimal, the peak, coming after the winter floods down the Gila, created havoc in the Imperial Valley.

Emett's multiple activities were almost more than the family could handle. He was away so often that the other members were forced to assume some of his responsibilities, but they failed to operate at his level of efficiency. No one had inspected the two inch Manila line for possible deterioration despite its having weathered for almost six years. There was little travel in the summer and as it was between seasons for sheep drives, the ferry had remained idle and unchecked. The result was the same as John D.

Lee had experienced in 1873. The heavy runoff accumulated driftwood and trash against the upstream beam, increased the pressure, and broke the boat loose from the mooring. As soon as she hit the current head-on, she started to bounce and the aging line parted. Everything was lost and the ferry was inoperable for weeks.[42]

Jim Emett realized that the Manila line had been false economy, and he resolved to replace it with another steel cable. In the interim, any travelers could be crossed in the skiff, as they likely would have been anyway until the high water went down. He made a list of needs and set out for Brown's sawmill and Kanab. At Jacob Lake, he left an order for gunwale timbers and planks for a new ferryboat, then went on to town where he intended to use the Woolley-Bowman connections to order five hundred feet of one-inch steel cable from ZCMI in Salt Lake City.

A consultation with Woolley changed Emett's plans abruptly. Creation of the U.S. Forest Service had brought red tape to Buckskin Mountain, and Woolley, after discussing the matter of the trail franchise with Forest Supervisor Lorum Pratt, realized that his firm would be forced to obtain official permission to construct the trail that now was nearing completion. Politically astute, he contacted Senator Sutherland, who passed the request on to Gifford Pinchot. Then he began rounding up support in Arizona by inviting Attorney General E. S. Clark (one of the company's incorporators) to gather some influential friends and attend a fall hunt. Clark suggested Mark Smith, Arizona politician and perennial delegate to Congress; associate Richard Sloan; and T. J. Norton, solicitor for the Santa Fe Railroad, also be invited.[43]

While all this had been taking place, Woolley, using stationery with the Bowman & Company letterhead, ordered five hundred feet of steel cable and a cage six by ten by six and one-half feet to be used for transporting people and horses across the Colorado River in Grand Canyon. He also ordered a sixteen-foot rowboat to facilitate installation of the cable. The wily stake president added Emett's cable to the order and, realizing the value of personal contact with Utah's political leaders, accompanied Emett to Salt Lake City on a multiple assignment.[44] This not only would save the freight bill but would add several birds to the transportation company's bag. They started north with a full agenda and arrived in the capital August 15.

After placing his order for the added cable and arranging to take both with them when they left town, Woolley and Emett started on several rounds of lobbying. The first stop was at the *Deseret News* where they related the story of the new trail from the North Rim to the Colorado River and the aerial tram by which the partners proposed to transport tourists across the river. The newspaper gave it a good play and thus achieved publicity for the Grand Canyon Transportation Company, as well as paving the way for future financial backing if it became necessary. The story caught the imagination of newsmen, and dispatches were sent around the country, which produced additional interest in Arizona. The *Coconino Sun* printed them on

August 12. When the first broadside hit the streets, Woolley called on both United States senators with two objectives in mind. The first was to promote tourism by bringing prominent men to the area. He had planned well, timing an invitation to a deer hunt to coincide with the politicians' whistle-stop campaign tour to southern Utah. Then Emett launched an attack against the Bureau of Indian Affairs about a matter that would be attractive to the politicians because of the vote-getting possibilities.

It was simple economics. Utah growers produced an excess of sheep that Arizona consumers were anxious to buy, but the Bureau was impeding the purchases by levying a fee on all animals crossing the reservation. The tax could be eliminated or modified by pressure in Washington. Sheep were collected in central and southern Utah during the spring and fall months and driven along the route used to colonize Arizona. Feed and water were scarce once the bands left the Virgin River drainage. At the ferry, Emett charged two and a half cents to cross each animal, taking as many at a time as could be crowded into the boat. The Colorado provided their first and last good drink until they reached the Flagstaff area. They were on the reservation when they crossed the river and didn't leave it until passing the Little Colorado. This distance required three to four days. If the band happened to be headed for the eastern range, it would be on Indian land almost to Winslow. The Indian agent demanded fifty cents for every hundred sheep and twenty-five cents each for horses for each twenty-four hours they were on the reservation. The charges bit into the profit of the venture and it was not clear how the collected money was to be used. The sheepmen charged the agent with graft, while those in Utah accused him of having anti-Mormon bias that hurt their business. It was expected that fifty thousand head would travel the route in 1905.[45]

Emett explained the situation to Senators Reed Smoot and George Sutherland, then—possibly at their suggestion—publicized the matter in the Salt Lake City newspapers. The two coils of cable were loaded on his wagon and the men pulled out of town later in August. They had the assurances of Senator Smoot, Congressman Joseph Howell, James Clove, and Lewis T. Cannon that they would avail themselves of the invitation to behold the marvelous country in person.[46] The trip had been eminently successful.

Back in southern Utah, Emett paused in Kanab, where he decided to ask for a continuance in his case since the September term would conflict with the congressional visits. He then dropped one coil of cable at the trailhead and returned to the ferry to find the replacement boat nearly complete. It was just in time because the fall sheep drives were about to begin. There was, however, some bad news, too. During the July meeting of the Coconino County Board of Equalization, the assessor had increased the number of Emett's taxable cattle from twenty-five to one hundred. The value rose from $258.75 to $1,035. At the same time, the Saunders herds increased from four thousand to seven thousand head—a value change from $41,400 to $72,450. Both figures actually were favorable to the owners because each had a greater head count, yet both protested, Saunders through his faithful agent Edgar L. Clark.[47]

The first result of Emett's lobbying effort appeared August 11 when Matthew M. Murphy, superintendent of the Western Navajo Agency, issued a compromise on the stock fee. He reduced the charge to twenty-five cents per hundred sheep between Lee's Ferry and Willow Spring, provided this portion was crossed within six days; otherwise the old rate would apply. There would be no charge for the leg between Willow Spring and the Little Colorado River provided it was crossed within six days. Sheepmen must keep their drives within a half-mile of the pioneer road, and no Indian water could be used by non-reservation sheep. Horse and cattle fees remained the same.[48]

Besides the original charge against Jim and Bill Emett of stealing a cow, the grand jury had returned an indictment of horse stealing against George and Bill. The Emetts spent the third week of September attending court in Flagstaff. B. F. Saunders, not knowing that Emett was requesting a postponement, came to town for the same purpose and was chagrined when all cases were bound over to the April term. He took the train back to Salt Lake City while the Emetts turned their wagon toward the ferry. Jim had told the *Coconino Sun* editor that the Bright Angel Trail would be completed in 1905. This was published but the promise was premature.

Meanwhile, the members of the Smoot-Howell party held a series of political rallies as they traveled south. They arrived in Kanab on Tuesday, September 26, as did the Arizona political contingent, and such a gala spirit prevailed that school was dismissed for the day. Woolley conducted them all to the North Rim forests, where Emett joined the party. They hunted deer on Greenland Point, enjoyed the spectacular scenery, and returned home raving about the beauty of the place. The publicity did not hurt the Grand Canyon Transportation Company a bit.

It was fortunate that the new ferryboat was operable in September because Frank Beasley and his herder, Jose Chavez, appeared near the end of the month with forty-five hundred sheep.[49] Almost five days were required to cross them, and feed was so scarce that the herders split the band. Jose proceeded with the ones crossed first. Beasley complained that the slow speed of each round trip extended the time of crossings, and Jim began thinking about making another improvement. That winter, he rigged a pulley to a deadman on the right bank, attached a one-inch line through it to the boat, and hitched the other end to a horse that pulled the boat back to the right bank while plodding parallel to the stream. Jim wanted to use horsepower to increase the boat's speed both ways, but the present usage did not warrant keeping animals on each bank, and the length of rope needed to pull both directions from one side would be too cumbersome to be practical. At least he had decreased a round trip time by half.

By this time most of the certified teachers in the county had either spent a term at Lee's Ferry or refused to do so. When it began to appear that the Coconino superintendency could not provide a teacher for the fall term, Jim Emett took matters into his own hands. He learned of a man who held temporary accreditation in District 6 at Fredonia. His name was John David Leigh and he normally was a Utah resident, but border-hopping was utilized as convenience dictated. Between Dee Woolley and Emett, he was persuaded to come to Lee's Ferry. Superintendent Amundsen cooperated by keeping him on the county payroll, although at a lesser salary than his predecessors. Leigh opened the term on October 9, 1905, with a class of eight girls and one boy.[50]

Jim brought Emma Jane with him when he took his annual Thanksgiving turkeys to Flagstaff in November. This time, he remained two weeks in town taking care of a number of items, but chiefly working with defense attorneys for the forthcoming trials. He found time to stop at the newspaper office to dispense tidbits pertaining to the new trail and cable tram. He related how the five hundred–foot cable was at the rim and would be snaked eighteen miles down the trail to the river on about twenty pack animals. He also said that the trail would be completed in a few weeks, an exaggeration as the work already had been shut down for the winter.[51] A delayed result of the visit in town was made public late in January. County Assessor Ralph Cameron appointed James S. Emett as his deputy who would assess all property in the county north of the Colorado River. It is safe to say that the appointment did not set well with Saunders.[52]

For the past two years Robert Walton, one of the largest sheep dealers in northern Arizona, had trailed several thousand head from Utah to his range near Flagstaff. He believed that the high volume of business should entitle him to lower ferry rates than the standard two and one-half cents per head. Carrying a letter of introduction from B. F. Saunders, he had discussed the matter with church Presiding Bishop William B. Preston in June 1905, but the meeting was inconclusive. He detailed the situation again in a letter several months later, accompanied by one from Saunders sustaining his views. In short, Walton contended that Emett would do well if he reduced the fee to one cent per head. A normal load was forty to fifty sheep, which meant that the operator would receive only forty to fifty cents per round trip—a ridiculous wage even in 1905.

Church President Joseph F. Smith wrote to E. D. Woolley on January 10, 1906, enclosing the Walton and Saunders letters. He added a postscript to say that church authorities had not heard from Brother Emett for a long time and had no idea of the state of their property at Lee's Ferry. Things certainly had changed since the days of Warren Johnson, but then so had the contract. The stake president and Emett responded immediately upon receipt of the letter. Woolley and his second counselor, J. H. Johnson, defended Emett's work and his charges, saying that he deserved a pension instead of complaints for maintaining a vital link in such a remote and uncivilized location. Emett wrote a detailed explanation of his improvements during the past decade and the present state of his business. He noted that his price for crossing sheep was cheaper than Brother Johnson's charge of three cents per head, and he closed with his opinion that the complaints against him were politically motivated by the Indian agent who charged the sheepmen for crossing the reservation. He said that he had circulated petitions in Coconino County and in Kane, Garfield, and Iron Counties in Utah for the Indian Service to grant a right-of-way two miles wide across the reservation where livestock could travel tax-free. He gave no indication of reducing his ferriage.[53]

Domestic troubles in a Kanab family led to a Lee's Ferry tragedy in mid-February 1906. After two children had been born to them, Emily Nash Crosby and Taylor "Bud" Crosby separated. The English-born wife went to California as the court awarded custody of the children to their father with the stipulation that they not be taken from the estate. Crosby had been making two trips a week carrying the mail to Lee's Ferry, and in the fall of 1905, he disobeyed the court order when he took Eula and Glen to stay with the Emetts. Realizing that he was answerable to the sheriff, he remained in Fredonia. His children lived with Sarah and John Emett in their cabin by the creek. Eula, the older of the two, attended school, but Glen, being only four, spent the time in the cabin.

There are three versions of the tragedy of February 13, 1906, all by people who were there at the time. According to Solena (Lena) Emett Bennett, John came in from hunting quail and laid his shotgun on the bed. His three and one-half year old son, Ray, knocked the gun over; it discharged, hitting the Crosby boy in the head. Lena said it happened during the noon hour when Miss Wingert was teaching. This version is not completely accurate because Glen Crosby's death and funeral dates are recorded at the Kanab Cemetery office. It is known that John David Leigh taught at Lee's Ferry from October 9, 1905, to March 23, 1906, and Wingert did not teach there until 1908. Lena, seventy-five years old at the interview, was trying to remember something that happened sixty years before. Ed Wooley recalled the "official Emett version" of the event: John stood a loaded .30–30 in the corner of the cabin, Ray began playing with it, and he shot Glen in the head. But Ed Wooley said the truth was that a man—who shall not be named here—was drunk, annoyed at Glen's crying, picked up the gun and shot him in the head, saying "I'll shut the little … up."[54] Whatever happened, a rider carried news of the shooting to Kanab, and Bud's twin brothers, William and Jake Crosby, picked up the little boy's body and brought it back to Kanab packed in snow from Buckskin Mountain.

The Emett trials were called in Flagstaff between April 9 and 14, 1906. B. F. Saunders and the Pierce family were on hand. Jim had been indicted on two counts by the Grand Jury. Bill was indicted on one count and was found not guilty on the thirteenth, while his father's two cases were continued over to the fall term in September.[55] The presiding judge was Richard E. Sloan, who was destined to become Arizona's last territorial governor three years later. At this time, he was a territorial supreme court judge, appointed by President McKinley in 1897, and reappointed by President Roosevelt in 1902 and 1906. Besides his interest in legal matters, Sloan was an adroit politician. The family arrived home just in time to celebrate the birth of a daughter, Jennieve [sic] to Sarah and John Emett on April 17. With mother and child doing well, and Bill cleared of his larceny charge, it seemed that things were breaking favorably.

Jim Emett countered the Bar Z staking of Emett Spring on May 10 when he and Coconino County Recorder Harry Hibben located the Hibben Lode. This mining claim took in a small spring about a mile northwest of Jacob's Pools. Emett's control of this higher-elevation spring posed a threat to the Bar Z lower-elevation outlet and served his purpose even better than Emett Spring, except that Bar Z riders now knew when their enemy was there. As a consequence, Dimmick continually kept at least one cowpuncher at the lower pools.[56]

The runoff in the Colorado was even higher in 1906 than it had been the previous year. The June flood was the greatest known to the old residents in the vicinity of Needles; the river was six miles wide and ferryboats threaded their way through the treetops when coming in for a landing. The peak at Yuma was 116,000 cubic feet per second on June 20.[57] Sometime during the high water period, another tragedy occurred at Lee's Ferry. The resident Navajo brothers frequently crossed the river to get the mailbag from Tuba City, and the Navajo carrier often spent the night with them. Jim Emett had instructed them to use the rowboat, never the ferry. On this occasion the water was too high to swim the horse, and the brothers could not resist the impulse to show off before their tribesman. They disobeyed Hosteen Emett and launched the ferry at about 4 P.M. It seemed so simple when the *bilagana* operated the boat, but the brothers did not realize that even experienced men were very careful when the river was high. They nosed the boat into the stream and the strong current hit the beam before they let the aft block out. The boat bounced about three times, then was inundated. The anchor on the reservation side pulled out and everything was swept downstream. The younger brother drowned and the older one barely made it to shore. All was lost—boat, hardware, and cable.[58] The surviving Navajo was so guilt-ridden over being a party to his brother's death that he left Emett's employ and returned to the reservation.

Once again Emett built a new ferryboat and replaced the cable with his own funds. This was the third boat lost during his tenure, and the first fatality, but the fault was not his and he felt more exasperated than culpable. He had no trouble obtaining Navajo employees because it was common knowledge that Hosteen Emett consistently provided good food and was sympathetic to Indians. The replacement for the brothers was a small, wiry Navajo they named "Little Johnny." He was good with livestock, rode well, and spoke and understood English. He had no desire to farm the plot of the departed brothers but willingly helped the Emetts in their agricultural activities. He built a hogan near the blacksmith shop where he slept and he ate with the family. He learned to use the rowboat and frequently crossed to pick up the mail sack and bring the carrier back with him to spend the night.

It was July, and J. D. Newman attempted what most sheepmen would not have dared—he started south from the Utah highlands in midsummer with eight hundred head. It was hot and dry, and Bar Z had the water at House Rock and the Pools restricted to use by their own stock. The band had been dry for three days when it rounded Five Mile Point, and the herders knew what the animals did not—that they soon would be able to drink their fill at the Colorado River. Most of the sheep never made it. They caught the scent of the water and broke into a bleating mass, stampeding toward that which they craved. The herders and dogs were powerless to head them off or redirect the charge. In about a mile, the lead animals reached the rim at Cathedral Wash. Stopping was impossible, and the ones behind crowded the leaders over the three hundred foot cliff. In a matter of minutes, most of the band were dead.[59] Newman and his Mexican herders accepted the loss as total, went to Emett's to relate the tragedy, crossed the river, and moved on to Flagstaff.

Jim Emett couldn't sleep that night. He rode out the next morning to the scene of the debacle and found many of the animals still alive. He dashed back to the ranch and organized a salvage operation composed of himself, his two sons, and two hired men—at that time the entire work force. They rescued approximately one-quarter of the band and revived them at the ranch. Jim sent a letter to Harry Hibben describing the salvage. Hibben contacted Newman who sent herders to get the animals. The Emetts say that Jim received nothing for his efforts, not even an expression of thanks.

Dimmick and Emett were adversaries in more ways than on the range. When notice was posted of the primary election to be held in the Fredonia precinct, Charles Dimmick was listed as inspector for the Democrats, J. S. Emett as judge for the Republicans.[60] Once again Saunders and his witnesses made the long journey to Flagstaff to attend the fall court sessions, and once again the effort was in vain; the Emett cases were postponed to the spring sitting.[61] The cattleman was beginning to wonder if he could get justice in Arizona. The local newspapers adopted a populist tone, emphasizing that Saunders was a rich, out-of-state owner picking on a local citizen.

David Leigh completed the spring teaching term on March 23, 1906, and promised to return in the fall. He did, but not to teach school; instead, he married his former student Julia Emett on November 6, two weeks before her twentieth birthday. The couple departed to live in Utah and Lee's Ferry District 11 again was left without a teacher. Emett blamed himself for the school situation, but so many things had been going on that he was as much a victim as anyone. He prepared for his court appearance in April and September, built a new ferryboat and installed a new cable, rescued two hundred sheep from Marble Canyon, and fulfilled his duty with the Grand Canyon Transportation Company, which claimed all of his time.

He was the only one of the group with expertise in this work and he spent considerable time there. The trail down Bright Angel Creek had been completed in the spring; it now was possible to get pack animals safely to the river. A boat had been packed in and the cable was hung, but the tram still was under construction in Salt Lake City.

Emett was an excellent blacksmith, having learned the craft from his father. John Nielson's giant bellows and forge had been left in the shop when the Johnsons moved, and Jim found the outfit handy. He forged many of his own tools, did work for travelers, and made everything except the sheaves for his own ferry. In anticipation of a tourist boom when the tram was completed, he considered purchasing the church's interest in the ferry property. When they closed the tram operation down for the winter, he had Dee Woolley write President Smith asking if the property could be bought, and if so at what price.[62] The inquiry appears to have made the brethren suspicious, and their reply five days later declined to name a price until they had more information. They reminded Woolley that Brother Emett had neglected to keep them informed of business done at the ferry. If he had kept such an account, they asked for a copy. They also asked for Woolley's own estimate of the property's value and what Emett would be willing to give for it.[63] It should be pointed out that Woolley failed to mention anything about the anticipated tourist boom.

Emett had been too busy to take his usual load of turkeys to Flagstaff for Thanksgiving, but he made up for it at Christmas. He and Emma Jane hit town on December 24 and sold his entire load at two dollars per bird. He had more on his mind to discuss there than his forthcoming trial in the spring—namely, his now desperate school situation. Superintendent Amundsen had been replaced by J. E. Jones, father of Willie who had taught at Lee's Ferry in the spring of 1904. Jones apologized for his predecessor's not having procured a teacher for District 11 but said there were none to be had. Under the circumstances, it was easy to persuade him to take care of the Arizona certification if Emett could obtain a Utah teacher.

Jim Emett spent most of January 1907 making the rounds of the little Mormon towns in southern Utah. Ultimately he found a teacher in the person of his niece, Maud Bigler, who thought she could fill the bill for sixty-five dollars a month. Being a relative, she would board free. She opened school late, on February 18, but ran it until July 24 to make up for the lost time.[64] Emett's father, Moses Simpson Emett, died on April 5 at Fredonia, but Jim was unable to attend the funeral because he was in Flagstaff where his trial had finally begun.

The proceedings at the trial were rather unusual. The plaintiffs were Saunders and Charlie Dimmick; the three members of the Pierce family who signed the original complaints had gone elsewhere and there was not much of a case without their testimony. The defense attorneys were Edward M. Doe and Reese M. Ling of Prescott, the latter a hunting companion of Judge

Sloan. Counsel for Saunders was Henry F. Ashurst, T. A. Flynn, and Judge A. C. Baker of Phoenix. The defense produced a number of witnesses who testified that Emett was in Fredonia on or about the time the offense allegedly was committed and that he remained there until after the election in November 1904. These witnesses included Asa Judd, E. D. Woolley, David Ryder [sic], Elizabeth Hamblin, Emma Jane Emett, John Lay, George Bybe, Ashton Nebeker, and R. R. Church. The most influential testimony was given in the form of a deposition by William J. Watson, who had been a Flagstaff resident for fifteen years and a member of the city council. He had owned a plumbing business there but sold it and moved to Los Angeles in the summer of 1906. His deposition said that he was a guest of the Emetts on the date of the alleged crime and stated that the slaughtered cow bore Emett's brand. He also said that he accompanied Emett to Fredonia and remained there with him until after the election. No deposition from the Pierces was available. After two days, the case went to the jury, which deliberated for two hours and returned a verdict of not guilty.[65] The remaining cases against the Emetts were dismissed as the evidence was similar in all of them. It was estimated that the proceedings cost Saunders about ten thousand dollars and cost Coconino County several thousand more. Under the circumstances, both should have saved their money.

Charles Jesse "Buffalo" Jones had reversed his activity of trying to make the American bison extinct to that of preserving the species. In searching for the ultimate buffalo ranch, he went to Kanab in July 1905 and met with Woolley and Emett, who agreed to show him the Buckskin range. The plateau appeared perfect and on January 2, 1906, Jones received a federal permit to establish a Kaibab range for "buffalo and other big game animals."[66] On November 28, 1906, President Roosevelt proclaimed a Grand Canyon Game Preserve in the Grand Canyon Forest Reserve. Significantly, the bill protected the game animals but not the predators that controlled their numbers.

The day after Emett's trial opened, Buffalo Jones and a thirty-five-year old New York dentist who aspired to be a writer got off the train at Flagstaff. The greenhorn's name was Pearl Zane Grey, but he had dropped the first given name. They obtained hotel rooms and went immediately to attend the trial. Jones undoubtedly had been kept abreast of events by Woolley because it was not by chance that the timing worked out as it did. When the Emett wagons pulled out later in the week, Jones and Grey accompanied them. To say that Zane Grey was smitten by both Jim Emett and Buffalo Jones is putting it mildly, but then life itself in this wild country bowled him over. He saw danger, excitement, and romance in everything. He was intrigued by tales of outlaws and was impressed by Emett's skill with firearms, the rope, and stock-handling. He saw all things as either good or bad, black or white, and there was no room in his mind for the middle area. Before they reached the Colorado River, Grey was convinced that both Emett and Jones were residual knights of the frontier west and that he was entering an area that civilization had not penetrated. As a prudent easterner, he slept with a loaded pearl-handled revolver under his pillow.[67]

If Grey was impressed with the vastness of the Painted Desert, Emett's charge at the Tanner Crossing on the Little Colorado River, and the imposing Echo Cliffs, he was nearly smitten dumb by the big Colorado River and Emett's ferryboat. He perceived a sinister aspect of the stream that few people felt. He was afraid of the river when he first saw it and he never lost that fear. He didn't trust the ferryboat or man's ability to prevail over this muddy torrent in the desert.

As it had been pre-planned for Jones and Grey to arrive in Flagstaff at the time of Emett's trial so they would have transportation to the ferry, it also had been planned for Emett to furnish riding and pack horses, a wrangler, and himself to act as guide for a three-week lion hunt on the Kaibab. Emett would receive five dollars per day, with Jones and Grey furnishing food for the men and grain for the animals.[68] After a suitable rest and near the end of the third week in April, stock was assembled and Emett, Jones, Grey, and Little Johnny set out for Buckskin Mountain. They picked up Jim Owens at his cabin, and during the ensuing days they killed several cougars. They took Jones and Grey to the Shinumo Crossing where Bill Bass met them in a rowboat and packed them to his camp on the South Rim.[69] The three then took the stock back. At this time, Jim Emett had been to the Colorado River at both the Bright Angel and Bass crossings, which was more than any other single Mormon had done in the interior of Grand Canyon to date.

Before parting at the river, Grey arranged to return to Lee's Ferry later in the summer. He had eastern commitments he must fulfill, but his first trip west had overwhelmed him. He was tremendously impressed with Jim Emett and the ferry and was inspired to write there. Emett met him at the appointed time in Flagstaff and brought him home. He was given a downstairs room where he could close the door and not be disturbed, although sometimes Clara or the boys rowed him across the river where he would remain all day, writing in longhand. Fearful of both the ferry and river, he never expressed a desire to row himself across.

Grey called Emma Jane "Mother" and got along well with everyone except Bill Emett. An instant antipathy had sprung up between them at their first meeting and it never mellowed. When Grey wrote his book *Heritage of the Desert*, he based one of the main characters, August Nabb, on Jim Emett, and Nabb's son "Snap" on Bill, making the latter something of a villain. Jim told stories of his experiences and general lore of the country which Grey absorbed like a sponge. He included the story of Newman's sheep stampede in his novel. He learned the local place names and Emett's attitude toward the Bar Z. He derived his outlaw chief, Holderness, from Charlie Dimmick, although the physical description of the outlaw chief was considerably different from the model. He wrote of Fredonia as "White Sage," borrowing this name from the flat at the western base of Buckskin Mountain. His first few western books were the very synthesis of an author being overwhelmed by an environment and its people. Grey spent several weeks with the Emetts and completed the rough draft of his book, then Jim took him to Flagstaff where he caught the train for California. From there he thanked the family for their hospitality and sent Bessie a copy of *Black Beauty.*[70]

The desire of the First Presidency to obtain a copy of Emett's ferry business ledger did not produce results for the simple reason that Jim did not keep records. Early in the summer of 1907 they again requested a report through Stake President Woolley, who discussed the matter with the ferry proprietor when he came to town. The two men composed the answer and one of Woolley's daughters typed it. This letter differed from the one of eighteen months before; Emett now had built three new ferryboats, and he proposed selling the ferry interests to B. F. Saunders for ten thousand dollars. Of course, he said his offer was subject to church approval, but he placed the value of his interest at five thousand dollars.[71] Travel, he reported, had fallen off so extensively that he had been forced to resort to trading with the Indians, raising cattle, and importing sheep from Utah to Arizona; in fact, had it not been for the ferriage for crossing sheep, it would not have been possible for him to remain there. He noted that it was unfair to keep his children isolated any longer, and he expressed his desire to sell out or be released from the mission.

The truth was that Emett, now nearing fifty-seven, was becoming tired of the constant struggle with the harsh environment. Of his daughters, Janey's marriage had failed, and the ferry was no place to meet another prospective husband. Clara, now twenty-five, had wasted her youth doing a man's work at the ranch and had experienced little of the social life so important to a young woman. Julia had married a man considerably older than herself, but Rose, Susie, Lena, and Bessie, as well as Janey's Eva and Cora, were entering their precious teen years and facing the same bleak prospect that had confronted Clara. Yes, it was time to return to civilization; he had no intention of repeating Warren Johnson's sacrifice of family for his mission.

Runoff in the Colorado River was high in 1907. There were fourteen days in June—the seventeenth through the thirtieth when the flow exceeded 100,000 cubic feet per second, with the river peaking at 115,000 cubic feet per second during the last four days of the month. The high water continued through July, every day up to the twentieth passing the century mark.[72] The Emetts began to wonder if the river flow ever would subside.

Jim Emett's reply to the First Presidency had been weighed carefully. On July 25, they advised Woolley to pursue the matter with Saunders at his convenience and to stop at church headquarters to discuss the matter with them the next time he was in the city.[73] Thus, they expressed interest but not an eagerness. Saunders spent more time in Salt Lake City than elsewhere, but he was not contacted by the Presiding Bishopric. The Bar Z owner returned to Flagstaff on August 30 and appeared before the Board of Equalization to protest his taxes. Evidently Emett kept track of the head count on the range better than had the former appointees who ventured into the remote region from Flagstaff.[74]

Charles S. Russell made an indirect pitch for publicity in a letter to the *Arizona Daily Journal Miner* of Prescott (reprinted in the *Coconino Sun* on May 9, 1907). The story related how Russell and Bert Loper planned to travel in two steel boats from Green River, Utah, to Needles, California. The distance was stated to be three hundred twenty miles—which might have been a tipoff to somebody's knowledge of the project, the true distance being just under eight hundred miles. The purpose of the trip was said to be placer and lode prospecting, but the real objective was to make a pictorial record that the two men hoped to sell. Loper and Russell, accompanied by Edwin R. Monett, left Green River on September 20.[75] Their photographic equipment consisted of a box camera that got wet in Cataract Canyon when Loper's boat became hung up on a rock. At Hite, they sent the camera out to be repaired. Loper waited at Hite for the camera while Russell and Monett prospected leisurely through Glen Canyon. All three agreed to meet at Lee's Ferry on December 1.

Although the camera was received at Hite on November 20, Loper was in no hurry to rejoin his companions and push into Grand Canyon. Russell and Monett waited two weeks beyond the appointed time, but when Loper failed to appear by December 13, they resumed the trip by themselves. They reached Needles on New Year's Day having achieved none of their objectives. Loper finally arrived at Lee's Ferry at 3:00 P.M. on January 8, 1908, to find—as he may have anticipated—that his partners had gone on without him.[76] He availed himself of Emett hospitality for almost two weeks, including a trip to Kanab, but on the twentieth Emett offered him a job by asking him to bid on digging sixteen hundred feet of new ditch. Loper went through the motion of looking it over but concluded that the task would require too much time and he had better go back up the river. He rationalized that he would complete the trip through Grand Canyon that fall. Chauvinistically, he remarked that Emett tried to talk him into staying at the ferry because he probably had a girl he wanted him to marry. As it turned out, Loper wore the stigma of fearing the Grand Canyon rapids for more then three decades, and it was not until 1939 that he finally proved himself by running every rapid on his first traverse.

The flow of Utah sheep into Arizona decreased in the fall of 1907 due to the scarcity of the animals. W. C. Bayless spent several weeks and covered many miles before he could accumulate the size of band he wanted for his range near Prescott. He ultimately collected several thousand head and crossed at Lee's Ferry late in September. L. C. McCulloch either did not work as hard or was not as lucky a month later because he barely collected enough to make his trip worthwhile.[77]

Jim and Emma Jane Emett took the usual load of turkeys to Flagstaff, arriving on November 27, the day before Thanksgiving. He could have sold three times as many turkeys as he had, such was the demand. The *Coconino Sun* described the turkey shoot set up by Elmer and Charles Jones at which Jim's birds were the guests of honor: "Three turkeys were set up in a line at a distance of about 230 yards and about 50 yards apart. Some good shooting was done. It was so arranged that the marksman had to hit the turkey above the legs in order to secure the same. Among the marksmen were Robert Arnold, who killed ten turkeys on Thursday, and J. W. Francis who, during the two days, killed 13 turkeys. The affair was enjoyed by all who witnessed it except the turkeys who were very gamey."[78]

Emett was not the only one having second thoughts about life on the Arizona Strip. Another was B. F. Saunders, who had become disillusioned regarding his operation there after the end of the Emett trials; he is said to have declared that he would not do business in a country that condoned such thievery. As soon as he returned to Salt Lake City, he came to an understanding with Ora Haley and began looking for a buyer. It did not take long to find one in the person of a fellow cattleman who also ran Herefords, Edwin J. Marshall.

The E. J. Marshall Corporation was based in California, its main headquarters a forty-two thousand–acre spread in Santa Barbara County called "Rancho de Jesús y Maria." Marshall owned two large ranches in Texas, and his Palomas Ranch in Chihuahua consisting of two million acres extended along the United States border for two hundred miles. Smaller ranches were operated in the Salt River Valley of Arizona and the Imperial and Chino Valleys in California. He ran Durhams at Palomas, but otherwise his spread was known as a "whiteface outfit." His general manager was an astute Texan named Henry S. Stephenson. Marshall set up the Grand Canyon Cattle Company, incorporated under the laws of California, for the express purpose of buying out Saunders. He bought all improvements on the land as of June 30, 1907, the range from Cane Beds to Soap Creek, all water rights held through mining claims, and the VT and Bar Z brands. Several months were required to work out the details, but the papers were signed on December 3, 1907.[79] Charlie Dimmick remained as foreman and the same hands continued working, but the shrewd Stephenson involved himself more as time went on.

The fall arrived with no school teacher at the ferry. Maud Bigler had ended her term on the Mormon holiday of July 24. Teaching became a weary grind as summers at the ferry usually were oppressive and the little cabin was poorly ventilated. If county officials were trying to send Emett a message, he didn't turn out to be a good receiver. He continued to haunt the superintendent's office until, in self defense, Jones made a greater effort. At last, and apparently with the help of Jim Emett, Miss Laura Amanda Wingate of Pennsylvania opened school in January 1908. Some difficulty in Flagstaff prevented her being put on the payroll and Emett paid her first two months' salary, although he later was reimbursed.[80] She taught school through June 19 and at its close noted that three of her students—

Rose, Susie, and Lena Emett—had completed the eighth grade. This simple achievement was the most noteworthy academic feat in the ten-year history of District 11.

Zane Grey repeated his Kaibab trip in 1908.[81] Met by Buffalo Jones in Flagstaff on March 20, the two spent a night with the Emetts and pressed on to Jim Owens' cabin on the mountain. They did the identical things they had done the previous year but it was not the same; Emett could not be with them. They went to the same places, concentrating on Owens' favorite lion country—the Powell Plateau. He now was paid twenty dollars in bounties for each dead cougar. Again, Grey was taken to the river via the Shinumo Trail where Bass met him and escorted him to his camp.[82]

Little progress had been made on the tram project in 1907 because of Emett's trial, the ensuing pack trip with Grey, the need for the principals to attend to individual business, and the late delivery of the disassembled tram cage. However, the main difficulty was a lack of ready cash to hire labor. Emett had money but no impulse to bankroll the project beyond the financial input from his partners. Hoyt was unable to advance the hundred dollars and even took the examination for a job in the Forest Service to better support his family. The enterprise was on dead center and had ceased to move. The problem was solved on May 3, 1908, when Woolley's son-in-law David D. Rust accepted a contract to manage the company, agreeing for seventy-five dollars per month to repair the trail washout, complete the tram, and construct a trail south to the river.[83] The financial picture brightened when Jesse Knight of Provo invested five thousand dollars for a like number of shares. Up to now, Emett had been the dominant force in the project and it had taken more of his time than he should have given; he was free to concentrate on his personal business.

The Emetts figured that the transition in Bar Z ownership was a good time to claim some marginal water sources, so in late July Bill Emett filed on Soap Creek and Cottonwood Spring on the bench west of the tributary. These sources were on the eastern edge of the Bar Z range. The filing was reported by both the *Coconino Sun* and *Flagstaff Gem*, but there was no immediate reaction from the company.[84]

One day Ring came up missing and could not be found. George rode after a southbound wagon in case he had followed it, but the occupants had not seen him. Little Johnny was spending a few days with his family on the reservation and they knew that Ring had not accompanied him. Finally, one of the girls found the dog, dead in Little Johnny's hogan. They concluded that he had eaten poisoned bait set out for coyotes. That night tears were shed, John buried the dog beside the hogan, and the girls put flowers on the grave. Ring received more of a funeral than had John Kitchen.

A boy was born to Sarah and John Emett on September 17, 1908. He was named John Henry. The mother came through the ordeal with little trouble and Emma Jane served as midwife. Sarah no longer even thought of returning to Escalante for that service, but her brother Ed came down to help out until she fully recovered. Miss Tillie Mary Penny became the next school teacher for District 11, opening the fall term November 2 for a class of two boys and seven girls. Her salary was seventy dollars per month, as Laura Wingert's had been.[85]

Near the end of the month, a black family from Alabama crossed the river at Lee's Ferry. They were not the first African Americans to pass here, but they were the first seen by the Emett children. William Reed, his wife, and four children were seeking work in Arizona. They obviously didn't have much and Jim forgave them the ferriage. Their horse died near Tanner Tank, probably from drinking bad water, and that left the family stranded without food. An Indian brought news of their adversity to Tuba City and a rescue party brought them in. Mrs. Reed, far advanced in pregnancy, gave birth to her fifth child en route to Flagstaff, where they arrived on October 16.[86]

The ferryboat sank that fall, a victim of hard treatment. It was less than three years old, but the untreated wood was rotten and the craft leaked badly. For once, the cable was as good as ever. Emett took a list of lumber needs to Brown's sawmill at Jacob lake and arranged for his men to freight the material to the foot of the mountain. It was picked up by Jim and Ed Wooley, and shortly thereafter was transformed into a ferryboat.[87]

Later that month, John Emett arrived home with some horses that he had obtained from farther north. The animals decided to return to their home range and had made a good start before John realized they were gone. He grabbed a little food, saddled a horse, and set out after them, expecting to return next day at the latest. He was gone several days, however. The weather was cold, and having taken no bedroll, he spent the nights rolled up in his saddle blanket. When he returned to the ferry, he had a very bad cold as a result of the exposure.

Torrential rains hit the region in January 1909. The storm took out the Kanab dam, leaving the community without culinary water.[88] Some of the more enterprising citizens hooked teams to sleds and hauled water from Cave Lakes, selling it for twenty-five cents per barrel. Dee Woolley, having great faith in Jim Emett's ability to solve problems, sent him a message saying his help in the crisis would be appreciated. Bill was away but Jim and George left at once for the stricken town, leaving the ailing John and Little Johnny at the ranch.[89]

The weather became bitter cold, and John's condition did not improve. By the third week of January he had developed pneumonia, and in two days, on January 27, he was dead. For the first time since the family had lived at the ferry, there was no man on the place except Little Johnny. Clara offered to ride to Cane Ranch for help but her mother said, "No, because then I would have you to worry about." They sat tight and hoped that husband and son would return early. The temperatures had hovered close to zero for more than a month, and the ground was frozen. For the women, digging a grave was almost impossible, so they hauled ice from the river and packed it around the body, hoping the men would come. Adhering to the custom of the times, Emma Jane kept a kerosene lamp burning day and night in the south downstairs window, but Little Johnny would not enter the house while it was lit; he remained on the red shale slope west of the house. After the third day, Emma Jane said they could wait no longer. Janey and Clara built a coffin and dug a grave in the floor of the cellar—the only ground that was not frozen. John Taylor Emett was buried there without benefit of a service because no one holding the priesthood was present.

After an absence of ten days, Emett and his son returned. Jim was filled with remorse for not having been present when he was needed. He was aware of John's weaknesses, but he had loved his son and had tried to help him. His grief was so intense that he finally unburdened himself in a letter to the editor of the *Coconino Sun*, who printed it and a eulogy to life at Lee's Ferry in the issue of Friday, March 5, 1909:

Jim's letter follows:

Lee's Ferry, February 13, 1909

Friend John: I am writing to convey to you the sad news of the death of my son, John. He contracted a severe cold last fall which developed into quick consumption. His death occurred January 27. The most grievous part of it was that I was away at Kanab, and only the women folks were at home when he died. They made a coffin and buried him. John, it was one of the trials of my life to meet my heartbroken family on my return.

Hoping all is well with you and yours, I remain

Your friend
James S Emett

It was meaty stuff, material that Zane Grey could have used to advantage, and it impressed the readers.

Both Clara and Lena claimed that Jim and George re-interred John in the cemetery after the ground had thawed. Ed Wooley disagreed, saying the body was left in the cellar while the tombstone was placed at the head of an empty grave in the cemetery. In any event, the stone was inscribed in error: the year was 1910 instead of 1909.[90]

Miss Penny closed the school term on March 19, having had a constant class of two boys and seven girls. All of the children were Emetts except Janey Chamberlain's Eva and Cora. Jim had only one, Bessie; Sarah, the new widow, and Bill Emett each had three. The count was even less a month later as Ed Wooley went to the ferry and took his sister Sarah and her four children to live in Escalante.[91] Her future at the ferry was bleak but at age twenty-seven, even with four children, she had a chance to remarry elsewhere.

The winter of 1908–1909 was wet in the Colorado watershed. The runoff began later than usual but was prolonged well past the average crest. The river peaked at Yuma on June 24 at 149,500 cubic feet per second and had a sustained flow of more than 100,000 cubic feet per second from June 17 through July 10. During the period of big water, the ferryboat broke free from its mooring and was carried downstream. Fortunately, it hugged the right bank and was discovered circling in the large eddy at the lower ferry site, where Jim roped it and secured it to shore. When the river went down, he and George hitched a team to the craft and skidded it back to the crossing where it was put into use as if the interruption had not occurred.[92]

Henry Stephenson soon saw what Brigham Young had realized fifty years before—control of the crossing was vital to his operation. At the same time, Emett realized what B. F. Saunders could verify—that his presence had a certain nuisance value to the Bar Z. It was arranged to open negotiations for the sale of the ranch and ferry to the cattle company, and Jim Emett was called to Salt Lake City in mid-August.

While he was away much of the southwest was hit by record rainfall. The Zuni River basin suffered a series of storms from July 21 to September 6 that resulted in the heaviest floods on record. The Zuni dam was washed out on September 6; the Kanab dam went out at midnight on August 31; the Santa Clara gage three miles southwest of St. George showed a record runoff.[93] At the same time, the gages at Virgin, Escalante, and Ferron were washed out. Glen Canyon was especially hard hit, and thick red water poured down the drainage. It was estimated that 150,000 acre feet flowed out of the San Juan basin on September 5 and 6. The Colorado rose so fast that the Emetts knew the ferry was in danger. Emma Jane, Janey, Clara, and Little Johnny went to the crossing to keep the drift cleared from the ferryboat.

While they were watching the ferryboat, a tremendous flood swept down the Pahreah and cut them off from the ranch. They were isolated for forty-eight hours without food except for one watermelon. The four took turns keeping the boat cleared and taking refuge in the old fort. The flood reached almost to the ranch house and the cemetery, as the children remaining there talked of putting the family valuables in blankets and toting them up the shale slope. When the water receded, the fields were covered with a thick layer of mud, and a large silt bar had been deposited at the mouth of the creek.[94]

Agreement between officials of the Church of Jesus Christ of Latter-day Saints and the Grand Canyon Cattle Company for sale of Lee's Ferry was concluded in Salt Lake City on August 18, 1909. Trustee Joseph F. Smith released all claims for the payment of $1,750. No mention of Emett's rights was made.[95] Emett notified his friends in Flagstaff that the sale of Lee's Ferry was imminent, and on September 6, 1909, School District 11 was discontinued.[96] Emett executed a similar deed for the same amount at Kanab on

September 11 before Notary Public John W. Glazier. He quit claimed all improvements along the Pahreah River, including water rights, dams, ditches, and land consisting of about two hundred unsurveyed acres. He kept his livestock, wagons, harness, household furniture, and personal effects.[97] Emett then made his nuisance value known when he squeezed an extra thousand dollars out of the cattle company to release his water rights and improvements at Soap Creek, including his rock house, the Hibben Lode and Millsite claims, and Cottonwood Spring.[98] This quit claim deed was signed in Kanab before Notary Public Glazier. E. D. Woolley participated in all discussions and signed as witness to two of the three deeds.

The Grand Canyon Cattle Company now controlled the range from Cane Beds to Lee's Ferry. Emett received $2,750, and the church got $1,750.[99] Although nothing was written into the deed about his vacating the premises, Emett lost no time in doing so. He had arranged to settle on some property at Annabella, near the home of Joseph Staker, and he wanted his remaining school-age children to begin the fall term there. The family pulled out early in October with everything loaded in five wagons. Janey and Clara were two of the teamsters, and Brother Button and his two sons drove the twenty-five head of cattle.[100]

For the first time since its beginning, the ferry was not controlled by Mormons but by outsiders. The facility had served its purpose when the need existed. The crossing no longer represented, or was in fact, the sole conduit between Mother Utah and the Arizona settlements. The railroad and telegraph, although circuitous, were quicker and more efficient than using the difficult wagon track over the bottleneck. They diminished the importance of the crossing just as the ferry had made the Ute Ford obsolete.

9

Charles H. Spencer

Although the Emett incubus no longer tormented the Bar Z, the cattle company was out of its element in operating the ferry and ranch at the mouth of Pahreah Canyon. Foreman Charlie Dimmick sent Dave Rider, a reliable straw boss, to Lee's Ferry before the Emetts departed. This smoothed the transition for both sides. Rider, a member of a pioneer Kanab family, knew Emett well and had testified for him at his trial, yet Rider was a trusted Bar Z hand. Rider ran the detested operation for a few days, then turned it over to his younger brother Rowland, who wasn't even on the Bar Z payroll, then returned to his range in southeastern House Rock Valley.

Rowland Rider was the lone occupant of Lee's Ferry when Nathaniel T. Galloway, Julius F. Stone, Raymond A. Cogswell, and Seymour S. Dubendorff arrived at the original ferry landing at 12:35 P.M. on October 27, 1909. Stone had sent Emett a check for fifty dollars and asked him to have sufficient provisions on hand to resupply his river party for ten days. Emett had confirmed receipt of the money and said he would have the food or leave it in a cache at the east end of the fort. No cache or message from him was found, however, and the party shoved off the following day on reduced rations that they hoped would last until they reached the trail at the Rust tram.[1] Before the Stone expedition left, four prospectors from Searchlight, Nevada, arrived en route to the Wright Bar; news of George Wright's work with a spoon had spread farther than he ever imagined. The prospectors and the cowboy watched the party shove off, and Rider even galloped his horse along the river to the lower ferry as they ran Pahreah Riffle.

At the end of the month, Dimmick sent Nate Petty and Johnny Evans to the ferry with some bulls to be ranged in Pahreah Canyon. The pair then took over the operation of ranch and ferry, allowing Rider's return to his brother's spread. The Bar Z men disliked working at Lee's Ferry, a fact well known to the foreman. Dave Rider passed along Jim Emett's recommendation that the Johnson boys be hired to take over the work. It sounded like the solution to a growing problem and Dimmick immediately wrote to Jeremiah Johnson, who was living in Wyoming.

The poverty-stricken Johnsons were little more than sharecroppers without crops. The twenty-one members of the family had normal needs but no income and few assets; other families were in the same situation. John J. Simmons, chaplain of the contingent from Morgan County, controlled the finances of the Mormon colony and operated the official store. He extended credit as he saw fit, charged whatever interest he pleased, and doubled as community banker. Common morality never appeared to hinder Simmons in his business dealings; Jerry and Frank Johnson worked under them all and, according to the latter, not only worked "for nothing" but concluded the relationship owing Simmons money.[2] Most of the Mormons were polygamists or believed in the principles of plural marriage. Exceptions such as Frank and Rhoda Johnson and Jerry's wife Annie were in the minority. In 1907 Jerry began thinking of taking a second wife, his eye having been caught by Pearly, Simmons' daughter. Annie didn't relish the idea at all; in fact, she opposed it violently. When it became apparent in the summer of 1907 that she had no voice in the matter, she went on a hunger strike and died a bitter death on October 4, allegedly of typhoid fever. She left four children, the youngest only two years old. Jerry and Pearly were married in Salt Lake City on October 8, 1908, and only Annie's untimely death prevented Jerry from committing bigamy.[3]

The Johnson boys managed to keep almost even financially but neither was getting ahead. When Jerry received Charlie Dimmick's letter in November 1910, it was as though Christmas has arrived early; there was no doubt he would accept. The Bar Z foreman wanted them there by February, but it was impossible for them both to make this date as Frank owed Simmons several hundred dollars and wanted to clear the debt before he left. Jerry was in the same position, but he had no such qualms and left in January 1910, taking Frank's wife Rhoda and her four children with him. It was thirty-five degrees below zero and snowing when they boarded the train at Gailand, Wyoming. Frank went to the coal mine at Gebo to earn some money.

Jerry Johnson dropped Rhoda and the children at her mother's home in Kanab, and by the first of February, he was on the Bar Z payroll being paid fifty dollars per month and his board for doing what he knew best. Johnny Evans and Nate Petty were tending the place when he arrived. Evans returned to Cane and Petty stayed for three weeks to help complete a new flume in the ranch irrigation system. By month's end, Jerry was living in his father's old house, piddling at minor tasks around the ranch, and taking care of what little ferrying there was. Altogether, he liked everything about his job except the absence of his wife. Life at Lee's Ferry certainly was better than what he had experienced in Wyoming.

In 1905, a man who would have a profound effect on Lee's Ferry for a number of years started a mining promotion near the San Juan River. Charles Harvey Spencer was more than an expert teamster; he was a member of the vanishing breed of bullwhackers, and his feats of getting oxen to do what other teamsters couldn't were told and retold for decades. Spencer became interested in gold mining while freighting supplies and equipment to the camps on the San Juan during the 1892 excitement. He was obsessed with the fact that gold was present, but it was too fine to be collected. At this point, his knowledge of mining was confined to what he had picked up by watching miners and itinerant prospectors in Utah and Colorado. Somehow, he came to the conclusion that gold originated in the massive red stratum called the Wingate Sandstone.

Although Spencer had little schooling, he was quick to learn and possessed the ability to present the positive side of a subject in such glowing terms that his listeners accepted his point of view. He picked up and used catchwords and terms in his conversations which convinced neophytes that this colorful westerner was a diamond in the rough. He wasn't objective in his logic or deduction but bent his talents toward persuading others to his position. He was hardy, would perform his share of strenuous labor, and never sought the easy way. His personal needs were small; he could subsist for long periods on beans, coffee, and chewing tobacco. He impressed many as being an unrecognized expert on the verge of striking it rich. Charlie and his elder brother George accumulated a modest grubstake, some animals, and in the fall of 1905 followed the trail of the bullwhackers from Mancos to Clayhill Crossing. They prospected, rough-staked several claims, and did assessment work for three years, then found some investors in the middle west. Their project grew in magnitude to the extent that in November 1908 he brought Denver mining engineer John H. Marks and his young associate Albert H. Jones to survey and stake the claims.

The oil boom at Mexican Hat resulted in a steel bridge being built over the San Juan, but even this improvement did not hide the fact that the Spencer mining activities were in a remote area and transportation would make any operation there very expensive. Nevertheless, the project survived on a start-and-stop basis until June 1909 when better assay tests revealed the gold content of the Wingate Sandstone had no commercial value. The operation was closed and Spencer went to Chicago to obtain more venture capital. Previous investors refused to provide additional funds and his promotion appeared to be at a dead end. Then he met Dr. Herbert A. Parkyn. The two men answered each other's needs and a symbiotic relationship developed that lasted several years.

Parkyn, a promoter in his own right, provided access to new venture capital. When the operation became reactivated in December 1909, a reputable Chicago engineer, W. H. Bradley, was placed in charge of the assays, but the results were identical to those of the previous assayer. Samples Bradley had taken of the Chinle Formation, which underlies the Wingate, tested higher. Moreover, the "San Juan silts," as the Chinle was called locally, were easy to mine hydraulically and would not have to be crushed and reduced to powder. The tests called for a second look at the project and the backers advanced additional capital.

The Spencer brothers, Marks, Jones, Arthur C. Waller, and three wranglers left Dolores, Colorado, in April 1910 to examine the deposits of silts and the prospects of sluicing them with water from the San Juan River. While they were engaged in this assessment, a party of four strangers—two white men with two Navajo guides—came into camp. The Anglos were John C. Tipton and John M. Clark. Tipton had been a government employee at Tuba City during the winter of 1892–93 when Wright made his Glen Canyon strike. After the excitement died down, he had packed up the Sand Trail and prospected the Glen Canyon benches, but failed to find a route to the Wright Bar from the right-bank drainage. Now, he and Clark were attempting to reach the Wright Bar to culminate an overland prospecting tour of the left-bank drainage. According to the mining records in Flagstaff, the Pure Gold claim had lapsed and had not been patented.

After supper, the Spencer men explained their own project of sluicing the blue silts and noted that the exposures were isolated and fuel for pumping water was an unsolved problem. Tipton immediately suggested that their project be moved to Lee's Ferry, where the silt formation was exposed on both sides of the Colorado, river water was available, and large deposits of coal were on the bench upstream. Transportation would be less of a problem than if they remained in their remote location because of the good road from Flagstaff. Before the men turned in, they decided to travel overland to Lee's Ferry.

The outfit had to be lightened. Four days were devoted to packing extra supplies, wagons, teams, and equipment to the Wetherill and Colville trading post at Oljeto, from where they finally departed on May 2. They headed back to Red Rock cabin on the San Juan to pick up two of the crew, then struck southwesterly to Copper and Nakai Canyons. An Indian trail took them over Piute Mesa, into and out of Piute Canyon, and along the southeastern flank of Navajo Mountain. Tipton's Navajo reached the end of the country he knew and on May 6 he obtained another guide (for six dollars per day) who was familiar with the area they were entering. The new pilot took them into Navajo Creek, which they descended to Kaibito Creek to strike the ancient trail that Jacob Hamblin had followed to Oraibi. But when it began to bear south, they continued nearly due west past Leche-E Rock to the Echo Cliffs.

They descended a large sand dune a couple of miles above Lee's Ferry, and on the night of May 9 they camped beside the Colorado River, noting with satisfaction that the blue silts were visible just above each bank. It was a remarkable odyssey, one that white men never had made before.[4] The final leg, called the "Sandslide Trail," provided access for Navajo flocks from summer to winter range. The next day they went down river where Tipton got the ferryman's attention by the time-proven method of firing his pistol. Jerry Johnson and his cowpuncher helper, A. F. Ballard, ferried them to the right bank. At the ranch, Jerry invited them to help themselves to the garden and ripening apricots. They pitched camp beside the ranch house.

Charles H. Spencer and Howard Mayrant with the Spencer wagon train, Oljeto Trading Post, 1910 (*A. H. Jones photograph, P. T. Reilly Collection, Cline Library, Northern Arizona University*).

In his diary, Jones noted that about fourteen acres of alfalfa yielded five cuttings and a total of a hundred fifty tons of hay in a season. Jerry proved to be a goldmine of information; he told them how to find the Sand Trail and about Stanton and his two boats that remained behind the fort. Spencer listened to all he had to say but apparently never wondered why Stanton went broke. In the morning, the Spencer brothers, Marks, Tipton, and Clark went up Pahreah Canyon and ascended the Sand Trail to locate the coal deposits and Wright Bar. Jones sent the Navajo guide to Tuba City for more supplies and purchased ten pounds of honey and some dried fruit from Johnson to augment the provisions that remained.

Henry S. Stephenson began to involve himself in peripheral details concerning the Grand Canyon Cattle Company. Although he directed the broad operation of all Marshall's ranches, he now concentrated on making Bar Z the efficient business he felt it could become. This meant improving the road to Flagstaff and getting rid of ferry responsibility. Accordingly, he spent considerable time in Flagstaff cultivating political powers. The first evidence of his maneuvering appeared in the *Coconino Sun* on March 11, 1910, when Coconino County Superintendent of Roads A. J. Diamond, responding to a petition for a county-operated ferry, said that Lee's Ferry provided the only access to the valuable Arizona Strip, that the road should be improved, and that a bridge should eventually be installed. Three days later, District Attorney X. N. Steeves wrote an open letter to the editors of the other papers, pointing out that if Arizona expected to retain political control of the valuable strip, Lee's Ferry would have to be maintained and a competent operator kept in charge.[5] It was a crafty exercise to forestall possible future criticism and to mold public opinion on an issue that probably already had been decided.

Stephenson initiated discussions of ferry operations with the county supervisors and, on April 4, with board-appointed member W. G. Dickinson. Early in May, Stephenson and Dimmick went to Flagstaff to conclude the deal; they returned on the afternoon of May 11. Dimmick was not happy to find the itinerant prospectors ensconced at the ranch. He had virtually told them to clear out when Stephenson, feeling expansive, overruled him and told them to make themselves at home.[6] The act did not set well with Dimmick, who regarded it as poor judgment. The general manager and his foreman departed early in the morning, leaving everything in the hands of Jerry Johnson, who was noted for being generous to a fault.

Late that afternoon the Spencer pack outfit returned to the ranch after locating what they thought was coal. They failed to find an overland route to Wright Bar, but they had seen enough to justify setting up operations at Lee's Ferry and abandoning the San Juan claims. There was one fly in the ointment; somewhere on the plateau Tipton had removed his vest containing his train ticket to Los Angeles and more than a hundred dollars, laid it on a rock, and had left it. He said he was sure he could find it but had to return to the bench. The rest of the party proceeded without him.

The next day, Charlie Spencer, Marks, Clark, and Art Waller left for Flagstaff, planning to stop first at Tuba City to arrange for supplies. The river was high and rising, and the ferry dipped water on both crossings. They met the Navajo guide returning from Tuba City, and Spencer sent a note by him to Jones giving him instructions to follow as soon as the grub was received. Jones recorded them in his journal, and it was clear that Spencer intended to get full value from the young engineer as well as revealing his own plans:

1. Find nearest coal to river, at best available point for a dredge.
2. Find good coal beds for extensive development.
3. Tie coal deposits to boundary line between Utah and Arizona.
4. Retrace line from 138 mile post to bluffs above river and build suitable mound of stone that may be distinguished from river below.
5. Tri [triangulate] in points and gulches to give a fairly accurate map of the country and tie survey to state line.
6. Make water locations in Utah and Arizona at boundary line and send notes to Marks.
7. Make sketch maps of country as far as possible, showing trails, water holes, etc.
8. Mark trails by monuments where ever the opportunity offers.
9. Clean out water holes with shovel and wall up.
10. Bring out samples of coal if possible.

11. Make accurate measurements for tram lines or find some method
of transporting coal to the river.[7]

A Navajo teamster delivered the supplies at noon on May 18. A pair of his
dogs had destroyed two sides of bacon, but the remaining food was acceptable. The river was higher every day and they dared not bring the team and
wagon over.

On May 19, Jones, Tipton and his Navajo guide, George Spencer,
Harry Wetsel, James Carter, and George Smith ascended the Sand Trail to
the Glen Canyon benchlands. Albert Jones not only was a capable engineer
and surveyor, he was adept at trail finding and traversing strange, rough
country. He and his crew were gone three weeks, during which they found
four of the monuments marking the line between Utah and Arizona. They
ran base lines and triangulated the prominent topography, sometimes giving the features names that are different from the ones in use today. They
crossed Wahweap, Warm, Cane, Last Chance, and Rock Creeks, then
ascended to the top of the Kaiparowits Plateau, followed a trail along its
northeast rim, and came down to the Escalante desert. They returned by
way of Escalante, Henrieville, Pahreah, and the Sand Trail to Lee's Ferry,
arriving on June 8. They had found a twenty inch seam of coal and staked a
great many placer claims. Jones noted the extensive outcroppings of blue
silts at Pahreah village. One thing they didn't find was an overland route to
the Wright Bar, but Tipton and the Navajo left them on May 23 to make an
additional search.

Ostensibly partners in the Wright Bar, the flip of a coin determined
that Tipton was to have the upper half and Spencer the lower. After leaving
Jones, Tipton next appeared in Flagstaff on June 10 when he recorded
eleven mining claims and stated they had been located on May 19, 20, 21,
and 25.[8] Jones was unaware that Tipton had located anything up to their
parting. The claims were all recorded in the names of Tipton and his seven
partners; no mention was made of Charlie Spencer. The Wright Bar claims
1 through 4, amounting to one hundred sixty acres, were said to have been
located on May 20—the day Tipton was searching for his vest. He located
them as being one and one-half miles southwest of Navajo Creek, on the
west bank of the Colorado, which indicates that he had not revealed everything to Spencer or Jones. By this time, both men realized that the
Colorado River was the key not only to the Wright Bar but to all placer
claims in Glen Canyon, and each apparently resolved to obtain a boat without revealing his plans to the other. A double double-cross was underway.

Evidently Tipton and Clark had devised a plan and the former
immediately took the train to Los Angeles to carry out his part. Spencer's
party arrived in Flagstaff on May 19, the same day Jones had left the ferry
for his overland survey. Spencer also had a plan and he kept the wires hot
to Chicago. He learned that a gasoline launch, slated for use on the San
Juan, was in Gallup along with W. H. Bradley and D. H. McDermid, who

had accompanied the boat west. Marks took the train to Denver and Spencer went with him as far as Gallup. After arranging for the boat to be shipped to Flagstaff, the three men returned, and on June 4 started for the ferry, leaving Waller to follow with the launch. Spencer left his companions at Tuba City and went on to Oljeto to get the teams headed for Lee's Ferry.

When Jones returned to the ferry on June 8, he found Henry Stephenson, Charlie Dimmick, and George W. Ballentine, vice-president and general manager of the Denver Union Stockyard, spending the night before going on to Flagstaff. Stephenson told Jones that Coconino County had taken over the ferry and intended to install a new cable and boat; in fact, A. J. Diamond had spent several days there taking note of needs. Stephenson was rather sure of himself as it was not until June 6 that the supervisors had instructed the county clerk to draw up the deed and issue a payment warrant to the Grand Canyon Cattle Company. They devised a single-sheet contract listing ferry prices, conditions for crossing, and releasing the county of any responsibility in the event of an accident. All those wanting to cross would be required to sign this form. One thousand copies were printed and delivered to the cattle company, which would continue to operate the ferry. Red tape had come to Lee's Ferry.

FERRY PASSENGER AGREEMENT

Lee's Ferry, ___ 191_

For and in consideration of the county of Coconino Territory of Arizona; permitting and allowing the undersigned to transport himself livestock and personal effects at this time across the Colorado River, by its ferry boat at said place, the undersigned agrees to assume, and does hereby assume all risk and liability both to himself and property, that may in any way arise by reason of such transportation, and hereby releases, and forever holds harmless, said county of Coconino, from all liability in any way arising or growing out of any loss of, or injury in any way arising by reason of such above mentioned transportation in said Ferry Boat or in any way connected therewith.

The fees charged for transportation over the Ferry are solely for the cost of maintaining said Ferry for the accommodation of the traveling public, and travelers are requested (under the guidance of the Ferryman) to assist him in all possible ways to make a safe crossing. The Ferryman is hereby ordered to collect the following fees for transport on the Ferry.

Wagon and team 2 horses, $3.00
Saddle horse and rider, $1.50
Pack horse with saddle horse and rider, $0.75
Sheep and goats per head, $0.05

The fee for crossing 50 head to be minimum charge
Cattle, Horses and Mules per head, $0.25
The fee for crossing 6 head to be minimum charge

The Ferryman is hereby instructed to see that any party or parties wishing transportation over said Ferry, sign one of these contracts before entering boat.

All fees due and payable in advance.

Signature of party or parties wishing transportation: _____
By order of the Board of Supervisors of Coconino County, Arizona in regular business session on the 6th day of June A.D. 1910.[9]

There is no record that anyone ever signed the agreement.

Arthur Waller hired the livery operator, Tom Wagner, and a boy to help freight the launch, and the four-up team left Flagstaff on June 10. The ten-horsepower inboard launch, referred to here as the *Canopy*, was probably the most peculiar looking load yet to head across the desert. It had been an excursion boat operating on the Mississippi River out of Muscatine, Iowa, and was donated by H. W. Huttig, one of the financial backers of Spencer's Black Sand Gold Recovery Company. The boat was eighteen feet in length, with a green and white striped canopy covering the aft fifteen feet, and a scalloped valance extending around the periphery. Curtains of the same striped canvas could enclose the passenger compartment during adverse weather. Waller drew the curtains to keep the dust out, and before they reached the Tanner Crossing a band of antelope came near to examine the strange apparition. It could have passed as a veritable howdah for harem beauties.[10]

Meanwhile, Jones had sent mail by Stephenson and continued staking claims around the ferry. Wherever possible, he located the four corners of 160 acres, or 40 acres to each quarter. During this period he staked claims for 25,600 acres. He also triangulated the river at the crossing and found that Al Diamond's measurement for the new cable was a hundred feet short. By June 12, their provisions were exhausted, their animals were getting into the garden and alfalfa, and the men clearly were overstaying their welcome, even to Jerry Johnson. They decided to leave for Tuba City the next morning. When Jones and his men pulled into Tuba City on June 15, they found Bradley and McDermid waiting for Spencer to return from Oljeto. The pair provided the latest news, the main elements of which were that boilers and other machinery were in transit by rail to Flagstaff and Waller was on the road with a power launch. The operation appeared to be going forward, especially when Charlie Spencer and Pres Apperson came in that night.

Waller did not detour to Tuba City but continued on the old pioneer road, and the crew, except for the Spencer brothers who remained at

Attempting to launch the *Canopy* at Lee's Ferry, June 20, 1910 (*P. T. Reilly Collection, Cline Library, Northern Arizona University*).

the temporary Tuba City headquarters, caught up with him on June 17. They got the *Canopy* to the river the following day but left the rig on the dugway when one wheel ran over the edge. They nearly lost the entire outfit but, as it was almost dark, wisely unhitched the horses and camped on the left bank across from the fort. In the morning, Waller dug a graduated lead-track and they worked the wagon back onto the road. When the launch was unloaded they saw that she was old, dirty, and in need of a complete refurbishing. They began overhauling her while waiting for Spencer and additional supplies. They also built a ramada and tent for cook George Smith. Realizing that a smaller skiff was desirable, Jones and Bradley set about to design it. They had no material, their grub was running low, and there was no sign of Spencer. Morale fell. Harry Wetzel quit on June 17; Nick Carter and George Smith followed him to Flagstaff on the twenty-fourth. According to the Jones journal, those remaining had little to do but think derogatory things about Charlie Spencer.

To make matters worse, more of the crew from Oljeto drifted in along with several men from Colorado whom Spencer had hired. Three of the newcomers—Earl Nungesser, Oliver Richardson, and William R. Adams—brought their wives. The Richardsons even had an eight-year-old son, and the camp began to take on the elements of a family enterprise. They all camped among the willows on the left bank, behind the original ferry landing and across from the old fort. Adams' wife took over the duties of the departed cook. This place was referred to as "The Willows" or "Camp Willows."

Meanwhile, Frank Johnson had cleared his debt to Simmons in Wyoming and returned to Kanab. Dimmick put him on the payroll starting

July 11 at forty dollars per month plus board for himself and family. His wife Rhoda not only cooked for the Johnsons but for any Bar Z personnel who happened to be there. Frank was delighted to have returned to his birthplace, to have a dependable payday, and to not be cheated out of his earnings. This was the first time he had seen the cable-ferry at the new site and the changes in the irrigation system. Officially, he was in charge of the ranch and Jerry was in charge of the ferry, but the brothers helped each other in everything.

Two boilers, some accessories, and a pipe dredge were delivered to Flagstaff late in June.[11] This was the signal for which Spencer had been waiting; he dispatched a load of supplies for the men at the ferry and sent instructions for Waller to return to town and escort the equipment to camp. In the interim, Bradley and Jones had designed a boat to aid the operation and they began cutting out ribs and planking. Spencer's men had helped themselves to the ferryboat without bothering Johnson, and the happy-go-lucky Jerry saw no harm in their doing so. July was a month of achievement for Spencer's men. The renovated *Canopy* was launched on the sixteenth and the Bradley boat was placed in the water soon after. Charlie and the remaining crew with teams from Oljeto pulled in on the twelfth, while Art Waller came five days later.

On July 1, a man and his wife, whose names weren't recorded, arrived from the south. The narrow dugway had unnerved them both and they went into camp a short distance from the Spencer crew. Later that evening, the man said his wife was in labor and asked if a doctor was available. There was none, of course, but the three women helped deliver a baby boy. Next day, the family was crossed by the Spencer men and the new parents were as frightened of the boat and river as they had been of the dugway.[12]

Spencer, Bradley, Jones, and four helpers went upriver in the *Canopy* on July 21, surveying general river conditions, and staking the entire Wright Bar as far as Warm Creek. McDermid, who was Huttig's nephew, had operated the boat on the Mississippi and was the pilot. Although the engine was rated at ten horsepower, its actual output was, according to one of the crew, "three-dog power." They returned late that afternoon and next morning Spencer headed for Flagstaff to keep an appointment.[13] He returned on July 31 with Thomas J. Lovett, the inventor and manufacturer of a pipe dredge, an associate and potential investor named Hoskins, and a new employee going under an assumed name.

Richard William Thomas was the new employee, but few ever learned his true name. He was sober, industrious, a good mechanic, and respected by both his co-workers and foreman. He had lived in Bisbee, held a good job, and had a better than average home. One thing he had, but wished he didn't, was a nagging wife. He had seen considerable labor strife during the previous few years but it was as nothing compared to the domestic strife he experienced at home. He finally decided that his marriage was beyond salvage and the best thing was to leave town quietly without argument. In the spring of 1910, he left everything for his wife, retaining only the clothes on his back and what he carried in a single handbag. He confided in no one and eventually found his way to Flagstaff, broke and in need of a job. Chance brought him into contact with a one-time telegrapher named Frank Watson, a recipient of Flagstaff's outdoor relief program. Thomas stayed with Watson for several weeks and picked up a little money at odd jobs, but he could not find work commensurate with his skills. Late in July he met Charlie Spencer, who was soliciting help in a saloon, and Thomas agreed to go to work for the Black Sand Gold Recovery Company under the name of his benefactor, "Frank Watson." Thomas served as teamster, cook, and wrangler when he left town with Spencer, Lovett, and Hoskins on July 28.[14]

The crew had set up one of the two boilers on the left-bank flat, but not one of the men was skilled in assembly or operation of the rig. The work languished until Watson appeared. Fuel would remain a problem pending their obtaining a dependable supply of coal. For the time being, Art Waller gathered driftwood in the skiff. It was just about an all-day job to keep the cook supplied with firewood, so the driftwood pile for the boiler grew hardly at all. Lovett saw that with plumbing hookups and the fuel problem unsolved, they were at least a month from operating the pipe dredge. He decided to return to Chicago; Bradley and Hoskins elected to accompany him to Flagstaff on August 7. Spencer's planning methods were illustrated when, at about 5 P.M. on August 6, he told Jones that a team would be going to Flagstaff in the morning and he wanted a list of lumber needed to build a barge twelve feet by twelve feet. The barge had not even been designed and Spencer had no idea what his request entailed, but Jones worked until 3 A.M. and had the list ready for Pres Apperson. Pres returned with the lumber in ten days.

Tipton's plans were progressing more smoothly as a sleek sixteen-foot inboard powerboat was set on the Flagstaff depot dock on August 6.[15] Tipton and a new associate, O. B. Landon, arrived from Los Angeles and soon made arrangements to freight boat, supplies, and themselves to Lee's Ferry. The craft, called the *Mullins Boat*, was well suited for Tipton's purpose: simple transportation up and down the river. There was little space for freight, but then he did not have a large outfit. They reached the ferry in mid-month and the two men started up the river on the sixteenth.

On August 11, 1910, the first discharge measurement of the Colorado River was taken at Lee's Ferry. A. H. Jones, civil engineer of Denver, handled the transit and recorded the figures while A. C. Waller worked the rod and released the floats. The cross-section was taken from the ferryboat, the floats being released every twenty feet and timed over a two hundred fifty foot course.[16] They calculated the discharge to be 10,398 cubic feet per second.

Besides commandeering the ferryboat at will, the Spencer men had appropriated the boats stored behind the fort that Jerry Johnson attributed to Stanton. One was made serviceable and, with the *Canopy* and

Bradley Boat, now constituted a three-craft fleet. On August 18, Charlie Spencer sent Jones, Waller, and four others upriver in all three boats. The *Canopy*, carrying one hundred sixty-eight gallons of gasoline, pushed the Stanton boat and towed the *Bradley Boat* on a fifty-foot line. Their objective was to locate claims and to purchase the Stanton dredge for which Spencer gave Jones four hundred dollars. It was a peculiar appearing fleet—and the *Canopy's* curtains had not been drawn. Spencer had Jones stake the entire Wright Bar in his name the previous month, despite his commitment to split it, and said he would settle with Tipton later. Tipton and Landon found the location notices, removed them, and replaced them with his own, pre-dated to May. He then handed Jones the Spencer notices when the two river parties met above the bar on August 20. Jones realized that if the claims should ever amount to anything, litigation would be rampant.[17]

"Disaster Day" occurred on August 21 when the Stanton skiff, carrying the food, kitchen, and bedrolls, swamped as it rounded a rock above Mile 31. The two passengers, Nutter and Wiley, were rescued, but most of the supplies were lost. The towline wrapped around the propeller of the *Canopy* and the engine died, but Jones and Waller in the *Bradley Boat* and Tipton in the *Mullins Boat* salvaged everything that floated. They dried things out, had dinner, and decided that Waller and Wiley should take the skiff back to the ferry. The two started out about 3 P.M. with a few crackers and some candy and arrived at camp the following day. Tipton also turned back, probably to his claim on the Wright Bar, but Jones, Barnes, Nutter, and McDermid continued upriver in the *Canopy* and *Bradley Boat*. They augmented their meager supplies with fish, meeting success by dynamiting them with giant powder caps but getting better results with a six-shooter. They had to tow the boats up some of the minor rapids. Jones staked claims wherever the blue clay was close to the river. Barnes spotted an oil seep and they staked claims on that location.

At Mile 105 on August 27, they broke one of the two propeller blades and were forced to start back, surveying claims as they went down to the mouth of the San Juan River. The food shortage helped Barnes and McDermid decide to make a run for Lee's Ferry. Jones and Nutter arrived in the *Bradley Boat* by dinner time on September 1, only to find Spencer and all of the animals gone and the crew out of supplies. Jones was relieved that his job had come to an end; he was thoroughly disgusted at the manner in which the venture had been managed. Spencer had prepared for his leaving by importing a cousin, Charles E. Woodman, to replace him. Woodman had some engineering experience and could handle a transit, so Jones did not feel that his departure would inconvenience the operation. As the *Bradley Boat* was being tied up, he saw that A. J. "Jack" Diamond and his teamster, James Brinkerhoff (a son of Bishop David Brinkerhoff), were starting back to Flagstaff in their two wagons after delivering a new skiff, cable, and necessary fittings for the county ferry. Tipton and Landon had arranged to ride to town with them and Jones decided to join the party. He read his mail, loaded his gear on a mare borrowed from Jerry Johnson, and he and Art Waller set out on foot for Diamond's camp at Navajo Spring. Waller went along to return Jerry's horse.

The Diamond outfit met Charlie Spencer, Tom Lovett, Harold Parkyn, and a potential investor, J. V. Daniels, between The Gap and the Tuba City turnoff. This was Parkyn's first visit to the object of his investment, and Lovett was there to solve the problems of the pipe dredge which, thus far, had not been successful. The two groups didn't spend much time visiting and Jones didn't volunteer the information that he had all of the location notices in his duffel bag.[18]

Things now began to move swiftly for the Black Sand Gold Recovery Company. Twelve head of oxen arrived in Flagstaff from Dolores, and the head whacker, Howard Mayrant, set up camp at the big fill on the edge of town. More oxen were expected and Mayrant began making additional yokes and oxbows while he awaited a shipment of freight from the east.[19] The Lovett pipe dredge and one boiler had been set up on the left bank about forty feet from the river, but what little alluvium was sucked up had failed to carry recoverable colors. It was decided that due to the sweep of the current this location was not likely to be productive. They should relocate the dredge in the river on the outer edge of the curve. They relocated their camp on the right side on September 10–11, with the old fort being taken over for a mess hall; two tents alongside served as the cook's commissary.

The pump, boiler, and engines were in place by September 13.[20] It was apparent, even when the dredge was in place on the left bank, that the operation as it was conceived could not become functional until the fuel problem was solved. Tipton's boat, by simple contrast, had revealed the inadequacies of the *Canopy*. Everyone agreed that a more powerful and dependable launch was a necessity. Such a boat was shipped to Flagstaff early in September and it was sent on to the river by mid-September.[21]

Spencer saw the fuel problem in simple terms. He proposed to develop a trail to the coal deposits and bring coal down on pack animals. Parkyn wasn't too sure that this was the best solution and thought the issue should be presented to those who had advanced the money. This disagreement revealed the dichotomy between field manager Spencer and the men who bankrolled the project. Spencer, of course, wanted unlimited funds to dispense as he saw fit, but Parkyn and his group were unwilling to write a blank check.

Jones, with Spencer's approval, had turned the bookkeeping chore over to Waller in May. Art kept the men's time—a rather pointless function because Spencer had no regular payday. Occasionally a man could pry an advance out of Spencer, but the need had to be convincing. Indians were given one dollar per day plus their board, and they came and went with regularity. Spencer disliked paper work, never made lists in preference to verbal requests; he sent teamsters to Flagstaff to purchase supplies from memory.

They liked to go to town and visit the saloons, sometimes returning half drunk and with only partially filled orders. When the camp had supplies, there were three meals a day, each consisting of salt pork, beans, bread, canned tomatoes, and coffee. Sometimes they had dried prunes or apples, and Spencer bought an occasional sheep or beef from the Navajos. Parkyn had hired Waller early in 1910, and Art originally met Spencer by appointment in the Denver office of John H. Marks. From the very first, Charlie considered Waller to be a spy in Parkyn's employ and went out of his way to assign him jobs that removed him from the center of operations. This placed the books in an intermittent condition, a situation that suited Spencer.

When Jerry Johnson heard that Spencer wanted a more direct route to the plateau and the coal deposits, he told him about the old Indian trail that wound up the cliffs above the ferry. Improving it would result in a better way to the Glen Canyon bench as there wasn't much anyone could do to amend the Sand Trail. This was just what Spencer wanted; he put a pair of men to work on the project in September. Charlie liked to claim later that his mule Pete found the way to traverse the cliffs, but there is no doubt that the trail was known and used by white men for more than forty years before Spencer ever saw Lee's Ferry. Art Waller was assigned to this difficult job, but Spencer had other plans for him.

The largest sheep drive in recent years came to the ferry in late August 1910. Charles Woolfolk had gathered 4,100 yearling wethers and 1,000 yearling ewes in Utah and was taking them to his Flagstaff ranch. Art Waller photographed the animals as they traipsed to the river. Jerry and Frank Johnson worked three and one-half days crossing the band. Fortunately for Woolfolk, the county supervisors had reduced the crossing fee in July to two and one-half cents per head, but even this did not escape Spencer's notice as a potential source of income. The sheepman and his band reached Flagstaff on October 3.[22]

With the immediate priorities established, Parkyn, Lovett, and Daniels decided to return home. They left for Flagstaff with Spencer, Waller, and Stevenson on October 11; Waller and Stevenson rode their horses, night-herded, and cooked. After their arrival three days later, Spencer and Waller went to Greenbaugh's sawmill and ordered a supply of lumber for the new barge and other needs at the river. Waller then went to Mayrant's camp on the edge of town, and the three visitors took the train east while Spencer and Stevenson returned to Lee's Ferry with the team.

Mayrant, assisted by Willis Cronkhite and Ed Keane, had their two wagons heavily loaded with two inch planks, timbers, and some lighter lumber when they left the mill on October 18. They had a total of fifteen yoke of oxen but less than half were considered "broke." These animals were placed at the wheel, swing, and lead positions with bronco steers sandwiched between them. Ordinarily, five yoke would have pulled either load, but this was a chance to break in the inexperienced animals, and there were not enough broken animals to pull both wagons. Considerable time was lost each morning getting the steers to the yoke and hitched; each one was an individual problem. Once underway, however, they went along at an adequate pace, usually making six to eight miles per day. They reached the head of the dugway on November 6 after nineteen strenuous days. The men didn't dare take the long strings over the dugway's sharp curves. They divided the lumber into smaller loads and took it the remaining distance by mules. Mayrant and his men returned with empty wagons.

Prior to their arrival, Spencer sent Frank Barnes into town to keep an appointment, a result of Dr. Parkyn's promotion. Parkyn had arranged for H. N. Jackson, said to be a mining expert, and four potential investors to get to Flagstaff on a certain date, and for a Thomas Flyer automobile with an experienced driver to come there from the west coast to meet them. Barnes, an ex-U.S. Navy man with a good mechanical background, and the imported driver, T. A. Costa, were to take the group to the ferry. The visitors were pleasantly surprised to find that the last leg of their trip would be made in the latest model automobile. Little did they know that this was the first time a horseless carriage had ventured as far as the Little Colorado, to say nothing of being the first over the Tanner Crossing. Barnes had instructions not to attempt a crossing if the river was flowing. People were excited about automobiles after the big Los Angeles-to-Phoenix race that had ended Monday morning, November 7, at the fairgrounds before eight thousand fans. Parkyn's timing had been masterful.

Costa estimated his gross load of seven men, baggage, extra gasoline, tires, and tools at close to a ton when he left Flagstaff shortly after 1 P.M. on November 12. The narrow high-pressure tires didn't handle the sand too well, but the Thomas Flyer finally got across the Little Colorado River with everyone except the driver pushing. They chugged into Tuba City at 9 P.M. where they spent the night. After an early start, they arrived at the head of the dugway seven hours later. Costa examined the narrow road and refused to take the machine farther. Barnes walked the distance and Spencer sent a wagon over for the last short leg. The excursion was a waste of time as the project was not far enough along to allow definite conclusions; if the alluvium proved to carry the values Spencer claimed, the proposed mining method was logical. After two full days, both the expert and the potential investors had seen enough. Costa started the return trip at 6 A.M. on the sixteenth. They reached Flagstaff the same day, covering the distance in ten hours and forty-five minutes, a phenomenal time over a rough wagon road, and the driver basked in the glow of praise for his skill and daring.[23]

Costa was instructed to make a return trip the following day carrying a load of freight, but he did not get away until November 18. This time his luck was not so good; he hit the Tanner Crossing too hard and broke the kingpin for the right wheel. There was nothing to be done beyond praying there would be no rain to put a flood down the Little Colorado River. They sat there for three days until Mayrant and his oxen came along on the twenty-first. Fortunately, the wagon beds had been removed and the lumber was loaded directly on the wagon frames. They removed the entire front axle, hoisted the front end of the car onto the rear axle of the wagon, and lashed it down. Mayrant and his twelve oxen towed the crippled Flyer in to Flagstaff, arriving on the twenty-ninth.[24] One of the oldest means of transportation had rescued the newest.

Meanwhile, the crew at the ferry wondered why Costa and the car did not make the return trip; it was the main subject of conversation during the card game after supper. The matter was not lost on the Navajo workmen, as young Art Waller recorded:

> The automobile that went to Flag a week ago hasn't shown yet and every night the conversation centers on it and what has happened to it.
>
> Old Hosteen Seh said "What do they all talk about 'come back' all a time?"
>
> Charlie told him and he was quiet for a while, then he came out with the following:
>
> "If you will give me $100, I'll go to my hogan and get my beltone (rifle) and then I'll go to Flagstaff and bring the fire wagon son of a bitch back whether he wants to come or not."[25]

This was Waller's last observation at Lee's Ferry for more than four months as he and George Spencer were sent on a multiple mission to the San Juan country and southwestern Colorado. A lone man, John Palmer, was guarding considerable equipment at Red Rock cabin and Oljeto. At the San Juan, George Spencer was to inventory this equipment and determine what could be used at Lee's Ferry. Waller was to winter the company's horses at the Lamb Ranch in the McElmo Valley. Thus Charlie got rid of the man he considered to be Parkyn's spy and replaced him with his own man, Bill Switzer, clerk to the Coconino County supervisors. Bill Switzer got a friend, George Fleming, to take his place at the board meetings during his absence. Bill had learned of the opening through his brother-in-law, A. J. Diamond.

Jerry Johnson was frustrated by his wife's refusal to join him at Lee's Ferry. He finally convinced himself that Pearly would join him for the winter and see how she liked southern Utah. He sent her some money and then asked Charlie Dimmick to lend him a team so he could pick her up at Marysvale, the end of the railroad. Charlie granted him paid leave and loaned him a four-up team in case she had considerable luggage. Jerry was there at the agreed time, but she did not appear. He hung around for three days and then, sick at heart, reluctantly turned homeward.

Henry Stephenson did not approve of Dimmick's generosity and let him know about it. For his part, Dimmick didn't like the general manager's continual interference in his operation and decided it was time to move on. He told Stephenson he would stay until the end of the year, and that three months' notice would allow plenty of time to find a replacement.

For some time, Stephenson had reasoned that the company might be better off in Mormon country with a Mormon foreman. He made good use of his contacts before settling on Eph Mansfield of Beaver. Eph, a devout Saint, had spent his life in the cattle business and was noted for being exceptionally honest. He agreed to take the job at the beginning of 1911.

Some weeks before Dimmick departed, he had Frank Johnson apply for the job of postmaster and reactivated the Lee's Ferry Post Office. The appointment came through on January 13, 1911, and the Bar Z ranch house, which Frank's father had built in 1886, once again served as post office. The schedule was not serviced by pony express, but it was considerably better than a two hundred fifty mile round trip to and from the mailbox. The delivery was in two stages, from one outpost on the reservation to another even more remote. Mail arrived at Tuba City from Flagstaff on Sunday, Tuesday, and Friday and left Tuba City for Flagstaff on Monday, Wednesday, and Saturday. Carriers departed Tuba for Lee's Ferry on Monday and started the return trip on Thursday. The carrier was a Navajo who used the mail sack as a cushion in the old-style Navajo saddle.[26] The schedule was not iron-bound, however, and varied at convenience.

The year 1911 was a banner year for the Spencer promotion. More changes took place at the ferry and surrounding country than had occurred up to this time. Charlie Spencer would give anyone a job but still never had enough labor for what he wanted to accomplish. He started out by importing Eugene Spencer, his younger brother, to act as his foreman. Eugene was not particularly knowledgeable about the work, but he learned by leaning on the reliable Frank Watson. While he was loyal to his brother, he was disliked by most of the men. Shortly after the advent of spring, work intensified on the Indian trail above the ferry. Charlie took two of the men to examine the twenty-inch coal vein that Jones had visited above the center fork of Cane Creek. He concluded that it would not be practical to work this deposit since it was located above a cliff; building a road would be too costly and difficult. Exploring farther, they located a relatively approachable deposit in one of the heads of Warm Creek about twelve miles above the Cottonwoods and four miles above a good spring. After this discovery, they followed Warm Creek to the Colorado and ascertained that a wagon road could be hacked out with little labor.

At this time, Spencer envisioned a camp for coal miners at The Cottonwoods. He accumulated a stock pile there, packing it overland to the new trail head and down to the ferry. If the investors ever obtained a boat that could carry any kind of payload, the coal could be moved on down to the river and put on board. He notified Parkyn, and before the year was out it was decided to construct quarters for the coal camp at The Cottonwoods.

Thus it was that jobs became available and there was a constant flow of men to Lee's Ferry. At the beginning of the year Spencer had crews improving the trail and dugway, building a barge for use with the Lovett pipe dredge, and constructing rock buildings at the ferry. Other crews were doing similar work at The Cottonwoods and building a road from there to the mouth of Warm Creek. In addition, Howard Mayrant in the Flagstaff camp was breaking bronco steers and making yokes and hoops. The operation was much more extensive than Stanton's had ever been.

The successful employment of Jerry and Frank by Bar Z prompted an influx of more Johnsons from Wyoming. Their half-brother LeRoy, barely twenty-two, returned to Kanab with his mother in July 1910. He went to work for Bar Z on January 10, 1911, helping his brothers at the Lee's Ferry ranch. Warren Elmer Johnson, not quite twenty-one and full brother to Jerry and Frank, returned in February 1911 but remained in Kanab. The flow of Johnsons was in danger of being reversed when Jerry, unable to persuade Pearly to join him, talked of returning to Wyoming.

During the winter, the Spencer men continued to help themselves to the ferry, and the easy-going Jerry made no objection. Eugene Spencer knew no more about the river than he did about his brother's work, but he gave orders in a dictatorial manner. He had observed Jerry's caution in operating the ferry and concluded Jerry was afraid of the river. When the flow was low, the Spencer men kept both falls equal and pulled the boat across rapidly with the hand line. Eugene saw no reason for Jerry's caution in letting out the aft fall before he hit the main current and told him so. In fact, he went further and said Jerry was afraid, and a couple of his sycophants echoed him. Eugene ordered the men to use his method of crossing because it was faster. Their criticism didn't bother Jerry; he continued to use the time-proven discretion in crossing travelers, the Spencer men took themselves across as they saw fit. The county supervisors had no inkling that anyone other than Jerry was operating the ferry.

March was noted for being a time of widely ranging discharges in the Colorado River. In March 1902, the minimum flow at Yuma was 5,340 cubic feet per second, but three years later it peaked at 111,000 cubic feet per second.[27] In March 1911, the river started out like a lamb at 7,590 cubic feet per second, but by mid-month the flow had more than quadrupled. On March 14, the Yuma gage read 34,900 cubic feet per second, and the discharge was close to this amount at the ferry on March 9, 1911. Frank Watson's letter to Charlie Spencer, who was at Flagstaff at the time, tells what took place when five men with a team and wagon attempted a crossing to do some improvement work on the dugway:

Lees Ferry, March 10th, 1911.

Dear Friend Charley:
    Yesterday while trying to cross the Ferry we had a very sad accident. The Ferry sank and poor "Pres" was drowned. We have dragged all along, but have found no signs of him, and am afraid that we will never find him, as the River is running very swift. We have taken the old ferry up, and put it on a new cable, so as to start Bill out

in the morning for Flagstaff. We had to take the old cable down, in order to get it out of the way. The Johnson boys came over and we made the change. There were Pres, Bill, John, Aul, and myself, and as we got about the centre of the current, the water ran over the side of the boat. John and I were on the South end pulling on the hand line. Pres was making the blocks fast after letting them out. Aul was standing near him. Bill was on the seat in the wagon. The next thing the boat took a lunge and it jerked John and myself, about ten feet clear of the Ferry. I seen Pres climbing the block ropes; the next lunge it made, the boat went clear under, and Bill, horses and wagon were washed off the boat. Aul swam ashore, Bill got hold of two boards and floated down stream, and Aul hollered as he was swimming and after he got ashore for Art, Ed, and Bob, who had crossed with a row-boat and were going to work on the dugway. They had not got far. They came back and picked Bill up, just above where the barge is anchored, and while they were doing this, Pres, John and myself, were hanging and being jerked, fully ten feet or more, up and down; sometimes down in the water and then way up in the air. John seen Pres after he got on the cable. I had in some way got my left arm over the cable and the hand line over my arm, so that I was fast and could not get loose. John was hanging on the hand line just to the left of me during this tim [time]. The cable had slipped about ten feet around the deadman on the North side of the river and it was throwing us higher every time the boat went down, and came up. Then the boat made another lunge. This time the rope in the blocks on the ends that Pres was on, broke and released the strain on the cable, and we dropped about ten or twelve feet into the river. It seemed to me that I went straight down feet first, six or seven feet in the water. When I came up, I saw John. He looked to be thirty or forty feet away and swimming all right, and just about the same distance ahead of John, I was sure that I saw Pres. When I got to shore, I heard Aul say, "Pres is drowned," we [you] will probably see Bill, and he will tell you all about it. The team and wagon went down the river. Every body here feels awful bad, for all of us boys liked Pres. I will close for this time.

Hoping to see you soo [soon]: I am

Very truly yours
F. D. Watson[28]

Watson's letter describing the accident is the only extant eyewitness account. It does not pinpoint the cause, which was Eugene Spencer's instruction to let both falls out equally and pull the ferry across with the handline. Both Jerry and Frank Johnson agreed that Eugene's method of placing the ferryboat beam-on to the fast current was dangerous except in very low water. Jerry was indirectly to blame for abrogating his job responsibility and allowing the men to use the boat as they pleased. Five days later, Jerry quit his job and went to Wyoming to get his wife. Frank now had charge of both ranch and ferry, although at present there was no boat. Mansfield raised his salary to fifty dollars a month and instructed Roy to assist him.

Art Waller brought the company's horses to the ferry about a week after Apperson's death. He participated in the general work underway at the time until May when he was called upon to go to Denver for Dr. Parkyn. He made the long ride to Flagstaff, boarded his horse at a livery stable, and took the train. After his duty was discharged, he continued east to his father's home in New Jersey where he remained a few months before returning to Denver. His connection with the mining company was interrupted for about eighteen months.

Prospects never appeared brighter for the Spencer promotion. Charlie went to Chicago late in February to meet with all the backers. The decision was made to replace the Black Sand Gold Recovery Company with a new syndicate under the more favorable laws of South Dakota. The American Placer Corporation had its head office in Pierre, but the sub-office was Parkyn's old address of the Marquette Building in Chicago. The new corporation was formed April 22, 1911, and gave notice in the *Coconino Sun* on July 14 of doing business in Arizona. Considerable money was pledged to meet every need. A negative aspect, as far as Charlie was concerned, was that Parkyn and the financial backers were making decisions without his approval.

Mayrant had about seventy-five work cattle at his camp by the end of 1910, and in late January, he freighted two boilers, a large hydraulic pump, and 1,250 feet of lumber to the ferry. He was gone forty days, returning in mid-March. He had been lucky; a short time after the ox train crossed the Little Colorado a flood had roared down the channel and water was said to have been ten feet deep at the Tanner Crossing. His experience justified a feeling of satisfaction when the *Coconino Sun* announced that $90,000 had been appropriated for a bridge to be built over that unpredictable stream, hopefully to be started that spring.[29] Later in March, the Pierce amalgamator, other placer processing equipment, and one hundred twenty-five additional work cattle arrived in Flagstaff. The company now had almost two hundred head in Mayrant's camp, an indication of the extensive nature of the proposed operation.

Zane Grey had been corresponding with Dave Rust regarding a pack trip out of Lee's Ferry. When Rust heard of the ferry's loss, he immediately notified the novelist that the trip was off. Grey's response revealed his inner fears of the river: "I'm 'some' glad we weren't on that old ferry boat when she went down. It always scared me stiff when I got on it .... Well, that knocks the Lee's Ferry trip out for me."[30] Grey and C. A. McLain, editor and manager of *Popular Magazine*, arrived in Flagstaff on April 14, hired guide Al Doyle, and packed into the recently discovered Rainbow Bridge.[31]

When Spencer read Watson's letter about the ferry accident, he reflected and arranged through Switzer to meet with the county supervisors.

As a result, he agreed to restore ferry service on a cooperative basis; the county was to furnish lumber and a new cable. He would provide labor to build the boat and hang the cable. Moreover, Spencer convinced the majority of the board to take the custodianship of the ferry from the cattle company and give it to him at the end of June. The fee, now up to $75, would be extra cash to Spencer because most of his men received no wages. The Flagstaff Lumber Company charged the county $160.88 for pine timbers and planks. The ferry, built in July, was a replica of the last Emett boat.

Dr. Parkyn appears to have had good connections on the west coast because he arranged for chemical and mining engineer Dr. Julius Koebig to visit Lee's Ferry in April to advise on the use of the Pierce amalgamator. Koebig was there on April 25 when a telegram notified him that on the previous day his nineteen-year-old-daughter had been assaulted and badly hurt in the family's Los Angeles home. Mayrant took the company's best horse and rode to the ferry in thirty-one hours, losing five hours in Tuba City when he was unable to obtain a fresh mount. Koebig was persuaded to remain since his departure could not help his daughter, and Spencer agreed to speed on to him any reports received in Flagstaff. As it turned out, the girl recovered from a severe pistol-whipping. The assailant, an unemployed sailor named John Edwards, was apprehended, confessed, and within a week was sentenced to life imprisonment.[32]

Everything did not go well for the corporation, and most of the bad breaks resulted from ignorance and inefficiency. The Lovett pipe dredge was rigged between two barges along the right bank in mid-May when silt from the rising river clogged the pumps. By day's end, the dredge was stuck in the silt; they decided to leave it until the next morning. Unfortunately, the water continued to rise and Tom Lovett's brainchild appeared to be a victim of the river. This shut down the operation temporarily while Spencer went to Chicago to consult with Lovett, Parkyn, and his cohorts.[33] Charlie came back with a reversing procedure that salvaged the pipe dredge.

Spencer had start-up authority and news of future plans, which convinced the crew as well as the Flagstaff merchants that the company intended to spend more money to keep the operation functioning. The construction programs shifted into high gear and everyone exuded optimism. Bill Switzer gave a very rosy report to the *Coconino Sun* that appeared on June 2. He stated that the company would spend half a million dollars, the latest machinery was being installed, and a fleet of automobiles would be placed in service as soon as the bridge was built across the Little Colorado. He spoke of a railroad being planned to run to the ferry, and referred to valuable copper deposits and vast coal fields nearby, as well as fertile acres of farmland. Bill Switzer had certainly absorbed a goodly amount of that Spencer imagery.

If the blind led the blind at the river, a similar deficiency was taking place in the corporate management. The dichotomy between the men writing the checks and the field manager resulted in chaos. The Lovett pipe dredge was written off as a non-producer; they decided to concentrate on washing the blue silts through the Pierce amalgamator. Against Spencer's recommendation to transport the coal by pack animal and wagon, the officers voted to order a stern-wheeler steamboat. The plan was to freight the fuel to the mouth of Warm Creek and move it by river-barge to Lee's Ferry. Significantly, no one thought of hiring a steam engineer to determine the power needed to run against the current.

The contract went to the well-known firm of Schultze, Robertson, Schultze of San Francisco, a company that was experienced in building stern-wheelers for the bay and river traffic of California but had never built a boat to contend with a strong current. The order called for a stern-wheeler 72 feet in length, a beam of 20 feet, with a 4-foot depth. The boiler was to be 72 inches in diameter by 120 inches long. There were to be two engines 8 inches by 40 inches, rated at 174-pound boiler pressure. The two horizontally-mounted steam cylinders, one on each side, were 18 inches from the hull. The paddlewheel was 12 feet in diameter and length, with twelve 10-inch blades. The deck of the pilot house compartment was 12 feet above the keel, and the smokestack was 27 feet above the deck.[34] The boat would have been adequate on the near sea-level waters of the Sacramento or San Joaquin Rivers, and no one told the firm building it that the current of the Colorado was any different. The decision to build the boat appears to have been made by the directors over mild dissent from Spencer, who by this time felt the operation was getting away from him. To overcome his opposition, the officers named the boat after him—the *Charles H. Spencer*.

Mayrant's weaknesses were known to his wife. When his sojourn in Arizona lengthened and he sent no money home, she decided she had better join him. With her two daughters, her son-in-law, and a grandchild, she arrived in Flagstaff on April 9. Howard Mayrant was a good bullwhacker but a poor family man. Spencer paid his saloon bills and occasionally gave him a few dollars which he spent in the local bordellos. Mrs. Mayrant soon got on top of the situation and decreed that her husband should have a regular payday or go elsewhere. She lined him up with a job in Prescott late that summer and delivered Spencer an ultimatum to pay him regularly or he would quit. Charlie couldn't accede to her demand because he did not always have money available, and such an act would set a precedent for the other men. Consequently, the Mayrants went to Prescott and Spencer moved Willis Cronkhite up to replace Howard.

Although Frank Johnson had a good job and a dependable payday, there were many demands on his resources. He supported his brother Price on a church mission to the southern states, and now he received a letter from Jerry asking for money to bring his wife to Arizona. Jerry had not found success in Wyoming. When he arrived in March he thought he would stay, so he rented forty acres from John Simmons, his father-in-law. He raised a fine crop of hay that summer, but Simmons took it all to apply on an old debt and Jerry was left where he had been when he went to Arizona.

Frank sent Jerry some money and Jerry brought Pearly back with him. He did not have the effrontery to ask Mansfield for his old job; in July, he went to work for Spencer to operate the newly-completed ferry. He knew that Spencer was not paying his men, but naively thought he could get his wages from the county.

Early in July, the American Placer Corporation received a large railroad shipment at Flagstaff, including several heavy-duty freight wagons and a steel-hull powerboat twenty-six feet long called the *Violet Louise*. The craft's engine was rated at thirty to forty horsepower (depending on the informant) and was the most powerful of its kind in those waters up to this date. With Mayrant gone, Bill Switzer assembled the shipment for the ferry under direction of the master bullwhacker, Charlie Spencer. The teams pulled out of the Flagstaff camp on the morning of July 18.

Territorial historian Sharlot Hall had hired Al Doyle of Flagstaff to guide her on a tour of the Arizona Strip, which was a long cherished ambition of Hall's. Their light wagon left town on July 23. A day later they passed the Spencer ox trains at their noon stop and were told they would reach the Tanner Crossing that evening. The river was roaring with runoff from summer rains but the skies were clearing and the pair had hopes that the flow would decrease to allow their crossing. Charlie and his wagon got in about dark and echoed the expectation. Spencer waited until noon before he risked a crossing, and even then it was hazardous with water up to the wagon beds. After his outfit was across, two riders tied lariats to Doyle's wagon to augment the power of the team, and Sharlot got the thrill of her life as the muddy water splashed around her feet. The Navajo mail carrier came along and told them Moenkopi Wash was running bank-to-bank. He then switched his pony into the flood but had to pull his feet onto the animals back in mid-channel.

The whackers decided to shoe some of the sore-footed steers on the right bank as Doyle and Hall pressed on. That night, they camped amid the Chinle hillocks on Moenkopi Wash where he and Miller Herlinger had scattered the ashes of artist Frank Sauerwein a few weeks before. The Moenkopi had a more impressive flow than the Little Colorado River, and they spent two days attempting to find a crossing, then went to the Indian school at Tuba City. After visiting the Hopi village of Moenkopi and Sam Preston's trading post, they set out again on July 30. They had lunch at Moenave and camped that night at Willow Spring.

Next morning they passed the advanced units of the Spencer ox train, which were worn and muddy from their crossing of the Moenkopi. They all reached the Colorado River on August 2, where Sharlot was brought over by Spencer's men in a small gasoline boat. The ferry conveyed Doyle and the wagon across and they pitched camp under a large pear tree at the Bar Z ranch. Sharlot rested and visited the mining operations as Doyle recruited the team. The vanguard of the ox train appeared Sunday morning, August 6, and Sharlot got someone to cross her and her camera

The Spencer barges and the *Violet Louise* in Glen Canyon, 1911 (*P. T. Reilly Collection, Cline Library, Northern Arizona University*).

in the launch. She then walked back on the dugway to photograph the oxen. The new boat was too long to make the sharp dugway curves; it was shunted down the lower-crossing dugway and unloaded at the landing. Next day she watched the *Violet Louise* run up the Pahreah Riffle and reported that the boat navigated the rough water "like a seabird."

The *Violet Louise* was put to work immediately. Four of the new wagons were loaded on two thirty-foot barges fastened tandem. Remembering how the *Canopy* had gotten the tow rope wound around its propeller, they lashed the lead barge alongside the powerboat. The wagons were filled with bedrolls, supplies, and work equipment. Sharlot photographed the rig and watched it depart upriver; it didn't falter as it passed from sight. That afternoon, Jerry Johnson rowed her a few miles into Glen Canyon in a duplication of the Galloway-James excursion of 1897, drifting back after dark. Sharlot was rapidly getting the feel of this wild country. She and Doyle started out for Fredonia on August 9.[35] Her observations and camera preserved a vital part of strip history that otherwise would have gone unrecorded.

Charlie's transportation plans received a shot in the arm on July 31 when the contract to build the bridge across the Little Colorado River was given to the Midland Bridge Company of Kansas City. The *Coconino Sun* reported the good news in the August 4 issue and announced the cost as eighty-four thousand dollars. At long last the unpredictable stream would be neutralized, and those living north of the Tanner Crossing would feel that their comings and goings could be made with more dependability.

The stern-wheeler steamboat was completed in San Francisco by the end of August, disassembled, and loaded for shipment by rail. The master shipwright, Herman Rosenfelt, left San Francisco on the evening of September 7 to supervise the assembly; he was gone for six months and two days. The components, filling two freight cars, were unloaded at Marysvale in mid-September, where Spencer had eight ox trains waiting. The ox trains made the trip from the end of the railroad to the mouth of Warm Creek in fifteen to thirty-nine days, depending on their loads, and the ship began to take shape early in November.

Although Congress had dissolved the Perpetual Emigrating Company in 1887, the Saints still managed to bring converts or potential converts to this country by private subscription. A twenty-five-year-old Welshman named Albert E. Leach made it to America through the proselyting zeal of relatives in Kanab, where he arrived in July 1911. Informed by LeRoy Johnson that Spencer was hiring, Leach got a ride to Lee's Ferry and went to work improving the trail. When they found out he was a coal miner and knew how to handle powder, he was put in charge of the trail-building phase.

Summer rains were heavier than usual in 1911 and they intensified by the end of September. The Virgin, Escalante, and Yuma gage readings suggest that a sudden rise came out of Glen Canyon at that time, which almost cost the county another ferryboat. The men awoke one morning to find the river roaring and the ferry perilously close to the strong current, fastened only by the falls to the sheaves. The anchor post was submerged and the line was out of sight even if it had been fastened. Something had to be done quickly, and Spencer called for volunteers. Only Bert Leach stepped forward, but then Frank Watson said he would go also. Both men tied ropes around their waists and were played out as they swam to the boat. Once on board, the ferry was pulled to shore and secured.[36] Bert's performance brought him status in the camp.

The ferry rescue saved embarrassment in several places. Bill Switzer, at a September board meeting, read a report to the supervisors that he had witnessed heavy loads being crossed on the new ferryboat and considered it to be the answer to the county's needs for an indefinite period. Should they approve the report, Spencer would be relieved of further responsibility, although he agreed to make and install loading-aprons provided they furnished the material. If there was criticism of Bill's service to two masters at the same time, it did not come to light. Spencer's men installed the loading aprons, and the supervisors gave him a warrant for $156.61 at their meeting of September 5. Up to this time the aprons were considered an integral part of each ferryboat, not an add-on extra. The warrant included the $75 that Charlie was paid for operating the ferry, but the bill was not itemized. It was within $5 of the $160.88 that the Flagstaff Lumber Company received for furnishing material for the entire ferry.

Sometime during 1911, Spencer got the idea that the Chinle contained free mercury, probably from processing the blue silts over the plates of the Pierce amalgamator. Several flasks of the "quick" had been brought in, and Charlie even related to Sharlot Hall how he had discovered the metal's presence in the formation and developed a process for extracting it. She reported that he had already collected sixty pounds, which, if true, would have exceeded the value of all the gold that both Stanton and Spencer ever gathered in the Glen Canyon area. From this time on, Charlie began to promote the recovery of mercury almost as much as he enthused over the paltering of gold, even though he was aware that free mercury is rarely found.

John Palmer brought the last of Spencer's usable equipment from the San Juan in July after Mayrant quit. Spencer was recruiting all the men he could find who had bullwhacking experience and when Palmer told him his two brothers qualified, it wasn't difficult for him to get his back wages and take the train to Clovis, New Mexico, to get them. On their return, all three brothers were sent to Marysvale where Jesse and DeWitt loaded two large boilers and freighted them to Lee's Ferry.

Palmer met Spencer, Parkyn, and two Englishmen, whom Parkyn had rounded up as potential investors, and packed them via Antimony, Widstoe, Cannonville, Pahreah (where Spencer had a crew at work), the Clark Bench, Cottonwood Camp on Warm Creek, and the coal mine, then down the unfinished trail to Lee's Ferry. The Englishmen—Lord Hugh Grovenor and George Massey Baresford—remained at the ferry for several days looking over the operation. Unfortunately for Parkyn—or fortunately for the Englishmen—they knew two of the workmen, Ed Saughton and Pat Vorhies, whom Parkyn had sent out from Chicago. Possibly the doctor had used them in previous promotions, and by their presence here the quarry became wary. According to Palmer, one of the Englishmen said, "Oh, I say, Charlie, if there is so much gold here, how is it that it hasn't been found?" Saughton spiked the quicksilver part of the promotion by showing Lord Grovenor the hidden flask of mercury, the hole in the cork, and the straps that fastened it to one's leg.

Frank Johnson said that Jerry saw Spencer filing the edge of a twenty dollar gold coin and salting the filings in some dirt to be panned. The Englishman examined the gold bits with a magnifying glass and noted the sharp edges which would not have been present in placer gold; he said nothing. The next day, Parkyn and Spencer accompanied their guests to El Tovar at Grand Canyon so they could board the train for Chicago. John Palmer once again did the packing, but this time a couple of wranglers named Gordon and Reed were taken along to service the whims of the visitors. On their trip from Marysvale, a hard rain had wet the bedrolls and Lord Grovenor told Palmer to dry his blankets before the fire. The independent packer, surprised at being ordered to perform such service, refused. Even the addition of servants failed to entice the British investors; they evaded the bait and had a free outing in the west at the company's expense.[37]

Parkyn returned to the ferry to oversee the operation in the interests of the backers. His presence brought an element of bureaucracy to the operation without adding to its efficiency. If Spencer failed to utilize company money to the best advantage, Parkyn did not improve the situation as he had little experience in such matters. He did, however, have opinions and he expressed them, much to Spencer's annoyance. He took his talents to every phase of the program, from trail and building construction to operation of the Pierce amalgamator. The men realized the situation and ostensibly followed instruction from him and Eugene Spencer, but actually were advised by Frank Watson.

Bert Leach—called "Teddy" by his bosses—gave a good example of how too much supervision hindered the work. In Wales, Leach had learned to be economical with powder, to place charges where they did the most good. He followed this practice in trail construction until one day he returned to camp and Parkyn said, "Teddy, you didn't roll many rocks today." Leach made no reply but thought that if his work was being judged by the amount of rocks rolled down the slope, he would comply. After that he rolled many rocks without benefiting the trail, and Parkyn's touch can be discerned today, even considering washouts and the passing of time.[38]

Massive building programs now were nearing completion at Lee's Ferry and Cottonwood camp. Eugene Spencer supervised the operation at Warm Creek, which entailed digging coal in Tibbet Canyon, stockpiling it at the camp, and erecting stone buildings for a mess hall, bunkhouse, and storage. Herman Rosenfelt had charge of assembling the stern-wheeler, and Eugene had sense enough not to interfere. A tent camp, with a cook, was maintained at the river, but this would be active only until the boat was built. Work crews went to the coal mine when needed as it was four miles past the last water, while another crew hauled rock and worked in camp. Stone corrals were built at both Warm Creek and the ferry to contain the draft animals.

The men lived in tents at the ferry until the bunkhouses were built. The old fort-trading post was used as a mess hall, and the workmen added a twenty-six-foot extension on its west end to accommodate a cook and food supplies. The first building to be completed was the ten and one-half by twenty–foot structure west of the fort that became the company office. Bill Switzer held sway there, attending to the books and assays—such as they were. The new mess hall was completed shortly after the office building, as was the cook's quarters-supply room. The former was twenty feet wide and three times as long, while the latter was thirteen by twenty feet and located on the slope off the northeast corner of the mess hall. In all there were eight buildings in addition to the old fort, spread over eight hundred feet as in a small village.

Spencer had filed mining claims over mining claims, some of which overlapped the property rights of the Grand Canyon Cattle Company. Jones had staked the entire banks in the ferry vicinity during the previous year, and in the spring and summer of 1911 Spencer staked the Chinle exposures well into Pahreah Canyon. Besides holding the ground on which his improvements stood, Spencer made a practice of filing claims in the names of his principal investors. He located sixty-three claims on the Pahreah River alone and eight claims around Soap Creek between April 24 and June 6, 1911.[39] If the paper made those with venture capital happy, Charlie kept them content.

The heavy rains in late September made everyone connected with the enterprise realize that the immediate environment was not to be taken lightly and that tragedy could strike unexpectedly. Late one afternoon, a Spencer ox train of two wagons drawn by ten yoke of oxen was bringing a load of coal down to Cottonwood Camp. The weather was threatening and Charlie had a horseman ride about a mile behind to bring word in case a flash flood struck. It had showered intermittently most of the day but the rain became steady as the heart of the east-moving storm hit the upper drainage. Suddenly the rear-guard horseman appeared, shouting that a flood was upon them. The bullwhips cracked but the oxen could not be hurried; they continued their steady plod. The canyon walls were too steep for the poor dumb beasts but not for man. There was no time to unhitch them or remove the yokes as the men scrambled to save themselves. A wall of water that Eugene Spencer said was twelve to fifteen feet high bore down at express-train speed, a tree riding the crest. Charlie had pulled the team out of the heart of the wash, but the tree caught the rear wheel of the trailing wagon (hitched tandem) and dragged the entire outfit into the flood. The ten animals and both wagons were swept fifteen miles to the Colorado and flushed on downstream. The carcass of a large bull and one yoke lodged on the Pahreah delta was found, but nothing more. The coal wagon was a new four-inch Bain with roller bearings. Charlie, always feeling empathy for the livestock, was disconsolate.[40] Fortunately, the stern-wheeler was being assembled on a sand bar on the downstream side of the mouth of Warm Creek and was only brushed by the flood. The men, however, were isolated at the site.

On September 8, the *Coconino Sun* printed the news that F. S. Breen had received a letter from the Kolb brothers at Green River, Wyoming, saying they intended to begin a river trip on the sixth. They departed two days later—the second trip since Flavell's in 1896, and only the third after Powell's 1869 traverse, to begin the journey so close to the stream's head.[41] They prevailed over the rigors of Cataract Canyon and pulled in at Dandy Crossing on the first day of November. Although the post office was even more remote than the one at Lee's Ferry, they found several letters awaiting them and they took time to write a few themselves. One, to the editor of the *Coconino Sun* was printed in the November 17 issue (the same day the brothers climbed from Bright Angel Creek to their home on the South

Rim). After leaving John Hite's hospitality, the Kolbs visited Bert Loper at Red Canyon and Cass Hite at Ticaboo on their way downstream.

On about noon on November 6, they observed sixteen men assembling the internal timbers of a large steamboat at the mouth of Warm Creek. One of the workmen was Bill Wilson whom they had known in Flagstaff. The dinner gong sounded as they landed and they ate with the crew. Emery Kolb took a picture of the men and their work, then they departed for the ferry, about twenty-eight miles away.[42] After four hours of hard rowing, the brothers landed at the Spencer dredge just as the cook banged the triangle to announce that supper was ready. For the second time that day, they were the guests of the American Placer Corporation. Finishing the substantial meal, they walked over to the Bar Z ranch house to pick up their mail. Postmaster Frank Johnson informed them that their friend Dave Rust had waited several days for their arrival, leaving only the day before. Rust had taught Galloway's boating technique to the Kolbs, which contributed to their successful trip through the canyons.

Foreman Watson invited the brothers to use the workshop for any needed boat repairs and offered use of a room for their photographic developing. He asked them to keep a sharp watch for the body of Pres Apperson. He told them that the great rise in late September had caused the river to come up forty-five feet at the ferry—an indication that Watson did not have the ability to estimate distance. The *Edith* and *Defiance* were ready by the end of their first full day at the camp, so there was time for the Kolbs to examine the Lovett pipe dredge, the Pierce amalgamator, and to take a picture of the operation. They departed on the morning of December 9 as the forty workmen and a skeptical Navajo mail carrier watched them negotiate the Pahreah Riffle.

Babbitt and Preston secured the contract to freight six hundred tons of steel for the new bridge over the Little Colorado, and by late November had set up a temporary camp and trading post on the left bench. Wagon "traffic" between Flagstaff and the site was several times that between there and the ferry. Even so, Spencer turned in $68 as ferriage for the months of July, August, and September. He even paid $13 in tolls for company use of the ferry in October.[43] If the people of Utah still held any hopes of acquiring the Arizona Strip, their aspirations received the coup de grace in 1911. Sharlot Hall crossed the Colorado on both the Lee and Scanlon ferries and encircled the Grand Canyon in an even wider arc than had Jacob Hamblin. Her account aroused public interest in the remote lands in the northern parts of Coconino and Mohave Counties. The Little Colorado River bridge and the Spencer promotion at Lee's Ferry and Warm Creek added to the general opinion that the strip had a rosy future. The *Coconino Sun* now ran editorials extolling the value of the area and calling for another bridge to cross the Colorado.[44]

Despite the optimism in Coconino County, the investors of the American Placer Corporation were becoming impatient for returns on their money. In a letter of December 20, 1911, W. H. Bradley told A. H. Jones, "The company has spent $150,000 since June 1910 and has very little to show for it. A change of management will be made."[45] Clearly the investors' patience was wearing thin. If the present setup did not produce a return, it was unlikely that even Spencer's glib tongue could keep the project functioning.

Interest was no less keen among the gleaners of Glen Canyon gravels regarding the building of the stern-wheeler at Warm Creek and the big-scale operation of the American Placer Corporation. River traffic increased almost as much as the flow of wagons between Flagstaff and the Little Colorado. Among those who boated down river for personal impressions were Bert Seaboldt and his two employees Bert Loper and George Meiss. They pulled into the mouth of Warm Creek on the morning of December 21, saw the steamboat being framed, and, as had the Kolbs, went on to Lee's Ferry. They pitched camp nearby and became acquainted with the foreman, Frank Watson. In a few days the weather turned bitter cold and ice began running in the river. Watson invited them to move into one of the empty buildings, for which they were grateful. They examined the dredge operation and bought fruit, honey, and groceries from Frank Johnson at the ranch. They ate Christmas dinner with the Spencer crew—a welcome relief from their plain river fare. They gathered wood during the day and whiled away the evenings playing solo and poker with the men. All the while it became colder and ice soon choked the river, making their decision to remain where they were appear logical through rationalization. For several days the river was frozen solid and men crossed on foot.

Charlie Spencer came in from Cottonwood Camp on January 30 and said the steamer would not reach the ferry for at least a week, so the two men decided not to wait for it. That evening they enjoyed a final poker game, Loper ending his card-playing twelve dollars and fifty cents in the hole. They had a good breakfast in the company boarding house on the last day of January and departed upstream that afternoon.[46] Reaching Warm Creek on February 3, they saw that Charlie's estimate of the boat's completion day had not been understated. They obtained some flour, a chunk of beef, a plank from which to make a new pair of oars, and resumed their journey the following afternoon.

Early in the fall of 1911, Spencer had appeared before the county supervisors claiming that the ferryboat was inadequate to transport the heavy equipment he planned to bring to Lee's Ferry. He asked them to build a barge that could haul what the ferry couldn't. Charlie's real purpose in getting the barge built was not to transport material across the river but to use it to haul coal from Warm Creek to the ferry. It was slated to be pushed up and down the river by the new stern-wheeler. The board agreed, possibly with an assist from Bill Switzer. The county not only paid for the lumber but gave Charlie a warrant to cover the labor of the construction. Bill Switzer had not put all of his eggs in one basket: he ran for the position of county treasurer and won. He held on to his job with Spencer, however, but now divided his time between the two. By planning carefully he managed to be where he was most needed, and no one questioned his dual role.

Since the capable Albert Jones no longer was connected with his operation, Spencer had no one with the ability to stress and design a barge. Thrown together by several would-be carpenters, the barge was constructed from two-inch planks, but the gunwales also were only two by twelve. The craft was built upside-down so the planks could be nailed to the bottom. When it was complete, the men muscled it on its beam and let it fall; it broke in the middle under its own weight. The weak gunwales were repaired with splints of more two inch planks.[47] Finally launched, the empty barge was taken by the *Violet Louise* to Warm Creek where eventually it was loaded with coal. It was a difficult trip that barely succeeded.

When Spencer returned from Warm Creek at the end of January, he brought the disturbing information that the smokestack of the sternwheeler was too high to clear the ferry cable. Nobody thought of berthing the boat above the landing, so they set to work raising the cable. The right bank was relatively easy; they simply raised the cribbing. The south anchorage was another matter and the absence of a knowledgeable person affected the outcome. As no one realized the necessity of keeping the cable ninety degrees to the current, the men found it convenient to move the anchor post about fifty feet upstream while raising it to suit their need. This placed the cable at an angle to the thrust of the current. Northbound crossings were easier, but when the boat was southbound it was virtually impossible to bring it to shore except by excessive manpower. This didn't bother Spencer, however, as he had plenty of labor.

It was questionable whether Goebel would complete the Little Colorado River bridge ahead of Rosenfelt's assembly of the stern-wheeler, but the shipwright finished his job late in February while Goebel still had a month to go. The United States maritime inspectors approved the hull and boiler and then helped launch the craft from the sand bar. Rosenfelt made a few adjustments, fired up the boiler, and ran the boat off the mouth of the tributary. Spencer assembled a crew to operate the stern-wheeler and sent them upstream in the *Violet Louise*. Even though the spring rise had not started, and the silt content of the river was below normal, the bearings had to be re-babbited en route. Fortunately a mechanic named Staats was along. The other three were Pete Hanna, who supposedly had steamboat experience on the Mississippi River, Al Byers, a new employee from Flagstaff, and Leach. Rosenfelt familiarized the crew with the boat and its operation and left for San Francisco.

Hanna put enough coal on board that he estimated would suffice for a round trip. He backed out into the current and headed upriver. Despite calling for more steam, the pilot could not get the boat more than one hundred yards above the mouth of the tributary. The men looked at each other and wondered how she would ever push the empty barge if she

The *Charles H. Spencer* docked at Lee's Ferry, 1912. From left to right, captain
Pete Hanna, unidentified man, "Rip Van Winkle" Schneider, "Smitty" Smith,
Lee's ferryman Jerry Johnson, Bert Leach, and Al Byers (*Emery Kolb Collection,
Cline Library, Northern Arizona University*).

couldn't make way against the current itself. Pete Hanna then swung the
craft back into the cove, had the barge lashed alongside, and headed downstream on a flow of less than eight thousand cubic feet per second, but he
had no idea at the time how this volume related to the river's extremes.[48]

Aided by the use of long poles in the hands of Teddy Leach and Al
Byers, and occasionally by reversing the paddlewheel at sharp bends,
Hanna guided the *Charles H. Spencer* and the barge to her mooring place
that afternoon. The trip had taken a little over six hours and she had come
bow-first all the way. Fuel consumption was normal and there was plenty of
coal for the return trip. But the skipper's report that the boat was underpowered and had not been able to buck the current at Warm Creek raised
feelings of apprehension in everyone. Spencer resolved to test the boat's
power by pushing the empty barge as soon as it was unloaded. This
required about three days.

It was amazing how the news traveled: everybody in the region
wanted to see the large steamboat. Miners, prospectors, and trappers came
by boat down Glen Canyon. "One-eye" Smithy came down from Hite early
in January and waited patiently for two months. Indians rode over from as

far away as Tuba City, while cowpunchers came from Cane and House Rock. Even townspeople from Flagstaff and Kanab journeyed to see the new craft. They examined the boat minutely, posed on the deck for pictures, and questioned the crew. The company had received valuable publicity when it imported the Thomas Flyer, yet there was no effort made to capitalize on the maiden run of the stern-wheeler. Possibly the news that the boat was a failure was disseminated shortly after her arrival at the ferry.

The bargeload of coal was the only positive thing about the boat trip. Fuel shortages had hampered the entire mining operation and the smaller boilers rarely ran for more than a half day; the two large ones were in position but had never been hooked up. If the operation could function on a sustained basis by receiving sufficient coal, it would put boilers, pumps, the Lovett dredge, and the amalgamators to work. By the time the coal was unloaded and hauled to the boilers, the spring rise had set in, nearly doubling the flow on which the boat had arrived. Hanna and the crew fired up the boiler and headed upstream. The boat made progress but so slowly that it became clear she never could move the barge against the current. After struggling for more than two hours, the *Charles H. Spencer* could not surmount the bend one and one-half miles above the ferry landing. When they lashed the barge alongside, she failed to move at all once she was out in the main current. That night the entire crew was engulfed in gloom.

With this disastrous turn of events, the whole operation was suspended. Koebig returned to Los Angeles; Spencer rode to Flagstaff and took the train to Chicago. After Charlie Spencer was gone, Bill Switzer noticed that a bottle of amalgam had been left in his office, and thinking that it had been forgotten, took it with him when he returned to Flagstaff, then sent it on to the main office in Chicago. The amalgam was the product from the concentration plates and presumably contained the gold that would be recovered in a Chicago laboratory.[49] The amalgam tested as poorly as the stern-wheeler had, and even Parkyn saw no hope of continuing the operation. The investors refused to spend another dime.

After twenty-two months, Charlie Spencer's dream at Lee's Ferry exploded. When he returned later in March, most of his workmen had left, realizing that waiting for their pay was useless. Numerous bills remained unpaid in Flagstaff and would never be collected. The scene at Lee's Ferry had been changed, it seemed, forever, but now the place no longer bustled with activity. The eight forlorn stone buildings might have been a deserted village in a forsaken hinterland, the four cold boilers were the remains of an industry that had moved elsewhere, and the inactive stern-wheeler, rocking gently at her mooring, was a derelict from another age. Unlike Stanton, Charlie Spencer would return to Lee's Ferry many more times.

10

The Aftermath

CHARLIE SPENCER'S ABILITY TO PAINT A ROSY PICTURE NEVER DESERTED HIM as he tried to reassemble the pieces of his broken enterprise. He undoubtedly stretched the truth by telling his creditors that the shutdown was only temporary, and he promised to remember those who stood by him. The truth was, he had little money, no credit, and most of his workforce had gone elsewhere. But Charlie still had faith in the blue silt and his ability to generate backing to mine the Chinle Formation. Only a handful of workers remained, the ones willing to take a chance as long as Spencer fed them. Among those who hung on were John and Jesse Palmer, Bill Adams, Bob Billings, Nick Van, Fred Austin, Noan Apperson, and Frank Watson; Bert Leach and Jerry Johnson stayed for a while. Charlie had a persuasive approach: "We have this thing figured out and we need your help. If it develops, you'll have a good job."[1] Already, he was thinking of another promotion based farther upstream on the Pahreah River. John Palmer packed considerable equipment to Pahreah over several months and remained there to ride herd on it. Spencer had big plans; he even ordered five-inch pipe cut into packable lengths and transported along with hand tools and the contents of the machine shop.

Cash was Spencer's immediate problem. His only income was the $75 that the county paid him monthly as custodian of the ferry, plus auxiliary sums he wangled from time to time for work on the road or ferry. The money he turned in as ferriage never came close to his salary as custodian. He did not personally work as ferryman and dispensed a few dollars among his men just to keep some of them around. Bookkeeping was nonexistent. Bill Switzer knew the project was dead and remained in Flagstaff. Charlie settled what he could with his workmen by dispensing company equipment in lieu of wages. According to Frank Johnson, Spencer owed Jerry Johnson about $800 but never paid a cent; Jerry finally settled for a wagon and team. John Palmer claimed he was owed $1,500 one time, $2,000 another, but he received nothing. Nick Van persuaded Spencer to give him a bill of sale for two wagons, six horses, and two mules to prevent other creditors from claiming them. When the danger of attachment had passed, Charlie asked

Charles H. Spencer, no date (*P. T. Reilly Collection, Cline Library, Northern Arizona University*).

Van why he didn't return the property and Nick is reported to have said, "Don't you think I have sense enough to mind my own business?"

Spencer supposedly had four thousand pounds of mercury in seventy-six pound flasks for use on the plates of the Pierce amalgamator. He cached these under the bench in the assay office but was observed by Fred Austin who, with Jesse Palmer, removed and buried the flasks under the corral gate. Austin is said to have double-crossed Jesse, removed the flasks secretly and sold them on the open market. Apocryphal? Probably, but it is known that the company had a large number of flasks and there was no known accounting of them. Legend tells of Indians observing a team straining to pull an apparently empty wagon over the dugway.[2]

Spencer's work force diminished as the food supply was exhausted. According to Frank Johnson, Spencer owed the cattle company about six hundred dollars when Stephenson cut off his credit. Previously the miners had obtained hay, lumber, vegetables, and honey whenever there was a need and Frank merely added it to the account. The ranch had proven to be a convenient supermarket until the flow was stopped, and now the plight of the men hanging on would become serious. When it was definite that the operation was dead, Jerry Johnson unsuccessfully attempted to get his back wages. He then quit his non-paying job of ferryman early in April and went to Wyoming in another effort to persuade his wife to come south. The ferry was left without an operator, although Leach crossed a few who appeared. Bert Leach saw the handwriting on the wall, and though he was single at the time, he told Spencer that his wife was in desperate need of funds in New York City. Charlie gave him some money and Bert left for Wales, where he remained until 1914.

As fate would have it, the bridge over the Little Colorado River was completed in mid-March and formally accepted by acting Chief Engineer John Granville on March 22, 1912. If Spencer held bitter thoughts regarding his troubles at the Tanner Crossing, he could take comfort in the knowledge that Moenkopi Wash still was unbridged, even though his need had passed.

Sid Wilson was a Texas cowboy who, when he left the William F. Cody Wild West Show, went to work for the Double O outfit near Seligman in 1910. Early in 1912, he bought three Army artillery wagons at Peach Springs and set out in one of them to look for a ranch. He arrived at Lee's Ferry and took a job packing for Charlie Spencer, moving equipment from Lee's Ferry to Cottonwood Camp. On one such trip, he was ascending the trail when the stern-wheeler pulled away from her mooring and headed slowly upstream. She failed to get past the first bend and turned back downstream before Wilson was half-way up the trail. He saw this happen a second time, but on that occasion the steamer got somewhat farther, yet was headed for her mooring again before he topped out. He did not know who was on board.[3] Wilson's observation indicates that although the *Charles H. Spencer* never returned to Warm Creek, at least two more attempts were made and possibly these have become mistaken over the years with actual round trips.

To feed the few remaining workers, Charlie Spencer decided to plant a garden on the small bench across the creek from the ranch house and to preempt Bar Z water. He obtained a quantity of seed packets from Flagstaff and when Frank made a trip to Kanab, the men moved in to take advantage of the more pliable and less experienced LeRoy Johnson. Quickly they cleared and leveled the plot, then ran a line of five-inch pipe to the ranch ditch. LeRoy's protests were brushed aside. Frank returned in about five days and was told the story. He rode to Cane and laid the problem in the lap of Eph Mansfield who, after reflecting overnight, told him not to go out of his way to cause trouble, to do what he thought best, but not to let Spencer have water when it was needed at the ranch.

Frank Johnson put a dam across the miners' diversion and turned the water onto the alfalfa. This brought three Spencer men on the double and a minor confrontation ensued. They tried to bluff him, but Frank stood his ground and warned them to leave his dam alone. After that they came to the ranch and asked if they could have a little water, a request usually granted. Spencer's drifters were no better at farming than they were at building rock houses or barges; they failed to raise a crop. Frank took a look at their plot and noted that the melon seed had been planted in hills twelve to fourteen inches high where the water could not possibly reach the roots. Nothing came up and the first minor flood took out the pipeline, ending their adventure in farming.

In March, Spencer audaciously presented his bill to the county supervisors for raising the ferry cable to clear the smokestack of the steamer that couldn't go upriver, but they deferred action on it. On July 1, the board issued a warrant for $841 against the road fund in favor of the American Placer Corporation.[4] It is doubtful that any of the company officers ever learned about it, but the money was a godsend to Charlie. The taxpayers were not asked their opinions.

With Leach's departure coming on top of Jerry Johnson's defection, Spencer knew that to keep his salary as custodian coming he must have a dependable ferryman. He approached Frank Johnson who was still operating the ranch for the cattle company. Frank agreed to take the job if Spencer would endorse the county check directly to him. Charlie consented and even gave him the first check. Then two months went by without payment and Frank took matters into his own hands. He collected the kitchen utensils, a tent, a blacksmith outfit, and other articles as ransom. When Spencer came around, Jerry told him what Frank had done and said he would return everything when he was paid. Later in the year, Spencer finally settled for his keeping such equipment as would satisfy the unpaid claim.

The 1912 runoff in the Colorado basin changed the immediate landscape at Lee's Ferry more than in any year since Caucasian settlement. It began in March and was sustained with only minor decreases until it reached 102,300 cubic feet per second on June 5, peaked at Yuma on June 22 at 244,000 cubic feet per second, and was 108,500 cubic feet per second on June 24. For almost three weeks the river flow exceeded 100,000 cubic feet per second, and it came down only gradually.[5] The protracted high flow deposited great quantities of sediment along the Pahreah delta and across the mouth of that tributary; massive deposits were left along the length of the Colorado River. At the same time, the Pahreah watershed received no significant precipitation, certainly not enough to enable the creek to reestablish its channel through the siltbank. Instead, it followed the course of least resistance and flowed southwest behind the siltbank, ultimately to capture the lower part of the first channel along the right side of the delta and to move its mouth nearly a mile downstream.[6]

Agnes Spencer, Charlie's first wife, died in Denver on June 12, 1912. Art Waller was working as a draftsman for an engineering firm. He learned of Mrs. Spencer's death when Charlie suddenly appeared at the office and asked him to be a pall bearer. Waller agreed, and after the funeral Spencer unfolded his plan for Pahreah and asked Art to join him. Preferring an outdoor life to one in the office, Waller accepted even though he was aware that his paydays likely would come to an end. He said he wanted to complete the job on which he was working and it would be about six weeks before he could leave. Spencer and Waller took the train to Flagstaff, picked up Charlie's younger brother Ernest, and Sam Day, then all four rode to Lee's Ferry. At the time, Spencer still had half a dozen men hanging on plus considerable equipment that he was moving to Pahreah as fast as John Palmer could pack it. After a short stay at the ferry, they went up the Spencer Trail and reached Pahreah townsite on the second day. They found Bert Parkyn and his wife, who had left Chicago to get away from the criticism of the other creditors. The doctor had hopes of recouping the losses sustained at Lee's Ferry.

Charlie Spencer gave another example of his persuasive ability on October 19, 1912. He got Frank Johnson to resign as postmaster of Lee's Ferry so that Charlie could succeed him. Spencer not only became postmaster but remained as custodian of the ferry, even though his residence was Pahreah, almost fifty miles upstream. Several Spencer employees confirmed that Charlie regularly sent a man on horseback to carry his mail to Lee's Ferry, from where a Navajo carrier took it to Tuba City and on to Flagstaff. His act takes on added dimensions because Pahreah had postmasters continuously from 1893 until 1915: Effie Adams, appointed June 19, 1911, and Maud Apperson, appointed on August 31, 1912.[7]

Two more Johnson boys—Price and Jody—returned from Wyoming in 1912. Jerry later wrote Frank for some money because he wanted to bring his Pearly with him. Frank responded in true brotherly fashion, and Jerry arrived with a pregnant Pearly in mid-August. Both Jody and Jerry were put on the Bar Z payroll, the latter helping Frank at the ferry, the former assigned to oversee the horse herd at South Canyon. LeRoy Johnson went off the payroll as Jerry went on, indicating a familial sharing of jobs. Before LeRoy left, Frank decided to correct Spencer's mislocation of the left ferry anchorage. He no longer had Spencer's manpower to pull the boat to the left landing and he wanted to make the repair while LeRoy could help. Choosing a solid ledge about fifty feet upstream, they drilled a hole ten feet deep. The anchor itself was a ten-inch pipe reinforced with an eight-inch pipe inside and both packed with sand. The cable was one and one-quarter inches in diameter and six hundred feet long. By using two heavy block-and-tackles and a quantity of one-half-inch cable, they moved the main cable to the new anchor.

Pearly Johnson refused to live at the ferry, so Jerry was forced to quit at the end of November and take her back to Wyoming. As 1912 came to an end, Frank and his family were alone at the river, operating the Bar Z ranch for which he was paid and the ferry for which Spencer was paid. Eph Mansfield solved the labor problem when he sent Tom Caffall with his wife Allie and infant daughter to Lee's Ferry on April 23, 1913. Caffall was a farmer, not a cowboy, and would be more useful at the ranch than on the range. Too, he could help Frank operate the ferry. He received a rude breaking in.

It was before mid-June and the river was near its peak when a south-bound traveler appeared and asked to be crossed. Frank was apprehensive due to the high water, but he reluctantly consented when the man urged him. As he was about to shove off, Caffall came up and climbed aboard. About forty feet from the left bank, after the forward fall had been let out to bring the boat in squarely to shore, the boat grounded and could not be budged. Frank took a coiled line and got in the skiff, playing the rope out as he rowed to shore while sitting on the end of the coil. Just as he was ready to step out of the skiff, the traveler pulled the line, which fell in the river, and the ferryboat began moving toward midstream. When it hit the current beam-on, it began to dip and the water poured over the upstream gunwale. Tom moved to the downstream side as the boat dipped a second time and water poured completely over the deck. At that instant the cable broke close to the left anchor and came down where Tom had been standing a moment before, jamming itself on the corner of the ferry; it barely missed Frank and the rowboat. The right anchor held and the ferry was swung as on a tether toward the right bank. Frank crossed in the skiff and then wilted.

Three days passed before Frank felt like jousting with the river again. Finally, he took the light wagon apart and in three or four trips had it on the left bank, and he swam the horses one at a time. When the traveler resumed his journey, he carried word of the mishap to the county officials. Frank then requested payment for operating the ferry, thus revealing that Spencer was collecting the money without doing the work. According to county records, Spencer had turned in $224.98 in Lee's Ferry tolls after the fiscal year ended on June 30, 1913. In the same period, he had collected in custodian and spe-cial-service warrants a sum of $1,741.63, netting him $1,516.65. Outside of endorsing one $75 check to Frank Johnson and dispensing a minimal sum to Bert Leach, it was clear profit with no physical labor.

Frank also told county officials that he was leaving to take care of some personal business and there would be no one at the river to cross trav-elers, even in the skiff.[8] But before he left, he and Caffall made a pair of sweeps and put fulcrum-posts on the ferryboat. County officials sent Charlie Greene, a one-time helper to the county road superintendent, to take care of travelers at the ferry until other arrangements could be made. Greene worked from July 19 to August 3; he could not handle crossings in the skiff and returned to Flagstaff. In September, he received a warrant for

From left to right, Tom, Nell, and Allie Caffall; Bill Langton; and Charles H. Spencer, seated in the harness shed at Lee's Ferry, summer 1913 (*A. C. Waller photograph, P. T. Reilly Collection, Cline Library, Northern Arizona University*).

$37.50 as pay for the sixteen days he had put in. County officials also sent George McCormick and his team to haul contractors Wilson and Coffin to Lee's Ferry in an effort to salvage the cable. They worked about a week but were not successful breaking it loose from the silt. They finally cut it and recommended ordering a new one. The firm's effort cost the taxpayers $166.20. In the meeting of August 4, 1913, the county supervisors took the custodianship of the ferry from C. H. Spencer and gave it to the Grand Canyon Cattle Company. The contract was to run for five years and pay $75 per month.

Despite the draining of his resources, Frank had accumulated a little money and intended to purchase a homestead or a place at Hurricane. Jerry had brought Pearly back again and found property at Hurricane that she liked better than at Lee's Ferry. With the cable out of commission and Caffall to care for the crops, Frank felt justified in taking some time off. He was gone for six weeks, returning in mid-August. He missed a notable visitor.

After the debacle of the 1912 presidential election, Theodore Roosevelt planned a hunting trip on the Kaibab and a pack trip to Rainbow Bridge with his sons Quentin and Archie, and his nephew Nicholas. The latter made arrangements with Dave Rust to provide a guide, packer, cook, wrangler, pack outfit, and riding stock. Dave obtained the services of Scott Dunham, who agreed to meet the Roosevelts and Jesse Cummings of Mesa, who would serve as packer, cook, and wrangler, at the Rust tram on July 15. Meanwhile, E. J. Marshall and his general manager Henry Stephenson had arranged to bring a cattle-buying customer, George W. Ballentine of Denver, to the Rust tram on the same day, and had requested Eph Mansfield to meet them there with saddle horses. Both parties spent the night of July 14 at El Tovar and then used Fred Harvey mules to reach the tram, but the Roosevelt group started earlier and got there one-half hour sooner.

Aged Eph Mansfield managed to crank the cage over to the north side and was quite surprised when the Roosevelts stepped out instead of his employers and their guest. He was overjoyed, however, to meet President Roosevelt, and he inquired if they had seen the party he was expecting. The Roosevelts were just as curious regarding the whereabouts of their guide and saddle horses. As they discussed the matter, a shot was fired on the south side to signal the arrival of the Bar Z party. This time the Roosevelts, Nicholas, Quentin, and Archie winched the cable car across the river and then back with Marshall, Stephenson, and Ballentine aboard. Both groups were delighted at the coincidence and Stephenson suggested they all remain at Camp Rust that evening and get an early morning start for the rim, more than a vertical mile above them. That night the former president and the general manager talked until late about hunting, ranching, and United States relations with Mexico—the latter a subject of deep concern to the cattle barons.

There were not enough horses to go around, so Nicholas, Archie, and Jesse Cummings started on foot at 2:45 A.M. Those on mounts caught them in a few hours and they all topped out together. They found Scott Dunham at the trailhead, preparing to start for the river; somehow, he had confused the dates. Roosevelt paid him off and decided to get along without him. Stephenson and Uncle Jimmy Owens loaned them some stock, and the old lion hunter guided them for two weeks of hunting. On August 1, they started for House Rock Valley, guided by Lester Dalton, a Bar Z cowboy. They camped that night at Jacob's Pools and next day were welcomed by the Caffalls at Lee's Ferry. Tom was given a note signed by Eph Mansfield, but not written by him, asking that the Roosevelts be given chickens, produce, or anything they needed. Allie Caffall was impressed by the former president's display of affection when he put his arm around Quentin as they walked to the melon patch.[9]

Nicholas Roosevelt had arranged with Lorenzo Hubbell to have an outfit meet them at the ferry and conduct them to the Wetherill post at Kayenta. They were pleased to learn that he had sent a Navajo cook and a Mexican teamster in a good wagon with four mules for their use. The outfit had arrived two days previously and was encamped on the river's left bank. The party remained over Sunday, but crossed most of the outfit that afternoon in order to make an early start on Monday morning. Tom Caffall and Lester Dalton loaded the ferry and manned the sweeps. As the work was progressing, Teddy Roosevelt sat with Allie Caffall, thanked her for their hospitality, and issued a standing invitation to have dinner with him at the White House. He said, "If I don't live there, you will be just as welcome at Oyster Bay."[10]

Former President Theodore Roosevelt chopping wood at Lee's Ferry, 1912 (*P. T. Reilly Collection, Cline Library, Northern Arizona University*).

Frank Johnson returned to work a few days after the Roosevelts had crossed, but it was not a happy homecoming. He and Tom Caffall had a disagreement about farming procedures and their relationship became strained; possibly Frank considered Tom to be overbearing and he no longer felt comfortable in the house that his father built. It was his nature to avoid a confrontation if possible, so he decided to let Tom operate the ranch while he managed the ferry. During the fall of 1913, he began building a log cabin at the ferry landing, but construction progressed slowly because of his frequent comings and goings. In September, he filed on a homestead at Short Creek while Jerry and his family were living at Hurricane. However, Jerry helped him build the ferryman's house, which was livable before spring. Eph Mansfield gave a twenty-five dollar Christmas bonus to four Bar Z employees, including Frank and Tom. Relations were healed somewhat by Christmas Day as they took their families in two skiffs and rowed into Glen Canyon. According to Allie Caffall, they floated back to the ferry in a light snowstorm.

Charlie Spencer's need for money was more acute than at any time in his life. The Lee's Ferry Post Office was discontinued on January 31, 1914, and afterwards mail came from Tuba City and Kanab about once a month. The Spencer promotion at Pahreah never got off the ground and was completely dead by the end of 1914 with no resources to pay a caretaker. Charlie was in and out of Lee's Ferry often, gathering some of his old ox yokes for the trading posts to sell to tourists. In January 1914, the Coconino County supervisors finally received a new cable from the Monson, Dunnigan, Ryan Company at a cost of $111.30. Charlie Spencer proved that he still had some influence when he wangled the contract to freight the cable and fittings to the ferry for a fee of $490 and another warrant of $432.75 for road work.[11] It was remarkable how he continued to reap inflated rewards from the taxpayers of Coconino County.

Frank Johnson's intermittent attendance as ferryman failed to provide service when needed, and Mansfield persuaded Jerry Johnson to help out. Jerry took the children by his first wife and went to the ferry in late January. He worked through June, made periodic trips to Hurricane, and was aided by Frank, who made the Bar Z payroll in February, March, and June. Both brothers left Bar Z employ at that time to work on their own land at Hurricane and Short Creek.

Tom Caffall came down with typhoid fever in April 1914, and Allie, with the help of Jerry's twelve-year-old daughter Wilma, managed to get him to the doctor in Kanab. He is thought to have picked up the disease by drinking from the polluted Pahreah River. Mansfield sent Nate Petty and Carl Antille to replace Caffall and operate the ferry, but this work was demeaning to the cowboys and nobody was satisfied. Petty and Antille held on until August, when Eph Mansfield sent Tom and Blanche Richards to help the Caffalls, who had just returned. At the same time, Eph persuaded Frank and Jerry to alternate as ferry operators. Both were capable, and he didn't care which one was there so long as one of them was. He turned the county check over to them and they shared it as they saw fit. By splitting the ferry responsibilities, Jerry and Frank took care of the job yet each spent time at his second home. Too, Frank always had things to do on his homestead at Short Creek— a natural camping place between the ferry and Hurricane—and both brothers usually spent at least one night there as they went back and forth.

While Caffall was away at Jacob's Pools for supplies on April 26, his wife and the Richards had retired when, close to midnight, Allie was awakened by someone scratching at the screen. She sat up, saw the figure of a man, and screamed. Tommy Richards dressed and came downstairs. The man was one of two who had ridden bicycles out of Utah and were headed south. His companion had bedded down in the field but this fellow was hungry and wanted a good meal. He grumbled at the bread and milk Tommy set out and was asked if he expected chicken at midnight. He ate everything in sight, then took the offered blanket and slept in the hay. Next morning the women fed the men a good breakfast and they went on to the ferry. Johnson had seen a dromedary cross there in 1879, and he had seen bicycles before, but had never known of one being used for such an extended trip. No fee was specified for this mode of travel, so he charged each man one dollar for being crossed.[12]

Although two dozen automobiles were said to have been driven to the opening of the bridge across the Little Colorado in 1912, few cars ventured beyond that point, even to Tuba City. The narrow tread of the high-pressure tires simply was not designed for travel on the wagon roads in this sandy country. Nevertheless, an automobile came out of Utah, surmounted the grades of Buckskin Mountain and the Badger sand to arrive at the ferry on August 22, 1914. One of the Johnson boys crossed the car and driver, then watched as they chugged along the dugway where Costa had drawn the line, and continued south. The ferriage was three dollars, the same as for a wagon. On November 4, another daring driver repeated the trip, and by late 1915 several cars had crossed in a single month.[13]

Tom Caffall's mother died at Cannonville on November 21, and Art Waller, who had gone to work there for Bishop Henderson after the Spencer enterprise folded, volunteered to carry the tidings to the ferry. He made most of his ride during the daylight but hit the head of the trail that Spencer's crew had "improved" on a dark, moonless night. He managed to come down by giving the horse his head and hanging on to his tail. He had planned to break the bad news gently, but blurted it out instead.

After the failure of his promotion at Pahreah Charlie Spencer turned to water development in the San Francisco Peaks. As a base for a new corporation, he and a companion, with two saddle and three pack horses, crossed at Lee's Ferry on March 15, 1915. The pair staked thirty-two claims between the ferry and Jacob's Pools, even jumping water sources that the Bar Z had used for years. They crossed again on the twenty-seventh and headed for Flagstaff to record their millsites and water rights.[14] They paid no ferriage either time, although they might have promised to pay in the future.

On June 6, Dr. Herbert E. Gregory, with three companions, four saddle and four pack horses, crossed the river at Lee's Ferry and went into camp on the right bank. This was the beginning of field work that ultimately led to a classic publication on the geology of the region.[15] They went up the Spencer Trail the next day and duplicated part of the trip Jones and George Spencer had made in 1910. The geologists, however, found the region unmarked by trails. Possibly their recognition-level was equivalent to that of the Spaniards, Domínguez and Escalante.

Despite the lapse of a quarter-century, the Mormon wounds resulting from the Woodruff Manifesto had not healed completely. For a while the question that burned in Mormondom was "When will the manifesto be repealed?" It wasn't, but as time went on the great majority of Saints followed the stated policies of the church and remained in good standing. A minority of the brethren clung to pre-manifesto views, however, charging that the plurality of wives was a God-given tenet of the faith and the true Mormon would not abandon any part of the plan that assured eternal salvation. They further charged that the manifesto was not a revelation from God but a surrender to the federal government in order to retain church property and gain statehood for Utah. But not all of the separatists thought alike on the question, and the dissidents broke into a number of splinter groups, each claiming to represent the pure teaching of Joseph Smith. By 1913, several of those nonconformists had settled at Short Creek, practically on the Utah-Arizona border. A few orthodox Mormons, attracted by the land and water, settled there among them.

Just as Warren Johnson had not accepted the manifesto as having been directed at him, his eldest son clung to the Mormon social structure under which he was raised. Except for his first wife's preference for death rather than sharing her husband with another woman, Jerry probably would have become a bigamist in 1908. In sharp contrast, his full brother Frank believed in the orthodox Church of Jesus Christ of Latter-day Saints. Jerry not only was attracted to splinter-group fundamentalism, but he added his own interpretations. Furthermore, he tried to impose his outdated beliefs on his blood brothers and sisters, an act that eventually split the Johnsons between orthodoxy and heterodoxy. The problem that Warren Johnson had failed to solve in life returned to haunt his posterity after his death. Five of the six remaining Johnson boys were in monogamous marriages by the end of 1914: Warren Elmer married Miss Viola Spencer on August 26, 1913; Price W. married Miss Esther C. Heaton on September 17, 1914; and LeRoy S. married Miss Josephine Ford on December 10, 1914.[16] Jerry and Frank already were married, and Jody would not end his bachelorhood until 1920. But for the time being, the Johnson heterodoxy was all pre-manifesto iconoclastic rhetoric.

Early in September the Coconino County supervisors indicated their concern for travelers finding their way in the northland by having road signs with mileages erected between Flagstaff and Lee's Ferry. The Automobile Club of Southern California obtained the contract, then billed the county $1,000; they received a warrant for $872, which apparently was satisfactory.[17] On December 2, 1914, the supervisors formally appointed Jerry Johnson as the Lee's Ferry custodian and raised his salary to $100 per month, effective from August 1.[18] Stephenson signed a waiver to allow direct payment, as the contract with the cattle company had not expired.

River runners continued to pass Lee's Ferry, whether the Johnsons knew it or not. If J. H. Hummel paused at Lee's Ferry when he traversed the drainage from Green River, Utah, to Bright Angel Creek in late August and September, he did not impress the Johnsons enough to be remembered. In any event, he left no record there and the first anyone knew of his presence was when he startled some tourists at Bright Angel on December 2. Charlie Russell, on a repeat river trip, and Goddard Quist arrived at the ferry on December 12 and spent the night. Their two wood-hulled boats were sheathed with galvanized iron—the second to be used by any river runner in Cataract, Glen, Marble, or Grand canyons. Not being as adept as Flavell or Galloway, the men sank one boat at Bright Angel, pulled the *Ross Wheeler* up on the talus near the Bass Cable, and walked out on the Bass Trail.[19]

During the fall of 1914, Stephenson gave his approval to the installation of a trading counter in the large kitchen of the Johnson house.

Navajos often came there to obtain staple groceries for which they usually paid with blankets. Although many were taken in this trade, their disposal has not been recorded. Stephenson and Mansfield frequently remained overnight at the ranch house as they traveled between Cane and Flagstaff. Eph and the Caffalls, being devout Mormons, always knelt at the breakfast table for morning prayers. Mansfield explained this to the general manager, thinking he might join them. Instead, he said, "That's all right, go ahead." He then sat at the table and read a newspaper while the others communed with the Lord.[20]

By mid-April of 1915, the Caffalls had accumulated enough money to purchase a home, and they left the Lee's Ferry ranch. Tom had been on the Bar Z payroll two years. Tom and Blanche Richards operated the ranch for the remainder of the year, assisted by Carl Antille whom Eph Mansfield sent from Cane. Jerry Johnson and several members of his first family lived in the cabin at the ferry. Pearly seemed more or less content to live at Hurricane and had a child born there in February 1915.

Stephenson began to juggle his herds in 1915. His discussion of Mexican politics with Roosevelt had not been casual; he and Marshall were concerned about the future of the Palomas Ranch and whether large American holdings would be protected in the ebb and flow of the volatile Mexican upheaval. Although Pancho Villa and his ragtag army commandeered cattle and especially horses as needed, they paid for them in gold, which was more than the Mexican or United States armies did. After Obregon defeated Villa in April 1915, it appeared that the United States would recognize Carranza as president with possible serious consequences for American-owned mines and ranches. The fear became reality in October, but the cattle company's management had guessed correctly and had arranged to decrease the Palomas herd. Some of their Mexican cattle were moved to Bar Z, and the cattle on that range were dispersed elsewhere.

In June, Stephenson had four thousand head removed from the House Rock-Kaibab range and driven to the railroad at Flagstaff. Mansfield wanted to swim the herd at Lee's Ferry as there was no feed on either side of the river to sustain them while a week of ferrying was underway. He and Frank Johnson selected the site above the ferry where the right-hand wall was relatively close to the bank and the water was quiet. They ferried about a hundred head to the left bank where they could be seen by the remainder. Eph made the mistake of trying to move the herd into the water when the sun was in the west, bouncing its rays directly into the eyes of the animals. They would not enter the river, but the riders urged those in the rear forward and a number were drowned. Frank finally convinced Eph that he was not doing it correctly. The cattle should be put in the water early in the morning when the sun was behind them. The operation went like clockwork shortly after daylight next morning. The small herd was bawling on the left shore, Frank was in the rowboat to prevent the animals from heading downstream, and the main herd willingly entered the river. Years afterward, Frank recalled the sight with great satisfaction—the white faces, seemingly without end, slanted across the river. But the previous afternoon effort had cost more than a hundred steers.

In September the Bar Z drove 1,100 cattle to Flagstaff, followed by a shipment of 1,253 head in November. The total crossing at Lee's Ferry in 1915 was 6,239 head, with about 100 charged to experience.[21] The shipments however were not all outbound. In September the Bar Z bought 3,000 Durham heifers from Palomas. Stephenson applied for a permit from the Forest Service to drive them to House Rock Valley, but was refused after local cattlemen protested. How the astute manager got around this roadblock has not been revealed, but he did, and 1,910 of the Durhams were on the Bar Z range in October.[22] The other third went to another of the company's ranches.

Tommy and Blanche Richards left the ranch at the end of February 1916. Mansfield persuaded Frank Johnson to take over its operation, assisted by Carl Antille—an arrangement not relished by the Mormon. Nevertheless, Frank started the job in March and he and Jerry helped each other at both ranch and ferry. When Antille quit in mid-May, the brothers had everything to themselves.

The Christmas issue of the *Coconino Sun* had an article about a proposed highway from Mexico to Canada, slated to cross the Colorado on a bridge at Lee's Ferry. This project was not aborted; late in 1937 it came to full birth as Highway 89 after nearly a quarter-century. In 1915, the ferry operation cost Coconino County about three times as much as it took in. The custodian's salary was one hundred dollars per month; tolls rarely exceeded twenty-five dollars. Jerry Johnson was the officially designated custodian from August 1, 1914, to June 1, 1918, but Frank was on the job at least half of this period. The brothers had no trouble in dividing the salary and both were honest in collecting and turning in ferry fees. The county officials were aware of the trade-offs but felt as Mansfield did about the matter. Jerry was unanimously re-appointed at the beginning of 1916. The tolls for the fiscal year ending June 30, 1916, amounted to $241.

Frank remembered how, early in 1916, he and Jerry found the ferryboat had sunk during the night. The planks had rotted and given away, allowing the offshore end of the boat to submerge. As repairs were out of the question, they decided to use the old, smaller boat that had been forsaken on the bank because of its size. Getting it floated took considerable labor as it had been abandoned on a steep slope. After several days of digging, they got the boat to the water, transferred the tackle, then realized that the sunken ferry blocked the landing. The derelict could not be moved, so they close-hauled the small boat and berthed it on the upstream beam. They did not even impart news of the change to the county officials, although Stephenson and Mansfield knew of it.

After more than thirty-eight years, the Arizona experience turned sour for pioneer Joseph Fish. His father-in-law and leader Jesse N. Smith had died in 1906, and the failure of the eleventh Woodruff dam on February 16, 1915, prompted his return to Utah. It took a year to wind up his affairs, dispose of his property, and gather his outfit. With his wife and five children he left Woodruff on April 12, 1916, with all of their possessions loaded on three wagons. They reached the left-bank of the Colorado on the twenty-second but found it too late to get across. Jerry and Frank crossed them the following day and invited them to camp at the ranch.[23] Although Fish had done considerable traveling between Utah and Arizona during his life in the south, he still noted many changes not only at the ferry but at the old watering places on the pioneer road. But some things had not changed; he was forced to double-team several times on the new road over Buckskin Mountain. This was his last trip over the route of migration. He died a decade later, never again leaving Utah.

Some progress was being made in the country, as Hubert Richardson, in 1916, built a trading post near the new bridge at the Little Colorado. Later the bridge and town were named after Senator Ralph H. Cameron, and a post office was established there in 1924. The long haul from Flagstaff now could be made without a side-trip to Tuba City. Stephenson began traveling by auto in December 1915; his vehicle was the last to be carried on the ferry that sank. Any car or wagon had to be positioned close to the center of the small ferry, and the crossing was precarious at best. In high water, neither Jerry nor Frank Johnson dared to take the risk. Most traffic was made by Indians trading blankets for food staples at the Bar Z ranch house. According to the ferry ledger, six autos crossed at Lee's Ferry in 1916.

One of Charlie Spencer's better schemes was his water-collection plan in the San Francisco Peaks. He proposed to construct a series of concrete catchment troughs, pipe the snowmelt to bentonite-lined craters that were natural reservoirs, and disperse the precious water to Flagstaff and as far away as Grand Canyon. His main prospective client was the Santa Fe Railroad, and he initiated correspondence with G. W. Harris, chief engineer. Harris gave the death knell to Charlie's plan on August 30, 1915, when he rejected it "due to prohibitive expense to develop."[24] The indefatigable Spencer did not roll over with this setback; on November 3, he formed the Coconino Water Development and Stock Company under the laws of Arizona. The assets were the thirty-two water rights and mill sites between Lee's Ferry and Soap Creek, but none had been developed and all had lapsed. Spencer did not like the regulations of a public utility company and, near the end of 1916, he issued a prospectus of a new operation, calling it the Northern Arizona Livestock and Ranch Company, which was never incorporated.

The appearance of his new company coincided with his finding a new source of venture capital—R. N. Burgess of San Francisco. The Coconino Water Development and Stock Company was reorganized on January 6, 1917, with Burgess agreeing to advance seventy thousand dollars.

From left to right, Pearl, Byron, Harold, Annie, and Jerry Johnson at the Johnson ranch house, 1917 (*P. T. Reilly Collection, Cline Library, Northern Arizona University*).

Charlie emphasized that his assets included four large boilers in place at Lee's Ferry, eight stone buildings at both the ferry and Warm Creek, mining claims, equipment, and cabins at Pahreah. The steamer, now resting at an oblique angle and mostly out of water, was not mentioned, but the thirty-two water claims were regarded as valid. If Spencer realized that his claimed assets were invalid, he gave no indication.

Jerry Johnson was unanimously reappointed custodian of Lee's Ferry at the board meeting of January 12, 1917, and Frank managed the ranch for the cattle company. The brothers operated as they had in the past, helping each other with the labors of both. They continued to travel between Lee's Ferry and Hurricane, each time—Jerry especially—anticipating a layover at Short Creek. Jerry's preaching and his brand of pre-manifesto religion divided the family. Price, Elmer, LeRoy, and his elder sister Lizzie agreed with Jerry; Lizzie was even stronger in fundamentalist beliefs. She and her husband O. F. Colvin had been advised to move to Short Creek in 1914 by highly respected David H. Cannon. Not all citizens of Short Creek were polygamists, but they all believed in the fundamentalist doctrine relating to plural marriage. Mary, Frank, and Jody opposed Jerry's views and resisted his arguments. Lydia wavered between the two, vacillating first to one side, then the other. The division was not along the lines of Warren Johnson's first and second families, as Mary, LeRoy, and Jody were Permelia's children; Jerry, Frank, Lydia, Price, and Elmer were Samantha's. There was much inter-family proselyting as each faction tried to change the views of the other.

A milestone of sorts was achieved on May 16, 1917, when D. W. Hopkins accompanied Dolph Andruss of Bluff, Utah, in the latter's Maxwell roadster on a tour from Colorado to St. George. Unaware that the Zahn brothers had driven an air-cooled Franklin from Los Angeles to their camp at Mile 42 on the San Juan River in September 1915, Hopkins claimed theirs was the first automobile trip through Monument Valley. He even coined the term "Monumental Highway" and documented the trip with photographs along the way, and later he presented albums of the trek to Indian traders who had provided hospitality.[25] Jerry Johnson was so impressed that he gave free ferriage to the car.

Henry Stephenson probably crossed the river in the Bar Z car more than any other traveler. He became exasperated at the time required to position his vehicle in the correct place on the small ferry. He appeared before the Coconino County supervisors during their monthly meeting on April 3, 1918, to explain the problem. When Henry spoke, people listened, and in no time at all the supervisors authorized the county engineer to draw plans and construct a new ferryboat with dimensions of fourteen by forty feet.[26] County Engineer J. B. Wright drew the plan and had the required material delivered to the ferry. He built the boat with the aid of Frank Johnson, who was custodian at the time.

The residents of Flagstaff apparently were no more qualified to design a ferryboat than those of Salt Lake City, and the county engineer just as obdurate in taking advice from the ferryman as had been the ecclesiastics of Utah. Wright's plan called for a scow that would have been acceptable for use on a calm-water lake but not on the Colorado River. The gunwales were too shallow, the sides too box-straight with no flare. Frank wanted deeper gunwales and flared beams, especially on the upstream side so the current would slide under the boat instead of over and into it. Wright was inflexible, insisting they follow the plan. The engineer remained until the bottom planks were spiked to the gunwales, and the craft was turned over and floated. They installed the anchor bolts and rings, pulled it up to the cable, and hooked up the block and tackles. Then Wright returned to Flagstaff, leaving Frank the job of installing the deck.

As soon as Wright was out of sight, Frank modified the craft more to his liking. Using gussets and extra planks, he provided flare by making a false beam to deflect the water downward; thus, the man who had received less than three months of schooling improved the design of the county engineer. Frank had no way of making deeper gunwales, and this boat, even with the flare, dipped water on all but the lowest flows. Frank even built a corral in the center of the boat so the livestock could not crowd to the ends when water washed aboard, but he knew the craft's deficiencies and was very careful in its operation.[27]

Jerry Johnson, succumbing to his wife's pressure, had not been at the ferry for several months and submitted his resignation as custodian. The supervisors accepted it with regret at their June meeting and unanimously approved the application of Frank Johnson, starting June 1, 1918. At this time, the salary was raised to one hundred ten dollars per month.[28] Navajos now exceeded Caucasians in ferry crossings and autos outnumbered wagons. Riders and men on foot were not unusual, but over all there wasn't much traffic. The number of cars varied from one to six per month, although on August 17, 1918, two automobiles crossed on the same day. On October 7, the first motorcycle was ferried for a dollar fifty.

After the entry of the United States into World War I on April 6, 1917, some stockmen decided to move onto the Bar Z range. Bill Shumway led the way by squatting on a waterhole on House Rock Wash about five miles south of Jacob's Pools. He called his spread the "Bar Quarter Circle F." Shumway sold the place to the four Pratt brothers: Ernest, Orson, Lorum, and Elwin. Another squatter was Tyson L. Bean. With his wife and two sons, he came in on the road from Flagstaff and crossed the ferry on November 4, 1917. He had one hundred cattle, a wagon, an auto, and a .30–.30. He, too, settled on House Rock wash nearly two miles downstream from the Pratts and named his ranch "The Bean Hole." The Bar Z cattlemen did not move him. The Beans were a tough family. Tyson, a strong two hundred pounder, didn't back off from anybody. The men all packed six-guns, and Mrs. Bean could ride, rope, and swear with any cowboy. Bean made occasional trips to Flagstaff, and it was rumored that on his return he usually had the carcass of a Navajo calf in his car. Moreover, it was suspected that the main item in the family's diet was Bar Z beef. If this was true, they were too clever to be caught.

The United States Forest Service began to question the unlimited ranging of Bar Z stock on federal lands, and Stephenson saw it was only a matter of time before herd size must be reduced. He and Marshall had clout but preferred to settle their problems locally whenever possible. To reduce their herds, Bar Z resumed the cattle drives in the fall of 1918 with 1,113 head being crossed on November 14. By this time, Mansfield had learned the technique of getting large herds across the river. They ferried 309 cattle, 37 horses, and the chuck wagon on the afternoon before, using them as bait on the left bank. Early next morning, the others were driven into the water and they swam across with no difficulty, hitting the trail to Flagstaff by midmorning. The ferry bill was $76.20.[29]

LeRoy Johnson was put on the Bar Z payroll in November, taking the place of Jerry who now was active at Hurricane. Eph Mansfield generously allowed the Johnson boys to switch jobs as they saw fit, for he had no intention of forcing his regular cowboys to become ranch hands and ferrymen. Jody Johnson was discharged from the Army and joined the Bar Z in July 1919. His main job was working with the horse herd at South Canyon, breeding mares, cutting pine poles for corrals, and keeping the waterholes open. The company had nearly five hundred head, including stallions, geldings, mares, colts, and mules. The animals were trailed to Lee's Ferry for the winter and ranged along the Pahreah River.

As an illustration of the high regard the Indians still held for Warren Johnson, Jody related how in 1919 he was riding from South Canyon to the ferry, and met an elderly Navajo en route. They exchanged names and Jody said he was Ba'hazoona Begay (son of Ba'hazoona). The Navajo embraced him, took a bracelet from his arm, put it on Jody's, and patted him on the back.[30] During his first winter at Lee's Ferry, Jody noted a constant flow of Indians to buy supplies. They usually camped a day or two beside the fence at the lower alfalfa field. He saw them mixing bread dough by squirting water from the mouth as needed. If the dough still was too stiff, they simply ran to the creek for another mouthful.

According to the Mansfield ledger, Carl Antille worked periodically for the Bar Z from November 1914 to September 1918, part of this time as a helper at the ferry. An unpopular man, he was judged to be a marginal cowboy and was laid off when work became slack. Mansfield assigned him the job of developing Navajo Spring in anticipation of the November drive to Flagstaff. Antille was paid $296.50 for this work; then Eph found out he had slaughtered Bar Z beef for himself and a companion named Frank Geer. On September 24, Mansfield had them arrested and charged with rustling. The case was scheduled to be heard on October 5, but it was postponed and the pair were released on bail. Both men pleaded guilty on January 11, 1919, and were let off with a two year suspended sentence.[31] Geer started to mend his ways but Antille wanted revenge on Bar Z.

Another ex-employee who carried a grudge against the company was Jim Cook. He came to the strip from Texas early in the summer of 1912 and worked for Mansfield until June 20. He evidently was impressed with the way Charlie Spencer was spending money on his promotion at the ferry, because he quit the cow outfit and became a non-working miner. Cook appears to have thought that Spencer owed him several months' wages when the American Placer Corporation ceased to operate, as he disappeared for a while then took up residence in the Spencer mess hall in 1916. He claimed some of the Spencer machinery in 1917 when Elmer Johnson came down from the Kaibab to liberate one of Charlie's steam pumps that he and Price wanted for a sawmill they were starting. At this time, Cook tried to involve Johnson in a land colonization scheme he had devised for the Bar Z range, claiming the range was being used illegally and was open to settlement. A lengthy argument took place, but Elmer finally went off with the pump. Nobody knew what Cook did for a living; he squatted there with a husband-less Kanab girl and her fatherless child, apparently hoping Spencer would appear and dispute his possession.

Charlie Spencer used the backing provided by Nate Burgess to revitalize his various projects. Besides the Great Western Cattle and Sheep Company, organized under the laws of California, he formed the Arizona Cattle and Sheep Company, organized under the laws of Delaware and with a home office listed as Parkyn's address in Chicago. By now, Parkyn's role was that of a non-participating friend. The assets for both companies, together with the buildings and equipment at Lee's Ferry, Cottonwood Camp, and Pahreah, were the thirty-two lapsed water rights that had been filed in March 1915. Charlie renewed these on March 30, 1918, purely as a paper asset. Burgess never met Spencer's full financial needs and doled out what he did in a parsimonious manner.

Spencer's main interest now was an irrigation scheme with dams on the Pahreah and its tributaries. He had attracted the services of a drinking water engineer, John Calhoun, who claimed to be a great-grandson of the nineteenth century states' rights advocate. Calhoun was a capable engineer with a fondness for good food and drink, but he could rough it with the most rugged of westerners. He had his own transit and level and knew how to use them. By June of 1919, he had run levels for the Pahreah Reservoir and determined that it would hold 115,210 acre feet. A dam was proposed for the narrows just above the mouth of Cottonwood Canyon, but the site was questionable geologically as the base was not sound. Had Spencer's dam been built, the Bar Z ranch in the mouth of the canyon would have reverted to desert. At the same time, two of his old employees, the Moon brothers, who were working for the Arizona Lumber and Timber Company of Flagstaff, listened to the promoter's siren song. Charlie Moon quit a paying job to do pick and shovel work for the promise of a better, future position on the San Francisco Peaks irrigation project. Even his enemies had to admit that Charlie Spencer was persuasive.

The Grand Canyon Cattle Company started its annual drive to Flagstaff late in November. The crossing was unusual in that Mansfield drove a car instead of riding a horse, and the entire outfit was ferried. On December 1, 1919, Jerry and Frank Johnson finished ferrying 1,030 cattle, 34 horses, and the Mansfield auto for a total charge of $215.80.[32] This was something of an experiment as it turned out that the labor in taking alfalfa to the animals held on the left bank while ferrying was underway exceeded the cost of the few animals that might be lost to the river if they swam across. However, the practice of ferrying the cattle was not abandoned and was repeated for small herds.

Both Jerry Johnson and Carl Antille applied for the Lee's Ferry custodian job on December 1; Jerry was appointed without any discussion.[33] It was well known that the work was relatively easy due to the sparse travel, and although he was not the epitome of dependability, Jerry was capable. There were complaints about the irregular service, however, since he still took time off periodically for trips to Hurricane. In the county supervisors meeting of February 2, Jerry finally was removed and the Grand Canyon Cattle Company was given the custodianship. Eph Mansfield had been glad to put up with the Johnson boys because their work was superior, even if he didn't know who was doing it at a given time. They were not demanding and Bar Z got a better return on their labor than if only one man was hired and the others were barred from the ranch. Jim Cook, giving

Frank and Jerry Johnson, July 20, 1919 (*P. T. Reilly Collection, Cline Library, Northern Arizona University*).

his residence as Lee's Ferry, applied for the custodian's job in April, but the officials deferred making a change and he drifted away in a few months.

The fall of 1920 marked the gathering of the Johnson clan at Lee's Ferry. Frank was there most of the time and his son Lile came in even before he was put on the Bar Z payroll, helping his father from August through November. Jody was employed in May, while Jerry was back and forth as was his wont. With Eph Mansfield's liberal attitude toward them, closing his eyes to a strict accounting, Elmer and Price, with their families, also moved there later in the year. They helped on all labor and made garden plots of their own. It was the nearest thing to a Johnson enclave since 1890.

But the year also saw the appearance of future Lee's Ferry residents who were not Johnsons or even Mormons. The first of these was Hawaii-born Frank Dodge. After his discharge from the armed services in late 1919, Dodge decided to head west and look for a homestead. At least he rationalized that was his reason; actually he was seeking adventure. In January 1920 he was working as a timber helper at Miami's Inspiration Mine. He earned $5.85 per day, which he considered generous for common labor, but he quit after six weeks because the work force seemed to be the remnants of the Bisbee deportation, carrying on a constant "God damn Rockefeller" and "God damn Carnegie" attitude. He hoofed it to Cooley (now McNary) and found work as a carpenter. When he had a little money in his jeans—and not liking the cold weather—he quit and started walking to Flagstaff. He was camped under the Mogollon Rim near Pine when he learned it was fifty-seven miles to his destination. He left his camp at 4 A.M. the next morning and pulled into Flagstaff at 11 P.M. of the same day.

Dodge spent a few days in town, where he received a box of personal gear that had been shipped from Hilo. He got a ride on the mail stage to Tuba City, where he bought a jenny and her yearling colt from a Navajo sheep herder for six dollars. He put his pack on the jenny, wrapped his bedroll around the colt, and set off on foot. He met Buck Lowrey at The Gap and helped him on his inventory of trade goods. In a day or two he moved on, armed with a stick containing a nail protruding from the end that he used as a prod to increase the pace of his thoroughbreds. It was near mid-May when he rang the Emett school bell at the end of the dugway. In due time, Frank Johnson appeared and hollered across that someone had sabotaged the ferry cable by loosening the clamps and allowing it to sag almost to the river. Dodge turned his burros out to graze and helped make the repairs. He crossed on May 16, and the ferriage for one pack animal, one loose animal, and one footman amounted to a dollar twenty-five.[34] Dodge camped at the ferry for a few days and evidently acquired a feeling for the place. Had there been any activity there he probably would have remained. Instead, he prodded his burros toward Buckskin Mountain and went to work for the Forest Service.

The 1920 runoff was the Colorado's highest since 1884, peaking at 190,000 cubic feet per second at Yuma. Crossing, especially with this particular ferryboat, was dangerous in such high water and Frank was increasingly careful. He ferried a team and wagon along with two loose head on June 1, but had no more business until June 29 when a man in an auto wanted passage. In the following week, two more autos braved the river and the dugway. September proved to be a month of unprecedented automobile travel over Lee's Ferry. On the seventh, four cars crossed in one day—

the first time this had ever happened. Jerry noted in the record book the makes as being a Buick, a Studebaker, an Elgin, and a Dodge. But it was a month of Fords as fourteen crossed, four on the twenty-first alone.

The fall of 1920 brought more non-Mormon residents to the ferry and set the stage for others. When Sid Wilson had packed for Spencer in 1912–13, he spotted a potential ranch site about four and one-half miles up the Pahreah. He had ridden up the creek for a closer look and was elated to find a good spring at the base of a large sand dune. He never forgot the site and resolved that some day he would return and claim his ranch. He rode for Double O until 1917, then married and acquired a stepson, Don Blockberger, who was serving on the destroyer *Whipple* in the Atlantic. Sid's ranch became reality to his wife Mary even before she had seen it, and she imparted her enthusiasm in letters to Blockberger. In turn, Don talked about his "folks' ranch in Arizona" to his friend Owen Clark, chief water tender on the *Whipple*. Both men were alert to acquire a business or make a deal when they were released from the Navy.

During their leave that fall, Don and Owen came to Arizona, met Sid, and all three went to Pahreah Canyon to inspect the dream ranch site. Owen liked what he saw and agreed to become a partner and to send money to help make it a reality.[35] He and Don returned to the Navy while Sid brought Mary and baby Margie Jean to the ferry, set up housekeeping in the Spencer mess hall, and prepared to carve out the homestead. The Wilsons made no effort to farm but lived "cowboy style" on beef, biscuits, and black coffee three times a day.

Mansfield had sent Charlie Lewis, the Bar Z handyman, to the Lee's Ferry ranch at the beginning of the summer. Charlie did anything asked of him from wrangling stock, cutting hay, or building water troughs. He was dependable and Eph knew that now there was no danger of the ferry and ranching being left unattended by the peregrinating Johnsons.

Meanwhile, Frank Dodge worked all summer for the Forest Service until they began cutting back for winter. Then, hearing that Bar Z planned to drive cattle to Flagstaff, he obtained a job with Mansfield on September 28. For the first time, he learned that when the Bar Z cowboys had visited his camp between Jacob's Pools and House Rock, someone had noticed the "U.S." on his army mess kit and the "USGS" on one of the old Powell topographic sheets. Even as late as 1920, strangers were looked upon with suspicion, and the men figured he either was evading the sheriff, spying on poachers for the Forest Service, or spying on rustlers for the stock association. The word had been passed along, "Look out for the guy with the burros." Frank put the rumor to rest, realizing he was lucky he hadn't been drygulched without knowing why.

Stephenson now was reversing the flow of the Bar Z herds. Conditions in Mexico appeared to have stabilized, while the Forest Service was squeezing the company to reduce its herds on the Kaibab summer range. Mansfield and his men, including Dodge, left Cane early on October

22 with about 1,650 head. The first stop was Jacob's Pools where the cattle were watered, but at the next stop, Soap Creek, some of the stock refused to drink. They reached the ferry near evening of the twenty-fourth, and the cattle had their first full drink since Jacob's Pools. The herd was urged into the river early on the twenty-fifth and almost all got across safely. About ten animals were bogged down and lost, so Eph Mansfield ordered the remainder ferried, along with his car, the chuck wagon, and thirty-four head of horses. The ferriage amounted to $72.20. The herd reached Flagstaff three weeks out of Cane. After the outfit returned to headquarters, Frank Dodge worked two weeks more. He drew his pay on November 23, rode to Kanab and spent a few days, then decided to winter at the ferry. He reached there early in December and took over one of the Spencer cabins for a residence.

Rumors began to fly that big things were about to take place at the ferry. Reports had circulated since E. C. LaRue's exploratory work there in 1916,[36] but now items appeared regularly in the newspapers. Spencer was promoting at Pahreah and Flagstaff. He now revived the Lee's Ferry project in November and sent Walter Parker and two Navajos to do assessment work on his old claims. Spencer and his golden tongue even talked Sid Wilson and Lile Johnson into helping to retain the claims. Sid already maintained that Charlie owed him more than five hundred dollars in wages from the original promotion, and he was holding some of his equipment to insure payment.

As soon as he put Parker and his crew to work digging in the Chinle, Spencer returned to Flagstaff, visited the recorder's office, and began writing letters. His latest emphasis was on oil and gas. He claimed to have put a shaft down thirty-three feet and two weeks later it was full of gas. He said he then found tremendous volumes of gas escaping along the river at this point. He alleged that he had gone into Marble Canyon and found a sixty-foot stratum of Casper oil shale and evidence of a major oil field. As usual, he needed expense money and wanted some experts to examine the find. He sent identical letters to R. J. Billings of Denver and Nathan B. Moran of San Francisco. Another letter with slightly different wording, but the same general content, was sent to V. E. Gillilan of Chanute, Kansas. Nor did he neglect his old investors H. W. Huttig of Muscatine, Iowa, and Bert Parkyn of Chicago, who had intriguing pitches directed at them. Parkyn was given copies of the optimistic reports by A. L. Field and N. D. Ingham regarding the possibilities of land, cattle, water, and farming in the Pahreah country. In addition, Spencer noted that big money was backing a drilling project north of the Kaiparowits Plateau. He then resorted to an old technique: he enclosed two location notices made out in the recipients' names.[37]

The magnet that attracted all this interest, of course, was the interstate wrangling over the division of the West's last waterhole—the Colorado River. By this time, the sides had been drawn. The four upper-basin states of Utah, Wyoming, Colorado, and New Mexico—where the water originated—were pitted against the three lower-basin states of California, Arizona, and

Nevada—where the water was used. On Christmas Day, 1920, the *Coconino Sun* printed an article stating that the Southern California Edison Company was planning a 2.5 million horsepower project on the Colorado, and naturally Lee's Ferry would become a center for the construction.

Even the Coconino County supervisors caught the fever. In the January 3, 1921, meeting, they retained Frank Johnson as ferry custodian and sent him a new skiff. At the same time they sent their chairman Frank Garing, County Engineer J. B. Wright, Road Commission employees Charlie Greene and Lester Power, and a cook and helper to locate a bridge site over Marble Canyon. The new skiff was lashed to the top of Wright's car when they chugged out of Flagstaff. The custodian happened to be doing road work near the head of the dugway when the Garing-Wright car arrived. Frank climbed into the skiff for the ride to the ferry landing, enabling him to claim in later years that he came to the ferry by boat at a higher elevation than any other man in history. After crossing they informed Frank of their mission.

Wright had been told that Johnson knew the location of the railroad site located forty years before. He asked and was given instructions for finding it. It was almost a week before the party returned to the ranch reporting no success. Frank got in the car with them and drove to Five Mile Point. A short walk brought them to the rim and he pointed out some light excavations on the opposite rim. They then found several stakes which had been put there in April 1881 by the Sevier Valley Railway engineers to indicate the approach. Wright set up his transit and triangulated the distance across. Frank said that the Marble Canyon Bridge later was built exactly at this place.[38]

Permits for Bar Z cattle on the Kaibab summer range were reduced drastically in 1921, necessitating a spring herd reduction before the animals were moved to the highlands. Stephenson accompanied Mansfield on the drive, each in his own car. Early in March, the chuck-and-bedroll wagons, 2 teams, 31 horses, and 16 cowboys left Cane with 1,412 Herefords. The drive reached the ferry on March 12, where the cowboys fed the animals alfalfa and held them above the landing. By the time almost a third of the herd had swam the river, 6 steers were lost by becoming bogged down, and Stephenson ordered the remainder to be ferried. The bill for the outfit and 1,093 cattle came to $293.40.[39]

Jeff Slade, said to be a "jack" Mormon from the Eager country and fleeing from trouble, came to the strip in the winter of 1920–21. He had a small herd of about thirty head, and the animals carried several brands. Although his ownership appeared suspicious, Sid Wilson bought the cattle and the A Cross brand, which he claimed to own. Slade went to work for Bar Z on February 28 but quit when the drive reached Flagstaff. Sid had a good business going by trading cattle and horses to the Navajos for blankets which he in turn traded to the Mormons for more horses. He didn't like to see his profits decreased by ferriage costs, so he usually gave Frank or Jerry

Johnson five dollars to let him use the ferry to cross his stock. One such instance was entered in the ferry book on March 16, 1921.

Representatives of the Southern California Edison Company were in and out of Lee's Ferry so often that winter that everyone knew something was about to unfold. Little tidbits of information were dispensed by the strangers, and Frank Dodge learned that the Edison company and the U.S. Geological Survey were on the verge of collaborating on a Colorado River project. Having done level work for Claude Birdseye in the Hawaiian Islands ten years previously, Dodge wanted to get in on the ground floor, so he wrote to the USGS office in Sacramento asking for a job. Back came a reply telling him to see a Mr. H. A. Schenck at the Commercial Hotel in Flagstaff on May 1, 1921.

11

Water

Wrangling over the West's "last water hole" dominated the early 1920s at Lee's Ferry. The problem started in southern California and the solutions developed into interstate dissensions. For millennia, the Colorado River moved topsoil from its drainage basin to its delta in the Gulf of California. The river's silt content was very high; annually, it moved a total of 170 million cubic yards—or 105,000 acre feet—of sediment. The effect of this alluvial deposition changed the topography of the delta because the river's velocity slowed, meandering increased, and deposition increased near sea level. Occasionally, and especially during the annual flood season, the channel through the delta rose to a higher elevation than the surrounding country. Because the western edge of the delta sloped downward into the Salton Sink, a remnant depression of the Sea of Cortez with a maximum depth of 248 feet below sea level, the potential for a natural catastrophe was high.[1]

In recent geologic times, the Salton Sink became a thirty-mile extension of the Colorado Desert, the sub-sea level portion lying from nine miles south of the border northward to Indio. At the turn of the century it was known as the Imperial Valley and contained thousands of acres of good agricultural land that needed only water to provide a twelve-month growing season. The western edge of the delta is cut by an overflow-channel called the Alamo River, which curved northward and at times fed river water into the deepest part of the Salton Sink. Several other overflow-channels cut the southwestern edge of the fan, drained into the Rio Hardy and ultimately fed back into the main stem and the Gulf. Farmers grasped the fact that these overflow-channels could provide gravity-fed water to the lower lands and needed only to be controlled to be used.

Mormons were the first major Caucasian irrigators in the West and certainly were the first large-scale water appropriators since the Hohokam's extensive canal system along the Gila River, in central Arizona, in the fourteenth century. When the first contingent of Mormons arrived in the Salt Lake Valley in July 1847, water immediately was turned onto the land, marking the beginning of reclamation projects in the West and launching the doctrine of Prior Appropriation. Other Saints built dams and diverted water for crops in 1854 at Black's Fork, Wyoming, Fort Harmony on Ash Creek, and on the Santa Clara River in southern Utah.[2]

The first gravity diversion of Colorado River water was made by Samuel Blythe in the Palo Verde Valley in 1877, and a town now honors his memory by carrying his name. About seventy miles downstream, Yuma farmers began using water from the Colorado in the 1890s, while an equal distance to the west, some progressive developers conceived the idea of placing a headgate in the Colorado and running water to the thirsty acres below. Charles Rockwood, Anthony Heber, and others formed the California Development Company in 1896 to bring the water to the desert and create farmland. Three years later an irrigation expert named George Chaffey joined them. He succeeded in building a headgate and cutting a canal on May 4, 1901. Chaffey's headgate was in the United States, but to avoid a topographical obstacle he went into Mexico, intersected an old overflow-channel of the Alamo River, and followed it to his objective. In short order, four hundred miles of distributing secondary canals were built and about a hundred thousand acres were made irrigable.

President Roosevelt signed the Reclamation Act into law in June 1902 and three weeks later Secretary of the Interior Hitchcock established the Reclamation Service. The stated purpose of the Reclamation Service was to bring water to naturally arid lands that needed only irrigation to become farmland. New towns such as Brawley, Holtville, Imperial, and El Centro sprang from the barren desert, and the Imperial Valley was named. By early 1903, the population of the area had tripled, the Southern Pacific Railroad was extended to the town of Imperial, and the Reclamation Service engineers were challenging the right of the California Development Company to use Colorado River water.

Anthony Heber went to Washington to lobby for a bill to legalize the diversion. The Reclamation Service opposed him and killed the legislation. Heber left the capitol threatening to obtain his irrigation water south of the border. He did in July 1904, but at a stiff price: Mexico demanded and got half of the diverted water for use on the farmlands in her portion of the Imperial Valley. Ironically, Harry Chandler, owner of the *Los Angeles Times*, and a group of Los Angeles developers owned more than eight hundred thousand acres of Mexican land that would benefit from the agreement. Nevertheless, the Mexican Cut was made in 1904, and in only four miles intersected the Chaffey Canal, effectively bypassing an area that had been prone to fill with silt.

All went well until the Gila River went on a rampage in February 1905. Four consecutive crests came down, the last of which on March 18 washed out the headgate and sent the entire Colorado River pouring down the irrigation channel into the lower-elevation Salton Sink. For eighteen months, before the washout was finally closed at the Mexican Cut on November 3, 1906, water poured into the Imperial Valley forming the Salton Sea. Other levee breaks occurred in early December and February 1907 but were plugged through the herculean efforts of Harry T. Cory and the Southern Pacific Railroad Company. It was said that President E. H. Harriman spent three million dollars to put the Colorado back in her channel.

The Reclamation Service built the Laguna Dam just above Yuma and the mouth of the Gila River in 1909. This first dam on the Colorado benefited the farmers on both sides of the river; however, it was a low structure, provided only irrigation water, and did nothing to control the floods that were a constant threat. The following year, the Colorado preempted another of its old flood channels, the Bee River, and poured the entire output down it to Volcano Lake. As the impounded waters crept northward, the Imperial farmers constructed new levees and asked President Taft for help. Congress appropriated a million dollars for flood control and built the Ockerson Levee. This was the first recognition by the federal government of the destructive river's potential menace.

But the next flood wasted the expenditure and took out the entire twenty-five mile levee, allowing the river to pour once again into Volcano Lake. In 1911 the farmers took matters into their own hands and organized the Imperial Irrigation District, at that time the largest single agricultural unit in the world. The original California Development Company still owned the headgate at the Mexican Cut, the canal, and associated levees south of the border. The new organization bought these rights in 1916 and although the stockholders now controlled their own water, they continually encountered *la mordida* (the bite) every time they were forced to do maintenance or repair work in Mexico. Bribery was, and still is, a way of life among underpaid Mexican officials and was a constant irritant to the Americans. The persistent petty tributes and time delays led to agitation for an "All American Canal."

On January 22, 1916, the Gila flooded again, inundating Yuma. The floodwaters spread upstream to Laguna Dam. Already there were calls for the federal government to alleviate the flood menace and to build the All American Canal. The ensuing political struggle found an aggressive Imperial farmer, Mark Rose, and the company's legal counsel, Phil Swing, opposing the *Los Angeles Times* syndicate that wanted the present situation to continue for the benefit of its Mexican and Chinese tenants. As long as the Imperial Valley received its water from the Mexican Cut, the Chandler interests made money, and the *Times* fought the idea of the proposed canal at every turn. But Swing and Rose convinced Arthur Powell Davis, chief engineer for the Reclamation Service, that the All American Canal, a protective dam, and a storage reservoir should be built on the Colorado River.

This water proposal in the lower Colorado River region caused apprehension among the water experts in the states where the water originated. They saw their rights threatened by the water-user states, mainly California. Their fears were justified. Wyoming consumers were embargoed from further use of the waters of the North Platte when the Pathfinder Dam, which mainly benefited Nebraska, was built in 1904. Likewise, the government placed an embargo on any further upstream irrigation on the Rio Grande when the Elephant Butte Dam was planned in 1907. Water users in Colorado and upper New Mexico were outraged that their rights had been made secondary to those in the lower Rio Grande Valley in New Mexico and Texas. Thus the seven states in the Colorado River drainage basin were divided naturally into those of the upper basin—Utah, Wyoming, Colorado, and New Mexico—against those of the lower basin—California, Arizona, and Nevada.

On January 18, 1919, a group of governors, senators, water experts, and hydraulic-engineers met in Salt Lake City to discuss the problem. The issue was how to protect the downstream users while preserving the future rights of the states where the water originated. The outcome could have been predicted; a resolution was passed that Colorado River development should start at the headwaters and follow downstream—essentially the view of the upper basin states.

A later meeting was held at Los Angeles where the California delegates controlled the proceedings, and another resolution was passed to investigate the possibilities of building the All American Canal and a control dam at Boulder Canyon. This was more to the liking of the lower basin states and against that of the upstream group. However, attendees at another meeting in Denver in January 1921 saw the advantage swing the other way when it was decided to settle all matters on a vote by states. Here the upper basin prevailed, always by a count of four to three. At this time the very capable representative from Colorado, Delph Carpenter, promulgated the idea that an interstate compact should be agreed to by all participants before any authorization should be delegated to the Reclamation Service.

Early in 1921, the seven state legislatures passed enabling acts to allow the framing of the Colorado River Compact, and Congress concurred in August that this action was proper. Each state now selected a representative to uphold its interest. The Kinkaid Act, passed in May 1920, authorized and directed the Secretary of the Interior to examine and report on the conditions existing along the lower Colorado River and the possible irrigation development of Imperial Valley. This involved the Reclamation Service and the U.S. Geological Survey, along with input from various interested private parties. The report presented by Arthur P. Davis, now director of the Reclamation Service, reiterated his views, derived from long personal study and other sources, that a high dam should be built in Black or Boulder Canyon, with hydroelectric power generated to pay for it, and the All American Canal should follow.

There were more than two adversaries in the scramble for the Colorado's water. Arizona Territorial Engineer James B. Girand was on the ground before any of them and had applied for a license to build a dam in the lower granite gorge just above Diamond Creek. The walls in the inner gorge, however, were too low to allow construction of a high dam with a necessary large reservoir. Eugene C. LaRue of the U.S. Geological Survey wanted the dam at Glen Canyon site number 1, near Lee's Ferry. He was relatively unconcerned about the All American Canal and opposed the ideas of Reclamation Commissioner Davis, who had a splendid grasp of the overall problem. The Southern California Edison Company and the Southern Sierra Power Company, representing private interests, were concerned with hydroelectric power generation but were opposed by the Los Angeles Metropolitan Water and Power District and the Chandler syndicate. The Edison Company and the U.S. Geological Survey cooperated well in their mutual areas, but Edison and the Reclamation Service operations overlapped and sooner or later one would have to give way to the other. The *Los Angeles Times,* wanting to perpetuate its favorable water situation in Mexico, sniped at the others from the sidelines but inflicted no wound of any consequence. All delegation members were aware that the upper basin states dominated the irrigation committees in both houses of Congress and would have to be reckoned with before a final solution could be resolved.

The contents of the Davis report became known even before initial copies were passed out to state water commissions in July 1921. Possibly the Southern California Edison Company had inside information or made a shrewd guess regarding the conclusions, because its representatives filed on power sites and survey parties were sent into the field in April 1921. Harry A. Schenck and George Harriquet of the Edison Company arrived at Lee's Ferry on April 29 to arrange with Sid Wilson to pack survey parties into the back country. They left their car on the left bank and crossed in the rowboat. Wilson was up the Pahreah working on his ranch but his wife assured the visitors that they would be accommodated. Schenck brought the mail, which consisted of packages for J. W. Calhoun, Spencer's drinking water engineer on the Pahreah River project. They then recrossed the river and drove back to Flagstaff.[3]

Entry of the surveyors, engineers, and hydrologists into the area promised to be an economic godsend. The people of the Arizona Strip had always been cash-poor, and tourism had yet to get started except at Grand Canyon. The cattle company could have hired several times the number of men that could be used, and it was only through Mansfield's charitable nature that he put as many on the payroll as he did. The bulk of the money in circulation had its origin in the payrolls of the Forest Service and the cattle outfit. The ferry custodian earned one hundred and twenty-five dollars per month and the help at the ranch gleaned whatever Eph Mansfield chose to pay. The rest of the people were hanging on; some raised such garden truck as they could, lived on husbanded savings, or did without. It was generally conceded that Bar Z beef and poached deer filled many an empty belly, while Sid Wilson was known to "go up the creek to get a wild one"—a euphemism for shooting one of the many feral burros. Now, hopes were high that jobs would be available.

Optimism was sustained on May 6, 1921, when fourteen Edison Company men in two cars arrived at the ferry landing. The party, headed by

Chief Engineer Harry W. Dennis, included Vice President G. E. Ward, H. A. Barre, H. A. Schenck, and F. H. Ducker. They set up a camp. In the morning, Sid Wilson provided horses and guided several of the men up the Spencer Trail to the narrow neck overlooking LaRue's damsite at Mile 4.6. They started down the trail at 4:25 P.M. and reached the river forty minutes later. The next day, Dennis triangulated the river to determine the length of a cable needed for a gaging station, and on May 8, LaRue set up a temporary staff gage on the right bank below the Spencer buildings.[4] Thus began the federal stream-gaging era at Lee's Ferry. The county profited financially by four dollars when Frank Johnson crossed fourteen footmen, even though he apparently couldn't add or multiply well. Schenck started running levels from a camp twenty-four miles out of Flagstaff on May 31, with Frank Dodge recording for one of the two instruments. Schenck noted that at this time the telephone line stopped at The Gap. They reached a reference point near the present gage well on June 10 and another phase of the work was history.[5]

A near tragedy occurred on June 6. The handline—one-half inch cable—was held together by a large square knot in mid-river. This knot was a source of annoyance to the ferryman as the falls between the ferryboat and the sheaves invariably caught on it and stopped the boat. Frank Johnson decided to replace the handline since there was plenty of cable available. It was fastened solidly at the left anchorage, its elevation controlled by a cranked drum on the right bank. Frank, with Jerry's help, put the new cable on the ferry and crossed the river where he fastened it to the old one so that Jerry could crank both to his side. The operation went smoothly and after it was concluded Frank prepared to re-cross.

The river, rising rapidly, was several feet higher than when they had started. The increased flow directed fast water at the landing, and Frank knew he could not untie the line and get aboard the boat before it would be swept toward midstream. Accordingly, he fixed the line so he could pull it loose from the ferryboat, but he had no time to take up the forward fall before the boat began to dip. He was helpless as the bow went under and the aft end rose in the air. The craft was fourteen by forty feet; Frank clung to the high inshore end and waited. The cable was creaking, the boat groaning, and he was peering down into a twenty feet deep hole of swirling, muddy water, expecting something to break loose any second. Suddenly, something did give way and the boat came up. The rebound of the cable was terrific, knocking nine logs off the crib and breaking the other pulley. The ferryboat, now full of water, was loose and being carried toward Marble Canyon. Frank grabbed the only loose plank in the deck and used it for a paddle. He got to within a hundred feet of the shore when he saw some inundated willows that allowed him to take the line and slip into the water, which only came to his armpits and became shallower as he approached the shore. Jerry reached him in the rowboat as he tied up.

The cable had sagged nearly to the river and snagged a large tree. The cribbing had to be replaced, the cable raised, and the ferryboat towed one-half mile upstream to the crossing. Three Bar Z riders came along and Frank obtained their help to get the boat back to the landing, which required half of the next day. To cut the tree, Frank tied a rope to the pulley of a snatch block, fastened safety lines to a saw and ax, and Jerry played out the line as Frank and the snatch block slid down the cable. When the tree was cut free, the cable rebounded, but Frank held on. Jerry, sitting on top of the cribbing, could not brace himself enough to pull his brother up the sloping cable, so Frank "cooned" his way backwards to the crib. With the aid of five- and three-ton chain blocks, twenty-four cable clamps, and a length of three-quarter inch cable, they raised the main cable to the rebuilt crib and the ferry was back in business. Frank paid Mansfield twelve dollars for the labor of his men in towing the boat upstream, and he gave Jerry twenty dollars for his three days' work. The payments came out of the accumulated ferry fees and were so noted in the ferry book.[6]

The Colorado, as if disdainful of human efforts to measure and ultimately tame her, went on a rampage. The discharge between June 13 and 23 was unprecedented for more than thirty-five years and topped the temporary gage. Stakes were set to mark each day's flow, and on the twenty-fourth were correlated to another gage designated number 1, but the method was not totally satisfactory and the readings are now considered to be unreliable. Nonetheless, they recorded a peak discharge of 181,000 cubic feet per second on the eighteenth.[7]

The Edison Company maintained a policy of spreading employment among the local residents to the best of its ability, even when some of the help was sub-marginal. The survey party was in the field for the remainder of the year, and during that time eight local residents and two semi-citizens from Cannonville were given jobs. Sid Wilson did the packing, Jerry Johnson was boatman, Frank Johnson and his son Adolpha served as rodmen. Elmer Johnson worked on the gage and proved to have latent talent for hydrology. Frank Dodge was the first rodman, but Frank Johnson's nephew, Delmer Spencer, also served in this capacity. Squire Mangum and Wallace Henderson, the pair from Cannonville, later packed and cooked. Price Johnson worked as a utility man and general flunky. Originally hired to sit in the bow of the boat and "show them where the rocks ain't," he loaded, unloaded, and repaired boats, carried messages, helped the cook, and even served as cook when the man imported for that job quit. In anticipation of large trucks bringing heavy loads to the ferry, Schenck hired Jerry Johnson and Sid Wilson to work on the road. As this employment promised cash, development of Wilson's Pahreah Ranch was postponed.

An Edison Company survey party under A. T. Fowler and V. E. Leech arrived at noon on July 6 and set up camp at the ferry landing. Its job was to make a topographic map upstream from the ferry and to survey the tributaries along the Glen Canyon benches to determine the reservoir line resulting from a proposed dam. The survey was started from the benchmark that had been set at the ferry landing and was an extension of the levels

Schenck had run from Flagstaff. Orientation was by solar plane-table chart. A truck arrived on July 13 with an eighteen-foot open boat containing an Evinrude outboard motor. As in the case of the *Violet Louise*, it was taken down the lower-crossing dugway and launched at the foot of Pahreah Riffle. Like the *Canopy* and the *Charles H. Spencer*, it had insufficient power and failed to make headway against the rapid, even with full throttle and five men rowing; they finally lined the boat to the ferry landing. In about a week, the silt had ruined the bearings and they had to be replaced.

The entire crew was called upon July 25 to pull a cable across the river to support gage readings. This cable was located about three-tenths of a mile upstream from the ferry and almost a mile above the dugway gage. Eventually the profile of the riverbed was taken here, the river height and velocity were measured, and discharges were calculated. The Lee's Ferry gaging station was established officially on August 3, 1921, the first discharge measurement being made by Roger Rice, C. W. Sopp, and W. E. Johnson and referenced to a permanent staff gage.[8] E. C. LaRue and Elmer Johnson repeated the recordings on the fifth and seventh.

The Edison activity at Lee's Ferry generated intense claim filing. Even the local people got into the act, with Sid Wilson, Jerry and Frank Johnson setting claims. Walter Parker and John W. Calhoun filed numerous claims in the names of themselves, C. H. Spencer, H. A. Parkyn, W. R. and R. S. Hackney, J. W. and F. C. Rockwell, and various Flagstaff friends such as W. H. Switzer, F. M. Gold, Lee Doyle, C. B. Wilson, W. H. Campbell, and J. H. Crawford. Rockwell and Hackney had investment money in the Pahreah project, and Spencer still hoped to entice more money from Parkyn; the Flagstaff people were covered for purposes of influence gathering.

On August 6, another boat arrived at the head of the dugway. This one was larger than her unnamed, underpowered predecessor. Called the *Navajo*, she had a four-cylinder inboard engine that also was underpowered. As in the case of the first boat, everybody turned out to help her down the lower dugway. It was quite a chore; the truck had to be backed down the steep grade since there wasn't room at its foot for maneuvering. Like the other craft, she had to be helped up the riffle. On the eleventh, LaRue, Gerdine, Fowler, Schenck, Ellsworth Kolb, Dodge, and five others started upriver; Price Johnson sat in the bow to watch for rocks. They returned the next afternoon, having made only eighteen miles in two days—far too slow for servicing the survey from the river. However, the two underpowered boats had to be used until one was refitted with adequate power.

James E. Klohr served in the Seventh Cavalry from 1913 to April 1919, first in the Philippines, then in the United States and Mexico. He was in the West Column under Blackjack Pershing on the punitive expedition into Mexico after the Columbus raid and went through the entire campaign. When his hitch was over, he married a vivacious girl named Christina and headed west across New Mexico. They landed in Flagstaff in May 1921, where Klohr found a job as barn boss for a mule outfit west of town. Jim and

The *Navajo* on the dugway at Lee's Ferry, August 6, 1921 (*courtesy of Southern California Edison Company, #7894*).

Christina left Flagstaff late in August, driving north in an old buckboard and looking for a homestead. They crossed at Lee's Ferry, talked to Mary Wilson and a few Edison men, and camped at the ranch through the courtesy of Charlie Lewis. They went on as far as Tuweep where Jim climbed Mt. Trumbull on September 17. He was impressed with the range and thought the grass resembled a wheat field. No water was available for filing, however, so they turned back. When they reached Lee's Ferry in early October, they became acquainted with Sid Wilson who bought their mules and buckboard for sixty dollars. The Klohrs rode to Flagstaff on the Edison Company truck and Jim found a harvest job at Turkey Tanks. During the fall, Wilson sent word that Jim could do well by returning to the ferry and working for the Edison Company.

On August 20, the Edison Company appointed Irving G. Cockroft as hydrographer at Lee's Ferry. Cockroft and his wife Margery arrived on September 5 and took up residence in the old fort. The following day, he and Elmer Johnson made their first discharge measurement. By month's end, he was the permanent-resident engineer, assisted by W. E. Johnson. They were employees of the Edison Company which furnished and installed all equipment except current meters and bore the entire cost of the operation. The work progressed under a cooperative agreement with the U.S. Geological Survey which acted in an advisory capacity, furnished the current meters, and compiled and checked the data.

With the two powerboats providing everything except power, the burden of supplying the two survey parties fell upon Sid Wilson and his pack animals. Jerry Johnson dismantled the engine at one of the river camps, found a broken part, and walked overland to the ferry where a new one was sent for in Flagstaff. Jerry grew tired of tinkering with the temperamental motors and quit on September 7. He returned to the ranch and was replaced by his brother Frank. This was the standard operating procedure for the interchangeable Johnsons. On September 1, Sid Wilson and geologist Kirk Bryan threw the mail down to the river camp from the rim, there being no way to descend at that particular place.

On September 4, Junker, who cooked, and Fritz Erlinger, his flunky, found their jobs too isolated and the hours too irregular, so they quit. Fowler promoted Price Johnson to cook—probably the most serious mistake he made on the entire job. Even Price's brothers laughed about his effort, or lack of it, because if he knew anything about the art, he failed to show it. Price's idea of a job performance was to open a number of cans, put a spoon in each, and set them on a plank. The men helped themselves to the open cans and when they finished eating, Price put the plates and utensils in a bucket of cold water. They soaked all day while he retired to some shady place and read the Book of Mormon. When he heard the crew nearing camp he hurriedly removed the plates, air-swished them semi-dry, placed them on the plank, and opened more cans. Later it was ascertained that he rarely got a bucket of fresh water but used the same one for several days. The men marveled at his digestion when they saw him take a pint jar of strawberry preserves, eat half of it with a spoon, fill the jar with condensed milk, stir it up, and eat the rest of it.

An accident that could have had serious consequences occurred on September 19. Chief Engineer Dennis was directing the mounting of a winch on the gaging car and had brought it to the north anchorage. At about 3 P.M., he sent Irv Cockroft and Elmer Johnson across in the cable car to the south anchor. An eyebolt gave way when they were over mid-river, plunging men, cable, and car into the water. Three of those on shore rushed for the skiff and rescued the swimmers and car canopy about a thousand feet downstream, landing at the ferry. Wilson was just coming down the trail from Fowler's camp on Wahweap and he rushed over to lend a hand, as did Roger Rice. The cable car and cable were on the river bottom. Aided by a set of triple blocks, the seven men got the car and cable to the surface by sundown, and in two days' time, the gaging station returned to normal operation.[9]

On September 12 William R. Chenoweth and his group of geologists and surveyors, which included the Kolb brothers as boatmen, left Green River, Utah, to make a plan and profile of the Green and Colorado Rivers down to Lee's Ferry. On October 5, at the mouth of the San Juan, they met the Trimble-Miser party, which had done the same thing for the lower 144 miles of the San Juan River.[10] They pulled into Lee's Ferry on

October 8 and tied into Schenck's line from Flagstaff, and closure was within 0.4 feet of perfect.

As the river parties arrived at Lee's Ferry, Pete Ducker and Bill Marrs were preparing to start upriver in the *Navajo*. The wear and tear on bearings and propellers had been excessive and the boat was now refitted with a sixteen-blade paddlewheel five-feet in diameter. The *Navajo* returned on the afternoon of August 10 after a running time of thirteen hours to cover the 28.85 miles to Warm Greek. This was 2.22 miles per hour; obviously the paddlewheel was not the answer. The operators finally concluded that the blades were too close together, and in 1922 this wheel was replaced with a twelve-blade unit of the same diameter.

Sid Wilson was constantly on the go. He not only packed in food, men, and the mail, but he moved camp from one location to another. There was some turnover in personnel as the hours were long and Sundays were not observed. The men went out before sunup and came back after sunset, sometimes walking eight or nine miles before starting work. Rodmen had the most strenuous job because they had to go where the others didn't. Frank Dodge and Adolpha Johnson were the most adept, and the only rodmen to last the entire job.

Harry Schenck, after running the levels from Flagstaff and helping on various jobs at or near the ferry, became the Edison personnel manager operating at the ferry. He went to Flagstaff with each truck—which was at least twice a week—to recruit new employees. According to Dodge, he would head for Black's Bar and "Spitting Corner" to make a general announcement to the men of leisure that he was hiring. Rarely did he return to camp with more employees than had quit and gone back to town.

Surveys of Ferry Swale, Wahweap, and Warm Creek were completed, the latter at the 3,900-foot level, on October 20. The farther the spike camps got from Lee's Ferry, the harder it was on Sid Wilson. He no sooner arrived at an outpost with a load of supplies than he had to move camp to the next outpost and return for more supplies. James E. Mahoney went to work for the Edison Company on October 9, and three days later Sid brought him and Delmer Spencer to Leech's camp at the Spencer cabins on Warm Creek. Both were listed as rodmen and were broken in by working the Cottonwood Canyon drainage out of the Warm Creek camp. This meant long walks to and from work as the camps had to be located where water was available.

It was from the Cottonwood camp that Fowler found the spring eight miles upstream where Spencer's miners had obtained water. Two miles beyond was Tibbet Canyon, and the coal mine another two miles up that tributary. The coal vein was eight inches wide at best, casting doubt on the promoter's ability to mine sufficient coal to fuel the operation.[11] Leech described the distance problem well in his notebook. Sid arrived with supplies on Sunday, November 13. He moved part of the camp to Last Chance Creek the next day, and the second load on the fifteenth. By this time, the spike camp was in such rough country and so far removed that a round trip from Lee's Ferry took four days. Thanksgiving in 1921 fell on November 24, but it was just another work day to the surveyors. The long hours made everybody tired and grouchy.

Wilson got in on November 26, shortly after the crew hit camp. It had been another long, hard day and no one helped him unload. He had been in the saddle since daylight and interpreted this departure from the usual custom as being deliberate. He finished the job by himself, taking his bedroll, his .30–30, and the mailbag to the spot where he had decided to sleep. There are two eye-witness accounts of what happened next, and they differ only slightly. Mahoney reached for the mailbag and Sid snarled, "Leave her sit." Mahoney wanted his mail and ignored the warning. Sid grabbed his rifle, pumped a cartridge into the chamber and got to his feet in one motion, saying "I'll kill the first son-of-a-bitch that moves."

Not one did.

Mahoney drew back and said, "I guess you win."

Sid replied, "Damn right I win."

Mahoney retorted, "You wouldn't have if you didn't have that gun."

Sid flung the rifle aside and charged. Mahoney grabbed a short-handled shovel and stood ready as Sid drew up, then turned away.[12]

The mail was distributed.

Leech took no action and everybody turned in. Next day, Wilson moved camp in two loads to lower Rock Creek, then started back to the ferry. He returned with more supplies on the last day of November, and in the morning moved camp about five miles above the mouth. That night Leech paid him off and said the party would backpack to the Colorado River and return to the ferry by boat. Undoubtedly the Mahoney episode had resulted in Sid's firing, but it was done at the crew's convenience. The same day that Sid arrived at Rock Creek, Leech had seen Trimble and his party who had worked upriver after completing the San Juan Canyon survey.[13]

Leech's last camp on Rock Creek was close to the base camp of Lige Moore and the cattlemen of the Cannonville-Henrieville area, whose range was the Glen Canyon benches between the Kaiparowits Plateau and the Echo Cliffs. Leech gave the boys a day off on Sunday, December 4, and they all watched the cowboys cutting and branding. At the same time, he arranged with two of the local hands, Wallace Henderson and Squire Mangum, to appear at the ferry with six pack horses to complete the survey of the country that eventually would be flooded in Navajo and Kaibetoh Creeks. This work was completed by the end of the year.

Sid Wilson liked Jim Klohr and, when he returned from Rock Creek, sent another message to him to come to the ferry if his seasonal job had expired and he had not found another. Klohr was out of work and he knew the Flagstaff winters were more severe than those in southern Texas, so he and Chris returned to the ferry in mid-December and settled down in one of the old Spencer buildings. Jim rode with Sid for about three months, "prospecting." According to Frank Johnson and Delmer Spencer, Sid's "prospecting" as well as his packing for Edison included the gathering of long-eared calves on the open range and hiding them in isolated draws. After accumulating a few he would take them down the Sand Trail and turn them on the range near his ranch. The cattlemen who ran stock on that range suspected what was taking place but couldn't prove it.

As stated by Sid and Jim, however, Lige Moore was rustling from his fellow cattlemen and blaming Sid. The range was too rough to allow wagons in, so the roundup was conducted by packing. Moore allegedly did what he accused Wilson of doing; he gathered unmarked calves and hid them out until the roundup was over, then returned and branded them "Flying M" with his own ear crop. Moore had a large number of cattle, seemingly more than could be charged to natural increase. Wilford Clark of Cannonville— an impeccably honest and outspoken man—said everybody stole from everybody else and both Wilson and Moore were suspected. The big outfits such as Bar Z were the usual victims, but separating an unbranded calf from its mother was considered no more serious than chicken stealing, and all small operators suffered loss and enjoyed gain.

When the survey job came to an end at Tuba City, the two Mormon packers went to the ferry while Fowler, Dodge, Leech, and Spencer took the stage to Flagstaff, arriving in a snowstorm on January 3, 1922. Dodge had about a thousand dollars in uncashed checks in his jeans and thought he needed a vacation. He went to Phoenix for a couple of weeks, took the train to Los Angeles, and was back in Flagstaff by month's end. There he met John W. Calhoun, Charlie Spencer's engineer on the Pahreah project, who talked him into joining them. Spencer was in Los Angeles raising money and the prospects were high that they would all have good jobs. Calhoun needed help running levels for the reservoir that would be impounded behind the dam in the narrows and for a ditch to carry water to the Clark Bench. There was money immediately for salaries.

At the ferry, Calhoun recruited three new employees—Dodge as rodman, Klohr as cook, and Wilson as the packer who would furnish the horses for them all. They set up a good camp in Cottonwood Canyon, built a juniper windbreak, and passed the winter reading magazines. Once a week Calhoun and Dodge would run a few lines. Owen Clark finished his hitch in the Navy, retired, and in August 1922 came to the ferry to help on the ranch. Wilson convinced him to join Calhoun for the time being, and brought him up to the camp. Clark had scarcely settled down when Spencer's funds were exhausted. Charlie Spencer failed to find more and the work force scattered. Dodge collected the few horses he had on the range, threw in with a pair of cowpunchers headed for Tuweep Valley, and bummed around for a year. Wilson returned to his horse-blanket trading with the Navajos and Mormons. Owen Clark and Jim Klohr wrangled Sid's stock on the bench, then returned to the ferry where they and J. H. Crawford did assessment work on the Spencer claims.

During this period of intense activity at the river, the residents of the ranch were reverting to the past. Being Warren Johnson's eldest son, Jerry was regarded as the family head. Never noted for his leadership or reasoning power, he saw the gathering of the Johnsons at the old ranch as a sign from God to revert to the social structure that prevailed when his father held sway. The fact that his views were opposed to present church policy did not appear to bother him. Frank and Jody, however, were not to be moved. The latter left the employ of the cattle company in May 1920 rather than endure the constant arguments with Jerry. Frank maintained his orthodox views, as did Price's wife, Esther. Mary Johnson Judd, in Fredonia, and Frank's son Adolpha conformed to official practice. Charlie Lewis, a confirmed bachelor and conventional Mormon, tolerated Jerry's heresy. Although Jerry's wife Pearly encouraged her husband in his religious reversion, she rarely came to the ferry. Lydia, married to fundamentalist Isaac Carling Spencer, also believed in polygamy.

The non-Mormon element at the river was aware of affairs at the ranch but did not know enough of the Mormon religion to realize what was underway. The presence of the Gentiles, plus the opposition to orthodox doctrine, consolidated the fundamentalists into the belief that the survival of the "true Israel" was in their hands. The men at the ranch got along with those at the river even as they looked down on them as semi-heathens. Those at the river regarded the Johnsons with amused indifference, even designating Price and Elmer as "the Prayers." The custodianship was in Frank's name but he, Jerry, Elmer, and Price might operate the ferry at any given time. The county supervisors considered the ferry to be in the hands of "the Johnson boys," regardless of who cashed the check.

The arrival of the Edison men at Flagstaff generated a tremendous amount of publicity. The *Coconino Sun* printed an article about some phase of the development in almost every issue, and those writing the copy were not too concerned with accuracy. Once, the paper had Schenck's party preparing to run levels for a railroad to Lee's Ferry. A week later, an item appeared announcing the start of a large hydroelectric project there and that another project was being considered at Diamond Creek. The most accurate article appeared on June 24, 1921, when it stated that the river would be surveyed, maps made, and a gaging station established at the ferry. Remarks by members of the Federal Power Commission and the Edison Company were printed and discussed editorially.

It was assumed that a dam soon would be built, and location sites were hot issues. Edison Company president John B. Miller, in September, expressed his opinion that the dam to control the Colorado River should be located in Glen Canyon, above Lee's Ferry. Other sites under consideration were at Diamond Creek and Boulder Canyon, the latter favored by the Los Angeles power interests. Edison's vice-president George C. Ward was quoted as saying that if his company was granted a federal license to build the dam in Glen Canyon, they would construct a crushed rock road from

Flagstaff to Lee's Ferry. This would benefit tourism on the North Rim, an area now fully appreciated by Arizona's more southern citizens.

When the Southwest Conference ended its fourth meeting at Riverside, California, in December 1921, the lines of the power struggle were definite. Southern California championed the cause of the Imperial Valley through public power development and was pitted against the upper basin states, Arizona, and the Edison Company. Public sentiment against the "California power grab" began to build and it persisted for more than a quarter century.

Pressure to build a bridge across the Colorado River near Lee's Ferry intensified. Navajo Reservation Superintendent Stephen Janus, who had collaborated with Senator Ralph Cameron to get the bridge constructed across the Little Colorado, stated that the Lee's Ferry Bridge was proposed by the Bureau of Indian Affairs, which wanted itself, the state, and the county to each bear one third of the cost. Janus kept the issue alive and, in March 1922, arranged for federal engineer Herbert Deacon to accompany him, county engineer J. B. Wright, and Supervisor Campbell to the site that Frank Johnson had shown Wright five years previously. The fact that the location originally had been selected by the Denver and Rio Grande Railway engineers was enough to carry the day and the quartet endorsed it without reservation, but Frank Johnson's role wasn't mentioned.

In mid-December 1921 President Harding appointed Herbert Hoover to head the Colorado River Commission. The first meeting was held in Washington on January 26, 1922, and the sides were drawn. Delph Carpenter headed the upper basin states; Winfield S. Norviel, an able Phoenix water attorney, was Arizona's representative. Nothing was resolved and a second meeting was scheduled in Phoenix. The Colorado lived up to its reputation as a rogue when on May 22 it broke through the levees at Blythe, increasing the calls for flood control. On June 5, the Supreme Court, in the case of Wyoming versus Colorado, rendered a decision in favor of Prior Appropriation. This was a setback for the upper basin states who realized that California now was in the driver's seat. Even the upper basin states were acutely aware that a deal had to be struck.

At the ferry, Irving Cockroft and Elmer Johnson were feeling their way in gaging the Colorado's flow. On March 18, 1922, they used a one-hundred-pound weight for the first time and found that, despite the weight, the line made a ten to eleven degree angle in the swift water. The Edison Company leased one acre of land from the Navajos on the left-bank flat across from the fort on April 11. Signed with the Department of the Interior, the lease would run for five years and be renewable. The purpose of the lease was to build a boathouse, and it appeared the company intended to store a number of unused boats there for protection. At this time, building a dam upriver seemed assured.

Chris Klohr, now eight months pregnant, was taken to Flagstaff late in May, where Jim put her on the train for El Paso. While in town, he visited the newspaper office and gave a glowing account of Charlie Spencer's plan to dam Pahreah River and bring twenty-five hundred acres of desert under cultivation.[14] Strangely, he made no mention of Spencer's activity at Lee's Ferry.

Cockroft listened to the Johnson stories of past high-water years, and when Jerry mentioned the notch he had cut in the peach tree to mark the crest of the 1884 flood, he decided to run levels from it to the benchmark at the gaging station. He and Elmer, with Jerry's assistance, did this on June 7, 1922. By correlating this mark to a rating curve established from the 1922 flood, Cockroft calculated a discharge in the vicinity of 225,000 to 300,000 cubic feet per second for the 1884 peak. The figure wasn't very accurate but it was the best that could be obtained after thirty-eight years.[15]

The 1922 runoff was spectacular although not as high as in the previous year. It began building late in April, gained 2,000 to 7,000 cubic feet per second each day through May, and hit 106,000 cubic feet per second on May 28. At this stage the river was in the dugway road, had backed above the Pahreah crossing on the Kanab road and was two feet over it one mile downstream. It peaked at 119,000 cubic feet per second on the thirty-first and remained there until June 2. During this span, the river was running in the dugway road and the gage height read 19.87 feet before the gage was torn loose. Because of alternating warm and cool weather in the watershed, the river fluctuated through June, thereafter declining gradually to 52,000 cubic feet per second on July 1. From the beginning of April through the end of July, 12.3 million acre-feet of water was discharged past Lee's Ferry. For the entire water year—October 1, 1921, through September 30, 1922—the runoff was 16.4 million acre-feet. Even at that, the runoff was below those of preceding water years (18.9 and 20.5 million acre-feet respectively). Unfortunately, the antecedent decade of anomalously high discharge gave a distorted picture of the Colorado's ability to provide water and it unduly influenced political decisions being made.[16]

Cockroft and Elmer Johnson earned their pay during this high water period, but all was not running smoothly between the two hydrographers. Elmer disliked Cockroft's authoritative manner, words were exchanged, and each man preferred to work independently of the other. Johnson measured by himself on July 4, 8, and 11—the latter being his last as he resigned at the end of the day. For several weeks thereafter Cockroft worked alone.

A change also occurred at the ranch. Frank Johnson had grown weary of the endless harangues about polygamy by his brothers and resolved to leave his birthplace to escape their apostasy. He wrote his resignation as custodian and gave it to Price, who agreed to turn it in to the county supervisors along with his own application to assume the job. Price's appointment was effective on August 1, 1922. Frank returned to what he considered to be the more wholesome environment of Hurricane and never came back to the ferry except for visits.

Price had operated the ferry periodically for several years. His first job as official ferryman was as impressive as any in the past. He crossed, among others, Arizona Governor Thomas Campbell and his wife; the state's first representative to Congress, Carl T. Hayden; and the state water commissioner and delegate to the Colorado Water Commission, Winfield S. Norviel. Roger C. Rice, U.S. Geological Survey district chief for Arizona, and his wife and staff also were along. The three carloads of officials had come to Flagstaff late in July, and when they headed for Lee's Ferry on Monday morning, July 31, the party had more than doubled. Included in the group were local Coconino County political leaders who wanted to get into the dam and bridge act: Fred Garing, chairman of the county supervisors; W. H. Campbell, board member; Miss Virginia M. Lockett, school superintendent; L. B. Mullen, president of Northern Arizona Normal School (now Northern Arizona University); Dr. Felix Manning, county health officer, and his wife, Dr. R. C. Raymond; Pat J. Moran, the Babbitt Brothers' credit manager; and an influential visitor from Winslow named M. S. Gilmore. Four more cars were added to the caravan, three of them taxis. It was the largest automobile procession to pass over the Emett dugway. The party camped on the left-bank flat while the governor inspected the gage station. It was planned to get an early start next morning to inspect LaRue's choice for the damsite from the rim.

After crossing the party on August 1, Price attached himself to it, and Irv Cockroft led the way up the trail. The day was hot and not everybody carried a canteen. The governor's wife and Mrs. Manning wore long skirts, but Miss Lockett donned hiking britches. At the top, LaRue's plan for a rock-filled dam was discussed. He had proposed that both canyon walls be blasted simultaneously to create a dam—a most unprofessional plan for an engineer of his supposed caliber. The men walked across the narrow neck and rolled sandstone boulders down the slope. The rocks proved to be very friable, breaking into fragments in a short distance and raising doubt that a dam would be feasible in that formation.[17]

While the climbers were gone, Margery Cockroft worried about a menu because Irv had told her he was inviting the party to lunch. No one had bothered to inform them of the impending visit, or preparations could have been made. All of their supplies were either hauled in from Flagstaff or raised at the ranch; if a shortage suddenly occurred, the nearest trading post was at The Gap, fifty miles away. Margery decided that pot luck was the best they could expect after the strenuous climb. She didn't have much choice until she remembered a sack of jerky Irv had bought from the Navajos. She had no fresh beef but decided to make a dish that she and her husband had concocted called "Lee's Ferry goulash." She ground the venison, used eggs, onions, olive oil, garlic, tomato sauce, cheese and spices, and put the concoction on the stove. When the perspiring people dragged themselves into the fort, they were greeted with a captivating aroma. Served with a salad, coffee, home-made bread, and cake for dessert, the meal was a success.[18]

After lunch the governor's party re-crossed the river, made the tortuous drive over the dugway, and visited the proposed bridge site. The general conclusion was that the federal government should build the bridge here and that Glen Canyon was a better site for a dam than Boulder Canyon. Congressman Hayden did not want to eliminate J. B. Girand's Diamond Creek location, but they all agreed that keeping both dam abutments in Arizona would benefit the state more than if the dam were shared with Nevada or California.

Its population had increased to the extent that a Lee's Ferry precinct was established, with the polling place located at the Grand Canyon Cattle Company ranch house. The primary election was scheduled for September 12, and the appointment of six precinct officials provided a feeling of maturity that had not existed previously at the ferry. J. W. Calhoun was inspector, I. G. Cockroft and Jerry Johnson were judges, Mrs. Jerry Johnson and Mrs. Sidney Wilson were clerks, and Mrs. I. G. Cockroft was named marshal. The notice was printed, according to law, in the *Coconino Sun* on August 11, 1922.

Irv Cockroft finally was given an assistant on August 2. The new man, John T. Stone, helped take the readings on the third and fifth before coming down with severe abdominal pains. Cockroft took him to the hospital in Flagstaff, but his appendix had ruptured and peritonitis set in. He died on August 25 after only two days of active service. During her husband's absence, Margery read the gage on August 14, 19, 20, and 23.

Hoover's Colorado Commission had held successive meetings in Phoenix, Salt Lake City, and Denver, all without progress in reaching an agreement. Each state held out for unrestricted use of river water within her borders. At the fourth meeting, Hoover took Carl Hayden's recommendation that the next one be scheduled after the November election. The politically-minded Arizona congressman knew that no representative could be conciliatory and lay his party open to criticism by a provincial electorate before a poll. The next commission meeting was scheduled to open in Santa Fe on November 9, and the lower basin interests realized that if they could crack the united front of the upper basin they would be in control. Utah was regarded as a pivotal state and the weakest link in the Rocky Mountain alliance. The Church of Jesus Christ of Latter-day Saints dominated Utah politics, and any wooing of that state would involve church leaders. This led to an interesting lobbying effort in September.

E. C. LaRue put a trip together that aimed at breaking the upper basin front and advancing his own choice of damsite at the expense of the Boulder Canyon advocates. He had traveled hundreds of river miles in various parts of the drainage, located several potential damsites, and was an acknowledged river authority. He favored Glen Canyon for the location of the control dam on the Colorado despite the prevailing opinion among Department of Interior agencies that Boulder Canyon was superior.

LaRue's party consisted of H. W. Dennis, chief engineer of the Southern California Edison Company; Herman Stabler, chief engineer of the USGS Land Certification Board; Colonel Claude H. Birdseye, chief engineer of the USGS Topographic Branch; A. P. Davis, director of the Reclamation Service; Charles P. Kayler, an engineer with Union Pacific Railroad; John A. Widtsoe, an apostle of Church of Jesus Christ of Latter-day Saints and an irrigation and farm expert; R. E. Caldwell, Utah state engineer and representative to the Colorado River Commission; Clarence C. Stetson, executive secretary of the Colorado River Commission; Franklin Thomas, professor of civil engineering, California Institute of Technology; Robert D. Young, president of Sevier Stake; Thomas G. Wimmer, head boatman; Andy Wimmer, his son and helper; Lewis R. Freeman, boatman; Lute C. Ramsauer, boatman; W. H. Ramsauer, his brother and helper; and W. W. Jones, boatman.

Four sixteen-foot open boats were furnished by the Edison Company. The boatmen and helpers started upstream from Lee's Ferry on August 17, 1922, intending to reach Hall's Crossing before the passengers arrived there on September 7. Although the boats were heavily loaded and had only a few inches of freeboard, they were pushed along by outboard motors and reached their destination with time to spare.

The guests started by train from Salt Lake City, transferred to autos at the end of the line, and drove to the Bowns ranch from where they made the last leg in two four-up wagons. The party shoved off on schedule on the eighth and enjoyed a glorious eight-day river trip of one hundred nineteen miles. They climbed to the rim at Hole in the Rock and Warm Creek, walked up to Rainbow Bridge and wrote their names in the register book. They sang songs, had water fights, and in general became little boys again. They also looked at and discussed damsites before landing briefly at LaRue's Glen Canyon site number 2. Here some skullduggery took place. After a cursory explanation, LaRue hurried the two boats containing the distinguished guests five miles downstream to his favored Glen Canyon site number 1. The other boats held back, apparently taking their time. It really wasn't important as they were loaded with the kitchen and camp gear, and the occupants were not involved in the considerations.

Besides convincing the Utah men of his views, LaRue hoped to steer Davis from his option of either Boulder or Black Canyon to his preferred site 4.6 miles above Lee's Ferry. Davis knew that LaRue had planned to make a major pitch for his choice and had brought along a large map to illustrate his presentation. The map was huge—one foot on paper being scaled to one mile of Glen Canyon. The river loop was shown, as were the 3,500-foot tunnels and spillway. The powerhouse was pictured where the Spencer buildings now stood.

LaRue had landed his audience in the shade of the right-bank cliff at Mile 4.6, unrolled his impressive map, and launched a learned and technical dissertation on the merits of his pet project when two boatloads of "pirates" bore down on them. Someone had used beet juice to paint the Jolly Roger on a dish towel and it flew at the bow. The buccaneers wore bandana headbands and rings cut from tin cans hung from their ears and noses; they held knives between clenched jaws, sang "Fifteen Men on a Deadman's Chest" and other appropriate ditties, and demanded extra rations and rum. Their arrival broke up LaRue's presentation. Davis revealed his hand in the affair by singing "I am the Pirate King" which he had sung in "The Pirates of Penzance" during his college days. LaRue tried to pick up the technical thread of his presentation but the levity continued and he failed; at last, he rolled up his map and admitted he had been scuttled by the Davis pirates.

The group continued downstream and made a last camp on the right bank at the ferry, landing on September 16. The apostle and some companions walked down to the ranch where Price Johnson dispensed melons, grapes, apples, almonds, and misinformation. Widtsoe had a good grasp of pioneer history and was delighted to meet a son of Warren Johnson, whose years of faithful service had not been forgotten.

Next morning, the party got an early start going up the Spencer Trail to duplicate the governor's climb of the previous month. Dr. Widtsoe toed out in one hour and thirty-five minutes—not bad for the forty-nine-year-old man of letters. It was Sunday and he combined his deep religious feelings with an objective appreciation of the magnificent vista. All first-time visitors were more impressed with LaRue's choice for a damsite as seen from the rim than from the river, and this time Davis did not interfere. After a group picture was taken, the men began descending when they saw fit, Widtsoe and Caldwell coming down in forty-five minutes.

Price Johnson, having volunteered to take them to town, had spent the morning pumping up the tires of his old jalopy. He must have counted on Divine Guidance due to the apostle's presence. It turned out to be a rash offer because, when they finally departed at 4 P.M., they had a blowout in less than a mile and were forced to walk back. The apostle recorded that he had a "long serious talk" with Price, but if he perceived the ferryman's polygamous views he made no mention of it. They reached camp about dark and, finding the survey truck had just pulled in, decided to take it to Flagstaff the next day.

While they were crossing their equipment in the morning and it appeared they would not get away before noon, Irv Cockroft made the mistake of inviting the entire party to lunch before discussing it with his wife. As usual, the supplies on hand did not warrant such an invitation. Margery was out of jerky, but she was resourceful. She dashed over to the ranch and obtained a quantity of asparagus, which grew abundantly along the irrigation ditches. She had just baked bread and fortunately had a fresh jar of mayonnaise. Her menu consisted of asparagus sandwiches and coffee. Engineer Dennis remarked that he had never heard of asparagus sandwiches but he thought they were very good. Margery confessed that she hadn't either but necessity gave birth to invention.[19]

After disbanding in Flagstaff, some of the party went on to view the site at Diamond Creek, where they met J. B. Girand and the W. S. Norviel. Diamond Creek also was in the news because of a grandiose plan advanced by a veteran developer, George H. Maxwell of Phoenix. He advocated the construction of a control dam in Glen Canyon, another high dam in western Grand Canyon, and a tunnel to divert water to the desert in the Topock area. This would benefit Arizona and California, but was so impractical as to be ludicrous. After Diamond Creek, the men visited the Boulder Canyon site and took a boat down river to Black Canyon, where Davis gave a presentation that wasn't disrupted by pirates. They looked at the Eagle Rock damsite at Mile 397 and at Bull's Head at Mile 421 and did not think much of either. The group disbanded at Needles, and this trip constituted the last investigation before the Commission met at Santa Fe.

Sid Wilson did not participate with either party of rim climbers. He and Blockburger were busy making improvements on the ranch site up the Pahreah, using liberally the material, such as old pipe for corral posts and a part of the cabin, left by the Charlie Spencer promotion. That fall, Sid and Jerry began dismantling the upper structure of the Spencer steamboat, dividing the lumber between them. Sid used his share for his cabin's flooring and interior sides, while Jerry hauled his portion to Hurricane. Jerry traded his first house and lot in Hurricane for a Dodge panel truck, and he had acquired another lot and was building a house. Sid used the twelve two-by- ten paddlewheel blades for cabin rafters, and a length of Spencer's six-inch pipe for the ridgepole. He stretched cowhides over the rafters, placed willows above them, and put a layer of shale on top of the branches. He dragged long poles up the canyon and lashed them to the hides over the eaves. These kept the shale from washing over the drip line and added stability to the roof. Some observers commented that the cowhides had been placed hair-side up, effectively concealing the brands.[20]

The Bar Z, waging a losing battle with the squatters of House Rock Valley and the Forest Service on the Kaibab, further reduced its herds. Eph Mansfield had made known his intention to retire at the end of the year 1921, and Stephenson tapped the Forest Service for one of its bright young men to replace him. Delmar McCuistion joined the outfit in October and learned what he could in three months. It made no difference that a former ranger now was foreman of the cattle company; permit restrictions continued. Two herds were crossed in the fall of 1922 and driven to the loading chutes at Flagstaff. The first, which Stephenson said consisted of 1,140 head, required four days to ferry and was on the reservation side on October 28. The general manager browbeat the ferryman on both the head count and ferriage; the herd actually numbered more than 1,400 head plus 40 horses and 11 riders. The ferriage, even on 1,140 head, would have come to $285, but Stephenson paid only $238. A smaller herd of 725 cattle, 39 horses, and a wagon and team were crossed on November 25 and 26; the total ferriage came to $63.75.[21] Price Johnson was no match for the sharp manager.

The Colorado Commission met at Santa Fe on November 9 and as usual the wrangling was over basic issues. Nobody knew how much water the drainage produced from one decade to another, and exceptionally high

runoff in recent years tended to generate the belief that the system produced more than it actually did. The lower basin states leaned toward a
higher figure and wanted a guarantee by the upper basin group that the
output would be divided equitably. If the upper basin could get a compact
that allowed them to guarantee a smaller discharge, these member states
would have more water for themselves as well as having their rights legalized. The Fall-Davis report had settled on an average flow of 16.4 million
acre-feet, and division of this amount was the crux of the dispute.

The upper basin refused to settle for half of the average flow but
finally compromised on Hoover's suggestion of 7.5 million acre-feet for
each. Then Norviel said he would sign if Arizona withheld the output of the
Gila River or was granted a special compensation of 1.0 million acre-feet if
the Gila should be included. Colorado's Delph Carpenter protested but
ultimately agreed. The Colorado River Compact was signed on November
24, 1922, with the upper basin getting 7.5 million and the lower basin guaranteed 8.5 million acre-feet. The Compact, in effect, guaranteed the rights
of the upper basin states and made no mention of a control dam and storage reservoir or the All American Canal. The document was flawed further;
it failed to mention that Arizona was to get the extra 1.0 million acre-feet
and instead allocated that additional amount to the entire lower basin. The
weakness of the California representative had caused Norviel to fight alone
for the rights of the lower basin while establishing a basis for years of litigation that approached armed conflict.

By definition the two basins were divided at Compact Point, a hypo-
thetical location one mile downstream from the mouth of the Pahreah
River.[22] For this reason, it was necessary to install a gage on that stream to
record the discharge, as its drainage was part of the upper basin. Legal
technicalities prevented this for almost a year. Early in August 1922, Roger
C. Rice, district engineer of the U.S. Geological Survey, and H. W. Dennis,
chief engineer of the Edison Company, agreed to build a stilling well for the
Colorado River gaging station. They chose a location on the left bank near
the end of the dugway. The Shinarump conglomerate was prominent here
and the velocity was fast enough to discourage sedimentation; the conglomerate would provide a firm foundation for the well. The work was headed by
F. C. Egbert, a USGS hydraulic engineer, assisted by Dennis, who arrived
October 10. The well was completed December 16, and a continuous water-
stage recorder was installed on January 19, 1923. A new vertical staff-gage
also was installed on the side of the well and set to an arbitrary datum tied
to sea level by the Coast and Geodetic Survey in 1921.[23]

The Edison Company appeared optimistic that it would receive a
federal license to construct Glen Canyon dam. The large boathouse built
on the left flat in 1922 now housed a number of motorboats. Core drilling
had been completed at the Glen Canyon site number 1 on January 20, and
D. A. Dudley had set and adjusted the automatic recorder. The ferry was a
veritable beehive of activity.

After Charlie Spencer's money ran out, Jim Klohr and Owen Clark took care of Sid's horses on the bench, but when the weather turned cold, they trailed the stock to the ranch up Pahreah Canyon. Clark remained there to help improve the place while Klohr went to Flagstaff, where he consulted County Attorney Frank M. Gold regarding the back wages owed by Spencer. He was told that even if he got in the long line of creditors, it was unlikely he would receive anything. He found employment in town as a cook and was so engaged when he received a letter from Cockroft offering him the job of assistant hydrographer. He decided to accept and telegraphed some money to Chris. The Klohrs arrived on the Edison truck late in January 1923 and set up housekeeping in the Spencer bunkhouse.

According to Klohr, Cockroft left no doubt about the relations between himself and his assistant. He told him he "didn't want any familiarity" and he expected to be saluted each day.[24] Having spent several years in the Army, Jim was used to the practice and while aware that it was uncalled for here, complied with the request to keep the peace. Klohr started on the new job on January 30, 1923. Roger Rice had visited the station earlier to observe the new recorder functioning in the gage well.

Tom Campbell, a Republican, had been defeated by G. W. P. Hunt, a Democrat, for the Arizona governorship, and Hunt was not in favor of the compact negotiated by the rival party. It was necessary that the legislature of each signatory state ratify the agreement, and six of them did before the end of April. Arizona was a holdout, refusing to have anything to do with it. (Arizona did not ratify the compact until 1944.) The opposition was led by the old reclamation champion, George Maxwell, who proposed to water more than two million acres in central Arizona by means of a tunnel and a high-line canal from a reservoir on the Colorado River at Diamond Creek. He stumped all over the state making speeches, and more than any other man was responsible for the development of a populist attitude about the Colorado River. Just as Arizona belatedly had come to recognize the value of the strip, her citizens now discovered what the Colorado's water meant to them.

Maxwell published a leaflet which stated that if Boulder Dam were built, "the construction profit goes to Las Vegas; the franchise goes to Nevada; the power goes to Los Angeles; the water goes to Mexico; and Arizona goes to hell." It was true that the compact gave the upper basin states a guaranteed supply of water, and a congressional authorization for Boulder Dam and the All American Canal would give California all she wanted, while Arizona received nothing. Throughout the state popular sentiment was against the "California Scheme."

The Lee's Ferry Post Office had been re-established on August 12, 1922, with Margery Cockroft as postmaster. She was the sixth person to hold the job. She selected the American Placer Corporation's office building as the post office and Irv made a sign that so stated. Her tenure wasn't long, however. Irv Cockroft planned to leave Lee's Ferry by mid-summer of 1923 and had notified the post office officials accordingly. The volume of mail had not been as high as expected, hence the Lee's Ferry post office was discontinued March 15, 1923. Mail service to the historic crossing, with two interruptions, had lasted less than forty-two years, the final span little more than seven months.

In early 1923 Frank Dodge came back to Buckskin Mountain and went across the Kaibab Trail to Grand Canyon Village. There, Emery Kolb told him that his old friend Colonel Claude Birdseye was planning a survey down the river from Lee's Ferry next year. Frank Dodge immediately wrote for a place on the crew and was accepted. In the meantime, he threw in with a roaming cowpuncher supposedly named Shorty Robinson. Frank claimed to have bought a horse from Ranger Bert Lauzon, bringing his head count to five while Shorty had two. They then headed for Cameron and Lee's Ferry, aiming to spend the winter in Nankoweap Canyon.[25] They crossed the river on November 22, 1922, and are so recorded in the ferry book. They went over the Bar Z range and down into the Nankoweap basin and spent December and January living on venison and exploring.

Coming out of Grand Canyon, they had an encounter at a Bar Z line camp that cannot be accurately described because the accounts of Dodge and Ernie Appling are diametrically opposed.[26] Whether the two saddle tramps rode off with Ernie's big bay, Two Step, isn't very important but the horse disappeared and Appling thought the dust cloud they raised was larger than their outfit warranted. They continued up House Rock Valley, crossed the divide, and in due time hit the Pahreah River, which they followed upstream to Cannonville. Here they obtained supplies—possibly by horse-trading—and rode out over the Clark bench to the Spencer Trail and Lee's Ferry. They spent a few days with Sid Wilson and Jim Klohr, then crossed the river on February 7, paying no ferriage because they were broke.

On May 4, the *Coconino Sun* printed an article relating that numerous horses had disappeared and Sheriff Campbell had just returned from a trip to the Panguitch area searching for them. Martin Buggeln, Pete Berry, Bert Lauzon, and Sanford Rowe were among the losers. Sid Wilson confirmed that Lauzon's horse had crossed the ferry but the unfazed owner had claimed he bought the animal. The sheriff noted that two years before the ferryman was instructed to keep a record of every animal crossed on the ferry, but this had not been done.

Price Johnson suddenly resigned as custodian on May 7. Accompanying his resignation was the application of Owen Clark for the position. The county supervisors accepted both at the same time.[27] The salary remained at one hundred and twenty-five dollars per month. Apparently with money in his pocket, Price decided it was time to bring his wife Esther and their seven-year-old son Owen to the ranch. Elmer Johnson operated the ferry from November 22, 1922, to May 12, 1923, at which time he received notice of Clark's appointment and turned it over to him. Owen instituted a new wrinkle in the ferry record-keeping by noting with a simple "N" or "S" which direction the one being ferried was headed.

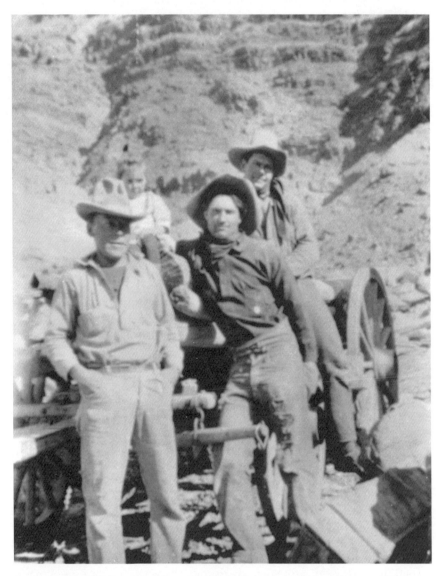

Owen Clark, Sid Wilson, and Don Blockberger at Lee's Ferry, February 1923
(*Hazel Bowlen photograph, from the Klohr Collection, P. T. Reilly Collection, Cline Library, Northern Arizona University*).

May also brought a near tragedy. Two school teachers and a Navajo guide had come across the reservation from Rainbow Bridge to the Sandslide Trail.[28] They descended the sand dune to the Stanton Road and went out toward Flagstaff without crossing the river. Near Navajo Spring they found an old man with a broken leg who would have died if no one happened to come along. One of the women returned to the ferry to enlist help. Cockroft had the only car but wasn't keen on making the long drive. The teachers paid him eighty-five dollars to take the old man to town. He asked Don Blockburger to help him, and the ferry book lists their crossing on May 11, but paying no ferriage. Coconino County records show that Warrant Number 432 for eighty dollars was issued to I. G. Cockroft on June 4, 1923, charged to road services. According to Jim Klohr, Cockroft was paid double for being a good Samaritan, and he gave Blockburger nothing.[29]

Owen Clark had barely two months' experience to his credit when deterioration of the equipment caught up with him. Late in 1921, Frank Johnson had requested replacement of several items, including sheaves, from the county engineer, but nothing came of it. The feeling among county officials was to make the old equipment do until the bridge was built. Dr. Harold S. Colton came to the ferry with the intention of crossing, but when he was about to drive on board he noticed the equipment was so rickety that he declined, returned the way he had come, and took the long way around by way of Kingman and Topock to reach the North Rim.[30]

Two new Studebakers carrying three adults and five youths pulled in from the Kaibab at about 3:30 in the afternoon of July 16, 1923. It was hot, the Cockrofts were swimming in the river in front of the fort, and the river was running 38,200 cubic feet per second. Irv, being road inspector and required to record vehicle license numbers, went up to the landing to obtain them. Clark had both cars run on board, and he cast off. Near mid-river the rig suddenly stopped. The forward sheave had split, locking the ferry in the swiftest part of the current. Cockroft got in his canoe, paddled to the ferry and transferred to the skiff that always accompanied the large scow. The five boys came aboard and one took the line from the canoe. The skiff had no oarlocks so had to be paddled. As they headed for shore, two adult passengers jumped into the water, swam to the skiff, and hung on to the stern. Cockroft, with one paddle, couldn't make much headway hauling himself and five passengers and towing two swimmers and a canoe. He missed the eddy below the Spencer steamer and when he saw he would also miss the next one, he took the line, jumped overboard, and swam to shore. As he pulled his cargo in, the other sheave gave way, the ferry tilted, then boat and machines were submerged. Clark and the remaining passenger swam to shore.

The travelers lost everything, including their transportation and camp gear. They were shown every consideration and were driven to Flagstaff, where they took the train for their homes in Minneapolis. Later, they put in a claim to the county for $4,519.66, but it was rejected in the

November 5 meeting. A lawsuit was filed, and a final settlement of $2,000 was made.[31] F. A. Bean, Jr., of the International Milling Company recommended Irving G. Cockroft for a Carnegie medal, but when the episode was investigated it was decided that the rescue was due to the efforts of several people and the award was denied.

Cockroft perceived a shift of control to the rating sheet from that of 1922, and he took the problem to the USGS office in Tucson. This brought D. A. Dudley to the ferry early in July to instruct the hydrographers in the proper use of the static method of soundings to resolve the problem. As Cockroft's tenure was nearing its end, Dudley worked chiefly with Klohr, instructing him from the basics to the most advanced techniques.

Birdseye assembled the Grand Canyon survey party in Flagstaff on July 15. They started for the ferry three days later, taking a new eighteen-foot boat that overhung the truck bed. They arrived the following day and made camp in the Edison boathouse. Here the three boats from the 1921 survey of Cataract and Glen Canyons were stored in the boathouse, and they would be refurbished to accompany the new boat on the Grand Canyon trip. While preparations were being made, Birdseye and Burchard connected the end of the Glen Canyon survey to the gage well, which had been designated "mile zero" for the downstream measurement. The gage well, opposite the old mouth of the Pahreah River, was determined to be 0.62 mile from the benchmark where the 1922 survey ended. Birdseye then ran his measurement down the left bank to a point below the lower dugway, where it would be picked up when the surveyors started down river.[32]

Jim Klohr probably had lost a day when he wrote the notation on the gage graph that the Birdseye party started downstream on July 31.[33] Both Freeman and Dodge claim the start was made August 1.[34] At any rate, nine men in four heavily loaded boats and Dodge in the canvas boat named the *Mohave* ran the Pahreah Riffle about 10 A.M. Thus began the measurement of the last great unsurveyed river canyon in the United States. August 1 was Dodge's birthday, and Margery Cockroft baked a cake, which her husband delivered from his canoe.

The surveyors camped the first night at Badger Creek Rapid. According to the *Coconino Sun* of August 3, a group of spectators watched from the Badger overlook as the party ran the first major rapid. The observers included Emery Kolb's wife and daughter; Birdseye's son, his cousin who was the ground contact; the Cockrofts; and C. E. Fisk of Grand Canyon. Evidently this was the first of many future mass viewings from this site by the spectator phase of river-running. They spent the second night at Soap Creek, on the right-hand beach near the foot of the rapid. It was at this camp, about 9:15 P.M. Arizona time on August 2, that they learned of Warren G. Harding's death in San Francisco. The radio reception was clear and was received less than an hour after the president's demise. The dispatch came from Los Angeles and was heard at Soap Creek as soon as at Flagstaff.[35] This helped usher the Arizona Strip into modern times and disproved the widely accepted theory that radio waves did not penetrate into deep recesses of the canyon country.

A number of Flagstaff people who had come to watch the Birdseye expedition start downstream remained over to obtain some fish—a custom since the Spencer promotion. Charlie had left several boxes of dynamite, rolls of fuse, and caps. His men had often dynamited the eddy for fish, and the Johnson boys took up the habit. The river had an inexhaustible supply, the Johnsons were accommodating, and the citizens of Flagstaff, including city and county officials, took advantage of the situation.[36]

In their board meeting of August 6, the Coconino County supervisors voted to visit the ferry, investigate the recent accident, and settle on a replacement ferryboat. They did this near mid-month and decided Clark was not to blame as the accident had resulted from deterioration of the equipment. At the same time, notice of the special election to be held December 4 was posted, with the Grand Canyon Cattle Company ranch house designated the polling place. The previous election had illustrated how easy it was to pick up extra money by serving as precinct officials, and the local residents jumped at the chance to do so. For this particular balloting, O. R. Clark was named inspector; I. G. Cockroft and Jerry Johnson were judges; Mrs. Jerry Johnson and Mrs. Sidney Wilson were clerks; and Mrs. I. G. Cockroft was marshal.

Cockroft and Klohr made their last reading together on July 25; from that time on, Jim was the hydrographer and did most of the work by himself. Possibly Cockroft oversaw the operation, as he remained in residence while waiting for reassignment. On August 9, a new method of ferry crossings was achieved. A car showed up and the driver insisted he had to get across although the ferry was out of commission and a new one was not even being constructed. Clark, Klohr, and Wilson talked the matter over and decided to cross the car suspended from the gaging cable, if the driver was willing. He was, but declined to ride while the vehicle made the trip. The car was balanced on four points, hoisted close to the sheave clevis by a heavy-duty block and tackle, and started over the river. A rope had been attached to it and the coil taken across by the men in the skiff. The load coasted easily to mid-river but had to be pulled uphill to the other bank. There was no set fee for such a service so Owen charged seven dollars.

The U.S. Geological Survey assumed full control of the Lee's Ferry gaging station on November 1, 1923. The Cockrofts remained until after the election, probably to collect their fees. They held the ferry's first garage sale before leaving; Klohr bought forty dollars worth—all he could afford— and Cockroft burned the rest. The furniture was all home-made—a willow bedstead, tables and chairs made from boxes—all crude but sufficient. With no ferry available when they departed on September 5, the Cockrofts headed west over the Kaibab on the two-rut road which was rough and washed out in places, requiring repair work to be passable. On some stretches they spent an hour covering one mile. They drove to St. George,

Las Vegas, Searchlight, crossed the Colorado at Topock, and reached the U. S. Geological Survey office in Tucson on September 13.[37]

Jim Klohr moved his family into the vacated fort. The Spencer addition on the west side was a bedroom; the Edison Company had put a roof over this portion when the boathouse was being constructed. The east end containing the fireplace was used as a living room and the middle area served as the kitchen. Cockroft had added a ramada and built a cellar and an outhouse. His wife had planted a small vegetable garden at the fort, watering it with buckets of river water. If the men who built the fort in 1874 could have returned to see the evolution of their handiwork, they would have been surprised.

The Klohr family was about to retire at 9:30 P.M. on September 19 when Jim noticed the sound of the river was unusually loud. He went down to his boat landing and discovered the water had come up several feet from its level at sundown. It was still rising and he re-tied his four boats, which now were several feet offshore and ready to break loose. As he pulled them farther up on the beach, the river's roar increased and heavy drift appeared. By 11 P.M. the river was solid with driftwood; some of the logs seeming to be eighty feet long with the appearance of just having been uprooted. Klohr remained there until about 1 A.M. when the flood apparently crested. He was unable to cross the river until noon of the twentieth. The gage indicated a rise of 13.5 to 14 feet.[38]

The Birdseye party was hit by the same flood at Lava Falls, enlarged by substantial inflow from the Little Colorado River. They recorded an initial rise of fourteen feet on August 20, plus eight more feet the following day. They assumed from its color that the water came from the Little Colorado and reached 125,000 cubic feet per second.[39] Klohr's report indicates that a good portion of the flood poured down the main stem. The peak later was adjusted downwards to 117,000 cubic feet per second.

Al Simms of Lake Mary was given the contract to build the new ferry, and it was launched on September 28. The total cost was $1,087.05.[40] The Grand Canyon Cattle Company started moving another large herd to Flagstaff in late October, arriving at the ferry on the twenty-eighth. Stephenson had kept track of the ferryboat construction and timed his arrival accordingly, as this drive was to be ferried. Swimming the herds had always resulted in some loss, and the general manager disliked losing a single cow. Ferrying the animals was hard work for everybody concerned. Feed on either side of the river was no better now than it had been forty years earlier. Some of the cattle were held at the ranch where there was plenty of alfalfa and water; they were driven to a holding corral at the ferry as fast as they could be loaded and taken across. Other hands took hay across the river to suffice until the herd could be moved out. The ferryman worked hardest of all, from daylight to dark. He not only had to help load but to cast off, handle the lines, and tie up. Then it was a rush back to the right bank for another load.

Sometime during the operation, Stephenson became aware that Clark was counting the cattle as they boarded and keeping track of the total number crossed. Previous ferrymen never had done this but had accepted Stephenson's head count of the total herd, which always was lower than the actual number. The ensuing argument was one-sided: when the manager threatened to have him fired for doubting his word, Clark hit him. There was no fight as Stephenson backed off. At the close of the job, Clark's tally stood at 1,746 cattle, 36 horses, 2 wagons, and 1 car. The ferriage amounted to $335.10.[41] True to his word, Stephenson tried to have Clark discharged when he reached Flagstaff.

The Bar Z drive registered another first in that two cars of movie cameramen picked up the herd in House Rock Valley and obtained selected shots along the way. A male lead named Roy Stewart supposedly helped gather the cattle and appeared at several places along the drive. The director tried to induce Stephenson to swim some of the cattle across the Colorado but was turned down.[42] Stephenson had no sooner loaded the cattle at Flagstaff when the outfit returned to House Rock Valley to make another drive. Again, the movie cameramen were on hand but Eph Mansfield and Frank Johnson were not, and the attempt to swim some of the cattle for the cameras never got started. On November 22, Clark ferried the entire outfit of 1,586 cattle, 28 horses, 1 four-up wagon, 1 two-up wagon, and Stephenson's car for a ferry fee of $324.20.[43] Henry Stephenson had not let the matter of the ferryman drop; he was merely biding his time.

He soon learned, however, that he was not dealing with one of the trusting, naive Johnsons. In fact, Clark was aware of the manager's efforts to have him fired, so he took the battle to him. He notified Harvey K. Meyer, superintendent of the Western Navajo Agency, that the Bar Z had crossed a total of 3,332 cattle at Lee's Ferry and logically the same number had been trailed through the reservation to Flagstaff. Stephenson had reported that 2,146 cattle crossed the reservation in 1923 and he had paid for that number. Meyer took up the matter of the 1,186 unreported head with him and appears to have obtained a settlement.[44]

Stephenson made one more effort to have Clark discharged. This time he worked through the State Livestock Sanitary Board in Phoenix, but that body passed the request summarily back to the Coconino County supervisors. They refused, stating that Owen Clark had turned in more ferry fees in seven months than any previous custodian had in a year.[45] Everyone now was aware that the Grand Canyon Cattle Company was drawing its operation to a close and they saw no reason to accommodate an undependable departing resident instead of backing a faithful employee.

Governor Hunt made a loop trip from Topock across the Arizona Strip to Lee's Ferry in mid-October to publicize the need for two new bridges—one west of Grand Canyon, and the other at or near Lee's Ferry. He was accompanied by State Game Warden G. M. Willard and a forestry expert, S. B. Locke, who were to examine the deer situation on the Kaibab. The main concern was that the killing of cougars had allowed the mule deer to multiply to an estimated 25,000, while another 8,000 animals were expected to be added this year through natural increase. At the same time, range permits had been reduced from 11,000 to 5,600 head of cattle, and pressure was mounting from all quarters to solve the deer problem.[46]

Charles Lewis, the Bar Z handyman who managed the Lee's Ferry ranch, would always remember the year of 1923. He had been subpoenaed to testify in Phoenix on a federal case involving his company. He told Jim Klohr that he saw his first train on this trip—even rode on it—and ate his first banana.[47] The year ended on a high note for Coconino County when Congressman Carl Hayden sent Joe Richel, clerk of the Board of Supervisors, a letter stating that he had introduced a bill to construct a bridge at the selected site below Lee's Ferry. The cost was to be split between the federal government, on behalf of the Navajo Indians, and the State of Arizona.[48]

Not all strip residents were in agreement on the bridge location. A noisy group of Fredonia citizens claimed that a bridge linking their town with Seligman, crossing the Colorado between Toroweap and Prospect Valleys, would be of more benefit to them than one at Lee's Ferry. Vulcan's Anvil (Mile 177.8) was even suggested as the base for a pier. Other Fredonia citizens opposed the western site, claiming that Lee's Ferry was much preferred. The matter was put to rest when it was pointed out that the western bridge would not benefit the Navajos and other funding would have to be found. Carl Hayden, E. C. LaRue, USGS Director George Otis Smith, Interior Secretary Herbert Work, and nearly everyone in Coconino County smothered the drive for a change and kept the bridge at Lee's Ferry.[49]

The U.S. Geological Survey wisely established a policy of having two men stationed at Lee's Ferry during the period of high water. Jim Klohr's assistant I. G. "Rudy" Kasel arrived on April 1, 1924, and moved into the fort with the hydrographer. It turned out that the runoff for this year was lower than normal, reading only 72,800 cubic feet per second on June 18. The two hydrographers worked together until Klohr went on vacation the first two weeks of August. On his return, Kasel moved to another station and once again Klohr worked alone.

Meanwhile, argument regarding the Colorado River Compact continued and Arizona still refused to ratify the document. Popular sentiment in the state favored Glen Canyon site number 1 despite the fact that no irrigation water could be utilized from the reservoir. State jingoism was rampant and directed at California, with the location for the control dam still in the air. Girand, in December 1923, started drilling at Diamond Creek under a preliminary permit. In the summer of 1924, Federal Judge F. C. Jacobs granted a permanent injunction against construction of the thirty-six million dollar Diamond Creek project.

The controversy aroused more public interest in the Arizona Strip and travel there increased. Automobiles now outnumbered wagons. In

Cable-driven ferryboat bearing automobiles at the lower crossing, ca. 1920s (*A. R. Hromatka photograph, Woodruff Collection, P. T. Reilly Collection, Cline Library, Northern Arizona University*).

April twenty-three cars, one band of loose stock, one wagon, and four Indians crossed at the ferry. In May, the count was thirty-nine cars and seven teams. Although National Park Service personnel had crossed previously, the first car registered to the service made the crossing May 18, 1924, paying three dollars for the privilege.[50] The ranger evidently was driving to the North Rim to assess the critical deer situation. More cars crossed in August—fifty-five—than in any other month up to this time. Travel fell off only slightly in the fall, with fifty-one cars crossing in September and forty-seven in October. These records all were broken in December due to the promotion of the Kaibab deer drive; a total of sixty-nine cars crossed, mostly on passes issued by the Coconino County supervisors.

The deer drive came about because of man's tinkering with the balance of nature and general wildlife mismanagement. Intense hunting of the cougar had resulted in a near depletion of the animals. Lions are predators whose chief prey is deer. When the numbers of predators decreased, the quantity of deer increased and soon there was not enough browse to sustain them. The problem became acute before it was recognized, and by then no one knew what to do about it.

One man who thought he had the answer was George McCormick of Flagstaff. While there were thousands of deer on the North Rim—and

Ferryboat with automobile and passenger, 1926 (*Emily D. Boyer Collection, P. T. Reilly Collection, Cline Library, Northern Arizona University*).

they were starving—those on the South Rim had been hunted to the point of scarcity and there was plenty of browse. George conceived the idea of driving some of the North Rim deer to specified areas on the southern range, much as Australian rabbit-drives had been conducted. He knew the area well, having mined along the Butte Fault, searched for John D. Lee's fictitious gold mine, and been in and out of the canyon by trail. He proposed rounding up the animals, channeling them by drift fences to the Nankoweap Trail, along the Horsethief route through the canyon, and up the Tanner Trail to the South Rim. His idea received great local support from the time of its proposal.

Governor Hunt, in October, authorized a state contract to be written for McCormick to deliver between three and eight thousand animals. George was to receive two dollars and fifty cents for each deer and the drive was to take place in December. It even was planned for the animals to be driven up the Tanner Trail on a Sunday so that people could witness the spectacle. One-fourth of the herd was to remain at the south rim, another fourth was to be driven to the San Francisco Peaks, and the others were to be taken to areas southeast and southwest of Flagstaff. Indians and cowboys were to be the drivers, but anyone could participate. The Lasky motion picture company paid one thousand dollars for the film rights, and guaranteed to give McComick one dollar a head for those shown in the picture.

The famous and near-famous rushed to climb on the deer-drive train. It was a promoter's dream, enough to send a chamber of commerce president into ecstasy. Zane Grey was to write the story; Lee Doyle, who had guided Sharlot Hall through the strip in 1911, was the official outfitter; Buck Lowrey, the trader at The Gap, was slated to manage the Indian detachment; Sid Wilson was signed to provide horses; and a subscription was circulated in Flagstaff to give McCormick a thousand dollars to drive the deer through the city streets. The only dissenting voice was that of Lorum Pratt, Jr., of Fredonia who opined that the plan could not possibly succeed.

The original date of November 10 was re-scheduled to December 16—a risky thing to do, as the residents should have known. A three-mile drift fence consisting of six-foot hog wire was built to funnel the deer into the trail at Saddle Mountain. It was estimated that thirty thousand deer were in the immediate area, and they were baited with apples, potatoes, and salt. At last all was ready and a steady stream of participants began crossing the ferry. Among them were Zane Grey and his Japanese valet who requested lodging from Jim Klohr. Klohr took them in but they had to sleep in the kitchen. Grey used a canvas folding cot while the valet wrapped himself in a blanket spread upon newspapers on the floor. It had turned bitter cold—fifteen degrees below zero—and Jim told Grey he would be better off on the floor beside the valet, but the author brushed off the suggestion. When they awoke in the morning, Grey was on the floor and the Japanese valet was shivering on the cot. The Lasky camera crews were not so lucky, finding scant protection in one of the old Spencer buildings.

When the drivers gathered at the designated place on the morning of December 14, the temperature had dropped to twenty degrees below zero. It began to snow and a howling gale set in; visibility was reduced to fifty feet. The six Lasky camera crews were set up at advantageous positions even though the operators couldn't see anything to photograph. When the actual drive started at 2:30 P.M. on the sixteenth, it was twenty-two degrees below zero and snowing hard with already knee-to-waist deep snow on the ground. There were about one hundred twenty-five drivers armed with cowbells and six-shooters loaded with blanks.

There were plenty of deer before the drivers, but the animals faded between them or cleared the six-foot fence as if it were not there. When the men reached the trail head not a single animal was to be seen. The drive was an utter failure and only one deer was transferred to the South Rim—a fawn that was driven around the canyon and over the ferry in the car of Ranger Fred Johnson and his wife, Tiny.[51]

A comparison of the discharge records at Lee's Ferry, Topock, and Yuma indicated that ferry readings generally were too low, while those made at Topock were too high. As a result of the disparity, a general investigation was made. Jerry Johnson had stated that the great flood of 1884 was two feet above the high-water mark of 1921. This led Dickinson and Jim

Klohr, on September 22, 1924, to run new levels from the mark on Jerry's peach tree to bench mark number 38.[52]

    Bar Z made its last cattle drive to Flagstaff in November, completing a two-day crossing on the twelfth. This time Owen Clark counted only 660 cows, 163 calves, 13 saddle horses, 22 loose horses, and 1 four-up wagon. Stephenson did not bother to attend the crossing or the drive. Clark hired Jerry Johnson to help cross the stock.[53] Everybody knew that the Grand Canyon Cattle Company was closing its operations on the House Rock-Kaibab range and an era was coming to an end. There was much conjecture about what would happen to the range rights and the fate of the Lee's Ferry ranch.

12

Change and Reversion

I N NORTHERN ARIZONA, 1923 IS BEST KNOWN FOR THE END OF THE BAR Z
Ranch. E. J. Marshall's bankers forced the liquidation of the ranch holdings
in House Rock Valley, but it was the canny general manager who figured
out the best disposal of the Lee's Ferry ranch. Stephenson knew that
Charlie Lewis had good rapport with the Johnson boys and that Jerry did
not have the imagination to initiate any large-scale operation without stimu-
lation. It appears that he planted the idea with Lewis, who then transferred
it to Jerry over a period of several months.

The general concept was that Warren Johnson's sons should own
the ranch their father had managed for the church for more than two
decades. The church should advance the money, and Jerry should file on
the land for a homestead. The land had never been legally surveyed and
the cattle company had only a right-of-use title. If Jerry had both rights in
his name, the title would be iron clad. Although there were other complications that Jerry's simple reasoning did not recognize, this is exactly what
developed over a lengthy period. The Johnsons lived in poverty, existing
mostly on what they raised at the ranch. All of them held various jobs with
the county, the cattle company, and the Edison Company at one time or
another but had quit to return to the agrarian existence with their relatives
at the ranch. The lack of a steady income was sorely felt, but they realized
that they couldn't have everything and would have to endure some discom-
forts if they were to return to the Mormon world of 1880. They concurred
that if the men could pick up occasional jobs from the county, they could
get by and reduce contamination by outsiders to a minimum.

Although they were not consciously aware of it, the Johnsons were
raising their children exactly as they had been brought up. The youngsters
were wary of strangers, and even when familiar river gagers came to the
ranch, they would fade behind a corner or dive into the bushes and disap-
pear like a covey of quail. Social ease was an unrecognized term and if they
were not actually taught to avoid those not of their ilk, they nevertheless did
so. Balanced diets were unknown, as was any inclination toward variety.
According to Owen Johnson, they lived on asparagus in the spring, melons
in the summer, and bread and gravy the rest of the time. Sometimes the

men would throw a stick of dynamite into the eddy and they would augment their diet with a fish fry.

At the same time, a peculiar means of female identification came into use. Since nearly everyone at the ranch was named Johnson, they avoided confusion by using the given names of their husbands and the title "Miz." Thus, Pearly was Miz Jerry, Viola was Miz Elmer, Esther was Miz Price; the Gentile women were Miz Jimmy and Miz Sid. Chris Klohr even heard Johnson women refer to each other in this manner rather than by the normal first name or "Sister Johnson"—at least when speaking to her.

All the local inhabitants looked forward to county elections, not for political results but for the fees paid for officiating at them. The 1922 action had shown the way; the primary election of October 10, 1924, and the general election of November 4 had convinced all Lee's Ferry residents that being an election official was an easy way to garner a few dollars. On the last two, J. E. Klohr was inspector, Elmer Johnson and O. R. Clark were judges, Mrs. Elmer Johnson and Sid Wilson were clerks, and Christina Klohr was marshal. Affiliation with the two parties was divided and electioneering was nonexistent unless campaigners came out from Flagstaff.

The winter of 1924–25 was unusually severe. The river was frozen one hundred and fifty feet out from each shore by Christmas Day, and by New Year's Eve there was only a narrow strip of open water in midstream. An ice jam started forming on January 1, and the river was frozen over except at the Pahreah Riffle. On the ninth, the station was inoperative with the stilling well and recorder frozen in place. Several Navajos with saddle horses and pack mules crossed on the ice January 15—the first time this had been possible since 1912.[1] Later that day, the Klohrs crossed the ice on foot from one bank to the other. A channel opened at the ferry crossing on the thirtieth and the ice began moving down river on February 2.

Owen Clark was reappointed ferry custodian in early January, but it turned out to be his last month in that capacity. The reason for his termination or resignation still is not clear; perhaps the influence of Henry Stephenson caught up with him or the hand of local politics was felt. At any rate, Clark was out and a new man, Chester A. Moon, who had worked for Charlie Spencer at both Lee's Ferry and Pahreah, was appointed. Clark turned to working periodically for the U.S. Geological Survey. After Spencer's various promotions had failed, Moon had drifted to Bisbee and found work in the copper pits. In due time, he met and married a miner's daughter whom he called "Sweeter." Considerably younger than her husband, she called him "Papacito." Evidently she agreed to the marriage in order to find a way out of the dead-end mining town, and the pair came to Flagstaff where Moon had friends. Somehow, he was appointed custodian of Lee's Ferry, effective February 1, 1925, despite his record of never having officially operated the ferry. The salary was still a hundred and twenty-five dollars per month. The couple moved into Frank Johnson's old cabin at the crossing.

Jerry not only accepted Charlie Lewis' suggestions, but he added something that had not occurred to the handyman. He now saw the ranch as the perfect place to put his religious views into practice, to build his version of the pre-manifesto society, to create a polygamous commune. But his plan was known only to himself, Price, and Elmer. He went to Salt Lake City and presented to Anthony W. Ivins the proposition that several of Warren Johnson's sons—including Frank, who knew nothing about the scheme—wanted to own and operate the ranch as had their father. They did not want outside interests to acquire the property, but they had no money. The Johnsons wanted the church to make the down payment; they would make the succeeding ones and repay the original investment. Ivins, first counselor to President Heber J. Grant, was a man whose opinions and recommendations carried great weight. He was sympathetic to Jerry's request and taken in by the presentation.

Ivins had been well acquainted with Johnson's father, knowing him as a man of good judgment, great faith, and high moral integrity. Assuming that the son had the same character as his father, he recommended that the church advance the four thousand dollars needed to buy out the Grand Canyon Cattle Company. This was done on May 25, 1925.[2] Considerable trust was involved; the ranch was in Jerry's name and the church held an unsecured debt against him. It is not known who suggested the subdivision plan, but Jerry probably remembered the little cabins his father had built for the benefit of trysting polygamists. The plan evolved slowly because it started with only himself, Elmer, and Price. They needed several more anti-manifesto nonconformists who were willing to live the life they preached. The final realization would be a fundamentalist commune, its people housed in apartments or cell-like dwellings, and the cultivated land divided into parcels among the participating families.

Frank Johnson had lived in Hurricane since leaving the ferry in 1922. He went on a church mission to Washington state in December 1924, and while there received a letter from Jerry telling of the plan for the Johnson brothers to purchase the ranch and saying Frank's name was used to advance the cause with Ivins. Frank was known for his integrity and devotion, which undoubtedly had figured in the decision. After several letter exchanges, Frank agreed to help pay off the place and to participate in the subdivision plan providing he got the parcel by the lane. Jerry agreed; everything now was in order and the plan incubated.

The first birth at Lee's Ferry in fifteen years occurred on April 21 when Elmer and Viola Johnson became the parents of a daughter they named Mae.

Klohr went to Flagstaff on April 2 and returned two days later with D. A. Dudley and D. H. Barber. They bought a new friction-type float wheel for the automatic recorder and installed it the following day. Barber, a civil service engineer, was assigned to help during the flood season; he moved into the fort with the Klohrs. Dudley remained but a few days, working with

Jim Klohr at Lee's Ferry Post Office, 1924 (*P. T. Reilly Collection, Cline Library, Northern Arizona University*).

the hydrographers to refine the measuring techniques. W. E. Dickinson, who had replaced R. C. Rice as district chief at Tucson at the end of 1923, visited the station in May and reviewed the entire procedure. On June 12 the hydrographers set a bronze-tablet benchmark in a large sandstone boulder eight feet west of the southwest corner of the fort. After establishing the elevation of this benchmark, they ran levels to the mark on the peach tree that had served as a refuge for Jerry's cottontail in 1884.

Klohr went on vacation the first two weeks of August and then took charge of the Topock gage on the Colorado River. It was USGS policy to rotate the hydrographers between the various stations—a procedure that pleased everyone. Barber worked alone for several weeks. Dickinson decided to discontinue use of a resident hydrographer on September 30. Jerry and Elmer Johnson were hired to read the gages and change the tapes for the rest of the year, aided by occasional visits from Dudley and Baumgartner.

At this time, Dave Rust had a profitable tourist business going in Glen Canyon that included visits to Rainbow Bridge; his trips ended at Lee's Ferry. One such party landed there on the morning of August 10 and a Dr. F. I. Proctor hired Jerry Johnson to drive him to El Tovar. When they arrived at the South Rim, Proctor asked the charge, then doubled it. Jerry was so enthused at the tourist's generosity that he wrote Rust to tell him about it.[3]

The Johnson brothers all realized they had been short-changed when they were young in not having a school at the ferry. The influx of outsiders in the summer of 1921 caused a redoubling of efforts to start a new school, but the number of potential students was too small to interest the county and the attempt failed. Jerry managed to start an unofficial school in the fall of 1921, using the old Spencer bunkhouse between the Wilson residence and the river for a schoolhouse. Several teachers were brought in from Fredonia and Kanab, but they were not qualified, the inducement was low, and they didn't stay long. The Johnsons paid what they could accumulate among themselves, which wasn't much. There were no books or equipment although they "borrowed" some from the Fredonia District. Price's son Owen, who attended, recalled how the students would watch Sid Wilson bring his packstring down the Spencer Trail while class was in progress.[4] The sessions became irregular and finally were abandoned altogether due to the inability to hold and pay teachers.

Now, four years later, Jerry, Elmer, and Price all had children of school age and their need for a school was real. They petitioned the county supervisors in the spring of 1925 to establish a district at Lee's Ferry, promising to meet or exceed the minimum number of students required. The board approved the request on June 1, 1925. The old District Number 11 had been absorbed in county growth, so a new number—twenty-six—was assigned and school was scheduled to open October 5. School Superintendent Acker certified Jerry and Elmer as the trustees of District 26 on August 6.[5]

As when Jim Emett was ferryman, a teacher willing to go to such a remote place was hard to find. Jerry Johnson was wooing a polygamist woman at Draper—he possibly had already married her—when he met Ruby A. Huish in Bountiful. He persuaded her to come to the ferry and she reluctantly consented to teach one more year before she married. She was not certified in Arizona but Jerry was sure she could qualify. He told her nothing about the polygamous activity and she assumed she would be working with the children of orthodox Mormons.[6] Ruby was given a trial certificate and paid a salary of one hundred forty dollars per month; had she held Arizona credentials the pay would have been one hundred sixty. She was employed for eight months but was allowed to teach on Saturdays so the term could be completed prior to May 1 rather than the usual June 30, due to the warm weather and the primitive nature of the district. Ruby boarded with the Spencers, who lived in John Emett's old house by the creek at the end of the lane. Her schoolhouse was the one-room cabin Jim Emett had rebuilt with Warren Johnson's logs and timbers from the *Nellie* mining boat.

Jerry knew that the number of school-age children at the ranch was slightly under the minimum required for a county district, but he juggled things a bit and fate helped him at the opportune time. First, he induced his sister Lydia and her husband Isaac Carling Spencer to bring their family to the ranch from Glendale. Both Spencers were fundamentalist to the core and didn't have to be coaxed. They brought three children to the school, and Spencer even became involved in Jerry's communal land parceling. Carling Spencer's house served as a town hall for the fundamentalist meetings, of which there were many. The lucky break came in the form of an early snowfall that shut down travel over Buckskin Mountain just after Cleve and Leo LeBaron with their families had come from Mexico en route to Utah. Leo put his two children in school at the ranch while he tarried two weeks at the ferry waiting for the snow to melt.

The school started from scratch with no books or equipment. The total budget was broken down in the following manner: salary, $1,120.00; supplies, $35.04; janitor, $60.00; fuel, $65.00; building, $24.50; and equipment, $152.95. The head count of fourteen pupils—five boys and nine girls—satisfied Superintendent Charlotte Acker, who was sympathetic to the plight of the remote county residents. Students' ages were five to twelve and they were in grades one through seven. Everything, of course, was in the one-room cabin and each child absorbed some of the others' lessons. It did not take Ruby long to realize that she was in the midst of a microcosm of Mormon society from the 1850s. She was subjected to great pressure to leave her church and join them, but she rejected their proselyting.

Besides working as resident observers for the Geological Survey, Jerry and Elmer Johnson maintained the road for several miles on both sides of the river, drawing county warrants for their work. Frank had returned from his mission to the Northwest and obtained a job delivering mail between Hurricane and Kanab. He did not visit the ferry until late in the fall, and when he did he was very upset to find that Jerry had reneged on the agreed-to land allotment. Instead of Johnson's six sons sharing the cultivated land, Roy and Jody were missing while Cleve LeBaron and Carling Spencer had taken their places. The parcel promised to Frank had been given to LeBaron; Elmer and Carling Spencer had the lots adjoining it on the other side of the lane; Jerry had the piece on which his father's house stood; and Frank was given the lower part of the alfalfa field that had been eaten away by Pahreah floods. Frank withdrew from the scheme on the spot. He notified church authorities of his action and the reason for it.[7]

Sweeter's father, Waddy T. Ligon, decided to visit his daughter and son-in-law late in October. He was seventy-three years old and rather feeble. He had built a box-like cabin on the back of an old Model T Ford, his concept of an early camper. Ligon made the long trip from Bisbee in acceptable fashion but had been too weak to crank his car after stopping at the Gap Trading Post on October 28. He started up the dugway approach and attempted to shift into a lower gear but only succeeded in killing the engine. When he failed to set the brake, the car backed a few feet, the outside wheels went over the edge and the vehicle slid sideways into a ravine. It struck bottom and wedged against the other side, pinning the old man inside. Ligon remained there until Harvey K. Meyer, superintendent of the Western Navajo Reservation, and a couple of companions came by. They were returning from a hunting trip on the Kaibab and heading for Tuba City. Ascertaining the man was dead, and not knowing his identity, they went on to Cameron and telephoned the sheriff in Flagstaff.

Meanwhile, someone else came by, saw the truck and the body, and brought word to the ferryman. Moon got Elmer, who was alone at the ranch, and the two of them went to the scene of the accident. Moon recognized him at once, saying, "It's my father-in-law." They removed the body and took it to the ranch. At that time the Johnsons were tearing down their father's two-story house to get lumber to build the commune cabins. The east wing was practically disassembled and they used some of the lumber to build a coffin. They buried Ligon at once, with Elmer officiating at the service. Sweeter told him he could have the car if he could salvage it. He did, with the aid of a team, and learned to drive in this vehicle. He used it for several years before selling it in Salt Lake City.[8]

Wrangling over the site of the proposed control dam on the Colorado remained heated. President Coolidge came out for a high dam at or near Boulder Canyon in the 1924 campaign, and the move helped him carry California. Arizona still refused to ratify the Colorado River Compact, maintaining that E. C. LaRue's Glen Canyon site number 1 was the best location. The U.S. Senate committee on irrigation and reclamation was sent west to inspect the various sites and report the findings. They examined the Boulder and Black Canyon sites first, then came to Flagstaff on November 7. Most of the committee members, including Chairman McNary of Oregon, had made up their minds beforehand and failed to look at Glen Canyon, but Senators W. L. Jones of Washington and H. F. Ashurst of Arizona joined Commissioner D. E. Carpenter of Colorado, Colorado Attorney General W. L. Boatright, Santa Fe officials, Governor Hunt of Arizona, Mayor L. W. Cress of Flagstaff, and a host of reporters and interested citizens when a caravan of cars left Flagstaff en route to the ferry. The Edison Company made its boathouse available to the party, and the mayor had sent three men out earlier to prepare a good meal. On Sunday morning, the Edison powerboat took the visitors upriver to the damsite. The chief reaction came from Senator Jones, who murmured, "The site is very inaccessible." The visitors then lunched at the boathouse and returned to Flagstaff. The major sites—at least two of them—had been inspected.[9]

When 1925 came to an end, two, and possibly three, of the Johnsons had second wives. Price married Helen Hull, and Elmer had taken Artemisia Shumway, both on Christmas Day. If Jerry had married a second wife, as Frank claimed, he kept her at Draper and it is not known if he ever brought her to the ferry. His brothers, however, did bring theirs and, together with Carling Spencer, set off a baby boom that lasted until 1933.

Sid Wilson and Owen Clark were running a surprisingly large number of stock up Pahreah Canyon. The snug ranch house was a better dwelling than the Spencer messhall where Mary remained. They had good corrals and about twenty thriving fruit trees. It was rumored over a wide area that Wilson was rustling, especially from the Glen Canyon bench range. He generally had little use for Mormons, and they had little use for him. In fact, his honesty was more or less decided on the basis of creed— Gentiles vouched for his integrity while the Saints, including the fundamentalists, denied it. The cattlemen who ran stock on the Pahreah and Wahweap benches knew they were losing cattle and preferred to believe Wilson was the culprit instead of their colleague Lige Moore.

They had good reason to stay clear of Moore, however, because it was generally accepted that he had been a gunman for the Hashknife outfit along the Little Colorado. He came to Utah in 1890 and over the years had demonstrated his prowess with a six gun. Nobody cared to challenge either his speed or accuracy. In 1925, he was a vigorous seventy-five years of age, and his skill was respected by all. Sid Wilson, too, was reported to be a gunman and was said to have killed a man in a shootout. Unlike Moore, Wilson had never demonstrated his skill in public. He usually wore a six gun on the range, had a .30–.30 in a saddle scabbard, and always carried field glasses. Nearly every cowboy wore a six shooter, but few packed rifles except when wolves were killing cattle.

Late in 1925, the Mormon cattlemen convinced Hy Barton, sheriff of Garfield County, and Jake Crosby, sheriff of Kane County, to investigate the alleged cattle thefts and particularly the activities of Sid Wilson. One of the plaintiffs, Elijah Moore, agreed to accompany them. They rendezvoused with Crosby at Adairville on January 4, 1926, left a cache of food and grain, then rode to Thousand Pockets near the rim of the Echo Cliffs overlooking

Pahreah Canyon. Sid Wilson's ranch was about a mile southwest of their vantage point and they had field glasses, pistols, and rifles. They spied for almost three weeks before seeing any activity. Three riders came up from the river, left two pack mules at the Wilson corral, and went on up the canyon. In about an hour and one-half, they reappeared, driving a small herd of cattle. They branded some of the animals, butchered another, loaded the meat and hide on the mules and went down the canyon.

Next morning the lawmen broke camp, rode to the Spencer Trail, and descended to the river. As they were pitching camp near the cable anchor and cooking their dinner, Chester Moon made several visits and appeared agitated. Wilson had spotted them coming down the trail and shortly after they unpacked, Wilson, Clark, and Appling walked into their camp. Barton made introductions and remarked that he knew Lige Moore was present although he had never met him. Lige's gun was in its holster hung on his saddle forty feet away. Sid is said to have held his gun on Lige, slapped his face and accused him of snooping out of his territory. Moore replied that he was unarmed but if Sid would allow him to get his gun they would see who could draw faster and shoot better. As he turned to get his gunbelt, Sid unbuckled his and laid it on a rock.

What happened next depends on who is telling the story. Jake Crosby said that Lige slapped and scratched Sid's face, humiliating him, and Moore and the sheriff then rode up to Sid's ranch to inspect the cattle. They allegedly found two with altered brands. Ernie Appling claimed that Sid's act of removing his gunbelt and laying his weapon aside diffused the tension, and after more discussion the visitors packed and went up the trail. Mormons brand Sid a coward for refusing to fight, and are divided on who slapped whom. One thing is apparent: the confrontation was between Sid and Lige; the two sheriffs, Clark, Appling, and Moon were spectators.[10]

Jerry Johnson's star reached its zenith on January 24, 1926, when Heber J. Meeks, president of the Kanab Stake, set him apart as presiding elder of the Lee's Ferry Branch of Fredonia Ward of Kanab Stake. At the same time, Annie Spencer was set apart as branch clerk.[11] But his euphoria was short-lived, as almost immediately rumors began to circulate that the people at the ferry were living in blatant polygamy. Many of the Saints did not openly espouse plural marriage but were sympathetic to those who did, and they would not blow the whistle on practitioners unless they proved to be an embarrassment to the orthodox church. In a few months, proselyting by the polygamists among the orthodox families had become so irritating that local church authorities were forced to act. On June 15 members of the bishopric and stake presidency went to Lee's Ferry to investigate. Price Johnson was away at the time, which is the only reason he did not become involved.

They could not close their eyes to what they found. The people there admitted the practice and even argued the righteousness of their cause. There was no choice but to disorganize the branch.[12] The matter was discussed thoroughly by the highest local authorities and three weeks later a course of action was determined. On July 6 complaints were drawn against Jerry and Pearly Johnson and Elmer, Viola, and Artemisia Johnson; Bishop Will T. Henderson of Cannonville served the complaints at Lee's Ferry on July 12. All were ordered to appear before the stake high council at 8:30 P.M. on July 25, 1926. Elmer appeared at the specified time and pleaded guilty for all of the accused. Granted permission to state the reasons for their behavior, he quoted scripture and personal beliefs, but President Meeks declined to argue the case. At the close of the meeting, a unanimous vote to excommunicate all five was passed.[13]

Jerry Johnson's purchase of the ranch had been a sub rosa deal, the price on the deed being "for ten dollars and other valuable considerations." Actually, the church paid out a thousand dollars, and Jerry promised to pay the remainder of the total price at the rate of a thousand per year for three years, and eventually repay the money the church had previously invested. He was unable to make the second payment, however, and so notified the Presiding Bishopric. The brethren in Salt Lake City deemed it best to pay off the Grand Canyon Cattle Company and secure their investment as best they could. On August 19, Jerry and his wife deeded to the church the ranch they had never really owned.[14] The situation was loaded with potential embarrassment for church authorities, who now held title to a property that was being used by known polygamists who had just been excommunicated. Counselor Ivins must have been disappointed to learn that sons do not always have the integrity of their fathers.

At a meeting of the stake presidency and high council held in Kanab on August 22, the excommunications were discussed. Church authorities reiterated their firm stand against plural marriages; violators would not be tolerated. Joseph S. Johnson, orthodox brother to the apostates, expressed his grief for his misguided kin, hoped they would see their mistakes, and come back into the fold.[15] He and Frank, ever steadfast in their faith, retained personal love for the errant ones, but the religious split remained in the Johnson family past the deaths of the principals.

After the Lige Moore episode, Sid Wilson became so obnoxious to the polygamists at the ranch that they held a prayer circle and asked the Lord to remove him. Even Ruby Huish attended and joined the request.[16] Sheriffs Barton and Crosby wrote warrants for Sid's arrest and sent them to Flagstaff for the Coconino County sheriff to serve. Warrants also were issued for Owen Clark, as he had been one of the riders when they were spied on from the Echo escarpment. Sid had been brought to trial in June 1924 on a similar charge, but the case was dismissed at a cost of $274.40 for witnesses.[17] The county authorities had no desire to repeat this, and they had little sympathy for the stock problems in Utah, as it was generally agreed that Utah cattlemen were grazing their herds illegally on the strip.

Wilson's Flagstaff friends tipped him off that a deputy might appear in a few days to take him in. Armed with this knowledge, Sid watched the dugway and when a figure appeared from the south early in

March he went into hiding until the traveler's identity was ascertained. He had arranged a signal with Mary whereby she would hang a white sheet on the clothesline if the traveler was a friend or an Indian blanket if he was a deputy who had come to take him away. Alas for human frailty; one of them got the signals mixed and Sid remained high in the rocks all day even though it actually was safe to show himself.

He had kept a snatch-block and puller hidden in the rocks on each side of the river for a couple of years, thus assuring that he could cross the Colorado without using the ferry.[18] After all lamps were extinguished, he crossed the river on the gage cable and walked to Navajo Spring. He had some horses in the area and knew that they came for water just before midnight. He caught one of the animals, made a surcingle, and rode to Cedar Ridge, where Preacher Shine Smith gave him breakfast and drove him to Lowrey's at The Gap. Buck Lowrey took him to Flagstaff, where he boarded the eastbound train and made a fresh start at Albuquerque, sending for Mary and Margy Jean soon afterward, but leaving his equipment with Owen Clark.[19]

Prior to this, a young man who went by the name of Dick Smith had come to Lee's Ferry from the jurisdiction of the St. George sheriff. It was rumored that his real name was Cunningham and he had the record of a chronic lawbreaker, although he acted like a drifting cowboy. He pre-empted one of the Spencer buildings and did some riding with Sid and Owen. Soon after Sid's hasty departure, a deputy did show up; finding that his quarry had left the country, he took Owen Clark and Dick Smith to Flagstaff instead. There really was no case against either one and they were released shortly.

The first school year for District 26 ended on April 30, 1926, and with it the tenure of Ruby Huish as a Lee's Ferry teacher. The two LeBaron children had withdrawn after two weeks of the opening but the remaining eleven students finished the term, and Ronald Spencer's entry later increased the size of the class to twelve. This was acceptable to county officials. The next semester began on September 6 with teacher Alice W. Lee, a Tempe Normal School graduate. She was recruited by Superintendent Acker, an act appreciated by Jerry Johnson. The children in school where from three families, those of Jerry and Elmer Johnson and Carling Spencer. The latter, however, withdrew his four children at the end of October when he moved to Mexico.

After resigning from the ferry job early in 1925, Owen Clark had learned the river-gaging procedure from Jim Klohr and had been used as an assistant hydrographer at various stations. He did not work steadily and had some free time to care for the stock he and Sid owned as partners. It was thought best to sell the jointly-owned cattle. That fall, Clark gathered the stock and trailed them to Cedar City in a snowstorm. He sold them to John Adams, who had a little spread high on the Sandhills. Adams gave him a check for fourteen hundred dollars and Clark just had time to get to

Mexican Hat to work for the Geological Survey. He did not attempt to cash it for three months; when he did, the check bounced. Adams claimed the brands had been altered and the cattle would not pass inspection and had been seized; therefore, he had stopped payment.[20]

December 13, 1926, was a day of mixed blessings for Jerry Johnson, and the bad part came first. He and Chester Moon crossed the river early to do some road work near Red Point when they saw a large column of smoke coming from the ferry area. Fearing that only the Johnson house could cause a pillar of that magnitude, they hurried back and found the forty-year-old house was a mass of smouldering embers. Pearly and the children were safe. Only a small table and sewing machine had been saved outside of the clothes on their backs. The fire had started in the kitchen and the women and children were unable to extinguish it.

Warren Johnson's house was not a total loss as the east wing had been torn down and the lumber used in the new building program. Two cabins were complete and another under way. Personal loss was greatest; even the bedding was burnt, and it was nearly December. Jerry's friends from Flagstaff to Hurricane came to the family's rescue with donations of food, clothing, and money. There was a marked difference between the way Jeremiah Johnson and John D. Lee were treated after their excommunications; Jerry received none of the hostility that had been directed at Lee. Kanab Ward, which had excommunicated him a few months previously, raised about fifty dollars for his benefit.[21]

Blue Monday turned rosy that afternoon when a crew of General Land Office surveyors pulled in and pitched camp. Jerry Johnson, Sid Wilson, and Buck Lowrey, in 1922, had requested that the land be surveyed so they could file homestead entries and gain legal titles. It had taken a long time but the subdivision was about to commence. The work was headed by United States Surveyor William E. Hiester who had an associate named Otis O. Gould. The country was rough and some of it had to be triangulated. The township was completed on March 5, 1927, including section 22 to the north that contained Sid Wilson's claim.[22] One thing neither Sid nor Jerry knew was that their potential homestead entries were within the power-site withdrawal Number 446 by Executive Order of September 5, 1914, and Number 605 of April 28, 1917. It would be necessary for the Federal Power Commission to approve any entry within the affected area. Apparently Wilson had abandoned his location, but Jerry and Lowrey were still eager to file their entries.

A complication arose late that winter when Dick Smith, the drifter, victimized both Sid Wilson and Chester Moon. Admittedly, life in an old cabin by the Colorado River was dull for Sweeter; her husband was twenty-five years older than she, and the young cowboy offered her things Moon could not and probably never would. Smith and Sweeter ran off together while Moon was doing road work on the reservation. Not only did Smith take the ferryman's wife, but while Clark was gaging on the San Juan, Smith took most of Wilson's equipment that had been left in Clark's care.

The middle-aged ferryman was devastated by his wife's treachery and almost went into shock when the full realization hit him. He knew that his marriage had been a December-May affair, but he was happy in the cabin by the ferry landing and had thought Sweeter was also. He no longer cared to live at the scene of his disappointment and resigned effective April 1, 1927. He had been a good ferryman and an honest one, having turned in $751 for 1926. When the county supervisors met on April 4, they accepted his resignation with regret and appointed Jerry Johnson. A letter which they had never delivered to Moon was written on March 25, 1927, and given to Jerry. It directed the custodian to pass the officials of the State Highway Department free of charge while the bridge was being constructed and a part of the road realigned.[23] By this time, the bridge was certain to be built; the only question was when.

Jubilation had run high in Flagstaff on February 4, 1926, when Representative Carl Hayden dispatched the following telegram:

Washington, D. C. Feb. 4
Coconino Sun, Flagstaff, Arizona

House has just adopted item in urgent deficiency bill appropriating one hundred thousand dollars for Lees Ferry bridge to be available when Arizona legislature appropriates like amount.

Carl Hayden[24]

Congressional wrangling set in when Senator Cameron opposed taking money from the Indian fund to pay for the federal portion of the bridge; he preferred it to come from the general fund.

As the debate continued in Washington, publicity was generated in Arizona, and one who decided to get in on the ground floor was Indian trader David Crockett Lowrey at The Gap. Known as "Buck" by his associates, Lowrey had learned the trading business at Kaibitoh from his friend Tobe Turpin. He had first heard rumors of the bridge in 1924 and resolved to be open for business when the construction started. He obtained his license to trade at Marble Canyon on January 25, 1925, but kept it under wraps until the bridge project was closer to reality. The aforementioned publicity convinced him that the time was ripe, and he transferred his residence to Lee's Ferry in the summer of 1926, moving into Wilson's place with Owen Clark and setting up a trading post. Until he was sure of the bridge site and where the new section of road would be located, he traded and stockpiled building materials.

A state highway survey crew under Percy Jones set up camp at Navajo Spring in late February 1927. They located the selected bridge site, then laid out one and one-half miles of new road that joined the pioneer track leading to the ferry. Marble Canyon was triangulated from east to west side. After two or three weeks of work on the east side of the river, they moved to Lee's Ferry and set up camp by the old fort. Again the bridge approach was connected to the pioneer ruts and the new section of road was staked. The entire job required a stay of six weeks, after which the surveyors moved out in mid-April.[25]

Lowrey began building his lodge on the west side of Marble Canyon where the new road to cross the bridge branched from the pioneer track. He used native rock from the cliffs and hauled lumber and hardware from Flagstaff. The cutoff from the ferry road was already staked, thus solving the problem of location. As soon as the survey was made he would have a legal description and could file a homestead entry. He kept close track of the subdivision as it proceeded.

Budget problems for the funding of the bridge were resolved and four bids were received on June 7, 1927. The lowest bid, offered by the Kansas City Structural Steel Company, was accepted ten days later. A heavy compressor and other excavating equipment were worried over the dugway and across the Colorado during the high water period. Actual excavation was started on the west rim on June 23, mainly to test the stability of the rock. It was slow, dangerous work and was expected to take weeks to complete.

The trustee-in-trust paid off Jerry Johnson's mortgage in full on July 11, 1927, and received a quit-claim deed from the Grand Canyon Cattle Company.[26] A day later, the three-boat Clyde Eddy party of thirteen men, a cub bear, and a dog landed at Lee's Ferry. They had started from Green River, Utah, on June 27, but the rigors of Cataract Canyon, combined with poor leadership, resulted in the withdrawal of three crewmen. Nate Galloway's son Parley furnished the river experience that had gotten the party this far, as the rest of the men were raw recruits. There had been no reason to make the trip except to satisfy the whim of the leader to run a dangerous river. Eddy hired Jerry Johnson to haul eight of the men to Kanab, and while they were gone the bear bit Price's son Owen on the leg, giving him a lifetime scar. They started downstream on the eighteenth but lost another of the crew as McGregory became terrified at the thought of entering Marble Canyon and deserted.[27]

When Miss Lee's school term ended on April 15, 1927, there were only seven children enrolled—those of Jerry and Elmer. Price's and Carling Spencer's families were elsewhere. But the fall quarter opened on September 6 with fifteen students; Price had returned to the ranch and contributed four, and the Lowreys' seven-year old Virginia was enrolled. The new teacher, Iona Davie, was a graduate of Northern Arizona Teachers College.

Both bridge footing excavations were finished by November. The crew moved to the left rim after completing the work on the west side. Moving the heavy equipment taxed both men and ferryboat, and the weight didn't help the walled-up portions of the dugway. The impending winter weather and the lack of adequate housing for the workmen brought bridge construction to a temporary halt. Buck Lowrey was making good progress in building his lodge. He applied for a post office even though he would be at

Lee's Ferry until the bridge was completed. The appointment of Florence Lowrey as postmaster of Marble Canyon was dated October 12, 1927.[28]

Hollywood gave its inestimable touch to river-running when the Pathé-Bray party of thirteen men and six boats left Green River, Utah, on November 8.[29] The former USGS hydraulic engineer E. C. LaRue was technical adviser and in charge, while Frank Dodge was head boatman. Dodge saw to it that his pal Owen Clark was signed as a boatman, and he would have added Cockroft but Margery said it was too dangerous. Of course there were a director, two cameramen, a cook, and two publicity men. The "expedition" reached Lee's Ferry on schedule in twenty-one days, but not before the publicity men had put out the rumor that the so-called "explorers" were overdue, lost in the canyons, or had met disaster. The only trouble the crew actually had was in getting paid with checks that carried two signatures. They managed to have an Army plane fly the canyons searching for them, but if the pilot spotted the boats, his sighting was suppressed.

The crowning touch was to have Clyde Eddy, who had recently ended his traverse at Needles, come out from New York to help in the "rescue." Eddy's ego caused him to jump at the chance to aid in the supposed rescue and he took the first train west. He and George McCormick left Flagstaff on November 24 with a driver who was taking a truckload of supplies to the ferry. At Cedar Ridge, they reached "Gables Camp," a radio publicity station set up by the movie company to dispense information about the explorers to a supposedly eager world. Preacher Smith, then enjoying the hospitality of the trading post, willingly lent his presence to whatever activity was underway and dispensed local lore to the visitors. There was a role for everyone.

Eddy went on to Lee's Ferry the next day and arranged to board with the Lowreys until the river party should appear and resume its progress downstream. He also learned that the terrified McGregory had not returned to the ferry in July, but probably had started walking toward Kanab. His fate never was learned. Florence Lowrey confided to Eddy that Buck probably would build a trading post on the east side of the Colorado as the Indians did not like to cross the river to trade. They attributed this to fear but the ferriage might have had something to do with it. Eddy visited the Lee's Ferry school on November 28 and gave the children a talk on world travel. The teacher and fifteen pupils no doubt constituted the smallest audience to which the renowned adventurer ever spoke, but it went off well for everyone.[30]

The well-fed river party's arrival on schedule shortly after noon of November 30 demolished the publicity that the starving explorers were lost in the desolate canyon. The crewmen were paid with checks signed only by Mrs. Bray, not co-signed by the Pathé treasurer as required. Knowing that they would not be honored, the men went on the ferry's first strike. It did not last long, however, as LaRue promised to intercede to see that they were paid and the men agreed to move on to Bright Angel.[31]

From left to right, Shine Smith, Buck Lowrey, and Clyde Eddy, November 1927
(*P. T. Reilly Collection, Cline Library, Northern Arizona University*).

Thirteen men, including Clyde Eddy, departed downstream on the morning of December 3. George McCormick resignedly rode the truck back to Flagstaff instead of a boat down the river. The publicity experts had led Elmer and Price to expect good jobs on the project but somehow they did not materialize. The unsophisticated Johnsons had never dealt with men who said things they didn't mean and were easily taken in by glib strangers. The Johnson boys heard nothing more of the promised jobs, and Coconino County realized no ferriage from the many crossings made by the specious visitors.

Buck Lowrey, with Owen Clark's help, made excellent progress on the lodge that winter. It now appeared certain that he would complete it before the bridge was finished, although the construction was slowed somewhat when Owen was given steady employment as the resident recorder at the Lee's Ferry gaging station. His appointment was dated January 7, 1928, and he made his first measurement a week later. Previously, he had only worked part time as needed. Florence Lowrey's prediction to Eddy came true. With the lodge having such a good start, Buck and son David, helped at times by Owen and several Navajos, built a trading post about a quarter-mile from the east bridge abutment. Buck had Navajos collect rock while he and David did the masonry. The post was finished and doing business early in March 1928. Of course, there was only so much labor available, and work on the lodge ceased while the trading post was completed. The Navajos cooperated because they would not have to cross the river. Besides the Indian trade, the post was patronized by steel workers who had moved in to begin assembly of the bridge cantilevers.

At this time, the ranch was utilized almost as it had been in Warren Johnson's time. Jerry took care of the orchard, vineyard, and garden, as well as a small amount of alfalfa—no longer the crop it once had been due to decreased demand. Carling Spencer farmed the middle ranch until he went to Mexico, while Elmer and Price worked the upper field, raising mostly melons. There were fifteen children in school and almost as many who did not attend, bringing the ranch population to more than thirty. Two of Frank's sons, Adolpha and Glenn, the former's wife Marva, and their son Milo, had come to the ferry in January after trapping in Soap Creek. The magnet was work to be had at the bridge.

The U.S. Geological Survey also generated employment in December and January when a new gage cable was installed and A-frame supports were built. All of the Johnsons obtained jobs, along with six Navajos. Walter J. Stevens and Orin Spencer ram-rodded the work and received the highest wages—$5 per day—the Johnson boys and S. C. Black were paid $4.50, and the Navajos were paid $3. Jerry and Elmer were terminated as gage observers on March 31, and John A. Baumgartner arrived early in April to help Owen Clark during the high water season. Baumgartner, a capable engineer, soon detected certain discrepancies in Clark's measurements. After checking all the evidence, they found that the new cable sagged a foot closer to the water when the sun expanded the steel. This, of course, provided a different sectional profile and had to be taken into consideration.[32]

As the weather moderated, work was resumed by building the forms for the bridge footings. The concrete pedestals on the left rim were poured on March 9, and those on the west rim were poured on April 5. Most of the Johnsons obtained jobs that did not require particular expertise. Jerry operated the compressor that furnished power to the jackhammers and riveters as the east cantilever arched over the gorge. Elmer and Price worked at form building and removal or wherever they were needed. A camp for the steel workers was established on the east rim, although some of the men bunked in the old Spencer office building at the ferry.

Besides becoming a trading post and boarding house, the Spencer mess hall did a brisk business serving meals. Florence Lowrey not only fed travelers but several bridge workers as well. Marva Johnson helped when she was needed and was always available. After the new trading post opened, Buck or David Lowrey had to be present. The Indians usually required agonizingly long times to conduct simple transactions, and Buck was not as patient as most traders found it necessary to be. An elderly Navajo couple lived up the creek where they raised a small garden. The woman made blankets and when prospective buyers wanted to purchase one, she refused, saying she had to sell to Lowrey. Buck didn't like to extend credit but he did so occasionally and needed blankets to insure his being paid. Sometimes there were confrontations. Once, Marva went to the trading post and found Buck holding an axe handle, his back to the wall, and facing several Navajos. He told her to "get out quick" and she did. Apparently the incident ended peacefully.

The population of Lee's Ferry was curiously divided. A bridge worker named McGowan and his wife boarded at the ranch. They were not Mormons and had no opinion on the manifesto problem, so no attempt was made to persuade them. Realizing that their most likely converts were children of polygamous families, the Johnsons made little effort to proselytize outsiders to any form of their religion. The Lowrey family and Owen Clark lived in the Spencer mess hall; state inspector Woody Claypool boarded with them, sleeping in the cook's quarters, which Buck used for paying guests; visiting engineer Baumgartner and his wife lived in the fort.

Adolpha and Marva were subjected to intense pressure, especially by Pearly, to join the polygamists, but they resisted. As a result, Dolph was relegated to running the ferry, and he worked on the bridge only when extra help was needed. He and his wife lived in his father's old cabin at the ferry and avoided the ranch as much as possible. They associated more with the non-Mormon Baumgartners and McGowans than the apostate Mormons. Thus, the fort and the Spencer buildings housed the Gentile population while the ranch was a small nonconformist enclave existing with the toleration of both Mormon and non-Mormon society.

The ferry record book, filled long ago, had not been replaced. Crossing records now were kept on loose sheets of paper fastened to a clip board, and those were periodically sent to Flagstaff. The loose-leaf sheets have never been found and presumably were destroyed. The crossing contract forms, which had been instituted in 1910 when the county took over the ferry, had very limited use and were not reprinted.

Iona Davie closed her spring term on April 20 with fifteen students. Enrollment had been up to seventeen when Lawrence and John Lee attended before their father's work at the bridge ended. Even fifteen pupils overtaxed the old school house and led to Elmer's making a deal with the school superintendency to build a new one; he offered to furnish the labor if the county would furnish the material. His technique was similar to that of Charlie Spencer in constructing the ferryboat that his men had operated illegally and lost. Unlike Charlie, he did not exact as much of a kickback, but at the same time he had an ulterior motive that Charlie didn't: the Johnsons wanted a larger building that could double for a meeting house.

Elmer Johnson worked another angle that would have had Spencer's approval. He agreed to dispose of all the scrap lumber at the bridge, and then—demonstrating a degree of sophistication not possessed by other members of the family—he bribed the form-construction foreman to discard good lumber with the scrap. All of the wood was hauled to the ranch to be used in various phases of the cabin and school construction. The county ultimately paid $170 for the new building, plus $91.27 for repairs.[33] At the same time, the Johnsons received county warrants for working on the road which was maintained reasonably well. The new school house, a ten-room apartment, and four cabins were built with scrap lumber and what was recycled from the Johnson house.

The old Mormon adversary, Sid Wilson, had not forgotten his possessions and livestock left at the ferry and on the Pahreah range when he made his sudden departure in 1926. Figuring his trouble with the law had blown over, he returned in May. He was visibly upset when he found he had been robbed and couldn't believe that the man he befriended had taken advantage of him. Instead, he thought Owen Clark had sold the saddles and other gear and pocketed the money. Clark couldn't convince him that he had been on the San Juan when Smith absconded with his property and Moon's wife. When Buck Lowrey confirmed Clark's story, Wilson threatened to shoot them both. Not wanting trouble with his old friend, Buck contacted the sheriff.

Deputy Sheriff Art Vandivier and Under Sheriff Durwood L. McKinney got the drop on Sid Wilson when he stepped off the ferry on May 29, and they hauled him to Flagstaff the following day. Vandivier had used the two-year-old warrant instigated by Utah Sheriffs Crosby and Barton. Chris Klohr, then in Flagstaff for the birth of her third child while Jim tended the Topock gage, visited Sid in jail and helped convince him that Buck and Owen were blameless for his losses. After a few days' incarceration, he cooled down and promised to behave himself if allowed to retrieve his stock. The sheriff agreed to this and released him. He returned to the ferry and gathered seventeen mules and thirty-six horses.

Dolph Johnson ferried a third of the band on each of three trips. The river was still high, the stock became frightened when the boat hit the current and water splashed over the side. The animals crowded to the aft end while some jumped overboard and swam. After the difficult crossing was completed, Sid trailed the herd to Ganado where he sold them to the Navajos. This was Sid Wilson's last visit to the ferry; he left his share of the Pahreah ranch to be disposed of by Owen Clark as he saw fit.[34]

Buck Lowrey was not the only one who envisioned the corridor to the strip becoming a major tourist route. Hubert Richardson began building a two-story hotel beside his trading post at Cameron in the spring of 1928. In midsummer, a newly-formed firm, calling itself the Lee's Ferry Stage Line Company, applied for a franchise to provide service between Flagstaff and Fredonia. The application was scheduled to come before the Arizona Corporation Commission at Phoenix on July 30.[35]

The river peaked early in 1928, reaching 113,000 cubic feet per second on June 2 and 3. During the peak, a Los Angeles photographer, Leonard Poole, and a Flagstaff publisher, L. D. Brower, accompanied Cy Perkins of the state Highway Department to the bridge site. Poole and

Brower went to Lee's Ferry to get some pictures from the left rim. The river was running over the road and Jerry advised against taking the ferry but offered use of a rowboat instead. They accepted and started across. When past midstream, Brower lost an oar and the men were panic stricken. As luck would have it, the boat became caught in a large eddy just above the fort and they circled for over an hour before reaching the right bank. Poole got his pictures and they made the return crossing without incident after borrowing another oar. Dolph and Marva Johnson regarded them as "New York cowboys."[36]

The river was running 85,600 cubic feet per second on June 7 when Royce Deans and his Navajo helper Lewis (Nez) Tsinnie arrived close to noon. They drove a wire-cage panel Ford and had taken a load of Navajo rugs across to Othello C. Bowman in Kanab. Marva had lunch ready, but Dolph said he would eat after the crossing. Woody Claypool had prevailed upon Dolph for the use of the skiff, and the safety device was tied up on the left bank when the trio shoved off. Making the crossing without difficulty, Dolph let the forward fall out as far as the left one to avoid a silt bar. He had scrambled ashore with the line when the strong current caught the boat and began moving it toward midstream. He dug his heels in but couldn't hold it. When he reached the water, he went hand-over-hand back to the boat to crank up the forward windlass so the current would push the boat back to the left bank. Deans or Tsinnie could have done this had they been familiar with the operation, but both remained frozen into immobility.

Marva, holding son Milo by the hand, was watching from the right bank as Dolph reached the ferryboat. The pulleys were creaking, the upstream beam was under water, and the deck was tilted to a dangerously steep angle, taking the full force of the current. When the cable let loose, everything went out of sight. She never saw her husband or Deans again, but after a few moments, she observed the motionless Navajo floating downstream.

Marva was completely helpless, could only clutch her child's hand as she strained to see that which common sense told her she wouldn't. Finally realizing that Dolph was lost, she turned and started back to relate the sad tidings. The Baumgartners were the only ones at home and they solaced her as best they could. She went on to the ranch where the wives were coldly disinterested as if satisfied that the young couple was being repaid for not accepting their brand of religion. Only Price's first wife, Esther, and Urban Colvin were sympathetic and the sixteen-year-old boy offered to take the news to Frank, then living at Hurricane. Urban left immediately, relating the loss of the ferry and the drownings as he traveled. He rode all night before stopping to rest at Short Creek. There Frank's fourth son, Glenn, saw him and learned that his brother was dead. He took the news on to his father.[37]

While most of the ranch people gave no comfort to the grieving young widow, Earl W. "Daddy" Parker appeared the next morning to

Adolpha Johnson, the last ferryman, who drowned in the wreck of the last ferry, (*P. T. Reilly Collection, Cline Library, Northern Arizona University*).

express sympathy and offer help. Parker had homesteaded about three miles southeast of House Rock ranch and was rumored to be bootlegging to the Indians, using his small stock operation merely as a front. But he had a good heart and now came forward with an offer of aid when avowedly religious people withdrew. Owen Clark and Virginia Lowrey carried word of the tragedy to the Babbitt post at Cedar Ridge, for the wives of both men were there. Deans also left a son of less than five months; Tsinnie left a widow.

Frank and Rhoda Johnson immediately departed for the ferry. They met Marva and Milo east of House Rock ranch as they were returning to her parents' home in Leamington. Frank learned the details of Dolph's death, then inquired about the polygamous situation at the ranch. She related how second wife Helen served as "helper" to Esther, as did Artemisia to Viola, although the former had a "chicken coop" fixed up rather well for her own quarters. He went on to the ferry to check for himself and resolved to return when the river was lower to search for his son's body.

News of the lost ferryboat reached Flagstaff on the evening of the same day and was printed in the *Coconino Sun* on June 8. At that time the boat was barely visible, swinging on the cable in the eddy. It was suggested that County Engineer J. B. Wright hurry there with a block and tackle to salvage the craft, but he was not sufficiently motivated to make the attempt that soon. After several meetings with the county supervisors, Wright did go to see if the Edison scow could be repaired as a temporary replacement. He found this to be impractical and when told that the bridge would be ready for use by the first of October, recommended against reestablishing ferry service.[38] The supervisors concurred in their meeting of July 2.

This decision brought ferry service at the historic crossing to an end. To be sure, there were several motor and row boats capable of crossing people and small loads, but until the bridge was completed, nothing floated that was large enough to ferry a wagon or an automobile. Service had been available from January 11, 1873, to June 7, 1928—a total of fifty-five years and four days less than five months. There had been interruptions—sometimes for several weeks—and at least fourteen ferryboats were used. The average life of each ferryboat was less than four years.

Marva was gone by the time Wright made his investigation, so he failed to interview the only adult witness to the tragedy. He obtained several second-hand versions of the accident and carried back the impression that the men had been swept into the river by the cable and the boat hadn't capsized until late that night. Thus is legend made.

Florence Lowrey's cousin, sixteen-year-old Bonner Blanton, came out to spend the summer and provide what help he could. He arrived the day after the accident and later recalled that the corner of the ferryboat could be seen turning slowly in the eddy. He remembered that Buck was operating the trading post on the reservation side of Marble Canyon, the walls of his lodge on the west side were half up, and the west cantilever of the bridge arched out over the gorge.[39] Bonner and David, both about the same age, were a great help to the overworked Buck.

Another tragedy occurred on Tuesday morning, June 12. The east cantilever was nearly complete when Lafe McDaniels, one of the high steel men from Kansas City, missed his footing and fell about four hundred and seventy-five feet into the river. Safety nets had not been installed because of the fear they would catch fire from hot rivets. The badly shaken crew took the rest of the day off in a visual search for the body. Four steel workers quit at once, believing the job was jinxed.[40] Not since Brown, Hansbrough, and Richards were lost in 1889 had the Colorado claimed so many lives in such a short time. The east cantilever was completed June 15, arching three hundred and eight feet from the rim. A tower was erected at the end and a cableway installed to the west rim. Deliveries were accelerated, all steel was on site in July, and work on the right cantilever started immediately.

The summer of 1928 saw a remarkable lobbying effort bear fruit. The upper basin states and Arizona had been successful in keeping the Swing-Johnson Boulder Dam bill bottled up in Congress. Adroit maneuvering cleared it through the powerful House Rules Committee. In May, the bill passed the House, Senators Ashurst and Cameron, aided by Utah Senators Reed Smoot and William King, filibustered it in the Senate. In the second Arizona filibuster, the session adjourned without a vote. Congressman Phil Swing knew he must neutralize the Utah senators in their support of the Arizona position. When the Union Pacific Railroad opened its Grand Canyon lodge on the north rim, Representative Swing was one of the dignitaries in the bus cavalcade from Cedar City. The buses also carried President Heber J. Grant and First Counselor Ivins of the Church of Jesus Christ of Latter-day Saints. Before they reached the canyon rim, Swing had secured a promise from Ivins that he would have Senator King's support and Senator Smoot would not oppose him.[41]

The Senate took up the Swing-Johnson bill in December. After a half-dozen amendments offered by King were accepted by the Californians, and six days of debate during which Senator Phipps of Colorado offered an amendment giving the Golden State 4.4 million acre-feet of water, the Arizona delegates admitted defeat and the bill was passed on December 14. The House agreed to the Senate amendments and President Calvin Coolidge signed the bill into law on the twenty-first. The Boulder (actually Black Canyon) site had prevailed over LaRue's Glen Canyon location, and Lee's Ferry was destined to remain as it was—at least for the foreseeable future.

Frank Johnson had the support of his brothers when he returned to search for Dolph's body. On July 23, 1928, four men shoved off from Lee's Ferry in two open boats; Jody and Frank worked the left bank while Elmer and Roy examined the right shore. They made portages at Three Mile Wash and Badger Creek Rapid and found Deans' body at the head of Soap Creek Rapid. Deans had worn overalls with a leather belt around the waist; this belt, combined with tightly packed silt, kept the dead man's wallet in his pocket. Inside were Bowman's payment for the rugs (a check for $1,061.08 and two notes of $500 each), $35 in bills, and a small notebook. They buried the body along with an explanatory note at the foot of the cliff about two hundred yards from the river. They had food and bedrolls and camped that night on the beach. Frank walked down to Mile 12, then gave up the search. The brothers clambered up Soap Creek, walked back to the bridge site, and rode to the ranch with Jerry after quitting time. Home again in Hurricane on the twenty-ninth, Frank wrote to the county supervisors, telling of finding the body and offering to return the effects at their direction.[42]

The west cantilever, constructed faster than its mate, was completed on August 11. Before the two were joined, the gap was covered with planks and several people crossed on foot, including Inspector Woody Claypool, Buck Lowrey, and his daughter Mamie. There was a gap of nine inches when the screws were started on the morning of the twelfth, but it was not until 5:30 P.M. that both sides were bearing on the center pin. It was necessary to continue the screwing operation for another four hours, due to the contraction of the steel by falling temperature. At last there was no possibility of the toggles again taking the load of the spans. Now the crew went to work dismantling the erection traveler, changing the tie-back steel into approach spans, and setting the floor system on the main span. The steel work was finished and the crew moved out on October 30, 1928. All that remained was to make the approach fills, build the forms, place the reinforcing steel, and pour the concrete floor. Jerry had operated the compressor during the steel assembly; when his job came to an end, he succumbed to Pearly's pressure and took his family to Hurricane. Pearly resigned as a school trustee and Price was certified to fill the vacancy on September 7.[43]

School District 26 had operated for three years with a like number of teachers. Iona Davie chose not to return and none of the other Arizona teachers wanted to work under the now-known conditions. Jerry was instrumental in procuring the services of Joseph T. Wilkinson, a graduate of the University of Utah, but not accredited in Arizona. Superintendent B. K. Best took care of that and school opened in September. Twelve students attended regularly, but that number went as high as seventeen. Jerry's children transferred to Hurricane, but others named Cox, Lang, Spencer, and Siebecker took their places.

Buck Lowrey knew his lodge had to have water. He questioned the Johnson brothers and learned that Warren Johnson had ranged cattle on the bench below the Vermilion Cliffs and utilized Phantom and Four Mile Springs for his stock. He and David explored and found that the latter was his closest water source, about three miles away. He purchased the necessary pipe and two large galvanized tanks; by dint of Lowrey and Navajo labor, the pipeline inched down to the tanks at the foot of the red shale. In time, the name Four Mile Springs was discarded in favor of "Lowery Spring."

Elmer and Price Johnson contracted to furnish the sand and gravel for the concrete pavement of the bridge. They knew of a nearby deposit just

Navajo Bridge, at the time unnamed, nearing completion, 1928 (*Owen Johnson Collection, P. T. Reilly Collection, Cline Library, Northern Arizona University*).

east of the bridge, and they had an old truck to transport it. They stockpiled a supply while the forms were being set, ultimately furnishing seven hundred yards. The bridge floor was made in six equal sections that were placed to distribute the weight without generating undue stress on the diagonal bracing. A traveling bucket, with wheels guided on the steel curbs and a frame spanning the roadway, was designed by the contractor. The concrete deck was completed December 9. It was cured with wet sawdust obtained from Flagstaff, while water was hauled from Navajo Spring, only four miles away.

The temporary approaches were complete by the time the concrete was poured, and the bridge was opened to traffic on January 12, 1929. The permanent approaches were completed before the bridge was dedicated on June 14 and 15. The construction statistics are as follows: excavation, 9,048 cubic yards; concrete, 503 cubic yards; structural steel, 2,087,043 pounds; reinforcing steel, 81,412 pounds; cost of bridge, about $341,000; and the cost of one mile of approaches, $50,000. The height of bridge deck was 467 feet above river, depending on river stage.[44] When the construction was complete, Price Johnson transported the foreman, Joe Gordon, to Flagstaff. During his three-day absence, Roy went to Cameron to telephone the sad news that Price's young son Calvin Marshall Johnson had died on December 14. The child was buried near his kin in the cemetery.

Glen R. and Bessie Hyde landed their Salmon River scow at Lee's Ferry on November 7 and camped on the beach. They talked with the residents and said they were on a honeymoon trip, having married on April 12. They had left Green River, Utah, on October 20, 1928, intending to go through to Needles. Bessie appears to have been the first woman to navigate all of Cataract and Glen Canyons. The scow had no oars but Hyde guided it by standing in the center and using sweeps which were inserted between fulcrums at the bow and stern. The boat was the most peculiar craft ever to appear on this section of the river. It resembled a miniature ferryboat, fifteen feet long with a five-foot beam. Both ends were square to the beams, although they sloped up at the bottom. The sides were unusually high; the interior was open. Price tried to dissuade the couple from continuing the trip by relating the recent deaths and how his brothers had barely been able to climb out at Soap Creek after finding the trader's body. Glen dismissed the advice, but his wife was impressed with the gravity of their venture. They left next morning and Glen was nearly knocked overboard in the Pahreah Riffle before they disappeared into the canyon.[45] Two days after the Hydes departed, Price followed Buck Lowrey's example and recorded a claim on the water at Badger Creek. He had filed a homestead on the road to Kanab in 1927, and now he had the water.[46]

On the advice of Earl Boyer, the trader at Cedar Ridge, Emily Deans filed a claim against Coconino County on May 23. Represented by staff attorney C. B. Wilson, she asked for twenty thousand dollars, charging the ferryboat and equipment were defective and the operator was inexperienced. The suit was rejected by the County Superior Court, and the appeal was rejected by the Supreme Court in Phoenix the following year. Emily Deans had gone to Los Angeles shortly after she learned of her husband's death and did not return to Cedar Ridge until March 1929. During her absence she was in communication with Earl Boyer who wanted her to come back.

Late in January, Boyer arranged with the Johnsons to help him recover the body of his young assistant. Frank, Jody, and Roy were no longer there, but Elmer had been present and Price agreed to help. They started out early on January 27, 1929. They let a rope down the cliff, anchored it securely, then went around to the south fork of Soap Creek. They followed down toward the river and when some distance from it, came upon the footprints of two people whom they judged to be the Hydes. Evidently Soap Creek Rapid had raised some doubt about the young couple's ability to surmount such hazards and they almost abandoned the trip before returning to the river. The trio dug up Deans' body, tied it to a board, and attached the unit in a yoke hookup to the rope. Returning to the rim, they hoisted the body to the top. It was a simple but ingenious and strenuous operation. Price Johnson drove to Flagstaff on February 4 and gave the story of the body recovery to the editor of the *Coconino Sun* who ran it on the eighth. He emphasized that the tracks of the Hydes were seen about three miles from the river, but the couple had changed their minds about abandoning the trip.

Earl Boyer took Deans's remains back to Cedar Ridge. On February 3, Royce E. Deans was interred on the Cedar Ridge divide beside the "paint pot," a beautiful exposure of Chinle Formation that the dead man had admired. Preacher Smith conducted the service, which was attended by Earl Boyer, Joe Lee, Floyd Boyle (the replacement assistant trader), and several Indians. A broken shovel was left at the grave, Navajo style. Ketosh, the Tuba City blacksmith, made a wide frame to protect the grave from livestock, and a bronze tablet was erected in February 1929.[47] Deans was the only victim of the ferry's last tragedy to be memorialized. Emily returned to Cedar Ridge to keep house for the bachelor trader Boyle and married him on December 11, 1929.

As the bridge neared completion it became apparent that an official name for it had to be chosen. The titles used most frequently were "Grand Canyon Bridge" and "Lee's Ferry Bridge;" the final name of "Navajo Bridge" wasn't mentioned. Everyone had an opinion and advanced fervent reasons to substantiate it. Discussion reached a peak in the fall of 1928 and it proved to be the most dissentious subject to have come before the public in years. The Arizona Highway Department announced the name would be Grand Canyon Bridge, pointing out that the structure was not at Lee's Ferry; this fanned the controversy and it burst into open flame. Lame-duck Governor Hunt came out for Lee's Ferry Bridge, as did Senator Ashurst. The latter added that the road passing over it should be called "the Mormon Highway" in honor of the Saints' migration to Arizona.[48] The Flagstaff Chamber of Commerce, Congressman Lewis A. Douglas, and the Indian Service concurred.

Even the *Los Angeles Times* got into the act, claiming that Lee's Ferry (with use of the apostrophe) was best as the old timers resented the other name. Some Arizona people suddenly switched to be on the opposite side of the *Times,* a hated California newspaper. The *Tucson Citizen* upheld the Highway Department's choice, saying it would help advertize the Grand Canyon. The leading editorial in the *Coconino Sun* of November 3 attacked both the name and the Tucson newspaper for backing it. Many organizations in the state, and especially those in northern Arizona, came out for Lee's Ferry Bridge—some using the apostrophe, some not. Several service clubs, the National Park Service, the U.S. Indian Service, officials of the Santa Fe Railroad, and the Fred Harvey Company signed a letter requesting Governor-elect John C. Phillips to ask for legislation officially naming the structure the Lee's Ferry Bridge.[49]

Flagstaff pioneer T. A. Riordan took the matter up with P. G. Spilsbury of the Arizona Industrial Congress on October 15, saying the use of the name Grand Canyon Bridge was the "work of ghouls" and would offend the residents of northern Arizona. He pointed out that the historical value of Tanner Crossing was lost when the Cameron Bridge was constructed, and the same thing was happening at Lee's Ferry. He declared that names are derived from tradition, not the reverse. A member of the commission answered him on the eighteenth, rebutting his case. Riordan ended the exchange on November 23, bloody but unbowed. Will C. Barnes, secretary of the Board on Geographic Names in Washington, wrote the

Coconino Sun on February 15;. he suggested dropping the possessive and using "Lee Ferry Bridge." In a letter to Governor Phillips, Horace M. Albright, Director of the National Park Service, urged that "Lees Ferry Bridge" be retained. He claimed that having Grand Canyon Bridge over Marble Canyon would confound tourists into thinking the bridge actually was over the Grand Canyon.[50]

The controversy did not die down. In the spring of 1929, Mormon Church President Heber J. Grant addressed a joint session of the Arizona Legislature and asked that the bridge not be named after Lee. He pointed out that John D. Lee had been there for a short time only and it would be more fitting to perpetuate the name of Warren M. Johnson who had operated the ferry for more than twenty years.[51] Church policy at that time was that Lee was a "non-person." The situation smoldered as nothing was done officially. When the bridge was opened to traffic on January 12, 1929, however, a large bronze plate was fastened to the approach sides of the guardrails which read "Grand Canyon Bridge."

Buck Lowery worked so hard between lodge-building, operating the trading post, and bringing water from the spring that he suffered a breakdown. The immediate cause was uremic poisoning and heart trouble but the underlying cause was hard work. He recovered and pushed ahead as vigorously as ever, and his Vermilion Cliffs Lodge was opened before the dedication.[52] The bridge was scheduled to be dedicated June 1, 1929, but this date conflicted with the Mormon conference in Salt Lake City and the Shrine convention held at Grand Canyon that tied up all Fred Harvey cars. It was postponed to June 14 and 15.

Still unsettled, the name controversy carried over to the official program that announced the dedication of the Grand Canyon Bridge, and Governor George H. Dern of Utah used that name in the write-up he made for the pamphlet. Arizona Governor Phillips straddled the fence with political adroitness, referring to "the bridge" three times without using a name. Bridge Engineer Ralph A. Hoffman, the Arizona Highway Commission, and E. O. Whitman of the Arizona Industrial Congress all used Grand Canyon Bridge. Walter Runke, superintendent of the Western Navajo Indian Reservation and state senator from Coconino County, referred to the structure as Lee's Ferry Bridge. Attorney Frank Gold of Flagstaff wrote a thumbnail history of Lee's Ferry that was more comprehensive than any other up to that time.

The temperature was insufferably high when the dedication ceremonies began at 1:30 P.M. on June 14. The Lowrey lodge was in business, but totally unprepared for the number of people who were present. The *Coconino Sun* stated that 7,000 individuals attended and 1,217 automobiles were in sight from one vantage point, with many parked along the road to the Pahreah Canyon. In addition, there were between 1,000 and 2,000 Indians representing several tribes.

The governors of Arizona, Utah, New Mexico, and Nevada attended, as did Heber J. Grant and Anthony W. Ivins, Archie and Nicholas

Dedication of Navajo Bridge, at the time called either Grand Canyon or Lee's Ferry Bridge, June 14, 1929 (*used by permission, Utah State Historical Society, all rights reserved*).

Roosevelt, Lewis R. Freeman of the *New York Times*, Phil Townsend Hanna of the Southern California Automobile Club, Harry Carr of the *Los Angeles Times*, representatives of the *Denver Post*, the Associated Press, the Hearst Newspapers, United Press, and dozens of other writers and photographers. Bands from the Indian School of Phoenix, Winslow High School, and Dixie College were brought in, the latter group playing for the dance held outside at night. The Indian band was the best of the three, led by David Black Hoop, a Sioux, who conducted with his index finger.[53]

Lowrey had two large water tanks that were fed from his spring. The inlet kept one full and carried a sign, "Water." It was always pure and sanitary. The second tank caught the overflow of the first and its sign read "Private." The Lowreys and the household used this tank for dips. Water was short and there was a steady line of visitors waiting to fill waterbags, canteens, fruit jars, and pans. Human nature being what it is, some tourists got the idea that the tank marked "Private" held the choice water and they filled their drinking containers from the Lowrey swimming water.

Unmarried members of the Dixie College band bunked in Lowrey's house, which was stacked with cases of soda pop. The water shortage caused the boys to help themselves frequently, and as a bottle was emptied it was shoved back in the case. Lowrey came out to get a case, saw the many empties and said, "Gosh, we're sure selling soda pop," little realizing that the empty bottles represented a loss instead of a profit.

Florence Lowrey and the cook became so harried that they made no effort to follow a menu; mulligan stew was served three times a day. Buck's watermelons went for two-fifty each. Mamie wore a large squash blossom necklace that tinkled when she moved and the tourists had visions of ice. Of course, there wasn't a bit of ice on the place but the cook told her to always wear the necklace when serving, as it was good psychology.[54]

Governor Phillips cut the ribbon, the four governors and important people spoke, bands played, and there was a symbolic marriage of "Miss Southwest," played by Betty Kastner of Prescott, and "Mr. Northwest," played by Kenneth Judd of Fredonia; Bishop Heber J. Meeks of Kanab officiated. There were solos, trios, and the Yavapai Cowboy Quartet. That evening, Navajo and Hopi tribal dances were presented, directed by C. L. Walker, then superintendent of the Western Navajo Agency. There were horse races, a choir program, and a pageant of six plays. The affair undoubtedly was the largest ever held in northern Arizona up to that time, and it allowed the Chamber of Commerce publicity men to run wild. It lacked only one thing—a funeral ceremony for the pioneer ferry.

13

The Polygamists

ALTHOUGH THE OPENING OF THE BRIDGE OVER MARBLE CANYON INCREASED travel to the Arizona Strip, the five-mile primitive dirt road to Lee's Ferry remained as rough as ever. The ranch in the mouth of Pahreah Canyon was more isolated than it had been when the ferry was in operation. Some travelers even failed to notice the two ruts that turned off toward the east—a situation that suited the people of the ranch. Engineers connected with river gaging used the road more than anyone. The resident hydrographer had support during high water—usually from April to July—and the assistant did the work when the resident took his annual leave. Other hydraulic engineers or the chief from Tucson often visited. Owen Clark was the resident hydrographer in 1929, assisted during high-water by Joe Gatewood. The hydrographer had duties elsewhere as well; Clark sometimes worked at Mexican Hat on the San Juan River; other stations were at Moenkopi Wash, Clear Creek, Chevelon Creek; and there were Little Colorado River stations at Grand Falls, Holbrook, and Woodruff.

Recognizing that the Grand Canyon Bridge opened Arizona to insect invasion from the north, state officials made plans to inspect vehicles before they reached the agriculturally important areas to the south. In 1929, a frame building inspection station built near the Lowrey trading post was manned by Halbert E. Woodruff for the Arizona Commission of Agriculture and Horticulture. The Highway Department had a rock building that was used as a warehouse on the same side of the road, making this—aside from Fredonia and Lee's Ferry—one of the more built-up areas on the Arizona Strip. Traffic increased to the point that one man could not handle the load, so Lavern Thayer, and later Finis H. McCaleb were sent to speed the flow of traffic. Both single, Woodruff and Thayer spent their spare time at the Lowrey lodge, the attractions being Buck Lowery's older daughter and her cousin. The inspectors appeared so official in their uniforms that during a visit John D. Rockefeller asked Buck Lowrey if they were special guards hired for his benefit. Woodruff pressed his suit and finally popped the question to Mamie Lowery. Although she was only a junior at Flagstaff High School, Mamie and Halbert were married on July 20, 1930, with Preacher Shine Smith conducting the ceremony. The young couple built a rock house

Owen Clark and dog at Lee's Ferry, 1930 (*M. B. Scott photograph, P. T. Reilly Collection, Cline Library, Northern Arizona University*).

across from the station and lived there until Governor George W. P. Hunt discontinued the entry inspections a year later.

Isaac Carling Spencer and his second family returned from Mexico in the fall of 1928 and resumed farming at the ranch. Along with the families of Price and Elmer Johnson, Victor Cox and his wife Neta (sister to Price's second wife) had two children, as did the Langs. All were fundamentalist in belief and practice except Price's first wife, Esther, and all were related by blood or marriage. As Professor DeMotte had noted in 1872, the ranch in the mouth of Pahreah Canyon excelled as "an out of the way place," and the residents could put their beliefs into practice with little fear of being bothered. Price planned to start a ranch at Badger Creek and sell gas to the travelers. He would not get first crack at the northbound traffic, but he could offer gas and oil to those headed south and compete with Lowrey on a modest scale. His first hurdle was to get title to his homestead.[1]

In July 1929, Jerry Johnson took steps to file a homestead entry on the Lee's Ferry ranch. He had no idea how to go about this and sought advice from Heber T. Meeks, president of Kanab Stake. As the land office was in Phoenix, Meeks enlisted the help of J. R. Price, president of the Maricopa Stake, who had the business acumen to employ the law firm of Gibbs & Gibbs, specialists in state and federal land causes. The situation was more tangled than the lawyers realized, but Jerry authorized them to act for him and on August 19, 1929, they applied for a homestead entry. Unknown to the attorneys, Jerry's claim was weakened by the fact that he no longer lived continually on the land, and both Heber Meeks and J. R. Price had different ideas of how best to proceed.[2] Nearly three weeks later, on September 6, Jerry emulated his brother Price and filed for water rights.

Joseph Wilkinson had seventeen students when school opened on September 16. The new schoolhouse was usable even though it was not completely finished. Its larger size was a noted improvement over the old log cabin, allowing the adults to use it as a meeting hall several times a week as well as Sundays. Meetings called to discuss secular matters were combined with religious fervor and devout prayers. According to the hydrographer there at the time, school was taught by a man and wife named Wilkins who conducted a "playpen type of classroom that stressed fundamentalist religion more than basic education." Mrs. Wilkinson was ignored in the official county records until she taught in her own name a few years later. Why the teachers used Wilkinson officially and Wilkins locally is not known. On the same day the fall term opened, a girl was born to Artemisia and Elmer Johnson. The child was named Viola after Elmer's first wife. A few months later, on April 8, 1930, Viola gave birth to her tenth child, a boy named Warren Marshall. The production of children at Lee's Ferry now was more reliable than any given agricultural crop.

The U.S. Geological Survey kept its gaging stations up to date, maintaining and upgrading them as necessary. In December 1929, J. A. Baumgartner, R. E. Cook, and Jay Pague came to Lee's Ferry to supplement the upper cable anchors. The temperature was near zero but, as Cook later noted, having his men pour concrete in these temperatures never bothered Dickinson. The work was completed early in January.

During a meeting in Kanab on December 7, 1929, President Meeks read letters from the Presiding Bishopric saying that it planned to sell the ranch at Lee's Ferry.[3] No doubt church officials were aware of the fundamentalist doctrines being practiced there, realized the potential for embarrassment, and were inviting offers to transfer ownership. But first, they wanted and needed a patented title if one could be obtained. The fact that Jerry Johnson's homestead claim was within the power-site withdrawals not only complicated the matter but added to the red tape connected with it. Jerry received a press copy of a letter addressed to the Registrar of the Phoenix Land Office, dated November 11, 1929, from the acting commissioner of the General Land Office, affirming the rejection of his homestead application because of the power-site reserve. The law firm was bypassed and it was six weeks before Jerry let them know. The lawyers were irritated at the General Land Office for ignoring them and were disgusted with Jerry for his failure to notify them immediately. B. H. Gibbs was familiar with the technical aspects of the law and, on December 29, he fired off a letter to the commissioner pointing out the errors in the government's position. Gibbs resolved that the government agencies should follow the law in considering his client's claim.

On January 28, 1930, the commissioner of the General Land Office called for an investigation to determine if the applicant had been a bona fide settler upon the land during the dates of the withdrawals. The inquiry was assigned to General Land Office mining engineer W. R. Sholes, who made his survey in March. Sholes visited the property on the thirteenth, interviewed Elmer, later talked to Jerry at Hurricane, and secured their affidavits. He also interviewed Buck Lowrey, W. E. Hamblin, and W. M. Brown of Kanab, all of whom corroborated Jerry's declaration. He examined the records in the office of the Presiding Bishopric in Salt Lake City and found the deeds, notes, and other records of previous transactions, then verified them in the office of the Coconino County Recorder.

Sholes concluded that the only time Jeremiah Johnson could claim undisputed ownership of the land was between May 25, 1925, and August 19, 1926, and he had not done so. Therefore, he recommended that the homestead claim not be allowed for the following reasons:

1. That the entryman did not settle on the land for his own benefit but for the use and benefit of the Grand Canyon Cattle Company, its successors and assigns.
2. That the entryman was not a bona fide settler on the land prior to the dates of the Power Site Withdrawals numbers 446 and 605.
3. That claimant did not file application within the required time.
4. That the application was not made for the use and benefit of the entryman but for the use and benefit of Heber J. Grant, Trustee, or his successors or assigns.[4]

The adverse report was not sent to Jerry or his lawyers. Impatient at not hearing of the claim's progress, the attorneys on August 25 requested a status statement from the General Land Office Commissioner in Washington. This letter elicited a reply from Assistant Commissioner John H. Edwards, who stated that the attorney's letter of December 27, 1929, had been treated as an appeal that would be considered in regular docket order about the middle of October.

At the same time, Edwards passed the buck to the Federal Power Commission, requesting that body to consider the propriety of restoring the tract to entry subject to the provisions and limitations of section 24 of the Federal Water Power Act. On December 5, 1930, the executive secretary advised the Secretary of the Interior that the Federal Power Commission had determined the value of said land would not be injured or destroyed for the purpose of power development by location, entry, or selection under the provisions of the Federal Water Power Act, and that no further action would be taken. On December 13, 1930, the Department of the Interior reversed the previous decision and allowed Jerry Johnson's claim to advance through established procedure, and all interested parties were so notified. There were forms to fill out, affidavits of witnesses to be obtained, and publication notices to be made, but the lawyers guided Jerry through the legal phase that he did not understand, and on January 28, 1931, the three-year process was initiated. The government agencies, however, did not give up easily; on September 25, 1931, Archie D. Ryan, chief of Field Division of the General Land Office, had the application stamped to withhold the final certificate until a field investigation had been made.

Joseph Wilkinson became the first Lee's Ferry school teacher to repeat a hitch when he completed his second term on April 25, 1930. He had taught, aided by his wife, from the fall of 1928 through the spring of 1930 before deciding to return to Cane Beds. Their fundamentalist attitudes had given them good rapport with both parents and children, and they were missed. Conditions changed abruptly when the county obtained the services of Margaret Anderson, a graduate of Arizona State Teachers College and veteran instructor in Coconino County. She was the wife of Hugh Anderson who ran cattle in House Rock Valley, and she brought her son Oscar to the class. She believed in teaching basic education, was not a Mormon, and tolerated no fundamental theology in her classroom. Although she was never as popular as the Wilkinson team, the residents must have realized that their children were receiving better instruction than before. She had a total of fourteen students, ten of whom were Johnsons, three Allreds, and her own son, when school opened on September 1, 1930. Anderson's class put on a Halloween program for an audience of sixteen adults including parents, Hugh Anderson, the Scotts, and Preacher Smith. Nothing like this had taken place at the ferry since the days of Sadie Staker.

Lydia Johnson Spencer sustained her husband's action in marrying sixteen-year-old Sylvia Allred, and when Carling Spencer brought her to Lee's Ferry, the local church authorities were faced with a painful choice. They wrestled with the problem for some months, but on July 29, 1930, Lydia was excommunicated. She even went to the ferry and acted as midwife when Sylvia's first child was born on July 26, 1929—a boy named Marden Carling. She did the same when Lucius Henry was born on January 23, 1931. At this time, Carling Spencer was fifty-one years of age. Tragedy struck again on March 10, 1931, when the infant baby Lucius Henry died of unknown causes and was buried at Lee's Ferry.

The irrepressible Charlie Spencer had found two men who were interested in mining and had capital. The prospective investors, John B. Treadwell of Los Angeles and A. Barclay of Flagstaff, visited the area several times during the winter of 1930–31 and filed many claims in the Chinle Formation at Soap and Badger Creeks, Lee's Ferry, and in Pahreah Canyon about a mile above the Sid Wilson ranch.[5] The claims at Lee's Ferry took in the Chinle outcrops north of the buildings that were built in 1911, and any mining operation would interfere with the gaging station. The hydrographers kept the Tucson office informed of the situation.

Spencer envisioned an operation even farther afield and looked at the shales near Kayenta. According to the "Kayenta News" section of the

Coconino Sun of January 2, 1931, Spencer, F. A. Freeman of Beverly Hills, F. A. Stearns of Los Angeles, and Pat H. M. Flattum of Alhambra, California, ate Christmas Eve dinner at the Wetherill Kayenta trading post. Spencer was attempting to interest Freeman in the Chinle Formation at the San Juan River while Stearns and Flattum were enlisting Wetherill's help in changing Rainbow Bridge National Monument into a national park.

Both groups spent several days in the area pursuing their separate interests. Spencer and Freeman were back in Flagstaff in mid-January where they checked into the Monte Vista Hotel, the town's newest and most elegant establishment. Freeman undoubtedly was paying the bills or Spencer would have gone to a cheaper place. This chance act set up far-reaching consequences for the ferry because of personnel changes at the hotel. Hazel Barbeau, a pretty waitress in the Fred Harvey system, had been captain of her co-workers in the dining room at El Tovar at the South Rim. She later worked in the Harvey House at Williams, and after the depression caused cutbacks, she found employment at the Monte Vista coffee shop in September of 1930. Hotel manager George Hellig was her former boss.

Leo E. Weaver had come to Phoenix in 1919 and lived on a twenty-acre farm at Seventh and Osborn. He sold Cadillacs for Ed Babbitt and in time leased the old Lazy RC Ranch on the outskirts of Wickenburg. He started his first guest ranch about 1924; Leo claimed that he introduced "guest ranch" to replace the expression "dude ranch." His wife, Nellie Foerster Weaver, was the talent behind what success he had and perceived that a year-around operation should replace the six-month winter season that opened in October and closed in May. This meant acquiring a summer ranch in the high country. On November 6, 1928, Harold S. Colton, his wife Mary, and their son Joseph were Leo's guests at Wickenburg. Before the winter was out, Weaver had made a deal for the M. I. Powers Ranch north of Flagstaff, which Colton owned. The acquisition gave Leo a continuous operation, because he opened one place as soon as he closed the other, often taking guests with him. Both ranches were called "Circle Flying W," although he ran cattle at neither.

Weaver's world fell apart on May 12, 1929, when Nellie Weaver was killed and their fourteen-year-old daughter Billie was injured in an automobile accident eight miles west of Flagstaff. Nellie had been hurrying to close the Wickenburg ranch as Leo was opening the Powers place. The Great Depression ruined the tourist business, especially that of marginal guest ranch operations. Without Nellie's management Leo was unable to make money and on April 30, 1930, deeded his equity to W. L. Richards, the Wickenburg merchant to whom he was indebted.

Weaver got a job as secretary of the Flagstaff Chamber of Commerce. A personable man, he was well suited for the position, having the natural ability to promote the rosy side of anything and stir enthusiasm in his listeners. Although he could accentuate the positive, he was blind to the negative and on the whole quite impractical. In the course of his work, he dropped into the Monte Vista and recognized Hazel Barbeau as the attractive girl who had worked at El Tovar in the summer of 1928. He returned repeatedly and they began dating. Leo was considered very eligible by most unmarried women; he dressed in elegant western clothes, was rugged in appearance, and made feminine hearts flutter. In August 1930, he and Billie led the parade of the Fox Film Rodeo and were very much in the public eye.

George Hellig saw greener pastures elsewhere and Leo wanted to earn more money, so Leo became manager of the Monte Vista Hotel on January 1, 1931. Thus he checked in C. H. Spencer and F. A. Freeman on January 15. After dinner that evening, Spencer held court in the hotel lobby, speaking mostly to Freeman but not ignoring the gathering circle around him. He romanticized eloquently on the development of his prospect at Lee's Ferry, moved on to the history of the place, his former project there, and the amount of money he had expended. Leo Weaver was as taken in by the golden words of the master promoter as anyone within range of his voice. He didn't care for the mining phase of the place, but the lush ranch at the mouth of Pahreah Canyon appeared to be the ideal location to replace the Wickenburg ranch. Also, it was much closer to his summer ranch in Flagstaff. Weaver resolved to examine the property at his first opportunity. A gifted promoter had been hustled by a truly talented one.

Hazel Barbeau sensed the development of her romance with Leo and on January 6 filed for divorce from John Inman, the man she had married three years previously. The marriage ultimately was dissolved and she legally resumed her maiden name, which she was already using. The fires of romance had singed Leo just as deeply, but his needs were different. Whereas Hazel searched for security and good living, he required a mate who was practical where he was impractical, a manager who attended to details when he dismissed them airily, a helper who made an operation work behind the scenes while he played the grand show on center stage. But he had more than romance on his mind; a year-around guest facility was his first priority. On January 21, 1931, Colton deeded the old Powers ranch to Leo Weaver;[6] a week later, Leo signed a mortgage to Colton.[7] In effect, Weaver bought the ranch for twenty-six hundred dollars and had the property in his name without paying a cent. Then, on May 13, 1931, he and Hazel Barbeau married in Gallup, New Mexico.

Meanwhile, Stearns and Flattum took in the sights out of Kayenta for four days, and when they left the trading post, John Wetherill had agreed to join them in the effort to go up the Colorado to Rainbow Bridge. The small boat could not carry three men, extra gas, and the outfit, so Stearns remained at the Lowrey lodge while Flattum and Wetherill tackled the ice floes and river currents with a small, steel-clad skiff and a fourteen-horsepower Indian outboard motor. A little group was on hand to see them off on January 4, 1931, and Preacher Smith handed them a notebook in which to write a record of the expedition.[8] The trip was a huge success in spite of the ice floes. They not only reached Rainbow Bridge but packed in additional gasoline from Rainbow Lodge and went as far as Hole in the Rock. They started downstream on the twentieth and found the going much easier, landing at Lee's Ferry at dusk two days later. They were greeted by Marion Scott and his wife, who invited them to dinner. Flattum's little outboard had proven to be more efficient than any previous power unit.

Although Jerry Johnson's land claim was progressing normally through the maze of red tape, he lived in Hurricane, subsisting on a job with the highway department. He assumed the role of an absentee landlord and visited the ranch enough to oversee his vested interests. Elmer and Price Johnson, along with Carling Spencer and their families, actually lived on the property, farming in the traditional Mormon manner that returned a living but little else.

Marion B. Scott and his wife first arrived at Lee's Ferry on April 1, 1930. He and D. H. Barber helped measure during the high water season, then Scott succeeded Owen Clark as resident hydrographer in July. Clark moved to the Grand Canyon gage, and Scott worked alone until Barber joined him on April 13, 1931, before the spring rise. Charlie McDonald showed up a few days later and for the rest of the summer the crew took care of the Lee's Ferry gage as well as those at Moenkopi Wash, the Little Colorado River, and Mexican Hat. McDonald became resident hydrographer in July.

Buck Lowrey heard the rumors that the ranch was available and he asked Heber Meeks on April 13 if he could lease the property with the option of buying it. He noted that its assets had deteriorated due to neglect—an indirect criticism of the Johnsons. The stake president stalled Lowrey by saying that he would consult church officials and pass on their reactions; he then sent Lowrey's letter to the Presiding Bishopric in Salt Lake City.[9]

Charlie Spencer's promotional net ensnared Treadwell, a retired mining engineer who had been involved in the winter claim-staking. His plan appeared logical, aspiring to salvage vast quantities of mercury that he said had been expended in recovering the flower gold in 1911. No one was around to dispute his statements of what had taken place twenty years before, so Treadwell decided to investigate. Two businesses—the Spencer Mining Company of Flagstaff, capitalized at $500,000, and the Treadwell Mining Corporation, capitalized at $100,000—were incorporated under Arizona law on February 27, 1931. The incorporators of both firms were Spencer, Treadwell, Barclay, D. S. Cook of Pasadena, and J. F. Guyton of Los Angeles. The investors were small businessmen who put in from $1,000 to $5,000 after listening to Spencer's rosy promotion. Charlie also claimed the Chinle Formation was loaded with free mercury far in excess of what had been lost in 1911. Treadwell knew that mercury was refined from cinnabar and was rarely found in a pure state, but he didn't argue the point. He was curious enough to bring a set of amalgamating tables to Lee's Ferry to explore the prospect. About a dozen men with two trucks and trailer-loads of equipment arrived at the site on March 5 and settled in the three west-ernmost buildings that had been Spencer's 1911 office and laboratory, the old fort, and the structure Sid Wilson had used as a tackroom.

Among the work crew were three Nelsons: Pete, Al, and the for-mer's wife Ada. Al worked as a laborer and drove the truck while Pete and Ada ran a boarding house for the crew in the old fort. Pete Nelson's real name was Nielson, and he had attempted to become an outlaw around the turn of the century. According to Charles Kelly, he was one of the twelve most wanted men on the list of Governor H. M. Wells, with a five hundred dollar reward for his capture. After a fiasco in this line, he concluded that he was not smart enough to be an outlaw and decided to go straight. When "Gunplay" Maxwell was killed in 1904, Pete married his widow, Ada. Now they were in a new country, trying to make a living in another one of Charlie Spencer's tenuous enterprises.

Spencer hired Elmer and Price Johnson to help set up the tables and sluice troughs and do the manual labor. Price foolishly quit a sure day job with the highway department to join Spencer, whose payment of wages was uncertain at best. One of the old pumps, which was made to run again, brought water to the head of the sluice. Charlie worked on the high ground shoveling the shale into the trough where it was washed down to the tables. To Treadwell's surprise, a small amount of mercury was recovered.

For some unaccountable reason, Spencer had to go to Flagstaff. Before leaving he cautioned the Johnsons not to do any mining while he was away. As soon as the promoter was out of sight, Treadwell got the brothers to make another run. The result was negative and Treadwell judged that Spencer somehow had salted the ground even as they watched. Price then allegedly found a bottle of mercury with a hole in the cork and two leather straps that they assumed had been used to fasten the bottle upside down to Charlie's leg. A vigorous shake would deposit mercury on the ground, which would be shoveled into the trough and washed down to the tables. Treadwell disassembled his tables and was gone before Spencer returned. The promo-tion collapsed and all the men except the Nelsons drifted away.[10]

Spencer's venture had two notable consequences. The Lowreys, impressed that mining was about to boom, staked claims as fast as they could. By March 24, 1932, they had located thirty-two lode claims to protect Buck's homestead, and almost as many along the Chinle Formation on Soap Creek.[11] Lowrey's reaction to Spencer's activity was minor compared to that of U.S. Geological Survey District Engineer W. E. Dickinson. Knowing the effect any active mining operation would have on the gaging station, he immediately contacted State Water Commissioner Frank P. Trott and the USGS Chief Hydraulic Engineer in Washington. After making its circuitous rounds through the various interested agencies, the problem wound up in the lap of Archie D. Ryan, chief of the Field Division. He assigned George G. Bywater, General Land Office mining engineer, to investigate the matter and report on it.

Bywater was in the field on July 5 and 6 and tendered his report on the eleventh. As the promotion was dead when he was there, he said there was no immediate danger to the gaging station but suggested the hydrographer should notify his superior if the operation became active. He noted that the Lillian claims numbers one and two were within the power-withdrawals and would affect the survey work. He also disclosed how Charlie Spencer allegedly had salted the ground and said that the deposit contained no mercury whatsoever. He even quoted the opinions of two independent engineers, whom Treadwell had hired, that the deposits were barren of mercury. He recommended that the spring near the upper ferry, which had been used by the survey for culinary purposes, be withdrawn for the benefit of the gaging station.[12] This was done through the Public Water Reserve No. 107, approved April 8, 1932.

Grover Cleveland LeBaron and his two wives and children arrived at Lee's Ferry early in the summer of 1931. Cleve LeBaron had not been successful in Chihuahua and, emulating Carling Spencer, had followed his father-in-law to settle on the ranch of another father-in-law. If this is confusing, it can be charged to the peculiar relationships resulting from polygamous households. LeBaron's first wife was Jerry Johnson's eldest daughter Alice; his second wife was Annie, the daughter of Carling Spencer, whose first wife Lydia was Jerry's full sister. Both Carling and Cleve knew that Jerry could not say no to anyone, that he was lax in conducting his affairs, that taxes on the ranch had not been paid for several years, and that he was attempting to claim his homestead without living on the land. Elmer and Price were more aggressive than Jerry, but neither claimed a share of the ranch. Opportunity appeared to be knocking for both newcomers.

Jerry put in an appearance often enough so that it could not be said he wasn't living there, although he was seldom at any one place very long. At this time, Price farmed the upper field and attempted to build a living quarters at Badger Creek. By a stretch of imagination, the efforts could be called "improvements." Carling Spencer farmed the middle field and Cleve LeBaron took over Jerry's part of the lower ranch, which he worked with Elmer. Pearly's attitude about living at the ferry was known from there to Hurricane; no one expected her husband to live at the ranch, but church officials did not know this.

They were jolted to reality in June 1932 when they received Jerry's letter from Hurricane. They were astounded to learn that he had moved there, had not yet made final proof on the quarter section because he didn't have the necessary fifty dollars, and that two poor families from Mexico had settled at the ranch and refused to vacate (if indeed they had been asked to do so). The Presiding Bishopric told him in no uncertain terms that he had jeopardized his title to the ranch. The same mail carried copies of Jerry's letter, their reply, and a letter to President Meeks asking him to ride herd on the irresponsible fellow. Meeks gave Jerry a good dressing down, which hurt Jerry's feelings but got the message across. He wrote to the Presiding Bishopric on June 26 saying that his wife had rejoined him at the ranch after school was out at Hurricane, inferring that he and his wife had been living apart in the interests of the church, and that he had not deserted his homestead. This was patently false but it eased his conscience.

The Presiding Bishopric had grown weary of Jerry's continued expressions of loyalty and goodwill, his lackadaisical attitude about gaining title to the ranch in order to discharge his obligation to the church, and his inability to recognize the best course of action to advance their mutual interests. When necessary to write, they addressed him as "Dear Brother," yet they knew he had been excommunicated. They wanted nothing to do with this well-meaning rustic, including correspondence, and turned the matter over to Zions Securities Corporation, advised by attorney Fred C. Bush. This church agency was to deal directly with Gibbs & Gibbs, and all third parties were to be eliminated, including Johnson and Stake Presidents Price and Meeks.[13] The bishopric sent a check for the filing fees to the Phoenix attorneys with instructions for them to deal directly with Zions Securities.

The little pocket of fundamentalists was a throwback to the 1880s. Everyone knew that polygamy was practiced at Lee's Ferry, but the secular authorities ignored the situation. Although he was a fundamentalist polygamous Mormon, Cleve LeBaron was different both in character and attitude. He was more aggressive than the others; they never really trusted him, and a note of discord attended him. He was not above slanting facts to present a favorable lean to his interests, and he schemed to gain his ends. He was a living example of why the United Order had failed to survive.

On the other hand, Carling Spencer was industrious, scrupulous, and a good neighbor to Indian, Mormon, and Gentile alike. He was cooperation personified and represented the type that could have built a more perfect cooperative society except for his views on marriage. Elmer Johnson, the most sophisticated member of his clan, was the quiet leader at the ranch. He was pragmatic to a degree and blended equally well with both the fundamentalist and Gentile worlds with which he dealt. Price Johnson, attempting to prove up on his Badger Creek homestead, had three children in school at the ferry, although, like Jerry, he came and went constantly. He kept a wife at each place but usually attended meetings in the new schoolhouse at Lee's Ferry.

Jerry liked the prestige of being in communication with the Presiding Bishopric of the church and sometimes made long trips merely to display his latest letter. He avowed sympathy with fundamentalist doctrine, but no one could verify that he was a practicing polygamist. None of his children attended school at the ferry, and he was back and forth so often that he failed to accomplish much at either place.

The Monte Vista Hotel was owned by the Flagstaff Community Hotel Company whose stockholders were all local businessmen. The board of directors held its annual meeting on July 17, 1931, reelected board members, and expressed its pleasure with the management of Leo Weaver.

This sentiment soon changed through the pressure and political influence of some people from Phoenix, who went to the high country to escape the summer heat. The sons of a prominent Phoenix family brought girls and whiskey to the Monte Vista, became intoxicated, and threw bottles from the windows at pedestrians on the street. People complained and Leo threw the drunks out. Harsh words were exchanged and one young man bragged that he would get him fired. Weaver told him to go ahead. The youth telephoned his influential father, who contacted the publisher of the *Coconino Sun*. In due time, a board meeting was called to discuss firing the manager. One faction stood for appeasement of the prominent Phoenician whose feathers had been ruffled, while the Babbitts, C. B. Wilson, Bill Switzer, T. S. Riordan, and Colton backed Weaver to the hilt. The pro-Weaver faction won, but he was disappointed that the board had not backed him fully and felt that he would be thrown to the wolves at the first opportunity.

After taking Hazel on a two-week vacation to the Indian country that fall, Leo resigned from the Monte Vista and took charge of guest entertainment for Johnny O'Farrell, then managing Babbitt's Tuba City Trading Post. Among O'Farrell's guests was artist Lillian Wilhelm Robertson, a niece of Zane Grey. Before marrying Jesse Smith, she had lived at Tuba City and painted the surrounding area. One of her paintings was used to illustrate the dust jacket for Grey's *Heritage of the Desert*, and Leo learned about "The Oasis," Grey's name for the ranch in the mouth of the Pahreah. This bit of romance renewed his interest in the place described by Charlie Spencer, and he was stirred anew to see the historic setting.

The old ranch was going through another period of turmoil. The capable non-Mormon Margaret Anderson had encountered more than her share of problems in attempting to teach basic education to her fundamentalist students. The parents expected the county teacher to accept a literal interpretation of their Mormon theology and to include religious doctrine in the class work, but Anderson refused. The continuing controversy was so deeply rooted that Margaret elected to teach elsewhere when her term ended on May 1, 1931. Jerry prevailed upon Mary W. Wilkinson to return to District 26 for the next semester that opened on August 31. Once again the fundamentalist playpen-type of school was in session and the polygamists were happy. Sister Wilkins had thirteen students who claimed more mothers than they did fathers.

If any one thing was more certain than another at Lee's Ferry, it was the birthing of children. On November 29, 1931, Artemisia was born to Elmer and Viola. Five days later, on December 4, Price and his second wife had a girl whom they named Neta. Then on February 28, 1932, Clarence Orson, their third child, was born to Carling Spencer and his young wife Sylvia. His first wife Lydia journeyed from Glendale to deliver the teenager's baby.

Early in March, a spring drizzle had set in when Leo and Hazel Weaver first visited the ranch at Lee's Ferry. The gray day added to Hazel's repugnance at what she saw. There were more women than men, and a multitude of children, all existing in abject poverty. To her, there appeared to be no hope, no ambition, and no effort being made to improve their miserable condition. The general impression could be called favorable, however, compared to her feelings when she peered into the cabin of Carling Spencer. His young wife and her new baby were lying on a pallet on the floor. The rain was leaking through the roof and dripping onto the dirty quilt that covered them. Sylvia appeared younger than her seventeen years as she cradled her infant toward a dry spot. Hazel became absolutely sick as she realized the hopelessness of the situation, and then Carling told Leo in emphatic terms that his property was not for sale. She had seen enough and suggested they leave.

They did, but went only to Buck Lowrey's lodge where they spent the night. Leo did not share his wife's views; in the morning, he returned alone to the ranch. The rain had stopped and his optimistic eyes saw possibilities in the place. He had a nose-to-nose confrontation with Carling Spencer and was ordered off the property. The Weavers returned to Tuba City, but Leo could not get the site out of his mind and made plans to investigate further.[14]

When the Scotts left in July 1931, Charlie and Doris McDonald moved into the more choice quarters in the west end of the stream-gager residence and settled down for a quiet winter. Besides taking care of the Lee's Ferry and Pahreah readings, the hydrographer serviced the gages as far away as Woodruff and Silver Creek, a round trip requiring several days and made every other week. The hydrographer thus spent only half of his time at the ferry. The circuit gave them a break in the routine, enabled them to spend a night or two in Winslow or Holbrook and to bring back enough supplies to last until the next excursion. Upon returning from such a tour in September, they were surprised to find some laborers had taken over the residence. Charlie Spencer had sent the men there to work, telling them the buildings were his. Assuming that McDonald's supplies belonged to the mining company, the crew had made liberal use of them. They had attempted to haul water from the spring and damaged the tank trailer. The couple's personal things had been piled to one side, but a locked survey file cabinet was intact.

McDonald convinced them that they had broken into a government operation and the men reluctantly moved into the harness shop. They cooked outside over an open fire and set up a laboratory in the old fort. Seeking gold and quicksilver, they built new sluice boxes and began sluicing the previous tailings from the Chinle Formation. Charlie Spencer was in and out frequently while this was going on. He and his associates located about fifty placer claims at Lee's Ferry and in upper Marble Canyon during the first two weeks of October. These were recorded at Flagstaff on February 1, 1932.[15] However, since wages and additional supplies were not forthcoming, the labor corps did not last long and departed early in November.

McDonald kept Dickinson informed of the Spencer intrusions, and the district engineer reported them to the chief hydraulic engineer in Washington. McDonald was told not to tolerate the intruders and to keep them away from government property. The problem appeared to have solved itself when the labor force left, but Spencer continued to haunt the area.

The Great Depression intensified prospecting and many would-be miners took to the field. According to McDonald, one such was J. D. Stegler, an elderly man of about sixty who ran Glen Canyon in a crude home-made boat and oars, left his name and the date of "Sept 14, 1931" in a large arch-like cave at Mile 17.4, then came on down to Lee's Ferry. Pickings could not have been encouraging because he left his boat on the beach and went out on the stage.

After Frank Dodge had completed the Pathé-Bray project at the end of 1927, he spent an adventurous four years ranging from Seattle, Black Canyon, the Columbia River, Nevada, sniping on the Feather River in California, Mono Lake, and trail-building in Grand Canyon. Finding himself in Los Angeles and unable to obtain a job, he decided to ride out the depression in one of the unoccupied cabins at Lee's Ferry. He had no idea that the site had been set aside as a stream-gaging station, nor did he know that Charlie Spencer's efforts to revive his promotion had created an atmosphere that was unfavorable to strangers.

Dodge arrived there on November 23, 1932, introduced himself to Charlie McDonald and asked which cabin was not being used. The river gager had heard of Dodge, knew he had lived at the ferry and worked for the survey, but he remembered Dickinson's instruction to admit no strangers. On being told he could not stay, Frank hunkered down in the lee of his old cabin to think things over, as Charlie consulted with Doris McDonald. After a while, he was told that he could squat there temporarily. Breathing a silent "thank you" to Doris, Frank moved into his former quarters and began thinking of improving his home. For the next five years he was employed intermittently by the U.S. Geological Survey as an observer, laborer, and recorder, receiving pay that ranged from forty cents an hour to a hundred and fifty dollars per month.[16]

The prospecting boom enabled Dodge to acquire a fleet of three boats from would-be miners who ran Glen Canyon and reached the ferry with no funds to remove the craft. Frank purchased two of them, with outboard motors, for pittances, while one was given to him outright. He earned enough from USGS to keep supplied with beans and gasoline, and he envisioned operating a tourist business running customers up to Rainbow Bridge. This was the first motorized attempt to wrangle tourists at Lee's Ferry and some trips were made, but no business records exist.

Neal Johnson, a "Jack Mormon" who carried the self-imposed title of "Captain," arrived about the same time as Dodge. Neal brought a motor boat on a trailer to the ferry at the invitation of Elmer, who appears to have accepted the grandiose rumors the young man circulated about himself.

He claimed to have an inherited interest in the "Bibby Ranch" at Tropic and to be an expert on placer mining; he also said he would soon run Dodge off the river, start a tourist business to Rainbow Bridge, and manage the ranch into a big operation. He had four-flusher written all over him and fooled no one except Elmer, who saw the braggart as being the answer to his people's greatest need. The captain settled down at the ranch to bring his expertise into use.

Although he had lost his labor crew, Charlie Spencer had not been idle. He found new associates, some of whom had funds on a small scale, and one promoter-type who gave the impression that he had considerable money and influence. The small investors were J. R. Cranet, R. J. Winn, and F. D. and W. H. Irons. Nearly one hundred additional claims were recorded at Flagstaff later in February 1932, all in the names of the above plus C. H. Spencer, his daughter Muriel, and her husband H. S. Pope.[17] Ada and Pete Nelson again set up a boarding facility for the miners in one of Charlie's old buildings.

The real power behind the promotion, besides Spencer, was M. V. Styles, who assertedly held leases from Spencer and Irons for the purpose of recovering gold and mercury from the blue marl. Two workmen arrived on April 29 with a truckload of equipment. After a confrontation with McDonald, Styles declared that the power reserve was no longer valid and they had a right to the buildings through their mining claims. The previous group had left some equipment in the Spencer addition to the old fort, and since McDonald had some private property stored there, he had padlocked it. He told Styles he could remove the mining equipment but could not use the place as a laboratory. Styles threatened to break in.

Styles left and McDonald gave Dodge the key to the locked room, authorizing him to allow the miners to remove their equipment if they should come while he was measuring or away. Styles returned later, accompanied by Buck Lowrey, and told Dodge he was in a hurry to get something from the storeroom. Once in, he said he had decided to stay and would not leave. Dodge, having an intense loyalty to the survey, did not hesitate to throw him out, then relocked the door. The aggressive miner went to Flagstaff and swore out a warrant for Dodge's arrest, charging him with assault and battery. The service was made by Deputy Sheriff D. C. Lowrey, who appeared at Dodge's door with a six-shooter on his hip. Amused by the show of force, Dodge shamed Buck for showing up with a gun and said he would willingly accompany him to town. Frank had only ten dollars, so McDonald wrote a check which he gave to Lowrey to pay a fine if necessary. Then, he hurriedly wrote Dickinson about the affair and gave the letter to Dodge to be mailed as soon as he reached town. Dodge was convicted of assault and battery, was given a thirty-day suspended sentence, and was released on a fifty dollar bail pending the outcome of the threatened lawsuit for ownership of the cabins. Both Dodge and Lowrey were home on May 3.[18]

Dickinson then passed the trespass problem on to Chief Hydraulic Engineer N. C. Grover in Washington and sent several letters to McDonald directing him to hold fast and deny access to the miners. Unfortunately, Grover had no immediate solution to the matter, but he informed Dickinson that the Bywater Report, dated July 11, 1931, and given to the district engineer on April 20, 1932, must be kept confidential. It declared that all land on the north bank of the Colorado within one-quarter mile of the spring had been included in Public Water Reserve Number 107 by interpretation number 160, approved April 3, 1932. This did little to promote a feeling of security in Dickinson.

Styles did not file his lawsuit to determine ownership of the buildings. Instead, he went to Tucson and discussed the matter with Dickinson. He rejected the district chief's contention that his claims were in conflict with Public Power Reserve Number 107 and inferred that he had the influence to override the withdrawal if it did. He stressed the depression and how the activity would stimulate the local economy. His presentation was so effective that Dickinson caved in and did an about-face. He and Styles concluded a gentlemen's agreement in which the miners would occupy the present three Spencer buildings at Lee's Ferry without objection from the Geological Survey, and they in turn would respect the rights and privileges of that agency and not interfere with its function. Dickinson then informed Grover of the arrangement and requested that some airtight arrangement be concluded to protect survey interests. At the same time he instructed McDonald to be cooperative, show the miners every consideration, and asked for the return of his previous letters that charged otherwise. McDonald did as he was requested.[19]

Spencer's samples proved to be enticingly good—as long as he helped gather them—showing fine flower gold and pure mercury to be present. Evidently Styles became suspicious because the mercury was pure instead of contained in cinnabar. A small button of gold was recovered, but it was not sufficient to pay the grub bill. Styles left, followed by the others, and the operation lapsed into limbo. Spencer was so in need of funds that he gathered eight or ten of his old discarded ox yokes and peddled them at the trading posts to be resold to tourists.

Lola Johnson, sixteen-years old, was told that she must marry Neal Johnson, her father's choice for economic reasons, but whom she did not like. She took her problem to Doris McDonald, who advised that she did not have to marry anyone she didn't love. Lola said, "Yes, father has decreed it." She withdrew from school in March and on the appointed day, Elmer started with the young couple to Flagstaff. They never passed the bridge but stopped the car and threshed the matter out. Lola refused to go through with it and the trio returned to the ranch. Doris' advice had been taken, at least for the nonce.[20] Doris became pregnant before Charlie's tour of duty was completed and returned to civilization early in the summer of 1932. The polygamists, with so little personal resources, scraped together a bit of money and bought the unborn baby a pair of shoes. Most of their own children were barefooted.[21]

The spring of 1932 brought several changes to the area. After the Spencer-Treadwell project became inactive in April 1931, the three Nelsons hung on and lived in the old fort as long as they could. Al got a job with the Christensen Brothers Construction Company on LeFebre Ridge. When the snows of winter closed the project, he returned to cook at Buck Lowrey's lodge. Pete and Ada made a deal with the polygamists at the ranch to exchange labor for food.

Pete heard about the Wilson ranch up Pahreah Canyon, and he went to see it. The people at the Lee's Ferry ranch had stripped the place of everything usable, but he liked the site and obtained Owen Clark's address through the hydrographer. Owen came up from Yuma and although his property right was tenuous at best, he and Nelson made some kind of a deal. Nobody appeared to know where Sid Wilson was, but the place had never been patented and the title of both partners was questionable. Pete later said he paid fifty dollars and nine head of horses for the ranch.[22]

Ada planted morning glories around the cabin while Pete made the place livable. He cleared out the spring, which yielded plenty of good water. The corrals were in usable condition and the Nelsons began to think about acquiring some cattle, but they had no funds to buy them. Pete went up the Sand Trail and rode the tributaries as far as Rock Creek, noting the feral horses on the range. He captured several of the animals, broke them, and traded some to the Navajos after his own needs were met. He saw unbranded cattle on the remote range but left them alone.

Captain Neal Johnson invited Charlie McDonald to accompany him upstream in his outboard-powered boat in April, and the hydrographer accepted. They went as far as the Ute Ford, where Johnson had been previously because he pointed out the steps that had been cut in Navajo (Padre) Canyon. They came down to Gunsight Bar where they emulated George Wright by scooping gravel out of the cross-bedded sandstone, obtaining some coarse colors. The engine failed and they started downstream with oars when night and a storm arrived simultaneously. Taking refuge beneath an overhang, they spent the night, returning on oars to the ferry the following day. McDonald showed the gold to Styles, who pronounced it genuine.

When it became definite that Black Canyon had superseded Glen Canyon as a damsite, the interest of the Southern California Edison Company in the Lee's Ferry area declined. The company had allowed its lease of one acre from the Department of the Interior to expire on March 31, 1932. The fire insurance on the boathouse and the *Navajo* had been discontinued and both were given to Carling Spencer after he had tendered an offer of three dollars for the shed.[23] Thus, the problem of disposal was painless for the company. Carling used the galvanized corrugated sheets to re-roof his cabin, and the studs came in handy in a dozen places. He now authorized Captain Johnson to operate the *Navajo* if he could get it started. The paddlewheel was gone, but they re-installed the shaft and six-teen-inch propeller. Neal got the engine running and they launched the boat. Then they learned what the Edison men had known in 1921—the power was insufficient to buck the current. Carling eventually sold the *Navajo* to truck-driver Hazel Hopkins, who hauled her to Lake Mary and sank her there. The paddlewheel was left on the flat.

Meanwhile, a scramble for ownership of the ranch was underway. Buck Lowrey had grown weary of waiting for an answer to his offer to lease or buy the property. In January 1932 he wrote directly to Church President Heber J. Grant, noting that a hundred and ninety dollars in delinquent taxes were due and that the Pahreah River was claiming some of the best land.[24] Jerry had told the Presiding Bishopric that he had a deed to the property, whereas he had simply complied with each step and thought reception of the deed was imminent. Jerry made an arrangement with LeBaron to take over his interest in the ranch on the remote possibility that Cleve could obtain a federal loan to pay the church. Jerry hoped to emerge from the deal with a few acres in his own name, the debt to the church satisfied, and his two sons-in-law as land owners. It was a typical Jeremiah Johnson scheme: far-fetched and totally impractical with little chance of success.

Zions Securities Corporation stalled Lowrey by referring him back to Jerry because Heber Meeks had expressed his opinion that Lowrey had no more wherewithal to purchase the place than LeBaron. The Presiding Bishopric then notified Jerry to mail the patent directly to that office with-out recording it and to provide a legal description of the parcel he wished to retain, whereupon they would prepare a deed accordingly. They sent a copy of Jerry's letter to LeBaron and asked him what he was prepared to pay.[25] A series of letters followed. Lowrey stalled by asking about title and water rights, and he charged the present occupants with wantonly cutting magnificent trees for firewood. Jerry hedged on the unpaid taxes, and LeBaron asked for a sale price, defended his Pahreah dams, and inferred he could make a down payment.

The Presiding Bishopric didn't care whether Lowrey or LeBaron was the purchaser so long as the church corporation received the $4,057.04 it had advanced to Jerry. President Meeks was asked to act as agent and get the buyer and seller together, with the latter receiving any money beyond the invested sum. Jerry had not forwarded the final receipt or the legal description of the parcel he wished to retain, although it had been several weeks since he was asked to do so. On April 7, the Presiding Bishopric sent a carefully worded warranty deed to Meeks, asking that it be signed by Jeremiah Johnson and his wife. The deed transferred the entire one hun-dred sixty acres to the church corporation and made no mention of any acreage to be retained by the signee. Jerry and Pearly signed the instrument on May 16, 1932, and Meeks sent it to Salt Lake City the following day.[26]

Purchasing the ranch developed into a struggle between Buck Lowrey and Cleve LeBaron. Each made and refuted charges brought by the other, but neither had the money to make a deal. When it became apparent that Jerry did not know whether or not he had received the final certificate for the homestead, John Wells made inquiry of the Coconino County recorder, with negative results. Jerry then revealed his ignorance by asking U.S. Commissioner Asa W. Judd in Fredonia to give the legal description of the ranch to President Meeks.

While this comedy of errors was taking place, another distracting element was injected. Neal Johnson, still trying to marry Lola, had evaluated the ranch situation and offered a solution that would benefit him if it were accepted. The scheme was exposed when President Meeks visited the property and presented his findings to the Presiding Bishopric.[27] Meeks noted in his report that the residents of the ranch were excommunicated and living in polygamy. The Johnsons were intending to move away, but Cleve LeBaron and Carling Spencer were determined to stay and were depending on the commitment of Neal, who claimed to be an ex-serviceman and the recipient of a government pension. His inheritance had changed from the Tropic ranch to property in Phoenix and California and some government securities, and he intended to borrow on these assets to pay the taxes and buy the ranch. Neal said he was a member of the Third Ward in Salt Lake City. He intended to marry Lola next week, but Meeks advised Elmer not to allow the marriage until Neal's record could be verified. He was not impressed with the self-proclaimed captain's story. Meeks agreed with Lowrey's statement that the property had suffered from neglect.

Church officials expressed no concern with Neal Johnson, the deals he might arrange with the excommunicates, or his impending marriage to one of their daughters; if Lola married outside the church, that was her affair. Their only interest was in the final certificate that would confirm their ownership of the Lee's Ferry property. One person's money was as good as another's.

Unknown to anyone outside of the federal government, Claude H. Birdseye of the U.S. Geological Survey informed the commissioner of the General Land Office that granting the homestead requested by Jeremiah Johnson would be detrimental to the Lee's Ferry gaging station. Survey officials were concerned because the Pahreah River gaging station and access road were near the center of Jerry's claim, he conceivably could deny access.[28] It was unlikely that he would assume such an attitude, but subsequent owners might not be as amenable.

Through all this, the stream-gaging work continued. Wilbur Heckler visited from Tucson and helped McDonald take measurements in January; he returned for high-water duty on April 1, 1932, with Joe Gatewood. Although the preceding years had very low runoff, 1932 peaked at just under 100,000 cubic feet per second. The McDonalds went on vacation the last two weeks of August, and Heckler only had Frank Dodge, who was more or less in steady residence, working as needed. When the McDonalds returned, Heckler took his vacation. In two weeks, he showed up

Streamgager's residence at Lee's Ferry, 1931 (*W. L. Heckler photograph, P. T. Reilly Collection, Cline Library, Northern Arizona University*).

again, now married, and when his bride, Lela, got out of the car, she nearly stepped on a five-foot gopher snake, making her reception unforgettable.

The only income available to the people at the ranch was that generated by School District Number 26. Mary Wilkinson, now serving her second consecutive hitch, received one hundred thirty-five dollars a month, and she pumped part of that into local pockets for board. The county paid for janitorial service, travel expenses in school interests, and for fuel to keep the students warm during winter months. Plenty of wood was available on the Pahreah delta, although it had to be collected, cut into stove lengths, and hauled to the schoolhouse. Janitor duty and wood gathering were considered porkbarrel jobs which were dispensed by the vote of the three school board trustees.

The brethren wanted the prestige of having the government hydrographer on the board. In October 1931, they induced Charlie MacDonald to join Elmer Johnson and Cleve LeBaron as board members. Charlie soon learned that he was only window dressing, as Elmer and Cleve voted together and ran the district to suit themselves; they split the jobs and schemed to overspend the budget. McDonald protested, and knowing that he was due for reassignment, made the protest stronger by resigning on September 10, 1932.[29] This was a blow to Elmer and Cleve, but they shrugged it off, hoping to induce his replacement to join the board.

Elmer's wife, Artemisia, never having recovered from a miscarriage, died on May 4, 1932. Despite having been excommunicated, she was buried in her temple clothes, a fact that upset the Kanab Stake authorities.[30] Elmer was aware of the community's attitude toward Neal Johnson, and Lola had won the first round with her father, but Elmer persisted in his efforts to persuade her to follow his wishes. The argument had developed into a test of will between father and daughter. He had exerted all the pressure he could muster, evidently accepting Neal's profession of belief in the fundamentalist cause and realizing that his daughter would not be likely to acquire an orthodox Mormon for a husband. She finally consented, and Neal and Lola were married in a civil ceremony, and Elmer appeared to be satisfied even if Lola wasn't.

Attempting to curry favor with Lola's parents, Neal Johnson located the Mesken Bar No. 1 and 2 claims in the names of himself and W. E. and Viola Johnson on August 23.[31] Aware that Elmer intended to move to Short Creek, and that one of the three trustee positions would then be open, Neal continued on to Flagstaff to visit School Superintendent Bessie Kidd Best in her home. He misrepresented the situation at the ranch to his advantage and somehow he managed to talk Best into appointing him to fill Elmer's unexpired term as trustee. Despite his big talk, he intended to cut himself into a split of the school budget. When he returned to the ferry and announced that he now had a voice in decision making, he opened a conflict with Cleve LeBaron, the only member of the previous board still in residence.

The anti-Neal faction included every resident in the area except Lola, who had to appear neutral. Twelve of them petitioned Superintendent Best to appoint I. C. Spencer and A. E. Nelson to fill the trustee vacancies. The same mail carried a personal letter from LeBaron, who expressed general dissatisfaction with Neal's appointment and enclosed some advance vouchers to be signed.[32] Three days later, Cleve received official notification that Neal was a member of the board of trustees for District 26. Only McDonald had resigned in writing; W. E. Johnson had not and technically was still a board member. Neal had filled McDonald's place. This prompted a return letter from LeBaron, pointing out quite logically that neither W. E. Johnson nor McDonald lived at Lee's Ferry. If Johnson was still on the board, then so was McDonald and there was no vacancy. He reiterated that no resident had confidence in Neal; all of them accused him of lies, deception, misrepresentation, and moral turpitude. Moreover, Cleve charged that Neal was hiding out at Lee's Ferry to escape a bootlegging charge.[33] Apparently the protest did no good; if the superintendent knew she had made a mistake, she did not acknowledge it. She probably did not expect much of a representative from Lee's Ferry and therefore was not disappointed in Neal Johnson.

The following day Neal wrote Superintendent Best and brought the conflict with LeBaron into the open. He exposed the petty squabbling over janitorial work, wood hauling, and made an ill-disguised bribe for her good will by offering her father a river trip to Rainbow Bridge, along with a job building cabins for use by his expected tourist trade. The crude letter would not have earned a passing grade for a fifth grade student.[34] Elmer Johnson submitted his official resignation on October 29, but the superintendent had already called an election for his replacement four days earlier. All nine votes were cast for Buck Lowrey, because there was no other candidate. Apparently absent, Neal did not vote, but his enemies did.[35] The officials now were LeBaron, Johnson, and Lowrey, each of whom disliked the other two.

While the wretched social pot boiled at the ranch, Charlie Spencer made another run at taking possession of his old buildings. Early in November, he appeared at the ferry with two companions. His intentions were to salvage his abandoned pumps and other machinery for sale to a Chicago group that intended to revive the mining venture. Wilbur Heckler, now the resident hydrographer, was about to leave on his bimonthly inspection of the Little Colorado River gages when Spencer decided to store the refurbished machinery in his old blacksmith shop that the survey used as a garage for Wilbur's car. The hydrographer ordered Spencer off the property, but Spencer refused to go unless Wilbur produced a court order. Wilbur cautioned Dodge not to use force, and he departed for Flagstaff.

Heckler notified Dickinson and requested firm instructions before he returned to the ferry on November 9. Dickinson telegraphed Grover in Washington, then followed up with a copy of Heckler's letter and a plea for action to end the intrusions for good. Spencer had been a thorn in the side of the survey for several years, with the Treadwell and Styles phases proving to be major threats to the gaging station. Grover telegraphed that appropriate proceedings were being instituted.[36]

The commissioner of the General Land Office, C. C. Moore, ordered that adverse proceedings be initiated against all Spencer-Treadwell claims at Lee's Ferry, on the Pahreah River, and at Soap and Badger Creeks. The request was transmitted from the Secretary of the Interior to the Attorney General and, from there, to the District Attorney for Arizona. The action did not deter Spencer because the papers had not been served; he returned with two possible investors just before Christmas and with another early in January.

Administrative Geologist Julien D. Sears confirmed that on November 16, 1931, the lands claimed by the Johnson homestead entry had been classed as being non-oil and non-gas bearing. A year later A. J. Bauerschmidt and G. G. Frazier made a field investigation in which Jerry Johnson was interviewed. He naively informed them that he intended to deed the property to the church as soon as he received the patent. The two geologists then went to the Presiding Bishopric and discussed the matter with Joseph Eckersley, who convinced them that the church did not want the land but only the return of the money that had been loaned. The government men appeared to be satisfied and recommended that the patent be issued to Jeremiah Johnson.[37] If Brother Eckersley had been given to profanity, he could not be blamed for cursing Jerry's stupidity under his breath.

Possibly the government assault on Spencer's mining interests, along with the favorable report, softened the stand against the Johnson homestead claim because on January 10, 1933, Archie D. Ryan, General

Land Office chief of field division, wrote N. G. Grover, "Personally I see no objection so far to the issuance of a patent on the Johnson homestead …" and suggested he notify the commissioner's office to withdraw the USGS protest.[38] The assistant commissioner, on January 17, recommended the final certificate be issued but suspended for a period of sixty days from this date. The stall on Jerry's homestead claim appeared to be dying of old age, but the legal case to void the Treadwell-Spencer mining claims was just getting started.

President Herbert Hoover, in what has been described as his last official act before leaving office, signed papers creating the U.S. Government Reserve at Lee's Ferry on January 18, 1933. The order was effective against any asserted rights or claims initiated subsequent to the date of withdrawal, but it did not control valid antecedent claims. Therefore, until the court determined the legality of his claims, Spencer came and went as he pleased. He and potential investors Ford and Surber pitched tents near the old saddle barn and spent most of the month salvaging the water pump from the steamboat and refurbishing other abandoned machinery. Heckler informed Dickinson, who passed the information on to Grover.

Early in February, Dickinson raised the issue with Grover of just what Public Water Reserve No. 107, effective April 8, 1932, was meant to cover, and for whom. The Hiester survey of 1927 subdivided the township containing the Johnson and Lowrey homestead claims, but did not subdivide the one to the east. Unfortunately, the fort, all but one of the Spencer buildings, and the spring appeared to be in Section 18, Township 40 North, Range 8 East. Dickinson claimed misuse of the spring by trespassers, knowing it was on unsurveyed land.

The Pahreah River was always a problem. If flooding appeared likely, the hydrographers were accustomed to leaving a vehicle on the right bank so they would not be isolated for trips to Flagstaff or the Little Colorado River gages. Wilbur Heckler returned from such a trip to find the stream had flooded while he was away. It was close to midnight, he was anxious to turn in, and an examination by his headlights made him think he could cross the creek. This was a mistake, because he became stuck in midstream. After working for half an hour to extricate the car, he was joined by Carling Spencer who had heard him struggling from his cabin at the end of the lane. "I. C.," as he was called by the gagers, hitched up his team and pulled the car out. Wilbur tried to pay him but he would not accept a cent. This was typical of Carling Spencer; several of the hydrographers, Ed Fisher, and others claimed the old man was the best neighbor they ever had.

Most of the river gagers enjoyed very good relations with the fundamentalists and considered them to be remarkably self-sufficient. The polygamists had little money but were generous with their produce. Melons were raised in great quantity and several were packed in straw and buried in barrels each year. These were unearthed during the winter, and the brethren took great pleasure in delivering a large watermelon to the hydrographer at Christmas. The Klohrs, Scotts, McDonalds, and Hecklers all retained happy memories of ranch people going out of their way to be good neighbors.

Carling Spencer, Elmer Johnson, and Cleve LeBaron had reduced the delinquent taxes to forty-five dollars by the end of 1932. Church officials made no objection, apparently considering that taking care of the taxes was the least they could do for being allowed to live there rent-free. Jerry's irresponsibility and vacillation between forming an island oasis of polygamy and discharging his financial obligation to the church allowed Spencer and LeBaron to feel they had a legitimate interest in the place. Cleve felt this way especially, since he had taken over the interests of both Jerry and Elmer. He now bombarded the Presiding Bishopric with requests to sell him the ranch on credit.

In the fall of 1932, Neal Johnson was returning to the ferry, towing his boat on its trailer, when within one and one-half miles of the ranch, the car stalled. Unable to get it restarted, he walked back to Lowrey's for help. While he was gone, someone torched the entire outfit. Designating a suspect was difficult since he was so universally disliked. After it was brought home so forcefully that he had no support in the trustee squabble, he left. Neal returned a few days before Christmas with the story that President Meeks had authorized him to take over parts of the ranch. He produced nothing to substantiate this but through sheer arrogance began to assert himself. A confrontation led LeBaron to seek confirmation from Meeks. When it did not come, Johnson was ignored by LeBaron and Lowrey. On March 10, eleven local residents petitioned the school superintendent for a recall election, and on the twenty-first, he was given the legal choice of defending his conduct and going through with the ballot or resigning. Thus, the local citizens disposed of the Neal Johnson problem.

On March 28, 1933, Gibbs & Gibbs obtained a copy of the final certificate for Jerry's homestead. They passed the good news on to him and also sent a copy of the letter to the Presiding Bishopric. The patent was approved May 3 and transmitted on the twenty-third. Jerry did not have the $26.75 final payment, but the church officials told him they would pay it and presumably they did. They sent him one deed transferring ownership to Heber Meeks and another assigning title from Meeks to the Corporation of the Presiding Bishopric. Jerry and Pearly executed their deed to Meeks on September 9, 1933, and three days later Meeks and his wife deeded the Lee's Ferry ranch to the church.[39] It had been a long, difficult struggle to reclaim partial security for the investment Anthony Ivins had made in Warren Johnson's posterity, but by this time the counselor had gone to his reward. The church now held title to the property but it was doubtful whether it would ever get the money back that had been expended.

Wilbur Heckler was the resident hydrographer from the fall of 1932 until December 16, 1934. Frank Dodge helped when needed and Howard S. Leak arrived in May for high-water duty. The 1933 runoff turned out to be about average, peaking slightly under 80,000 cubic feet per second, and Heckler was alone again after June 26. Dodge came and went as his maverick nature dictated. Subsequent to his last pretense of refurbishing the abandoned mining machinery, Charlie Spencer disappeared. He found more small investors, because on March 27, 1933, two men named Winn and McGinnis arrived to join George Wilson in setting up some experimental machinery for recovering gold and mercury. Wilson, a holdover from the Styles venture, was the pitchman for Spencer's supposed assets. Heckler passed this development on to Dickinson, who relayed it to Archie Ryan.[40]

Meanwhile, Ryan reported that the mining activity had not interfered with the Lee's Ferry gaging station. He recommended to the United States Attorney for Arizona that no further action be taken until the validity of the mining claims could be determined.[41] The Attorney General passed the problem on to the Secretary of the Interior Harold Ickes, who called for the latest opinion from those affected as to whether an injunction was still needed. Several rounds of buck passing between Washington, Tucson, and Lee's Ferry carried the question into May. At mid-month, the Spencer-Treadwell-Styles claims were declared null and void.[42] The United States Attorney dropped his proposed suit and the case was closed. Lack of further Spencer activity appears to have prompted the decision.

The state of Arizona launched some long-delayed road improvements in the spring of 1933. Julius Irion brought a survey crew to relocate the pioneer road from the west end of the new bridge to the foot of Buckskin Mountain in House Rock Valley. In places, they merely removed the kinks from the wagon road, but generally the new location was up to a quarter of a mile farther from the base of the Vermilion Cliffs. The Vickers Company followed behind with the road work.[43]

The three Fisher brothers—Ernie, Ed, and George—were raised in Colorado as stockmen. They could ride anything, and in 1923 they trailed about three dozen head of horses into Vernal where they put on a rodeo. They were successful and continued giving shows in a circuit of Utah towns. After completing the season at Cedar City, Ed and George wintered the stock on the Arizona Strip out of St. George. They continued putting on small-town rodeos through the fall of 1925, then sold the stock and went to work as cowhands.

Ed Fisher was riding for an outfit south of Seligman in the spring of 1933 when he decided to acquire a ranch and some range. He had accumulated several hundred dollars, was single, and he quit his job in spite of the Great Depression. In May, he took the train to Flagstaff, went to the Pine Hotel, and discussed his ambition with the proprietor, who recommended trying the range around Lee's Ferry. Ed had known Peter Nelson in Colorado, heard that he lived in the vicinity, and decided to look him up after he had talked the matter over with George, who was then living in Kanab.

Unknown to Ed, the stage he boarded in Flagstaff was driven by a one-time cowboy named Riley Baker; two other passengers were Maggie Jackson and Ada Nelson. Maggie was the widow of old-time cattleman I. M. Jackson, who was impressed with the economic potential of the strip and was dickering with Price Johnson to purchase his Badger homestead. Ada, Pete's wife, was working at Lowrey's and left the vehicle at the trading post. After the stage pulled out of Marble Canyon, the driver told Ed "That woman is Nelson's wife." Ed went on to Kanab only to learn that his brother was riding in the House Rock Valley and that he had passed him. He obtained a horse and rode back, meeting Jerry Johnson in the Vickers camp at Badger Creek; Jerry said he could find the Nelsons at the ferry. The reunion there was genial and they soon got down to business.

Pete held grazing rights to two sections and parts of two more but had no money to stock the range. He tried to get Ed to stock it for him, but the cowboy declined, knowing Pete's penchant for jumping range. Ed did, however, buy two good horses from him for $75. The next day, they rode up Pahreah Canyon to look at Pete's ranch. Ed liked it and they began dickering, finally settling on a price of $500. He paid $100 in cash and signed three notes for the remaining $400. Being a newcomer, he was apprehensive that Alex Cram or Billy Mackelprang might dispute his claim, so he hurried to get stock on his range. He knew he could buy weaners for $11, and learned that by dealing through Joe Lee—then at The Gap with J. C. Brown—Indian cattle could be bought for $15 and a dry cow brought $12. He took a bag of silver coins, paid Joe Lee $2 a head commission, and came back with 26 animals. His savings now were reduced to $1 but he had a ranch on which he owed money and a few head of stock. It was a poor year and cattle did not thrive on the open range. That fall, Ed paid Pete off at the rate of 50¢ on the dollar, making the total cost of his ranch $300.

Things had not been going well for Price Johnson. He had refused to join Buck Lowrey and Dode Burch of House Rock in maintaining a price of 50¢ a gallon for gasoline, retailing instead for 35¢. One night while he was away, somebody pumped his underground tank dry and left it containing ashes and dirt. Already operating on a shoestring and bypassed by the road relocation, Price was broken by the theft. On July 6, 1933, he sold his homestead to Margaret Jackson for $250.[44] Aside from the one and one-half miles of fence and two hundred feet of two-inch pipe from Badger Creek to his flimsy dwelling, Price's improvements were not worth salvaging. The survey had placed the new road about five hundred feet southeast of the pioneer track, so Maggie, with advice from Riley Baker, began construction of a new way station on the relocated highway.

Price's relinquishment of his Badger homestead and his retreat to Short Creek marked the first time in many years that some Johnson did not call Lee's Ferry or the immediate area home. The region's demographics revealed that an influx of non-Mormons had replaced the one-time population of all Saints. Two excommunicates, Cleve LeBaron and Carling

Spencer, with their families, hung on at the ranch in which they had no legal interest. Ed Fisher ran stock four and one-half miles up Pahreah Canyon from a ranch in which he had a tenuous right-of-use equity. Lela and Wilbur Heckler, along with Frank Dodge, represented the U.S. Geological Survey. Milt Winn and William George Wilson lived in one of Charlie Spencer's stone buildings as non-paid caretakers of Spencer's imaginary mining interests. Al Nelson cooked at Buck Lowrey's lodge while his wife and children lived in another Spencer cabin, and two of their boys attended Mary Wilkinson's school. The Lowrey family and, frequently, Preacher Smith dispensed meals, lodging, and gasoline at Buck's Vermilion Cliffs Lodge. Maggie Jackson and Riley Baker were living at Badger Creek and building a tourist facility on the newly located roadway. The Vickers Construction camp also was at Badger Creek with an uncertain number of employees. Blanche and Bill Russell were building a colorful tourist trap among the large boulders where the pioneer and relocated roads crossed Soap Creek. Mary and George Fisher lived in a cabin beside the creek two hundred yards north.

The Russells had visited Kanab as tourists in the summer of 1930. They became paying guests of Dean Cutler, whose rental at House Rock was about to expire; Bar Z caretaker Charlie Lewis refused to grant him a lease because of his alleged bootlegging to the Indians. While hunting, Bill Russell was impressed with the setting at Soap Creek and brought his wife to see it. They decided to homestead the site and Cutler set them up with two tent houses. Using Navajo labor, they built cabins against the large boulders and sold meals, wine, home brew, and gasoline. Blanche arranged for the place to become a bus stop. It was rumored that she had been a madam on San Francisco's Barbary Coast and had retired here for a simpler life. Several residents contemporary to her period have said that she imported prostitutes from Flagstaff for the weekend benefit of the road construction workers.

Buck Lowrey was granted the patent to his homestead on March 2, 1933, and it was recorded on the twenty-eighth.[45] Although the road was graded, it was not paved. A surprisingly large number of cars traveled it and Buck had a thriving business. He was not an astute manager, however, and did little to reduce his debt. In March 1929, he borrowed $10,000 from Lorenzo Hubbell, Jr., for three years at eight percent interest. Nothing had been paid on either interest or principal. In addition, his $1,100 debt to the J. D. Halstead Lumber Company of Flagstaff was not reduced nor the interest paid. Lowrey grossed about $15,000 each year, but he was weak in accounting and budgeting.

Federal budget problems in 1933 caused the position of resident hydrographer to be temporarily discontinued. Wilbur Heckler, re-assigned, left on December 16 and went to Tucson. The station was attended by a capable observer, Betty Jo Games, who with her husband and son arrived at the ferry with Dwight Doolittle and two other prospectors. Bobby Games had worked with Dodge at Black Canyon in 1930 when Colonel Birdseye

D. C. "Buck" Lowrey at the original Vermilion Cliffs (later Marble Canyon) Lodge, ca. 1930s (*Woodruff Collection, P. T. Reilly Collection, Cline Library, Northern Arizona University*).

was measuring contours. Dodge was off on another survey job, but the Games family moved into Frank Johnson's old cabin at the upper ferry. While Bobby and his companions prospected lower Glen Canyon, Betty Jo checked each gaging station daily. They wangled food at the ranch and, in exchange, helped water the fields. Engineers from the Tucson office visited the station three times between December 17, 1933, and April 1, 1934. On the latter, Marion Scott arrived to serve a second hitch as resident hydrographer. Dodge returned in the spring to assist when needed, which wasn't often because 1934 was an all-time low water year. The runoff peaked on May 16 at 24,700 cubic feet per second and never reached 20,000 during June—usually when the peak occurred.

Charlie Spencer's two caretakers starved out. Milt Winn, a retired druggist, went to southern Arizona. George Wilson obtained a job with Buck Lowrey pumping gas at the trading post. The depression had so tightened the field of venture capital that even the great promoter was unable to find backers. Under the circumstances, Charlie did not appear at his favorite scene of past undertakings.

The church corporation now had a clear title to the ranch in the mouth of Pahreah Canyon. Although officials were eager to reclaim some of the poor investment, they allowed it to remain in limbo for several months. Near the end of 1933, the news leaked that the property was available at a very good price. As might be expected, two citizens of Salt Lake City—attorney Keith Holbrook and his partner, James Courtney—picked up the disclosure and hurried south early in 1934. They examined the property and discussed its purchase with Heber Meeks on their way home, offering him $2,000. The stake president wrote Bishop Wells of their proposal and stated that the bid was all the property was worth in its present condition. The church now had $4,083.79 invested in the property.[46]

Holbrook and Courtney met with church representatives on January 8 and tendered an offer of $2,000 for the ranch, with $200 down, the balance at 6 percent, and payments of $200 per year. Some dickering followed. On February 6, the parties settled on a net price of $2,000 for the Jeremiah Johnson homestead, with $500 down payment and $200 paid annually and an interest of 7 percent in deferred payments. The deal went for naught as the prospective buyers failed to come up with the down payment. The Presiding Bishopric gave them until April 5 to raise the money, then called the deal off.

The appearance and big talk of the pair from Salt Lake City convinced LeBaron and Spencer that time was running out for them. Church officials at this time also thought the sale was certain, and they notified Jerry that his kindred had thirty days to vacate. Jerry promised to relinquish some of the buildings and give possession of the land if his people could remain until the school term was complete. He could not correlate the fact that he had received a quit-claim deed from the Grand Canyon Cattle Company for 200 acres, which included the upper ranch and was outside of his homestead, with the simple truth that his homestead entry gave him title to only 160 acres. If the church sold the patented land, he proposed to move LeBaron and Spencer to the upper ranch where they could claim homesteads, and he expected the church to give him some kind of title.[47]

The assumption generated letters from both LeBaron and Spencer to Bishop Wells. Cleve pleaded for the opportunity to buy the ranch on time, pay what he could by November, and obtain a federal loan. Carling merely itemized his improvements and said he had a canceled check to prove he had paid $270 as his share of the purchase price. Jerry attempted to appear benevolent and cooperative both to church officials and his sons-in-law, but he only succeeded in reinforcing himself as a well-meaning incompetent [48]

Buck Lowrey now got into the act, motivated chiefly by his dislike of the polygamists and seeing an opportunity to help remove them from the locality. In a letter to church authorities, he lamented that he was unable to obtain answers to his inquiries regarding the ranch. He offered a down payment of $1,000 with a note for the balance at a reasonable rate of interest. His offer was conditioned on the church's providing title, giving immediate possession, and ejecting those now living on the property. He noted that six acres of the best land had been lost to floods of recent years and that another torrent would cut through the heart of the property and make it worthless. He concluded with the statement that the open practice of polygamy there outraged the decent people of the general community and they expected the church to take the lead in bringing it to an end.[49]

Lowrey's letter was effective. Four days later, the Presiding Bishopric notified LeBaron and Spencer to vacate the premises by May 1,

1934; copies also were sent to Jerry Johnson. They replied to Lowrey April 11, stating that they thought $3,000 was a low price for the property and offered to carry the balance at 7 percent after a down payment of one-third. Buck, not knowing that Holbrook and Courtney had received an even lower price and better terms, countered with an offer of $2,500. It was accepted on April 20.[50]

Cleve LeBaron now became desperate and wrote a pleading, yet threatening, letter to the Presiding Bishopric on April 23. He probably realized he had no legal claim to the ranch, so he reverted to distortion of past relationships, asked for favorable purchase terms, and concluded by questioning the ethics used in the case, noting that school would not be out until May 18. He reiterated his determination to fight for his rights. The intractable LeBaron let Lowrey know that he had no intention of vacating the ranch; he would go to court to prevent his removal and would seek damages if he were ejected. He engaged attorney C. B. Wilson of Flagstaff to draw up the agreement that he claimed Jerry had made with him and tender it to Jeremiah and Pearly Johnson to be signed. An aide presented the document to them at Hurricane on May 13. It was rejected and Jerry immediately wrote the Presiding Bishopric regarding the episode and offered his services to straighten out the affair.

Cleve's perversity worked more to Lowrey's advantage than his own. Faced with responding with a down payment of $1,000 to the acceptance of his offer, and not having the money, Buck stalled. He stated the water rights were not a matter of record; the tenants refused to vacate and he did not want to become involved in the eviction.[51] He then followed this on May 15 with an offer to reduce his down payment to $600 because of the need for immediate repair of the neglected ranch; even this proposition was conditioned by his obtaining possession without legal difficulties with LeBaron. He reiterated his eagerness to purchase the property on the revised terms.[52] Joseph Eckersley countered Lowrey's objections by noting that the water rights were mentioned specifically in the deeds of title on October 2, 1909, and on August 4, 1925. Further, he guaranteed that Lowrey would have peaceable possession. At the same time, he requested Jerry to advise LeBaron that he would testify against him if the case went to court.[53]

Sylvester Q. Cannon, by telegram on May 22, accepted Lowrey's revised terms, then mailed a duplicate contract to him that embodied the terms agreed upon. The letter rejected Buck's charge that LeBaron and Spencer were church members because they had been excommunicated. They could be removed by the local prosecuting officer on complaint and at church expense. The same mail carried a letter to LeBaron denying his claims to the property and telling him that arrangements had been made to evict him if he refused to leave peaceably.

Carling Spencer saw the hopelessness of their position. Upon being told by Jerry that he would sustain the church's position in court if necessary, Carling agreed to depart, and Jerry helped him resettle at Short

Creek. Jerry continued on to Hurricane where, on May 24, he wrote the Presiding Bishopric that Spencer had left but LeBaron still was adamant against leaving. Jerry was hopeful that a change in Cleve's attitude was forthcoming and concluded with the statement that Buck Lowrey had been looking for a chance to get a whack at LeBaron for some time. Had the men in the church office been more familiar with the local situation, they might have looked closer at the potential purchaser.

The shoe now was on Lowrey's foot, and he squirmed at the fit. On May 31, he put the sale in abeyance until he was free to take possession without being a party to evicting the LeBaron family. He also wrote to the state water commissioner to ascertain the exact water rights for the ranch. On the same day, Cleve wrote John Wells that he was vacating the ranch on June 15 but the church owed him $1,060 for his crop, improvements, and taxes paid. He also attempted to shame the officials for the "raw deal" given him. Upon receipt of the welcome information, the church agent transmitted the news to Lowrey and urged him to return the signed contract with his check for $600.

Buck received a reply from the state water commissioner that if water from Pahreah River had been used to irrigate the ranch for the past fifty years without a period of five consecutive years of non-use, the office would recognize and confirm the water right. Forms for statement and proof of claimant were enclosed.[54] Lowrey waited until LeBaron's date for vacating had passed. On June 18, he wrote Eckersley to tell him that his trespasser was still there but appeared to be preparing to move. Cleve, however, was dismantling some of the buildings and evidently planning to use the lumber wherever he relocated; the contract called for transfer of the improvements. Lowery also raised the issue of a right-of-way to the Geological Survey withdrawal, noting it had not been mentioned. He enclosed the letter and forms from the Arizona water commissioner, suggesting the church apply for use of the one hundred and twenty miner's inches of water. Lastly, he provided the name of attorney F. L. Russell of Flagstaff to handle the eviction of LeBaron if needed.[55]

LeBaron and his two families left the ranch June 23 and resettled at New Harmony. Lowrey did not take possession, nor did he sign the contract or return it with his down payment to the Presiding Bishopric. He waited four days, then wrote Eckersley that water had not been on the place for more than a month, the ditch headgate had been taken out by a flood, the planted crop was a total loss, and the fruit trees and other shrubbery would be dead in ten days. He stated the ranch was in such poor condition that he could not accept it at the price offered. Lowery said it would require the work of four men and a team over eight days to put the water back in the ditch; he would arrange to have this done if the church would bear the expense.[56]

Thus, Buck Lowrey ended his bid to purchase the Lee's Ferry Ranch. It is doubtful that he ever had the down payment or was sincere in his offer. He merely used his role as a prospective buyer to remove the polygamists he detested. LeBaron later charged that Lowrey paid back taxes in an attempt to acquire the property through delinquency. It also was charged that he made prejudicial statements regarding the ranch to divert other buyers. The Presiding Bishopric sent him a registered letter on August 30 calling on him to desist and to return the contract, its copy, and proof of water rights.[57] Buck did so in part without comment in September, but evidently kept the contract copy as proof of the offered price.

If Lowrey was successful in dispersing the polygamists from Lee's Ferry, Jeremiah Johnson's attempt to resurrect his father's trysting cabins into a self-contained colony of polygamists was an utter failure. His abortive effort came to naught because of his personal inadequacies, not because the potential for success was absent from the Mormon social structure. Others with more organizational ability had espoused the pre-manifesto cause, did not try to be all things to all men, and built a thriving aggregation that combined the early church ideas of the United Order and plural marriage. Several of those involved were his own brothers and sisters. The main consequence of Jerry's pathetic venture was tragic—he split his paternal family. Warren Johnson would have avoided that at all costs.

14

Paradise Canyon Ranch

As THE GREAT DEPRESSION CONTINUED, UNEMPLOYMENT EXCEEDED 15 percent. The money supply fell and auction sales for debt judgments were halted in several states. Few people had money to spend on anything except necessities. Real estate sales declined and were exceeded by foreclosures. It probably was the worst time the church could have chosen to reclaim its investment in the ranch at Lee's Ferry. Nevertheless, the property was put on the market for $3,000, $500 down, and the balance to be carried at 7 percent in deferred payments with a $450 annual reduction of the principal. Interest was widespread both in Utah and Arizona, but nobody came forward with a down payment.

If Buck Lowrey's effort to obtain the property at a reduced price had failed, it awoke the brethren in Salt Lake City to the unpleasant fact that the value of the property decreased the longer the ranch went unwatered. Jerry Johnson also realized this, and on June 15 from Hurricane, some one hundred forty miles away, he offered his services to save the place. Unable to learn Lowrey's intentions, the Presiding Bishopric, on the twenty-third, asked Jerry to go there, ascertain Lowrey's decision, and care for the place until it was sold. They pointed out that under the circumstances, it was the least he could do. Jerry responded two days later by asking for a loan of fifty dollars per month as his family was sick and destitute. The churchmen appear to have ignored his economic situation, and he finally wrote that if he did not hear from them by 2 P.M. of August 3, he would go to the ranch anyway. He went there authorized to evict trespassers and in three days, helped only by his son, had the water back in the ditch.[1]

Jerry's hopes were buoyed when a man from Phoenix, peddling melons to the Indians, offered to contract for two truckloads of melons per day in 1935. Visions of obtaining a federal loan to regain control of the ranch again filled his head, and he wrote to the church officials that if the place had not been sold, he would buy it. By this time his naivete evoked no surprise and they offered him the same deal they said had been tendered to Lowrey—three thousand dollars for the ranch.

The brethren asked Jerry to make a map of the ranch showing the acreage under cultivation, the crop being raised, the location of the 40 acres

372

outside of the 160-acre homestead, and whether there were any buildings on the 40 acres. The map was beyond Jerry's capability and he rendered it illegible; he promised to make another one but never did. They gave Jerry the crop from the 7 acres now under cultivation and said he could have the produce from the 8 acres lying within the homestead that now were idle. He informed them that all of the buildings were on the deeded land and stated that he needed help because the ranch was too much for one man. He asked if they had any objection to his bringing his brother Elmer to help him. The officials agreed to Elmer's presence but barred Carling Spencer and Cleve LeBaron. The brethren in the north had no idea how the 40 acres outside the patented quarter-section were related to the 160 acres. Meanwhile, a rumor was afoot that these 40 acres were open for entry, and ownership of that parcel could control the ditch to the ranch. The names of J. C. Black, J. S. McConaghy, and Babbitt were bandied about as being interested parties. Others were Carling Spencer, Buck Lowrey, and a partnership of Ed Fisher and Ned Smith, the Tuba City blacksmith.

Elmer joined Jerry in September 1934, and the Johnson brothers made plans to acquire the 40 acres comprising their father's upper ranch. They began building a cabin there and made overtures to purchase the land, unaware that the right-of-use deed received from the Grand Canyon Cattle Company was not equivalent to a deed for patented land. Jerry pursued the matter of obtaining a federal loan, ignoring the fact that he had no equity for collateral. Finally, on September 21, the Presiding Bishopric told him bluntly that he had no basis for obtaining a loan and they did not want to reawaken government interest in how Jerry's homestead came to be in church ownership. He was told unequivocally either to purchase the ranch on the terms offered or continue to occupy the premises, cultivate the land, and make the project a profitable investment until the place was sold.[2] Jerry never questioned his status on the property that once had been in his name.

Leo Weaver's interest in the ranch had not cooled. Fate had decreed a postponement of his plans to follow up immediately. Limited funds, always a Weaver handicap, prevented opening his Flagstaff ranch, the Circle Flying W. Instead, he leased it for the summer of 1932 to Kay Dewing, one of his affluent winter customers. That fall, Leo, Hazel, her sister Irene and husband Scotty made an inspection visit to Lee's Ferry. Carling Spencer was working up the canyon, and his absence probably prevented a violent confrontation. Traditional accounts tell us that Spencer learned of the visit at the end of the day and instead of sitting down to his supper, he buckled on a six-shooter and went to Lowrey's looking for the man he thought was trying to deprive him of his property. Fortunately the visitors had returned to Flagstaff, and the paranoid old polygamist was saved from committing a rash act.

Hazel Weaver began having headaches and dizzy spells during the summer of 1932. They increased in frequency that winter, and the Flagstaff doctors told her she was pregnant. She was sure she wasn't, so Leo decided to take her to Dr. Earl Tarr whom he had known in Phoenix and who now had a practice in Pasadena. A payment of six hundred dollars was due on the Flagstaff ranch on January 2, but Harold Colton, aware of Hazel's illness, did not push for the defrayal. Leo took his wife to California in February 1933 and rented a house in Glendale for March and April. Dr. Tarr diagnosed Hazel's ailment as a form of mastoid in which the infection was nearing her brain and would have killed her in another two weeks. The diagnosis was confirmed by a brilliant surgeon, Dr. Don Dryer, whose sister owed her life to Dr. Tarr. Hazel underwent a radical mastoid operation. It was risky but successful and Dr. Dryer charged only a nominal fee.

Leo was grateful and asked what he could do to repay Dr. Tarr. Tarr was chairman of a social program dealing with children of problem families, not necessarily impoverished or underprivileged, but those broken by divorce, alcohol, or career. His delinquent children usually had been affected by too much money, not too little, and many of the parents were associated with the Hollywood studios. Tarr asked Weaver to reopen his Flagstaff ranch and accept his young charges as paying guests. The manager was delighted to do so. The doctor's solution to Weaver's indebtedness not only would help those he fostered but resulted in a financial windfall for Leo.

Weaver opened the Circle Flying W in July 1933, playing host to twenty-three boys, four girls, and a scattering of adults. Among the guests were Allan Hale's two boys who were under the guidance of Darrell "Unk" Hyde. Unk had been Leo's guest at the Wickenburg ranch and was romantically interested in Kay Dewing. His sister, Hester Hyde Hately, was Kay's companion and was shepherding the two sons of movie star Victor McLaglan. Another boy in the group was Pete Ducker, Jr., the obese son of the man who had been at Lee's Ferry with the Edison crew in 1921–22. Esther H. Bowers, sister of Mrs. Walt Disney, had her two sons, Bill and the unruly Sam. "Essy," as she was called, was divorced from a very wealthy doctor and received more alimony than she could spend. She was a devotee of the "I Am" movement, one of the philosophical-religious groups that appear to flourish in the Golden State, and was an incessant reader of its publications. She was said to have given considerable money to the organization.

Leo Weaver was an imposing figure in the Tom Mix tradition. He stood an inch over 6 feet, weighed 175 pounds, had an erect bearing, and he dressed as a cross between a Hollywood cowboy, a gentleman gambler, and a big-time cattleman. Noted for his oversized western hats, he was called *Hastiin Ch'ah Tso* (Mr. Big Hat) by the Navajos. He wore expensive boots, belts, and kerchiefs in the traditional western motif, and he had a large turquoise nugget set in silver on the ring finger of his left hand. He seldom drank, but smoked incessantly. He was definite in his likes and dislikes and catalogued people as ".45 or .22 caliber," leaving no room for anyone between the extremes. He was stern but fair, and the youngsters loved him.

Leo Weaver at Grand Canyon, 1935 (*P. T. Reilly Collection, Cline Library, Northern Arizona University*).

The project was a success for all. The young people had the time of their lives, Dr. Tarr solved his problem, and the Weavers earned some badly needed money. More importantly, Leo told Unk Hyde about the operation of the two ranches. The wealthy bachelor with the delicate stomach expressed interest in his plan of a year-around guest operation. Weaver, however, had no time to develop his idea because business remained good.

As soon as the enthusiastic youngsters returned home, a group of Disney people became guests at the Circle Flying W. Unk remained, as did Essy, Bill, and Sam. Three Fergusons, Bill Cottrell, Hazel Sewell, and Jennie and Joe Grant came to Leo's cool forest home. Grant was a Disney artist who was so taken by the Weavers' pet fawn "Bucky" that he sketched her into the creature that animator Jake Day turned into "Bambi." Grant filled Leo's guest book with drawings of Bambi, Mickey Mouse, and Pluto, besides presenting his hosts with individual drawings of his creations and of Leo.

When the summer season ended at Flagstaff, Leo reverted to Wickenburg for a winter guest facility. He leased the Kay Bar Ranch for six months, starting from the first of November. Many of his old standbys helped make the winter season a success; and if his guest list ran low, he made quick trips to the Arizona Biltmore and replenished his supply. The colorful Leo induced many tourists to extend their stay and experience more of the real West than was offered by the Phoenix resorts. He was friendly with the management, who welcomed the imposing westerner.

Although the gross receipts were impressive, the Weavers did not make much money from the winter trade. Leo, always poor at business, depended on Hazel to keep the ranch turning a profit, but she lacked Nellie's ability. Consequently, they did little more than break even. Their prices were too low and their expenses were too high: Leo gave too much for what he charged. His guests invariably had a good time, and when the season closed on April 19, 1934, two of them accompanied him to the Circle Flying W near Flagstaff and remained for a month. Several of Dr. Tarr's boys returned and Leo had plenty of paying customers—again with indifferent profit. Unk returned also, and when Leo learned that the polygamists had been moved off the Lee's Ferry ranch and the place still was for sale, he induced Unk to back him. At the close of the summer season on September 24, he and Hyde went to Salt Lake City to discuss the matter with church leaders. The churchmen wanted to sell the property outright but the pair from the south wanted to lease the place with an option to buy it, and they returned to Flagstaff with the matter unresolved. Typically, Leo was thinking of expansion while still behind two payments of six hundred dollars to Colton.

Hyde was willing to back Leo financially but did not want to go into business with him, apparently having observed his loose operation. He agreed to provide the five hundred dollar down payment and be repaid in trade. He and Leo finally accepted the deal on church terms and notified Bishop John Wells on November 9 to prepare the contract. This was done the following day, along with the notation that caretaker Johnson had been instructed to give possession to Weaver and Hyde. In consideration of Jerry's service, they released to him right, title, and interest in the forty acres lying outside the patented homestead, with the understanding that he would settle with Spencer and LeBaron.[3] Jerry's reaction to this windfall was one of elation, as if he had received an inheritance.

He spread the news far and wide. Carling Spencer was so stirred that he enlisted J. M. Lauritzen of Short Creek to press his case of compensation for the improvements he had made there. Leo Weaver also was agitated, fearing that someone might claim a right-of-way through his property for access to the land up the canyon. The issue was argued thoroughly from November 1934 to April 1935, and many letters were exchanged between Salt Lake City, Short Creek, Marble Canyon, Flagstaff, and Phoenix before the views of the Presiding Bishopric were accepted. The crux of the problem was that Jerry Johnson, Carling Spencer, and the church officials did not know the legal description of the forty acres lying outside of the patented area. None of those interested in the property had seen a plat of it.

Weaver's timing appeared to be excellent. Flagstaff postmaster Walter Runke had announced that the first direct mail service to Utah would begin October 15, 1934. The link went from Flagstaff to Kanab via the Arizona-Utah Transportation Company that operated the bus line. Service was three times a week; the bus left Flagstaff on Monday, Wednesday, and Friday, and returned Tuesday, Thursday, and Saturday. Previously, a letter from Flagstaff went to Barstow, California, then northeast through Nevada to Lund, Utah, for a trip of more than five hundred miles.[4] Now it was delivered by Maggie Jackson's brother, Hazel Hopkins, who often drove the stage for Mr. Nye. After the Marble Canyon post office was discontinued on February 28, 1935, the mail was routed from Cameron. Hopkins threw the mailbag for Lowrey's and Lee's Ferry from the stage if no stop was made. The mailbag was picked up the same way, and whoever happened to be up from the ferry would make the delivery as a communal enterprise.

When Leo, Hazel, and Billie Weaver moved to the Lee's Ferry ranch in mid-November 1934, they selected the county schoolhouse for a residence because it was the soundest of the buildings. Since teacher Mary Wilkinson and the students had moved away, no provision was made for a fall term. School Superintendent Best so informed the Board of Supervisors in their meeting of January 7, 1935, and District 26 lapsed.[5] No immediate disposition was made of the building or equipment.

One day when Leo and Billie were up in the canyon, Hazel heard their police dog barking and stepped outside to ascertain the cause. She saw a man carrying a walking stick and went to calm the dog. Frank Dodge said he had come to introduce himself and to meet his new neighbors. She invited him in, prepared coffee, and they chatted until Leo came back. Before he returned to his cabin, Frank refused the offer of a job, explaining that his first allegiance was to the U.S. Geological Survey.

Weaver already had a rough idea of how he wanted to transform the one-time polygamy colony into a guest ranch, but getting it underway would entail more labor, much of it rough, than he could furnish. After Dodge's refusal, he offered jobs to Riley Baker and Ed Fisher; the latter accepted. The first priority was a well, as use of creek or ditch for culinary water was not endorsed by Hazel or Billie. That winter Ed dug a well eight feet square but hit the aquifer at twenty-four feet and could go no deeper by hand. The water quality was poor, being too heavily laden with salts to be potable, and the effort was wasted.

Weaver turned to his Indian friends and brought a Hopi named Poli Hungavi and his family to the ranch.[6] A prominent progressive from Moenkopi, Poli was able to procure more of his tribesmen when needed. Poli's first job was to gather stones, lay the foundation, and do the masonry work on the new Weaver ranch house. Foundation stones still marked the site of the old Johnson house, and Leo selected his location northeast of it, where the truck garden had existed sixty years before. As the polygamists had disdained masonry construction in favor of wood, a good supply of stone was waiting to be used. Poli started gathering and laying rock almost eight years to the day after the Johnson house had burned down.

During his time in Phoenix, Leo had visited the Wigwam resort in Litchfield Park and was impressed with its architectural style. He considered it the ultimate in southwestern elegance and was determined to pattern his ranch house after it, modified to suit Weaver's individuality. To help carry out this theme, he gathered relics and discarded items from the Spencer and pioneer periods. He accumulated Spencer ox yokes, broken wagon wheels from Lee Hill, and anything that would add color to his rustic headquarters.

The romance connected with any subject appealed to Leo more than the practical or historical aspects. He therefore had decided on a name for the ranch before he contracted for it. Undoubtedly he was influenced more by Zane Grey than the pioneer Mormons when he called his latest acquisition "Paradise Canyon Ranch." He arranged to have letterheads made almost as soon as he moved there. The only insignia missing was the turquoise horse logo he used on his mailbox, an item that was useless at Lee's Ferry or Marble Canyon.

Billie Weaver and David Lowrey had graduated in the same class at Flagstaff High School in May 1932. Now both were helping their fathers in their respective enterprises. Billie enthusiastically supported Leo's plan to eventually raise Anglo-Arabian horses. Leo had some good stock, including several standard-bred mares and geldings, and he had three prime milk cows that produced so much that Hazel made cottage cheese and fed it to the pigs and chickens. They had all the fresh-churned butter they could use. The Weaver feed bill, quite naturally, was enormous. Billie loved horses and spent much time riding; as soon as her chores were done she would saddle her mount and explore the immediate area. Over the succeeding years she covered considerable ground and made some interesting discoveries. Sometimes she went riding with David.

Weaver had purchased a new Ford pickup from Babbitt's when his wallet was full at the close of his successful 1934 season. The first of several misfortunes occurred early in 1935 when he parked the vehicle under a large cottonwood near the original school house. A violent wind broke a huge limb that crashed down on the bed, flattening it to the ground. Uninsured, the truck was a total loss. He had owned it only two months.[7]

Hester Hyde Hately planned to join her brother at Paradise Canyon Ranch in February. Hyde had simple tastes, lived on a bland diet, and had been accommodated there for several weeks. Weaver wasn't ready for more demanding guests but Unk's sister could not be refused; the only solution was to make some of the older buildings livable. They decided to clean up the original school house, move into it, and relinquish their present quarters to the guests. The old cabin was dirty and rat-infested, not having been used in a quarter-century. Cleaning it was a major job, but the rats were eliminated and Leo whitewashed the interior, chinked the logs, reworked the windows, installed a beaverboard ceiling, and built a closet. Hazel borrowed Mary Fisher's sewing machine to make curtains; Leo drew Indian designs on them, which Hazel carried out in colored yarn. They added Navajo rugs. When the renovation was concluded the result was very attractive. Leo's artistic nature touched everything.

On March 8, School Superintendent Best proposed that Weaver buy the county school house, and asked for his offer. No written reply has been found, so presumably he disregarded the proposal or handled it orally. On May 9 the supervisors instructed Best to sell the building for three hundred dollars. Leo countered by requesting the county to remove it from his property. The supervisors decided the structure wasn't worth salvaging, but they took the desks and other equipment for use at Fredonia. Leo got the building for nothing and eventually used the lumber in his own construction program. Thus, his main residence was built with lumber from the west wing of the old Johnson house and scrap wood from Navajo Bridge.

While the Weavers were struggling with their problems at Flagstaff in 1934, life went on in a more or less normal manner along the river. Frank Dodge attended a dance at Tuba City and while "under the influence" on June 20 he married a nurse who worked in the Indian hospital. The ceremony was performed by Reverend R. W. Johnson, and Frank recorded the document at Flagstaff the following day. He did not sober up for a day or two after that; when he did, he was greatly surprised and shocked to learn that Mattie Harris now was Mrs. Frank B. Dodge.[8] Mattie hoped the marriage would work and made several trips to the ferry in support of her ambition, but Frank would have none of it. He did not even treat her civilly.

On an exceedingly warm day in mid-July, eight men gathered at Lee's Ferry to resume an interrupted river trip. Several months earlier they had suspended their journey at the end of Glen Canyon because of cold weather. The group was "The Dusty Dozen," although they were fewer than a dozen. Their trip was unique because there was no designated leader; post-trip publicity released in the East referred to Clyde Eddy as the leader, and publicity in the West referred to Dr. Russell G. Frazier. Actually, Robert

"Bus" Hatch and Franklin Swain made the major decisions, but it was a rather loosely run, communal affair. The Colorado River was at a lower stage than for any previously attempted traverse of Grand Canyon. They shoved off July 19, 1934, on a flow of 1,530 cubic feet per second and went almost to Boulder Dam, then under construction. The highest river flow during their trip was 2,810 cubic feet per second.[9]

Marion Scott, who was resident hydrographer until November 19, 1934, noted that 2.09 inches of rain fell in about three hours on the evening of August 27. The deluge washed out most of the road between the gate and the spring, and floodwaters pouring down the Shinarump into the river deposited a point that projected about seventy feet from the right bank of the river. The debris temporarily shifted the current next to the gage on the left bank, but was washed downstream and the stage-discharge relation reverted to normal.[10] When Scott left, Frank Dodge became the observer, inspecting the gaging station every two days. Until the spring rise set in, an engineer from the Tucson office visited the station periodically to check with Dodge and note the condition of the equipment.

The relative inactivity at the gaging station was broken about 6:30 P.M. on April 22, 1934, when two vehicles turned up the canyon, into the lane, along the creek bank to the crossing, and proceeded on to the withdrawal area. The lead car was driven by R. Elton Cook, who was no stranger to Lee's Ferry, and the second car contained Sherman O. Decker, his wife of nine months, Ida, and a pregnant cat named Dixie. As the cars came to a stop in front of the old Spencer mess hall, Dodge charged out demanding to know the reason for their intrusion. He cooled down when told they were from Tucson and Decker was the new resident hydrographer. He even invited them to supper, an impromptu meal of canned vegetables, cold biscuits, peanut butter and coffee. Ida wrote that the dinner tasted heavenly. She was so discouraged that if the last few miles of the road had not been so rough, she would have gone back to Flagstaff. That night, she lay awake for hours, pondering how she could make the crude quarters livable. Sherm Decker and Cook made their first measurement next morning as Ida washed, cleaned, and unpacked.[11]

As soon as the government reserve became effective on January 18, 1933, Dickinson began planning improvements for the gaging-station operation and the prevention of subsequent intrusions by Charlie Spencer's seemingly endless mining promotions. Part of the plan involved the destruction of all Spencer buildings not in active use. Dickinson and the chief hydraulic engineer had discussed this matter with the solicitor of the Interior Department, who advised that demolition would prevent undesirable occupancy by future trespassers, but it should be done gradually and in such a manner as to provoke no opposition.[12]

John Baumgartner visited the station in March to survey and photograph each building. After the results were evaluated in Tucson, a renovation took place in June. A work crew was brought in to improve the interior of the old mess hall, which had been appropriated as the hydrographer's residence, and the building that Dodge used as a residence; they installed a new roof on the garage. A steel gate was placed where the conglomerate ledge came close to the river bank, and a new car for the upper cable was provided in September. In connection with this work, the men followed the example of Klohr, Clark, and Wilson by crossing a pickup on the gaging cable to gather willows along the left bank. Willow growth had been virtually eradicated on the right bank but still was luxuriant on the reservation side.

Dickinson sent Wilbur Heckler on another survey of facilities on February 19, 1935. Heckler photographed the various structures a second time, concentrating on those they could dismantle to discourage the miners from using the area. Leo Weaver's building program fit nicely into Dickinson's plan to be rid of Spencer for good; obviously Poli Hungavi needed more rock than could be salvaged from the Johnson foundation. Dickinson must have given the engineers some oral instructions that he didn't want recorded on paper. On the morning of April 25, they went to Weaver's to carry them out, proposing that he tear down certain Spencer buildings and use the rock for his own need. Those designated were the westernmost three between the road and the river, which the survey called the old school house, chicken house, and saddle barn, along with the Spencer addition to the fort.

Leo Weaver appeared agreeable and promised to start the job as soon as Milt Winn and George Wilson removed their personal property. Two days later, Decker discussed the matter with Wilson, who took care of the gas station at Lowrey's and helped in the trading post. George declined to honor the request unless presented with a court order. The Deckers were taking Cook to Flagstaff so he could catch the train for Tucson and discuss the matter of a court order with Dickinson. Meanwhile, Leo had second thoughts about tearing down the buildings; he took up the issue with Buck Lowrey, who advised against it. Fearing possible legal trouble from Spencer, Leo backed away from his original commitment and made one excuse after another when Decker pressed him to get started.

The Weavers had more winter guests than they were prepared to receive. Besides Unk Hyde and his sister Hester, there were Kay Dewing, Alle Griffin, and the Moore family. Hester was especially troublesome, demanding the best accommodations and that Hazel cage her cat. They lodged her in the Carling Spencer cabin, which met the needs of a polygamous family but not those of a Hollywood socialite. Taking guests into such primitive living quarters undoubtedly hurt Leo's reputation and cost him future business.

In due time, Jerry Johnson came to the ranch to discuss access to his forty acres. The conversation generated visions in Leo's mind of another polygamous enclave with bearded, overall-clad men and a multitude of ragged children, all detrimental to his business, and he refused the request. Jerry could not understand the reasons for the rebuff but declined to make trouble. He was piqued, however, and henceforth reacted unfavorably to the latest owner of his father's old farm.

Before Unk and Kay left Phoenix in March, he and Weaver legalized their partnership. The certificate was filed in Flagstaff March 7, 1935. But six months later, when Hyde became aware that the Weavers' debts were growing at an alarming rate, he dissolved the relationship. On September 4, Hyde sold his interest to Leo, leaving him full responsibility for the liabilities and the sole grantee with the consent of the Presiding Bishopric.[13] There were no guests at Paradise Canyon Ranch after March 11, and Leo seized the opportunity to block the lane and relocate the Pahreah crossing farther downstream. He thus eliminated an established road that had been used since the days of John D. Lee, but nobody protested and the new crossing was accepted.

Ed Fisher helped wrangle the guests, and when he learned that Weaver intended to shut down and move the stock to the Circle Flying W for the summer, he and his brother George took a lease on the winter ranch. In August, however, they decided they lacked the agricultural skills to make the ranch return a profit and so told Leo, who tore up the contract. George and Mary Fisher went to work at The Gap, and Ed returned to his ranch up the canyon. When the Taylor Grazing Act became effective in 1934, Ed Fisher had obtained one of the first permits, one good for one hundred twenty head. At the time he owned about half that number, but natural increase was enlarging his herd each year.

Because he expected above-normal runoff, Sherm Decker hired Dodge on May 28 for the highwater season. On June 10, the temperature was 110 degrees, the Colorado was flowing at 61,900 cubic feet per second, and Leo's new crossing was inundated. Dodge grumbled that he "wished Weaver was here" as the men moved the crossing a short distance upstream. Four days later, this, too, was flooded, and on the sixteenth, with the Colorado at 89,600 cubic feet per second, all three crossings of the Pahreah were too deep to drive across, The river peaked on June 18 at 101,800 cubic feet per second, the highest reading in six years. Luckily, they had left a car on the right bank of the creek and were not marooned.

Little is known about George Wilson except that he was born in England, had migrated to Nova Scotia, then came west about forty years before and became a United States citizen. He worked as a carpenter in Hollywood studios for about twenty-six years before he and Milt Winn became involved with Charlie Spencer. Wilson remained as an unpaid "caretaker" when the promotion failed, but he went to work for Buck Lowrey at the beginning of 1934 when Spencer didn't pay him. At age sixty-five, he slept in the back of the station, ate with the Lowreys, and fought to protect their resources.

It was about 10:30 P.M. at Lowrey's on Sunday, June 23, and Wilson intended to close the service station as soon as a customer left. A car carrying three men pulled in from the south and stopped at the pump. After the

George Wilson at the Marble Canyon gas station, June 1935 (*Woodruff Collection, P. T. Reilly Collection, Cline Library, Northern Arizona University*).

first car left, they purchased gasoline and soda pop and requested that air be put in a tire. George told them to drive to the hose while he got a flashlight. As he reached under the counter, the customer who had followed him in pulled a gun and announced it was a holdup. George knew there was only about twenty dollars in the till but instead of putting up his hands, he hit the robber with the flashlight. The bandit shot him, hitting him low in the abdomen. Wilson didn't fall but staggered into the back room to get a gun from under his pillow. The thief fired again, missed, and ran to the car, and the trio headed toward Buckskin Mountain in a cloud of dust. George got off one shot before they left.

It was decided quickly that Florence and Virginia Lowrey would drive the wounded man to Flagstaff. Merle "Peaches" Beard, the cook, and young Bonner Blanton would care for the lodge while Buck and David armed themselves and pursued the desperados. They failed to catch up with them. At Jacob Lake they telephoned Deputy Tom Jensen in Fredonia, who notified Sheriff Vandevier, who gathered a posse and drove toward Buckskin Mountain from the west. The bandits were intercepted about halfway to the mountain, but during an exchange of shots, they made a U-turn and headed back the way they had come. While out of sight of their pursuers, they turned off on the Ryan road, temporarily eluding the posse. The posse figured out what happened, blocked the road, and waited for daylight. Shortly after dawn, they caught up with the bandits near Pine Flat.

Their rifles were superior to the single .32-caliber pistol of the bandits. The getaway car was hit, one man was wounded, two fled in one direction, and the third ran in another.

The pair of fugitives caught a range horse that night, allowing the wounded man to ride while his partner led. They were captured without resistance at a water hole in the Big Siwash Canyon on Tuesday afternoon. The men were Albert White, age nineteen, and his wounded brother, Carl, seventeen, of Provo, Utah. Forest rangers took Carl Cox, age twenty-nine, of Seymore, Indiana, into custody near the sawmill at Three Lakes at about the same time. The suspects were taken to Flagstaff and brought to Wilson's bedside in the hospital. George identified Albert White as the man who shot him. They were jailed without bond. Ironically, Buck had met the White brothers a few years before when they were touring and had run out of funds. He had fed and housed them and provided enough money for them to return home.

Wilson died Wednesday night, with Buck Lowrey at his side. A coroner's jury brought in a verdict of culpable homicide against the trio, ruling that Wilson died of a gunshot wound inflicted by Albert White. They were indicted for burglary, robbery, and first degree murder. Three weeks later, Albert broke out of jail and started across country, keeping to the woods. He stole a car at the state highway camp in Doney Park and drove north. Tourists brought word of the escape to Marble Canyon, and one who dropped in for an early breakfast told of a lone man who had run out of gas north of Cedar Ridge and tried to trade his spare tire for fuel. Buck thought this man probably was the fugitive. Peaches and Bonner stopped all southbound traffic while Buck and David, each with a rifle, drove south to meet him.

Seeing a dust cloud near Bitter Springs, they parked by the road and assumed positions on opposite sides. The car was coming fast; the driver ignored the effort to flag him to a stop and tried to run Buck down, but the Lowreys shattered the windshield with a shot and Buck leaped aside. As the car went by, both fired again, Buck emptying his rifle. David turned his vehicle around to pursue. The fleeing car veered from side to side and finally swerved off the road and into a wash. White had been hit three times and was dead. David drove the stolen car a couple of miles, but the tie rod was bent and steering was difficult. Buck's car pushed it the rest of the way to Marble Canyon. They sent word by tourists going in both directions to notify the sheriff. The getaway car with its dead driver was towed behind the sheriff's car to Flagstaff the same day, where a coroner's jury came up with the following verdict: "Albert White, on July 21, 1935, came to his death by gun shots inflicted by D. C. Lowrey and David Lowrey, that his death was justifiable and we wish to commend said D. C. Lowrey and David Lowrey for having performed a real service to Coconino County and the state at large."[14] White's hat, with a bullet hole through the crown, hung on a nail in the gas station for a long time. As David later explained to Nora Cundell,

From left to right, Essy Bowers, Hazel Weaver, Leo Weaver (in car), Sherm Decker, Frank Dodge, Ann Forsythe, Sam Bowers, March 15, 1936 (*Ida B. Decker Collection, P. T. Reilly Collection, Cline Library, Northern Arizona University*).

they weren't proud of it but they wanted to warn other potential bandits should they get the same idea to hold up the place.

The Weavers had a moderately successful summer season at the Circle Flying W in 1935, but they failed to make enough to reduce the debt on the place. Besides several repeats, four customers stayed who were destined to have more impact than the average guests: Maud Johann, Ann Forsythe, Essy Bowers, and Rhoda Power. The first two were loners who came to the area to play cowgirl, and three of the four became involved in Leo's tangled finances, but there the resemblance ended. Maud was single, close to seventy-years old, and was short and dumpy; she could not ride well and was hard on a horse. Her home was in St. Louis, but she preferred ranch life in the West. She had money, which covered a multitude of sins as far as Leo was concerned. Ann Forsythe was the wife of a California banker. She lived in Levis and boots, talked and acted like a cowpuncher, and brought a year and one-half old Anglo-Arabian colt to board with Leo. She loved horses, rode well, and was generous in her payments. She could swear like a trooper and usually did. She added a touch of color to Leo's household that was not always appreciated by Hazel.

Essy Bowers wasn't particularly addicted to playing cowgirl or to ranch life, but she liked to read her "I Am" literature in the rustic, peaceful environment. Her main interest was educating and controlling her son, Sam. She quickly perceived that Leo could handle the boy, something she could not do, and saw Leo and his way of life as being Sam's salvation. Sam had a mind of his own and did not succumb to the Weaver charm as his mother did. Rhoda Power was an English writer who came to the American

West at every opportunity. She spent the summer of 1935 at San Ildefonso Pueblo near Santa Fe and wrote Leo that she intended to visit the Circle Flying W on August 12 and hoped he could take her to see the Snake Dance. Although she was not a customer at that time, she became a steady the following year and accompanied the Weavers from Flagstaff to Paradise Canyon Ranch, as did Ann, Maud, and Essy.

When it was apparent that he had to offer more and better guest facilities at Paradise Canyon Ranch, Leo knew he could not continue building his ranch house at Poli Hungavi's leisurely pace. During a lull in the summer operation, he turned to the Ortegas, whom he had employed at Wickenburg. They were a hard-working Mexican family consisting of a husband-less mother, Oldavina, her son in his late twenties, and two teenage daughters. They arrived late in the summer, and Leo settled them into the Carling Spencer cabin. The son assisted in building the house, and later the women helped Hazel care for the guests.

A. L. "Doc" Inglesby of Salt Lake City had formed a partnership with Frank Dodge on the prospect of running commercial river trips upstream to Rainbow Bridge and downstream to Badger Rapid. He had a Mullins power boat with a twenty-two horsepower outboard motor. They took a passenger named Emil Johnson on the first commercial trip upstream to Rainbow Bridge on April 12, 1933; ten hours were required to negotiate the sixty-eight and one-half miles. Dodge made a few more trips, but the public had not yet accepted river tourism and the venture did not catch on. The Dodge-Inglesby effort was the first serious attempt at river recreation based at Lee's Ferry. People were becoming more aware of the scenic values in western river canyons. On August 14, 1935, a river party of twelve boys came down from Hite and spent the night in the USGS garage.

On August 17 Dodge received a letter from LaRue appointing him head boatman of a river party to help the Fairchild Aerial Survey tie their photos to their ground control between Diamond Creek and Pearce Ferry. He left two days later for Los Angeles to assist in organizing the party. Since he no longer was available to observe the gages while Decker was visiting the Little Colorado River stations, Ortega was hired as observer in September. Inglesby came to the ferry on September 13 and was disgusted to find that Dodge had departed. He took his boat and would have taken the outboard motor but it was locked in Dodge's cabin, and Decker refused to say that he had the key.

Weaver had another iron in the fire to support his beleaguered ranch. Before he closed the Circle Flying W for the summer, he induced Essy to invest six thousand dollars of working capital in the business. Enlarging Leo's checking account by that much money was similar to sending a young boy into a candy store with a sackful of quarters. Did Weaver use this windfall to pay off Colton and the church to obtain clear title to his two ranches? Of course he didn't. He made no effort even to clear or reduce his long-standing debt to Babbitt's. Instead, he purchased a new

Buick sedan and bought two registered Arabian stallions from Chino Valley horse breeders. The well-bred animals were his pride and joy, whether he could afford them or not.

When Leo made the transition from the Circle Flying W to Paradise Canyon Ranch, he frequently had a summer guest go with him to the winter facility. Ann Forsythe was one such customer whose car he transported there before she arrived, leaving it in the care of Ortega. Unknown to the Mexican, Weaver had written down the mileage before returning to Flagstaff. When he brought another load to the Lee's Ferry, he took a second reading on the odometer and saw that the car had been driven extensively. He discharged Ortega on the spot, even though Leo needed his labor, and the Mexican left on October 6.

A small-scale re-enactment of Bar Z days occurred that fall when Ed Fisher, Walt Batty, and a couple of wranglers drove a small herd of two hundred and fifty cattle to Flagstaff for Billy Mackelprang. En route they met Leo Weaver driving his new Buick and appearing prosperous. At that moment he was.

A three-day celebration scheduled for October 11 was planned to honor the Mormon pioneers who had crossed at Lee's Ferry to colonize Arizona. It was promoted by George A. London, secretary of the Flagstaff Chamber of Commerce, whose letterhead carried the title "Immigration Commissioner of Coconino County." He secured the cooperation of the Mormon church; Miss Grace Sparks, secretary of the Yavapai Chamber of Commerce; and the Associated Civic Clubs of Southern Utah. London thought in expansive terms. He knew USGS planned to demolish the Spencer buildings, so he suggested using the Works Progress Administration to fund the construction of an auditorium large enough to seat a thousand people, plant shade trees, develop a water system, lay out campgrounds, and make the celebration an annual affair. Coconino County would improve and maintain the road to the ferry. In effect, London would turn the Lee's Ferry Gaging Station Reserve into a park that would be administered by the hydrographer.

When the Deckers returned on the afternoon of October 7 from their bi-monthly inspection of the Little Colorado gages, they found Frank Suffea, former owner of Flagstaff's Black Cat Cafe, camped beside the old saddle barn. He had what Ida described as "a nice trailer house"—possibly the first of its kind to visit the ferry. Two Kanab men arrived the following day to set up eating facilities for the coming celebration, but a fire destroyed their equipment. After a bit of an argument, Sherm allowed them to use the fort. Lela and Wilbur Heckler came in on the ninth, preceding the letter that informed the Deckers of their intended arrival. Wilbur had the assignment of observing the celebration for the survey.

The affair was very orderly and relatively quiet. The Utah Parks Service set up three dozen tents behind the old fort, each containing two cots with pads and renting for two dollars per night. Only half of them were used because many people brought their own bedding and slept on cots or on the ground. Indians from the Navajo, Hopi, and Paiute tribes camped nearby, displaying trade goods on blankets. Poli, arrayed in headband, turquoise, and silver, was the center of attention, although Preacher Smith was more active socially. Some visitors stayed at the Lowrey Lodge and Buck did a lively business. No camping was permitted east of the saddle barn and a sign on the gate prohibited the sale or use of alcoholic beverages.

Arizona Governor B. B. Mouer appeared on the afternoon of October 11 but left before dark without making a speech. Utah's Governor Henry M. Blood was represented by his secretary, N. L. Wilson. President Heber J. Grant was the star of the evening as he spoke of Jacob Hamblin, the late Anthony W. Ivins, and his own experiences as a missionary in Arizona during the 1880s; he didn't mention John D. Lee. Then the fiddlers broke out their instruments and a Brother Morrison of Richfield, who was an Arizona pioneer in 1880, called a series of square dances. Ida Decker counted eighty-eight whites and about sixty Indians; Heckler estimated the crowd to be one hundred twenty-five.

Saturday was the big day of the celebration, and three hundred people attended. A few genuine old timers were present, as were the children of others. Ettie Lee and her half-sister, Edna Lee Brimhall—both granddaughters of John D. Lee—were there, extolling the labors of their grandfather to all who would listen. Lee's grandson, Joe Lee, attracted much attention as a well-known trader. Speeches started in the afternoon and continued that evening. Sharlot Hall, naturally enough, spoke of women's roles during territorial days; as in the case of Heber Grant, she knew whereof she spoke. She was followed by Professor A. C. Peterson of Arizona State Teachers College who, as an eight-year-old boy, had crossed the ferry in a wagon driven by his widowed mother. Parley P. Willey and his wife Sarah Jane had crossed behind Lot Smith's wagon in 1876. Lot's son Willard R. Smith was there, as was James M., son of William J., Flake. Israel Call related life at Sunset with its communal dining hall presided over by Lot Smith.

Frank Johnson, now bishop of Hurricane's North Ward, took an interested group to the upper ferry site and showed Joel H. Roundy the rock that was instrumental in the 1876 drowning of his father. Brigham S. Young, who was an eyewitness to the drowning, related the story of the tragedy; Zadok Knapp Judd, Jr., also a witness, nodded his head in agreement as Young spoke. Brigham F. Duffin, who worked on the Emett dugway in 1899, spoke about road construction. The final speech of the evening was given by Frank Martinez, president of the Associated Civic Clubs of Southern Utah, who appealed for the paving of Highway 89 from Mexico to Canada, as had previous speakers.[15]

The celebrants left for their homes Sunday morning, and the ferry began returning to normal. The Deckers and Hecklers slept late, had a leisurely breakfast, and then walked up to the remains of the *Charles H. Spencer*, now fully exposed by seasonably low water. Ida and Lela climbed out on the boiler, and Wilbur took their picture. Wilbur completed his report for Dickinson that evening, and the next day he and Lela headed for Tucson. Four members of the Decker family arrived on November 26 to spend Thanksgiving with Sherm and Ida, who, as soon as she learned of the impending visit, had written out a list of groceries that Leo Weaver promised to bring from Flagstaff. Sleeping accommodations were stretched, so Sherm and his father slept in Dodge's cabin. The turkey dinner, prepared with all the trimmings, well could have been the most elegant meal served at the ferry since Stanton's Christmas feast of 1889.

On December 1, an event occurred that was common sixty years ago but now was rare: two Navajos with pack outfits arrived and went into camp at the foot of the Spencer Trail. Economic conditions had not changed as much for the Indian as for the white man. During the continuing depression, some tribesmen made long treks over desolate regions to conduct simple barter as one solution to pressing poverty. The natives topped out before 10 A.M. next morning and disappeared over the rim.

Dodge returned December 22. Restless as always, he remained until the day after Christmas, then left for Salt Lake City, Flagstaff, and Phoenix. He was back again by January 16 with the urge to buy a radio, and he asked the Deckers to accompany him to check the reception experienced by local owners in House Rock Valley. There were only two, and the survey was made on the afternoon of the twenty-ninth. Social visits in early 1936 had progressed considerably since pioneer days, yet retained the flavor of that era.

Their first stop was at Lowrey's to pick up the mail. Their second was at Soap Creek to leave some magazines with the Russells and enjoy a brief visit. In her diary, Ida noted that "Blanche Russell certainly is a hard-looking character." Dodge's main objective was seeing Pete and Ada Nelson, who lived in one of the cattle company's shacks at House Rock. They had a battery-powered Atwater-Kent that to them sounded pretty good. Ada fixed a supper of steak, fried potatoes, turnips, muffins, butter, peach preserves, and coffee, which was somewhat different from those of Bar Z days. After supper, they went over to another of the shacks where the Suerts lived. He was a topographer then working on Buckskin Mountain, and his family's radio was the product of a mail-order house. The listeners concurred that the Atwater-Kent was superior. When they returned home about ten o'clock that evening, Ida saw the living quarters at Lee's Ferry in a new light: they were luxurious compared to the House Rock shacks.

Essy and Sam spent the winter with the Weavers, providing needed income without realizing how vital their presence was to the shoestring operation. Essy was impressed with Leo as a person, his energy in improving his ranch, and his rosy plans for the future. She not only believed in his ability and integrity but saw her partnership with him as a probable solution to her problem with Sam, who was opposed to almost everything his mother thought and did. Essy interpreted his attitude towards Leo as being one of respect for the father figure Sam didn't have. She was grateful and amenable to Leo's silver tongue when he suggested she reconvey her recorded half of the Paradise Canyon Ranch to him. She had only his promise to see that she suffered no losses; the property would be in his name and thus he could obtain needed funds in a second mortgage. Filled with holiday spirit, she agreed.

On the first business day of 1936, Orinn C. Compton of the law firm of Wilson, Wood, and Compton wrote the Presiding Bishopric that Weaver needed an additional $1,500. Leo could obtain it from a local bank on a second mortgage if the property were in his name. The attorney stated that his client had made approximately $6,000 worth of permanent improvements since acquiring the place. This was not quite true, as the improvements were grossly over-valued, but everyone accepted Leo's estimate. At the same time, Leo purchased two policies that provided $2,000 of fire insurance on the new dwelling and $500 on the old barn, with mortgage clauses favoring the corporation of the church. This action was taken by a man who did not believe in insurance and carried none for himself. Of course, his behavior impressed the brethren and they responded favorably on January 9. On February 1, 1936, the Corporation of the Presiding Bishopric transferred the title of the property to Leo and Hazel Weaver and took a first mortgage of two thousand dollars on the place.[16]

The Paradise Canyon Lodge was completed in January 1936. The low, rectangular building had mortared rock walls, a stuccoed interior, a brick fireplace, a wood floor, and a beamed ceiling. It had a kitchen, dining room, living room, pantry, and a bathroom, whose single door opened from the outside. There were no bedrooms; guests would sleep in the school house or the Carling Spencer cabin. Joe Moore hauled the heavy planks for the dining table top directly from the mill at Flagstaff. Leo never made drawings and his products evolved as he went along. The proportions were achieved by fitting the article into the space. For lamp fixtures, Leo used the hubs of broken wagon wheels that he had scrounged from the Lee Hill road. Other wagon wheels and ox yokes were displayed appropriately to carry out the ranch theme. He removed the school bell that had been left atop the new school house and mounted it over the kitchen roof; the bellrope could be pulled from inside the house, enabling Hazel to call guests without going outside.

Weaver brought his gas-operated refrigerator and his piano from the Circle Flying W. The Steinway baby grand was placed in the living room, where it became the focal point of ranch evenings when guests would gather around after dinner to sing "Stormy Weather" and "Smoke Gets in Your Eyes." Leo didn't keep liquor on hand, but some guests brought their own. He was a fair pianist, had true pitch, and did his own tuning, but was so temperamental that he sometimes played all night to let off steam. He even wrote music but used his talent mostly to entertain his company.

Several guests visited the ranch that winter despite the poor facilities. Leo had plenty of good horses, and long rides were the main attraction.

Not having much variety in the offered recreation, he sometimes brought people to the gaging station. Occasionally, there were cookouts. On February 9, 1936, the Deckers joined Leo and Hazel, Ann Forsythe, Sam Bowers, and Kern Metzgar in a picnic supper at Navajo Spring. The menu was barbecued steaks, scalloped potatoes, deviled eggs, olives, bread, butter, gingerbread, and coffee—quite different from the pioneer meals served there sixty years before.

Although Leo had Essy's oral commitment to convey her share of the ranch to him, he had nothing on paper and nagged her to make it official. Sam opposed his mother and Leo on the move, and in the evening of February 14, a three-way argument developed into a rumpus. Next day Bowers left for the coast to consult her lawyer, Charles L. Nichols. She was back in a few days with the issue still unresolved. On February 21, with only Ann Forsythe at the ranch, the Weavers made a quick trip to Phoenix to explore the possibilities of obtaining a second mortgage on the ranch. Leo was sure of Essy's cooperation and was just as certain that the Phoenix bankers would see things his way. They had no qualms about leaving Ann to take care of the chores; she did not mind and carried on as if a part of the family.

That month a jarring note was thrust into the established relationships when it became known that the Lowreys had advertised their place for sale. The asking price was $33,000, with at least $17,000 as a cash down payment—the rumored amount of the mortgage. It was rather widely known that although Buck Lowrey was highly respected as a person, he was a poor business man. He had not reduced his original loan from Lorenzo Hubbell, nor had he paid anything on his debt to the J. D. Halstead Lumber Company, which now was in dire straits and pressing for payment. On June 18, 1936, a judgment was rendered against D. C. and F. L. Lowrey for the $1,098.81 lumber bill plus eight percent interest, $109.81 in attorney fees, and $18.60 in court costs. Buck simply did not have the money.

Leo Weaver had failed to make a single payment on the 160 acres that comprised the Circle Flying W. Colton put the property in Weaver's name on January 2, 1931, after the purchaser agreed to pay $600 on January 2, 1932, and signed four promissory notes of $500, each one due on that date annually through 1936 and bearing 8 percent interest. Leo used the ranch every summer but paid no principal or interest. The scheduled last payment passed with no word from the delinquent Weaver. On March 4, using his Paradise Canyon stationery, Leo wrote Colton, detailing his financial woes and promising a turnaround with the summer season. He even admitted the Bowers investment of $6,000. Colton merely noted "allowed interest to default" on the margin and filed the letter without questioning the allocation of Essy's money. He permitted Weaver to use the property, which had been returned to Colton's name on May 8, 1935.[17] Leo, regarding this only as a temporary setback, used the facility in 1935 and intended to do so in 1936, opening about June 1.

A variation of the usual cookout took place on Sunday, March 15, when the Weavers, Deckers, Dodge, Ann Forsythe, and Essy and Sam Bowers drove to Navajo Spring and hiked down the north fork of Jackass Canyon to Badger Creek Rapid. A rope was in place at the only difficult spot, indicating that others had made the trip before them. They packed food and roasted meat wrapped in bacon over a driftwood fire. Leo had learned of the jaunt from Buck Lowrey, who evidently had taken his guests on the same excursion.

The day after the Badger hike, Leo took Essy to his lawyer's office in Flagstaff and induced her to sign a document that canceled their previous arrangement and conveyed her half of the business to him.[18] He assumed all responsibility for debts and promised to repay her $6,000 with no interest in an elaborate arrangement based on potential business profits. Had Nichols seen this document, he would have advised her against signing it. When he finally did see the agreement, he exploded and dispatched a scathing letter inferring that she was not responsible and that Weaver was dishonest and had taken flagrant advantage of her. The allegation caused Essy to do some serious reconsidering. She asked Leo to nullify the agreement, he refused, and a violent argument ensued. She left in a huff on the morning of April 6.

A typical evening at the ferry might see the Deckers in Dodge's cabin listening to the radio, exchanging magazines, or conversing. Sometimes the three went to the Weaver's house, where they played bridge or listened to Leo. On February 27, Leo, Hazel, Billie, and Ann Forsythe visited the Deckers. Ida popped a large plate of corn, Leo read the old ferry book, and the others played bridge. It wasn't life in the fast lane but it sufficed. Ann was one of Leo's best customers. Knowledgeable in many subjects where the Weavers were ignorant, she debated bridge with Hazel and stock handling with him. She asked no special favors and would lend a hand whenever needed. Leo was overbearing with her but she took it in stride, realizing her hosts were not very professional.

Billie had spent the winter in Phoenix attending nursing school. She experienced some difficulty and returned to Paradise Canyon Ranch in late February saying she was not going back to the hospital. A month later, her father took her to the Grand Canyon, where he had arranged for her to work in the Hopi house for the summer. A late storm hit while he was there, stranding him. There was no stage or mail service out of Flagstaff for two days, and travel likewise was cut off from Utah.

On March 31, 1936, a stranger from Kayenta came to the ferry towing an empty trailer. He was scheduled to meet a party of four men who had put a boat in the San Juan at Mexican Hat, Utah, with the intention of running to Lee's Ferry. This was the first commercial river trip of Norman D. Nevills, who, for fifty dollars, had contracted to take "Husky" Hunt, Jake Irwin, and Charles Elkus on a scenic tour of the San Juan and Glen Canyons. The guide was inexperienced; despite his professions of being familiar with the canyons, he had never been downstream further than sixty-seven miles below the Mexican Hat bridge. His boat, a crude horse-trough affair made from the boards of an old outhouse and seams that were covered with strips cut from tin cans, leaked like a sieve. After the first two days, the trip was an adventure for all four men, and the pilot was as impressed as his charges. Naturally they did not arrive on time, so the Kayenta driver bunked with Dodge. When the party finally did pull in, Frank could not understand why they bothered to return the craft to Mexican Hat.[19] Nevertheless, this was the beginning of a thirteen-year career of commercial river running and a harbinger of things to come. Nevills was destined to expand commercial river running to other rivers and their canyons.[20]

Leo Weaver advertised himself as a horse trainer, but he did not really know stock and was only a mediocre rider. Ann had two Anglo-Arabian colts, and a customer from Philadelphia brought Weaver three more. Leo boarded them and "trained" the animals for seventy-five dollars per head per month. He had a copy of the Barry book, *How to Train Horses*, wore a pair of sharp Mexican spurs, and "dressed like a Hollywood cowboy." One little mare bucked him off as soon as he dug the sharp spurs into her. He went into the house and studied the book further, then tried again. He was bucked off three times and finally told his wife, "Hazel, it just isn't in that book what I'm doing wrong." He admitted at last that he was unable to break the horses and asked Ed Fisher to ride them at his ranch. Ed agreed and rode each of the five with no trouble. He even rode the little mare to Lowrey's, where Preacher Smith rode her and she didn't buck. Both owners paid Leo off but were very disappointed with his "horse training" and they spread the word. Ann resolved to leave at the end of April when she perceived that the training at Paradise Canyon was wasted effort. The Weavers lost a good customer permanently.

Soon after they had arrived the previous year, the Deckers, in exploring the old Spencer buildings, found enough dynamite in the powder magazine "to blow up the world." The Johnsons had dipped into the supply since 1912 when they wanted to go fishing, and Dodge continued the practice. People often came to the ferry for fish, and the word got around, but by now anglers also used rod and reel. On April 12, 1936, several cars rolled in and their occupants devoted the day to fishing. Sherm and Ida crossed the river in the cable car and walked up the Stanton road to the bend. They ate lunch in Hislop Cave where Ida was impressed with the 1889 carving and the lavender blooms of the tamarisks.

Dickinson authorized Sherm to purchase lumber and install a new floor in the gager's residence, which delighted Ida. The first of May brought Wilbur Heckler back to gage the river with Dodge until the Deckers returned from Flagstaff with the necessary materials. Their shopping list, filled May 4, included forty-five dollars worth of groceries and clothing, then Sherm spent eighty dollars of Uncle Sam's money for living room flooring, roofing paper for the porch, tools, and paint. Ann Forsythe had agreed to let the Deckers have her radio when she ended her stay. Sherm already had installed an aerial so it could be used immediately. It brought a touch of civilization to the job that raised Ida's spirits and made life there more bearable.

George and Mary Fisher were glad to care for the ranch after Leo ended his winter season and moved operations to the Circle Flying W in Flagstaff. They joined the Weavers, Deckers, and Dodge for a plebeian weiner roast at Navajo Spring on May 8. The Deckers invited the same group to a buffet supper on Mother's Day, after which they played bridge and rummy. The Weavers took only the horses; George fed chickens, milked the cows, and dispensed eggs and milk as usual.

Sherm Decker acceded to his wife's wishes during the ensuing weeks and agreed to work elsewhere. He made his last measurement with Dodge on July 13, then after a vacation, he took over the station at Willow Beach. Charlie McDonald became resident hydrographer on a temporary basis until Roy H. Monroe arrived on August 10. Possibly Dodge and Monroe did not hit it off, or the restless loner got the itch for salt water, because Frank Dodge ended his services as recorder on August 12 and headed for Port Isabel on the Texas gulf coast.[21]

On Memorial Day in 1936, Charles Kelly, a journalist from Salt Lake City, brought Robert B. Hildebrand to Lee's Ferry. Hildebrand had convinced him that as a boy he had spent a year with John D. Lee at the river crossing, and Kelly, thinking he had a scoop, took him there to obtain first-hand pioneer information. Hildebrand posed obligingly wherever Kelly requested, and at that time the writer had no idea which structures had originated with Lee or were built by his successors. Two of the pictures, which Kelly later printed in published articles, were the so-called "Lee cabin" and remnants of the upper ferry cribbing built to maintain the cable height. If Hildebrand had lived with Lee in 1875–76, it would have to have been in prison, because that's were Lee was except for four months between May 11 and September 24, 1876, when he was released on bail and traveling between his families.[22]

Land use to the average Mormon meant raising a crop or livestock. Allocation to any other activity was evidence the land was not being utilized as God intended. Thus it was that Jerry Johnson found it easy to listen to one of his brethren who had visited the place recently and concluded the ranch was being wasted. Still piqued over Weaver's denial of access to the upper forty acres, he wrote to the Presiding Bishopric in midsummer, stating his opinion and repeating his often-made declaration that he was prepared to take over the property. The officials made immediate reply, expressing surprise at his report and pointing out that the purchaser had paid one thousand dollars to date and was not delinquent in his contract. Moreover, they said they recently had received a letter from some Flagstaff attorneys who stated the buyer had greatly enhanced the property. Jerry then admitted his information was hearsay and he had not been there lately. Then he added that Hyde had withdrawn and Weaver was living at Flagstaff, having rented the ranch to a cowboy who was using it to pasture his horses.[23]

The Weavers had only a mediocre summer season at the Circle Flying W and failed to make enough to pull them out of their financial hole. They had some twenty-five guests during the entire season, but at thirty dollars per week, they barely took in enough to purchase food for people and livestock. Leo never carried a wallet; instead, he lived on credit and apparently thought some accounts were not meant to be paid. When he received a bill by mail he usually tossed it unopened into "File 13," his designation for the waste basket. He developed a peculiar attitude toward the Babbitt store based on his own warped logic. When guests arrived in Flagstaff, Leo headed them to Babbitt's and saw that a western outfit was purchased—boots, hat, shirts, and jeans. The guest paid in cash and Leo figured each sale built a balance for himself. The credit manager, Walter Bennett, did not agree on this and sent statements regularly. Just as regularly, Leo put them in File 13.[24]

When Essy Bowers finally found time to discuss her venture into the guest ranch business with her attorney, Nichols entered the fray with a vengeance. In late August, he met with Weaver and Compton to express his dissatisfaction with the previous agreements. Weaver offered to sell his equity to Bowers, but Nichols refused. Nichols then went to Salt Lake City and discussed the matter with Bishop John Wells. Upon returning to Los Angeles, he summarized the case in a letter to Wells and requested cooperation to protect the rights of his client. With this negative phase coming on top of the Johnson allegations, the Presiding Bishopric became suspicious of Weaver's operation, promised to collaborate in case the buyer defaulted, and immediately sent letters of reproach to Weaver and his Flagstaff lawyers.[25]

This sally brought a lengthy letter from Compton, who expressed surprise that the officials had accepted Nichols' story. He explained how Weaver operated winter guest facilities and maintained a caretaker at one place while he was at the other; the ranch at Lee's Ferry was not deserted in the summer. He enclosed a sixty dollar check representing the interest now due and said the regular payment of five hundred dollars would be made in November. He accused Nichols of trying to involve the church in a squeeze play on Weaver and concluded with a verification that his client was a man of excellent character and reputation. He invited church representatives to visit the ranch.[26] Compton's letter was an effective rebuttal; it evoked an expression of appreciation from the church and removed another burden from the back of the harassed Leo Weaver.

It was coincidental that two Londoners, neither of whom knew the other, should meet on the Arizona Strip in the fall of 1936. Rhoda Power came to the Circle Flying W early in September and stayed until the operation closed late in the month. She accompanied the Weavers to Paradise

Ed Fisher and David Lowrey at the Marble Canyon gas station, ca 1935–36 (*Ed Fisher photograph, P. T. Reilly Collection, Cline Library, Northern Arizona University*).

Canyon Ranch and remained until February. She immediately became infatuated with her hosts and their lifestyle. Rhoda brought temporary relief to Leo's struggling dude operation; she provided cash for his November payment to the church. Evidently unsecured, it could hardly be called a loan—it was more of a gift from the generous Britisher.

Artist Nora Cundell had returned to Lowrey's that fall for her third stay at Vermilion Cliffs Lodge and her second winter there. Besides being taken with the Lowrey family, she was smitten by the country and depicted it and its people in oils and drawings. After the two women became acquainted, they often would meet on horseback to ride together and have tea and dry toast at whichever place they concluded their jaunt. In an effort to give Nora a taste of what the country had to offer, the Lowreys planned for Ed Fisher to guide her on a pack trip to the Glen Canyon tributaries. Ed was wrangling hunters on the Buckskin when David appeared at the deer camp, but he consented to go as soon as the season closed.

As the outfit was being assembled, Ed Fisher and David Lowrey packed part of the six hundred pounds of grain up the Spencer Trail to their first night's camp, a cave-like overhang on the Echo bench. On November 25, Ed took Nora and David along a route once trod by Basketmaker sandals, Paiute moccasins, Spanish and then Mormon livestock, and the unshod horses of the Navajo, but to Nora the land was primordial and desolate as a wasteland on a forgotten continent. She and her companions could have been nomads, contemporary to Coleridge's Ancient Mariner, and the first ever to burst into this timeless wilderness of space and rock. Although widely traveled, she had never seen such country and never had she been so removed from the refinements of civilization. She loved every second of it and had the time of her life.

Ed continued past Cane Creek and turned up Last Chance. In the upper reaches, they cornered a mustang mare with two colts and succeeded in catching one of the youngsters, a beautiful black animal with a white star on his forehead. Ed broke him to trail in short order and presented him to Nora, who named him Windsor after her home. They rode on to Rock Creek and augmented their supplies with two poached deer as they retraced their steps. They returned to the lodge on December 11, having been out seventeen days.

Christmas Day 1936 was unlike any that Nora had ever experienced or even thought she might encounter. At 3:30 P.M., everybody at the lodge was basking in the afterglow of a fine turkey dinner when David caught two burglars who had broken into the trading post. The men were H. C. Smith, fifty-four, and Joe Hanson, twenty-six, who were down on their luck and thought the closed trading post offered easy pickings. David and Nora escorted them to the sheriff in Flagstaff. David drove Buck Lowrey's DeSoto, with Nora beside him; a pair of handcuffs and an automatic pistol lay between them, and a loaded rifle was in the back seat. The burglars' battered Chevrolet could make only twenty-five miles per hour, and they ran into snow an hour out of town. It was 11 P.M. before the pair were jailed. Nora, a respectable British spinster, spent Christmas night acting as assistant deputy sheriff in a play that could have been a scene in a wild west film.[27]

If Weaver's summer season had been disappointing, his winter season was disastrous. Besides Rhoda Power, the only other customers were two secretaries from San Francisco who spent the week of October 19 to 25 at Paradise Canyon Ranch. Preacher Smith, probably attracted by the presence of the young women, came over uninvited and attached himself to the household. Smith was in no manner self-supporting; he went from one establishment to another on the pretense of his self-styled ministry to the Indians. He had no skills and was of little help to anyone, but the traders were hospitable according to the custom of the time and region. His was just another mouth to feed. Leo's low rates demanded a high volume of business, but the Great Depression and his primitive facilities precluded realization of this necessity. He was broke and both of his ranches were listed among those with delinquent taxes.[28]

Three days after Christmas, Hazel found employment as a waitress at the Adams Hotel in Phoenix. Her meager pay and tips, plus Rhoda's board, were the Weaver income that winter. Early in December the Navajos predicted the area would experience the most severe winter in many years.[29] The prediction came true shortly after Christmas as one storm after another swept in from the coast. Temperatures plummeted, and travel came to a halt as a heavy snow closed all roads on January 8. The snow was more than six feet deep at Flagstaff and schools were closed. The situation was desperate on the reservation; many Indian livestock failed to survive. Cattle belonging to Billy Mackelprang and Ben Wilmot were dying at Soap Creek. There was no mail for two weeks.

Weaver's alfalfa supply ran so low that he turned the horses out on the range to conserve the feed for his milk cows. Then he ran out of wood, usually obtained as needed from the Pahreah delta. He couldn't find the horses and was forced to tow the wood wagon behind his Buick, which could not get off the road. His gathering became limited to what he could carry or drag over the rocks. As the month wore on and temperatures hovered below zero, everybody ran out of wood at once. The Pahreah delta had been a dependable source of firewood since the first settlement, but now the outlying ranchers and traders converged here as spokes to a hub from as far away as House Rock Valley and Cedar Ridge. Weaver counted eight loads going out as soon as a track was broken through the snow. Before long, the wood supply was decimated and local residents were bringing in short pieces that needed no cutting.

A track from Flagstaff was broken on January 22 when General Land Office surveyor Ben Kinsey brought seventeen men and nine trucks to the ferry. When Roy Monroe returned from the Little Colorado on the twenty-fifth, he took Dickinson's instructions literally and attempted to evict the surveyors, despite the fact that they all worked for the Department of the Interior. Kinsey laughed at him and proceeded to survey the west boundary of the reserve. Monroe refused to allow the surveyors to use the spring so they were forced to dip water from the river. Their trucks tore up the Pahreah crossing, making it impassable for Monroe's pickup so he left his vehicle on the west bank and walked the rest of the way to the residence.

Weaver came down with what they thought was the flu, but it was questionable whether he was ill, suffered from exposure, or was troubled because of his financial situation. At any rate, Rhoda took over as household head and was credited with curing him with a mixture of the remains of the Christmas brandy, lemon, sugar, and three aspirins. She pitched in more as a family member than paying guest; she cooked, milked, churned, cleaned, washed dishes, and even procured wood. She and Billie drove to Cameron and brought home eight bales of hay, two sacks of barley, and a quart of whiskey. Rhoda had adopted the Weavers just as Nora had become attached to the Lowreys.

Kinsey saved the day for Leo. His main service was in hauling supplies and mail to and from Flagstaff. Sometimes his entire crew ate at the ranch. Billie and Rhoda cooked, charging three dollars for dinner. In addition, Kinsey brought three gallons of milk each day at sixty cents per gallon. The temperatures remained below zero while residents and surveyors huddled around Leo's fireplace. It was so cold that Weaver found it impossible to cut steaks from a frozen quarter of beef; he finally attacked it with an ax to chop off a roast. Kinsey completed the survey on April 17, 1937, and the crew moved out two days later, leaving Monroe at peace and Weaver with less income.

Leo Weaver went from one financial tight spot to another, usually extricating himself with a loan from some friend. Strangely, he never modified his lifestyle or tried to reduce his bills; he used credit whenever possible, always getting deeper into debt. One possibility for a loan was a wealthy friend of both Leo and Rhoda, Rachel Lothrop, who wintered in Phoenix. Rhoda now became more deeply involved in Weaver finances. When she received a letter from Hazel broaching the subject of a another loan, she advised against it, saying she would ask Rachel to lend her the thousand dollars so she could invest in Leo's ranch. She obtained the money and sent it to Hazel, who put it in a Flagstaff bank for Leo to draw against. Temporarily flush, he had Hazel quit her job and return home.

Rhoda expected him to use the funds to build more guest cabins, his most pressing need. Leo didn't quite follow Rhoda's expectations. He had no customers, so as soon as the weather moderated he and Poli Hungavi tore down the country school house to build two bedrooms on the east end of the ranch house. As usual, he drew no plans but simply worked from his mental picture of the attachment. Both rooms were completed in April 1937. The ranch house now had the configuration of a T, the southeast room having a small ramada attached. It was an ill-fitting appendage from both inside and out.

Then Weaver hired a Short Creek driller to put down a well for culinary water. The well drillers hit the aquifer early, then continued to a depth of about two hundred feet to provide a good surplus area. Leo enclosed the well with a pump house on top of which he set a five hundred gallon water tank. When he fired up his gasoline pump and drew water, he was surprised to find it as alkaline and unpotable from this depth as was the surface water of the creek. Ignoring the fact that creek water had produced lush crops during the past century, he labeled the well a failure and refused to use it.

Buck Lowrey's finances were as poor as Leo Weaver's. Buck had been in debt longer and had been equally inept at discharging his indebtedness. On March 9, 1937, the Lowreys signed a quit claim deed to Lorenzo Hubbell for the entire homestead. Buck agreed to remain as manager until Hubbell found a capable replacement. The day was as sad for Lorenzo as it was for Buck; he didn't want the property, only the money he had invested.

Weaver had no guests after Rhoda's departure. What was worse, he had no reservations for summer activity, and even if he had, he lacked the effrontery to stall Colton yet again after his failure to deliver a single promised payment in five years. He was washed up at the Flagstaff ranch and his summer operation was dead. A few inquiries came in later than usual, so he leased Hade Church's Big Saddle deer camp on a contingency basis to accommodate them. He had new brochures made advertising Paradise Canyon Ranch, with an address of Marble Canyon, Arizona. Inside, he plugged his summer facility at Big Saddle on the North Rim of Grand Canyon. His prices were twenty-five dollars a week plus a dollar per day for a horse and a cowboy guide; Leo evidently did not himself believe what he had written to Colton the year previously. He had fewer than a dozen guests in July, none in August, but business picked up in September. However, he did not make much more than expenses and still was in poor financial condition when he had to vacate for the forthcoming deer season. Two guests, Mary and Raymond Browne of Long Island, helped him close Big Saddle and accompanied him to Paradise Canyon Ranch.

One of the guests at Big Saddle was Omer Mott, a wealthy playboy from Baltimore. After the day's ride was completed and supper finished, Leo and Omer would sit up late discussing Leo's reveries of operating big-time guest ranches. Leo thought he had another pigeon, as Mott led him to believe he would back him in building a cattle ranch, providing they could obtain range permits to start the business. Omer probably was not sincere and no doubt forgot the pipe dream as soon as he left, but Leo was susceptible to verbal commitments and believed him. He went into action as if the partnership already was reality. He knew that Ed Fisher held the only grazing permits for the Pahreah range and approached him asking to share them. Ed refused, pointing out that he was running cattle, and Leo wasn't. Becoming angry at the refusal, Leo said he would get his own and ram them through. Although he intended to fight him, Ed knew Weaver had influential friends in Flagstaff and realized he probably was outgunned. He finally gave him permission to run twenty-five head. When Weaver's plans failed to materialize, he kept the permits but paid nothing for them.

While still at Big Saddle, Leo wrote to Rhoda, now back at her BBC job in London, for another loan. He painted a bleak picture. The well was a failure, his additional rooms were empty, Essy and Babbitts were pressing him, and he could not meet the November payment to the church. Also, he needed a furnace to warm the ranch house. Rhoda replied that times were bad in England and it was impossible to interest anyone there to invest in an Arizona ranch. Then on October 9 she followed with another letter to say that she could not invest any more money in the ranch; she had sunk five hundred pounds with Leo, which was three-fourths of her life's savings. She questioned the need for a house furnace at that time, suggested he irrigate his field, raise his own grain, and use the money he intended to spend on facing the new addition with rock to pay the church. Her advice was so filled with common sense that it was a foregone conclusion Leo wouldn't take it.[30] When he received this bad news, he bowed to Babbitt pressure and signed an unsecured promissory note for $1,092.36. The firm was no closer to getting its money, but at least they had the debt on record.

Frank Dodge and Owen Clark returned to the Ferry in October with Ian Campbell, a geology professor from the California Institute of

Technology. Campbell, in conjunction with the Carnegie Institute, planned a geological trip through the Grand Canyon. He got the three Fairchild boats Dodge used in western Grand Canyon in 1935 and had stored them at the ferry the previous year when the trip was first planned. The seven-man, three-boat party shoved off October 11. The wife of Merrill F. Spencer, the third boatman who had been with Dodge on the Fairchild survey, piped them off with her harmonica. They asked her to play "Sailor Beware," but she didn't know the tune and compromised with "Nearer My God to Thee." There were four eminent geologists at the start, and Dr. Edwin D. McKee joined the party at the Bass Trail. So many samples were gathered that Owen Clark said "Taking a party of geologists through the canyon is the equivalent of fifteen years of normal erosion."[31]

The road from Flagstaff had been improved gradually after the bridge over Marble Canyon was dedicated. Work was done from Flagstaff to Cameron and then to The Gap and Cedar Ridge. Some stretches had asphalt surface treatment, others had an oil base. On July 26, 1935, the entire road was denoted a state highway, and by the end of 1937 U.S. Highway 89 had come into being. In October, the highway had thirty-nine miles of asphaltic treatment between Cedar Ridge north to the Kaibab National Forest; thirteen miles of base-course oiling between House Rock and Jacob Lake; and four miles of the same between Fredonia and the Utah line. Traffic was maintained on these fifty-six miles.[32] Andrew Amundsen would have been surprised at the changes wrought in sixty-four years.

Haldane "Buzz" Holmstrom did not always do things the easy way. It was dusk and the chill of winter was in the air when he pushed off alone from Green River, Wyoming, on October 4, 1937. He started late because he was nervous and knew he couldn't sleep. His destination was Boulder Dam, which he figured was about eleven hundred miles—and six weeks time—downstream. He planned to resupply himself at Jensen and Green River, Utah, Lee's Ferry, and Grand Canyon. On November 5, he drifted past the ferry and pulled in at a tributary ravine a short distance from Navajo Bridge. He needed supplies and intended to make minor repairs to his boat. The river was running only 6,160 cubic feet per second. Using a rough Indian trail, and helped by Ada Nelson and Shine Smith, Buzz spent two days packing the supplies he obtained from Buck Lowrey to the tiny beach. Then he shoved off again, hoping to catch the geological party someplace in Grand Canyon. On November 20, he caught the Campbell party at Diamond Creek and spent the afternoon and night with the geologists before going on alone. Frank Dodge was impressed favorably with both Holmstrom and the boat he had built.[33]

Late in the year, the USGS made a number of improvements at Lee's Ferry. On November 21, contractors Devine and Neilson began building a tank to store the good spring water. Alec Fischback came two days later to supervise the construction of pipelines to the gager's residence. The well was finished to a depth of about thirty-six feet and lined with con-

Shine Smith and Isabella Moseley at the Sid Wilson cabin, October 1936 (*Ed Fisher photograph, Wagener collection, P. T. Reilly Collection, Cline Library, Northern Arizona University*).

crete. The pump base was poured early in January. A septic tank was installed, and a six-by-nine-foot bathroom was added by extending the bedroom and living room walls. For the first time, a building at Lee's Ferry contained a lavatory, toilet, and shower, all properly drained to the septic tank. Charlie Spencer wouldn't have believed it. The work was completed by the end of January 1938.[34]

Weaver's fears, as expressed to Rhoda in September, were realized on October 25, 1937, when the Babbitt Brothers forced him to sign a second mortgage on the Paradise Canyon Ranch to secure his debt of $1,092.32. At the time, he stated he still owed the church corporation $1,000, which wasn't quite true as yet.[35] However, he scraped the bottom of the barrel and used the last of Rachel Lothrop's loan to make the payment on November 10. Now he owed $1,000, plus interest, and was in arrears on the taxes. Billie came to spend the holidays at the ranch and Leo decided to obtain what promotional work he could find in Phoenix. He got a job with Doc Pardee at the Arizona Biltmore planning riding activities for winter guests.

It was another harsh winter which, combined with the lack of ready cash, made life rough for Hazel and Billie. Had it not been for the survey men, it would have been even more difficult. They brought supplies from Flagstaff, exercising credit that might have been denied had Weaver appeared in person, and they performed other courtesies the women

Shine Smith at Vermilion Cliffs, or Marble Canyon, Lodge, no date (*W. L. Heckler photograph, P. T. Reilly Collection, Cline Library, Northern Arizona University*).

appreciated. But everything considered, the year 1938 started out as bleakly as any Hazel could remember.

Preacher Smith's favorite refuges were the Wetherills at Kayenta, the O'Farrells at The Gap, and the Lowreys at Marble Canyon. He usually went from one to another and thought nothing of being on the receiving end of western hospitality for two or three months at a time. While Leo was in Phoenix, Shine insisted on settling in at the ranch "to take care of Hazel and Billie." He could not and would not work, and seldom made the effort to back up his strong talk. When asked to help milk, he went to the wrong side of a steer. He was too lazy to gather or cut firewood and proved to be a greater liability than the rankest dude. Hazel and Billie hauled firewood from the delta and sawed it into stove lengths; Smith sat up half of the night reading his Bible and burning the wood they had cut. After a few days he began making suggestive remarks about Billie and David Lowrey. This angered both women and they asked him to leave. He did, with the air of an unappreciated martyr.[36] The Weaver women considered him not very representative of his calling.

Leo helped promote the spring rodeo at Phoenix and had a short visit with Nora and David, who had driven down from Marble Canyon for the event. After that, the weather became progressively warmer and the snowbirds returned north. Leo's job came to an end and he went back to Paradise Canyon Ranch.

Buck Lowrey received his last license for Indian trading at Marble Canyon on January 26, 1937, but since he deeded his homestead over to Hubbell on March 9, he had not bothered to apply for a 1938 license. Hubbell made it plain to him that he did not want the property but was in dire need of the money he had advanced on it. The Lowreys remained for more than a year as he was unable to find a buyer. Lorenzo Hubbell reluctantly informed Buck that he would assume ownership on May 1, 1938. The family went into immediate action. David took Nora on the long-promised camping trip to the Sandhills. Making the jaunt on short notice, the pair started from Marble Canyon in the afternoon, went up House Rock Valley to the divide, then ascended the Paria Plateau where they made camp. Next day, they walked to the rim in the vicinity of Soap Creek from where the Lowrey lodge was visible. They were back at Marble Canyon that evening, and Nora's last adventure with David was only a memory. A few days later, Hubbell's nephew, Bob, his wife, and Shine Smith appeared to take over the business. The Lowreys pulled out early next morning, Nora trailing after them in her car, followed by the loyal cook, Clarence, and his wife, who had waited tables. A decade and an era had come to an end.[37]

Another demographic change took place that spring when Ed Fisher sold his Pahreah Canyon ranch to his brother George. Ed went to California while George and Mary moved into the cabin in the canyon. George acquired Ed's range permits and made plans to increase the size of the herd.

The Weavers were in the same boat as the Lowreys. Hade Church offered the Big Saddle facility again for summer use, but Leo was broke and had no customers. He stayed at Lee's Ferry, hanging on as best he could. Some of the Indian traders also moved around. In 1934, Earl Boyer sold the Cedar Ridge post to Keith Warren, who remained until 1939. Leo's old friend Johnny O'Farrell had bought The Gap from J. C. Brown and still employed Joe Lee in the original post on the east side of the road. O'Farrell decided to build a new trading post on the west side of the highway, and somehow Leo and Poli became involved. They not only helped in the construction but Leo took on the job of framing Cora O'Farrell's large tapestry. He and the owner nearly came to blows over this project.

A landmark of sorts occurred on July 8, 1938, when a three-boat flotilla under Norm Nevills landed at Lee's Ferry. The party had left Green River, Utah, on June 20, had been treated roughly in Cataract Canyon, including the loss and recovery of a boat, and was hampered by inexperience and disharmony. The group included Elzada Clover and Lois Jotter, the first two women to go through Cataract, Marble, and Grand Canyons. After a five-day layover and the replacement of two boatmen, the revamped party shoved off again on the thirteenth. When the group cleared the Grand Wash Cliffs on August 1, commercial river running of the Colorado River through Grand Canyon had begun.[38]

On July 17, Dave and Nelson Rust landed and pitched camp on the beach below the Spencer buildings. They had left Hite on July 9 in two sixteen-foot canvas boats to show the glories of Glen Canyon to a pair of Princeton University men, Dr. L. F. H. Lowe and student Harold Hartshorne. Dave Rust by now had made so many trips down this canyon, and knew its history so well, that few passengers could appreciate the voluminous information to which they were exposed. When they had stopped at Music Temple, he noted that the metal box was void of the many papers containing the names of previous visitors except for the one listing the Frazier party of 1933.

With no business and little money, Weaver spent the summer doing desultory work around the ranch. It was about nine o clock in the evening and quite warm on August 22 when the dogs and cats became disturbed about something in the corner of the ramada. Leo, wearing only shorts and bedroom slippers, walked over to see what was bothering the animals, and stepped on a rattlesnake. The reptile struck him in a vein on the instep of his right foot. Hazel got the snakebite kit but in her haste and nervousness, broke the needle and lost the serum. She put a tourniquet on his foot but made it too tight. By the time she had him in the Buick, the leg had started to swell and his jaw started to lock. Then she started the car in high gear and nearly stalled at the ranch. Somehow she reached Marble Canyon, where Bob Lowery came to her aid by volunteering to drive them to Flagstaff.

The road still was not paved north of the Little Colorado but the telephone line extended to Cedar Ridge. Keith Warren called ahead to the O'Farrells at The Gap and the Richardsons at Cameron. Hubert Richardson alerted Dr. Creighton at Flagstaff that the Weavers were on the way and to have the serum ready. Earl Reed, who ran Gray Mountain, had a lookout and passed the word when they went by. Fred Moore opened his drug store for needed supplies and the hospital was ready when Bob drove up with an unconscious Leo at 11:30 P.M. His recovery was credited to a number of unselfish people who were willing to go out of the way to help a resident of the Arizona Strip. The Weavers remained at the Monte Vista for a week, then returned home at the end of the month. Billie obtained time off from her job at El Tovar and came with them.

Things looked up, temporarily at least, when a pair of secretaries from Los Angeles spent a week at Paradise Canyon. Hazel and Billie took Madeline Morneau and Helen Davies to the upper ferry crossing on October 3. They tied their horses under a cottonwood at Frank Johnson's old cabin, and the three younger women climbed up in the rocks. As they watched, the two Powell boats, *Emma Dean* and *Nellie Powell,* came around the bend with the ailing John F. Steward sitting in Major Powell's armchair that was fastened to the midships deck of the lead boat. Eighty-three-year-old Julius Stone was sitting in a similar armchair fastened to one of the three boats, and he was accompanied by six companions, among whom were Frank Swain, Charles Kelly, Doc Inglesby, and Dr. Russell Frazier.

The river voyagers had left Hite on September 21 and made a leisurely trip downstream, visiting the historic places and recording previous inscriptions. They stopped at Hole in the Rock, Music Temple, walked up to Rainbow Bridge, and on October 1 set a bronze plate on the sandstone wall to commemorate the ancient Ute Ford, which was referred to as "Crossing of the Fathers." Kelly and Frazier had not known the actual location of the ford until 1937 when they went upstream in a power boat, located the ford and verified it by finding the steps cut in the stone at Padre Creek. At the time, they thought they were the only ones who knew the true location, little realizing that Dave Rust had taken Utah Governor George H. Dern there on April 19, 1926, where he was photographed by his secretary, Oliver Grimes.[39]

After tying up, the party went into camp, then later made its way to the Weaver ranch. Leo was expected to arrive shortly, but the women made the men welcome, and Frank Swain accompanied Hazel when she drove to Marble Canyon to meet her husband. When he stepped off the bus, Swain stuck out his hand and said, "Mr. Weaver, we have taken over the ranch without firing a shot." For once, Leo was nonplused—he had never laid eyes on this strapping fellow and was painfully aware how close he was to losing control of the place so dear to his heart. Of course Frank had no idea of the situation or how seriously his remark might be taken. Hazel soon explained things and as they rode back to the ranch Leo invited the party to supper.

During the conversation that followed the evening meal, the travelers spoke about the places they had visited in Glen Canyon; frequent mention of Powell prompted Leo to ask if they knew anything about an old boat named *Nellie Powell.* Julius Stone replied that it was the boat abandoned here by the Major's second expedition in 1872. When Weaver announced he had found the old boat half-buried in the silt when he took over the ranch, the men started a mad rush to the door. Even though it was close to midnight, they grabbed lanterns and followed Leo as he led the way to the creek. Unfortunately the willows had been burnt that morning and everything above ground was consumed; only a few charred fragments of the boat were found. Next morning, they unearthed a three-foot section of the beam. Chief Naturalist E. D. McKee of Grand Canyon National Park later came to the ranch to pick up this fragment. It has been on exhibit at the South Rim ever since.

David Lowrey had shown the Huntington-Holladay inscription to Billie Weaver during one of their rides. After being told of its existence, Kelly and Frazier wanted to see it. Billie saddled three horses and led them up on the bench where the glyph was thoroughly photographed. By this time, the Johnson name "Phantom Spring" had not been preserved, and the Fisher brothers—for whom the spring ultimately was named—were not widely known. Kelly, not knowing about Clark Allen Huntington, stated unequivocally that Huntington and Holladay had visited the Lee's Ferry area in 1857.[40] After a three-day stay with the hospitable Weavers, all seven members signed the cowhide-covered guest book on October 7 and departed. A week later, Stone sent the Weavers an autographed copy of his book *Canyon Country* in appreciation of their hospitality. Leo thanked the old canyoneer for his gift and informed him that he had named a colt "Stoney" after him; unknowingly he had hit upon the industrialist's nickname.

Shortly before mid-month a three-man, two-boat party pulled into the ferry landing. Buzz Holmstrom, on his second transit of the canyons, carried a passenger, Willis D. Johnson. His boat, which he had built himself from Port Orford cedar and had taken through the year before, now was named *Julius F* after the respected dean of river runners. They were accompanied by *National Geographic Magazine* photographer Amos Burg, rowing the first inflatable rubber boat down the Green and Colorado Rivers. His boat, named the *Charlie*, was almost the size of a ten-man neoprene raft, although narrower in beam. The trio did not tarry but pushed on into Marble Canyon.[41]

Leo's hospitality to river runners continued when a French trio landed at Lee's Ferry late in November. Bernard and Genevieve de Colmont and Antoine de Seynes, all of Paris, had left Green River, Wyoming, on September 13, 1938, in three sixteen-foot kayaks. The beautiful, twenty-two-year-old Genevieve could handle the kayaks as well as the men and successfully took on the big water of the upper Green River. She was the first woman to run a boat from Green River to Lee's Ferry and the third woman to come through Cataract Canyon. Hazel and Leo made them welcome; they remained three days, signed the guest book, then caught the stage for Flagstaff.[42]

Despite his strapped financial condition, Weaver had not accepted a cent for his services to the river parties. His doctor and hospital bills reduced his checking account to the point that it was barely active. On October 16 he wrote the Presiding Bishopric regarding his misfortune and asked for a six-month extension of the November 10 payment. Since he had been prompt in his previous payments, the request was approved on October 20. But this was only a temporary convenience to him as his financial trail now took an unexpected turn. He was involved actively in a refinancing of his house of cards and his latest rescue, naturally enough, was to be made by another woman—Maud Johann, his guest of previous years. With a loan from Maud seemingly assured, he purchased on time a seven hundred dollar water heater from the Standard Oil Company. This expensive solution to a chronic problem improved living conditions.

Leo thanked the churchmen for their understanding and implied an early payment of the remaining balance. The talks with Maud were going rather well and, on November 13, he inquired for the entire balance as of December 10. He was told the payment of $1,160.85 would enable him to receive a deed. On December 9, Orinn Compton made a formal request to execute a release of mortgage and send it, with his note, to the Bank of Arizona at Flagstaff; the acknowledgment that the mortgage had been satisfied was dated December 15, 1938.[43] Weaver had been able to achieve this end by persuading Maud to loan him $3,500, whereby the church could be paid in full. The Babbitt Brothers, who held a second mortgage against the property, agreed to subrogate their claim provided Weaver paid $500 on his debt to them. He was to repay the Johann loan with $500 on December 6, 1939, and on the same date each year, until 1945. Leo was skating on thin ice as the claim of Esther H. Bowers was not even mentioned.[44] Both instruments were executed December 6, 1938.

He thus realized $1,839.15 when he walked out of his attorney's office and, as in the case of the windfall from Essy Bowers, one of his first acts was to buy some horses. These were a team of matched Percherons that Billy Mackelprang let him have for $500. He thought he needed the animals to carry out the next phase of his ranch development. The expenditure caused Hazel much anguish.

Leo Weaver and Poli Hungavi had built a small dam at the first point in Pahreah Canyon in the spring of 1935, but it was washed away immediately. He attributed the loss to the location, not knowing that Warren Johnson had done the same and had moved progressively upstream for his subsequent dams. This time he selected the same location that had proven best for the Mormons—nearly two miles up the Pahreah, just above the Emett tunnel. Poli and several of his tribesmen joined him in December and were augmented by the Percherons and a Fresno scraper. The dam was constructed along the lines of those built by his predecessors, except that he didn't use a tree trunk for a structural base. He used short logs, brush, rocks, and dirt to build a structure about ten feet thick at the base and almost eight feet high. It formed a fair-sized pond but let the water through. A Weaver touch was the addition of a short rock wall on which he set a float that opened and closed the headgate automatically. One thing he neglected to do was to install a screen to prevent debris from clogging the float. When the project was completed in mid-January 1939, he appeared to be in a position to raise his own feed and eliminate one of his major expenses.

Leo's spirits rose further when he received a letter from Ura Maud Dobbs, the girl who had spent a week at Paradise Canyon Ranch in the fall of 1936. She wanted to bring two underprivileged boys to the ranch in April. Leo quoted her a price of seventy-five dollars for all three that included the use of riding horses. He agreed to pick them up at Grand Canyon station, transport them to the ranch, and return them to the railroad for an additional fifteen dollars.

Whenever possible, Leo worked Grand Canyon much as he had the Arizona Biltmore to pick up guests who were wondering where to go next. He was not as successful as in Phoenix, but he became acquainted with Dr. Harold C. Bryant, acting superintendent of the National Park. Leo was prone to speak in expansive terms and issue invitations to visit his ranch when he thought there was little chance of acceptance. Bryant fooled him and appeared unexpectedly with a pair of eastern guests who were accustomed to the best of everything. It happened that Hazel was out of supplies, intending to replenish them in a day or so. She did the best she could but the impromptu visit was a disaster, leaving both parties convinced it should not be repeated.

Weaver planted alfalfa early in March and put a couple of irrigations down the ditch. The pond behind the dam was full and the automatic float appeared to control the headgate properly. The Hopi work force, except for Poli and his family, had returned to Moenkopi when Leo picked up Dobbs, Lee Newfield, and Richard Willis at Grand Canyon on April 2. The disadvantaged urban youngsters had the time of their lives, which fully rewarded Dobbs for bringing them to Paradise Canyon Ranch. Leo took them back to the South Rim on the eighth. They were the last paying guests to sign his register book. Influenced by the amount of work to be done when he had guests, Leo placed an order with a Flagstaff employment agency to procure a good couple for general work at the ranch. He needed help with such chores as feeding the animals, milking, collecting firewood, and irrigating. The woman was scheduled to relieve Hazel of cooking and household tasks. John R. Reed and his wife were sent to them early in April.

Shortly after Leo returned from Grand Canyon, the Pahreah River had a minor flow increase on March 23 and 24. The pond already was full when debris fouled the automatic gate float. The gate remained closed and water spilled over the dam face. Soon a breach appeared and the entire structure was washed away. The Weavers heard the water coming and they ran across the field, but there was nothing they could do but watch helplessly as the small flood poured down the channel.

Weaver was despondent, knowing that raising alfalfa was now out of the question, and he was too discouraged to rebuild the dam. He felt the same anguish that had struck Lee, Johnson, and Emett, but Leo lacked their determination to succeed despite nature's perversity. Shortly after

Easter he and Hazel went to Flagstaff to check on an alternative to guest ranching. The Highway 66 program had been launched in February, and County Supervisor Andy Matson, who also was head of the Flagstaff Chamber of Commerce, had too many jobs and urged Leo to give up the ranch and work with him in town. Leo agreed and bought a house, leaving John Reed in charge of the ranch.[45]

Dave Rust had devoted most of June to guiding the Freeman-Dodge party on a pack trip to the Thousand Lakes Plateau and the Henry Mountains. They started down the Colorado River from North Wash on February 21 and overtook Bert Loper's party two days later, camping with them at Hansen Creek. Considerable river lore was dispensed by the two guides. Rust pushed ahead in the morning and on the twenty-eighth stopped at the Ute Ford, where he noted that the Julius Stone plate, which had been placed there the previous October, was in the correct place. His party landed at Lee's Ferry late the following afternoon and pitched camp. Next day, they had lunch with Archie Hanson, who ran them up to Marble Canyon in order to catch the Santa Fe bus at 5:03 A.M. They were ready at the appointed time, sitting on thirteen pieces of luggage by the road, but the bus was four hours late.

Meanwhile, Essy's attorney, Charles Nichols, had learned of Leo's deal with Maud Johann and brought pressure for a settlement on behalf of his client. Hazel and Leo disagreed on their approach to the matter, and he sulked off to Paradise Canyon Ranch. He was there, pondering his troubles, when another party of river guests arrived on Independence Day. Bert Loper had guided USGS geologists Charles B. Hunt, Ralph Miller, and four others down Glen Canyon to Lee's Ferry. The men spent the night with Leo and intended to be gone by 10 A.M., but their host needed company and detained them until the next morning. Loper and the geologists finally signed the guest book and made their departure on the morning of the sixth.

Loper had different plans. He didn't accompany the Russell-Monett trip in 1908 as he had planned, but he intended to go through Grand Canyon, this time with Don Harris, who had parted ways with Norm Nevills at Lee's Ferry the previous year. Harris, Chet Klevin, and Bill Gibson left Hite on June 27 and tied up their boats at Lee's Ferry on the day the geologists were due to leave. Loper joined them and they shoved off on only 9,800 cubic feet per second; when they ended the trip as planned at Boulder Dam on July 21, the flow was 5,090. Next to the 1934 traverse, it was one of the lowest discharges on which a passage had been made before Glen Canyon Dam was finished in 1963, but in doing it they ran every rapid. Loper celebrated his seventieth birthday on the day they landed.[46]

Leo Weaver worked out his problems and returned to Flagstaff. If he ever came back to his beloved Paradise Canyon Ranch, the record has not been preserved. Attorney Charles Nichols brought him to heel and forced him to negotiate the claim of his client. After several acrimonious and difficult sessions, Leo yielded his last hold on his guest ranch dream;

on August 5, 1939, he signed his interests over to Bowers.[47] It was not an easy deal for her to accept because, to protect her original investment of $6,000, she must assume Leo's indebtedness to Maud Johann and the Babbitt Brothers, and she had to pay the delinquent taxes. Nichols bought the Johann note for $3,000 and on October 6, 1939, Essy signed a realty mortgage agreeing to pay $500 on April 6 and October 6, 1940, as well as similar amounts on the same dates of following years until the sum was paid.[48] Paradise Canyon Ranch now belonged to her, and Leo's financial house of cards was in shambles. She kept John Reed on as caretaker.

Was Leo Weaver born under an evil star, or was he the victim of his own poor judgment? He had more than one man's share of adversity, yet he failed in the same environment where his pioneer predecessors had thrived. Hazel had married him outside of her church, but to please her he converted to Catholicism in 1939. At the conclusion of the war, the Weavers moved to Placitas, New Mexico, where Leo served as executive secretary of the U.S. Highway 66 Association. He got lung cancer, probably as a result of his many years as a chronic smoker, and he died in Tucson on April 10, 1951, at age sixty-four. He was buried in his colorful western attire at Flagstaff, although Hazel was convinced that the undertaker stole his fancy lizard skin boots. But fate was not yet through with him. In a subsequent year, a clean-up minded priest had all of the old tombstones hauled away to the city dump, and today Leo Weaver rests in an unmarked grave in complete anonymity.

15

A Change in Priorities

WILBUR T. STUART DID NOT HAVE A TRANSPORTATION PROBLEM FOR THE two and one-half years he had been stationed at the Grand Canyon gaging station. Any place he went, whether to the USGS cable car on the Colorado River or the village on the South Rim, he was certain to be on foot. This changed when District Chief John H. Gardiner, who had succeeded W. E. Dickinson in 1938, assigned him to replace Archie Hanson at Lee's Ferry. Wilbur Stuart arranged to buy a new Ford coupe from a dealer in Williams and took delivery at the head of the Bright Angel Trail on June 22, 1939. He and his wife Florence drove to the ferry to case their new home, then went back to Flagstaff to spend the night. They were in Phoenix two days later where both obtained licenses to drive in Arizona. Hanson met the Stuarts in Flagstaff on July 25, returned with them to the ferry, and Stuart settled down as resident hydrographer.

Things were relatively quiet near Lee's Ferry. Lorenzo Hubbell's nephew had grown tired of operating the Vermilion Cliffs Lodge, so Lorenzo had obtained the services of J. H. "Bill" and Fredia Brownd to replace him. Brownd was a member of a Flagstaff business family. George and Mary Fisher lived up the canyon, John Reed, caretaker for Essy Bowers, worked as a laborer when the Survey improved the facilities. Hubert Hunter had come for high-water duty; because 1939 was a low-water year, he departed for good on June 23. Reed was resident observer during the hydrographer's absence, but he was not considered reliable and told fanciful stories regarding ferry history.

The Pahreah River flooded repeatedly in August. By the end of the month, the Weaver crossing was caked with mud and was impassable. When the Stuarts returned from the Little Colorado River on September 8, they found the creek had been up to 2,800 cubic feet per second, washing out the crossing. More heavy rains in the watershed sent a thirteen and one-half–foot crest down Pahreah Canyon, with 6,200 cubic feet per second recorded at the gaging station. The channel was deeply scoured and the road was washed out beyond normal repair. The crossing was abandoned, and Navajos were to build a temporary road located along the edge of the delta at one dollar per day. It was all shovel work because the silt had to be

412

removed to get down to gravel. A fork was washed in the low-water channel and almost bypassed the gage; Wilbur was forced to dig a trench to get water to the base. The roads north and west of the channel were washed out.

While the roads were impassable, Mary Fisher and Florence Stuart rode George's mules, Frankie and Johnny, to Marble Canyon to get the mail. The mail pouch, a canvas bag twelve by twenty-four inches and locked at one end, was usually found lying on the ground where the driver had thrown it. If a passenger got off the bus there, someone would bring the mailbag into the station.

Essy and Sam Bowers went into residence at the ranch in October. Essy kept Reed on because no one else was available. She expounded her "I Am" philosophy to anyone she could trap into listening. She had definite ideas and dispersed them readily. She told Wilbur Stuart that "no wonder there is so much trouble in the world with those bad Mormons buried in the ranch cemetery."[1] She considered red to be an "evil" color, disliked a negative or objective attitude, preferred the positive whether it was realistic or not. The owls hooting at night bothered her and she evolved the theory that they embodied the ghost of John D. Lee, so she had Reed uproot the sixty-year-old fruit trees in which they roosted. He pulled the trees out with the Percheron team she had taken over from Weaver, then dragged them to the creek bank in an effort to reduce erosion.

There was a bad drought during most of 1939, and Indian cattle could be obtained for twenty dollars a head. George Fisher bought what his resources would allow, then attempted to talk Stuart into backing him with a thousand dollars to procure more. But Stuart declined, knowing he would be going to another station after the runoff and would not be present to keep track of his investment. Essy picked up the cue and had Reed bring in several head in a stake-body truck. One cow had a spot rubbed raw from jostling; the sore became enlarged and infected with the hip bone protruding. Reed sold milk from this cow to the Stuarts until they refused to buy it. He then filled the hole with some unknown substance and tried to sell the animal, but found no buyers. He finally butchered the beast, cut out the infected quarter, and peddled the meat in Flagstaff.

Bowers frequently made trips in connection with the "I Am" movement. Upon returning unexpectedly early one time, she found Sam had brought in a girl and a Hollywood cowboy friend. She raised the roof, sent the pseudo cowboy to sleep at Fisher's, and drove the girl up to the stage stop at Marble Canyon. After receiving a tongue-lashing, Sam resolved to be more careful in the future, but not necessarily to mend his ways. Reed rebuilt the Pahreah dam, but December brought cold weather that caused icing and affected streamflow. Reed's dam, as had those of his predecessors, washed out in January 1940, leaving the ranch without irrigation water and bringing the hay-raising effort to a halt.

A prospector named Jack Saltz came down the river and set up a camp at Lee's Ferry. This was not unusual, but Saltz had no supplies and

Norman D. Nevills in Glen Canyon, June 9, 1949 (*P. T. Reilly Collection, Cline Library, Northern Arizona University*).

had been living off the land for several weeks. He said he had been working the "Chinese placers," probably referring to the site one hundred thirty miles up river where the three Japanese—Homma, Kemeda, and Inouye— had worked the previous year at Smith Bar. Stuart became acquainted with him and finally took him to Prescott, where an assayer's lab was located. He tried to buy him a meal but Saltz refused, saying restaurant food would be too rich for him after his long diet on indigenous fare.

George Fisher and Gerald Swapp planned to develop the range-land on the East Clark Bench by bringing water to the thirsty acres from Wahweap Creek. They gave Stuart a gold penknife to draw up the papers so they could file on the water rights. The scheme was interrupted by the war and did not come to fruition for almost a decade. Fisher was gone when the plan finally emerged, but Swapp brought the water up Judd Hollow from the Pahreah River before dying unexpectedly.[2]

The Survey began phasing out the field-trained hydrographers in the mid-1930s because there was an abundance of graduate engineers available for the jobs. Jim Klohr transferred to the Bureau of Reclamation in 1933; Frank Dodge left in 1936, aware that the technical part of the work was beyond his training, and Owen Clark was not rehired in 1937. The men with degrees did not always think that being a hydrographer was the limit of their talents. The clicks of the current meters were heard through head phones and counted manually on settings of one or five, depending on the speed of the current. Wilbur Stuart said, somewhat humorously, "All one needs to know to become a hydrographer is to stand in water up to his ass and be able to count by fives."[3]

The maintenance and improvement program carried over until 1940. George Fisher repaired the Pahreah crossing in late January, shoveling in several cubic yards of shale until the roadbed once again was on gravel. At the same time, Stuart hired Bob Hart to dig a sewer trench down to the river, and Survey sewage now discharged directly into the Colorado. They tried to deepen the well, but the point of refusal was met at three feet, or thirty-nine feet below the pump base. They also lost the aquifer at this depth.[4] Stuart transferred from the USGS Surface Water Branch to the Ground Water Branch and left the ferry on May 13; Quincy Cornelius replaced him. Three days later Cornelius drove to Santa Fe where he married Dorothy. He emulated Wilbur Heckler by bringing her to the ferry on the twenty-seventh.

Essy Bowers finally decided that her victory over Leo Weaver was not to her best interest. She lost enthusiasm early in the summer and moved on, leaving the Reed couple to take care of the ranch. His duties were light and the ranch never suffered when he acted as observer; he performed about the same on both jobs as neither interfered with the other. While Cornelius was checking the Little Colorado gages early in July, the recorder stopped functioning and Reed made "observations" for three days without noticing the trouble.

Norman Nevills, now established in the river tourist business, landed at the ferry on August 2, 1940. Seeking to retrace Major Powell's course, the three-boat party had left Green River, Wyoming, on June 20. Personnel changed slightly at Green River, Utah, when B. V. Deason withdrew temporarily while Barry Goldwater and Anne Rosner joined. The group had only two boatmen—Nevills and Del Reed. The third boat was rowed by one of the two sturdier passengers, either Hugh Cutler or

Goldwater. The party started downstream again August 4. Doris Nevills and Mildred Baker became the third and fourth women to traverse the Colorado River through Grand Canyon.[5] Doris also had the distinction of being the first pregnant woman to make this run.

Essy Bowers sold the ranch to Chester Augustus Griffin and his wife Ramona on October 25. Gus, who worked for the Indian Service and was stationed at Leupp, Arizona, had first heard of the ranch in the mouth of Pahreah Canyon from Richard Wetherill at Gallup in 1910. He agreed to pay $7,500 for the property, with $600 down and not less than $50 dollars per month beginning January 1, 1942. The payments would continue thereafter until November 1, 1945, at which time the balance was due.[6] He invested in it so that his son could farm the place. Warren Griffin took possession at the end of the month, and on November 23, he replaced Reed as observer.[7] The young man was much more satisfactory at both jobs than his predecessor, and Reed left the ferry. Riley Baker, now married to Maggie Jackson, received title to Price Johnson's Badger Creek homestead on November 7, 1940. His improvements were located on 77 and 21/100 acres and, although homespun, had evolved far from Price's facility. Johnson's ruins sat forlornly on the edge of the wash on the old pioneer road.

Meanwhile, Frank Dodge had holed up with Owen Clark on his Yuma citrus ranch. There he built an eighteen-foot sailboat which, in March 1938, he launched on Lake Mead. While there, Dodge built another craft—a small houseboat—and lived on it until the Park Service superintendent notified him that no more such residency would be allowed. An intensely patriotic man, Dodge thought it would be only a matter of time until the United States became involved in the war. He was fifty years of age now, and not the lad he once was, but after failing to be accepted by the Hawaii National Guard and as a gunner in the Canadian merchant marine, he wrote to USGS District Chief John H. Gardiner at Tucson and applied for a gaging job. The chief could see the handwriting on the wall; he knew he might lose most of his young engineers to the war effort, and he jumped at the chance to pick up the experienced Dodge. According to the Station History as recorded by Quincy Cornelius, Dodge arrived again at Lee's Ferry at 3:10 P.M. on January 24, 1941.[8] He settled in his old cabin and three days later began duty as resident observer, working with hydrographer Cornelius. His status was raised to high-water helper on May 6, a promotion that brought him more money.

Nevills brought parties down the San Juan and Colorado Rivers from Mexican Hat in May and June. Mid-July saw another Nevills party at the ferry for a trip through Grand Canyon. There were only three passengers, two boats and boatmen, and a canvas foldboat, similar to the kayaks of the French trio, that Alexander G. Grant, Jr., intended to row down the Colorado River. Grant had carried it under his Pullman berth in two handbags. Nevills picked him up at Thompson, Utah, and could not believe he actually had brought a boat. Assembled at the ferry, the canvas cover was stretched over a hickory frame to make a length of sixteen and one-half feet. Two eight-inch boards formed a vee forward of the cockpit that "Zee" called his "wave-splitter"; it did deflect some water. Balsa wood, five inflated beach balls, and eight inner tubes filled the interior for buoyancy. A large inner tube from Fifth Avenue bus tires was fastened to each beam as pontoons, which added to the stability although they didn't help the appearance. Grant used the Nevills boats as auxiliary support while Norm advised and directed the traverse. They shoved off July 15.[9] After the Grand Canyon run, he led a two-boat party from Mexican Hat to the ferry.

The remainder of 1941 was uneventful except that heavy fall rains occurred throughout the plateau watershed, causing the Colorado to exceed 80,000 cubic feet per second in October. But floods and local issues were forgotten when the Japanese attacked Pearl Harbor on December 7. Cornelius left for Grand Canyon and the Little Colorado gages on the first and did not return until 4 P.M. on the eighth. He serviced the Moenkopi gage last, had been on the road since daylight, and had heard no late news. Knowing that her husband would return that afternoon, Dorothy had invited Warren Griffin and Frank Dodge to dinner. As soon as the sun went down, radio reception improved and they tuned in to learn of the attack. The news electrified them all, but reactions of the two guests varied considerably.

Dodge was very disturbed. He had been born in Hawaii, his family was still there, and few citizens matched his patriotism. But young Griffin didn't want to hear the bombing details since he was of draft age; he wanted to remain at the ranch. The clash between the two was definite; they not only were polarized but were openly antagonistic.[10] By year's end, the war had caused abnormal reassignments. Dodge remained resident observer, but junior engineer R. B. Sanderson arrived on January 4, 1942, to replace Cornelius, who took him on a tour of the Grand Canyon and Little Colorado gages before departing January 11. The resident hydrographer's duties were greater now than they had been in the past because there were more stations to service and fewer men to do the work.

Early in 1943, Gus and Warren Griffin accomplished that which none of the ranch predecessors had been able to do: they whipped the Pahreah. The solution was simple; they placed a large gasoline-driven pump on a pallet above the creek and ran a six-inch hose from a pool to a flagstone-lined irrigation ditch. The only flaw in the technique was that the pump could not be operated when the stream was in flood, and crops sometimes required water when the creek was thick with sediment. On the whole, however, the pump was better than the many dams that had been built over the previous seventy years.

The Bureau of Reclamation sent the Smith-Moser reconnaissance party to the ferry in April to investigate the possibility of transferring Colorado River water into the Verde River drainage. On May 20, surveyors began running levels up the left bank for a proposed high-line canal to the Verde headwaters.[11]

Another jolt occurred on March 2, 1942, when Lorenzo Hubbell, Jr., died. His brother Ramon took over his interests, entangled as they were. The job was facilitated by the fact that the brothers had been close and each had a good working knowledge of the other's operations. One of the first changes was abolishing Buck Lowrey's name Vermilion Cliffs Lodge in favor of Marble Canyon Lodge. Hubbell's discard was Maggie Baker's salvage; she was glad to apply the placename to her Badger Creek enterprise.

Despite restrictions brought on by the war, Nevills managed to keep his young river-running business going. He made trips from Mexican Hat to Lee's Ferry on May 10 and 20 and June 1, 1942. The first was a two-boat party whereby he and Pres Walker conducted three passengers through one hundred ninety-two miles of spectacular canyon scenery. Two of the fares were Neill C. Wilson and Francis Farquhar of Pasadena; both men were destined to have future influence on the river. The second and third trips were one-boat parties, each with three passengers. The party that left Mexican Hat on June 1 included Stephen Moulton Fulmer and his wife Janice. Fulmer also was to have a river career ahead of him.[12]

The San Juan–Glen Canyon trips impressed most passengers favorably. Neill Wilson came home raving not only about the scenery but of Nevills and his ability. He was so enthusiastic that he convinced his friend and skiing companion, Otis Reed Marston, to accompany him on Nevills' forthcoming Grand Canyon trip. Accordingly, Wilson and his twelve-year-old son Bruce were joined by Marston and his sixteen-year-old son Garth. The quartet traveled by bus to Flagstaff, then took the 2:45 A.M. bus to Marble Canyon. Marston recorded arriving at the "Rainbow Bridge Lodge" at 5:20 A.M.[13] In his own words, few people ever started on a river trip with more inappropriate attire. His white flannels, deck shoes, and scarf were suitable for yachting on San Francisco Bay, but were decidedly out of place on the silty Colorado. The remaining two passengers were cameraman Ed Olson and boating enthusiast Ed Hudson. The latter was fated to make river history in seven years, and Marston was to collect it for the next thirty-seven. Nevills, Pres Walker, and Wayne McConkie rowed the three boats when they left the ferry at 10:30 A.M. on July 15, 1942.

Five days after the Nevills party headed downstream, a portion of river history from three previous decades fell victim to the war effort. The relatively high price paid for scrap metal motivated Riley Baker and his stepson to bring two trucks to the ferry and gather Charlie Spencer's old mining machinery. They had Dodge's blessing because he had no use for the promoter and would go out of his way to eradicate evidence of his presence at the ferry, especially if it aided the war effort. The scavengers worked for two days and left with full loads; Baker returned for another load on July 26. The only items remaining from the 1911 promotion were articles too large to be handled, such as the steam boilers.[14]

The divergent views on the war held by Frank Dodge and Warren Griffin grew wider as time went on. Dodge openly was critical of the young man and made no effort to hide his disdain. When Warren enlisted in the Coast Guard, the ranch once again was unoccupied. At about the same time, it was leaked that Dodge was indulging in the illegal practice of dynamiting fish. But his trouble wasn't even embarrassing; his appropriation of Spencer's powder for fishing had provided many a meal for Flagstaff citizens, reportedly even for officials. In Jerry Johnson's terminology, Dodge "took another whack at Charlie Spencer" when he began dismantling the three Spencer buildings that had been used during Charlie's promotion of the early 1930s. They were completely eradicated over a period of several months, and then Dodge went to work on the Spencer addition to the west end of the old fort. It was relatively safe to destroy these buildings since gasoline rationing prevented most public pleasure travel, and those who associated the buildings with Spencer, such as Buck Lowrey, had moved away. The better stones were put aside for use in facing the VTP building—a completely new quarters for housing visiting engineers or people of political importance.

Cabell, the area chief, and Dodge never became friendly. Cabell followed a strict code of behavior and took a dim view of Dodge's binges. He considered him to be an average worker when sober but utterly worthless when drunk. Consequently, the Lee's Ferry station caused Cabell extra work and he visited it more often than when Quincy Cornelius was there. Dodge always referred to his superior as "Mr. Cabell" in the station history writeups—his method of expressing disdain in the same manner that Clyde Eddy's river crew had referred to their leader as "Mr. Eddy." The war effectively shut down most activity at the remote location except Dodge's desultory river-gaging. He made one or two trips to Flagstaff each month for supplies and usually checked the Moenkopi gage on the way in, mailing the removed graph to the office. An exceptionally heavy downpour hit the area at sundown on October 10. When the storm passed, Dodge walked toward the lodge, repairing the washed-out road as he walked. The job took all day and he spent the night with Dick and Mable Ritchie, who had replaced the Brownds as managers. Next morning, he walked back to the ferry, smoothing out the rough places.

Elmer Johnson returned that fall to refurbish the dwelling at the upper ranch and make it liveable in time to plant a spring crop. He had fathered his sixteenth child in July and gave no reason for deciding to reside in so remote a location. He was over fifty and in no danger of being drafted. Jerry approved his brother's action, believing that he had a clear title to the forty acres. Jerry Johnson came to the upper ranch early in the spring to help Elmer put in a crop and get water to the field. He brought several of his children with him and what Leo Weaver had feared now was an actuality. However, there was no one at the ranch to be bothered.

Cabell made his final call of 1942 in late December and spent two full days helping Dodge, apparently in more ways than pertained to stream gaging. Frank recorded in the station history that "Mr. Cabell measured Paria Creek, I attended; He also gave me some miscellaneous help, both physical and mental"—presumably a euphemism for temperance advice.[15] Dodge's health had been deteriorating for the past few years; he took time off for a medical checkup in Flagstaff. The river was low, enabling one man to handle the gaging without danger. The hydrographers installed a new suspension cable at the upper site June 10. While playing around the recently deposited drift on June 18, children found the body of an Indian who supposedly had drowned in the high water. The man's identity, place of the tragedy, and burial of the remains are unknown.[16]

Charlie Spencer, now nearly seventy-one years of age, managed to find limited backing and in the fall set up exploratory operations at the abandoned Pahreah townsite. On September 29, two men named Brown and Segar appeared at the ferry to obtain samples of the Chinle Formation for testing in a Los Angeles laboratory. Undoubtedly, they were associated with Spencer, but they convinced Dodge they had no use for Charlie. If the samples proved to contain mercury, they proposed to set up a pilot plant to extract the mineral. Dodge, apparently unaware that Spencer had no legal right to mine in the withdrawn area, adopted a wait-and-see attitude while notifying Cabell. The strangers spent the night there, departed next morning and were seen no more, their scouting mission accomplished.

The war delayed the budding river business of Norman Nevills and he recorded no trips in 1943. Things picked up the following year. On May 26, 1944, he started from Mexican Hat with *Life Magazine* photographer Dimitri Kessel in a single boat, two-man party. The San Juan was flowing a respectable 14,500 cubic feet per second. When they entered the Colorado on the third day, they felt the heavy surge of 76,300 cubic feet per second. Nevills had his Mexican Hat to Lee's Ferry run programmed for seven days, which allowed a full day to visit Rainbow Bridge. His last night's camp was at a large, shallow cave that resembled the Great Arch of Zion. He called it Outlaw Cave, attributing the name in typical Nevills fashion to an outlaw named Neal Johnson who hid out there for several months and later was hanged in Nevada.[17] Norm developed such fiction for his river passengers. They ate it up, added their own embellishments, and in time even propagated some of the yarns into river lore.

No sooner was this trip completed than Nevills came down the San Juan River again. The passengers were recruited largely by Otis Marston, and they included his teen-age twin daughters. Others making the trip were freelance cameraman Ted Phillips and Nevills' daughter, twelve-year-old Joan, who probably was the youngest person to run that part of the river. The party of ten in three boats embarked at Mexican Hat on June 6 on 9,500 cubic feet per second. Nevills and McConkie rowed two of the boats while Marston alternated with two of his friends in operating the other. They entered the Colorado on the third day when it was running 65,000 cubic feet per second, experienced the standard Nevills tour, and landed at the ferry on June 12. This jaunt marked the advent of Marston as an oarsman on the Colorado River.

Nevills made an unusual fall trip from Mexican Hat to Lee's Ferry in September 1944. He preferred not to run at this time because of low water, but his Hollywood guests could go at no other time, and he needed the money. It was a Fox Movietone News project made up of editor Jack Darrock, cameraman Jack Kuehn with his assistant Ray Zeiss, Utah state publicity director Frank O'Brien, Utah state geologist Al Burenek, and Walter H. Koch, a mining engineer for the Bureau of Land Management. Nevills, Lynn Lyman, and Burenek rowed the three San Juan punts. They shoved off at Mexican Hat on the eighteenth on less than 800 cubic feet per second. One of the boats was pinned upon a rock in about twenty-five miles, resulting in the loss of a movie camera. Norm called the place "Eywmo Rapid" for the rest of his life, although no rapid was there. The Colorado flowed at about 3,400 cubic feet per second and had not changed much by the time they landed at the ferry. It was one of the all-time low-water runs for this stretch, but Hollywood's schedule had been held.[18]

Impressed by the fine crop of melons raised by Elmer and Jerry that summer, Price Johnson and his family joined them in the fall. Another reason was that the operation required two men and, as was his wont, Jerry spent so much time at Hurricane that Elmer frequently was forced to work alone.

Restricted travel made operation of the Marble Canyon Lodge even less attractive than the low volume of business caused by its remote location, and neither owner Ramon Hubbell nor the Richie couple was satisfied. Hubbell developed plans for a fresh approach that involved bringing in a new family to operate and expand the business. Arthur H. Greene was a homespun commoner from Colorado who exuded friendliness and hospitality. He operated a four-stool restaurant in Blanding, Utah, with his wife and three married daughters when the sons-in-law were called into their country's service. As the war dragged toward an end, he became associated with Ramon Hubbell at Ganado, working without wages to learn the business. He proved his worth and Hubbell sent him to Marble Canyon to operate the lodge and enlarge the facility. It was a fifty-fifty arrangement; Hubbell furnished the facilities and equipment, and Greene supplied the labor. Art and his wife, daughters Irene and Grace, the latter's husband, Bud Williams, and their children arrived at Marble Canyon in November 1944 to the distasteful task of telling the present managers that they were being replaced. They settled in and prepared for a post-war boom.

At the ferry, a large rockfall from just below the rim engulfed the right-hand anchorage of the upper gaging cable on December 19.[19] Subjected to such excess weight, the line became as tight as a bowstring and the vibration damaged the cable car. Dodge surveyed the situation and notified Cabell in the Flagstaff office. The sub-district chief came to the ferry January 9, 1945, and examined the condition with Dodge and Jerry Johnson. Jerry took the job of clearing the rocks at six dollars an hour. Jerry soon turned the job over to Price, who worked throughout February and uncovered the anchorage on March 10. He continued to work until he had removed all the rock and built a protective wall. Dodge and Cabell replaced the support hangers on the cable car and removed the excess sag in the cable by taking up thirteen inches in the bridge socket at the right anchor.[20]

The end of the war was in sight, but for some Americans the pent up urge for outdoor recreation could not wait for the armistice. Harry Aleson, while holed up in "My Home" in the mouth of Quartermaster Canyon, two hundred sixty miles below Lee's Ferry, was inspired to reverse the usual procedure and attempt upstream travel. He named his motorboat *Up Colorado* and reached Diamond Creek in May 1942. On August 1, he met the Nevills party at Mile 234 and towed the oar-powered boats across Lake Mead. He extended his upstream mark to Mile 218 the following year but failed to exceed it in the early spring of 1944. Meanwhile, Aleson's relations with Nevills had ruptured and he guided one of Norm's 1942 passengers, Ed Hudson, down Glen Canyon in April 1945. Later that month, he focused on Glen Canyon, and on the twenty-sixth he shoved off alone from Lee's Ferry. He left caches of food and fuel en route and reached Hite about noon of the thirtieth, having exceeded Dodge's effort of twelve years before by sixty miles. He even had four gallons of gasoline left in the tank.[21]

Nevills also had benefited from the public's reaction to restricted travel. Hostilities ended in Europe on May 9, 1945, and he started parties from Mexican Hat on June 4 and 17, each terminating at Lee's Ferry on the morning of the seventh day.[22] In July he led a party from Moab to Lee's Ferry, the first time this particular stretch of river had been negotiated in one trip. It was another Marston-organized outing that included his wife Margaret and their daughters. It was the fifth venture on the Colorado for Ed Hudson and his third with Norm. They traveled in three boats rowed by Nevills, McConkie, and Marston—his first as an oarsman on "big water." Cataract Canyon treated Nevills better than it had in the past, and they ran the forty-seven miles with relative ease.

One of his main objectives was to hike up Escalante River to visit a large natural bridge located nearly ten miles from the Colorado. The bridge, subsequently named Gregory, probably had been discovered by Llewellyn Harris in the 1880s, but was first made known by the USGS party under William R. Chenoweth in October 1921. Some claimed it was larger than Rainbow Bridge, although it had never been measured. Argument as to the bridge's size waxed hot at the bridge site, Nevills maintaining their perceptions were dwarfed by the immensity of the setting. Finally Marston announced he would settle the matter by measuring it and produced a six-foot roll tape and forty feet of twine. He used basic trigonometry to measure the bridge's length from its base. Nevills didn't believe it could be done as stated and he stalked downstream in a huff when the operation was underway.[23] Unfortunately this incident accentuated personal antagonism between the two that grew into open rupture within three years. Marston claimed Nevills was so upset that he rushed them to Lee's Ferry two days early and they missed some features they had counted on seeing.

Before the 1945 boating season closed, it was apparent that the Colorado system was on the verge of a great tourist boom. The surrender of Japan on August 16 revitalized the hopes of professionals and enthused the amateurs as gasoline rationing came to an end. It was clear that Lee's Ferry would become the evacuation point for those traversing Glen Canyon and the embarkation point for the ones heading downstream. Before the year was out, the Greene clan was augmented by the release from the armed services of Vern Baker and Earl Johnson, husbands of Art's daughters Ruth and Irene. In anticipation of increasing income from river tourism, Hubbell sent Greene an eighteen foot aluminum boat with a twenty-two horsepower outboard motor.

Marble Canyon was not the only place that anticipated a rosy future. The Yavapai Associates and the Associated Civic Clubs of Northern Arizona promoted their areas in glowing terms. Barry Goldwater acquired the Hubert Richardson interest in Rainbow Lodge and planned to reopen with Katherine and Bill Wilson as managers. The lodge had been closed three years. Babbitts bought out the Wetherill facilities at Kayenta and installed Bennett Hyde as manager. Johnny O'Farrell sold The Gap to Jack Owens, and his Copper Mine Trading Post to C. F. Thompson, who came from California—the place to which O'Farrell was retiring.

Art Greene borrowed a trick from the pioneer Mormons when he began questioning Indians about the location of little known features that would help the tourist trade. At the same time, he became a press agent for the region's scenic values by inviting leading photographers to exploit its spectacular erosion and deep colors. Local Indians told him about Paiute Cave, an unusual opening on a wash on the Marble Platform near the left rim and four miles south of the mouth of House Rock Wash. Greene and Bud Williams took Herb McLaughlin of Phoenix there on April 27, then repeated the visit with Joyce and Josef Muench on August 1, 1946.[24]

Earl Johnson became pilot of the Greene river excursions and made a few tourist trips to the mouth of Forbidden Canyon in the spring of 1946. The boat, however, was too small with insufficient power to make the venture pay, and this phase of river tourism languished. At the time, the Marble Canyon facility amounted to the old store and gas station on the north side of the highway, the lodge, and a pair of cabins on the south; all of the buildings on the reservation side of the river had been demolished. Art and Ramon agreed that the first order of business was to enlarge facilities for overnight guests.

Bill Wilson began advertising Rainbow Lodge in *Desert Magazine*, and in February Norm Nevills bought space to promote his Mexican Hat to Lee's Ferry trips that he made in April, May, and June. These trips became the heart of his operation. He did not gather a party for the Grand Canyon this year, but in midsummer Otis Marston put parties together and induced him to run trips on the Snake and Salmon Rivers in Idaho. Marston was a boatman on both trips.

In the summer of 1946 four innovative boats ran Glen Canyon. These boats, had they been seen by old-timers, would have made them wonder whether they had taken too many pulls from the camp jug. Professor George O. Bauwens of the University of Southern California College of Engineering designed an eighteen-foot boat of thin marine plywood and flexible tubing that could be folded into a compact bundle weighing sixty pounds and transported in the trunk of an ordinary automobile. The professor and three graduate students, each with his individual solution to the general problem of a design that stressed flexibility, a low center of gravity, and stability, built his own boat at a cost of thirty-five dollars and successfully negotiated the Colorado River from Hite to Lee's Ferry in ten days. Intelligence had obviated tradition and the need for guides.

USGS engineers did not like to have Dodge make measurements by himself as the results were not considered reliable.[25] His willingness to remain in residency during the war was appreciated; he was needed to keep the stilling wells open and the recorders functioning, but his river measurements could not be plotted with consistency. Thus it was that John T. Sanders was given use of the survey residence when he arrived there with Cabell on March 21. Sanders worked for the Bureau of Reclamation making surveys for a possible Glen Canyon dam. He made one measurement and irritated Dodge, who resented his occupation of the official residence. When Dodge learned Sanders was recording the official station history and ignoring him, he wrote a refutation and signed it with all the macho display of a little boy.[26] Sanders wasn't there long; he made one measurement with Cabell and one by himself before moving out.

Old times were revived late in the month when Jim Klohr arrived to become resident hydrographer. His wife Christina accompanied him. Jim not only was an accurate gager but he wrote splendid station histories, including more general data than had the average recorder. He revived the long-neglected practice in August, noting arrivals and departures and the conditions affecting the lives of the residents. Cabell was delighted to have a reliable resident engineer, and the choice couldn't have suited Dodge better. Frank now was fifty-five, his health had deteriorated, and he was not as self-sufficient as he had been. Klohr assumed the position at the beginning of the new fiscal year, July 1, and the old companions celebrated by measuring together. Dodge assisted throughout the month, but quit the U.S. Geological Survey for good on August 9 and departed for the coast. He had used the ferry as a refuge for more than a quarter century.

Torrential rains came the day after Dodge left and continued for two months. The Pahreah River flooded, knocked the cord from the float wheel, and washed out the crossing. The road to Marble Canyon was cut in several places—wherever it was crossed by a wash—and was impassable. Jim's river job now became road work, and he often shoveled during pouring rain. Even when he was able to reach Marble Canyon, he could not cross the creek in a car but was forced to wade and carry supplies on his back. The road was washed out between the residence and the garage, a distance of less than a hundred yards, and he could not drive along the creek's left bank. A massive downpour at the upper cable nearly rectified the rock slide of December 1940 by removing an estimated fifty cubic yards of debris from around the anchor, leaving the cable totally clear to the anchorage. Increased volume in the Colorado removed two-thirds of the slide that had projected into the river and caused a small riffle.[27]

A milestone was reached on September 17, 1946, when Utah Governor H. B. Maw cut the ribbon to open a new highway between Hanksville and Blanding. The key link was the Hite ferry, built and operated by Arthur L. Chaffin. The road was not paved but it bisected the upper half of some very rough country, and the Chaffin ferry was the only means of crossing the Colorado between Moab and Marble Canyon. During the program for an estimated three hundred fifty visitors, Harry Aleson announced that starting in the spring he would schedule commercial boat trips from Hite to Lee's Ferry.[28]

Another large front hit the region October 5, washing out the roads, flooding the Pahreah, and leaving a foot of snow on Buckskin Mountain. October also brought indications that large-scale plans were being hatched by government agencies. Don Harris and a party of U.S. Geological Survey engineers landed at the ferry on the seventeenth, having come by boat from Linwood, which was near the junction of Henry's Fork and the Green and close to the Wyoming-Utah state line. The trip had been made to investigate the flows of the system's tributaries. On the twenty-fifth, the Bureau of Reclamation began improving the road from the highway to the ferry. The work was completed by November 7 and relatively heavy loads could be transported to the Colorado River. The weak link was the Pahreah River ford, and another flood down that drainage in late October once again rendered it impassable. The day after the new road was completed, another heavy rain washed the ford out and sent masses of Chinle mud down the Pahreah to insure the impassibility of the crossing. Hoover Dam might have tamed the Colorado but the Pahreah was as wild as ever. In mid-December, several Bureau of Reclamation employees arrived with boats and barges to set up a base at the ferry. Surveyors began working up river toward the Glen Canyon damsite. There had not been so much activity here since the days of LaRue and the Edison Company.

Jerry Johnson, unable to dismiss his vision of operating the Lee's Ferry Ranch, made a deal with Gus Griffin to live rent-free on the property, care for it, and receive the full benefit of anything he raised. Griffin now felt more at ease than when the place was vacant. On November 7, Jerry moved into the cabin between the Weaver house and the cemetery and began planning for large-scale farming during the coming year. He was happy at having use of the place without its responsibility.

The winter of 1946–47 did not come close to the last one the Klohrs had experienced at Lee's Ferry. The crest at the gage well did not freeze until December 30, but after that, and for the next month, it froze solidly at night and thawed but slightly during the day. The Colorado was frozen along both banks and was thick with ice. Unlike Ida Decker, Chris did not accompany Jim when he serviced the Little Colorado gages but remained at Lee's Ferry to observe weather and river conditions. At this time the gaging stations at Lee's Ferry and Grand Falls were considered the most important in Arizona.[29]

Nora Cundell had driven an ambulance during the war and endured her share of hardship and deprivation, all the while longing to return to her beloved land of color. She wrote the Lowreys, now living in Flagstaff, to ask if they could recommend a place that would board her for a dollar a day. Restrictions on taking more than small amounts of currency out of Britain made it impossible for her to pay as a normal tourist. Buck brought her letter to Chris and Jim Klohr, who decided she could bunk in the old Spencer cook cabin and take her meals with them.

Nora answered the glad tidings by sailing in late February 1947. She visited friends in New York and Chicago, then took the train to Flagstaff. Buck and Florence Lowrey brought her to Lee's Ferry and turned her over to the Klohrs in April. She was happy, and although saddle horses were not available, she walked mornings and early evenings and painted all day. She and Chris went up the canyon and on the bench. She captured some subjects in watercolor, intending to do them in oil when she returned to England. The artist reversed her outbound journey in September, having achieved her greatest attainable ambition.

Late in January 1947, workmen began digging a well to serve as a water supply for the Bureau of Reclamation's base camp. The camp itself was partly built by the end of February, and loads of drilling equipment were trucked in during March. Operations were directed from the office in Salt Lake City and the site was visited by a pair of officials on March 23. Damsite investigation was under full steam by the end of the month and a canyon work camp was established on the right-hand willow bar several miles above the ferry.

The largest river party to date traversed Glen Canyon and landed at Lee's Ferry on April 5. Consisting of forty-six men and boys—most of them Boy Scouts from Salt Lake City—the company had come from Hite. Their passage marked the beginning of large-group exploitation of the canyon environment. The party leader must have been hard pressed to find suitable bed space for his charges in some camps, and from this time on the disposal of human waste became a major problem in the canyons.[30]

Norman Nevills left Mexican Hat with his first party of the 1947 season on May 1. The San Juan River was running 1,200 cubic feet per second, and the four boats had to be pushed off silt bars into the Colorado River, which was running 16,900 cubic feet per second. The river rose rapidly after May 4, gaining approximately 15,000 cubic feet per second each day. When Nevills passed the Glen Canyon damsite below the mouth of Wahweap Creek, the drill barge, positioned by a cable stretched across the river, was careening and trailing a hundred-foot wake. As the four-boat, twelve-person party landed at the ferry on the morning of May 7, the discharge had jumped to 47,400 cubic feet per second. Jim Klohr greeted them, as he did most parties, and recorded their arrival in the station history. The river rose to 56,800 cubic feet per second the following day. The debris, which now was heavy, accumulated against the upstream beam of the drill barge, just as it had with John D. Lee's ferry. The barge capsized and the cable broke, dumping the drill derrick, tools, and cores into the river. The Bureau of Reclamation temporarily suspended the operation due to high water.

River touring appeared to be catching on with the public. Nevills, now acknowledged as the only successful commercial operator, had additional trips from Mexican Hat to Lee's Ferry scheduled for May 10, 19, 28, and June 6. The planning was so close that he soon reduced the normal seven-day trip to six days, and he often spent a good part of the night driving the boats back to Mexican Hat. By this time, he was making more interesting stops than those made by any other group. He bestowed his own names where there were none, and in some cases imposed names for tributaries he did not know. Examples include Nasja Creek, which he called "Redbud," Navajo Valley, which he called "Twilight Canyon," and Cottonwood Gulch, which he said was "Seventy-seven Mile Canyon." Glen Canyon place names that he bestowed were Hidden Passage, Mystery Canyon, Labyrinth Canyon, and Outlaw Cave. A mortal enemy was instrumental in getting Mystery Canyon changed to Anasazi, the old Mormon Cottonwood Gulch now is called Reflection Canyon, and Outlaw Cave was discarded in favor of Galloway Cave during Norm's lifetime.[31]

War-surplus neoprene inflated craft, used for Colorado River trips through Glen Canyon, began appearing at Lee's Ferry. Easily procurable, they answered the needs of people who didn't have the time or ability to construct hard-hulled boats. Generally it was conceded that inflatables could be used in the quiet waters of Glen Canyon but were not sufficient to take on the rapids of Cataract, Marble, and Grand Canyons; the 1938 experience of Amos Burg was ignored. Nevills especially was disdainful of the war surplus rafts, maintaining that hard-hulled boats were superior for big-water commercial use and neoprene was for amateurs.

Nevills now had settled on July 12 as a starting date for his Grand Canyon boat trips. He preferred to run on a medium to low falling stage, regardless of the snowfall, or lack of it, in the Rockies. His parties assembled at the Marble Canyon Lodge a day or two before takeoff and had a final taste of relative luxury before roughing it for three weeks. He had built a new boat, the *Sandra*, and now had a fleet of four "cataract" boats. The 1947 party of twelve was accompanied by three guests as far as Badger Rapid, where they walked out via Jackass Canyon. They were Norm's wife Doris, Barry Goldwater, and his friend Bill Saufley.[32]

Glen Canyon continued to see heavy activity, mostly by private parties traveling the river trail to Rainbow Bridge and disembarking at Lee's Ferry. Jack Frost, who accompanied Norman Nevills on his first exploration of the San Juan in March 1934, made two trips from Mexican Hat in July 1947. Heavy rains in August more than doubled the Colorado's flow to 45,000 cubic feet per second, and the intake of mud caused many fish to die. Harry Aleson ran a party from Hite to the ferry in October and later in the month took a seven-man neoprene and a passenger from Green River, Utah, to Hite. His probably was the second inflatable to run Cataract Canyon.

In November 1947, the Survey remodeled Dodge's old house—an improved Spencer building—into a new sediment laboratory. A concrete floor, a sink, and shelves were added, together with a butane stove and a desk. At the same time a new hydrographer's residence, eighteen by thirty feet, was completed. It was made of rocks salvaged from the demolished Spencer buildings and was given a concrete floor, asphalt paper roof, new ceiling, and plastered interior. A modern bath with hot and cold running water was installed. It was furnished with a butane stove, refrigerator, water heater, an oil-heating stove, table and four chairs, sofa, twin beds with innerspring mattresses, pillows, and a chest of drawers. It was a far cry from Cockroft's willow and box furnishings. Another five-hundred gallon water-storage tank was installed alongside the existing one. Concrete floors were added to both the front and back porches of the old residence and a butane water heater was installed in the kitchen.

The Art Greene clan had worked hard to enlarge facilities at the lodge. An airstrip was hacked out south of the highway, and the gas station was enlarged to house a trading post and restaurant. They could not push river trips to Rainbow Bridge because their transportation was not suitable for commercial purposes. Hubbell had Seth Smith of Phoenix build a special flat-bottomed aluminum boat during the winter of 1947-48 and sent it out to Marble Canyon. It was air-driven by a one hundred fifty horsepower Franklin engine in an effort to neutralize the excessive wear of the silt on submerged bearings; steering was done by pivoting the engine. But it, too, proved to be underpowered. They made a few trips with passengers, but it took so long to reach the mouth of Forbidden Canyon that the efforts were regarded as failures. Hubbell then withdrew from the boating phase, leaving the Greenes to experiment as they pleased.

Art and his sons-in-law discussed the problem at length and finally had Seth Smith build another aluminum boat to their specifications. It had an inverted vee bottom, was 8 feet wide, 28 feet long, and 24 inches deep and was air-driven, this time by a 240-horsepower 1946 Lycoming engine. The propeller was too large for the engine and would not attain the required revolutions; it blew a valve in testing and made no trips. They replaced it with a 450-horsepower Pratt & Whitney radial engine and the boat would plane with a light load. Additional tests resulted in changing the centerline of thrust and adding an 18-inch airtank on the stern to prevent

From left to right, two paying passengers, Earl Johnson, Art Greene, and P. T. Reilly in Greene's airboat, June 25, 1952 (*P. T. Reilly Collection, Cline Library, Northern Arizona University*).

settling during planing. This boat was successful; it put the Greenes in the business of "hydro-herding" tourists to Rainbow Bridge.

Jerry and Price Johnson farmed the middle and upper ranches in 1947, raising sufficient melons to bring them eleven hundred dollars at one and one-half cents per pound. Indians and whites came to the ranch to pick up small quantities, and the Johnsons hauled loads of melons to the reservation. It was the most successful venture in private enterprise since this generation of Johnsons had occupied the ranch.

The year 1948 saw increased commercial traffic down the San Juan and Glen Canyon. As the number of neoprene raft parties increased dramatically, sanitation at the more popular bars such as the mouths of Lake and Forbidden Canyons became alarming problems. No agency maintained a set of ground rules and many travelers were novices at living in the open. Glen Canyon became a crowded river freeway through the heart of the rough country. Nevills ran a full schedule of trips from Mexican Hat, and started his usual Grand Canyon party from Lee's Ferry on July 12. The old ferry now saw more people leaving or entering the river than at any previous time in its history.

Anticipating the postwar tourist boom, Maggie and Riley Baker mortgaged their Badger Creek property in February 1945 to build necessary improvements. Unfortunately, the improvements were too homespun to attract customers from the more modern competition, and Marble

Canyon Lodge siphoned the bulk of the business. Their part of the boom amounted to little more than a pop. Yet a lean Texan, C. H. "Buck" Rodgers, thought the place had possibilities the Bakers didn't see and on May 21, 1948, he purchased the property.[33] Maggie and Riley remained as temporary proprietors since Buck Rodgers' other interests prevented him from taking immediate possession.

Charles Roemer, said to have been a Hungarian engineer, arrived by bus at Marble Canyon Lodge on October 19. He was carrying an uninflated six-man life raft wrapped in a blanket, but he had no oars, paddles, supplies, or safety equipment. He purchased a sack of dry onions, some raisins, and two loaves of bread, then caught a ride to the ferry. He embarked on the river next morning and started downstream. Tourists saw him float past the suspension bridge at Bright Angel on the twenty-fourth, but no one ever saw him again. It was a spectacular way to commit suicide.

The winter of 1948–1949 was very severe with snow blocking many roads on the reservation. Air drops of food for both people and animals were made to alleviate suffering, as ground traffic was restricted to keeping major highways open. The snowpack in the Rockies was unusually heavy and all indicators pointed to an above average runoff.

One of the region's most ardent admirers paid a final visit in May 1949. It is not known whether Nora Cundell was aware that a malignancy was spreading in her body when she came to Lee's Ferry in 1947, but if she was, she kept it to herself. She died in England on August 3, 1948, at age fifty-nine, having stipulated that her ashes be deposited in the land closest to her heart. Her sister and brother-in-law, Vi and Charles Eaton, brought the remains and a small brass plate to Marble Canyon. About two dozen people were present when Preacher Smith gave a brief eulogy and scattered her ashes on the chocolate-colored Moenkopi shale. Nora Lucy Mobray Cundell had returned to her beloved land of color. The Greenes later installed the brass plate on the large boulder beside which the service was held.[34]

River tourist traffic was almost as high as the runoff. Both the Green and Colorado watersheds had heavy snowpacks and the melt was extended by a later than normal spring. The river peaked at Lee's Ferry on June 22 at 115,300 cubic feet per second. Nevills ran a full schedule of San Juan trips that ended at the ferry; Aleson, now backed by wealthy wheat farmer Charlie Larabee, made several trips. The greatest increase came from private parties, who ran Glen Canyon without benefit of guides. The ferry was the exit point, and more people visited in 1949 than had colonized Arizona in 1876.

Lee's Ferry was the point of embarkation for three parties that went through Grand Canyon that summer. The first of these started downstream on June 12; Ed Hudson and four companions drove the *Esmeralda II* to Lake Mead in five days—the first motorboat to make the traverse. Their main objective was to deposit gasoline caches at strategic places in conjunction with an effort to make an upstream run. Although the upstream attempt failed, the party contributed numbers ninety-nine, one hundred, and one hundred one to have gone all the way through Grand Canyon in eighty years of river running. The second was a four-boat, eight-person party in which Bert Loper, Don Harris, Jack Brennan, and Harry Aleson each carried one passenger. It was planned for Loper to celebrate his eightieth birthday at the end of the trip. Instead, on July 8 the old man capsized after a possible heart attack twenty-four and one-half miles below the ferry, and lost his life. Harry Aleson took the first ten-man life raft through Grand Canyon on this occasion. Norm Nevills made his seventh traverse of the canyon by leading a four-boat, twelve-person party to Lake Mead. It was an uneventful passage during which they looked for, but failed to find, Loper's body.[35]

A legacy of Essy Bowers and her "I Am" cult appeared at the ranch in June. Eighteen of the rank and file who claimed membership in the sect came supposedly with the intention of forming a colony at Mesken Bar. They did not accept the fact that she had sold the ranch on contract, and claimed the right to use the place's resources. With no means of sustenance, they set up a camp in the willows across the Pahreah and helped themselves to Jerry Johnson's truck garden, and he, always generous to a fault, made no effort to deny them. The group had been there about a month and had exhausted the supplies when Gus Griffin, based at the Leupp facility, had occasion to visit Kaibito. After finishing his business, he went to the ranch to see how Johnson was getting along and learned of the uninvited visitors. Incensed at the abuse of Jerry's generosity, he went to The Gap and telephoned Sheriff Francis at Flagstaff. Gus and the sheriff rounded up all eighteen, took them to town, and told them to "get going." This ended the drain on the supplies but it made no difference because nothing was left. Moreover, Jerry had a severe hernia; he was alone and in no condition to shift for himself.

A minor flood came down the Pahreah on July 11 while the Klohrs were in Tucson. Glen Johnson went to check the gage and found Jerry weak from hunger, not having eaten for several days. His hernia was troubling him and his only resource was a barrel of creek water for drinking. He had crawled to some shade on the bank of the stream when the gager came upon him. Glen made him comfortable in his cabin, gave him something to eat, and got word of his situation to Harold Bogan, who telephoned Jerry's half-brother Jody in Kanab.

Jody borrowed a friend's pickup and, accompanied by his son and Jerry's brother Elmer, picked him up on July 14. They arranged for his son Warren to meet them in Zion and take his father to the Iron County Hospital at Cedar City. He was admitted on the sixteenth, appeared to be recovering, but succumbed to peritonitis from a strangulated hernia on the twenty-seventh. Although Jerry was not born at the ferry, and did not die there, he didn't miss either by very much and it is certain that his heart was bound inextricably to the place where he spent most of his life.[36] His death ended Johnson residency at the ranch that had begun in 1875.

Norman and Doris Nevills died when their plane crashed at Mexican Hat on September 19, 1949. Two of his boatmen, Frank Wright and Jim Rigg, purchased the assets of the estate and continued the trips under the name "Mexican Hat Expeditions." River trips definitely had moved from the expedition stage to ordinary commercial ventures, but nobody quibbled the point and the river-traveling public preferred to believe it was participating in something more glamorous than it actually was. The new operators followed the Nevills format when the 1950 season began.

Up to this time, relations between Ramon Hubbell and Art Greene had been very cordial. The failure of the two experimental boats to make profitable upstream trips to Forbidden Canyon, along with Greene's success after Hubbell's withdrawal from this phase, caused Ramon to propose an adjustment to their agreement. The split had been fifty-fifty, but Ramon Hubbell wanted a higher percentage or to share equally in the river. The impasse was resolved that fall when the Greenes concluded a deal with the Hade Church family for the Russell property at Soap Creek. They learned in time that their purchase did not include the creek itself, so they began building their new facility a quarter-mile down the road on the north side of the highway. Water was trucked by tank from Navajo Spring.

Hubbell was experiencing a cash-flow problem when the Greenes moved, and their departure triggered his decision to liquidate some of the company holdings. He sold one hundred acres of land near Winslow and five trading posts to Kyle Bayles, a Winslow attorney and land developer. Marble Canyon was one of the assets that changed ownership and, along with the Winslow acreages, remained in Bayles' hands as he quickly re-sold the other four trading posts. He operated the Marble Canyon Lodge with his own manager, sent supplies out from Winslow, and visited the place monthly.

Glen Canyon continued to be the waterway bearing the heaviest traffic, and some rivermen prophesied that uncontrolled sanitation would lead to disease outbreaks of epidemic proportions. The beautiful plunge pools were used for swimming and even bathing, yet others drank from them. Some people considered it safe to drink from small tributary streams that ran in the depths of narrow sandstone gorges, ignoring the fact that others also waded upstream in ventures of exploration. Although many travelers arrived at Lee's Ferry with dysentery, more serious ailments failed to appear.

Wright and Rigg ran a full schedule of San Juan trips and kept the traditional Nevills departure date of July 12 to traverse Grand Canyon. Thirty days before, again leaving on June 12, Ed Hudson and his *Esmeralda II*, with O. R. Marston in a stock Chris Craft nineteen-foot cruiser, attempted to repeat the 1949 feat. Human error defeated the *Esmeralda II*.[37] After abandoning the boat, the owner and his son were airlifted out of the canyon less than a hundred miles below Lee's Ferry, as Marston took the rest of the party to Lake Mead. The year 1950 added only seven names to those who made the Grand traverse—barely more than half those of the preceding year.

Glen E. Johnson replaced Jim Klohr as resident hydrographer in May 1949, but Jim remained on the job until March 1951, when he was replaced by E. P. Croft. Klohr, his gaging days over, then became a field engineer out of the Tucson office. His tenure at Lee's Ferry had been longer than Dodge's. Improvements were steady and not confined to technical equipment. In May 1950 the stones from Charlie Spencer's old buildings were incorporated in a new building for housing guests. Only sixteen by nineteen feet, it consisted of a bedroom, closet, and a modern bathroom connected to a common septic tank and leaching field. That fall, a new outside gage rod was installed on the gage well to allow the 8 A.M. gage height to be read by telescope from the residence area. This saved crossing the river to take the reading, although the recorder still had to be serviced.

E. C. LaRue's old dream, a Glen Canyon dam, had never died but merely slumbered. The Bureau of Reclamation was confident that obtaining Congressional approval for the project was only a matter of time. As the political pot bubbled, the main activity at the ferry consisted of people leaving or embarking on the river and the normal stream-gaging work.

The Art Greene clan built a tourist facility, which they called "Cliff Dwellers," just west of Soap Creek. They offered a traveler lodging, meals, sundry groceries, and a service station that gathered the bulk of the southbound business. Although Marble Canyon remained a strong competitor, sales were hampered by a succession of managers, few of whom remained more than three months. Nevertheless, the new cabins on the south side of the road that the Greenes had begun were completed on February 24, 1950, and the facility began remaining open twenty-four hours to meet the competition. Lowrey Spring could not provide sufficient output for full operation so water was hauled from Navajo Spring. Thus, with both Marble Canyon and Cliff Dwellers drawing from this source—never copious at best—there was not enough left for the Indians. The water was on the Navajo Reservation and as early as December 1949, rumors were circulated that Navajo Spring would be closed to commercial withdrawals.

Buck Rodgers assumed active operation of Vermilion Cliffs at the end of June 1950 as Riley and Maggie Baker moved to their ranch near Kingman. At the same time, the business of all three establishments was helped by an influx of prospectors searching for uranium. Hundreds of claims were filed during the next five years, and large sums of money changed hands, some of them in tax write-off schemes. Art Greene benefited in one such sale and the claim eventually was deeded back to him without out a shovel of earth being moved. There were two major prospects, the "Sam" on the bench near Lowrey Spring and the "Lehneer" across the creek from Sid Wilson's old ranch. Two other claims were developed in Shinarump channels from which ore was mined; the "Red Wing," about four miles up the creek, and "El Pequito," nearly a mile due west of the Griffin ranch house. Only the latter ever shipped ore.[38] The main effect of the uranium boom in this area was a financial shot in the arm for the struggling businesses along the base of the Vermilion Cliffs. Even a "shoot 'em up" movie was made but apparently never released.[39]

Jerry Johnson's death left the Griffin ranch open to vandalism. Gus feared that the many people scrambling around the ledges with Geiger counters would take advantage of the vacant ranch, and he made a deal with an old cowboy, Claude Delbridge of Winslow, to live at the place. Claude, a bachelor, had about thirty head of horses which he could run on the Pahreah range using the permits that Leo Weaver had wangled out of Ed Fisher. Delbridge was a character who would have delighted Zane Grey. He played the fiddle, was familiar with the classics—even had a small library of good books—quoted scripture, and could discuss Bach and Beethoven. He was not alcoholic but enjoyed a casual drink and went on an occasional binge. He moved into an old cabin between the blacksmith shop and the river, but when the cabin burned down he changed to the cabin that mistakenly was—and still is—attributed to John D. Lee. He was a good caretaker for almost a decade but never attempted to farm.

River touring picked up considerably in 1951. Traffic continued to be heavy in Glen Canyon, and Art Greene's air-driven boat made repeated trips to Forbidden Canyon. Approximately four thousand people had visited Rainbow Bridge from the time of its official discovery in 1909 through the end of World War II, most of them having come overland either from Kayenta or Rainbow Lodge. During the five years following the war, when river traffic increased so dramatically, nearly thirty-five hundred visits were recorded in the register book. Overland trips still were made, but the major assault now was by boat from the Colorado River, both downstream and upstream from Lee's Ferry.

Grand Canyon traverses increased to twenty-nine in 1951, almost three times the greatest previous number—ten—in 1927. Two parties of these canyoneers deserve special attention. Brothers Jim and Bob Rigg, who had two and one previous traverses to their credit, made a speed run in a standard Nevills sadiron. They left Lee's Ferry at 5:30 A.M. on June 9 on a favorable flow of 43,000 cubic feet per second. Alternating at the oars, they did not stop until they reached Mile 108.2 at 7:15 P.M. After some badly needed sleep, they resumed their journey at 6:15 A.M. on a slightly falling river, rowing for seventy-one miles, where they spent ten minutes examining Lava Falls. They ran the rapid successfully on the left and rowed on, clearing Diamond Creek at dusk. The last rapids were run by the light of a scant quarter-moon, and then it became difficult to keep their boat in the middle of the canyon-bound waters of Lake Mead. They judged they landed about Mile 255 at 12:30 A.M. on the eleventh. They departed at 6:15 A.M., cleared the Grand Wash Cliffs at 10:30, and met Bill Belknap in a power boat about a mile off Pearce Ferry less than an hour later. Total elapsed time was fifty-two hours and forty-one minutes. It was a remarkable feat that could only have been done by young men in good physical condition.[40]

The other group that merits attention was put together by Dock Marston, who led five power craft on a Grand Canyon traverse. There were fourteen men in the five boats that left Lee's Ferry on June 8. Three of the motorboats were inboards, and two were outboards; the latter, driven by Rod Sanderson and Jimmy Jordan, were the first outboard motors to power boats through Grand Canyon. The party was on Lake Mead on June 19.[41] The remaining canyoneers were members of commercial parties who accomplished nothing except a traverse—for a price.

Sometime during the uranium boom, vandals burned the cabin built by Sid Wilson and Owen Clark. Inadvertently, they also destroyed part of the sternwheeler *Charles H. Spencer* and the cowhides that Lige Moore had wanted so badly to examine. Evidently the arsonists coveted the long pipe Sid had liberated from Spencer's mining equipment and used for a ridgepole, because no trace of it was found in the charred remains. The finger of suspicion pointed to those working in the Lehneer or Red Wing claims, but nobody cared enough to pursue the matter.

With the success of the Hudson and Marston experiments using power fresh in mind, Wright and Rigg added two twenty-one foot inboard motor cruisers to their fleet of oar-powered craft. Late delivery of the stock units almost scuttled the schedule, but the two partners left Lee's Ferry about noon on May 27, 1952, with a modicum of paying passengers and freeloaders. The river flow was a favorable 58,100 cubic feet per second, which changed but little when they reached Separation Canyon at 7:15 P.M. on the twenty-ninth. The venture was a success in every way except financial. Jim Rigg took one of the cruisers to accompany the oar-powered trip in July, but the combination did not prove to be practical. Although a few additional trips were made through 1955, the public never accepted the quick runs by motorboat and this phase declined to the point that it finally was eliminated.

The year 1952 also saw the first traverse of Grand Canyon by Georgie White, who rowed a ten-man raft from Lee's Ferry to Lake Mead. After gaining experience and learning the places of interest on the San Juan and Glen Canyon from Harry Aleson, Georgie then launched herself in the guide business with "share the expense" prices. She plowed her profits back into the enterprise and soon was running her ten-man rafts on all popular stretches of the river system. A good grasp of the value of television publicity brought her a volume of business that had eluded Nevills and his successors. Her low prices made Georgie's style of canyoneering popular with the large segment of the public that could not afford the prices of her predecessors. She thus appropriated the bulk of the river business and instigated large parties in the canyons. Nineteen first Grand Canyon traverses were recorded in 1952, all but two of which were commercial ventures.

Despite below-average runoff in 1953, the combination of commercial, non-commercial, and technical river trips resulted in a total of thirty-one traverses, the most to date for any given year. The winter of

1953–54 was even milder than the preceding one and the entire upper-basin watershed was deficient in snowpack, resulting in a runoff almost as low as in 1914. Peaking early, the river registered 33,800 cubic feet per second at Lee's Ferry on May 26. Despite the projected low water and the cancellation of some scheduled traverses, two parties—among several—made complete runs to Lake Mead and set a pattern for future river running.

Forecasts predicting the low runoff, plus his own scheduled trips on the Green and Yampa, caused Bus Hatch to leave Lee's Ferry on April twenty-fourth, accompanied by his capable boatman Sylvester "Smus" Allen, Frank Hatch, and eight customers. Bus had experimented with U.S. Army bridge-pontoons on the Yampa and upper Green and concluded that if he could take one through the Grand Canyon, he could use it anywhere. When the party shoved off from Lee's Ferry it utilized a twenty-eight foot neoprene pontoon and a ten-man life raft, each pushed along by an outboard motor. Despite wrapping the pontoon around the island at Bedrock Rapid, the trip was successful and the landing at Temple Bar on May 2, 1954, marked the first of hundreds of traverses by this type of craft.[42] This marked the onset of the hydraulic tour-bus exploitation of Grand Canyon—the large payload-vehicle of the commercial operators.

An interesting story associated with the Hatch trip is that of Les "Buckethead" Jones and his ambition to make a solo run through Grand Canyon. Essentially a loner, Les was a professional boatman for Bus Hatch until he was fired (by not being rehired) because of his strange behavior toward the paying customers. When on his own, he developed a canoe with oarlocks mounted on outriggers. By employing oars instead of paddles, he could generate more power, yet his craft was not stable in big water. He then devised an arrangement to house a movie camera inside of a lard pail that was mounted on a football helmet; the lard pail kept the camera dry and had a window for the lens. The camera was set in motion by squeezing and releasing a rubber bulb held in his mouth, thus allowing him to work the oars and take movies simultaneously—and providing him with a nickname unique in river annals. A capsize in the same rapid that took the life of Bert Loper nearly cost Jones his life in 1953, but he saved the canoe and most of his outfit and continued down river without the burden of his bucket. In fact, he never used it again. When he reached Bright Angel he mothballed his equipment for the season and went up the trail. Learning that Hatch planned to run a pontoon and a ten-man through the Canyon in 1954, Jones left Bright Angel a day or two ahead of the commercial party, using it as a safety factor to support his "solo" run. When Bus had his difficulty at Bedrock, Jones was instrumental in salvaging the outfit and continued just ahead for the rest of the trip.[43]

Ideas sometimes make their appearances in diffused places almost simultaneously. Two members of the Aspen, Colorado, Ski Patrol, Chuck Bolte and Earl Eaton, conceived the idea of running a bridge-pontoon neoprene raft from Aspen to Boulder Dam. Such a run would take them about forty miles from Roaring Fork to Glenwood Canyon and the Colorado River. They knew they would encounter some rough going in Westwater, Cataract, Marble, and Grand Canyons but had faith that the thirty-foot pontoon, which was named *Driftwood*, a seventy-five horsepower outboard, a smaller auxiliary motor, and a drum of gasoline would carry them through. Although they were young and good outdoorsmen, they lacked river experience. They left Aspen barely a month after Bus Hatch shoved off from Lee's Ferry, and after three weeks and a loss of nearly forty-eight hundred feet in elevation arrived at the pioneer crossing.

While replenishing supplies and re-moisturizing their dehydrated bodies, they met Leroy R. Byers and Carl Gage, a pair of young uranium prospectors from Los Angeles. A deal was struck whereby the four joined forces for the final leg to Lake Mead. Being unaware that the National Park Service required a permit to pass through Grand Canyon, not having one, and upon being told that a sheriff would appear next morning to stop them from continuing the trip, they spent the afternoon getting supplies loaded. It was nearly dark when they shoved off. Although they did not always know where they were or what was coming up, they cleared the Grand Wash Cliffs and tied up at Lake Mead Marina on July 11. The full journey covered about eight hundred sixty-five miles and the novices had less trouble than the trip led by professionals.[44] Moreover, two of the men had no lifejackets but improvised by lashing air mattresses around their waists.

The two pontoon trips in 1954 sent a message that few commercial operators failed to read. It was clear that, combined with outboard motors, the neoprene monsters could carry a larger payload and recover from boating errors with fewer consequences than any type of craft that had appeared on the river. All that remained was to regulate the specter of unlimited exploitation of Grand Canyon now looming on the horizon, and solve several other problems pertaining to human intrusion. Solution of these problems was several years in coming and the arrival was made possible in a roundabout manner.

LaRue's dream of a major dam in the sandstone world of Glen Canyon had undergone two serious investigations by the Bureau of Reclamation, which needed the project to keep its employees functioning. Helped by proponents of federal projects who desired the resultant economic benefits, politicians counted votes and lined up on one side or the other. Opposition was provided by several conservationist groups who resisted the building of any additional dams on the entire Green-Colorado system.

In 1948, the four upper-basin states agreed on the division of their share of the water under the Colorado River Compact. This meant that storage reservoirs would be needed to catch and hold surplus water in the high-runoff years to insure that the lower basin would receive its allotment in dry years. It was the next logical step after the lower basin problem had been solved by the high dam in Black Canyon. After several years of wrangling, which ranged from local areas to state capitols and Washington, the issue was resolved when the conservationists withdrew their opposition to a dam in Glen Canyon if their political foes would insure the preservation of Echo Park and the Yampa River. The trade-off was not quite that simple; the Colorado River Storage Project Act also provided for major dams at Flaming Gorge on the Green River, Curencanti on the Gunnison River, and Navajo on the San Juan River, plus eleven upper-basin irrigation projects. The entire bill authorized an expenditure of 760 million federal dollars. The House of Representatives and the Senate approved the measure on March 28, 1956, and President Eisenhower signed it April 11. Preliminary work began immediately and seven months later, on October 15, the president pressed a telegraph key in the White House setting off symbolic blasts at Glen Canyon and Flaming Gorge to signify the start of the projects.

An era's end was in sight and the once little-known and difficult canyon country was about to be invaded by hordes of motorized tourists. Glen Canyon's days were numbered, and even Lee's Ferry would never be the same. LaRue would not have been entirely pleased, although his argument for a key dam at Glen Canyon was vindicated in part. Even after the Boulder Canyon project was settled in 1926, LaRue was clamoring for total development and was in conflict with his superior, A. P. Davis. Muzzled by U.S. Geological Survey Director George Otis Smith in June 1925, he found his position untenable and resigned a year later to join a private engineering firm. He died in 1948 before it was politically expedient to adopt his views or acknowledge his contribution to the development of the Colorado River. It was just as well because, as in the case of John D. Lee, LaRue filled a need and then became expendable.

16

Big Brother Takes Over

EVEN BEFORE CONGRESS APPROVED THE FATEFUL BILL AUTHORIZING THE Colorado River Storage Project, men were gambling on how the dice would fall and preparing for the future they were betting would come. Aerial photography covered the country in 1951; the field checks of new topographic maps were made in 1953 and 1954. The cartographers were housed at Art Greene's Cliff Dwellers establishment on both occasions. Art turned on all his homespun personality and was able to examine the surveyors' maps. Thus he had advance choice and filed on five school sections at the 3,840-foot level one-half mile west of Wahweap Creek, west of the Colorado River, before the preliminary work got underway at either the damsite or the potential townsite on Manson Mesa, east of the river. Even when full, the reservoir behind the dam would not rise above the 3,700-foot level, so the properties Greene filed on would be safe from inundation—and they had excellent views. Art repeated the gamble of Buck Lowrey, albeit in a more complicated situation with higher stakes.

Reaching his future development was not easy. Greene had to travel west to Jacob Lake and Kanab where the pavement ended. Two sandy ruts bore eastward toward old Pahreah townsite; the Cockscombs were crossed at Catstairs Canyon. The relatively good ruts ended at the Pahreah River, where he changed to a jeep as the road grew progressively worse. Just as the sand became impassable, even for a jeep, he had an Army surplus halftrack vehicle to traverse the final leg to Wahweap. Approximately one hundred sixty miles were required to cover an airline distance of twenty-five miles.

The Greenes purchased several old Forest Service cabins and hauled them to the school sections with the halftrack, intending to convert them to motel units. Two Navajo masons were hired to face the shacks with native rock, while food was provided by an old English actor named Joe Breiting, who dispensed meals from a ten by fourteen foot tent. Joe interspersed his flapjacks and beans with bits from Gilbert and Sullivan, Hamlet, or Macbeth. Wood and water were hauled in. A single-hole outhouse, open to the north and east, gave the occupant panoramic views of the Kaiparowits, Gunsight, Navajo Mountain, and Tower Butte. The luxurious views of undisturbed plateau scenery, of course, were only temporary.

439

Wahweap was the first commercial enterprise on either side of the river in the immediate area.[1] On the east side of the Colorado, a rough road left the pavement at The Gap and went north to Copper Mine, where another sandy track had been scraped out to Manson Mesa and the future townsite for the dam builders. However, the road of the future was to start at Bitter Springs and head toward Antelope Pass, which was a more direct route to the mesa. Although a few workmen were camped at the future townsite, not an electric light could be seen from the Wahweap side in 1956.

By December 1956, a full-fledged struggle by land developers was underway. Utah interests wanted a town built in Utah, close to the damsite. Flagstaff people became upset at the proposal, holding out for a town in Arizona on the east side of the river. All land between Glen Canyon damsite and the Utah border was owned by the federal government or the state of Arizona and had been reserved by the Bureau of Reclamation, except for the five sections of state land that were leased to Art Greene. On December 8, 1956, State Land Commissioner Roger Ernst stated that the Greene leases would be canceled at the Bureau's request.[2] This possibility failed to deter Greene, who proceeded with his building program. The location of the damsite dictated the construction town to be built close by in Arizona. Utah developers were mollified by a promise of several development sites in their state when the reservoir was a fact. Early in 1957, it was announced that Manson Mesa would be the location of the federal government construction town and that it would be named after John C. Page, commissioner of the Bureau of Reclamation from 1936 to 1943.[3]

Blasting at the damsite necessitated closing the Colorado River to navigation from Mile 18 to Lee's Ferry on January 5, 1957. Simultaneously, a dirt road was constructed to Cane Creek, where boats coming through Glen Canyon had to exit; this was the first time, except when the river was frozen, that traffic had been cut, decreasing tourist usage of Lee's Ferry. The closure halted the Greene boat trips to Rainbow Bridge from Lee's Ferry. A week later the post office was re-established at Marble Canyon, with Elmer A. Whelan as postmaster. Commercial interests from Flagstaff, Fredonia, and Kanab were optimistic that an economic wave of prosperity was about to wash this part of the Arizona Strip.

In late April, the prime contract to build Glen Canyon Dam was awarded to Merritt-Chapman and Scott Corporation, and in a few days work started on the Glen Canyon Bridge. When it became apparent that rim-to-rim access was needed, a steel cable-link mesh footbridge was built. Suspended 700 feet above the river, and 1,280 feet long, it allowed a view of the river with every step—not a facility for one afflicted with acrophobia. It was completed in November, but some of the workmen were never able to use it.

The question of whether the Colorado River Compact had allotted more water than the drainage system provided began to nag some hydrographers. On April 25, 1956, the level of Lake Mead fell to an all-time low of 1,083 feet above sea level. The current was all the way into Iceberg Canyon, while silty water and masses of driftwood extended to Sandy Point.[4] In contrast, the Colorado River at Lee's Ferry peaked on June 12, 1957, at a discharge of 126,000 cubic feet per second. This influx of runoff brought the level of Lake Mead up nearly seventy feet on July 1, 1957. It was a last defiant growl from the muddy giant before enduring another shackle; the 1957 flood was the biggest of the last half of the twentieth century.[5]

Gus Griffin retired from the Indian Service and on March 6, 1958, he and his wife Ramona opened the Weaver house for their residence. Claude Delbridge, now nearing eighty, continued to live in one of the cabins, while his horses ran free on the bench and in the canyon. Both Claude and the Griffins were glad to have company. The ferry was not as lonely as it had been, since it was visited in season by river runners and the resident hydrographer came and went as needed. But the place had barely been discovered by the American tourist.

Griffin's occupation of his ranch ended the intermittent residency of one of Lee's Ferry's more colorful characters. Jerry Johnson had become acquainted with Willard Dale in Hurricane and, as was his nature, invited him to visit "my farm" at the ferry. Dale, also known as "Red Wolf" and "Golden Jesus," was a throwback to an earlier time. He wore dirty buckskins, his red hair hung to his shoulders, he was seldom seen without his rifle, and he was a prodigious walker and hunter. His steel-rimmed glasses were exceptionally thick, but he was an excellent marksman and was adept at living off the land. He came to Hurricane to dance with the Paiutes during their two-week powwow, poached to feed himself, and avoided most other people. He lived in what the local residents called "the Outlaw Shack," one of the old outbuildings on the Griffin ranch. He related some rather wild tales that no one openly disputed. He imposed on Jerry Johnson but backed off from tangling with Gus Griffin.

In the spring of 1958, Gaylord L. Staveley, now married to Joan, the elder of the two Nevills daughters, launched a campaign to have the reservoir behind Glen Dam named "Lake Nevills." He compiled a dossier on his late father-in-law's accomplishments and made extensive mailings, but his efforts really never got off the ground. On November 18, 1959, the Department of the Interior announced that the impounded body of water would be named "Lake Powell" in honor of Major John Wesley Powell, leader of the first two exploring parties into Glen Canyon. On April 18, 1958, the Glen Canyon National Recreation Area was established by agreement with the Bureau of Reclamation, to be administered by the National Park Service. Already plans were underway to promote certain areas for development, among them Wahweap, Hall's Crossing, Bullfrog, Hite, and Lee's Ferry. It was even rumored that the Navajo Nation planned a resort on the reservation side of the reservoir.[6]

E. C. Moore was among those rushing to get in on the ground floor of the boom the commercial interests considered to be upon them. He leased a parcel from Kyle Bayles and constructed a block building east of the Marble Canyon installation. Started July 1, the place became known as the "Dinty Moore Steak House." The boom did not materialize as Moore expected and he defaulted; eventually the building was razed. Leo Weaver's relocated crossing of the Pahreah River continued to be periodically impassable due to frequent flooding. On September 12, 1958, the Pahreah River flooded with a peak of 11,500 cubic feet per second, and the annual runoff that year was among the highest yields of the century.

The right diversion tunnel had been completed on October 1, 1956. Twenty-eight months later, on February 11, 1959, the Colorado was forced into a new channel for more than one-half mile. The factors that made this possible were the diversion tunnel and two coffer dams, which enabled the excavation work for the dam's base to begin. Nine days later, on February 20, 1959, the Glen Canyon Bridge was dedicated and opened to the public. An area that was considered most difficult for Mormon pioneers to cross now had two great bridges over the Colorado within twenty miles of each other.[7]

Later that spring, Claude Delbridge returned to Winslow. The aged Texas cowboy had spent eight years at the Griffin ranch, but he was too old to live at such an isolated location. Unable to round up his stock, he left them on the open range by right of the permits Leo Weaver had wangled out of Ed Fisher. Having no heirs and feeling that his days were short, Claude gave the herd to Dave Branch, who had befriended him. North of the San Francisco Peaks, Ed Fisher was running the 77 Ranch for Hubert Richardson; he advised the young cowboy to get a bill of sale from Delbridge and he would help him gather the animals. In December 1960, Ed and Dave came for the Delbridge horses. The Indians had been running them and had captured the colts; the remaining animals were wild. The two men were out fifteen days but finally got them trailing along the ledge. They brought them off the bench at Badger Creek and drove them to the Vaughn-Robinson corral near Soap Creek. They split the herd, each getting fifteen head.[8] Now, the range around Lee's Ferry had no livestock for the first time since J. D. Lee arrived.

Hank Young had been managing Marble Canyon Lodge when Fisher and Branch went to gather the stock, but he either had quit or been discharged when they brought the herd down. Kyle Bayles had died from a sudden heart attack in 1959, leaving his estate to his three daughters. They operated in unison for a year but it did not work out, so they split the assets three ways. The middle daughter, Jane Foster, was practicing law in California, and emerged from the settlement with the Marble Canyon property as part of her share. With a law degree from the University of Missouri, and having passed her bar examination in California, the astute young woman looked her acquisition over and concluded she had three major problems to solve—water, power, and waste disposal. As she went to work, it was clear that a new breed of management had taken over.

Dam construction ground to a halt when a labor dispute over remote-area subsistence pay caused the work force to go on strike July 6,

1959. The men were out for 169 days, and Page took on the appearance of a ghost town. Many workers pulled their campers out of the trailer park and went touring; others took shorter trips such as to Lee's Ferry. Gus Griffin related how the strikers would pull into his yard and party into the small hours. Once he was awakened by a woman screaming and found her drunken companion beating her; Gus threw them off the property. Others had no qualms about pulling in to park under the large trees and trashing the place. This was the first time such problems had occurred at the ranch in its eighty-seven year history. The strike finally was settled on December 11, with the men agreeing to return to work on January 4, 1960, for an increase of fifty cents per hour in lieu of subsistence pay.[9]

For a brief period, residents of the Arizona Strip were called on to salvage light aircraft. On July 2, 1955, Art Greene and Earl Johnson were taking a group in their powerboat upriver to the mouth of Forbidden Canyon, where they walked to Rainbow Bridge. Included in the party were Ted Park and Ralph Gray, staff men for *National Geographic Magazine*. In lower Glen Canyon, a Piper Cub, its engine sputtering, flew over them and headed down river. The lone pilot, a prospector making a Geiger-counter check of the canyon for uranium, knew he was in trouble but he hoped to reach the dirt strip at Marble Canyon Lodge. His engine quit completely, and he tried to set his airplane down on the sandbar at the small tributary two miles above Lee's Ferry. He didn't quite make it and nosed over close to the left bank. The resourceful fellow floated down to the ferry and hitched a ride to Cliff Dwellers. Three days later, the river party returned and photographed the plane on her nose as they passed. Meanwhile the pilot contracted with Vern Baker to salvage the plane. Vern gambled that the job could be done regardless of time, and he set the price high.

Baker and Earl Johnson assembled three life rafts, two empty fifty-gallon oil drums, and several coils of rope. On July 6, they inched up to the Piper Cub, still on her nose in the river. They forced one life raft as far forward as they could, lashed it to the landing gear, then tied a line around the aft end of the fuselage. The power boat was used to pull the empennage down, pivoting it on the life raft lashed to the landing gear. They forced the tail section down into the water, then roped the two oil drums under the engine. Released, the empennage came up to allow the plane to float in a flight position. Placing another life raft under each wing tip as a safety measure, they towed the rig backward to the boat ramp at Lee's Ferry and pulled the plane on shore with the truck before noon. The pilot, chagrined that the job had been so easy, complained about the price. He hired someone else to haul the plane to Marble Canyon Lodge, where he cleaned it up and finally flew it out.[10] Resourcefulness had won the day.

Bob Vaughn and D. D. "Smoky" Robinson ran cattle between the Bean Hole and Soap Creek. On a crisp day in January 1960, Smoky was hunting strays on horseback along the Marble Rim when he passed some tire tracks. He thought nothing more about it until he rode back to the bunkhouse and realized he had never driven a pickup to that area. The next day he returned and was surprised to see the tracks of three wheels instead of two or four. He followed them to the rim and found an airplane upside down on a ledge, teetering on the brink. The plane had just missed a fifteen hundred foot plunge to the river at Mile 15. He came back just before dusk with Vern Baker and Ralph Haynes in a four-wheel drive equipped with a winch. Smoky lassoed the ship's tail section, and they used the truck to pull the small Cessna right-side up. They tied it down, piled rocks on the horizontal stabilizer, and returned home.

Using the radio-phone, Vern called in the plane's number to the sheriff in Flagstaff. Next morning, the owners flew in from Albuquerque, and the FBI arrived that afternoon. A thief had taken an extensive joy ride, feared the plane was becoming too hot to use, attempted to ditch it where it wouldn't be found easily, walked three miles to the highway, and hitched a ride. Deciding the plane was salvageable, the owners gave the job to Vern and Ralph on an hourly basis. After one day to gather equipment, they returned and removed the wings. They pulled the fuselage to the rim and tied it down, then hauled the wings and the empennage in a trailer to Cliff Dwellers Lodge. Next day, they brought the fuselage in by towing it backwards on its own wheels.[11] The plane flew again, thanks to the multiple skills of the people involved.

A Lee family reunion was held at the ferry in October 1961. The affair culminated at Navajo Bridge on the thirteenth, when an imposing granite monument was dedicated to John D. Lee. A granddaughter, Ettie Lee, promoted the event and a multitude of kinsmen came from far and wide. John D. Lee's eloquent biographer, Juanita Brooks, was the featured speaker. By this time, none of the descendants could say with certainty whether anything of their ancestor remained at Lee's Ferry except his name, although some attributed several current structures, including the Weaver house, to him.

James M. Eden, the first superintendent of Glen Canyon National Recreation Area, started the year 1960 with a small staff. John T. Mullady came over from Organ Pipe National Monument in March and a corps of rangers began to assemble. At this time, the role of the National Park Service was one of planning and preparation for the future while presenting a low public profile. In January 1962, the National Park Service became visible to the public at Lee's Ferry. Wahweap was the base headquarters from where ranger patrols radiated to Cane Creek and Hole in the Rock. John Mullady's force consisted of three rangers, one of whom, Ed Mazzer, patrolled to Lee's Ferry once a week. In February, two more rangers were added to the force. An outlying ranger station was set up at Cane Creek.

During April 1962, 654 river runners in thirty-seven hard hulls and a like number of inflatables either left or entered the river at Cane Creek. These people would have disembarked at Lee's Ferry had the river not been closed. Visitor usage increased as the boating season progressed. Rangers

counted 2,223 people at Cane Creek during the month of June and estimated that $170,000 had been derived locally from river tourism. From
April to September 12, 1962, 5,439 people visited Cane Creek, arriving
overland by car or via the river. The ranger station was closed on September
12, although daily patrols continued; two per week went to Lee's Ferry.

At 2 P.M. on March 13, 1963, the first diversion tunnel was necked
down to allow passage of only 1,000 cubic feet per second to flow downstream. Water was now being stored in Lake Powell reservoir, and the flow
of the Colorado River was completely regulated past Lee's Ferry. At the end
of March 10, the reservoir had risen to 3,233 feet above sea level.[12] By April
27, the coffer dam was fully inundated, and the reservoir was 145 feet deep
near the dam and extended eighty-five miles upstream.

May 1963 was a month of monumental importance to future visitor
use at Lee's Ferry. Wildlife officials made three plantings of seven- to nine-
inch rainbow trout in the Colorado River, each one week apart. One load
was placed in the river at the foot of the dam; the rest were planted at Lee's
Ferry. The fry were from the federal hatchery at Willow Beach, and each
planting consisted of 9,600 fish. Some "sportsmen" gathered at the plantings and took limits of the hatchery product before it could get the feel of
the new environment, but enough escaped to form the basis of another
attraction—a blue-ribbon trout industry. One million bass were planted on
May 23 but were not expected to do as well as the trout since the water temperature would become progressively colder as the reservoir deepened.

The Lee's Ferry Ranger Station opened on May 19 and consisted
of a trailer parked on a bench overlooking Two Mile. Edomo P. Mazzer
became the first resident subdistrict ranger. He recorded 424 visitors, five
boats, two rafts, and ten campers for the month.[13] A second trailer was
placed beside the first on June 7, when J. W. Gentless was assigned to the
ferry as a maintenance man. Visitation rose to 1,051 in 391 vehicles in June
and climbed steeply; July's count of 2,317 more than doubled June's.

The Pahreah River flooded seven times in August, once stranding
forty-seven people for one night. Thirty-four were stranded by the next
flood; thirteen of these crossed the swollen creek on the USGS cable. A
record breaking torrent came down on the last day of the month. Rains
were widespread; Wahweap Creek sent ten major floods down its channel.
Despite the August flooding, 1,361 visitors in 415 vehicles and 271 campers
came to the ferry, and 23 boats were launched.

The rising reservoir inundated the road at Padre Creek on
September 8, forcing the removal of the ranger station and launching facil-
ities to higher ground. The lake level reached 3,394 feet at month's end.
September also saw the topping out of Glen Canyon Dam. The Padre Creek
Ranger Station was disbanded and its equipment moved to Wahweap on
October 7. The road was closed entirely on October 28 when water inun-
dated the crossing at Wahweap Creek. This ended river running in Glen
Canyon. The reservoir level was up to 3,398 feet on October 31.

The National Park Service needed a reliable water supply to serve the influx of visitors to Lee's Ferry. Not knowing of Leo Weaver's well, which had been drilled in 1937, and not seeing the capped well-head, the Park Service contracted with a Taylor, Arizona, driller to sink a well just outside the ranch property in June 1963. It was drilled into the same aquifer as Leo's, and like his, proved to be unpotable. Park Service personnel were as surprised as Leo had been. For the last seven months of 1963, 6,383 people visited Lee's Ferry. Many were attracted by the fishing; in December, 89,080 catchable-size rainbow trout were planted between the dam and Lee's Ferry. With the now-clear flows of only 1,000 cubic feet per second, the once-mighty Colorado River resembled a babbling brook. At year's end, the water behind Glen Canyon Dam stood at 3409.8 feet, and the reservoir stretched 135 miles upstream to Red Canyon.

On January 1, 1964, a cooperative agreement between Utah and Arizona went into effect. Utah angling regulations were to be enforced on the entire lake, while Arizona regulations would govern fisherman on the river below the dam. For all practical purposes, this applied to Lee's Ferry and upstream, because very few sportsmen bothered to fish during a traverse of Grand Canyon. In February, a twenty-three-inch rainbow trout was caught at the ferry, but few people realized that monster fish might be caught anywhere downstream. In the month of March, 88,200 rainbow trout were released at the ferry in seven plants. On March 5, 10,000 fish that averaged ten inches in length were planted and were judged to be catchable immediately.[14]

The new year also saw the granting of a concession contract to Lee's Ferry, Inc. The company, said to have been formed by four old friends, was headed by Clay R. Garrison. Former governor of New Mexico John E. Miles and Harold J. Pavela were listed as vice-presidents; James R. Zentmeyer was the secretary-treasurer. Garrison applied for a liquor license in May, then moved a small trailer to the ferry and parked it up from the river bank on July 12. He stocked it the following day and made his first sale on the fifteenth. Garrison lived in Page and drove back and forth to Lee's Ferry to attend to weekend business. Mrs. J. W. Gentless, wife of the park maintenance man, took care of weekday sales. Plans supposedly called for the construction of a motel, restaurant, tackle shop, and boat rentals, but for the present it was a shoestring operation. One had the impression that a buyer for the concession would be greeted warmly.

High visitation forced the need for better roads and bridges at Lee's Ferry. Traffic counters were installed in March when concrete piers and embankment skirts were poured for a new bridge over the Pahreah River. The old outlaw was about to be shackled after man had put up with its periodic rampages for nearly a century. The Pahreah flooded at noon on April 4 and was impassable until the morning of the sixth, but it was the renegade's final act of inconvenience. The bridge was opened to traffic on the twenty-second.

The spring of 1964 saw the senseless destruction of Frank Johnson's cabin, which had been built at the upper ferry during the winter of 1913–14. Bishop Owen Johnson of Moccasin visited for old times' sake. The son of Price W. Johnson, Owen had attended school at Lee's Ferry and wanted to revisit the places familiar to him as a boy. As he started across the USGS Reserve, he was intercepted by hydrographer Larry Lopp and informed he was trespassing; a confrontation ensued and Lopp ordered him off the reserve. Johnson defied him and walked along the river bank to the object of his visit. Satisfied, he returned the same way and had no further encounter with the river gager. Next day, Lopp doused the old cabin with a gallon of gasoline and touched it off with a match.[15]

The National Park Service contracted for the construction of a picnic area consisting of twenty-eight units with sunshades, windbreaks, grills, tables, and a comfort station. Final inspection was made in April, and the facility was opened for use. It was located on a high gravel bar northwest of the Pahreah's mouth. The master plan called for two auxiliary campgrounds to be built at a later date if needed. The road, which for forty years had been considered a great improvement over the pioneer track that came down Two Mile Wash, was relocated below the campground and ran directly to the new bridge. The picnic area was landscaped with non-native Russian olive and locust trees.

Workmen installed a water tank of 150,000-gallon capacity high on the slope behind the development area. The tank was set unnecessarily on high steel girder legs, evidently to provide pressure to the sites below, but it could have been put on or near the ground because the location was at least a hundred feet above where the water would be used. The tank was completed in August, and a pump lifted water to it from the new well. The water's quality, however, was so poor that it required treatment before use.

In April, the road contractor poured street curbs for a future residential area of three units on the bluff west of the Pahreah River. The most startling addition was the frequently spaced, bright-red fire hydrants throughout the development area. All new installations were planned to be located above an elevation of 3,140 plus twenty feet, the predicted inundation level of a reservoir backed up by the proposed Marble Canyon Dam. Improvements also were being made below this elevation; a landing and boat-recovery ramp had been bulldozed, a steel-mesh mat installed, and a rock jetty extended from the right bank. Any river neophyte could have forecast the result—the steel-mesh mat was quickly silted-in from the eddy action caused by the jetty. The procedure had been carefully evaluated by the engineering corps and resulted in some red faces. At the time, the steel mat was judged to be a total loss.

State politics brought about other changes. Utah interests, not satisfied with the slow filling of the reservoir behind Glen Canyon Dam and the lack of developed facilities for their users, brought congressional pressure to bear on the Department of the Interior. This resulted in the premature closing of the dam gates on May 11, 1964, which allowed only 1,000 cubic feet per second to pass downstream.[16] The sustained low outflow had one favorable effect in that it exposed the hull of the *Charles H. Spencer*, allowing it to be measured on June 12, 1964. The hull was found to be intact and continuously connected from the bow plate to the aft rail of the paddlewheel well. The overall length turned out to be eighty-six and one-half feet, with a hull length of seventy-two feet and a beam of twenty-five feet.[17] The measurements agreed with those on the boat's blueprint and corrected the erroneous measurements, which had been quoted extensively, that shipwright Herman Rosenfelt testified to in the Riverbed case.

Gus Griffin had not had an easy time discharging his debt on the Lee's Ferry Ranch. He sold whatever assets he could to anyone who would buy them, including Jerry Johnson's old wagon, which he had taken in lieu of wages from Charlie Spencer, and several Spencer ox yokes. George Babbitt acquired the old blacksmith bellows that John R. Nielson had removed from the *Nellie*. The place, except for a couple of Spencer ox yokes, Leo Weaver's large table, the hand-made sideboard, the school bell, and the furnishings, almost was stripped by August 15, 1964, when the Griffins deeded the property to a syndicate for a hundred thousand dollars.[18] The six new owners were Denver and Jean F. Evans, Luhrs & Luhrs, Robert F. and Charlotte Brown, E. R. and Ione Fryer, Joseph Louis Refsnes, and Jack W. and Edythe Whiteman.

"Si" Fryer had been general superintendent of the Navajo Service in Window Rock, Arizona, for many years and was Griffin's superior in the Bureau of Indian Affairs. Fryer knew that Gus wanted to sell the ranch. Fryer was the grandson of Hyrum Smith Phelps, the leader of the second company to settle in the Salt River Valley, who crossed at Lee's Ferry on December 4, 1878, only three days after the birth of a son, Gove. Si had a sincere appreciation of the flavor of the place, even though he did not know what articles to ascribe to Weaver or subsequent occupants. He would have bought Gus out by himself had he been able, and he enlisted partners only to acquire the property with relatively little risk to each. The syndicate stated that its main purpose in purchasing the property was to raise seed that, due to the isolation, could not be contaminated by pollen from other farms. Actually, they planned to put in minimal improvements and hoped to double or triple their original investment by selling the place to the National Park Service or the concessionaire.[19]

Rumors were circulating that the stone buildings on the river flat were scheduled to be razed when the new residences were erected for U.S. Geological Survey and National Park Service personnel. These reports led to an unofficial survey of the buildings on October 6, 1964,[20] and a private effort to save the buildings. Several organizations were involved, including the National Park Service Regional Office at Santa Fe, the Arizona Historical Society at Tucson, and the Arizona Landmarks Commission at Phoenix. For a while it appeared that the various bureaucracies had grasped the problem and the demolition would be prevented.[21] Regional Historian William Brown visited the area on November 6 to consider the merits of having a historical evaluation made of the old buildings. This resulted in the Park Service arranging with Dr. C. Gregory Crampton to make a more thorough study on December 10–11, 1964.[22]

The new year of 1965 saw several changes at Lee's Ferry. Clay Garrison's store in the trailer was tended by the Snody brothers, Lyndel and Roy. It was open seven days a week from eight to five and did sporadic business. The Griffins vacated the ranch, and a month later Bob White left the custodianship of the Buffalo Ranch at South Canyon to become caretaker for the syndicate. Bids were opened for the new residences; the contract was awarded to an Albuquerque firm on February 25. The new ranger station was completed and furnished. During the last four days of January, Arizona Public Service Company used helicopters to survey the location of power lines to the ferry and Marble Canyon.

The ferry's tenth fatality occurred Sunday morning, February 21, 1965. The river was running 8,630 cubic feet per second, but the water coming out of the bottom of the reservoir was cold—about forty-seven degrees. Resident ranger Phil Martin and a visiting park ranger, Don Pledger, were riding Martin's canoe through Two Mile riffle when they capsized. Both men were good swimmers and were wearing life jackets. Pledger made it to shore but Martin didn't. His body was recovered at Cathedral Wash by Jack Blee, the resident hydrographer, and Bill Gentless. The burial took place at Grand Canyon on the twenty-fourth.[23] Martin was replaced as resident ranger by Richard E. Hoffman on March 10.

The increased number of visitors resulted in littering and some vandalism. A daily cleanup of beaches and roads was required, and a protective fence of hog wire and steel posts was placed around the old fort and trading post. The U.S. Geological Survey moved the lower cableway downstream to the gaging station opposite the new boat ramp. Fish stocking continued; ninety-five hundred rainbow trout seven and one half inches long were planted in the first quarter of the year. The monthly count of fishermen now numbered in the hundreds, a tenth of them using boats. The minimum elevation of the Lake Powell reservoir required to produce power at Glen Canyon Dam was 3,490 feet, and the lake was maintained at only one foot higher, resulting in a variable flow past Lee's Ferry.

The Dirty Devil and White Canyon bridges were finished in April 1965, creating another route between Moab and Marble Canyon. This remote, rough country no longer was the most isolated area in western United States. The new bridges were dedicated June 3, 1966, with Secretary of the Interior Stewart Udall and Utah Governor Calvin L. Rampton featured speakers.

Lee's Ferry, Inc., obtained its liquor license in April 1965, and almost immediately public drunkenness became a companion problem to littering and vandalism. The silted-in boat ramp continued to be a complaint of the boating public and was an embarrassment to the Park Service. In May, six commercial river tours departed Lee's Ferry on Grand Canyon trips. According to the ranger's count, 138 persons in 27 water craft were launched. A gasoline pump, installed at the concessionaire's trailer, was in use by the thirteenth, marking the first time such fuel was available at the no-longer-so-lonely dell.

The Park Service reported that 1,250 visitors came to Lee's Ferry during the 1965 Memorial Day weekend, and 15 boats were launched.[24] Two groups were removed from the area for obnoxious behavior. Intoxicated Indians were especially problematic. It was the policy to call Navajo Nation police in such cases and often they were not available in the northwestern part of the Navajo Reservation. The park ranger gave camp-fire talks and provided tours through the old fort and to the petrified forest when groups of sufficient size requested them. Aside from the heavy Memorial Day intrusion, 5,812 visitors were counted for the month. June's river runners exceeded those of May: 12 groups with a total of 321 people in 38 boats left Lee's Ferry. Nevills and Aleson would have licked their chops at the way river touring was taking off. Visitor count rose to 6,899 and the campground overflowed on seven nights, mostly because an angler caught a twenty-four-inch trout—a new record. However, some of the fish were observed with parasitic cysts.

On June 9, the ranch syndicate brought in a construction crew to fence the property and construct two ponds to hold Pahreah River water for irrigation. The ponds were dug west of the cemetery; both were lined with Chinle shale, which the owners figured was close enough to bentonite to serve as a seal. One thing they didn't count on was that water pumped out of the creek while it was in flood was so heavily laden with sediment that the outlet valves soon were clogged with silt and could not be used.

Twenty-five years after his first traverse of Grand Canyon with Norm Nevills, Senator Barry Goldwater, who had recently lost the presidential election, made another trip, this time with Gaylord Staveley. The Staveleys had bought Mexican Hat Expeditions on October 1, 1957, had renamed it "Canyoneers, Inc." in 1961, and operated with the same equipment used by Nevills. The party of sixteen included three of the senator's children and a son-in-law. A new facet to river running was introduced when a helicopter brought food, ice, and refreshments almost daily, and they even lifted the boats over Hance Rapid to save a lining job. The trip began July 1, 1965, and ended at Temple Bar on the sixteenth.[25]

The ranch owners complained that power lines from Glen Canyon Dam were detrimental to the area's scenic values and requested they be rerouted. This was done at considerable expense. The line reached customers at Lee's Ferry in August with individual hookups scheduled to be made in September. For the first time, power reached Lee's Ferry. The new residences were complete, except for power, by December, and Dick Hoffman moved furniture into the one slated for the resident ranger. On

January 5, 1966, the Lee's Ferry Station was upgraded from subdistrict to district ranger because of the relatively heavy visitor use. Arizona Public Service Company extended a power line to Cliff Dwellers on December 16, 1965, and the hookup was made the following day; the estimated cost was $100,000. The Greene's electric bill from that time to January 4, 1966, was $43.97 for 866 kilowatt hours. Their diesel plant in fifteen years had cost them approximately $10,113.[26]

In April, the concessionaire had put three used aluminum boats in service for rentals and acquired another five-horsepower outboard motor. Later, a nineteen-foot jet boat was brought in to provide river tours to the dam. However, no qualified operator was hired; if a customer appeared, anybody who was willing was pressed into service, even the hydrographer. Equipment failures were common, making it a rather haphazard operation. It was alleged that the concessionaire was bad-mouthing the Park Service to the general public and relations became strained.

By the fall of 1965, many large rainbow trout—seventeen to twenty inches in length—were caught. Problems with the new fishery began to appear; some of the trout were snake-like, with hooked snouts, indicating the number of fish was greater than the food supply. Several sizeable plantings had been made which accentuated the food shortage. River recreation continued to increase; the National Park Service counted 657 river runners leaving Lee's Ferry for Grand Canyon during the year and stopped several unauthorized and ill-equipped individuals from attempting a traverse. Although this count was the highest to date, it was a pale forerunner of things to come. Nearly forty thousand visitors came to Lee's Ferry in 1965—a fact that Allie Caffall, who thought the ferry was "the loneliest place in the world," would have found difficult to believe.[27]

For some time, the National Park Service had been pondering the acquisition of the ranch at Lee's Ferry, either by condemnation or purchase. An appraisal was requested, and on January 28, Superintendent Gustav Muehlenhaupt of Glen Canyon National Recreation Area brought H. B. Embach, senior member of the American Society of Appraisers, to the ranch. The report, dated February 18, 1966, stated that the property was worth the hundred thousand dollars the present owners had paid Gus Griffin. Embach stressed the scarcity of privately-owned property in the general area and the favorable location of this particular piece in his appraisal, especially if a direct road to Page were built. The report noted that Griffin had offered the ranch to Paul Jones, chairman of the Navajo Nation, but a negative appraisal by R. D. Bloxom made from an aerial inspection prevented further negotiations.[28]

Regional Historian Bill Brown had inspected the old fort for possible stabilization treatment the previous August, and in March 1966 the roof interior was sprayed with epoxy. Charles Pope, architect with historic building surveys, supervised the job and took accurate measurements of the building on the sixteenth.

For fifteen years, the National Park Service required permits for everyone seeking to traverse Grand Canyon via the Colorado River. Some people were unaware of this requirement, while others knew about it but attempted to sneak into Marble Canyon without being seen. Which group a man allegedly named "Dr. R. I. Maxon of Los Sierra, California" belonged to is not known, but his four-man, two-raft party was seen on April 3 and reported to the ranger at Lee's Ferry. Dick Hoffman stopped the illegal runners at Badger Creek Rapid, explained the consequences of an unauthorized traverse, and forced abortion of the trip. The men walked out at Jackass Canyon while a commercial outfit salvaged their equipment for a fee.[29]

Later in April, ranch caretaker White denied access to the cemetery to those who had kindred buried there, and the act was brought to the attention of the sheriff at Fredonia. For this and other alleged deficiencies, White was discharged on April 27. Workmen had discovered a set of dinosaur tracks near the foot of the dam during the fall of 1962. In the interval between the discovery of the prints and getting two geologists there to identify them, several of the eight were destroyed by workmen attempting to remove them for personal use. On the last day of April, Ranger Dick Hoffman found more tracks in a lens of limey mudstone near Mile 7, high above the river. Crowds continued to visit the ferry. On Memorial Day weekend of 1966, 1,874 non-residents were counted, 78 of them arriving by air in 34 planes. At the end of June, the total visitation for the first half of the year was 24,471, and 646 river runners had embarked on private or commercial trips.

Personnel changes in both government agencies now took place. Bill Gentless could not understand the slovenly nature of some visitors, who seemed to think they were entitled to litter at will and mess up the restrooms shortly after their daily cleaning; he refused to clean more often than scheduled. Complaints from the public were made in June and continued in July. Gentless was transferred to Wahweap on July 30 and replaced by Dick Cook.

Rangers were aware that local people were hunting illegally on National Park lands. Five bucks were known to have been killed on the bench below the cliffs, half the estimated total kill. The largest deer was an eight-pointer with a thirty-one inch spread.

The year marked a public kindling of interest in Pahreah Canyon. On May 17, the Coffin party of six arrived at the ferry to become the first known hikers to have traversed the canyon since John D. Lee and Sid Wilson. They took a little more than four days for the trip and told the ranger their jaunt would be published in the *Sierra Club Bulletin*. The traverse was repeated by Ralph W. Dietz, his wife Eileen, both of Ridgecrest, California; Patricia Esch of Aurora, Colorado; and Opal Norris of Kernville, California. They started on October 23, made several side trips, and reached the mouth on the twenty-ninth. They found an eighteen-inch aboriginal pot twenty-one inches high when they detoured to see the arch that Royce Knight had discovered previously from the air.[30] Dietz and his wife returned in October 1976 to guide nine others, including representatives from the Museum of Northern Arizona, the Bureau of Land Management, Park Ranger Joe Kastellic, and three interested individuals to recover the pot, which was then placed in the museum. The original Dietz party probably was the first group of non-residents to visit the feature now named Wrather Arch.[31] From 1966 on, hiking Pahreah Canyon exerted great appeal to back-packers. The trip became so popular that a ranger was stationed on the tributary south of Highway 89 on the road between Page and Kanab to register the hikers.

Late in the afternoon of a sunny January 31, 1967, a crime occurred that was very similar to the 1935 shooting of George Wilson. Bob Vaughn and Smoky Robinson were enjoying a beer in the Cliff Dwellers restaurant when a north-bound car pulled up to the gas pump. The Tillery brothers, two young black men from Philadelphia, needed gas and oil. Vern Baker went out to provide service. Apparently an incident about some spilled oil resulted in a minor controversy with racial overtones. Nineteen-year-old Daniel, a large end-wrench in his hip pocket, followed Baker into the store, ostensibly to purchase some canned goods. As soon as the proprietor turned to the shelf, Tillery hit him on the head with the wrench, putting the huskier man on the floor. He then went behind the counter and continued to beat him. The brothers fled after rifling the cash register.[32]

When Vern did not return to the restaurant, Bob Vaughn strolled out to the station to learn why and found Baker where he had fallen in a pool of blood. A speed run to Lee's Ferry resulted in Dick Hoffman using his radio to summon an aerial ambulance and notify the sheriff that the suspects were headed north. The unconscious Baker was airlifted to the hospital at Page, then to Phoenix. He lived but was never the same; his skull was as creased as a washboard. The Tillerys were apprehended near Fredonia, went to trial at Flagstaff on April 25, were found guilty on May 16, and were given lengthy sentences. They were released on good behavior after serving minimum periods, while Vern Baker's life was changed forever.

President Lyndon B. Johnson dedicated Glen Canyon Dam on September 22, 1966. The master of ceremonies was Secretary of the Interior Stewart L. Udall, descendant of David K. Udall, who had crossed at Lee's Ferry after being called to Arizona in 1880. Secretary Udall brought a party to the ferry on April 23, 1966, to evaluate the situation in case the site would be inundated by the proposed Marble Canyon Dam. The NPS boat ran the distinguished visitors into Glen Canyon to the foot of the dam, and evidently some decisive conclusions were reached. As the year wore on and the already firm conservationist stand strengthened, a different set of signals began to emanate from Washington. On November 25, the master-plan team came down the river from the dam and spent a day at the ferry. The main item of discussion was the preferred route for the planned highway from Wahweap to Lee's Ferry and the revision of existing plans if there should be no inundation of the ferry from the proposed reservoir.

On February 1, 1967, Secretary Udall announced that the administration had decided to abandon plans to build the Marble and Bridge Canyon dams but would proceed with the Central Arizona Project, extend Grand Canyon National Park boundaries to Lee's Ferry, and authorize five projects in Colorado and New Mexico. This last concession was a sop to the two upper-basin states; Utah already had three development sites on Lake Powell reservoir. This political compromise gave something to each of the interested groups. It was acceptable to northwest interests because it made no provision to transfer water from that area to the thirsty southland. As might be expected, the *Los Angeles Times* grumbled editorially and accused Udall of abandoning his regional solution.

Charlie Spencer was a genuine resident of Lee's Ferry and had contributed to its rich legacy. His stone buildings were a part of its historical heritage. Although Spencer no longer posed a threat—or even an annoyance—to the USGS operation, it was as difficult for the bureaucracy to change its intent to eradicate evidence of his presence there as it was to derail a runaway freight train. Arrangements had been made with the Atchison Construction Company, and Udall's announcement merely signaled the plan into motion. Demolition commenced on the morning of February 7, 1967; when the deed was done by noon of the eighth, considerable history had been vandalized. Even the two boilers, which had been freighted by ox teams from Flagstaff in 1910, were buried beneath the rubble. The USGS guest house was left standing.[33] No doubt it was a coincidence that an unusually heavy windstorm hit the following day, blowing over a house-trailer, damaging others, destroying sunshades, blowing boats off trailers, and sinking one of the concessionaire's boats.[34]

When Jane Foster assumed sole ownership of Marble Canyon Lodge in 1959, there were six employees—two couples and two Navajos. The gross income was between $30,000 and $40,000. In 1984, she grossed over $1 million dollars and employed thirty-two people, a quarter of them Navajos. In that year, the establishment had expanded to thirty-five units, and the proprietor was planning to restore the old Buck Lowrey lodge. Hers was the most notable success story of the Arizona Strip. However, it was not easy; she solved her problems one at a time, plowed her profits back into the business and allowed it to grow by its own resources. In 1967, she sank a well 540 feet, struck a good aquifer that flowed 1,100 gallons per hour, and ran a three-quarter mile pipeline to a 100,000 gallon storage tank. She obtained electrical power that same year, telephone service in 1971, and reduced her waste-disposal cost to about $100 per month.[35] Buck Lowrey would have been amazed at such management.

Relations between the National Park Service and the concessionaire had not improved, and the latter was considered to be dragging his feet in developing the site as he was contracted to do. Garrison appeared to be spending minimum funds as he waited for a purchaser of his concession. Such a person finally was found in Lee Sparks, owner of a Long Beach,

California, auto parts business. Sparks and his "Fort Lee Company" replaced Garrison's Lee's Ferry, Inc., on December 1, 1967. Development immediately picked up.

The new company was composed of Sparks, his son Tony Lee, and a son-in-law, David Boring. They lured head chef Jimmy Nasif from Roy Rogers' Apple Valley Inn to handle the culinary department. Nasif, glowing with high expectations, designed the kitchen and restaurant, and construction got underway in the spring. Plans were to build a first class motel and run charter trips through Grand Canyon. By midsummer, the motel consisted of several mobile homes set on blocks at the north edge of the flat. Nasif soon realized that he had misjudged the volume of people who would come to Lee's Ferry for haute cuisine and left for greener pastures. The high-grade restaurant degenerated into a fry-cook operation dispensing hamburgers, which suited the clientele.

As the only concessionaire based at the ferry, the Fort Lee Company had certain advantages over the other commercial operators. They even initiated new wrinkles to the business. In October 1968, they rafted customers to the mouth of the Little Colorado, where passengers and equipment were removed by helicopter. Fifteen-mile runs from the foot of Glen Dam to the ferry were begun in July 1971. The number of paying passengers increased yearly, amounting to 5,500 in 1974, only to be doubled the following year. After two years of running to the Little Colorado, the Fort Lee Company switched to eight-day trips to Diamond Creek. The passengers were returned to the ferry by bus.

Other commercial outfitters began their tours at Las Vegas or St. George, bussing passengers through Zion National Park or the Arizona Strip. This constituted interstate business and thus these companies avoided paying taxes to Arizona for the boat trips through Grand Canyon. It was sneaky but legal. The tremendous increase in visitation to Lee's Ferry was accompanied by a similar rise in river tourists. In the late 1960s, nearly 100 people embarked each day during the season. The head count rose to 200, then to 300. On June 17, 1972, alone, 324 people shoved off. By the end of July, more than 10,000 river runners had started downstream since March, and the final two months of the boating season continued at the same rate.

Such heavy usage presaged the same difficulties that had beset Glen Canyon after the Second World War. The National Park Service required all commercial operators and private parties to have permits, but behavior was largely unregulated in the canyon. The ranger posted a typhoid warning sign at the ferry in June 1972; diarrhea and symptoms of salmonella were common in most parties. In mid-July, Allan Steckler, U.S. Public Health Service, and Harry Downs, Coconino County Health Department, checked the concessionaire's facilities, and Steckler accompanied a river party to collect water samples and observe food handling in order to determine the cause of "river sickness," then pandemic on this portion of the Colorado.

In October, the river boatmen circulated a petition pointing out that too many people were allowed to depart each day. The eroding beaches were scarred by the remains of too many campfires, and human waste disposal was inadequate.[36] They recommended better sanitation for those handling food, camping restrictions, and fines for those found in violation. It was a worthy stand, but the Park Service was in no position to enforce such measures. Realization of the problems led to their over-reaction and the issuance of stringent—and in some cases absurd—regulations written by office personnel having no outdoor experience. Eventually, pretrip inspections at the ferry and ranger patrols on the river were established to ensure compliance. Even these were relaxed, boatmen monitored themselves, harmony reigned, and conditions improved.[37]

Personnel changes in this part of the Arizona Strip began at the close of the 1960s and continued for three years. The ranch syndicate had a succession of resident caretakers after White was discharged. Don Sealy of Vermilion Cliffs succeeded Verl Price in February 1971, who was followed by Steve Connolly in 1974. Ruth Baker, deprived of a fully functioning husband by the brutal attack, found the operation of Cliff Dwellers to be too much to handle. They retired to a less stressful life in Page, a move made possible by the hiring of Ray and Rowena Workman in April 1970. The Workmans proved to be excellent managers for several years, and the business prospered. The owners' refusal to keep salaries proportionate to inflation finally resulted in their leaving, and a succession of poor managers caused the place to decline. In February 1979, Cliff Dwellers Lodge was sold to the Charles DeWitz family, who put the establishment once again on a paying basis.

Buck Rogers had been subdividing his Badger Creek property for some time. Buyers began moving mobile homes on the parcels and landscaping them. He caught the water at a higher elevation before it picked up alkalinity from the saline Moenkopi Formation. The water was very good and the Badger Creek properties became the greenest places in this part of the strip. Buck met a tragic death in 1975, but his widow, Betty, continued their master plan.

Perry Thompson became resident ranger on October 3, 1970. Since the boating season was closed for the year, he had time to hike the surrounding country and gain first-hand knowledge of it. Routine public problems appeared, yet few preventive measures could be taken. In July 1972, two dozen members of the Phoenix chapter of the Dirty Dozen motorcycle gang pulled into the ferry campground, intimidated the other campers, and trashed the place. They left next morning for another friendship visit to Jacob Lake and a rendezvous with other members; telephone and radio warnings preceded them to every establishment along the line. Two years later, the performance was repeated by another group. Intoxicated Indians cutting tracks with pickups, or motorcyclists tearing up the talus slopes and beaches left unsightly evidence of their presence that had to be raked out. But the river and man's reaction to it caused the most concern.

For instance, in March 1971, a commercial raft got loose during the night but luckily got hung up about one-quarter mile below Navajo Bridge. Thompson led two boatmen down the old Navajo trail that Buzz Holmstrom had used to reach the river. They walked and waded along the bank to the unit and ran it up to Cathedral Wash. The rig was valued at fourteen hundred dollars. On April 6, three inexperienced boys cast off in a four-man raft. They lost their inflatable in Badger Creek Rapid but managed to reach shore safely. They took three days to hike upstream to Navajo Bridge—a distance of 3.6 miles—where their shouts alerted visitors to their predicament and the ranger was notified; he rescued them on the ninth.

Changes were occurring in the U.S. Geological Survey gaging mission at Lee's Ferry. Matthew Pierce became the last resident hydrographer May 1, 1971. Residency was discontinued on August 4, 1976. Periodic inspections still were made from Flagstaff and the visiting hydrologist stayed at a local motel. The USGS facilities were turned over to the National Park Service, ending over fifty years of on-site hydrographers at Lee's Ferry. Another major advance in stream gaging occurred when satellite telemetry was installed March 10, 1977. The USGS operation had come a long way in half a century.

On April 14, 1974, Easter services were held at the nearly obliterated aboriginal ruin that newcomers persisted in calling "Lee's Lookout." The ranger report stated that sixty-five people attended, which meant the gathering, of necessity, was very friendly, or at least closely packed.

Behind-the-scenes negotiations between the ranch syndicate and the National Park Service had been underway for several years. It was more or less apparent that the partnership, except for E. R. Fryer, had a sole interest in making the property return a profit on their investment. To simplify the complexities of their mutual ownership, the partners set up the Page Land and Cattle Company, an Arizona corporation based in the office of one of their number. The maneuvering included the threat of a lawsuit against the government, which was enough to make an ordinary minor bureaucrat quiver in his boots. No such action ensued, however, because the government forces caved in. On June 14, 1974, the ranch was sold to the National Park Service for $300,000—three times the value established by the Embach appraisal.[38] The property had come full circle, and if the ghosts of Jeremiah Johnson and Leo Weaver sighed among the cottonwoods, who could blame them? The syndicate had built some fences, constructed two reservoirs, planted a vineyard and an orchard of new trees, but the claimed improvements, added to the original purchase price, still allowed them more than double their investment.

Jack Whiteman heaped a final indignity on Leo Weaver the following August. Despite a deed that he signed stating that all "tenements, hereditaments, and appurtenances" were transferred to the National Park

Service, he was allowed to back a flatbed truck up to the house, where his crew stripped the place of its furnishings in three days. They took Jim Emett's school bell and Charlie Spencer's ox yokes. Leo's great dinner table was too large to be removed except through the south window. The old wood stove and his hand-made cupboard, chairs, and accessory tables were all removed; the flavor of the ranch house was irretrievably lost. A witness to the operation said that in his opinion: "the act was pure vandalism, motivated by greed and vindictiveness." He might have added that since the National Park Service had plenty of money, it could have employed an expert to write a deed in which there was no doubt that the furnishings went with the house. Si Fryer didn't learn of the despoiling for four years, but one look convinced him the place had been profaned beyond belief. He protested to Whiteman and inquired whether the removed items might be recovered for a restoration program.[39] His efforts came to naught.

Now that the Park Service owned and administered the Lee's Ferry ranch, the prime question was: what should they do with it? The Page Stake of the Church of Jesus Christ of Latter-day Saints received permission to farm the ranch on April 1, 1976. The project—to grow produce that could be used in the stake's relief program—was not successful, and the blame for the failure depends on who tells the story. National Park Service personnel claimed the stake sent unqualified young people with little or no farming experience to grow a crop; the Saints said the Park Service failed to produce water when it was needed. The stake relinquished the farming rights on December 31, 1977. Government experts claimed that years of using alkaline water from the Pahreah River had so impregnated the soil with salts that nothing could be produced until the fields had been thoroughly leached. The Park Service had tested both its own and the Weaver wells on August 4, 1976, and found the water to be very hard. Its well at that time was considered to be a total loss. Fortunately, the Lees, Johnsons, and Emetts were not aware of this condition, because they grew excellent crops despite the salts. Alfalfa, which thrives in alkaline soils, had not been successfully grown since World War I, mostly because the attempts to dam the Pahreah River for irrigation water had failed.

The Park Service found enough budget for an extensive renovation program during the winter of 1976–77. The old fort-trading post was stabilized, and its entire roof was treated. A vendor who specialized in restoring and stabilizing log cabins was given a contract to practice his craft on the Johnson and Brinkerhoff cabins. For several thousand dollars, he replaced four sill logs in each, as well as odd logs at random places in both, along with new daubing and chinking. The timbers from the *Nellie* were sound. A metal roof was installed on the Weaver house at a cost of $28,638.

The Fort Lee Company moved to Page in the spring of 1979, leaving the ferry without a concessionaire for the first time in fifteen years. The National Park Service was now the only occupant of the lands and buildings around Lee's Ferry. Improvements continued to be made, often at outrageous cost. The most egregious item, cost-wise, was the construction of a new restroom north of the boat ramp. The contractor constructed a slump-block building eighteen by thirty-six feet for $140,000. Historically, the freest-spending promoters between Cataract and Marble Canyons were Robert B. Stanton and Charles H. Spencer, but they were pikers compared to the Department of the Interior. Of course, the latter provides for many thousands of people, and the dollar has lost much of its purchasing power in three-quarters of a century. The National Park Service, besides being a big spender, appears to have destroyed more items of historical value than have the elements, while its efforts at preservation were minimal and expensive.

Epilogue

Richard D. Quartaroli

BORN TO PARENTS OF PIONEER STOCK IN DALLAS, TEXAS, ON JUNE 9, 1911, Plez Talmadge (P. T. or Pat) Reilly moved with them to southern California at two months old. Living in California except for a year in Idaho when he was thirteen, P. T. graduated from Los Angeles High School, where he met his future life partner, Mary Elizabeth (Susie) MacLean, in a pottery class. At the beginning of the Depression in 1930, Reilly worked at a gold mine promotion on the South Fork of the American River to earn money for liberal arts studies at California Christian College. A student athlete, he enjoyed competing in football, basketball, track, handball, and tennis.[1]

The Depression also found P. T. silver smithing, apprenticing at the Parker Machine Works, and field surveying for the U.S. General Land Office, the latter from August 1936 to June 1940. The GLO was one of the many agencies receiving federal money to create jobs and raise employment and, in this case, to increase field parties and reduce the huge backlog of land that needed surveying. P. T. had campaigned actively for the reelection of Congressman Thomas Ford, Democrat of Los Angeles, who sponsored him with the GLO. Reilly was a field assistant, or axeman, and knew little about surveying when hired, but having lived in the open, hunted, fished, felled big timber, and handled an axe, he had no trouble with the position, nor with advancing beyond it. From "dragging or pulling the chain" to reading the clinometer angles to serving as principal assistant, he moved quickly, efficiently, and conscientiously through hard work and mathematical study, and his duties were always above his rating.[2]

Having few expenses in the field, he saved some money. On New Year's Eve, 1937, P. T. and UCLA alum Susie MacLean married in Ventura, California. Shortly afterward, they purchased a lot in Studio City. P. T. designed their home at night in a GLO tent and Susie supervised construction. Because of his machine shop and tooling experience, Reilly began work at the Tooling Division of Lockheed Aircraft Corporation in July 1940, with only a weekend between jobs. Repeating his advancement with the GLO, after a few years he joined the management team in Burbank, where he remained until his retirement in 1969.

P. T. Reilly (at oars) and Edwin McKee on a Norm Nevills trip in 1949 (*P. T. Reilly Collection, Cline Library, Northern Arizona University*).

Seeing an ad in *Desert Magazine* for a seven-day, 191-mile Norman Nevills' trip on the San Juan and Colorado Rivers, P. T. and Susie booked the May 1, 1947, trip. Starting as a passenger, P. T. was soon rowing one of Nevills' sadiron boats. The trip put-in was at Mexican Hat, Utah; the take-out, on May 7, was at Lee's Ferry, Arizona, beginning Reilly's long association with the historic crossing. He noticed that Nevills' flare for a story did not always include correct information, especially concerning Lee's Ferry; thus began P. T.'s quest for historical accuracy.

Beginning in 1948, Nevills employed Reilly as a boatman. He rowed, during his vacations, the San Juan River and the upper Green River and completed his first Grand Canyon trip in 1949. Finishing a San Juan trip prior to the Grand Canyon run, he arrived at Lee's Ferry June 12, 1949, and encountered Otis Reed "Dock" Marston and Ed Hudson as their party readied for a downstream powerboat run. Both men also began with Nevills; Marston ran trips with him from 1942 to 1948. This was the initial on-river meeting between Reilly and Marston and, according to P. T., "Norm said to Dock, 'Why don't you take the oars of one of these boats (not his own) and run down with us?' Neither Frank Wright nor Jim Rigg made a move, so I spoke up and invited him to handle my boat. He accepted eagerly and got in." Dock and P. T. vary in their remembrances of their first run together down the Pahreah Riffle, which was not the last time they parried either.[3]

Commenting on why Reilly was a Nevills boatman in 1949 and Marston was not, Dock, in a 1964 interview by P. T., stated "I'll tell you, I applied for a job. I had a promise from Nevills, anytime I ever wanted to go on a trip through the Grand Canyon, all I had to do was ask for it. But there was some young upstart down there in North Hollywood who came along and got my job, so Nevills wouldn't let me go." In a 1976 interview, Dock further expounded on his replacement: "The firing. Oh well, what happened was that Pat Reilly had been with him on the San Juan stuff for a little bit ... why, he put Pat in my place." Reilly commented in 1985 on this 1976 interview: "It is not true that I asked to run the Grand. Jim Rigg was the newest boatman, joining Nevills in 1949. Both Frank Wright and I were with him in 1948. If anybody replaced Marston, it was Rigg, not Reilly."[4]

The 1949 trip earned Reilly number 109 on Marston's list of river runners who had completed their first traverse of the 277 river miles of Grand Canyon.[5] After Nevills and his wife, Doris, died in a plane crash in September 1949, Frank Wright and Jim Rigg purchased and operated Nevills Expeditions as Mexican Hat Expeditions. Reilly was a guest boatman for them during one Grand Canyon trip each year from 1950 through 1952. Susie Reilly completed her first traverse in 1951, making her number 126 and one of the first dozen women through Grand Canyon.[6] In 1953, P. T. designed and built two hard-hulled, dory-style boats, taking them through the Grand Canyon along with one other boat and eight people, including Susie.

Reilly led Grand Canyon river trips again each year from 1955 to 1959 and in 1962 and 1964. He was adamant that he never ran them as commercial trips; they were for his enjoyment and vacation. He invited friends and associates along to share the river and the canyon with him and Susie. He was also proud of the fact that he never ran the same boats twice but constantly worked on improving their construction, whether by changing the design or the materials. All changes were not for the better, but they eventually helped Reilly to achieve what he felt was the best boat for Grand Canyon.

Not all of P. T.'s fourteen Grand Canyon trips need attention here, but some surely do. Reilly's three trips from 1957 through 1959 are notable for being on extremely high water. Commercial river running had started to expand by this time, and most trips were in hard-hulled motor boats or military-surplus inflatable rafts. P. T. continued to row his wooden and fiberglass boats, even during the 1957 peak of over 125,000 cubic feet per second, the highest flow since 1927 and the highest-water rowing attempt of the Colorado River known.[7] These trips were not without their problems: broken oars, leaking fiberglass, boat flips, flooded campsites, a lost boat, hard-to-manage recoveries of boats and crew, and jammed driftwood on Lake Mead. The aforementioned events led P. T. to discontinue the 1957 trip at Bright Angel Creek, to abandon two boats at Lava Falls on the 1958 return trip, and to scuttle two boats at Pipe Creek in 1959. After boating on flows of up to 106,000 cubic feet per second in 1958, he stated in his trip log: "It is my considered opinion that a volume of 55,000–60,000 cfs is the top limit for consistently safe operations for controlled oar powered craft." At Pipe Creek in 1959, he noted: "Next I shove off the SUSIE and she rides the rapid as if I'm at the oars. She takes the laterals at a beautiful angle. She rounds the bend and my oar powered days have come to an end."

P. T. took newspaper and magazine journalist Martin Litton on his first trips through Grand Canyon, as a passenger in 1955 and as a boatman in 1956. A member of the Sierra Club's board of directors, Litton was instrumental in the fight against Congress, the Bureau of Reclamation, and Arizona in their failed bids to authorize and construct dams in Grand Canyon. Convincing P. T. to row again after a three-year retirement and no boats, Martin suggested for a 1962 trip that because of a lack of boat-building time, they order unfinished dory hulls from Oregon and finish them themselves. Because Litton and Reilly worked separately, the *Susie Too* and the *Portola* were slightly different, reflecting the personalities of their owners. With Brick Mortenson's *Flavell II*, the trip floated on an average of about 45,000 cubic feet per second,[8] what Reilly's log reports as "the easiest flow I have ever run ... The action of all our boats was good but the two dories are as much improved over the SUSIE R as the latter was over the Nevills sad-iron. The dories are the best craft for water in Marble-Grand that I have ever seen." The *Susie Too* presently resides in the courtyard at Grand Canyon National Park's Visitor Center with other historic river running craft.[9]

Knowing that the gates to Glen Canyon Dam would be closed in mid-1964, the Reilly party left Lee's Ferry April 27 on a pre-spring runoff flow of about 11,000 cubic feet per second. Below Whitmore Wash on May 12, they received a message from the chief park ranger in a note that Tuweap ranger John Riffey dropped from his airplane. It informed them that the dam's gates had been closed prematurely the day before and the river flow cut to 1,000 cubic feet per second, an unboatable level. Not wanting to abandon their equipment, they decided to race the falling river the next fifty miles to below the last rapid. The message instructed that "If you receive this note and do not wish to leave the river, one person stand alone and wave something white." Martin Litton literally tore the white shirt off his back to wave it at the overhead aircraft. In a caption to a Reilly photograph of Litton and his ripped shirt, P. T. wrote, "Martin wore his White Shirt of Honor with great pride and sacrificed it with a fitting sunrise ceremony to the River Monster on our last morning." Rowing as hard and as fast as they could for the next two days, the trip slogan from then on became "let's flush on down."[10]

With Reilly's help organizing and leading Colorado River trips in 1962 and 1964, François Leydet and the Sierra Club were able to publish in 1964 *Time and the River Flowing*. The Sierra Club placed a copy of the book on the chair of every senator and congressional representative, one weapon among many used to help preserve Grand Canyon.[11] Besides resulting in Leydet's classic book, the 1964 trip produced another important discovery for P. T. He was able to identify the location where Peter Hansbrough and Henry Richards lost their lives in Marble Canyon on July 15, 1889 on the Brown-Stanton expedition, a place long sought by Colorado River historians.[12]

In 1964, P. T. and Susie Reilly responded to rumors of continued destruction of the buildings at Lee's Ferry by joining forces with a National Park Service ranger on October 6 to conduct a complete survey of the structures. After involvement by several organizations, including the Park Service, a more thorough study occurred December 10–11. Recommendations from the report of January 1965 stated that "the evidences of the pioneer history of the river have remained undisturbed by modern development," and that "these remains are now threatened largely because the historic importance of the place is not appreciated."[13] Reilly has shown that destruction occurred before the statement and continued after the caveat. The National Historic Preservation Act became law on October 15, 1966, and thus improved the attitude regarding the structures at Lee's Ferry; however it did not forestall some destruction in 1967. In 1974, Congress listed the Lees Ferry Historic District on the National Register of Historic Places.[14]

The year 1964 also marks the beginning of Reilly's concerted effort at researching Lee's Ferry history by conducting and recording oral history interviews with anyone associated with the area. After the river trip, P. T. began the first of twenty years worth of recording, the recordings that form the crux of his manuscript. For although he meticulously researched virtually all written work concerning Lee's Ferry, the personal relationships of the people with the place became the heart of the story. Befriending his narrators, Reilly obtained other names and further leads, the evidence of which is found in his book's documentation. Many of the interviewees are no longer available to relate their stories.

P. T. also had other historic accomplishments, many of which resulted in publications. A friend and fellow member of the Los Angeles Adventurer's Club introduced Reilly in 1951 to Arthur Randall Sanger at a regular Thursday evening meeting. Sanger related a story of a heretofore unknown Grand Canyon traverse in 1903 that involved him, Elias Benjamin Woolley, and John Aaron King. P. T.'s article on the "ignored fifth" trip of "Hum" Woolley is still the definitive story of this amazing Colorado River expedition.[15] His "How Deadly Is Big Red?" is the basis for any study on deaths on the Colorado River.[16] Reilly's publications cover more than historical topics—they range from book reviews to articles on archaeology, anthropology, travertine formations, aerial discoveries, springs, and reservoirs. "Discovery of Keyhole Natural Bridge" documents P. T.'s April 16, 1956, use of aerial photography to make a modern rediscovery of a natural bridge up 140-Mile Canyon.[17] The Board on Geographic Names adopted Reilly's proposed name for this bridge as well as at least eighteen names he gave to other locations.

Reilly witnessed the immediate effects of the closing of the gates at Glen Canyon Dam in 1964 and the after effects in 1982 and in 1984 on a filmed reunion trip with Martin Litton and his dories.[18] P. T. and Susie accompanied John Hoffman, Emery Kolb's great-granddaughter Jennifer Lehnert, and boatman Art Gallenson on a 1982 Grand Canyon Expeditions history trip. Using a thirty-seven-foot motorized commercial raft, it was P. T.'s first and only river trip in anything other than a hard-hulled, oar-powered boat. Typical for him, Reilly kept a trip log and typed two pages of conclusions. "Change is certainly taking place. We don't notice it as much when we are in the midst of it but when we become detached for a lengthy period and return, it really strikes home. I was away from the river for eighteen years and the changes were monumental when I came back." After describing Glen Canyon Dam's effects regarding flow volumes, silt depletion, tamarisk invasion, and water quality, P. T. discussed an increase in the numbers of river runners. "Hance was an eye-opener for me. I never saw so many BFRs exposed [rocks revealed by the low, power-generating river flow from Glen Canyon Dam], and the 13 rigs and approximately 200 people at the head were more people than I saw in the canyon during my entire career, even including Georgie's large parties which I saw twice during the late 1950s and early 1960s." His stated opinion: "The simple fact is that this environment is too fragile to withstand the impact of 15,000 people annually, year after year."

In 1986, P. T. finished his Lee's Ferry manuscript after over twenty years of research and writing. Too lengthy at two volumes, reviewers were enthusiastic, but publishers were reluctant to go to press without some editing and shortening. Revision was one of the projects that was always on the back burner, and Reilly never did get to it. It seemed to some that he felt his major achievement had been accomplished, that if it never saw publication, his work still pleased him the way it was.[19] He was not idle, however, as researchers and historians were always contacting him for information. He also continued to add to his publication list, with a biographical article on Norman Nevills, a photographic essay on pre-Lake Powell Glen Canyon, and historical contributions on high-water boating and the location of the 1889 Hansbrough-Richards tragedy.[20]

Much has happened and continues to happen at Lee's Ferry and along the Colorado River since Reilly finished his manuscript in the mid-1980s. The boom in public demand for commercial and private river trips after the dam fight days of the 1960s has continued until the activity now includes over 16,000 recreational river runners departing each year from Lee's Ferry. That is, approximately 72 percent of the average annual total of over 23,000 recreational users on the Colorado River through the Grand Canyon embark from Lee's Ferry, a number which does not include around 5,000 commercial crew members, Park Service employees, and researchers.[21] Where Reilly rarely saw any other people on the river, increased use caused the Park Service to establish use limits in the early 1970s.[22] The National Park Service is currently involved in a multi-year review process of the 1980 Colorado River Management Plan (CRMP); in an attempt to alleviate crowding and contacts on the river, changes in launch procedures and numbers at Lee's Ferry will most likely occur.[23]

The National Park Service once again contracted a survey, this time of the Spencer steamboat specifically but also including Spencer's mining operations and a Lee's Ferry historic site evaluation. Published in 1987, the resulting report was comprehensive and provided management recommendations. Glen Canyon Dam operations adversely affect historical preservation when fluctuating flows cause constant wetting and drying of the steamboat and lead to its deterioration. In 1989, the *Charles H. Spencer* was listed as an individual property within the Lees Ferry Historic District, the same year that Secretary of the Interior Manuel Lujan ordered an environmental impact statement on the operations of Glen Canyon Dam.[24] The final EIS recommended minimum flows of 8,000 cubic feet per second from the dam to provide the best protection of the boat through constant submersion and a relatively stable sediment base level, consistent with what the National Park Service advocated. The report concluded that "the key to the situation today lies in preserving and interpreting the remaining features related not only to the Spencer mining operations, but also to the USGS years of survey and river monitoring at Lee's Ferry." Park Service recommendations for the Historic District include continued monitoring, continued stabilization and preservation, additional research, institution of a more comprehensive interpretive program, and no new developments.[25]

Reilly's 1964 "Permit to Traverse Colorado River" was one double-sided sheet, containing mostly data entries but with eleven conditions on the back. In 1982, P. T. noted that "each outfit is checked out by an NPS ranger at Lees Ferry to insure compliance with 20 pages of regulations"; regulations are much longer now with the almost-annual revision of the CRMP's "Commercial Operating Requirements" and "Noncommercial River Trip Regulations."[26] P. T. stated that "The NPS seems to be doing a good job at controlling litter as I saw less of it than I have seen from the camps" of others in the 1950s. Now a part of Park Service regulations, many "leave it as it is" practices were begun in the 1970s by river guides and outfitters who attempted to mitigate the increasing human impact on the riparian environment.

More than nineteen thousand trout fisherman annually congregate at Lee's Ferry. They boat upstream to the dam through the sixteen remaining miles of Glen Canyon, which support a multimillion-dollar, blue-ribbon trout fishery, a post-dam economic boon for the area.[27] Where once Lee's Ferry residents dynamited native fish for food, Glen Canyon Dam is now to be operated to minimize impact on native fish, among other purposes.[28] Selective withdrawal structures at the dam are being considered to increase mainstem water temperatures and thereby create new spawning populations of native fish; also being discussed is flooding of the Pahreah River mouth during spawning periods to more closely reflect pre-dam conditions.

The building of Glen Canyon Dam eliminated about 70 percent of the sediment in the Colorado River. The Pahreah River, which carried only .16 percent of the pre-dam river's volume but almost 5 percent of its sediment, now supplies the overwhelming majority of the sediment entering Marble Canyon, an important factor when considering beach replenishment in this reach.[29] Although the dam controls the flow of the Colorado, the Bureau of Reclamation is committed to reduce the chance of a spill to once every one hundred years.[30] Lake Powell filled in 1980 and overfilled in 1983, forcing the Bureau to release water through all eight turbines, four bypass jet tubes, and both spillways to achieve flows of over 90,000 cubic feet per second, more than the average peak and approaching the higher end of recorded pre-dam spring runoff.[31]

September 14, 1995, brought the official dedication of the second Navajo Bridge. Originally dedicated on June 14, 1929, the structure that replaced the ferry as a river crossing has now itself been replaced. With modern oversize and overweight vehicles traveling the nation's roads, Arizona Department of Transportation engineers determined that the 1929 Navajo Bridge was no longer adequate for the amount and size of the traffic. The original bridge has been closed to vehicles and is now open only to pedestrians, pedestrians who were once forbidden to walk on it. The new bridge approaches probably go through the sites of Buck Lowery's trading post and the Arizona inspection station. Highway 89, the main thoroughfare between northern Arizona and southern Utah, bypasses Lee's Ferry, passing over the Colorado River just downstream of Glen Canyon Dam on its route to Kanab. A new visitor center has been built near the old bridge on the west side of the river; memorial plaques to the Nevills and others have been moved from the area under the old bridge and given places of new prominence in the visitor's center courtyard.

P. T. Reilly "ran the last rapid," succumbing to congestive heart failure at home, on October 24, 1996.[32] Presenters at the "Grand Canyon: A Century of Change" gathering on November 6 dedicated the proceedings to P. T. for his contributions—by sharing his logs, observations, and photographs—to research of pre-dam river conditions.[33] To assist future historians and other researchers and in accord with his wishes, Elizabeth M. Reilly in 1997 donated P. T.'s vast collection of folders, books, and photographs from his "gold room" to Cline Library Special Collections and Archives Department at Northern Arizona University. That same year Susie once again pursued the publication of P. T.'s Lee's Ferry manuscript. Susie had been involved with P. T.'s research from the beginning, through the river trips and the interviews and by typing, editing, retyping, proofing, indexing, and offering all her support over the years. Her contribution to P. T.'s book cannot be denied.

Over thirty years have passed since P. T. began his research, over ten years since he finished writing. Great timing and determination on his part allow us to share the details of his efforts. This book will certainly increase anyone's knowledge of the Lee's Ferry area and its people and, it is hoped, provide enjoyment in the process. Susie Reilly particularly liked Pat's original closing paragraph. It is still a worthy ending. Publication of P. T.'s research helps to ensure that Lee's Ferry will be a place not just of the past but also of the present and of the future:

> Yesterday's Lee's Ferry was a pioneer crossing for an expanding people, the ranch a green oasis in a barren landscape. Tomorrow the ferry will continue to be what it is today—a recreation center for fishing, river-running, and hiking, its rich history a thing of the past.[34]

Chapter Notes

The following abbreviations are used in the chapter notes:

BYU	Brigham Young University, Provo, Utah
DC	Dixie College, St. George, Utah
LDS	Historical Department, Church of Jesus Christ of Latter-day Saints, Salt Lake City, Utah
NA	National Archives, College Park, Maryland
NAU	Cline Library Special Collections and Archives Department, Northern Arizona University, Flagstaff, Arizona
PTR	P. T. Reilly Collection, Cline Library, Northern Arizona University, Flagstaff, Arizona
UA	University of Arizona Special Collections, Tucson, Arizona
USHS	Utah State Historical Society, Salt Lake City, Utah
USGS	U.S. Geological Survey District Office, Tucson, Arizona

All cited interviews were between the cited person and P. T. Reilly. Unless otherwise noted, all documentation of interviews is in PTR.

Editor's Preface

1. One story of P. T. Reilly's exploits in Grand Canyon appears in Robert H. Webb, *Grand Canyon: A Century of Change* (Tucson: University of Arizona Press, 1996), 19. His version of his high-water boating appears in P. T. Reilly, "My High Water Experience in Marble and Grand Canyons," *Boatman's Quarterly Review* 10(2) (Spring 1997): 17–19.
2. E. B. Measeles, *Lee's Ferry* (Boulder, Colorado: Pruett Publishing, 1981); W. L. Rusho and C. G. Crampton, *Desert River Crossing: Historic Lee's Ferry on the Colorado River* (Salt Lake City: Peregrine Smith 1975).

Chapter 1

1. [*The Domínguez-Escalante Journal*, ed. T. J. Warner, trans. Fray A. Chavez (Salt Lake City: University of Utah Press, 1995). *Ed.*]
2. Although aboriginal petroglyphs are not decipherable literally, they were made at strategic places on well-traveled routes, just as modern humans erect billboards where many people will see them.

3. [Several biographies exist for Jacob Hamblin: P. Bailey, *Jacob Hamblin, Buckskin Apostle* (Los Angeles: Westernlore Press, 1948); P. H. Corbett, *Jacob Hamblin, Peacemaker* (Salt Lake City: Deseret Book Company, 1952); and Juanita Brooks, *Jacob Hamblin, Mormon Apostle to the Indians* (Salt Lake City: Howe Brothers Books, 1980). Also see L. H. Creer, *The Activities of Jacob Hamblin in the Region of the Colorado*, University of Utah Anthropological Paper no. 33 (Salt Lake City, 1958). *Ed.*]

4. Juanita Brooks, *The Mountain Meadows Massacre* (Norman: University of Oklahoma Press, 1962), 102. [In early September 1857, approximately 120 emigrants were killed at Mountain Meadows, a resting spot on the California Trail in southern Utah. Only the youngest children of the party were spared. It was later learned that the perpetrators were local Mormon militia men allied with Indians. *Ed.*]

5. Of the three Hopi mesas, the westernmost is designated Third, the middle is Second, and the easternmost First Mesa.

6. Progressive Hopi recognized the need for allies in the long struggle against their traditional enemies, the Navajos, but none appear to have perceived Mormon motivation for cultivating them.

7. Hamblin to Young, in "Journals and Letters of Jacob Hamblin," 71, BYU. Hamblin frequently had his letters written by better-educated brethren, which he signed.

8. *Annual Report of Commissioner of Indian Affairs*, 1870, 598, and 1875, 211.

9. Charles Kelly, ed., "Walter Clement Powell," *Utah Historical Quarterly* 16–17 (1948–49): 469, entry for November 5, 1872.

10. Conditions among the Hopi and the journey home are documented in the "Journal of Andrew S. Gibbons," LDS. See also James A. Little, *Jacob Hamblin: A Narrative* (Salt Lake City: Juvenile Instructor Office, 1991), 63.

11. Juanita Brooks, ed., "Journal of Thales H. Haskell," *Utah Historical Quarterly* 12 (1944): 570–95.

12. Shuichi Nagata, *Modern Transformations of Moenkopi Pueblo* (Urbana: University of Illinois Press, 1970), 32.

13. "Journal of Thales Haskell," 594, entry for March 5. Haskell forgot that 1860 was a leap year, so all of his dates after February 28 are one day off. He noted the Hopi raised cotton at Moenkopi.

14. Little, *Narrative*, 62.

15. "Diary of George A. Smith, Jr.," October 20, 1860, LDS. The young man wrote entries through September 16, but Hamblin carried on in Smith's name from October 10 through November 1.

16. Ibid., October 26, 1860.

17. Hamblin said three Hopi joined the trip and they crossed the Ute Ford on January 1, 1863. John Steele, who kept a journal during the trip (LDS) stated that four Hopi came to them and the crossing was made December 30, 1862. Since Hamblin told his story to Little about eighteen years after this episode, it could be assumed that his memory was not as accurate as Steele's journal. The fourth Hopi probably was Lye, a loner who traveled on his own. See Little, *Narrative*, 78–79.

18. James G. Bleak, Annals of the Southern Utah Mission, Book A: 112, LDS.

19. According to anthropologist David Brugge (Brugge to P. T. Reilly, March 15, 1968), the Navajo name for this trail is *Jadi Heabitiin*, which means Antelope

Trail. The Hopi name has not been ascertained. The trail ascends a landslide area, and parts of it can still be seen from Arizona Highway 89.

20. The expedition is well documented by Bleak. The original was found by A. K. Larson in Bleak's old desk in St. George, LDS, DC, PTR.

21. Bleak, Annals, Book A: 188, 191.

22. The Black Hawk War is well documented in Peter Gottfredson, *History of Indian Depredation in Utah* (Salt Lake City: Skelton Publishing Company, 1919); Bleak, Annals, Book A; A. F. Robinson, ed., *History of Kane County* (Salt Lake City: Utah Printing Company, 1970); and the William Palmer Collection in Southern Utah State College Library, Cedar City.

23. D. D. McArthur to Major R. Bentley, January 21, 1866, quoted in Bleak, Annals, A: 195.

24. Hamblin to Snow, November 21, 1870, quoted in Bleak, Annals, B: 65

25. This tragedy occurred in Paiute country and the arrows left in the bodies were identified as Paiute.

26. The expedition is well documented in C. G. Crampton and D. E. Miller, ed., "Journal of Two Campaigns by Utah Territorial Militia against the Navajo Indians, 1869," *Utah Historical Quarterly*, 29(2) (1961): 148–76. See also Jacob Gates to Brigham Young, St. George, February 28, 1869, in Brigham Young Incoming Letter File, LDS.

27. This trail saw sporadic use through the Lee, Johnson, Emett, and Spencer eras. Charles H. Spencer improved it in 1911–12. Its greatest use coincided with the influx of tourists, starting in the 1960s.

28. [Robinson, *History of Kane County*, 8–34. *Ed.*]

29. Hamblin and J. R. Young to George A. Smith, September 12, 1869, in Journal History, LDS.

30. "Diary of Horatio Morrill," USHS, and Little, *Narrative*, 93.

31. Bleak, Annals, B: 21.

32. Snow to Young, November 20, 1869, Brigham Young Incoming Letter file, LDS.

33. John H. Krenkel, ed., *The Life and Times of Joseph Fish, Mormon Pioneer* (Danville, Illinois: Interstate Printers, 1971), 122–25.

34. B. H. Roberts, *A Comprehensive History of the Church of Jesus Christ of Latter-day Saints*, vol. 5 (Salt Lake City: Deseret News Press, 1930), 327; Andrew Jenson, *Infancy of the Church: An Elaborate and Detailed Description of Persons, Places, and Incidents Connected with the Early Rise and Progress of the Church of Jesus Christ of Latter-day Saints* (Salt Lake City, 1899).

35. Brooks, *Mountain Meadows*.

36. [Two sources on the life of John D. Lee are Juanita Brooks, *John Doyle Lee, Zealot, Pioneer Builder, Scapegoat* (Glendale, California: A. H. Clark Company, 1961), and *A Mormon Chronicle, The Diaries of John D. Lee 1848–1876*, ed. Robert Glass Cleland and Juanita Brooks, 2 vols. (San Marino, California: the Huntington Library, 1955). See; Brooks, *Mountain Meadows*, 60–68, for limits to Lee's leadership. *Ed.*]

37. Thomas D. Brown, *Journal of the Southern Indian Mission*, ed. Juanita Brooks (Logan: Utah State University Press, 1972), 98–99.

38. Brooks, *Mountain Meadows*. See also "The Military as an Aid to Colonization in Utah," Case 1, Item 24, Cedar City Public Library.

39. Cleland and Brooks, *Diaries*, 2: 134.

40. [Robinson, *History of Kane County*, 20–22. *Ed.*]
41. [The journals of the first Powell expedition are given in chronological order in John Cooley, *The Great Unknown* (Flagstaff, Arizona: Northland Publishing, 1988). Powell's accounts, which merge his two expeditions and have some fictionalized sections, are J. W. Powell, *The Exploration of the Colorado River and Its Canyons* (New York: Dover Publications, 1961, reprint of the edition by Government Printing Office, Washington, 1875) and J. W. Powell, *Canyons of the Colorado* (Meadville: Flood and Vincent, 1895). Biographies of Powell are Wallace Stegner, *Beyond the Hundredth Meridian* (Boston: Houghton Mifflin Company, 1962), and W. C. Darrah, *Powell of the Colorado* (Princeton, New Jersey: Princeton University Press, 1951). *Ed.*]
42. W. C. Darrah, ed., "Journal of George Y. Bradley," *Utah Historical Quarterly* 15 (1947): 58, and W. C. Darrah, ed., "Journal of John C. Sumner," *Utah Historical Quarterly* 15 (1947): 118.
43. [Powell's version of what happened at Separation Rapid (Powell, *The Exploration*, 278–82) conflicts with other witnesses interviewed in Robert Brewster Stanton, *Colorado River Controversies*, ed. J. M. Chalfant (New York: Dodd, Mead & Co., 1932), 138–232. Another version claims the Howlands and Dunn were killed by Mormons, who mistook the trio for federal officers investigating the Mountain Meadows Massacre (W. P. Larsen, "The 'Letter,' or were the Powell men really killed by Indians?" *Canyon Legacy* 17 (1993): 12–19). *Ed.*]
44. Darrah, *Powell of the Colorado*, 152.
45. Cleland and Brooks, *Diaries*, 2: 135.
46. In 1852, Lee had selected the original site of Harmony with his own interests in mind. The site was too small for expansion, insuring he would gain control. The Indian missionaries under Rufus Allen who arrived later were very critical of the location. On May 19–20, 1854, President Young resolved the matter by moving the settlement four miles, where the communal farm was located. Politics and personal selfishness were not absent in the Mormon Kingdom of God. See Brown, *Journal*, 18, 19, 30, 31.
47. Cleland and Brooks, *Diaries*, 2: 139–40.
48. Hamblin, *Narrative*, 95. Jacob remembered this as being the spring of 1870, but his memory clearly was in error.
49. Hamblin to Young, September 30, 1870, LDS.
50. [The *Cañon Maid*, built in 1870, should not be confused with Powell's 1869 boat, the *Maid of the Cañon*. Powell, *The Exploration*, 120. *Ed.*]
51. Dr. J. H. Butchart identified the location from which Thomas Moran painted "The Chasm of the Colorado" in August 1873 and Jack Hillers took this photograph which later was used to make an engraving. It was printed in J. W. Powell, *Exploration of the Colorado River of the West and Its Tributaries Explored in 1869, 1870, 1871, and 1872* (Washington, D. C.: Government Printing Office, 1875), facing 195, and Powell, *The Exploration* (1961), 276. The view was taken about 1,400 feet below Muav Saddle, at the top of the Redwall, looking south by east to Dox Castle. Moran and another artist, Jack Colburn, were taken to the Kaibab by Powell in August 1873 (C. G. Crampton, ed., "Diary of Almon Harris Thompson," *Utah Historical Quarterly* 7 (1939): 114). The trail goes down Muav Canyon via Shinumo to the River and up Bass Canyon to Havasupai Point, where Bass built a tourist camp. The Shinumo

Trail north of the river and the Bass Trail on the south side constituted the main mid-canyon route.

52. Powell, *The Exploration*, 331–32.

53. Darrah, *Powell*, Corbett, *Jacob Hamblin*, and others insist on calling this man F. F. Bennett, possibly due to misinterpreting the captain's handwriting or an error in transcription. War Department records leave no doubt that his full name was Frank Tracy Bennett.

54. Robert W. Young, ed., *Navajo Yearbook* (Window Rock, Arizona: Bureau of Indian Affairs, 1960), 371.

55. Hamblin to Snow, November 21, 1870, in Erastus Snow File, LDS. Both Hamblin's and Bennett's letters are copied in Bleak, *Annals*, B: 160–68.

56. Roberts, *Comprehensive History*, 5: 353.

57. Cleland and Brooks, *Diaries*, 2: 143–44, 146.

58. Ibid., 146–47, November 22, 1870.

59. Ibid., 153–54, December 28, 1870.

60. Ibid., 154, January 3, 1871.

61. Journal History, April 13 and 24, July 25, 1871, LDS. Telesnimki also was known as Pulasimki and later as Coehenumon.

62. Bleak, Annals, B: 73–74.

63. No Navajo accounts are available, but Mormon versions of the affair were related to Powell's crew. See October 6, 1871, J. K. Hillers, *"Photographed All the Best Scenery," Jack Hillers' Diary of the Powell Expeditions, 1871–1875*, ed. Don D. Fowler (Salt Lake City: University of Utah Press, 1972), 85, and "Walter Clement Powell," 342. See also Bleak, Annals, B: 111–15. Lee (Cleland and Brooks, *Diaries*, 2: 331) said President Young let Jacob have seventy-five horses.

64. Hamblin to Snow, Kanab, September 13, 1871. Erastus Snow Papers, 1818–88, LDS.

65. "Walter Clement Powell," 356.

66. Cleland and Brooks, *Diaries*, 2: 174, November 10, 1871.

67. Polygamous wives often were seized and held as material witnesses to confront their husbands in court.

68. Cleland and Brooks, *Diaries*, 2: 175–76, 189.

69. [The name "Lonely Dell" typically is attributed to Emma; see Juanita Brooks, *Emma Lee* (Logan: Utah State University Press, 1975), 57. *Ed.*]

70. Lee's successor, Warren Johnson, found the Pahreah flats so limited for grazing that he built a trail to reach the bench below the Vermilion Cliffs. Also see Chapters 14 and 15.

71. Cleland and Brooks, *Diaries*, 2: 176–79.

72. Ibid., 179–80.

Chapter 2

1. Daniel Tyler, *A Concise History of the Mormon Battalion in the Mexican War 1846–1848* (Glorietta, New Mexico: The Rio Grande Press, 1964), 125–26, 240. Rachel also became the first white woman to cross the Colorado above the Gila since January 11, 1847.

2. Cleland and Brooks, *Diaries*, 2: 182–83.

3. Charles Kelly, ed., "Captain Francis Marion Bishop's Journal," *Utah Historical Quarterly* 15 (1947): 225.

4. Badger Creek and Soap Creek Rapids are eight and eleven miles, respectively, below Lee's Ferry. Badger Creek Rapid has egress via Jackass Canyon on the left; Soap Creek Rapid is accessible by its south fork.

5. Cleland and Brooks, *Diaries*, 2: 185–86.

6. This description was obtained from Frank T. Johnson, who was taught by his father, Warren M. Johnson. Originally a non-farmer, W. M. Johnson was instructed by Emma B. and John D. Lee. Lee said this dam was eight feet high and one hundred and fifteen feet long, per Cleland and Brooks, *Diaries*, 2: 202.

7. "Diary of A. H. Thompson," 60; "John F. Steward," ed. W. C. Darrah, *Utah Historical Quarterly* 16–17 (1948–49): 250; "Walter Clement Powell," 361; Cleland and Brooks, *Diaries*, 2: 193–94. Lee used the names John and Joseph interchangeably.

8. Cleland and Brooks, *Diaries*, 2: 198.

9. Ibid., 200.

10. Ibid., 202

11. The river probably was running over 100,000 cubic feet per second.

12. *Salt Lake Tribune*, July 29, 1872, 9, and J. H. Beadle, *Western Wilds and the Men Who Redeem Them* (Cincinnati: Jones Brothers and Company, 1877).

13. Cleland and Brooks, *Diaries*, 2: 206. July 24 marks the Mormon entry into the Salt Lake Valley. In those days, and for many years to follow, it was celebrated more than the Fourth of July.

14. See Bishop's 1871 river map in W. L. Rusho, ed., "Francis Bishop's 1871 River Maps," *Utah Historical Quarterly* 37 (1969): 212. None of Powell's cartographers translated the soft Paiute phonetics into its best English equivalent. The author has heard Phoenix radio and TV announcers pronounce this place name as they would the word for outcast. Many descendants of pioneer families still pronounce the name correctly. [Also see discussion in Robinson, *History of Kane County*, 488–89. *Ed.*]

15. The excursion is detailed in Elmo Scott Watson, ed., *The Professor Goes West: Illinois Wesleyan University Reports of Major John Wesley Powell's Explorations, 1867–1874* (Bloomington: Illinois Wesleyan University Press, 1954), 88–106.

16. Ibid., 98–100.

17. Cleland and Brooks, *Diaries*, 2: 209.

18. Brigham Young Incoming Letter File, 1872, LDS.

19. "Walter Clement Powell," October 13, 1872.

20. Ibid., October 16, 1872; Cleland and Brooks, *Diaries*, 2: 215.

21. Hamblin's first visit to Moenkopi and Moenave is detailed in "Walter Clement Powell," November 2, 3, and 5, 1872.

22. Ibid. This was the first time Hamblin had traveled from Moenave to Bitter Springs.

23. Ibid., November 10, 1872.

24. Cleland and Brooks, *Diaries*, 2: 216.

25. Ibid., 217.

26. Ibid., 219.

27. This description of ferry construction was furnished by Frank T. Johnson, who built or helped build several such boats. Ferries here changed little over the years except for the use of rails, more iron accessories, and much later, a cable.

28. Cleland and Brooks, *Diaries*, 2: 219.
29. Ibid., 222–23.
30. Ibid., 223.
31. Ibid., 227.
32. Roundy to Young, March 7, 1873, Roundy File, LDS.
33. Bleak, Annals, Book B: entry for January 18, 1873, and A. Karl Larson, *Erastus Beaman Snow* (Dugway, Utah: Pioneer Press, 1973), 446–47.
34. Horton D. Haight, Official Report of the Arizona Mission, LDS. See also "Journal of Jacob Miller," 83, LDS.
35. Cleland and Brooks, *Diaries*, 2: 231.
36. Ibid., 232.
37. Ibid., 233.
38. The road construction is related in Cleland and Brooks, *Diaries*, 2: 231–35, and "Life of Zadoc Knapp Judd, Jr.," 9, PTR.
39. Horton Haight Report to Brigham Young, August 4, 1873, LDS.
40. "Journal of Andrew Amundsen, 1873," LDS, USHS, PTR.
41. The arrangement between Tuba and Hamblin is well documented: "Journal of W. C. Powell," Arizona Mission, February 6–May 21, W. H. Solomon, clerk; "Journal of W. H. Solomon," June 9, 15, 1873, and March 30, 31, 1874 ; and Blythe to Young, April 8, 1874, LDS, PTR. Roundy Report to Young, March 7, 1673, and "Journal of James S. Brown, December 1875," LDS, also are pertinent to the Mormon advance into Arizona. [Also James H. McClintock, *Mormon Settlement in Arizona* (Tucson: University of Arizona Press, 1985), *Ed.*]
42. Cleland and Brooks, *Diaries*, 2: 240.
43. The child was Susan N. Robbins, age nine days, per "Journal of John H. Standifird," July 13, 1873, LDS. The seven men rode over forty miles for their baths.
44. Cleland and Brooks, *Diaries*, 2: 244.
45. Ibid., 246. There is no record of such a troop movement, so Roundy, at best, repeated hearsay, which he passed to Lee as fact. There is little doubt Roundy was jealous of Lee and tried to discredit him at every turn. Note that on January 3, 1871, there was verbal sparring between them and Lee stated that Roundy had attempted to influence President Young against him (Cleland and Brooks, *Diaries*, 2: 154).
46. Cleland and Brooks, *Diaries*, 2: 263. Footnote 1 (p. 339) states that the misinformation might have originated in Salt Lake City. The author disagrees.
47. Horton Haight to Brigham Young, August 4, 1873, LDS. This report, the journals of Amundsen, Solomon, Jacob Miller, Standifird, and John D. Lee are the basic documents of the 1873 Arizona Mission.
48. Cleland and Brooks, *Diaries*, 2: 287–90.
49. L. R. Murphy, *Frontier Trader–William F. Arny* (Tucson: University of Arizona Press, 1972), 208–9.
50. Capt. G. M. Wheeler, *Report of the United States Geological and Geographical Surveys west of the 100th Meridian*, vol. 1 (Washington, D. C.: Government Printing Office, 1874), 152–53, Annual Report 1874, Appendix EE; Cleland and Brooks, *Diaries*, 2: 302.
51. Cleland and Brooks, *Diaries*, 2: 306–7. This marked the beginning of the Lee–Hamblin feud.
52. Hamblin to Erastus Snow, September 13, 1871, LDS.

53. Hamblin to Young, September 19, 1873, LDS.

54. McClintock, *Mormon Settlement in Arizona*, 92.

55. Lee's letter has not been found, either among the Safford Papers in the Arizona Archives or in LDS. It is known that his letter to McDonald was delivered and he sent it on to President Young, per the A. F. McDonald letter folder, LDS.

56. Blythe to Young and G. A. Smith, January 20, 1874, LDS.

57. Arizona Mission, LDS. It is filed under the name of Hans J. Peterson but undoubtedly was written by clerk and mission historian W. H. Solomon, whose journal (LDS) and several of Blythe's letters to Brigham Young substantiate every phase.

58. The story of James Jackson was preserved by traditional information passed from Emma Lee to Warren Johnson to his son Frank T. Johnson, together with Arizona Mission and "Journal of W. H. Solomon." [Interestingly, Brooks, *Emma Lee*, does not mention the Jackson incident. *Ed.*]

59. The Jackson episode also is related in Blythe's letter to Brigham Young and G. A. Smith, dated "Lonely Dell Colerado Arizona March 13th, 1874" [sic], LDS.

60. Cleland and Brooks, *Diaries*, 2: 327–38.

61. Ibid., 329–32. This was the first major quarrel between Hamblin and Lee, and enmity was bitter from that time on.

62. Arizona Mission and "Journal of W. H. Solomon," March 15, 1874. Both entries are identical because Solomon wrote them, LDS.

63. Blythe to Young, April 8, 1874, LDS.

64. Cleland and Brooks, *Diaries*, 2: 150

65. Ibid., 338.

66. This letter is printed in Bleak, Annals, B: 235–37.

67. Joseph A. Young to President Brigham Young, April 23, 1874, LDS.

68. John D. Lee to an unidentified recipient (San Marino, California, Huntington Library). Lee might have written this letter to A. F. McDonald, knowing that through him it would ultimately reach Brigham Young. The address and first line of the original are too worn and torn to be legible. Juanita Brooks erroneously ascribed this letter to Lee's description of his diary entry of December 29, 1873. See Brooks typescript compared to the author's typescript of same letter, PTR.

69. John R. Young to President Brigham Young, May 21, 1874, LDS.

70. Bleak, Annals, B: 302–4.

71. Little, *Narrative*, 129–30.

72. A comprehensive discussion of Mormon cooperative movements, including the United Order, is found in Leonard J. Arrington, *Great Basin Kingdom, An Economic History of the Latter-day Saints* (Cambridge, Massachusetts: Harvard University Press, 1958), and Leonard J. Arrington, Feramorz Y. Fox, and Dean L. May, *Building the City of God* (Salt Lake City: Deseret Book Company, 1976). See also P. T. Reilly, "Kanab United Order: the President's Nephew and the Bishop," *Utah Historical Quarterly* 42(2)(1974): 153–59.

73. Andrew Jensen, *Church Chronology* (Salt Lake City: Deseret News, 1914), 93.

74. Krenkel, *Joseph Fish*, 154.

75. Ibid., 159, and "Journal of J. H. Standifird," July 16, 1875, LDS.

76. Brooks, *Mountain Meadows*, 191–94. The jury was divided with eight Mormons for acquittal and four Gentiles for conviction.

77. Statement signed by Amorah Lee Smithson at Lebanon, Arizona, February 18, 1930, in "Lee Gleanings," 32–33, PTR.

78. "Journal of Brigham Young, Jr.," June 11, 1876, LDS. See also the statement of Benjamin S. and Elvira M. Johnson, May 22, 1931, Mesa, Arizona, in "Lee Gleanings," 32–33, PTR.

79. *Deseret News* 25: 542.

80. Jeremiah Johnson claimed his father, Warren M. Johnson, Warren's two wives, and Emma and John D. Lee attended. The account was traditional and no date was provided.

81. John D. Lee to Emma Batchelor Lee, September 21, 1876, Henry E. Huntington Library, San Marino, California. Also in George Wharton James, *In and Around the Grand Canyon* (Boston: Little Brown and Company, 1900), 226–29.

82. Renkel, *Joseph Fish*, 59–60, 165–66. The reliable Joseph Fish plied U.S. Marshal William Nelson with liquor after Lee's conviction and was told that Nelson and Sumner Howard had been guided by Brigham Young in building the case against Lee. [Yet another version of the execution is Wes Larsen, "Folktales: JDL Survives His Execution," *Boatman's Quarterly Review*, 7(2) (1994): 28. *Ed.*]

83. "Journal of Anthony W. Ivins," I: 198, USHS.

84. Amorah Lee Smithson to Edna Lee Brimhall, February 8, 1930, in "Lee Gleanings," PTR.

Chapter 3

1. Little, *Narrative*, 134.

2. Cleland and Brooks, *Diaries*, 2: 424.

3. Bleak, Annals, B: 337.

4. P. T. Reilly, "Warren M. Johnson, Forgotten Saint," *Utah Historical Quarterly* 38(1) (1971): 19, and Reilly, "Kanab United Order."

5. Price W. Nelson, "Autobiography of Price W. Nelson," DC, relates that the people of Glendale did not like the United Order; the constant wrangling caused its breakup within the year. Frank Johnson told the author that his father did not look kindly on the Order. [See Robinson, *History of Kane County*, 420–44. *Ed.*]

6. Reilly, "Kanab United Order," 144–64. An opposing viewpoint is offered in Arrington, Fox, and May, *Building the City*.

7. Bleak, Annals, B: 399–400.

8. Brooks, *Mountain Meadows*, 206, 300.

9. In Little, *Narrative*, 134, Hamblin does not name his clients, merely saying he worked sixty days and earned three hundred dollars. Daniel Webster Jones, *Forty Years Among the Indians* (Salt Lake City: Juvenile Instructor's Office, 1890), 220–86, does not mention the incident. An objective account is contained in "Journal of Anthony W. Ivins," October 10, 1875, to April 1882, USHS.

10. *Salt Lake Daily Herald*, March 30, April 7, 15, 23, and May 23, 1876. The letters are dated March 1 and 9 and April 1, all from "Moencopie," April 19 from "Mow a Ya-Be," and May 15, 1876, from St. George.

11. Cleland and Brooks, *Diaries*, 2: 419.

12. "Diary of Allen Frost," August 8, 1875, BYU.

13. Johnson's children remembered his Navajo name as *Pahazuna* or "Laughing Man." Admittedly phonetic differentiation is difficult, especially between the sounds of "b" and "p." The Navajo word for laughter is *dich* and Laughing Man would be *Dichnizini*. Of course, a laughing man is happy. The author is indebted to J. Lee Correll, head of Research Section, Navajo Nation, Window Rock, Arizona, for this information.

14. Bleak, Annals, B: 428, December 28,1875.

15. Card file on Warren M. Johnson, LDS, and Journal History, October 10, 1875. His actual call is in the possession of a grandchild in Colorado City.

16. "Journal of James S. Brown," holographic original by George S. Tanner, January 21, 1876, USHS, PTR.

17. Ibid., and *Deseret Evening News,* January 21, 1876.

18. Interview, Louetta Brown Tanner, Salt Lake City, October 14, 1970, PTR.

19. A. J. Lucas letter, dated Kanab, March 4, 1876, *Deseret News,* March 29, 1876.

20. "Autobiography of Price W. Nelson," 24.

21. Cleland and Brooks, *Diaries,* 2: 424–25.

22. "Journal of John A. Blythe," USHS.

23. "Diary of Joseph H. Richards," March 22, 1876, UA.

24. Frihoff G. Nielson, *Journals of Frihoff G. Nielson, Pioneer Mormon Records,* three volumes (unknown city, privately published by son Frihoff Ellis Nielson., n. d.), March 19, 1876. [Ironically, Hamblin eventually moved to Arizona, died in Pleasanton, New Mexico, in 1886, and is buried in Alpine. See McClintock, *Mormon Settlement,* 86–87. *Ed.*]

25. *Journals of Frihoff G. Nielson,* March 28, 1876.

26. Ibid., April 1, 1876.

27. Ibid., April 10, 1876.

28. "Diary of James S. Brown." As George S. Tanner points out, Brown wrote both a journal and a diary.

29. Interview, Frank T. Johnson.

30. "Journal of Brigham Young, Jr.," 16, May 16, 1876, LDS.

31. Ibid., May 24, 1876.

32. In 1964, the author identified Roundy Rock from a photo in the *Deseret News,* October 14, 1935. On April 29, 1965, he took Frank T. Johnson and his wife, Ada Lee Johnson, to Lee's Ferry, where Frank pointed out the boulder that caused the ferryboat to careen. In subsequent years after the accident, several Roundys visited the ferry to obtain the story of their progenitor's death from Warren M. Johnson. He showed them the boulder which had been called "Roundy Rock" for many years. The descendants hoped to fasten a bronze plate on the rock, but this was never done. Instead, they used "wagon tar," or black paint, and there still were traces of the markings in 1965. The elevation of the top of Roundy Rock was established to a known discharge of 6,000 cubic feet per second when the Lee's Ferry gage read 7.5 feet. The differential corresponded to a gage height of 17.0 feet, which translated roughly to a volume of 83,000 cubic feet per second on May 24, 1876; Arnold J. Harms to P. T. Reilly, July 17, 1969, PTR.

33. The major documents pertaining to this tragedy are: Nuttall to Young, May 29, 1876 (*Deseret News,* June 7, 1876); W. D. Johnson to Editor, *Deseret News,* June 4, 1876; and Documentary history, LDS. W. D. Johnson was not present

and was not a witness. Probate of Lorenzo W. Roundy, Kane County, Kanab, Utah; Journal History, May 24, 1876; account of Thomas H. Lowe, who was present and gave his version on April 30, 1930, LDS; Little, *Narrative*, 135–36. Hamblin erroneously remembered the tragedy as having occurred May 28. "Diary of John Bushman," LDS; oral statements of Frank T. Johnson, Clara Emett Davis, and Solena Emett Bennett; Elizabeth Johnson Colvin, *Story of My Life* (Colorado City, Arizona: privately published, n. d.), 12, PTR.

34. Her father told Solena Emett Bennett that these papers were deeds that church authorities had issued to the settlers of the Little Colorado. If so, the act was a unique phase of land-title involvement by ecclesiastics in one territory for land in another to which they held no title.

35. Lorenzo Hill Hatch referred to the "Drowned Journal" and said the story of *The Rescuer* was therein or in his "Red Book." Despite a diligent search in the BYU archives, the "Drowned Journal" could not be located with his other volumes.

36. *Journals of Frihoff G. Nielson,* June 4, 1876.

37. Ibid., May 5 and June 25, 1876.

38. Will C. Barnes, *Arizona Place Names* (Tucson: University of Arizona, 1960), 163–64.

39. "Journal of Brigham Young, Jr.," June 7, 1876.

40. "Journal of Anthony W. Ivins," vol. 1, box 4, June 11, 1876, USHS.

41. Ibid., 89. See also "Journal of Brigham Young, Jr.," June 14, 1876.

42. Brigham Young and Daniel H. Wells to Elders Smith, Lake, Ballenger, and Allen, July 15, 1876, LDS.

43. The Aaron Johnsons returned to the cemetery in November 1911. Jerry Johnson showed them the unmarked grave and helped restore it, even toting a sandstone slab down from the slopes to serve as a headstone. Aaron and his two sons returned again at the end of June 1923, exhumed the remains, and set a simple marker containing the initials "W. J." Winifred's remains were reinterred at Mapleton Evergreen Cemetery. Her journey home had required forty-seven years. "Autobiography of Aaron Johnson," USHS; and Jay Haymond to P. T. Reilly, January 23, 1978, PTR.

44. Lot Smith to Brigham Young, July 7, 1876; B. Young and D. Wells to Smith, Lake, Ballenger and Allen, July 20, 1876, LDS.

45. *Journals of Frihoff G. Nielson,* August 19, 1876.

46. "Journal of Daniel H. McAllister," USHS.

47. First Presidency to Jacob Hamblin, December 15, 1876, BYU, PTR. See also Bleak, *Annals*, B: 464–65.

Chapter 4

1. John W. Young to Erastus Snow; J. W. Young, 1877 folder, Box 2, LDS.

2. *Deseret News*, February 28, 1877, 52.

3. The party's thirst was described in Little, *Narrative*, 84–85.

4. Documentation for the trip consists of "Diary of John Bushman" for 1877, and "Diary of May Hunt Larson"; David P. Kimball to John W. Young, September 12, 1877, also is pertinent (in J. W. Young, 1877 letter folder), LDS.

5. H. Pearce letter, September 15, 1878, LDS.

6. *Journals of Frihoff G. Nielson,* December 10, 1877.

7. J. W. Young, 1878–79 folder, Box 2, LDS.

8. J. W. Young, 1877 folder, Box 2, LDS.

9. This episode is recorded in "Journal of Anthony W. Ivins," October 10, 1875, to April 1882. See also Larson, *Erastus Beaman Snow,* 42–58.

10. John W. Young Collection, Box 2, folder 3, LDS.

11. Albert E. Smith, ed., "Thales Hastings Haskell, Pioneer-Scout-Explorer, Indian Missionary," *1847–1909* (Salt Lake City, unpublished manuscript, 1963), 48–49, LDS.

12. Lot Smith to John Taylor, March 29, 1878, LDS.

13. Kanab Stake was organized April 18, 1877, with Bishop L. John Nuttall designated stake president. After this time, low-level decisions affecting Lee's Ferry were made in Kanab rather than St. George.

14. Kanab Stake Historical Record 1877–1914, 5, LDS.

15. Larson, *Erastus Beaman Snow,* 57.

16. Jesse N. Smith, *Six Decades in the Early West* (Provo, Utah: J. N. Smith Family Association, 1932), September 14, 1878, and L. John Nuttall to Editor of *Deseret News,* September 14, 1878.

17. Smith, *Six Decades,* 224.

18. John Taylor Letterbook, LDS. Berardo's Station was at the mouth of the Puerco River, two miles east of present Holbrook.

19. Interview, E. Reeseman Fryer and O. N. Vance (grandchildren of H. S. Phelps).

20. French and his wife came to California from Boston in 1852, attracted by the gold boom. He was associated with several mines in the Mother Lode country, served in Company E of the Second California Cavalry, and was wounded in the Battle of Shiloh, resulting in his carrying a silver plate in his skull. He owned a large stock and grain farm in Tulare and had a son born there in 1865. After his wife died, he returned to his old love, prospecting and mining. He came to Silver Reef during the height of the boom but was too late to acquire worthwhile claims. He then decided to placer the gravels at Lee's Ferry and arrived there during the winter of 1878–79. [See also Brooks, *Emma Lee,* 98–99. *Ed.*]

21. "Journal of Wilford Woodruff," March 14, 1879, LDS.

22. "Journal of L. John Nuttall," April 21, 1879, LDS.

23. Lewis Allen (Wilford Woodruff) to John Taylor and Council, April 11, 1879, from "Mount Refuge, Severe Co., Utah.," LDS. The fictitious location was given in case the letter fell into the wrong hands.

24. "Journal of L. John Nuttall," April 24, 1879, LDS.

25. Lewis Allen (Wilford Woodruff) to President Taylor and Council from "Point Lookout, Colorado," May 9, 1879, LDS.

26. J. W. Young to John Taylor, May 1, 1879, LDS.

27. Emma Betchelor [sic] Lee to L. J. Nuttall (in W. M. Johnson's handwriting), dated "Lee's Ferry May 11/1879," in J. W. Young letter folder, LDS.

28. See Warranty and Quit Claim Deeds, transcribed from Yavapai Co., Coconino County, Arizona, Book l, 23, and J. W. Young to John Taylor, dated "Sunset, Apache Co. A. T.," June 2, 1878 [1879], LDS.

29. J. W. Young to John Taylor June 2, 1878 [1879].

30. "Journal of L. John Nuttall," May 17 and July 11, 1879.

31. Emma B. Lee and Franklin French were married by Judge Stinson at Snowflake on August 9, 1879, per Apache County Records, 35.
32. Colvin, *Story of My Life*, 17.
33. U.S. Postal Records.
34. *Journals of Frihoff G. Nielson*, June 10, 1879.
35. Interview, Vera A. Miller. Family members are divided on whether he spelled his name Neuman or Newman, and whether he died between Jacob's Pools and the ferry or at the river.
36. "Journal of L. John Nuttall," November 24, 1879.
37. W. M. Johnson to Erastus Snow, January 28, 1880, LDS.

Chapter 5

1. James Leithead to Erastus Snow, January 28, 1880, and L. John Nuttall to James Leithead, February 20, 1880, E. Snow and J. Taylor Letterbooks, LDS.
2. Nuttall to Warren Johnson, March 1, 1880, LDS.
3. "Journal of Wilford Woodruff," March 8 and 9, 1880, LDS.
4. Smith, *Six Decades*, April 13, 1880.
5. Johnson to L. J. Nuttall, May 12, 1880, Warren Johnson folder, LDS.
6. Nuttall to Johnson, May 25, 1880, John Taylor Letterbook, LDS.
7. W. M. Johnson to John Taylor, July 1, 1880, Warren Johnson folder, LDS.
8. F. M. Lyman, Kanab, Utah, October 8, 1880, to Editor, *Deseret News*, printed November 3, 1880, 631.
9. Gordon Chappell, *Colorado Rail Annual, 1970* (Golden: Colorado Railroad Museum, 1970), 61–62.
10. See Minutes of Board Meeting and Stockholders of Canaan Co-op for December 10, 1880, and January 5, 1881, DC; and John Taylor to W. M. Johnson, December 11, 1880, LDS.
11. Wilford Woodruff to Lot Smith, December 14, 1880, LDS.
12. Mrs. Clifford W. Dayton of Phoenix, Arizona, to P. T. Reilly, August 20, 1969, PTR.
13. W. M. Johnson to W. Woodruff, December 24, 1880, LDS.
14. Denver & Rio Grande Railroad, Annual Report, Colorado Railroad Museum Library, Golden, Colorado; W. M. Johnson to John Taylor, April 15, 1881, LDS.
15. L. J. Nuttall to J. Leithead, May 4, 1881, in Taylor Letterbook, Reel 5, vol. 5, 171; and Nuttall to Leithead, July 8, 1881, in Nuttall letter folder, LDS.
16. This spring is now called Fisher Spring after the brothers George and Ed Fisher who ran stock there in the 1930s. See Lee's Ferry 15' quadrangle, Sec.16 T40N R7E. Finding the spring was related by Frank Johnson.
17. The long point to which this trail gave access is now named Johnson Point; P. T. Reilly to J. U. Kilmartin, executive secretary, Domestic Geographic Names, USGS, March 23, 1969, and Decision List 6903, July through September 1969, 7.
18. "Diary of Allen Frost," July 21, noted that "Bro. Stillson started for the ferry with freight for the RR Surveyors last evening," BYU.
19. E. Snow and B. Young, Jr., to John Taylor, September 11, 1881, LDS.
20. *Journals of Frihoff G. Nielson*, 1, 276.
21. The description of running the ferryboat down to the lower crossing was developed from an interview with Mrs. Elizabeth Johnson Colvin at Colorado City, October 6, 1965.

22. Nuttall to Johnson, December 10, 1881, LDS.

23. Johnson to Taylor, December 21, 1881, LDS.

24. Taylor to Johnson, January 7, 1882, LDS.

25. W. M. Johnson diary, 1882, LDS, PTR. Original owned by Johnson's granddaughter, Mrs. Eletha Jacobsen.

26. Ibid.

27. D. Brinkerhoff to L. J. Nuttall, October 4, 1882, BYU.

28. "Diary of Brigham Young, Jr.," February 28, 1883, LDS.

29. G. Chappell, "Narrow Gage Transcontinental 1: Scenic Line of the World," *Colorado Rail Annual,* 1970, 74–75.

30. Johnson to Taylor, May 9, 1883, LDS. Evidently no northbound traveler came by for some time because Johnson's letter was not received in Salt Lake City until June 2.

31. Interview, Elizabeth Johnson Colvin, Colorado City, October 6, 1965.

32. Unpublished diaries of Mary E. and Melinda Johnson. Transcripts and photographs of the more legible parts of the originals are in PTR. Colvin interview, October 6, 1965.

33. Johnson to Taylor, April 3, 1884, LDS.

34. "Kanab Stake Historical Record," A: 65, LDS. Possibly the eruption of Krakatoa on August 26 and 27, which put more than four cubic miles of volcanic debris into the air, contributed to this unusually severe winter.

35. Johnson to Taylor, May 15, 1884, LDS.

36. This large rock is a limestone fragment of Kaibab Formation at the contact at river mile 1.0. It was paced at twenty-eight feet long by Carl Pederson in 1964 when the outflow at Glen Canyon Dam was 1,000 cubic feet per second. The author has observed that the rock is covered at a flow of 43,000 cubic feet per second. The rock was identified by Frank Johnson.

37. Nuttall to Johnson, May 9, 1884, LDS.

38. Johnson to Nuttall, June 2, 1884, LDS.

39. L. C. Mariger to Nuttall, June 10, 1884, LDS.

40. Johnson to Nuttall, June 14, 1884, LDS.

41. "Diary of Christian Lingo Christensen," 57. The author is grateful to Ann E. Christensen Hyde for use of the original diary, BYU.

42. John H. Gardiner, "Lee's Ferry," in Frank B. Dodge, *Saga of Frank B. Dodge* (Tuscon, 1944), 78, USGS; and any U.S. Geological Survey Water-Supply Paper, Part 9, Colorado River Basin, gage records for Lee's Ferry and Colorado River near Grand Canyon. [The most recent compilation of gaging records for these stations and for the Pahreah River appears in J. M. Garrett and D. J. Gellenbeck, *Basin Characteristics and Streamflow Statistics in Arizona as of 1989,* U.S. Geological Survey Water-Resources Investigations Report 91–4041 (1991), 32, 36, 133. *Ed.*] The date of July 7, 1884, accepted by the U.S. Geological Survey for the peak, appears to be in error and Christensen's diary reports that the true peak at Lee's Ferry occurred on June 18.

43. "Diary of C. L. Christensen," June 18, 1884, BYU.

44. Johnson to Taylor, July 30, 1884, LDS.

45. "History of William C. Allen," 7, UA.

46. "Diary of C. L. Christensen," 62.

47. Ibid., 63–64. See also Smith, *Six Decades,* 296–97, Krenkel, *Joseph Fish,* 259–61, and "Journal of John H. Standifird."

48. "Diary of C. L. Christensen," 64.
49. Taylor to Johnson, December 16, 1884, LDS.
50. Smith, *Six Decades*, 303
51. Ibid., 304.
52. Kanab Stake Historical Record A: 86, March 8, 1885.
53. Johnson to Taylor, April 21 and May 1885, LDS.
54. Johnson Ferry Records, PTR.
55. "Autobiography of Price W. Nelson," 44.
56. "Diary of C. L. Christensen," 87.
57. *Journals of Frihoff G. Nielson*, March 2, 1886.
58. The Clevenger case is detailed in *Arizona Weekly Champion*, February 5, 1887; *Arizona Weekly Journal-Miner*, June 1, 11, 18, and July 5, 1887, NAU. See also "Zadok Knapp Judd Reminisces," 26–27, PTR, "Autobiography of Price W. Nelson," 6–7, and John Roberts, "The fate of the Clevenger family," *Arizona Historical Review* 3(4) (January 1931): 88–96.
59. *Arizona Weekly Champion*, February 5, 1887.
60. Sheriff W. J. Mulverson to W. M. Johnson, April 13, 1887, in possession of Mrs. Eletha J. Jacobsen.
61. "Autobiography of William James Frazier McAllister," USHS; Colvin, *Story of My Life*, 56; Mary Johnson Judd, "Life History of Warren Marshall Johnson and Family," PTR.
62. "Diary of C. L. Christensen," 90.
63. Ibid., August 23, 1885, February 3, 1886, October 1, 1886.
64. Taylor to Johnson, March 25, 1887, LDS.
65. "Diary of Allen Frost," December 4, 1886.
66. Ibid., March 26–29, 1887.
67. *Arizona Weekly Champion*, August 13, 1887.

Chapter 6

1. This boy became the "Prophet" and President of the United Effort Plan, a communal trust of polygamous Colorado City. An autocratic leader, Johnson built the UEP into a multimillion dollar enterprise before dying November 25, 1986.
2. "Diary of Melinda Johnson," unpublished manuscript, original owned by Eletha J. Jacobsen, PTR.
3. Johnson to Woodruff, November 22, 1887; Woodruff to Johnson, December 7, 1887, LDS.
4. Smith, *Six Decades*, December 7, 1887, 345.
5. Woodruff to Hatch and Johnson, April 30, 1888, LDS; Johnson Ferry Records, PTR.
6. Warren Johnson Road Account Book. Original held by J. S. Johnson, Kanab, Utah, PTR.
7. "L. C. Mariger Journal," July 25 through August 9, 1888, LDS. Johnson Ferry Records, August 1, 1888, PTR.
8. Johnson Ferry Records, PTR. Adams went to Pine, Arizona, but moved elsewhere after a year or two.
9. Johnson's letter to Woodruff was dated December 19, 1888, and Woodruff's reply was dated January 3, 1889, LDS.

10. Johnson to Woodruff, January 28, 1889, LDS.

11. Woodruff to Johnson, February 11, 1889, LDS.

12. Ibid.

13. Documentation for the events of the Canyon Diablo robbery are the *Coconino Sun*, March 23, 1889; the diaries of Mary E. and Melinda Johnson; a description of the events at Cannonville by W. J. Henderson, one of the participants, PTR. W. C. Barnes, *Apaches and Longhorns* (Los Angeles: Ward Ritchie Press, 1941); W. C. Sparks, *The Apache Kid, A Bear Fight, and Other True Stories of the Old West* (Los Angeles: Skelton Publishing Company, 1926); Lot Smith to W. Woodruff, June 25, 1889, LDS.

14. Matt Warner, *Last of the Bandit Riders*, as told to Murray E. King (New York: Bonanza Books, 1940), 80–97.

15. Harvey Hardy, "A Long Ride with Matt Warner," *Frontier Times* (November 1964): 34–35, 61. Being familiar with Matt Warner's story and then with the Hardy yarn, the author checked them out with several of Johnson's children. They were unanimous in declaring both to be pure fiction. Joshua Swett was a squaw man who lived with a Paiute woman and two half-breed children in the canyon named for him, about five miles southwest of Hite. According to A. L. Chaffin, Cass Hite "invited Swett to leave the country" after horses began disappearing with regularity (a stock thief typically would have been shot). Josh accepted the kind invitation and dropped out of sight. A search of Nevada death records from 1911 through 1939 for both Sweat and Swett revealed that no person by that name had died in Clark County between those years. Under the circumstances it would appear that Warner was motivated by the Canyon Diablo train robbery, that he inspired Hardy, and that both yarns belong in western fiction. About ten miles west of Cedar City, nearly to Iron Mountain, are the Swett Hills. According to local tradition, a horse thief named Swett operated here for several years until a posse strung him up, thereby ending the thefts and giving the hills a name. He likely was buried on the spot because there is no record of a Swett burial in the Cedar City Cemetery. See the Desert Mound, Hite, and Mt. Hillers 15' quadrangle sheets.

16. Frank Johnson interview. Clark Allen Huntington, son of the famous Mormon scout Dimmick B. Huntington, was born December 6, 1831, at Watertown, N.Y. He entered the Salt Lake Valley on July 29, 1847. He was on the Elk Mountain Mission in 1855, was one of the twenty-seven strong young men picked by Brigham Young to help the Handcart company. He and two others were the three who carried members of the debilitated Martin company across the icy Sweetwater River on November 3, 1856. He married Rosanna Galloway on February 8, 1857. He and his brother Lot got into trouble over some horses, and Clark was convicted in the court of Elias Smith on March 19, 1860. He was released on a writ of habeas corpus April 3. His brother was killed by Porter Rockwell on January 16, 1862. Clark went to California where his last child was born. His wife died, the children scattered, and he returned to Utah in the late 1880s.

17. The author has seen this eddy in high water and can verify its size and length. It is located at Mile 1.5 in Glen Canyon and the eddy's strong current extends nearly the width of the river. At this place the river emerges from the sandstone walls of Glen Canyon and courses down the upper leg of the Echo Cliffs.

18. References for Nielson's activities and the *Nellie* are found in the testimony of Thomas Fotheringham in the *River Bed Case, USA vs. State of Utah*, 28: 4,975–4,993, or 2, 1,267, USHS; the diaries of Mary E. and Melinda Johnson; and interview with Frank T. Johnson, September 29, 1964.

19. [The stories of the Brown-Stanton Expedition are told in Robert Brewster Stanton, *Down the Colorado*, ed. D. L. Smith (Norman: University of Oklahoma Press, 1965), and R. B. Stanton, *The Colorado River Survey*, ed. D. L. Smith and C. G. Crampton (Salt Lake City: Howe Brothers, 1987). Also see David Lavender, *River Runners of the Grand Canyon* (Grand Canyon, Arizona: Grand Canyon Natural History Association, 1985), 22–32. *Ed.*]

20. "Diary of Melinda Johnson"; F. A. Nims, *The Photographer and the River*, ed. by Dwight L. Smith (Santa Fe: Stagecoach Press, 1967), 38.

21. Stanton, *Down the Colorado*, 71, and Stanton Field Notes, 1889–90.

22. P. T. Reilly, "How Deadly Is Big Red?" *Utah Historical Quarterly* 37(2) (Spring 1969): 254–56.

23. "Diary of Melinda Johnson."

24. No trace of Johnson's claim has been found, so it is not known if he recorded the ten acres that Jacob Hamblin first assigned to James Jackson and that he took over, or expanded the claim to include the ranch and ferry crossing as a protection of church interests.

25. Smith, *Six Decades*, 368–70.

26. Johnson Ferry Records, 1889, 13.

27. Both Stanton and Melinda Johnson recorded Stanton's arrival as December 23, but Nims, who agreed with his chief that they left Crescent Wash on December 10, wrote that it was December 21; Nims, *Photographer*, 60; Stanton, *Down the Colorado*, 107; "Diary of Melinda Johnson"; Stanton Field Notes, 1889–90, USHS. [In the editor's experience, Stanton was a better recorder than Nims. Stanton's diary (Stanton, *Colorado River Survey*, 112) clearly describes what happened. *Ed.*]

28. "Log of Leo G. Brown," National Park Service files, Grand Canyon National Park.

29. "Diary of Melinda Johnson."

30. On June 17, 1963, the author identified Stanton's exit route from House Rock Canyon at S$\frac{1}{2}$ SW$\frac{1}{4}$ SE$\frac{1}{4}$ of Sec 29 T36N R6E. J. H. Butchart and others confirmed its accessibility.

31. Stanton, *Down the Colorado*, 127. J. S. Johnson verified that McDonald's speech, while profane, was very picturesque in the use of metaphor.

32. The Nims episode is related in Stanton, *Down the Colorado*, 114–29; Stanton Field Notes 1889–90, USHS; Nims, *Photographer*, 63–67; and interview, F. T. Johnson, September 29, 1964. [Also see Stanton, *Colorado River Survey*, 122–27. *Ed.*]

33. *Journals of Frihoff G. Nielson*, 1: 530; Nims, *Photographer*, 66, and Johnson Ferry Records.

34. See Coconino County Mining Records transcribed from Yavapai County, Book 29, 307–10, 200, 256, 210–12. Flagstaff, Arizona.

35. Interview, Ben Swapp and Frank Johnson, St. George, April 27, 1965. The birds' longer flights were approximately one-half mile.

36. Mary E. Johnson Judd, "Story of Warren M. Johnson Family," and Almon Draper interview, May 23, 1968. These fish were either Colorado River

salmon, or Colorado squawfish, now nearly extinct. [Eradicated from the Grand Canyon, this fish has a new name, Colorado pikeminnow (*Ptychocheilus lucius*). William Stolzenburg, "How Much Water Does a River Need?: The Ebb and Flow of the Colorado Pikeminnow," *Nature Conservancy* 49 (2) (March–April 1999: 8–9, *Ed.*]

37. Mathias F. Cowley, *Wilford Woodruff, History of His Life and Labors* (Salt Lake City: Bookcraft, Inc., 1970), 568; Johnson Ferry Records.

38. *Journal of Abraham H. Cannon*, 13, September 17–21, 1890, and Kanab Stake Historical Record, Book A: No.10663, 205–6, LDS.

39. Woodruff to Johnson, October 13, 1890; Woodruff to James Jack, October 13, 1890, in First Presidency Reel 20, 23: 37–38, LDS.

40. E. A. Draper interview, May 23, 1968, Sunland, California; Colvin, *Story of My Life*; and Judd, "Story of Warren M. Johnson Family."

41. Clara B. Lee interview, Holbrook, Arizona, April 25–29, 1966; Clara B. Lee to P. T. Reilly, January 18, 1966; "Diary of Mary E. Johnson," PTR.

42. Kane County Mining Records, Book 1, 13–14.

43. "Journal of L. John Nuttall," 2, 228, 230, 240, 249, BYU.

44. The deaths of the Johnson children are well documented in "Diary of Mary E. Johnson"; Colvin, *Story of My Life*, 70–81; and interview of Erastus Almon Draper on May 23, 1968. Draper had his fifth birthday at the ferry just as the children were exposed to diphtheria, and he attended their funerals.

45. Asa W. Judd, "Account of Relief Party to Lee's Ferry by Kanab Bishopric in June 1891," PTR. This account and the "Diary of Mary E. Johnson" cover the period April 27 to July 6, 1891.

46. E. A. Draper interview, May 23, 1968.

47. Johnson to Woodruff, July 19, 1891, LDS. See also P. T. Reilly, "Warren Marshall Johnson, Forgotten Saint," *Utah Historical Quarterly* 39(1) (1971): 19.

48. First Presidency, Reel 20, 23: 853, LDS.

49. "Journal of Warren Foote," 259–60, courtesy of Mrs. Thurza Little, Cedar City, LDS.

50. E. A. Draper interview, May 23, 1968.

51. Coconino County Mines, Book 1, 42.

52. Ibid., 49–50

53. Journal History of Kanab Stake, LDS.

54. Polly A. Johnson to Mary E. J. Judd, July 19, 1892, PTR.

55. W. M. Johnson at Lee's Ferry to his family at Kanab, October 14, 1892, PTR.

56. It is lamentable that so little has been published about John W. Young. The most comprehensive item is an article by Charles L. Kelley, "Promoting Railroads and Statehood: John W. Young," *Utah Historical Quarterly* 45(3) (1977): 289–309. The best material is in the John W. Young file, LDS. A. M. Woodbury, Charles S. Peterson, George S. Tanner, Jesse N. Smith, Frihoff G. Nielson, and Joseph Fish all record interesting details.

57. This can was found June 7, 1928, by Frank J. Winess, assistant chief ranger, National Park Service; O. M. Carrol, NPS ranger, and C. E. Nash. The point was officially renamed Widforss Point on December 2, 1937, by the U.S. Board on Geographic Names; it is about two miles southwest of the North Rim Lodge. The main references to the Cody trip are A. M. Woodbury, "A History of Southern Utah and Its National Parks" *Utah Historical Quarterly* 12(3,4) (1944): 192. 190–91; *Coconino Sun*, November 10, 17, December 22,

1892; John M. Burke, *Buffalo Bill from Prairie to Palace: An Authentic History of the Wild West* (Chicago: Rand, McNally & Company, 1893); National Park Service Archives, Grand Canyon; and interview, Roy Woolley, May 32, 1969. When Woolley related the story of Cody's blessing, large tears rolled down his cheeks.

58. Stanton, *Down the Colorado*, 105, 107.
59. Coconino County Mines, Book 1, 194. Recorded January 6, 1893. Wright's use of the spoon to recover the gold was related by Frank T. Johnson.
60. Ibid., Book 1, 277, 278.
61. Permelia Johnson to Mary and Elizabeth in Kanab, September 25 and October 5, 1893; miscellaneous Johnson letters owned by Eletha Jacobsen, PTR. Wright's co-workers probably were employees, not partners. One undoubtedly was F. G. Faatz, as he told his family that he returned.
62. Kane County Deeds, Book G, 103
63. Smith, *Six Decades*, 397
64. Clara B. Lee interviews, April 25, 29, 1966.
65. Coconino County Recorder, *Marks and Brands*, 448.
66. This feature, now inundated by Lake Powell reservoir, resembled the Great Arch of Zion and was located on the right bank 17.4 miles above Lee's Ferry. Some river men called it "Outlaw Cave," others "Galloway Cave." See Chapter 14. [Also see P. T. Reilly, "The Lost World of Glen Canyon," *Utah Historical Quarterly* 63(2) (Spring 1995): 122–24. *Ed.*]
67. The author has seen and photographed the Wright and Galloway inscriptions. See also C. Gregory Crampton, *Historical Sites in Glen Canyon, Mouth of San Juan River to Lee's Ferry*, University of Utah Anthropological Papers no. 46 (1960), 89–92.
68. Faatz described the sight to his family, who attributed the seemingly small size of the grazing animals not to distance but to their being midgets.
69. Coconino County Deeds, Book 3, 9
70. Coconino County Mines, Book 1, 329–30.
71. Kane County Record, Book F, 682, 472, 474.
72. Coconino County Mines, Book 1, 370. Those notified were Wright's original grubstakers.
73. "Lorenzo H. Hatch Journal," 188, and Smith, *Six Decades*, 402.
74. Kane County Record, Book F, 473.
75. A copy of the handwritten inquest is in PTR. See also Frank T. Johnson interview, May 8, 1966, and Mrs. M. G. Chase of Alliance, Nebraska (McClurg's wife) to Judge N. G. Layton of Flagstaff, January 1, 1895, in Arizona State Archives; Box 986, Coconino County Miscellaneous Papers.
76. Kanab Stake Historical Records, Book 10663, 308, LDS.
77. The accident occurred just south of the state line about a hundred feet east of the present-day Buckskin Tavern, between Kanab, Utah, and Fredonia, Arizona.
78. Kanab Stake Historical Records, Book 10663, 309–10, LDS.
79. Warren M. Johnson File Card, LDS.
80. G. F. Gibbs, secretary, to Warren M. Johnson, February 4, 1896, in First Presidency Reel 25, 30: 176, LDS.
81. Johnson's ride was related by Frank T. Johnson in an interview June 27, 1964. See also Frederick S. Dellenbaugh, *A Canyon Voyage* (New York: G. P. Putnam's

Sons, 1908), 164–65; Frederick S. Dellenbaugh, *The Romance of the Colorado River* (New York: G. P. Putnam's Sons, 1902), Map C opposite 246; and USGS topographic quadrangle House Rock Spring.

82. Frank Tilton Johnson Biography, PTR.

83. [Record rainfall near Moab and Hanksville on September 22, 1896, caused the flood at Lee's Ferry; R. R. Woolley, *Cloudburst Floods in Utah, 1850–1938*, U.S. Geological Survey Water-Supply Paper 994 (1946), 94–95; and F. M. Tanner, *The Far Country, a Regional History of Moab and La Sal, Utah* (Salt Lake City: Olympus Publishing, 1976). *Ed.*]

84. Interview, F. T. Johnson, September 29, 1964. George Flavell, on September 30, 1896, noted that the river had been fifteen feet higher at Spanish Bottom [upstream from Cataract Canyon, *Ed.*] a few days before.

85. George F. Flavell, "Journal of the Panthon of Green River, Wyoming, 1896," PTR. [Subsequently published as George F. Flavell, *The Log of the Panthon*, ed. Neil B. Carmony and David E. Brown (Boulder, Colorado: Pruett Publishing, 1987), *Ed.*]

86. Coconino County Deeds, Book 4, 228–30. Recorded February 1, 1897.

87. Coconino County Leases, Book l, 69–70.

88. Frank T. and Joseph S. Johnson, in an interview on June 27, 1964, said that Warren Johnson was called to Canada. The author has found no record of such a call but if it was issued, it is probable that some local power wanted to obtain Cottonwood ranch. It was an old trick in some quarters to issue calls and take property over at bargain prices. It would have been criminal to call an invalid to such a bleak climate, but it is entirely possible that he was.

89. Charles A. Welch, *History of the Big Horn Basin: With Stories of Early Days, Sketches of Pioneers and Writings of the Author* (Salt Lake City: Deseret News, 1940), 47–97.

90. Permelia Johnson to Mary and Eli Judd, Byron, Wyoming, March 14, 1902. Original owned by Eletha Jacobsen, PTR.

Chapter 7

1. W. D. Oliphant to P. T. Reilly, July 27, 1966; interview, Blanche Mace, March 3, 1975, PTR.

2. Kanab United Order Minutes, Book, 42, LDS.

3. Winsor Castle Stock Growing Company Ledger B: 24,79, USHS.

4. Canaan Cooperative Stock Company Minutes, 84, DC.

5. Ibid., 98, 106, 112.

6. Ibid., January 3 and June 21, 1880.

7. Ibid., December 8 and 15, 1880.

8. Bishop W. D. Johnson to L. John Nuttall, August 17, 23, September 14, 27, October 4, 1882, in L. John Nuttall Collection, LDS.

9. Johnson to Nuttall, October 25, 1882, LDS.

10. Johnson to Nuttall, January 9, 1884, LDS.

11. Frank T. Johnson interview, April 29, 1965.

12. Interview, Amy Riggs Richards, Las Vegas, April 29, 1967.

13. Kanab Historical Record, Book D, 98, LDS.

14. Ibid., Book D 10653, 100–101, LDS.

15. Ibid.

16. Robinson, *History of Kane County*, 260.
17. "Journal of James L. Bunting," April 19 and May 19, 1895.
18. "1895 Journal of Abraham H. Cannon," 140, August 16, 1895, LDS. Agreement of May 8, 1895, between B. F. Saunders and Agent W. B. Preston, First Presidency Box 3 folder 4, LDS. Kane County Mining Claims, Book 1, 63–65, October 14, 1895.
19. Mohave County Quit Claim Deeds, Book 12, l.
20. Interview, Edward T. Lamb, May 10, 1967; Mohave County Deeds, Book l, 35
21. Kane County Mines, Book l, 73. [Also see Lavender, *River Runners*, 36–38. *Ed.*]
22. Kane County Agreements, Book G, 104–6.
23. Kane County, Sixth Judicial Court, Divorces, Minute Book A: 19–30; Kane County Recorder and Agreements, Book G, 1, 117.
24. Interviews, F. T. Johnson, April 29, 1965, and Clara E. Davis, October 8 and 9, 1964.
25. Kane County Mines, Book l, 61.
26. Ibid., 75–76; Frank T. Johnson testimony in the *River Bed Case* and interview. The claims were filed July 5, 1897.
27. *Winslow Mail*, March 20, 1897.
28. Ibid., July 31, August 14, 1897.
29. James, *In and Around the Grand Canyon*, 210–47.
30. Ibid., 226–27. Lee's letter was dated September 21, 1876.
31. *Winslow Mail*, November 20, 1897, 4. Clara B. Lee interview, April 25, 1956. Clara said the entire town of Winslow came to the French home to express sympathy. The social and political elite filled the house to overflowing; the common people crowded the porch, while the prostitutes and tramps occupied the yard. High and low had one thing in common: they all loved Emma. [See Brooks, *Emma Lee*, 97–108. *Ed.*]
32. James' photo of Mesken was used to promote W. A. Beck and D. A. Williams, *California, a History of the Golden State* (Garden City, New York: Double Day, 1972) and Time-Life Books, *The Miners* (New York: Time-Life Books, ca. 1976). James first printed Mesken's picture in James, *In and Around the Grand Canyon*, 233. The original glass plates are in the Southwest Museum.
33. James, *In and Around the Grand Canyon*, 234–38.
34. This phase of Stanton's activities is well documented in R. B. Stanton, *The Hoskaninni Papers*, ed. C. Gregory Crampton and Dwight L. Smith, University of Utah Anthropological Papers no. 54 (Salt Lake City, 1961).
35. Ibid., 12.
36. Julius F. Stone, *Canyon Country* (New York: G. P. Putnam's Sons, 1932), 265. Crampton, *Historical Sites in Glen Canyon*, 91–92, fig. 52. F. T. Johnson taped interview of September 19, 1964, and F. T. Johnson MS. 9–10. Crampton interpreted the date as "Oc 25/1897," but he saw it more than a decade after the author's first view in 1947 and the writing had deteriorated.
37. Stanton, *Hoskaninni Papers*, 47–49, and photo, 165.
38. Ibid., 50.
39. Kane County Court Records. Letter dated Kingman, Arizona, December l, 1897.
40. Interviews, F. T. Johnson and Clara E. Davis, September 29, October 8 and 9, 1964.
41. Post Office Records, General Services Administration.

42. Wilford Woodruff Letterbooks, First Presidency Reel 27, 32, 626, LDS. Memoranda for cable for Lee's Ferry was dated February 1, 1897.

43. "Diary of Sadie Staker," February 4, 1898, from former husband Osmond Olsen, PTR.

44. Wilford Woodruff Letterbooks, 626, 758, LDS.

45. Coconino County Wills.

46. Wilford Woodruff Letterbooks, 843, LDS.

47. *Coconino Sun*, April 16, 1898.

48. Certificate of Location and Plat of Lee's Ferry Toll Road, Coconino County Records, Book 1, 118.

49. Coconino County Probate Court, Docket 100, Estate of John G. Kitchen.

50. Kane County Recorder's Office, Book G, 124.

51. "Diary of Sadie Staker."

52. Kane County Deeds, Book F, 621, June 20, 1898.

53. Interview, J. E. Klohr, October 22, 23, 1964. Sadie Staker made no mention of Kitchen or his death in her diary but, according to her sisters, related it orally to her family. G. Frank Emett, son of George Emett, related detail about Kitchen's death and his father's ride to Kanab.

54. Emett claims against Kitchen estate, and J. E. Klohr interview.

55. "Diary of Sadie Staker," August 6, 1898.

56. Ibid., September l, 1898.

57. The grave spacing does not suggest that Pearl was buried at Lee's Ferry.

58. "Diary of Sadie Staker," October 16, 1898.

59. Lot Smith to W. Woodruff, March 5, 1889, LDS.

60. "Diary of Sadie Staker," October 28, 1898.

61. J. S. Emett to W. Woodruff, August 8, 1898, in Woodruff collection, Box 41, folder 17, LDS.

62. Secretary G. F. Gibbs to J. S. Emett, August 15, 1898, First Presidency Reel 28, 33: 329, LDS.

63. Warrant No. 807 to J. S. Emett, as noted in the quarterly report of Superintendent N. G. Layton, Coconino County School District. Layton also was probate judge.

64. Both Lydia Staker Peacock and Clara Emett Davis insisted there was no romantic involvement between Sadie Staker and Nathaniel Galloway, but Sadie eventually told her husband, Osmond Olsen, that Galloway asked her to marry him and promised to take her by boat through the Grand Canyon on a honeymoon. Sadie died December 7, 1931, and her husband later remarried. The second wife is alleged to have destroyed most of her pictures, although her sisters retained some.

65. Jim Emett recorded the child's birth during a subsequent trip to Flagstaff and remembered it as taking place on December 19, a day later than Sadie's record. According to Arizona Vital Statistics, Gladys Lamb was born at Lee's Ferry on December 19, 1898.

66. Kitchen estate.

67. Thomas Chamberlain, Jr., plaintiff, versus Emma Jane Chamberlain, defendant, September 18, 1901. Kane County Records.

68. Although Sadie Staker's diary is not specific on many things, its interpretation by the author leaves little doubt regarding the chronology of construction.

69. The road began in the residual shale covering the Kaibab Formation, gained approximately one hundred twenty-five feet through the lower member of the

Moenkopi Formation to a prominent ledge that divides the lower and upper members, and gradually worked down to a lower level that remained fairly constant where the gage well is now located.

70. Kitchen estate.
71. *Coconino Sun,* January 14, 1899.
72. Kane County Deeds Record, Book F, 668.
73. According to Clara Emett Davis, who witnessed the event, Sadie feigned the swoon because respectable young women were supposed to react in this manner to such excitement.
74. Kitchen estate.
75. Coconino County Deeds, Book 4. 564; Book 9, 480, 483; also see J. R. Burroughs, *Where the Old West Stayed Young* (New York: William Morrow and Company, 1962), 70–77.
76. "Diary of Sadie Staker," March 5, 1899.
77. Gibbs to Emett, August 11, 1899, First Presidency Reel 29, 34: 538, LDS.
78. Ibid., 640, 902, 932.
79. *The Weekly Gem* (Flagstaff), June 1, 1899. This news dispatch was sent by an unidentified C. E. Kunison, possibly one of those involved. Interviews, Clara E. Davis and Royal B. Woolley, October 8, 9, 1964, and May 31, 1969.
80. Interviews, John's sisters, Clara E. Davis, 1964, and Solena E. Bennett, October 13, 1965, and May 13, 1967.
81. Stanton, *Hoskaninni Papers*, 90–91. At that time Bullfrog also was called "Pine Alcove Creek."
82. R. B. Woolley and C. E. Davis interviews.
83. Stanton, *Hoskaninni Papers*, 105.
84. Ibid., 104, and testimony of Jeremiah Johnson in the *River Bed Case*, 2, 785–86.

Chapter 8

1. Senate Document 68, 56th Congress, last session.
2. Coconino County District Attorney E. S. Clark to Secretary of the Interior; *Coconino Sun-Democrat,* February 11, 1897.
3. Garfield County Court Records. [The Wooley family of Escalante has a different family name from the Woolley families of Kanab; see Nethella G. Woolsey, *The Escalante Story, 1875–1964* (Springville, Utah: Art City Publishing Company, 1964). *Ed.*]
4. The expedition is documented in the journals of Asa W. Kienke and Heber Magelby, and an interview of Royal B. Woolley (all members of the party); see also *The Brigham Young Alumnus* 8(6), November–December 1955, 8–11, *Brigham Young University: The First One Hundred Years* 1, 290–329, and *Brigham Young University: A House of Faith,* 10–13, BYU, and interview of R. B. Woolley, May 31, 1969, PTR.
5. Lorenzo Snow and George O. Cannon to Elder B. Cluff, Jr., March 12, 1900, in L. Snow Letterbooks, Reel 30, 35: 174, LDS.
6. H. E. Gregory and R. C. Moore, *The Kaiparowits Region,* U.S. Geological Survey Professional Paper 164 (1931), and the H. E. Gregory Notebook, 80, July 13, 1900, in Bishop Museum, Honolulu.
7. *Coconino Sun,* October 6, 1900; Clara Emett Davis interview, October 8, 1964.
8. Kitchen estate.
9. Kane County Register of Criminal Indictments, 33–34.

10. Coconino County Supervisors Minutes, Book 3, 30–11. Neither Clara nor Lena Bennet remembered the Hamblin or Wooley children attending school at Lee's Ferry.

11. Ibid., Book 4, 38, 188, 263

12. Daphne Overstreet, "The Man Who Told Time by the Trees," *The American West* 11(5) (1974): 28–29, 60–61.

13. Andrew Ellicott Douglass papers, Box 22, folder 1, UA.

14. Robinson, *History of Kane County*, 139. Apparently the editors of this book were unaware that the photographer was one of the most gifted scientists to visit Kanab. The picture is not credited.

15. Quarterly Report of Superintendent N. G. Layton, Arizona State Archives.

16. A. E. Douglass papers, Box 22, folder l, description for slide 100, UA.

17. Ibid., description for slide 90. [Also see Stephen E. Nash, "Time for Collaboration: A. E. Douglass, Archaeologists, and the Establishment of Tree-Ring Dating in the American Southwest"; Bryant Bannister, with Robert E. Hastings, Jr., and Jeff Bannister, "Remembering A. E. Douglass"; and "A.E. Douglass in the Southwest: A Photo Essay," *Journal of the Southwest* 40(3) (Autumn 1988): 261–305, 307–18, 319–32. *Ed.*]

18. Coconino County Supervisors Minutes, Book 3, 312–13, and *Coconino Sun*, December 3, 1901.

19. Copy of Warrant No. 1607, in Coconino County Quarterly Reports, Arizona State Archives.

20. Kitchen estate.

21. Kane County Register of Criminal Indictments, 33–34.

22. Coconino County Supervisors Minutes, Book 3, 329–30, 361.

23. Ed Wooley interview, May 4, 1966.

24. National Archives Record Group No. 75. See also *Coconino Sun*, November 15, 1902.

25. Post Office Records.

26. Coconino County School Records, Arizona State Archives, Warrants 1355 and 1412.

27. J. S. Emett to Harrison Conrad [sic], June 7, 1903, and Warrant 1475 in Coconino County School Records, Arizona State Archives.

28. Clara E. Davis interview, October 8, 1964, and *Coconino Sun*, May 9, 1903. [Also see T. Roosevelt, "I Have Come Here to See the Canyon," *The Ol' Pioneer, A Magazine of the Grand Canyon Pioneers Society* 8(7) (1997): 12–15. *Ed.*]

29. Coconino County Incorporations, Book 1, 494, and *Coconino Sun*, July 25, 1903.

30. The 1903 traverse led by "Hum" Woolley [not related to the other Woolleys discussed in the text. *Ed.*] is detailed in Arthur Sanger's diary, PTR; P. T. Reilly, "Who Was Elias B. Woolley, Fifth Riverrunner to Traverse the Colorado?" *Desert Magazine* 25(1) (December 1962): 22–36; P. T. Reilly, "To the Question Asked in Our January Issue: An Answer ... and a Rare Photo," *Desert Magazine* 25(10) (1962): 16–17; Clara E. Davis interview; and Arthur L. Chaffin letter to P. T. Reilly, January 9, 1962, PTR. [Also see Lavender, *River Runners*, 38–40, for a discussion of P. T. Reilly's role. *Ed.*]

31. Report of Superintendent Conrard for quarter ending March 31, 1904, and Warrants 1599 and 1604.

32. Coconino County school expenses and warrants. Emett also killed predators and collected bounties from the county.

33. Ibid. Telegram episode related by Solena E. Bennett.

34. Coconino County Mining Records, Book 5, 355–61.

35. Ed Wooley interview, May 4, 1966. Frank T. Johnson, although not present at the time, said Emett's procedure was common knowledge throughout the region for many years.

36. D. D. Rust Collection, Box 11, LDS.

37. Solena E. Bennet interview, October 13, 1965. Lena was thirteen years old at the time, seventy-four at time of this interview, and she thought the man's name was Tracy or Pierce. The list of students confirmed the surname.

38. 1905 Report of Lee's Ferry District 11, Arizona State Archives, Book 1, 494.

39. Coconino County Register of Actions, Book 1, 298–300. Files 286 and 288, 299; File 287; *Coconino Sun,* July 1 and 15, 1905.

40. Coconino County Mining Records, Book 3, 639.

41. *Coconino Sun,* March 11, 1905.

42. J. S. Emett to President J. F. Smith, January 16, 1905 [1906], and E. D. Woolley and Joel H. Johnson to President J. F. Smith, January 16, 1906. Both in Supporting Documents, National Park Service, Pipe Spring National Monument.

43. George Sutherland, May 6, and E. S. Clark, June 12, 1905, to E. D. Woolley. See also Overton W. Price to Lorum Pratt, May 29, 1905, in D. D. Rust Collection, Box 11, folders 5 and 6, LDS.

44. Bowman & Company to ZCMI, May 19, 1905; Thomas G. Webber, Secretary, ZCMI, to Bowman & Company, June 1, 1905; and Trent Engineering and Manufacturing Company to Woolley, August 22, 1905; in Rust Collection, Box 11, folder 6, LDS.

45. *Deseret Evening News,* August 15, 16, 1905; *Coconino Sun,* August 26, 1905

46. A. M. Woodbury, "The Kaibab and North Rim," *Utah Historical Quarterly* 12 (1944): 192.

47. *Coconino Sun,* August 5, September 2, 1905.

48. Murphy's decree was published in the *Coconino Sun,* August 26, 1905.

49. *Coconino Sun,* October 11, 1905; Clara E. Davis interview.

50. Coconino County School Records and Teachers Annual Report.

51. *Coconino Sun,* November 4, 25, December 9, 1905.

52. Ibid., January 27, 1906.

53. J. F. Smith to Kanab Stake Presidency, January 10, 1906, in First Presidency Reel 36, 41, 146, 156, LDS; and J. S. Emett to J. F. Smith, January 16, 1905 [1906], in Supporting Documents File, National Park Service, Pipe Spring National Monument.

54. Solena E. Bennett and Ed Wooley interviews; Kanab Historical Record, Book E, 96, LDS; Kanab Cemetery Records; Report of District 11 School Trustees, June 30, 1906. See also "Diary of Rebecca Elizabeth Howell Mace," January 1906 through December 1907, February 18, 1906, LDS.

55. Register of Actions, Fourth Judicial Court, Coconino County, Book l, 37, file 294; and *Coconino Sun,* April 14, 1906.

56. The Hibben Lode was recorded May 19, 1906, as being one and one half miles north of Jacob's Pools. It is to be found in the NW$\frac{1}{4}$ of Sec. 31 T39N R5E, per Coconino County Mines, Book 4, 374.

57. *Coconino Sun,* June 9, 30, 1906; *Surface Water Supply of the Colorado River Drainage Above Yuma,* U.S. Geological Survey Water-Supply Paper 211 (1908), 98.

58. Emett to Smith, June 21, 1907, LDS; Solena E. Bennett interview.

59. *Coconino Sun*, August 25, 1906; Clara E. Davis interview. The bones were still visible in 1970. Clara remembered that about three hundred and fifty animals were salvaged, while Emett's letter to Hibben quoted the number at four hundred and fifty. [Also see Rowland W. Rider, *The Roll Away Saloon, Cowboy Tales of the Arizona Strip*, as told to Deidre Murray Paulsen (Logan: Utah State University Press, 1985), 66–67. *Ed.*]

60. *Coconino Sun*, August 18, 1906.

61. Coconino County Register of Actions, Book 1, 307–8, and *Coconino Sun*, September 22, 29, 1906.

62. E. D. Woolley to J. F. Smith, November 18, 1906, in Supporting Documents, National Park Service, Pipe Spring National Monument.

63. J. F. Smith, John R. Winder, and Anthon H. Lund to E. D. Woolley, November 23, 1906; in Joseph F. Smith Letterbooks, Reel 37, vol. 42, 200, LDS.

64. Maud Bigler to J. E. Jones, February 22, 1907, Box 984, Coconino County School Records; Teachers Annual Reports for 1907, in boxes 783 and 784.

65. Coconino County Register of Actions, Book 1, 294–308, and *Coconino Sun*, April 14, 18, 1907.

66. O. N. Arrington Report, Arizona Game and Fish Commission, and S2732, 59th Congr., 40, 787.

67. Interview, D. D. Rust, October 8, 1960, Provo, Utah, PTR. [Zane Grey also changed the spelling of his last name from Gray to Grey; see G. M. Farley, *Zane Grey: A Documented Portrait* (Tuscaloosa, Alabama: Portals Press, 1986), 2. *Ed.*]

68. Zane Grey to D. D. Rust, February 15, 1911, in Rust Collection, Box 4, folder 7, LDS.

69. Grey's writings on his Kaibab adventures were wildly exaggerated and not dependable for reference but are described as well as he was able in Zane Grey, *Tales of Lonely Trails* (New York City: Harper & Brothers, 1922); Zane Grey, *Last of the Plainsmen* (New York City: Grosset & Dunlap, 1936), 3–140, 191–314; and Zane Grey, "The Man Who Influenced Me Most," *The American Magazine* 102 (August 1926): 52–55, 130–36. Several letters from Grey are in the Rust Collection, Box 4, LDS.

70. Clara Davis interview. Grey probably worked on *Last of the Plainsmen.*

71. Emett to Smith, June 21, 1907, LDS.

72. *Surface Water Supply of the United States, 1907–1908, Part IX, Colorado River Basin*, U.S. Geological Survey Water-Supply Paper 249 (1910), 41.

73. Joseph F. Smith Letterbooks, Reel 37, vol. 42: 901.

74. *Coconino Sun*, September 5, 1907.

75. [Lavender, *River Runners*, 44–47; Kim Crumbo, *A River Runner's Guide to the History of the Grand Canyon* (Boulder, Colorado: Johnson Books, 1981), 34–35. *Ed.*]

76. "Bert Loper's 1907–1908 Diary," The Huntington Library and PTR. Clara Russell Davis remembered Loper as being indolent and not as capable as her father in solving problems. A more sympathetic version of this episode may be found in Pearl Baker, *Trail on the Water* (Boulder, Colorado: Pruett Publishing, n. d.), 32–51.

77. *Coconino Sun*, October 7, November 14, 1907.

78. Ibid., December 5, 1907.

79. Coconino County Deeds, Book 33, 317–26.

80. Arizona Archives, Box 984, Warrants 285, 286, 468, 469, 470, 576. The last four for two hundred fifty dollars were to Emett.

81. Zane Grey in Lackawaxen, Pennsylvania, to Dave Rust in Orderville, March 4, 1908; in Rust Collection, Box 4, folder 7, LDS.

82. Grey to Rust, April 4, 1911, LDS.

83. Rust Collection, Box 5, folder 5, LDS.

84. *Coconino Sun,* July 31, 1908, and *Flagstaff Gem,* July 23, 1908.

85. Coconino County School Reports 1907–12, Teachers Annual Reports, Boxes 983, 984; Tillie Mary Penny to Jones, November 17, 1908, and A. C. Nelson to Jones, May 10, 1909.

86. *Coconino Sun,* October 9, 16, 1908; interview, Clara Davis.

87. Ed Wooley interview.

88. [Robinson, *History of Kane County,* 141; see R. H. Webb, S. S. Smith, and V. A. S. McCord, *Historic Channel Change of Kanab Creek, Southern Utah and Northern Arizona,* Grand Canyon Natural History Association Monograph 9 (1991). *Ed.*]

89. *Coconino Sun,* January 14, 1909; interviews, Clara Davis, Solena Bennett, and Agnes Johnson.

90. John's death and burial were described by Clara Davis, October 8, 1964, and Solena E. Bennett, October 13, 1965. Jim Emett's letter to John Francis was printed in the *Coconino Sun,* March 5, 1909. The tombstone was erected later and erroneously inscribed 1910. John's sisters were unaware of this error.

91. Ed Wooley interview.

92. *Surface Water Supply of the United States, 1909, Part IX, Colorado River Basin,* U.S. Geological Survey Water-Supply Paper 269 (1911), 47, and interview, Clara Davis.

93. [Woolley, *Cloudburst Floods,* 101. *Ed.*]

94. Interview, Solena Bennett; Water-Supply Paper 269, 83–85, 183–84, 187–91, 206–24, 214–15. Kanab Historical Record, Book E, 191.

95. Coconino County Deeds, Book 37, 285–87

96. Coconino County Supervisors Minutes, Book C5, 596.

97. Ibid., 286.

98. Ibid., 355.

99. Various fiction writers have quoted Emett receiving as much as sixty thousand dollars for the ferry property.

100. Clara Davis interview.

Chapter 9

1. Stone, *Canyon Country,* 83–84 and 89–91; "Nathaniel T. Galloway Diary," PTR. In 1930, Rowland Rider visited Stone in Columbus, Ohio. As they discussed their 1909 meeting, Rider told him an Indian teamster had arrived with the supplies two days after they departed, and Stone gave Rider a picture that Cogswell had taken of the cowboy on his horse beside the old fort on October 28, 1909. [See Rider, *Roll Away,* 66–68. *Ed.*]

2. Frank T. Johnson biography, 17–21.

3. The official cause of Annie's death was stated as typhoid fever, but Frank said she starved herself to death over grief at her husband's decision to take a second wife.

4. The Spencer operations are detailed by Albert H. Jones, "Spencer Mining Operation on the San Juan River in Glen Canyon, 1908–11," 1960 (collected by W. L. Rusho); "Daily Journal of A. H. Jones," May 2 to September 1, 1910; interview, A. H. Jones, May 20 and 21, 1969; and Arthur C. Waller interviews and correspondence, PTR.

5. The letter was published in the *Coconino Sun-Democrat*, April 21, 1910, and the *Flagstaff Gem*, March 24.

6. A. H. Jones interview May 20, 1969.

7. "Journal of A. H. Jones," 13. The wording clearly is that of Jones, as on May 20, 1969, he stated that Spencer had only gone through the third grade and at that time could barely write his name. He spoke "trading post Navajo" or "store talk" well enough to get by.

8. Coconino County Mines, Book 6, 442–53.

9. Minutes of the Board of Supervisors, Book C5, 474, June 10, 1910.

10. The boat never was named by its last users who simply referred to it as "the launch." Otis Marston, in the late 1960s, nicknamed it the *Canopy* and the appellation caught on with those few who knew its history.

11. *Coconino Sun*, July 1, 1910.

12. "Journal of A. H. Jones," and Jones to P. T. Reilly, August 22, 1969. An interesting item appeared in Paul Dean's column on B1 of the *Arizona Republic*, December 8, 1975; Bob Benner of 6312 W. Orange Dr., Glendale, Arizona, supposedly received a postcard addressed to "Dear Uncle Bob." It was postmarked Springville, Utah, and signed "Steve." It described how Steve's father was cremated and his ashes spread at Lee's Ferry. Benner does not know a Steve, nor anyone in Utah, and said he had sent the card on to Dean. Contacted by telephone the following day, Dean claimed to have sent the card to the correct address after receiving a telephone call, then discarded the number. The Glendale Benner was the only one by that name listed in the Phoenix area telephone books—suggesting that the subjects for daily columns sometimes become problems.

13. These operations are derived from the "Journal of A. H. Jones," the Arthur C. Waller Account Book, PTR, interviews and correspondence, and the *Coconino Sun*.

14. Biographical detail regarding Frank Watson was furnished by John W. Palmer interview and correspondence, and by Arthur C. Waller.

15. *Coconino Sun*, August 12, 1910.

16. The data for this measurement are contained in the A. H. Jones Field Book, PTR. The maximum surface velocity was 4.17 feet per second.

17. A. H. Jones to P. T. Reilly, September 26, 1967.

18. Jones to Reilly, February 14, 1968. See also Jones interview and "Review of Spencer Mining Operations," 8.

19. *Coconino Sun*, September 16, 1910.

20. A. C. Waller Account Book.

21. W. H. Bradley to A. H. Jones, September 27, 1910, and *Coconino Sun*, September 16, 1910.

22. *Coconino Sun*, August 5 and October 7, 1910; Frank T. Johnson and A. C. Waller interviews.

23. *Coconino Sun*, November 11 and December 2 and 23, 1910. The printer must have gone on a binge because the November dates were printed as December.

24. *Coconino Sun,* December 2, 1910.

25. Recorded by A. C. Waller on blank p. 81 of *Dine Bizad,* PTR.

26. Schedule found on p. 12 of the Waller Account Book.

27. *Summary of Records of Surface Waters at Base Stations in the Colorado River Basin, 1891–1938,* U.S. Geological Survey Water-Supply Paper 918 (1944), 246–47. At that time, the only gage on the main stem between the Green and Grand Junction and the river's mouth was at Yuma, and a discharge in that range would take five and one-half days to travel the 676 miles from Lee's Ferry to the gage; *Surface Water Supply of the United States, 1911, Part IX, Colorado River Basin,* U.S. Geological Survey Water-Supply Paper 309 (1914), 23.

28. Charlie Spencer gave Watson's original, which was typed on the backs of two sheets of Commercial Hotel stationery, to A. C. Waller, PTR.

29. *Coconino Sun,* March 17, 1911

30. Zane Grey to D. D. Rust, April 4, 1911; in D. D. Rust Collection, Box 4, folder 7, LDS.

31. *Coconino Sun,* Friday, April 21, 1911.

32. *Los Angeles Times,* April 25, April 27–28, and May 3, 1911; *Coconino Sun,* April 28 and May 5, 1911.

33. LeRoy Johnson at Lee's Ferry to his mother in Kanab, May 30, 1911. Original letter in possession of J. S. Johnson. This episode illustrates Spencer's dependence on his articulation and his indifference to needlessly spending company funds.

34. Dimensions obtained from original blueprints in C. H. Spencer Manuscript Collection, Cession No. 23, Museum of Northern Arizona. Hearsay has quoted the boat's length at ninety-two feet, probably a result of shipwright Herman Rosenfelt's faulty memory in the Riverbed Case. The hull actually was seventy-two feet while the total length to the end of the paddlewheel was eighty-six and one-half feet. [See also James E. Bradford and W. L. Rusho, *Submerged Cultural Resources Site Report: Charles H. Spencer's Mining Operation and Paddle Wheel Steamboat* ed. Toni Carrell (Santa Fe: Southwest Cultural Resources Center, National Park Service, 1987). *Ed.*]

35. Sharlot Hall's original diary is in the Sharlot Hall Museum, Prescott, Arizona. The entries are terse, written in pencil, and evidently were made as the trip progressed. She used this diary as a basic reference when she wrote a more detailed account for *Arizona, the New State Magazine,* published from October 1911 to April 1913. See *Sharlot Hall on the Arizona Strip,* ed. C. G. Crampton (Flagstaff, Arizona: Northland Press, 1975).

36. Bert Leach interview, June 25 and 26, 1964, confirmed by Frank Johnson. See also Water-Supply Paper 309: 197, 224, 23–24 for Escalante River, Virgin River, and Colorado River at Yuma readings.

37. John W. Palmer interviews, October 7, 1965, September 16, 1972, and his testimony in the *River Bed Case,* 2, 3,101–3,121; see also the *Coconino Sun,* November 24, 1911.

38. Bert Leach interview, June 25 and 26, 1964.

39. Coconino County Mining Records, Book 8, 88–150 and 158–65.

40. Eugene E. Spencer to Otis Marston, December 14, 1958; John W. Palmer to Arthur C. Waller, December 3, 1963, PTR; and *Coconino Sun,* November 3, 1911, reprint from *Kane County News.*

41. [The Galloway, Stone, Cogswell, and Dubendorff trip of 1908 also began at Green River Station, Wyoming. See Stone, *Canyon Country,* 45. *Ed.*]

42. Roy Johnson, Lee's Ferry, to his mother in Kanab, November 7, 1911, said the Kolbs were there. See also E. L. Kolb, *Through the Grand Canyon from Wyoming to Mexico* (New York: Macmillan, 1914), 171–72. In Kolb to P. T. Reilly, August 3, 1964, Emery Kolb said they were at the ferry on November 12, but this is unlikely as the brothers took eight days to reach Bright Angel, and Ellsworth recorded their arrival there November 16, 1911. [See also William C. Suran, ed., *The Papers and Journals Pertaining to the Kolb Brothers 1911–1912 Trip through the Canyons of the Green and Colorado Rivers* (n. p., 1989), 60. *Ed.*]

43. Minutes of Coconino County Supervisors Meetings for November 6 and December 4, 1911.

44. *Coconino Sun*, November 10, 1911.

45. W. H. Bradley to A. H. Jones December 20, 1911, in Bradley file of A. F. Jones. Also quoted in Jones "Review of Mining Operations."

46. "The Bert Loper Journal, 1911–12," PTR.

47. Bill Switzer witnessed this event and described it in a letter to J. E. and Chris Klohr, April 4, 1964, PTR.

48. Interview, A. E. Leach June 25 and 26, 1964, Kanab, Utah. See *Surface Water Supply of the United States, 1912, Part IX, Colorado River Basin*, U.S. Geological Survey Water-Supply Paper 329 (1915), 22–23. Frank T. Johnson concurred with Bert Leach's story.

49. W. H. Switzer to Jim and Chris Klohr, November 2, 1964, PTR.

Chapter 10

1. Interview, John W. Palmer, October 7, 1965.

2. A. C. Waller, John Palmer, Bert Leach, and Frank Johnson all conjectured about the fate of the mercury, and they concurred that Fred Austin was the most likely to have benefited.

3. Interview, Sid Wilson, Tombstone, Arizona, April 26 and 27, 1966.

4. Coconino County Supervisors Minutes, Book D6, 121, 128.

5. Water-Supply Paper 329, 22 (Colorado River at Yuma readings).

6. Both Frank T. and Price Johnson claimed the Pahreah moved its mouth downstream in 1912, although they did not understand why.

7. Post Office Records for Lee's Ferry and Pahreah.

8. *Coconino Sun*, July 4, 1913, reprint from Kane *County News*, and Frank Johnson biography, 24–25.

9. Interview, Allie Caffall Harker, September 3, 1966; see also Nicholas Roosevelt to P. T. Reilly, September 20 and October 29, 1967; Nicholas Roosevelt, *Theodore Roosevelt, The Man as I Knew Him* (New York: Dodd, Mead, 1967) chapter 11 gives details of the trip, as does *The Outlook*, October 11, 1913. Identical passages of this text appear in *The Works of Theodore Roosevelt*, vol. 3 (New York: C. Scribner's Sons, 1927), 204.

10. Interview, Allie Caffall Harker, September 3, 1966.

11. Coconino County Supervisors Minutes, Book D7, 10 and 3 for meetings of April 6, 1914 and February 2, 1914.

12. Ferry Book Records for Coconino County, UA.

13. Ibid.

14. Ibid., and Coconino County Millsites and Water Rights, Book 4, 150–51; see also Harold S. Colton, "Early Failure to Solve the Water Shortage," *Plateau* 29(2) (1956), 36–40.

15. Gregory and Moore, *The Kaiparowits Region.*
16. Marriage License Records, Kane Co., 70, 81, 85.
17. Coconino County Supervisors Minutes, Book D7, 39.
18. Ibid., 52.
19. [Lavender, *River Runners*, 50–54; Crumbo, *A River Runner's Guide*, 37. Russell and Monett were the first to use steel-skinned boats in the Grand Canyon, in 1907, although Lavender states they were wooden skinned over steel (Lavender, *River Runners*, 45). *Ed.*]
20. Interview, Allie Caffall Harker, September 3, 1966.
21. Mansfield ledger.
22. Ibid., and *Coconino Sun*, September 10, 1915.
23. Krenkel, *Life and Times of Joseph Fish*, 482.
24. Charles H. Spencer collection, Museum of Northern Arizona, folder 2. [Also see Valeen Tippetts Avery, *Free Running: Charlie Spencer and His Most Remarkable Water Project* (Flagstaff, Arizona: Flagstaff Corral of Westerners, 1981). *Ed.*]
25. The author is indebted to Emily Boyer, widow of Earl Boyer, one of the traders who accommodated the travelers and the recipient of one of the albums.
26. Coconino County Supervisors Minutes, Book D, 281.
27. F. T. Johnson biography, 28, and F. T. Johnson interview.
28. Coconino County Supervisors minutes, June 4, 1918, Book D, 289.
29. Ferry Record Book and Mansfield ledger.
30. Interview, J. S. Johnson, May 5, 1968.
31. Coconino County Superior Court Case 760, 379, and Case 909, 531.
32. Ferry Record Book, and F. T. Johnson interview.
33. Coconino County Supervisors Minutes, Book D7, 397, December l, 1919.
34. Ferry Record Book and Dodge, *Saga*, 26–28.
35. Sid Wilson's ranch was located on unsurveyed land in what became SW¼ of Sec. 34 T41N R7E.
36. [See Eugene Clyde LaRue, *Colorado River and Its Utilization*, U.S. Geological Survey Water-Supply Paper 395 (1916); and *Water Power and Flood Control of Colorado River below Green River, Utah*, U.S. Geological Survey Water-Supply Paper 556 (1925). *Ed.*]
37. Copies of this correspondence are found in the Charles H. Spencer collection, Accession No. 23, Museum of Northern Arizona, Flagstaff.
38. Interview, Frank T. Johnson, September 28 to 30, 1964, and F. T. Johnson biography, 29–30.
39. Ferry Record Book.

Chapter 11

1. [For overviews of Colorado River history, development, and politics, see Russell Martin, *A Story that Stands Like a Dam* (New York: Henry Holt, 1989); Joseph E. Stevens, *Hoover Dam* (Norman: University of Oklahoma Press, 1988); Marc Reisner, *Cadillac Desert* (New York: Penguin Books, 1986); and P. L. Fradkin, *A River No More: The Colorado River and The West* (Tucson: University of Arizona Press, 1984). *Ed.*]
2. [For reviews of early water developments, see Reisner, *Cadillac Desert*, and Fradkin, *River No More. Ed.*]
3. Southern California Edison Company Fieldbook No. 3191.
4. Ibid., No. 2451.

5. Ibid., No. 2455.

6. Ferry Record Book, under date of June 7, 1921, and the F. T. Johnson biography, 31–33.

7. Microfilm for Lee's Ferry history, Reel 1, USGS. *Surface Water Supply of the United States, 1922, Part IX, Colorado River Basin,* U.S. Geological Survey Water-Supply Paper 549 (1927); see also Microfilm Reel 1 for Lee's Ferry, USGS.

8. Ibid., 17, states this took place August 14 and was read by I. G. Cockroft and W. E. Johnson. Cockroft was not appointed resident hydrographer until August 20 and arrived there September 5.

9. H. W. Dennis accident account in Southern California Edison Company, Fieldbook No. 2451.

10. [R. E. Westwood, *Rough-Water Man* (Reno: University of Nevada Press, 1992), 51–70. *Ed.*]

11. Southern California Edison Company, Fieldbook No. 2540 under dates of October 13 and 15, 1921. Also see the Nipple Butte (Utah-Arizona) and Gunsight Butte (Utah) 15' quadrangle sheets. The coal mine was twelve miles above Cottonwood camp.

12. Interviews, Frank T. Johnson and Delmer Spencer, both of whom witnessed the episode.

13. Southern California Edison Company, Fieldbook No. 2540, and H. G. Miser, *The San Juan Canyon,* U.S. Geological Survey Water-Supply Paper 538 (1924).

14. *Coconino Sun,* May 26, 1922.

15. Readings were made twice a day at the Lee's Ferry gaging station, the first at 6 A.M. Regarding the 1884 flood stage, John H. Gardiner, in Dodge, *Saga,* 78, noted that LaRue changed the identity of the rescued animal from a rabbit to a cat because he had never heard of a rabbit taking to a tree. Both LaRue and Gardiner attributed the peak date at Lee's Ferry to the day it hit Yuma, never realizing that it could be refined to June 18, 1884, through the diary of C. L. Christensen.

16. [C. W. Stockton and G. C. Jacoby, Jr., *Long-Term Surface-Water Supply and Streamflow Trends in the Upper Colorado River Basin Based on Tree-Ring Analyses,* Lake Powell Research Project Bulletin no. 18 (Los Angeles: University of California, 1976). *Ed.*]

17. *Arizona Republican,* August 5, 1922, and *Coconino Sun,* August 4, 1922.

18. Margery Cockroft to P. T. Reilly, October 14, 1965.

19. Interview, Margery Cockroft, September 24, 1965. The entire trip is related by L. R. Freeman, *The Colorado River, Yesterday, To-day, and To-morrow* (New York: Dodd, Mead, and Company, 1923), 411–37, and L. R. Freeman, *Down the Grand Canyon* (New York: Dodd, Mead, and Company, 1924), 71–215; "Journal of John A Widtsoe," LDS; and A. R. Mortensen, ed., "A Journal of John A. Widtsoe," *Utah Historical Quarterly* 23(3) (1955): 195–231.

20. Interviews, Sid Wilson, at Tombstone, Arizona, April 26 and 27, 1966; Mary Ann Lang Johnson, at St. George, April 21, 1976. Jerry Johnson used the upper decking for the second-story floor of his house at 315 No. Main Street in Hurricane.

21. Ferry Record Book, October 28, November 25–26, 1922.

22. [Further confusing matters, this location is also known as Lee Ferry. See *Quality of Water, Colorado River Basin,* Progress Report 17 (U.S. Department of Interior, 1995), v. *Ed.*]

23. According to H. W. Dennis to W. E. Dickinson dated February 21, 1925, the stilling well cost $3,200, with material amounting to $750, labor approximately

$950, transportation about $1,000, and the remainder charged to miscellaneous items. Tech Data Reel No. 1, USGS.

24. Interview, J. E. Klohr, October 22 and 23, 1964.

25. Dodge, *Saga*, 33.

26. Ibid., 34, and interview, Ernie Appling, May 25, 1964.

27. Coconino County Supervisors Minutes, Book 8, 17.

28. The Sandslide Trail is not to be confused with the Sand Trail. [See map and text in Rusho and Crampton, *Desert River Crossing*, 128. *Ed.*] The former comes over a break in the Echo Cliffs and descends a large sand dune to the river. Navajos occasionally brought stock to the river throughout the Johnson and Emett periods, and later, a Navajo guided Spencer and his men over it in 1910; they nicknamed it "The Buzzard's Highline." The Sand Trail is some three miles up Pahreah Canyon and it surmounts the Echo Cliffs on the opposite side of the Colorado.

29. Interview, J. E. Klohr, October 22 and 23, 1964; Ferry Records; and Coconino County Supervisors Minutes, Book 8, 22–23.

30. Interview, Dr. H. S. Colton, October 1–2, 1964, Flagstaff.

31. Coconino County Supervisors Minutes, Book 8, 53; Margery Cockroft to Mrs. I. Cockroft, July 19, 1923, PTR. See Register of Actions, Coconino County 9, 194, F. A. Bean vs. Coconino County.

32. [Thus, there are two miles zero for mileage measurement, going upstream and downstream from the Lee's Ferry area. C.H. Birdseye, *Plan and Profile of Colorado River from Lees Ferry Ariz., to Black Canyon, Ariz.-Nev., and Virgin River, Nev.* (Washington, D.C. : U.S. Geological Survey, 1924), sheet A. This map shows 0.63 mile between the starts of the 1921 and 1923 surveys. Neither of the two miles zero accord with standard procedures of stream and tributary measurement; mile zero is usually designated at the mouth. *Ed.*]

33. Tech Data M/F, Reel 1, USGS.

34. Freeman, *Down the Colorado*, 316; Dodge, *Saga*, 36.

35. Freeman, *Down the Colorado*, 328–29.

36. Interviews with F. T. Johnson, Price Johnson, W. E. Johnson, Frank Dodge, and Margery Cockroft.

37. Interview, Mrs. I. G. Cockroft, September 24, 1965, and Tech Data M/F Reel 1, USGS.

38. Tech Data M/F Reel 11, USGS.

39. Freeman, *Down the Colorado*, 358–66.

40. *Coconino Sun*, October 5 and 12, 1923, and Ferry Record Book.

41. Ferry Record Book and Chris Klohr interview.

42. *Coconino Sun*, October 5, 1923.

43. Ferry Record Book.

44. H. K. Meyer to O. R. Clark, January 14, 1924, in Letters with the Coconino County Ferry Account Book.

45. *Coconino Sun*, January 25, 1924.

46. Ibid., October 19, 1923. [Also see John P. Russo, *The Kaibab North Deer Herd* (Phoenix: Arizona Game and Fish Department, 1964). *Ed.*]

47. J. E. Klohr interview, October 22 and 23, 1964.

48. Hayden's letter, dated December 20, 1923, was printed in *Coconino Sun*, December 28, 1923.

49. *Coconino Sun*, February 1 and 22, 1924.

50. Ferry Record Book.
51. See *Coconino Sun*, October 3, 24, 31; November 7, 14, 21, 28; December 5, 12, 19, 26, 1924; Ferry Record Book; interviews with Melvin McCormick, Chris and Jim Klohr, Sid Wilson, Jack Fuss, Mrs. (Fred Johnson) Del Averett, Bob Vaughn, Ernie Appling, Aldis Jensen; John E. Hogg, "The Deer Drive That Failed," *Touring Topics*, (May 1923): 10–13, 40.
52. They found the 1884 flood stage to be 3138.18 feet above sea level at Lee's Ferry.
53. Ferry Record Book.

Chapter 12

1. Tech Data Reel No. 2, USGS.
2. Coconino County Deeds, Book 53, 562; Frank T. Johnson biography, 35; Joseph Eckersley to Presiding Bishopric, March 6, 1934, LDS.
3. D. D. Rust Collection, Box 2, folder l, LDS.
4. Interview, Owen Johnson, October 8, 1964.
5. Minutes of Coconino County Supervisors, Book E8, Box 991, Arizona State Library and Archives.
6. Interview, Mrs. Joseph Reese Baird (nee Ruby Huish), Salt Lake City, June 5, 1969.
7. Interview, F. T. Johnson, September 29, 1964, and F. T. Johnson biography, 35.
8. Interview, W. E., P. W., and J. S. Johnson, Colorado City, May 16, 1974. See also *Coconino Sun*, November 6, 1925.
9. *Coconino Sun*, November 13, 1925.
10. Interviews, Wilson and Appling. A copy of the Jacob H. Crosby narrative is in PTR, and the author heard the incident related by a dozen people who were not there.
11. Kanab Stake Historical Record No. 10662, 1924–34, 61, LDS.
12. Kanab Stake Journal History, September 30, 1926, LDS.
13. Kanab Stake Historical Record, 1924–34, 76–78, LDS.
14. Coconino County Deeds, Book 55, 531.
15. Kanab Stake Historical Record, 1924–34, 80–81, LDS.
16. Interview, Annie Spencer LeBaron, May 17 and 18, 1974.
17. Coconino County Register of Actions, 12; Coconino County Court Minutes, Book 9, 246–49.
18. A snatch-block is a bosun seat hung from an open "C" clevis suspended from a sheave. Thus, one can slip the sheave over a cable, sit on the suspended seat, glide to the bottom of the sag, then use a puller to strong-arm himself to the other side.
19. Interview, Sid Wilson, April 26–27, 1966.
20. During an interview with Jim and Chris Klohr in October 1964, they related how Jim was gaging the Colorado River at Lee's Ferry in 1946 when John Adams arrived after dark. They took him in and fed him. After supper Adams related the early history of the ferry, including how Klohr and "Dixon" (Dickinson) had run the levels to Jerry's peach tree marking the 1884 flood, never realizing Jim's identity. He castigated Sid Wilson, mentioning that he had bought a small herd from him for fourteen hundred dollars. Realization

of his host's identity set in when Chris asked, "If you bought the cattle, how come the check bounced?"

21. Kanab Stake Reports, December 31, 1926.

22. Wilson's claim turned out to be in Sec. 34 T41N R7E. This was the only section that was surveyed in this township, and remained that way indefinitely.

23. Coconino County Supervisors Minutes, Book E8, 336 and 375.

24. *Coconino Sun*, February 5, 1926.

25. Interview, Page R. Thiers, February 4, 1982. Thiers was a surveyor on the job.

26. Coconino County Deeds, Book 56, 17.

27. The Eddy trip is documented in Clyde Eddy, *Down the World's Most Dangerous River* (New York: Frederick A. Stokes Company, 1929), and Oscar R. Jaeger, *The Great Grand Canyon Adventure: A Narrative of Rapid-Shooting on the Colorado, the World's Wildest River* (Dubuque, Iowa: privately published, 1932).

28. Post Office Records.

29. [Lavender, *River Runners*, 66–75. *Ed.*]

30. Arizona State Archives, Coconino County School District Records, School District No. 26.

31. This phase of the Pathé-Bray trip is described in Eddy, *Dangerous*, 273–93, and Dodge, *Saga*, 57.

32. Tech Data M/F Reel No. 2, USGS.

33. Arizona State Archives, Coconino County School District Records, District 26. Interview, W. E. Johnson.

34. *Coconino Sun*, June 1, 1928; interviews, Sid Wilson, Marva Johnson Whiting, and Chris Klohr.

35. *Coconino Sun*, May 18 and July 13, 1928.

36. Interview, Marva Johnson Whiting, September 28, 1972; *Coconino Sun*, June 8, 1928.

37. Whiting interview and F. T. Johnson biography. Marva was the only reliable witness to the accident as Milo was only two years old. Others claimed to have been present who were not.

38. *Coconino Sun*, July 6, 1928.

39. Bonner Blanton to P. T. Reilly, July 30, 1965.

40. *Coconino Sun*, June .

41. Remi Nadeau, *The Water Seekers* (New York: Doubleday, 1950), 215, and *The Colorado River Report* for March 1946, 59–67.

42. *Coconino Sun*, August 1, 1928.

43. Arizona Library and Archives, Coconino County School District 26, Box 991.

44. Bridge data obtained from *Official Program of the Dedication of Grand Canyon Bridge, Arizona,* June 14, 15, 1929, W. E. Johnson, PTR. [A framed architectural drawing in Marble Canyon Lodge states 467 feet, as does Buzz Belknap, *Grand Canyon River Guide* (Salt Lake City: Canyonlands Press, 1969). *Ed.*]

45. Interviews, Owen Johnson, October 8, 1964, and Price Johnson, October 5, 1965. Both were witnesses.

46. Coconino County Millsites and Water Rights, Book 5, 221.

47. Interviews, P. W. Johnson, October 5, 1965; F. T. and J. S. Johnson, May 16, 1974; Mrs. Earl Boyer (Emily Deans), July 17, 1973; *Coconino Sun*, February 8, 1929.

48. *Coconino Sun*, October 5, 1928.

49. Ibid., November 23, 1928.

50. Ibid., February 8, 1929. [Powell originally designated the first sixty miles of Grand Canyon as Marble Canyon; *The Exploration*, 261. *Ed.*]
51. Arizona Legislature Journal, 1929, 9th Session, 373. See also *Salt Lake Tribune*, March 9, 1929.
52. The Lowrey lodge originally was named Vermilion Cliffs Lodge. Ramon Hubbell renamed the place "Marble Canyon Lodge" in 1942.
53. Related by A. K. Larson, a member of the Dixie College Band.
54. *Coconino Sun*, May 24, June 7, 14, and 21, 1929. Interviews, Mr. and Mrs. A. K. Larson, May 7, 1968, and Mamie Lowrey Woodruff, April 27–28, 1974. Mamie Woodruff to P. T. Reilly, September 1, 1965.

Chapter 13

1. Price had filed on the water at Badger Creek on November 10, 1928, and he received his certification on June 26, 1929; Coconino County Millsites and Water Rights, Record No. 288 in Book 5, 291.
2. The homestead entry was for the E½ NW¼ and W½ NE¼ of Sec. 13 T40N, R7E. Heber J. Meeks to Presiding Bishopric, April 16, 1931; Presiding Bishopric to Heber J. Meeks, June 29, 1931; Fred C. Bush to Presiding Brethren, July 10, 1931. All in Presiding Bishopric Roll 51, folder 21, LDS. See also Jeremiah Johnson and B. H. Gibbs to Honorable Register, United States Land Office, Phoenix, Arizona, July 30, 1929 (received August 19, 1929) in Record Group 49 re Patent 106436, NA.
3. Kanab Stake Records, 226, LDS.
4. W. R. Sholes Report of H. E. 066377, April 24, 1930, in Record Group No. 49, NA.
5. Coconino County Mines, Book 13, 27–91.
6. Coconino County Deeds, Book 64, 274.
7. Coconino County Mortgages, Book 21, 67–69.
8. This journal, written by both Flattum and Wetherill, was published as "Early Trip up the Colorado from Lee's Ferry to Rainbow Bridge, January 1931," *Plateau* 34(2) (October 1961): 33–49.
9. The original letter in church files has a notation in the upper lefthand corner indicating it was answered July 3, 1931, but no copy was retained and Lowrey did not receive a written reply, so possibly it was done orally by Heber Meeks.
10. Interviews, Price Johnson, October 5, 1965, and C. C. McDonald, January 31, 1973. See also W. B. Scott to P. T. Reilly, April 8, 1973. This announced the abandonment of the quicksilver recovery scheme at Lee's Ferry "this week" on April 24, 1931. See also F. T. Johnson interview.
11. Coconino County Mines, Book 13, 110–40.
12. Bywater Report, July 11, 1931, and correspondence, NA.
13. Zions Securities Corp. to Gibbs and Gibbs, July 28, 1931, in Presiding Bishopric Roll 51, folder 21, LDS.
14. Interview, Hazel Weaver, May 1, 1976.
15. Coconino County Mines, Book 13, 145–65. See also interview, C. C. McDonald, January 31, 1973, for this Spencer episode.
16. Dodge, *Saga*, 68–69.
17. Coconino County Mines, Book 13, 241–307.
18. Interview, C. C. McDonald, January 31, 1973; C. C. McDonald to W. E. Dickinson, May 1, 1932; W. L. Heckler to W. E. Dickinson, May 3, 1932. Both letters in Record Group 57, NA.

19. McDonald interview, and Dickinson to Chief Hydraulic Engineer, May 11, 1932, NA.
20. Interview, Charlie and Doris McDonald, January 31, 1973.
21. Ibid., and Coconino County School Records for District 26, Arizona Archives.
22. Al Nelson claimed that Peter paid cash for the property right; interview with Al Nelson at Granite Dells, May 13, 1968.
23. H. W. Dennis to F. L. Hunt, October 20, 1931; V. T. Burke to H. W. Dennis, March 23, 1928; both in Southern California Edison Company files.
24. Presiding Bishopric, Reel 70, Box 23, folder 8, January 12, 1932.
25. Ibid., January 13, 1932. Copies of both letters went to Kanab Stake President Meeks.
26. Coconino County Deeds, Book 60, 345–46.
27. Presiding Bishopric, Reel 70, Box 23, folder 8, May 17, 1932, LDS.
28. C. H. Birdseye to Commissioner, General Land Office, July 30, 1932, NA.
29. McDonald interview.
30. Kanab Stake Historical Record 1924–34, No. 10662, 307, LDS.
31. Kane County Mining Records, Book 3, 122.
32. Coconino County School Records, District 26, September 23, 1932.
33. Ibid., September 26, 1932.
34. Ibid., September 27, 1932.
35. W. E. Johnson to Mrs. B. K. Best, October 29, 1932, Arizona Library and Archives, Box 991, and Tally Sheet for School District 26, Coconino County Superintendent's Office.
36. Telegram and letter dated November 5, 1932, NA.
37. Julian D. Sears to Commissioner, General Land Office, September 23, 1932; G. G. Frazier and A. J. Bauerschmidt, Jr., to same, November 21, 1932, NA. See also Joseph Eckersley to Presiding Bishopric, November 28, 1932, LDS.
38. Archie D. Ryan to N. C. Grover, January 10, 1932, NA.
39. Coconino County Deeds, Book 54, 339–40; Book 62, 321; Book 62, 320.
40. W. E. Dickinson to A. D. Ryan, April 13, 1933, NA.
41. C. Nathews and G. E. Wood to Attorney General, Washington, D. C., June 6, 1933, NA.
42. Commissioner Fred W. Johnson to Register, Phoenix, Arizona, July 31, 1933, NA.
43. Interview, Page Thiers, Phoenix, February 4, 1982.
44. Interview, Price Johnson, St. George, October 5, 1965; Coconino County Deeds, Book 68, 77. Price accused Buck Lowrey of the theft but said he was afraid to go for the sheriff.
45. Coconino County Deeds, Book 54, 331–32.
46. Heber J. Meeks to Bishop John Wells, January 6, 1934; and Joseph Eckersley to Presiding Bishopric, March 6, 1934, LDS.
47. Jeremiah Johnson to Presiding Bishopric, February 1, 1934, LDS.
48. Ibid., February 15 and 19, 1934, LDS.
49. D. C. Lowrey to Zions Securities Corporation, March 18, 1934, LDS.
50. Presiding Bishopric, March 22, 1934, to J. Johnson, I. C. Spencer, and G. C. LeBaron; to D. C. Lowrey, April 10 and 20, 1934, LDS.
51. D. C. Lowrey to John Wells, May 8, 1934, LDS.
52. D. C. Lowrey to Zions Securities Corporation, May 16, 1934, LDS.
53. J. Eckersley to D. C. "Buck" Lowrey and Jeremiah Johnson, May 17, 1934, LDS.

54. State Water Commissioner to D. C. Lowrey, June 5, 1934, LDS.
55. D. C. Lowrey to J. Eckersley, June 18, 1934, LDS.
56. Ibid., June 27, 1934, LDS.
57. Presiding Bishopric to D. C. Lowrey, August 30, 1934, LDS.

Chapter 14

1. Presiding Bishopric to Jeremiah Johnson, July 15, 23, 25, August 1, 3, 11, 1934, LDS.
2. Ibid., September 21, 1934.
3. Presiding Bishopric to S. W. Hyde and Leo Weaver, November 10, 1934, and to Jeremiah Johnson, November 8, 1934, LDS.
4. *Coconino Sun*, October 5, 1934.
5. Coconino County letter file re District 26, in School Superintendent's Office, Flagstaff, and *Coconino Sun*, January 11, 1935.
6. Hazel Weaver Jordan insisted the Hopi was Poli Hungavi, but the *Deseret News* of October 14, 1935, printed his picture and identified him as Pole Bayestewa, a grandson of Tuba. Glenn Bennion, who wrote the article, also identified one of the guests as "Miss Charlotte Hall of Prescott," who should have been Sharlot Hall.
7. Interview, Mrs. Hazel Weaver Jordan, December 23, 1964.
8. Coconino County Court Records, Book VIII, 401.
9. [Roy Webb, *Riverman, The Story of Bus Hatch* (Rock Springs, Wyoming: Labyrinth Publishing, 1989), 39–66. *Ed.*]
10. Station Summary for 1934, M/F Reel 4, USGS.
11. "Diary of Ida B. Decker," PTR.
12. W. E. Dickinson to Chief Hydraulic Engineer, October 7, 1935, NA.
13. Coconino County Record of Co-partnership, Book 21, 187 and 189; Assessments, Book 2, 626–27; Presiding Bishopric to Wilson, Wood, and Compton, September 12, 1935, LDS.
14. Coconino County Coroner's Inquest, July 21, 1935; *Coconino Sun*, June 28, July 5, 26, 1935. See also Nora Cundell, *Unsentimental Journey* (London: Methuen & Company, Ltd., 1940), 85–89. [Also see Kel M. Fox, "Murder at Marble Canyon," *Journal of Arizona History* 24(3) (Autumn 1983): 331-38. *Ed.*]
15. References for the celebration are found in the *Coconino Sun*, October 18, 1935; *Deseret News*, October 14, 1935; interviews, F. T. Johnson and Ada Lee Humphries Johnson; the report written by Wilbur Heckler for W. E. Dickinson, USGS District Chief, dated October 15, 1935, NA; and G. A. London to W. E. Dickinson, October 15, 1935.
16. Presiding Bishopric to Wilson, Wood, and Compton, and F. L. Decker to Sylvester W. Cannon, both January 2, 1936; Presiding Bishopric to Wilson, Wood, and Compton, January 9, 1936; and F. L. Decker to Presiding Bishopric, January 31, 1936. See Coconino County Realty Mortgages, Book 24, 336-38.
17. Coconino County Deeds, Book 62, 687, and Deeds, Book 64, 274. Colton related his sale of the ranch to P. T. Reilly and gave him a xerox copy of Weaver's original letter, PTR.
18. Coconino County Agreements, Book 3, 341-42.
19. "Diary of Ida B. Decker," March 31, 1936, and interview, Frank B. Dodge, October 3, 1953.

20. Besides the San Juan and seventy-eight miles of Glen Canyon, Nevills later ran the Snake, Salmon, in Idaho, the Green River, Cataract Canyon, all of Glen Canyon, and Grand Canyon. [Biographies of Nevills include P. T. Reilly, "Norman Nevills: White Water Man of the West" *Utah Historical Quarterly* 55(2) (Spring 1987): 181–200; William Cook, *The Wen, the Botany, and the Mexican Hat* (Orangevale, California: Callisto Books, 1987); and Nancy Nelson, *Any Time, Any Place, Any River* (Flagstaff, Arizona: Red Lake Books, 1991). *Ed.*]

21. These dates obtained from Station History. They do not agree with those quoted by John H. Gardiner in Appendix A of Dodge, *Saga*, but are believed to be more reliable.

22. Charles Kelly, "Lee's Ferry on the Colorado," *Desert Magazine* 7(1) (November 1943): 6, and Charles Kelly, "J. D. Lee's Lost Gold Mine," *Desert Magazine* 9(10) (August 1946): 9–10. The Lee cabin was built by Warren M. Johnson and David Brinkerhoff in 1881, rebuilt by Jim Emett during the winter of 1897–98 using the timbers of the old Nielson mining boat *Nellie*. The upper crossing and cable cribbing did not exist until 1899. During a visit in Kelly's home on May 17, 1967, the author asked him why he accepted Hildebrand's story. The reason turned out to be that on their way south Hildebrand knew every town that was coming up, and by Kelly's reasoning, was familiar with the route. Kelly died believing Hildebrand had told him the truth.

23. Presiding Bishopric from and to Jeremiah Johnson, July 20 and 29, July 23, 1936, LDS.

24. Interview, Hazel Weaver Jordan.

25. C. L. Nichols to Presiding Bishopric, September 14, 1936; Presiding Bishopric to C. L. Nichols, Wilson, Wood, and Compton, and Leo Weaver, all dated September 22, 1936, LDS.

26. Orinn C. Compton to John Wells, September 26, 1936. Presiding Bishopric, LDS.

27. Cundell, *Unsentimental Journey*, 155–58, and *Coconino Sun*, January l, 1937.

28. *Coconino Sun*, November 13, 1936, 11.

29. Ibid., December 4, 1936, 6.

30. Rhoda Power to Weavers, September 20 and October 9, 1937, in possession of Hazel Weaver Jordon Bray, PTR. In 1937, one pound sterling was worth $4.94, which meant Rhoda had blown $2,470 with Weaver.

31. "Diary of Ian Campbell," November 6, 1937, PTR. [Also see Lavender, *River Runners*, 86–93. *Ed.*]

32. *Flagstaff Journal*, October 23, 1937.

33. See diaries of Ian Campbell, Robert P. Sharp, and Haldane Holmstrom. Robert Ormond Case wrote the story of the Holmstrom odyssey in the *Saturday Evening Post* (February 26, 1938): 8–9, 34–40. See also Dodge, *Saga*, 71–72, PTR. [Also see Vince Welch, Cort Conley, and Brad Dimock, *The Doing of the Thing: The Brief Brilliant Whitewater Career of Buzz Holmstrom* (Flagstaff: Fretwater Press, 1998), note 31; and Buzz Holmstrom and Carnegie Cal-Tech Collections, both NAU. *Ed.*]

34. Station History, M/F Reel 6, USGS.

35. Coconino County Mortgages, Book 25, 211.

36. Interviews, Hazel Weaver Bray on two occasions.

37. Cundell, *Unsentimental Journey*, 227–44.

38. Norman D. Nevills 1938 Expedition Log, PTR.

39. David E. Miller, "The Great Salt Lake," *Utah Historical Quarterly* 27(3) (July 1959): 307; *Salt Lake Tribune*, May 9, 1926; Anthropological Paper 46: 9–18.

40. *Saturday Evening Post* (May 6, 1939): 20–21, 77–78, 81, 83; John W. Hilton, "Nuggets to Bullets at Castle Dome," *Desert Magazine* 7(12) (November 1943): 5–9; interview, Billie Weaver Bradney, March 26, 1978.

41. [Lavender, *River Runners*, 93–95; Welch, Conley, and Dimock, *The Doing of the Thing. Ed.*]

42. [Roy Webb, "Les Voyageurs sans Trace: The DeColment-DeSeyne Kayak Party of 1938," *Utah Historical Quarterly* 55(2) (Spring 1987), 167–80. *Ed.*]

43. Leo Weaver to Presiding Bishopric, October 20, 25; November 2, 16, 1938; Presiding Bishopric to Leo Weaver, October 25; November 21, 1938; Wilson, Wood, and Compton to Presiding Bishopric, December 9, 1938, LDS. Coconino County Realty Mortgages, Book 6, 137.

44. Coconino County Mortgages, Book 26, 75–76, and Agreements, Book 4, 75.

45. Interviews with Andy Matson, September 12, 1972, and Hazel Weaver Bray, September 7, 1972.

46. [Lavender, *River Runners*, 54–56. Loper's birthday was July 31, 1869; see Baker, *Trail on the Water*, 133. *Ed.*]

47. Coconino County Deeds, Book 59, 262.

48. Coconino County Mortgages, Book 26, 386.

Chapter 15

1. W. T. Stuart interview, May 24, 1974.

2. P. T. Reilly, "Historic Utilization of Paria River," *Utah Historical Quarterly* 45(2) (Spring 1977): 198–99.

3. Interview, W. T. Stuart, May 31, 1974.

4. Station History, M/F Reel 7, USGS.

5. Barry Goldwater, *A Delightful Journey: Down the Green and Colorado Rivers* (Tempe, Arizona: Arizona Historical Foundation, 1970). [They were also the first two women to boat from Green River, Wyoming, through the Grand Canyon. *Ed.*]

6. Coconino County Agreements, Book 4, 465–68, and interview with C. A. and Ramona Griffin at the ranch, October 4, 1964.

7. Station History, M/F Reel 7, USGS.

8. Ibid.

9. An objective account of the trip can be found in Alexander G. Grant, Jr., "Cockleshell on the Colorado: Through the Grand Canyon in a Foldboat," *Appalachia Magazine* 7(12) (December 1941): 485–94. A wildly exaggerated version appeared in Alexander "Zee" Grant, Jr., "I Tamed the World's Worst River," *Cavalier* 1(2) (January 1953): 36–39, 66–67. See P. T. Reilly to A. G. Grant, Jr. December 6, 1952 and Grant to Reilly, December 13, 1952. Grant was a fine sportsman; his foldboat is on display at Grand Canyon Visitors Center. He died December 26, 1971.

10. Quincy C. Cornelius to P. T. Reilly, August 26, 1974.

11. Ferry Station History, M/F Reel 7, USGS.

12. [These rather oblique statements refer to the fact that Farquhar later formally listed publications about Grand Canyon and Moulton Fulmer rowed numerous times through Grand Canyon, particularly with P. T. Reilly. *Ed.*]

13. "Diary of Otis Marston Grand Canyon Traverse, 1942," PTR.

14. Station History, M/F Reel 7, USGS.

15. Ibid., December 31, 1942.

16. Station History, M/F Reel 7, USGS.

17. Randall Henderson, "River Trail to Rainbow Bridge," *Desert Magazine* 8(11) (September 1945), 17–24.

18. Walter H. Koch, "Boat Trip on the San Juan," *Desert Magazine*, 10(5) (March 1952): 14–16; *Surface Water Supply of the United States, 1944, Part IX, Colorado River Basin*, U.S. Geological Survey Water-Supply Paper 1009 (1945), 20, 235; Norman Nevills, pers. commun., 1947–1949.

19. Station History, M/F Reel 8, USGS. Dodge failed to keep the station history from October 1943 to March 1946, but filled some of the break with single paragraph statements.

20. Roy E. Cabell to District Engineer, January 12, 1945 and March 13, 1945; M/F Reel 1, Station Analysis for 1945, USGS.

21. *Boulder City News*, Friday, May 18, 1945. Goldwater, *Delightful Journey*, 84–98.

22. Randall Henderson, "River Trail to Rainbow Bridge," *Desert Magazine* 8(11) (September 1945), 17–24; Alfred M. Bailey, "Desert River Through Navajo Land," *National Geographic Magazine* (August 1947): 149–72.

23. It was difficult for Nevills to accept the theory of Marston's measurement, as several years later he asked the author if it was possible. When assured that it was through simple triangulation, and after seeing the process diagramed, he grudgingly agreed that Marston was right.

24. P. T. Reilly, "The Refuge Cave," *The Masterkey* 47(2) (April-June 1973): 50.

25. W. L. Dickinson to R. H. Monroe, September 26, 1936, in Station History, USGS.

26. Station History for March 1946, USGS.

27. Ibid., August 1946.

28. "Utah: New Ferry at Historic Crossing," *Desert Magazine* 10(1) (November 1946): 27.

29. USGS District Chief J. J. Ligner to P. T. Reilly, October 20, 1964.

30. [Roy Webb, *Call of the Colorado* (Moscow: University of Idaho Press, 1994), 138–39. *Ed.*]

31. U.S. Board on Geographic Names, Decision List 6001, 50 (January–April 1961).

32. The traverse is described in Randall Henderson, "Grand Canyon Voyage," 4 parts in *Desert Magazine* 11(1) (November 1947): 4–10; 11(2) (December 1947): 7–12; 11(3) (January 1948): 9–14; 11(4) (February 1948): 9–16; also in log of Otis R. Marston, PTR.

33. Coconino County Mortgages, Book 29, 579–81.

34. [The plaque is visible on the north side of the road, about one-third mile from the 89A turnout. *Ed.*]

35. [Loper's body may have been found in 1975. See Ronald L. Ives, "People on the River: Bert Loper—the Last Chapter," *Journal of Arizona History* 17(1) (Spring 1976), 49–54. *Ed.*]

36. Interviews, J. H. Klohr, April 20, October 19 and 20, 1963; C. A. Griffin, October 4, 1964; J. S. Johnson, April 22, 1976; Cedar City Hospital records, PTR.

37. [Wright and Rigg's party, which included P.T. Reilly, salvaged the boat, which is at the South Rim, Grand Canyon National Park. See "Hard-Hulled Adventure: The Rescue of the Esmeralda," *Boatman's Quarterly Review* 10(2) (Spring 1997): 1, 31–33. *Ed.*]

38. David A. Phoenix, *Geology of the Lees Ferry Area, Coconino County, Arizona*, U.S. Geological Survey Bulletin 1137 (1963), 58–60, and Plate 3.

39. The latter part of the uranium rush is described accurately in Raymond W. Taylor and Samuel W. Taylor, *Uranium Fever* (New York: MacMillan, 1970). [See also Raye C. Ringholz, *Uranium Frenzy* (Albuquerque: University of New Mexico Press, 1989). *Ed.*]

40. Report, Rigg, Jr., to Otis Marston, June 23, 1951, Dock Marston Collection, Huntington Library, San Marino, California, and PTR.

41. O. R. Marston 1951 log, PTR.

42. [Webb, *Riverman*, 130; and Webb, *Call of the Colorado*, 85. *Ed.*]

43. [Leslie Allen Jones, *Whitewater Exploration and Mapping—Colorado Basin* (Midway, Utah: Western Whitewater, 1962). *Ed.*]

44. Eaton operated the motor on the river. Byers and Cage were swept overboard in one rapid but were pulled aboard by Bolte. They ran all the rapids. [A Bill Belknap photo shows the four men the day after their arrival. NAU.PH.86.4.113.6. *Ed.*]

Chapter 16

1. The author and his wife were the first guests of the Greenes on July 7 and 8, 1956. An autographed dollar bill was given in payment and still hangs in the installation now known as Wahweap Trailer Court.

2. *Los Angeles Times*, December 9, 1956.

3. [For a complete history of the construction of Glen Canyon Dam and Page, see Russell Martin, *A Story That Stands Like a Dam* (New York: Henry Holt and Company, 1989). *Ed.*]

4. The author's river party ended its 1956 traverse here on July 5, 1956.

5. *Surface Water Supply of the United States, 1958, Part 9, Colorado River Basin*, U.S. Geological Survey Water-Supply Paper 1563 (1960), 328.

6. [In 1999, the Navajos and NPS aimed to build a marina at Antelope Canyon. *Ed.*]

7. The Glen Canyon and Navajo Bridges are 19.5 river miles apart.

8. Interview, Ed Fisher, October 2–5, 1969.

9. [Martin, *Story that Stands*, 135, 146–55. *Ed.*]

10. Ralph Gray, "Three Roads to Rainbow," *National Geographic Magazine*, (April 1957): 547–60. A photo of the plane before it was salvaged appears on page 551.

11. Interviews, D. D. Robinson and Vern Baker, October 6, 1964.

12. Dodge, *Saga*, p.81.

13. Ranger Reports.

14. Ibid.

15. Interview, Larry Lopp, May 21, 1964. Lopp admitted that he destroyed the cabin under the described circumstances. Lopp made the same admission to Charles Kelly. See Kelly photo 16896 in Kelly Collection, USHS; see also interview, Owen Johnson, October 8, 1964.

16. [P. T. Reilly was in western Grand Canyon at the time. See François Leydet, *Time and the River Flowing: Grand Canyon* (San Francisco: Sierra Club-Ballantine Books, 1964), 117–20. *Ed.*]

17. The measurement was made by the author, hydrographer Jack Blee, and resident ranger Rodger Brask. A copy was given to William E. Brown, NPS Regional Historian on March 10, 1968.

18. Coconino County Deeds, Docket 226, 340–41.

19. Appraisal Report by H. B. Embach, February 18, 1966, and interview, E. R. Fryer, October 11, 1969, PTR.

20. The survey was made by P. T. and E. M. Reilly and ranger Philip Martin. A copy was sent to NPS Regional Historian W. E. Brown, March 10, 1968.

21. P. T. Reilly to Yndia Moore, October 19, 1964; D. E. Phillips to P. T. Reilly, November 18, 1964; Reilly to W. E. Brown, January 28, 1968; Brown to Reilly, February 1, 1967; Reilly to Brown, February 12, 1967; Brown to Reilly, February 22 and March 20, 1968. Copies are in the Harrison Research Center, Fair Oaks, California, USHS, PTR.

22. See Gregory Crampton and W. L. Rusho, "Lee's Ferry Historical Report," January 1965. Copies at Wahweap, Santa Fe, NM, PTR.

23. Reilly, "How Deadly Is Big Red?" 250, 254. The author now believes the 1884 deaths of Henry Roseley and his son were listed erroneously because they cannot be substantiated elsewhere, nor is Roseley's name on any church call list. Possibly Mrs. Wilkins confused Roseley with Roundy.

24. National Park Service, Monthly Ranger Reports.

25. *Arizona Republic,* July 11, 1965, 1. [See also K.C. Den Dooven, "We Ran a River," *Western Gateways* 6(1) (Winter 1996): 4–15, 43–45, 47; and 6(2) (Spring 1996): 28–32, 34–36. For an account of his last trip with this equipment, see Gaylord Staveley, *Broken Waters Sing: Rediscovering Two Great Rivers of the West* (Boston: Little, Brown and Company, 1971). *Ed.*]

26. Data furnished by Vern Baker.

27. Quoted in the H. B. Embach Appraisal Report, the exact number was 39,857; interview, Allie Harker, September 3, 1966.

28. Embach Appraisal Report, February 18, 1966, National Park Service Files, PTR. The report contained errors but was sufficient for its purpose.

29. Lee's Ferry Ranger Reports. "Los Sierra" appears to be a fictitious city.

30. Ranger Reports; P. T. Reilly to R. W. Dietz, June 3, 1974, and Dietz to Reilly, June 18, 1974.

31. Wrather Arch was officially named for William Embry Wrather, director of the U.S. Geological Survey from 1943–56. See Board on Geographic Names Decision List 6504, 6 (October through December 1965).

32. *Arizona Daily Sun,* May 2, 1967; interviews with Ruth Baker, Bob Vaughn, Smoky Robinson, and Ralph Haynes.

33. Obliteration Report, National Park Service, Santa Fe, N. M. (unavailable to the public). [Charlie Spencer's last visit to the Lee's Ferry region was in 1962–63, when he was in his nineties. He attempted to extract rhenium at Pahreah townsite; see Rusho and Crampton, *Desert River Crossing,* 79. *Ed.*]

34. Ranger Reports.

35. Interview, Jane Foster, April 3, 1984.

36. [For a review of the problems in Grand Canyon during the 1970s, see Robert Dolan, Alan Howard, and Art Gallenson, "Man's Impact on the Colorado River in the Grand Canyon," *American Scientist* 62 (1974): 392–401. *Ed.*]

37. [In the mid-1990s, the National Park Service required compliance with Coconino County Health Services mandates for commercial river outfitters and guides. *Ed.*]

38. Coconino County Deeds, Docket 511, 400–403.

39. E. R. "Si" Fryer to Jack Whiteman, August 10, 1978.

Epilogue

1. Unless otherwise noted, all information may be found in the Cline Library Special Collections and Archives Department, Northern Arizona University, which holds the P. T. Reilly Manuscript Collection, the P. T. Reilly Photographic Collection, and the P. T. Reilly oral history interviews (PTR).

2. For a history of the GLO, predecessor to the Bureau of Land Management, and Reilly's contributions see Lola Cazier, *Surveys and Surveyors of the Public Domain, 1785–1975* (Washington, D.C.: Department of the Interior, 1976).

3. Dock Marston Collection, Huntington Library, San Marino, California. Reilly material may be found in boxes 195 and 196 and consists of annual folders from pre-1948 to 1978. Reilly donated his copies of Marston correspondence to the Utah State Historical Society (E. M. Reilly to R. D. Quartaroli, August 21, 1998).

4. The Nevills pre-trip flyer listed neither Marston nor Rigg but Kent Frost as the prospective boatman.

5. Marston's lists of the first 206 river runners through the Grand Canyon from Lee's Ferry to the Grand Wash Cliffs appeared on two Christmas cards ca. 1952 and 1953. They are in PTR, with Reilly annotations. See also Goldwater, *Delightful Journey* (Tempe: Arizona Historical Foundation, 1970), 190–191, for a slightly different Marston list of the first 100.

6. Marston's list left off Leigh Lint's name in 1923, but included Nevills' daughter Sandra in 1940 *in utero* with mother Doris. If Sandra is left on, Susie is number 13, a baker's dozen instead of number 12.

7. Reilly, "My High Water Experience in Marble and Grand Canyons," 17; C.V. Abyssus, "High Water Redux," *The Confluence* 3(1) (Winter 1996):22; *Surface Water Supply of the United States 1957: Part 9 Colorado River Basin,* U.S. Geological Survey Water-Supply Paper 1513 (1959), 349. Reilly's trip log for 1957 indicates that the Colorado River flow peaked at the Lee's Ferry gage "@ 8:40 PM: 126,700," although his article states 126,000. Water-Supply Paper 1513 lists "maximum discharge during year, 126,000 cfs June 12" and "peak discharge June 12 (9 P.M.) 126,000 cfs."

8. "In my opinion, our 1962 trip provided the best flow for river running that I ever encountered; from June 25 through July 14 we averaged 45,500 cfs per day. This water level was pure pleasure," (Reilly, "My High Water Experience in Marble and Grand Canyons," 19). In the spring of 1996, the Bureau of Reclamation conducted a controlled flood from Glen Canyon Dam of 45,000 cubic feet per second for seven days. A safety study during the "flood" confirms Reilly's conclusions: "The information from the spring 1996 experimental flows indicates no greater risk of an accident than at other studied flow levels. The information gathered from the boater interviews suggests that while the 45,000 cfs flow presents certain risks and limits camps in some areas of the canyon, the flood flows enhanced the overall quality of the visitor experience." Linda M. Jalbert, "The Effects of the 1996 Beach/Habitat Building Flows on Observed and Reported Boating Accidents on the Colorado River in Grand Canyon National Park, Draft Report," (Grand Canyon: Grand Canyon National Park, December 1996), ii.

9. P. T. Reilly to R. D. Quartaroli, July 26, 1995, August 4, 1995, August 9, 1995; personal communication, M. Litton to R. D. Quartaroli, 1998. For construction

and evolution of the dory as used in Grand Canyon, see Clyde Martin Litton, "The Dory Story," *Sunset Magazine* (May 1968): 86–91; and Brad Dimock, "A Nest of Dories: A Meandering Inquiry into the Origins of the Grand Canyon Dory," *Hibernacle News 1994* ([Flagstaff, Arizona]: 1994), 6–13.

10. Leydet, *Time and the River Flowing*, 121–123. In 1965, Reilly sold his outfit to Martin Litton; Litton later incorporated his river trips into Grand Canyon Dories, a National Park Service licensed concessionaire (P. T. Reilly to R. D. Quartaroli; M. Litton to R. D. Quartaroli).

11. Ibid.

12. P. T. Reilly, "Search for the Site of the Hansbrough-Richards Tragedy," in Webb, *Grand Canyon: A Century of Change*, 19.

13. Crampton and Rusho, "Lee's Ferry Historical Report," 32–33.

14. Barry Mackintosh, *The National Historic Preservation Act and the National Park Service: A History* (Washington, D.C.: History Division, National Park Service, 1986), viii; *Operation of Glen Canyon Dam, Colorado River Storage Project, Arizona: Final Environmental Impact Statement* (Washington: Department of the Interior, March 1995), 140.

15. Reilly, "Who Was Elias B. Woolley?" 22–29, 31–36; "To the question asked in our January issue: An answer . . . and a rare photo," *Desert Magazine* 25(10) (October 1962): 16–17.

16. Reilly, "How Deadly Is Big Red?" 244–260. Dr. Thomas M. Myers, Grand Canyon National Park Clinic, is currently researching a monograph on accidents, injuries, and deaths on the Colorado River through Grand Canyon, building from Reilly's article (Flagstaff: Red Lake Books, in press).

17. P. T. Reilly, "Discovery of Keyhole Natural Bridge," *The Masterkey* 46(2) (April-June 1972): 61–70.

18. "Where God Lost His Boots!" KPNX TV12, Phoenix, Arizona, November 1984.

19. Personal communication, K. J. Underhill to R. D. Quartaroli, 1996.

20. "Norman Nevills: White Water Man of the West"; "The Lost World of Glen Canyon"; "My High Water Experience in Marble and Grand Canyons"; and "Search for the Site of the Hansbrough-Richards Tragedy."

21. "Grand Canyon National Park Colorado River Recreational Statistics by Calendar Year," through 1995, courtesy of Tom Martin, Grand Canyon Private Boaters Association.

22. Roderick Nash, "River Recreation: History and Future," in *Proceedings, Symposium River Recreation Management and Research* (Minneapolis: North Central Forest Experimentation Station, 1977), 2–7.

23. "Issues, Objectives, and NPS Statements: 1. Access and Allocation of Use; 2. Distribution and Volume of Use; 3. Noncommercial Permit System," *Colorado River Soundings* (Grand Canyon: Grand Canyon National Park, May 1998).

24. *Operation of Glen Canyon Dam*, 50, 141; Michael Collier, Robert H. Webb, and John C. Schmidt, "Colorado River: Multiple Mandates, Multiple Uses," in *Dams and Rivers: A Primer on the Downstream Effects of Dams* (Tucson: U.S. Geological Survey, June 1996), 71.

25. Bradford and Rusho, *Submerged Cultural Resources Site Report*, xix, 151-157; *Operation of Glen Canyon Dam*, 264–265, 270.

26. "Appendix C, Commercial Operating Requirements, 1998" and "Grand Canyon National Park Noncommercial River Trip Regulations 1996-1997"

are, respectively, 38 and 26 pages (Grand Canyon: Grand Canyon National Park, 1998, 1996).

27. Anglers who boat number 11,000, while 8,000 wade or fish from the bank (*Operation of Glen Canyon Dam*, 149).
28. Ibid., 42–43.
29. Collier, Webb, and Schmidt, "Colorado River: Multiple Mandates, Multiple Uses," 66, 78.
30. *Record of Decision: Operation of Glen Canyon Dam Final Environmental Impact Statement* (Washington: Department of the Interior, October 1996), Section VI. 3. "Flood Frequency Reduction Measures." Secretary of the Interior Bruce Babbitt, as the water manager for the Colorado River, signed the ROD October 9, 1996. This section states: "Under this commitment, the frequency of unanticipated floods in excess of 45,000 cubic feet per second will be reduced to an average of once in 100 years." The reduction is from previous estimates of one in 25 and one in 40; the 1983 spill was one in 20.
31. Collier, Webb, and Schmidt, "Colorado River: Multiple Mandates, Multiple Uses," 65, 70, 77; R. D. Quartaroli, personal experience as a river guide.
32. C. V. Abyssus, "River Runner/Historian P. T. Runs the Last Rapid," *Boatman's Quarterly Review* 10(1) (Winter 1996–97): 16–18; "Errata," *Boatman's Quarterly Review* 10(3) (Summer 1997): 6; personal communication, E.M. Reilly to K. J. Underhill, 1996.
33. C. V. Abyssus, "...recovering hippies and river rats...," *Boatman's Quarterly Review* 10(1) (Winter 1996–97): 26.
34. E. M. Reilly to R. D. Quartaroli, August 12, 1998.

Appendices

1
Children Born at Lee's Ferry

Child	Date of birth	Father	Mother	Wife No.
Francis Dell	January 17,1872	John D. Lee	Emma	17
Victoria Elizabeth	November 5, 1873	John D. Lee	Emma	17
Frank Tilton	August 3, 1878	Warren M. Johnson	Samantha	2
Gove	December 2, 1878	Hyrum S. Phelps	Elizabeth	2
Nancy	November 8, 1879	Warren M. Johnson	Permelia	1
Lydia Ann	April 3, 1880	Warren M. Johnson	Samantha	2
unnamed baby	December 18, 1880	Samuel Stowe	Mary Ellenor	1
Permelia	July 18, 1881	Warren M. Johnson	Permelia	1
William	March 25, 1882	David Brinkerhoff	Lydia Ann	1
Samantha	April 5, 1882	Warren M. Johnson	Samantha	2
Laura Alice	September 25, 1883	Warren M. Johnson	Permelia	1
Lucy	March 30, 1884	Warren M. Johnson	Samantha	2
Mark James	September 26, 1885	Price Nelson	Mary L.	1
Jonathan Smith	October 30, 1885	Warren M. Johnson	Permelia	1
Price William	February 2, 1886	Warren M. Johnson	Samantha	2
Price	February 16, 1886	David Brinkerhoff	Lydia Ann	1
Estella	December 25, 1887	Warren M. Johnson	Samantha	2
LeRoy Sunderland	June 12, 1888	Warren M. Johnson	Permelia	1
Steven Addison	November 11, 1889	John Addison Swapp	Martha	1
Warren Elmer	April 27, 1890	Warren M. Johnson	Samantha	2
Joseph Smith	March 28, 1891	Warren M. Johnson	Permelia	1
Gladys	December 18, 1898	William S. Lamb	Charlotte	1
William Glenn	April 11, 1901	Wm. Moses Emett	Mary Church	1
Lucy	June 9, 1902	John Taylor Emett	Sarah	1
Ray	July 6, 1903	John Taylor Emett	Sarah	1
Emodean	August 9, 1905	Wm. Moses Emett	Mary	1
Gennieve	April 17, 1906	John Taylor Emett	Sarah	1
John Henry	September 17, 1908	John Taylor Emett	Sarah	1
unknown	July 1, 1910 (per A.H. Jones, 7/2/10)			
Mae	April 21, 1925	Warren E. Johnson	Viola	1
Lucy	November 12, 1926	Warren E. Johnson	Viola	1
Calvin Marshall	May 12, 1928	Price W. Johnson	Esther	1
Annie Isabell	June 16, 1928	Warren E. Johnson	Viola	1
Marden Carling	July 26, 1929	Isaac C. Spencer	Sylvia	2

Viola	September 16, 1929	Warren E. Johnson	Artemesia	2
Esther	October 26, 1929	Price W. Johnson	Helen Hull	2
Warren	April 8, 1930	Warren E. Johnson	Viola	1
Lucius Henry	January 23, 1931	Isaac C. Spencer	Sylvia	2
Artemesia	November 29, 1931	Warren E. Johnson	Viola	1
Neta	December 4, 1931	Price W. Johnson	Helen Hull	2
Clarence Orson	February 28, 1932	Isaac C. Spencer	Sylvia	2
George Washington	July 17, 1933	Isaac C. Spencer	Sylvia	2

2
Deaths at Lee's Ferry

Date	Person	Cause
March 10, 1874	James Jackson	Blood poisoning
May 24, 1876	Lorenzo Wesley Roundy	Drowned ferry
December 18, 1880	Mary E. Stowe & baby	Childbirth
ca. 1880-81	Two Navajo Indians	Drowned crossing
June 5, 1883	William Brinkerhoff	14-month infant
May 17, 1891	Jonathan Smith Johnson	Diphtheria
June 11, 1891	Laura Alice Johnson	Diphtheria
June 15, 1891	Permelia Johnson	Diphtheria
July 5, 1891	Melinda Johnson	Diphtheria
July 13, 1898	John Green Kitchen	Probably euthanasia
ca. 1899	Two Navajo brothers	Drowned crossing
June 11, 1902	Lucy Emett	Infant death
February 13, 1906	Glen Crosby	Shot at ranch
January 27, 1909	John Taylor Emett	Pneumonia
March 9, 1911	Preston Apperson	Drowned ferry
October 28, 1925	Waddy Thompson Ligon	Dugway accident
June 7, 1928	Royce Elliott Deans	Drowned ferry
June 7, 1928	Adolpha Johnson	Drowned ferry
June 7, 1928	Lewis Nez Tsinnie	Drowned ferry
December 14, 1928	Calvin Marshall Johnson	Infant death
March 10, 1931	Lucius Henry Spencer	Infant death
ca. 1933	W. E. and Artemesia Johnson baby	Premature
Feb. 21, 1965	Philip D. Martin	Drowned at Two Mile
April 17, 1982	Glen Miller	Helicopter accident
April 17, 1982	Diane Doherty	Helicopter accident
April 17, 1982	Frank Novak	Helicopter accident
January 5, 1985	Albert Craig Smith	Drowned four miles upstream

3
Lee's Ferry
Proprietors, Ferrymen, and Custodians

1. A. H. Thompson, F. S. Dellenbaugh, W. C. Powell ferried Jacob Hamblin, three other Anglos, and nine Navajos in the *Nellie Powell* and *Emma Dean* on October 28, 1871.

2. John Doyle Lee and his wife Rachel provided ferry service on January 19, 1872, using the old Powell-Hamblin boat, *Cañon Maid*. Lee also used a home-made skiff and the abandoned *Nellie Powell* for sporadic ferry service until a ferryboat was built on January 11, 1873.
   A. James Jackson, 1873–March 1874.
   B. Juan Lorenzo Hubbell, April 3–June 16, 1873.

3. Emma Batchelor Lee, 1874–1879.
   A. William James "Billy" Lee, 1874–June 1879
   B. Warren M. Johnson, April 1, 1875–June 2, 1879

4. Joseph L. Foutz, June 2–November 30, 1879
   A. Warren M. Johnson

5. Warren M. Johnson, November 30, 1879–November 28, 1896
   A. Billy Lee, 1875–1879
   B. David Brinkerhoff, April 1881–February 26, 1886
   C. Andrew S. Gibbons, a few weeks in 1883
   D. Christian Lingo Christensen, October 30–November 24, 1884
   E. Price W. Nelson, summer 1885–August 12, 1886
   F. Brady Englestead
   G. John S. P. Adams, fall 1887–October 31, 1888
   H. Frank Ivie, 1888–1890
   I. William Clayton, 1888–1890
   J. John Addison Swapp, 1889–1891
   K. Jesús worked in 1891
   L. Almon Draper, fall 1890–August 1891
   M. Jeremiah Johnson, fall 1891–August 1898

6. James S. Emett November 28, 1896–September 11, 1909 (cable ferry ready for service March 5, 1899)
   A. Jeremiah Johnson, December 1895–August 1898
   B. Ed Mesken, June–November 1897
   C. John T. Emett, March 1897–December 1908
   D. William S. "Bill" Lamb, Fall 1898–June 1899
   E. Ed Wooley, summer 1904–summer 1906

7. Grand Canyon Cattle Company, September 1909–June 6, 1910
   A. Dave Rider, September 1909
   B. Nate Petty
   C. Johnny Evans
   D. Jeremiah Johnson, February 1–June 6, 1910

8. Coconino County bought the ferry on June 30, 1910, and appointed the following custodians:
   A. Jeremiah Johnson, June 6, 1910–April 1912
   B. Charles H. Spencer collected salary, got Jeremiah and Frank T. Johnson to operate ferry, August 1911–July 1913
   C. Bert Leach, March–April 1912
   D. Frank T. Johnson, April 1912–January 1914
   E. Charles A. Greene, July 19–August 3, 1913
   F. Grand Canyon Cattle Company, August 4, 1913–August 4, 1918
   G. Tom Caffall, July 1913–April 1915
   H. Jeremiah Johnson, January–June 1914
   I. Tommy Richards, April 1914–February, 28, 1916
   J. Johnson brothers, Jeremiah, Frank, Price, and Warren Elmer all operated the ferry and shared the salary regardless of which one was appointed custodian. Jeremiah and Frank alternated in holding the job until August 1, 1922
   K. Price W. Johnson, August 1, 1922–May 7, 1923
   L. W. E. (Elmer) Johnson, November 22, 1922–May 12, 1923
   M. Owen Clark, May 7, 1923–January 31, 1925
   N. Chester A. Moon, February 1, 1925–April 1, 1927
   O. Jeremiah Johnson, April 1, 1927–June 7, 1928
   P. Adolpha Johnson, January–June 7, 1928

4
Postmasters
Lees Ferry, Coconino County, Arizona
(established April 23, 1879, in Yavapai County)

Warren P. Johnson, appointed April 23, 1879
James S. Emett, appointed January 8, 1898
Clara Emett, appointed January 2, 1903
Frank T. Johnson, appointed January 13, 1911
Charles H. Spencer, appointed October 19, 1912

Discontinued January 31, 1914

Re-established August 12, 1922
Margery C. Cockroft, appointed August 12, 1922

Discontinued March 15, 1923

5
Schoolteachers

June 14, 1898	Miss Sadie Staker of Anabella, Utah, her salary paid by James S. Emett, began teaching at Lee's Ferry
January 23, 1899	Teacher's salary of $30 per month charged to Fredonia District 6
April 28, 1899	Last day of spring term; Staker returns to Utah
fall 1899	No teacher, no school
January 15–April 6, 1900	Tamar Stewart of Kanab
fall 1900–spring 1901	Mae Rogers, said to have been a member of the Mormon Tabernacle Choir in Salt Lake City (still on District 6 payroll)
July 1, 1901	J. S. Emett petitioned Coconino County Board of Supervisors for a school district at Lee's Ferry
October 7, 1901	Lee's Ferry School District No. 11 created
November 20, 1901–April 4, 1902	Alex J. McKay, transferred from Tuba City
fall 1902–spring 1903	Thomas W. Brookbank, transferred from Moenave
November 11, 1903–January 18, 1904	J. W. Tonnies taught two months and six days at Lee's Ferry
spring 1904	William C. Jones finished the term
fall 1904–spring 1905	L. L. Steward
fall 1905–spring 1906	John David Leigh of Utah
fall 1906–spring 1907	Maud Bigler of Utah
fall 1907–June 19,1908	Laura A. Wingert
November 2, 1908–March 17, 1909	Mary Tillie Penney of Kanosh, Utah
September 6, 1910	Lee's Ferry School District No. 11 discontinued
June 1, 1925	Lee's Ferry School District No. 26
October 5, 1925–April 16, 1926	Ruby A. Huish
September 6, 1926–April 15, 1927	Alice W. Lee
September 6, 1927–April 20, 1928	Iona Davie
fall 1928–spring 1929	Joseph T. Wilkinson
September 16, 1929–April 25, 1930	Joseph T. Wilkinson
September 1, 1930–May 1, 1931	Margaret Anderson
August 31, 1931–May 18, 1934	Mary W. Wilkinson
January 7, 1935	Lee's Ferry School District No. 26 lapsed

6
U.S. Geological Survey Resident Hydrographers at Lee's Ferry

August 11, 1910	Civil engineer Albert H. Jones, assisted by Arthur C. Waller, made the first discharge measurement of the Colorado River at Lee's Ferry.
May 6, 1921	Fourteen men under Southern California Edison Company chief engineer met USGS Hydraulic Engineer E. C. LaRue at Lee's Ferry.
May 8, 1921	LaRue staff gage installed on right bank above mouth of Pahreah River.
June 24, 1921	Lee's Ferry gaging station established by Roger C. Rice, John H. Gardiner, E. C. LaRue, and H. W. Dennis. Slope gage installed.
August 3, 1921	First discharge measurement by R. C. Rice, C. W. Sopp, and W.E. Johnson.
August 5-7, 1921	LaRue and W. E. Johnson measured.
August 20, 1921	I. G. Cockroft becomes first resident hydrographer at Lee's Ferry.
September 5, 1921	Cockrofts took up residence in the old fort assisted by W. E. Johnson.
June 7, 1922	Cockroft and W. E. Johnson, assisted by Jerry Johnson, ran levels from mark on peach tree reached by 1884 flood. They tied this to a benchmark.
August 1922	R. C. Rice and H. W. Dennis build stilling well.
December 16, 1922	Stilling well completed.
January 19, 1922	Continuous, automatic water-stage recorder and new vertical staff gage installed on well.
January 29, 1923	J. E. Klohr arrived to assist Cockroft, on payroll thirtieth.
August 1, 1923	J. E. Klohr became resident hydrographer after Cockroft's resignation.
September 1, 1923	USGS assumes full control of Lee's Ferry Station.
November 22, 1923	Pahreah gage station established as a result of the Colorado River Compact.
April 1, 1924	R. J. "Rudy" Kasel arrived to assist during high water. Remained until August 15, 1924.
September 22, 1924	W. E. Dickinson and J. E. Klohr ran levels from mark on Jerry Johnson's peach tree to BM No. 38.
February 1, 1925	Owen R. Clark quit job as ferryman to learn gaging procedure and worked part time as assistant.
April 1, 1925	D. H. Barber arrived to assist Klohr during high water.
July 1, 1925	D. H. Barber becomes resident hydrographer.

September 30, 1925	Residency discontinued. Barber had instructed Jerry and Elmer Johnson to be observers helped by visits from Dudley and Baumgartner.
April 17, 1927	D. H. Barber arrived for high-water duty, aided by observers Johnson, Johnson, and Clark.
December 1927– January 1928	R. Elton Cook, Baumgartner, and Jay Pague installed new A frame supports and gage cable.
January 7, 1928	Owen R. Clark put on steady, measured a week later.
March 31, 1928	J. and W. E. Johnson terminated as resident observers; Clark and Baumgartner became resident hydrographers. Discovered measurement discrepancies due to cable expansion in warm weather.
April 22, 1928	Baumgartner, assisted by Clark, resident hydrographers.
February 1929	Lower gage cable completed.
April 12, 1929	Cook and Clark were resident hydrographers until October l.
December 1929– January 1930	Cook, Baumgartner, Pague supplanted the upper cable anchorages.
April 1, 1930	Marion B. Scott became resident hydrographer, assisted by Clark and Barber.
April 1, 1931	C. C. McDonald arrived for high water duty.
April 13, 1931	D. H. Barber came for high water duty.
July 31, 1931	McDonald became resident hydrographer as Scott left.
November 23, 1931	F. B. Dodge arrived, allowed to stay.
January 1932	Wilbur L. Heckler arrived for high water duty.
September 12, 1932	W. L. Heckler became resident hydrographer as McDonald left.
January 18, 1933	U.S. Government Reserve created by President Hoover.
May 1933	Heckler helped by Dodge and Howard S. Leak.
December 16, 1933– January 12, 1934.	Residency discontinued. Betty Jo Games hired as observer, and Scott made three visits from Tucson.
April 1, 1934	M. B. Scott resident hydrographer with occasional help of Dodge. No high water in 1934.
November 19, 1934	W. L. Heckler resident hydrographer as Scott resigned in December.
April 23, 1934	R. E. Cook and S. Decker arrived. Decker became resident hydrographer as Cook did not stay.
October 11–13, 1935	W. L. Heckler was District Representative for the Pioneer celebration. Decker on duty at station.
May–June, 1936	Decker helped by Dodge during high water.
July 17, 1936	C. C. McDonald temporary resident hydrographer as Decker went to Willow Beach. Dodge helped.
August 12, 1936	Roy H. Monroe resident hydrographer as Dodge took boating job with Fairchild Survey.
March 1937	Archie J. Hanson, Junior Engineer, arrived for high water duty.
April 12, 1938	Fred Anderson arrived for high water duty.
June 24, 1938	A. J. Hanson resident hydrographer when Monroe took vacation.
November 23, 1938	Alex A. Fishback supervised construction of water supply and sanitary system.

December 21, 1938	Fishback was resident hydrographer through February 11, 1939, when Hanson took over after his leave of December 21, 1938 to February 11, 1939.
April 20, 1939	Hanson was resident hydrographer when Hunter arrived for high water duty.
July 25, 1939	W. T. Stuart became resident hydrographer as Hanson went to Grand Canyon.
May 1, 1940	Quincy Cornelius became resident hydrographer as Stuart transferred.
January 24, 1941	F. B. Dodge returned, became resident observer and caretaker at Lee's Ferry. Cornelius was resident hydrographer.
May 6, 1941	Dodge hired for high water duty.
January 4, 1942	R. B. Sanderson became resident. Cornelius and wife left a week later.
June 10, 1942	Weather Station reestablished.
June 25, 1942	F. B. Dodge became resident assistant field hydrographer as Sanderson returned to Tucson.
1942–1945	Dodge on duty as resident hydrographer.
July 1, 1946	J. E. Klohr became resident engineer, Dodge assisted.
August 9, 1946	F. B. Dodge resigned because of poor health.
May 1949	Glen E. Johnson replaced Klohr as resident hydrographer.
March 1951	E. P. Croft replaced Johnson.
May 1951	J. Akers was resident hydrographer.
October 1952	C. Cox was resident hydrographer.
August 1953	D. Trenck was resident hydrographer.
July 1954	D. Tidball was resident hydrographer.
September 1961	S. Jones was resident hydrographer.
August 1962	L. E. Lopp was resident hydrographer.
April 1964	J. Blee was resident hydrographer.
March 15, 1966	Larry Mann was resident hydrographer.
August 15, 1966	Fred Burke was resident hydrographer.
May 23, 1971	Matthew Pierce was resident hydrographer.
August 4, 1976	Residency discontinued; station serviced from Flagstaff. Facilities turned over to NPS.
March 10, 1977	Lee's Ferry Station equipped with satellite telemetry. Periodic inspections still made but visiting hydrologist stays at local motel.

7
Lee's Ferry Ownership

December 1871	Emma B. and John D. Lee took up residency at mouth of the Pahreah Canyon.
May 16, 1879	Emma B. Lee sold to John Taylor, trustee of Mormon Church.
November 28, 1896	Warren M. Johnson sold to Wilford Woodruff, trustee of Mormon Church.
November 28, 1896	Wilford Woodruff, trustee, leased to James S. Emett.
August 18, 1909	Joseph F. Smith, trustee of Mormon Church, sold to Grand Canyon Cattle Company.
September 11, 1909	James S. Emett et ux sold to Grand Canyon Cattle Company.
June 30, 1910	Grand Canyon Cattle Company sold Lee's Ferry boat and landing to Coconino County.
May 1925	Mormon Church advanced down payment to Jeremiah Johnson to purchase Lee's Ferry ranch from Grand Canyon Cattle Company.
May 25, 1925	Grand Canyon Cattle Company sold to Jeremiah Johnson.
August 19, 1926	Jeremiah and Pearly Johnson quit claim to Heber J. Grant, trustee of Mormon Church.
July 11, 1927	Grand Canyon Cattle Company quit claim to Heber J. Grant, trustee of Mormon Church, because Jeremiah Johnson failed to make payments
August 19, 1929	Jeremiah Johnson filed homestead claim.
September 6, 1929	Jeremiah Johnson filed for water rights.
January 28, 1931	Jeremiah Johnson homestead claim allowed.
May 16, 1932	Johnsons gave warranty deed to Mormon Church Presiding Bishopric.
May 23, 1933	USA granted Patent No.1064367 to Jeremiah Johnson.
September 9, 1933	Johnsons gave warranty deed to Heber J. Meeks.
September 12, 1933	Meeks gave warranty deed to Mormon Presiding Bishopric.
November 10, 1934	Presiding Bishopric deed sold to S. W. Hyde and Leo Weaver.
March 7, 1935	Leo Weaver and S. W. Hyde signed certificate of partnership.
September 4, 1935	Weaver-Hyde partnership dissolved. Weaver assumed all responsibilities.
February 1, 1936	Presiding Bishopric put title in name of Leo Weaver et ux and took first mortgage.
February 15, 1936	Presiding Bishopric deeded a portion of Lee's Ferry and water rights to Leo and Hazel Weaver.
March 16, 1936	Esther H. Bowers invested in Paradise Canyon ranch.
October 25, 1937	Weavers mortgaged Paradise Canyon ranch to Babbitt Brothers.

December 6,1938   Weavers mortgaged Paradise Canyon ranch to Maude Johann.

December 6, 1938   Babbitt Brothers subordinated their mortgage on basis of another loan from Maude Johann so that Mormon Church could be paid in full.

December 15, 1938   Presiding Bishopric acknowledged release of original mortgage.

August 5, 1939   Weavers gave warranty deed to Esther H. Bowers.

October 6, 1939   Esther H. Bowers paid Maude Johann to clear her claim.

October 25, 1940   Esther H. Bowers gave C. A. and R. Griffin agreement to purchase ranch.

January 1, 1946   Agreement extended five years from November 1, 1945.

April 12, 1957   Griffins leased twenty acres to W. Eakins.

July 24, 1958   Lease canceled.

August 15, 1964   C. A. & R. Griffin sold ranch to consortium.

June 11, 1974   Consortium sold Lee's Ferry ranch to National Park Service.

8

The National Park Service

March 1962	Weekly patrols to Lee's Ferry from Wahweap; subdistrict office started.

Park Rangers:

May 19, 1962	Edomo P. Mazzer, first sub-district ranger
October 1, 1963	Rodger Brask
September 11, 1964	Philip D. Martin
February 21, 1965	Philip Martin drowned at Two Mile
March 10, 1965	Richard E. Hoffman
January 5, 1966	Lee's Ferry Station upgraded from sub-district to district ranger
March 29, 1966	E. MacDougall Palmer
October 1, 1967	Joe Kastellic
October 3, 1970	Perry Thompson
Date not available	John Chapman
May 25, 1973	Jan Dick
Date not available	Wayne Landrum
January 15, 1978	Larry Dilts
November 2, 1980	Jerry Ballard
April 3, 1983	Jan Dick

Maintenance Employees:

June 7, 1963	G. W. Gentless
July 30, 1966	Dick Cook
July 27, 1969	Gerald G. Terry
March 30, 1975	Nannie Lee Terry went on payroll; had been helping her husband
January 6, 1985	Chester Mikus

Index

A

Adair, George, 21, 28, 48, 480n. 21, 23, 25
Adams, John, 320, 321, 502n. 20
Adams, John S. P., 55, 61, 107, 110
Adams, William R. "Bill," 224, 249
Aleson, Harry, 422, 425, 428, 431, 435, 450
Allen, Lewis. *See* Woodruff, Wilford
American Placer Corporation, 235, 238, 244, 245, 252, 267, 297
Amundsen, Andrew, 36
Amundsen, J. S., 194, 200, 204
Anderson, Hugh, 344
Anderson, Margaret, 344, 351
Anderson, Oliver, 44, 46
Andrus, James, 8, 147
Antelope Trail, Arizona, 7, 18, 31, 56, 470n. 19
Antille, Carl, 258, 261, 262, 267, 268
Apperson, Pres, 223, 226, 235, 244
Appling, Ernie, 298, 318
Arizona Cattle Company, 110
Arizona Mission, 36, 40, 43, 49, 60, 475n. 47, 476n. 57
Arizona Strip, 132, 185, 219
Arny, William F., 41
Ashurst, Henry Fountain, 196, 205, 317, 332, 336
Austin, Fred, 249, 250, 498n. 2
Ayers, George S., 160, 163

B

Babbitt Brothers, 244, 331, 351, 373, 378, 395, 400, 402, 408, 411, 423, 448
Badger Creek, Arizona, 26, 36, 45, 62, 72, 88, 166, 259, 335, 341, 349, 350, 361, 365, 366, 392, 416, 418, 429, 442, 456, 504n. 1

Badger Creek Rapid, Arizona, 156, 301, 332, 386, 392, 427, 452, 457, 474n. 4
Baker, Johnny, 132, 135
Baker, Maggie, 418, 429, 430, 433
Baker, Mildred, 416
Baker, Ruth, 456
Baker, Riley, 365, 366, 377, 416, 418, 429, 433, 430
Baker, Vern, 423, 443, 444, 453
Ballenger, Captain Jesse O., 60, 62, 63, 68, 69, 74
Ballenger's Camp (Brigham City), Utah, 68, 69, 74
Barboncito (Navajo spokesman), 18, 21
Bar Z Cattle Company, xiii, 174, 181, 185, 187, 191–96, 202–19 *passim*, 225, 232–310 *passim*, 366, 387, 389
Bass, William Wallace "Bill," 16, 206, 210, 260
Bass Trail, Arizona, 16, 260, 401, 472n. 51
Batchelor, Emma. *See* Lee, Emma Batchelor
Baumgartner, John A., 314, 326, 327, 329, 342, 380
Bayestewa, Pole, 506n. 6
Beadle, John H., 28
Beaman, E. O., 27
Bean, Tyson L., 266
Bean Hole, Arizona, 266, 443
Beaver, Utah, 9, 48, 51, 53, 114, 232
Belknap, Bill, 434, 510n. 44
Ben (Paiute guide), 28
Bennion, John R., 36, 37, 41
Bennett, David, 48, 49
Bennett, Frank Tracy, 17, 18, 21, 473n. 53
Bennett, Solena (Lena) Emett, xv, 37, 201, 210, 479n. 34, 493n. 37
Bennett, Walter, 395
Berry, Isabella, 8
Berry, Joseph, 8

Berry, Pete, 298
Berry, Robert, 8
Best Party, 130, 131, 134
bigamy. *See* polygamy
Big Horn Basin, Wyoming, 143
Bigler, Maud, 204, 209
Birdseye, Claude H., 274, 292, 298, 301, 302, 303, 358, 366
Bishop, Francis M., 14, 16, 18, 26, 27
Bishop, William K., 55
Bitter Springs, Arizona, 7, 31, 56, 69, 384, 440, 474n. 22
Black Hawk War, 7–8, 471n. 22
Black Sand Gold Recovery Company, 223, 226, 228, 235
Blanton, Bonner, 331, 383
Blockburger, Don, 271, 295, 299, 300
Blythe ferry, 42, 55, 63, 70, 80, 88
Blythe, John L., 42–50, 54–88 *passim*
Blythe, Samuel, 276, 289
boats. *See under specific types and names*
Bolte, Chuck, 436, 510n. 44
Boulder Dam, Arizona-Nevada, 297, 332, 380, 401, 410, 436. *See also* Hoover Dam
Bowers, Esther H. "Essy," 374, 385, 385, 386, 389, 391, 392, 395, 408, 411–13, 415, 416, 431
Bowers, Sam, 385, 389, 391, 392, 413
Boyer, Earl, 335–36, 404, 499n. 25
Bradley, W. H., 217, 221, 223–26, 245
Bradley Boat, 227
Brennan, Jack, 431
Bridge Canyon Dam, Arizona, 454
bridge-pontoons. *See* pontoon boats
bridges, proposed, 90, 92, 219, 244, 262, 273, 289, 291, 300, 304, 305. *See also* Navajo Bridge
Bright Angel Trail, Arizona, 199, 412
Brimhall, Edna Lee, xv, 388
Brinkerhoff, David, 91, 93–96, 101–5, 107, 110–12, 118, 131, 163, 227
Brinkerhoff, James, 227
Brinkerhoff, Lovina Lee "Aunt Vina," 131, 133, 135
Brinkerhoff, Lydia Ann, 91, 96
Brinkerhoff, Samuel, 149
Brookbank, Thomas W., 90, 189
Brooks, Frank S., 167; Camp Brooks, 157
Brooks, Juanita, xii, 444
Brown, Frank Mason, 115–18, 332, 464
Brown, James S., 58–63, 68, 74, 76
Brown, John F., 160, 164, 174, 176, 183, 191, 197, 211

Brown, Leo G., 19, 119, 122
Brown, Lora Ann, 84
Brown, Newman, 84, 90, 481n. 35
Brown, Rachel, 59, 60
Brown, William "Bill," 449, 451
Brownd, J. H. "Bill," 412, 419
Brownd, Freda, 412, 419
Bryant, Harold C., 409
Buckskin Mountain, Arizona, 6, 60, 192
Burg, Amos, 407, 427
Buzzard's Highline Trail, Arizona, 501n. 28. *See also* Sandslide Trail
Byers, Al, 246, 247
Byers, Leroy R., 437

C

Cabell, USGS Area Chief, 419–22, 424
Caffall, Allie, 254, 255, 256, 258, 261, 451
Caffall, Nell (infant daughter), 254, 255
Caffall, Tom, 254–59, 255, 261
Calhoun, John W., 268, 279, 282, 287, 292
California Development Company, 276, 277
Cameron, Arizona, 263, 328; bridge, 244, 246, 251, 258, 263; named, 289, 336; proposed, 235, 236, 239; post office, 263
Camp Rust, Arizona, 256
Campbell, Ian, 400, 401
Canaan Cooperative Stock Company, 89, 116, 147, 148, 151, 152, 481n. 10, 488n. 4
Canaan Ranch, 195
Cannon, George Q., 22, 58, 73, 74
Cannonville, Utah, 113, 189, 241, 259, 281, 286, 287, 298, 319
canoes, 300, 301, 436, 449
Cañonita, 21, 28, 29
Cañon Maid, 16, 18, 20, 22, 25
Canopy, 223–28, 224, 239, 282
Canyon Diablo, Arizona, 112, 113, 114
Cardinale, T. J. "Tim," *xiv*, xvi, 162
Carling, Elizabeth "Lizzie" Johnson, 124. *See also* Colvin, Elizabeth "Lizzie" Johnson; Johnson, Elizabeth "Lizzie"
cataract boats, 427
Cataract Canyon, Utah, 116, 134, 135, 208, 243, 260, 301, 323, 335, 405, 407, 422, 427, 428, 437, 459
Chaffin, Arthur L., 425
Chamberlain, Emma Jane "Janey" Emett. *See* Emett, Emma Jane "Janey"

Chamberlain, Thomas "Tom" Jr., 56, 126, 140, 150, 171, 171, 191, 490n. 67

Charles H. Spencer, 237, 247, 247, 248, 251, 282, 388, 435, 448, 459, 466, 497n. 33

Charlie, 407

Chenoweth, William R., 284, 422

Christensen, Ann, 99, 105

Christensen, Chris Lingo, 98, 99, 100, 101, 105, 106

Christensen, Severina, 105

Chuar ("Captain Frank" or "Frank", Paiute guide), 16, 28

Church of Jesus Christ of Latter-day Saints, x, xii, xv, 4–6, 8, 10, 17, 20, 22, 30, 32, 35, 43, 48, 51, 53, 62–64, 71, 73, 75, 76, 80, 81, 96, 100, 102, 106, 117, 125, 143, 145, 181, 213, 240, 259, 260, 275, 292, 293, 317, 318, 332, 336, 365, 458, 476n. 72

Circle Flying W Ranch, 345, 373, 374, 376, 382, 385–87, 390, 391, 394, 395

Clark, Georgie. *See* White, Georgie

Clark, Owen R., 271, 287, 297, 298, 299, 300, 302, 304, 309, 311, 317–20, 324–28, 331, 340, *341*, 347, 356, 381, 400, 401, 407, 415, 416, 435

Claypool, Woody, 327, 329, 333

Clayton, Will, 110, 112, 115

Clevenger, Samuel, 104, 107, 483n. 58

Cliff Dwellers Lodge, Arizona, 433, 439, 443, 444, 451, 453, 456

Clinger, James, 43, 48, 50

Clover, Elzada, 405

Cluff, Benjamin, Jr., 181

Cockroft, Irving G., 283, 284, 289, 290, 291, 294, 297, 300–3, 324, 428

Cockroft, Margery, 283, 291, 292, 294, 297, 301, 302, 324

Cody, William F. "Buffalo Bill," 132, 133, 134, 251, 486n. 57

Cogswell, Raymond, 215, 495n. 1, 497n. 41

Colorado, 33

Colorado, Grand Canyon Mining and Improvement Company. *See* Best Party

Colorado River, ix, xiii, 1, 6, 7, 28, 63, 196, 202, 207, 276, 282, 499n. 1; freezing of, 75, 89, 101, 123, 159, 160, 170, 178, 210, 245, 311, 346, 347, 426

Colorado River Commission, 289, 293

Colorado River Compact, 278, 296, 305, 316, 437, 440

Colorado River salmon, 96

Colorado River Storage Project, 438, 439

Colton, Harold S., 300, 345, 346, 351, 374, 376, 386, 391, 399, 400

Colvin, Elizabeth "Lizzie" Johnson, 264. *See also* Carling, Elizabeth "Lizzie" Johnson; Johnson, Elizabeth "Lizzie"

Colvin, O. F., 264

Colvin, Urban, 329

Compact Point, Arizona, 296. *See also* Lee Ferry, Arizona

Conrard, Harrison, 189, 190, 192, 194

Cook, R. Elton, 342, 380, 381

Costa, T. A., 230, 231

Crampton, C. Gregory, 449

Crosby, Glen, 201

Crosby, Jake, 144, 201, 317–19, 328

Crosby, Taylor "Bud," 153, 201

Crossing of the Fathers, Utah, 3, 406

Cundell, Nora Lucy Mobray, 384, 396, 397, 426, 430

D

Dale, Willard ("Golden Jesus" "Red Wolf") 441

Davie, Iona, 323, 327, 333

Davis, Arthur Powell, xiii, 277–79, 293–95, 438

Davis, Clara Emett. *See* Emett, Clara

Day, Henry, 37, 38, 40

Deans, Emily, 335, 336

Deans, Royce, 329, 331, 332, 335, 336

Decker, Ida, xv, 380, 387–89, 392, 393

Decker, Sherman O., xv, 380–82, 385, 386, 387, 389, 393, 394

de Colmont, Bernard, 407

de Colmont, Genevieve, 407

Delbridge, Claude, 434, 441, 442

Dellenbaugh, Frederick, 27, 28

DeMotte, Harvey C., 28, 29, 341

Dennis, Harry W., 280, 284, 292, 294, 296

Deseret News, 19, 53, 59, 71, 109, 125, 140, 197

de Seynes, Antoine, 407

Dewing, Kay, 373, 374, 381

Diamond Creek, Arizona, 278, 288, 292, 294, 295, 297, 305, 386, 401, 422, 434, 455

Dickinson, W. E., 314, 342, 348, 353–55, 361, 362, 364, 380, 381, 389, 393

Dimmick, Charlie, 195, 196, 202–4, 209, 215, 220, 222, 224, 231, 232

Dirty Devil River, Utah, 20, 21, 28, 157; bridge, 449

Dodds, Pardyn, 21, 22

Dodge, Frank B., 270–72, 274, 280–82, 285, 287, 298, 301, 324, 353, 354, 358, 361–4, 366, 367, 379–82, 385, 386, 389, 392–94, 400, 401, 415–22, 424

Domingo, Juan, 138

Domínguez-Escalante expedition, 2, 3

Don Cisneros. 3

dory boats, 462, 463, 465, 512n. 9

Douglass, Andrew Ellicott, 186–89, 194

Doyle, Al, 235, 238, 239

Draper, Erastus Almon, 125–30, 486n. 44

Driftwood, 437

Dubendorff, Seymour, 215, 497n. 41

Dunn, William, 13, 472n. 43

Dusty Dozen, 379

E

Eaton, Earl, 436, 510n. 44

Echo Cliffs, Arizona, 2, 3, 7, 9, 138, 188, 206, 218, 286, 317, 319, 396

Eddy, Clyde, 323–325, 325, 379, 503n. 27

Eden, James M., 444

Edison Company. *See* Southern California Edison Company

Edmunds Act, 100–2

Edmunds-Tucker Act, 106

Elkus, Charles, 392

Emett, Bessie, 183

Emett, Bill, 166, 178, 183, 186, 190, 196, 199, 201, 202, 206, 210–12

Emett, Clara, xv, 153, 154, 167, 171, 172, 176, 178, 185, 189, 190, 206, 207, 211–14

Emett, Emma Jane Lay, 145, 147, 150, 153, 166, 168, 170, 172, 175, 178, 181, 186, 191, 200, 204–6, 208, 210, 212, 213

Emett, Electa Jane Gruell, 150, 153, 166

Emett, Emma Jane "Janey," 150, 171, 212, 213, 214, 490n. 67

Emett, Electa Jane Westover, 145

Emett, G. Frank, 490n. 53

Emett, George, 165, 172, 196, 199, 211–13, 490n. 53

Emett, James Simpson "Jim," xiii, 64, 65, 67, 89, 126, 139, 140, 143, 145, *146*, 147–56, 160, 161, 163–74, 176–215,

479n. 34, 492n. 32, 493n. 35, 495n. 90

Emett, John Henry, 210

Emett, John Taylor, 147, 156, 160, 165, 177, 180, 183, 185, 188, 201, 201, 210–12, 495n. 90

Emett, Julia Mae, 183, 203, 207

Emett, Moses Mosia, 145, 148, 172

Emett, Pearl, 153, 166, 490n. 57

Emett, Ray, 201

Emett, Rose Nell, 150, 153, 166, 207, 210

Emett, Sarah Ellen Wooley, 180, 183, 185, 189, 201, 202, 210, 212

Emett, Sister (Tom's wife), 148

Emett, Solena "Lena." *See* Bennett, Solena Emett

Emett Spring, Arizona, 187, 193, 195, 196, 202

Emett, Tom. *See* Emmett, Thomas

Emma Dean, 24, 28, 29; replica, 406

Emmett, James, 145

Emmett, James Simpson. *See* Emett, James Simpson

Emmett, Moses Simpson, 145, 147, 204

Emmett, Thomas Carlos "Tom," 147, 148

Escalante River, Utah, 28, 422

Esmeralda II, 430, 432, 509n. 37

Evans. *See* Morell and Evans

F

Faatz, Friend Grant, 134–38, 487n. 68

Fairchild Aerial Survey, 386, 401

Farquhar, Francis, 418, 508n. 12

ferryboat construction and use, 33, 474n. 27; Blythe, 42; Brinkerhoff, 112; *Cañon Maid,* 16; Coconino County, 236, 265, 303; *Colorado,* 33; Emett and Woolley, 211; *Emma Dean,* 28; flatboats, 95; James Simpson Emett, 174, 176, 199; Leithead, 90; one-wagon ferry, 106. *See also under specific boat name*

Fish, Joseph, 52, 78, 100, 262, 263

Fisher, Ed, xv, 362, 364, 366, 373, 377, 382, 387, 393, *396,* 396, 400, 404, 407, 434, 442, 481n. 16

Fisher, George, 364, 366, 382, 394, 404, 407, 412, 413, 415, 481n. 16

Fisher Spring, Arizona. *See* Phantom Spring

Flagstaff, Arizona, 68, 110, 131, 137, 166, 173, 183, 184

flat-bottomed boats, 25, 71, 80, 83, 95, 428
Flattum, Pat H. M., 345–47, 504n. 8
Flavell, George F., 142, 260
Flavell II, 463
Forsythe, Ann, 385, 385, 387, 391–94
Fort Defiance, New Mexico, 6, 15, 16, 18, 20, 21, 26, 41, 43, 48, 50
Fort Hamblin, Utah, 145, 147
Foster, Jane, 442, 454
Foutz, Joseph L., 74, 81, 82, 84, 90, 172
Frazier, Russell G., 379, 405–7
Fredonia, Arizona, 102, 131, 183, 187, 200, 203, 314, 340
Freeman, F. A., 345, 346
Freeman, Lewis R., 293, 301, 338
French, Emma Batchelor Lee, 79, 83, 481n. 3. *See also* Lee, Emma Batchelor
French, Franklin Marquis, 78, 79, 80–83, 126, 155, 156, 157, 480n. 20, 481n. 31
Frost, Allen, 19, 57, 106, 481n. 18
Fryer, E. R. "Si," 448, 457, 458
Fullmer, Hannibal Octavius, 60, 63
Fulmer, Stephen Moulton, 418

G

Gage Rock, Arizona, 98
Gage, Carl, 437, 510n. 44
gages: Grand Canyon, 347, 417; Lee's Ferry, 280–82, 290–92, 296, 297, 301, 303, 314, 320, 326, 347, 352, 380, 386, 425, 431, 433; Little Colorado, 361, 362, 386, 387, 415, 417, 426; Moenkopi, 417, 419; Pahreah, 352, 413
Galloway Cave, Utah, 137, 157, 159, 427, 487nn. 66, 67. *See also* Johnson, Neal; Outlaw Cave
Galloway, Nathaniel "Nate," 137, 152–57, 157, 158, 159, 167, 169, 171–75, *171, 175,* 178, 215, 244, 260, 427, 490n. 64, 487nn. 66, 67, 497n. 41
Galloway, Parley, 323
Games, Betty Jo, 366, 367
Games, Bobby, 366, 367
Gap, the, Arizona, 228, 270, 280, 291, 308, 401, 403–5, 423, 431, 440
Gardiner, Robert, 49
Garrison, Clay R., 446, 454
Gentless, Bill, 449, 452
Geological Survey. *See* U. S. Geological Survey

Gibbons, Andrew S., 48, 50, 55, 71, 74, 89, 470n. 10
Gila River, Arizona-New Mexico, 47, 196, 275–77, 296
Girand, James B., 278, 292, 294, 305
Glen Canyon, Arizona-Utah, 2, 114, 134, 152, 167, 314, 428, 432
Glen Canyon Bridge, Arizona, 440, 442, 510n. 7
Glen Canyon Dam, Arizona, 410, 440, 445–47, 449, 450, 463, 465, 466
Glenn Placer claim, Utah, 152–56
Goff, Harper, *ii,* xvi, 1, 5, 9, *66, 121*
Goldwater, Barry, 415, 416, 423, 427, 450
Grand Canyon, Arizona, ix, 6, 75
Grand Canyon Bridge, Arizona. *See* bridges, proposed; Navajo Bridge
Grand Canyon Cattle Company, 209, 213, 214, 219, 222, 243, 255, 268, 292, 302, 304, 309, 312, 319, 326, 343, 368, 373
Grand Canyon Forest Reserve, Arizona, 182, 205
Grand Canyon Game Preserve, Arizona, 205
Grant, Alexander G. "Zee," Jr., 416, 417
Grant, Heber J., 95, 312, 332, 337–38, 343, 357, 388
Grant, Ulysses S., 10, 30, 32
Grass Valley, Utah, 43, 44, 47, 48, 50
Graves, Walter H., 14, 16, 18
Greene, Arthur H. "Art," 421, 423, 428–30, *429,* 432–34, 439, 440, 443, 445, 510n. 1
Grey, Zane, 205–7, 210, 235, 308, 351, 494nn. 67, 69
Gregory, Herbert E., 182, 259
Gregory Natural Bridge, Utah, 422

H

Haight, Horton D., 36–40, 57, 58
Haight, Isaac C., 19, 21, 23, 27, 35
Hall, Sharlot, 238–89, 241, 244, 388, 497n. 35
Hamblin, Benny, 33, 41
Hamblin, Jacob, xiii, 3–10, 13–23, 25–28, 30–38, 41–48, 50, 54–58, 61, 62, 64, 65, 67, 70–72, 74, 75, 82, 470nn. 3, 7, 15, 17, 472n. 48, 475n. 41, 476n. 61, 477n. 9, 478n. 33
Hamblin, Lyman, 9, 10, 29, 54
Hance Rapid, Arizona, 450, 465

Hanna, I. B., 182, 183
Hanna, Pete, 246, 247, *247*, 248
Hansbrough, Peter M., 116, 117, 464
Hardy, Harvey, 114, 484n. 15
Harker, Allie Caffall. *See* Caffall, Allie
Harmony, Utah, 13, 14, 16, 19, 370, 472n. 46
Harris, Don, 410, 425, 431
Haskell, Thales H., 5, 48, 50, 55, 58, 75
Hatch, Ira, 20, 21, 34, 37, 44, 46, 47, 50, 58, 110
Hatch, Lorenzo Hill, 64, 65, 67, 74, 75, 100, 138, 479n. 35
Hatch, Robert "Bus," 380, 436
Hately, Hester Hyde, 374, 379
Heckler, Wilbur L., 358, 361–63, 381, 387, 388, 393, 415,
Hiester, William E., 321, 367
Hillers, Jack, 22, 28–31, 472n. 51
Hislop, John, 120
Hislop Cave, Arizona, 393
Hite, Cass, 244, 484n. 15
Hite, Utah, 155, 157, 167, 178, 208, 247, 386, 405, 406, 410, 422, 424–26, 428, 441; ferry, 425
Hoffman, John, 465
Hoffman, Richard E. "Dick," 449, 450, 452, 453
Holladay, C. E., 114, 123, 127, 407
Holladay, Wilford, 148
Holmstrom, Haldane "Buzz," 401, 407, 457
Honeymoon Trail, Arizona-Utah, 56
Hoover Dam, Arizona-Nevada, 425. *See also* Boulder Dam
Horsethief route, 307. *See also* Nankoweap Trail, Tanner Trail
Hoskaninni Company, 166, 178
House Rock Spring, Arizona, 24, 26, 28, 36–38, 45, 62, 141, 195
Howland brothers, 13, 14, 472n. 43
Hoxie, R. L., 41
Hubbell, Juan Lorenzo, 35, 42
Hubbell, Lorenzo Jr., 256
Hubbell, Ramon, 418, 421, 423, 428, 432
Hudson, Ed, 418, 422, 430, 432, 435, 461
Huish, Ruby A., 315, 319, 320
Hungavi, Poli, 378, 381, 386, 388, 399, 405, 408, 409, 506n. 6
Hunt, "Husky," 392
Huntington, Clark Allen "Al," 114, 116, 119, 123, 124, 127, 130, 131, 133, 136–40, 143, 407, 484n. 16

Hyde, Darrell "Unk," 374, 375, 376, 379, 381, 382, 395
Hyde, Bessie, 334, 335
Hyde, Glen, 334, 335
Hyde, Hester, 374, 379, 381

I

Inglesby, A. L. "Doc," 386, 406
Irwin, Jake, 392
Ivie, Frank, 110, 112
Ivins, Anthony W., 53, 68, 133, 138, 170, 312, 319, 332

J

Jackson, James, 32, 35, 42, 44, 45, 476nn. 58, 59
Jackson, Margaret "Maggie," 365, 366, 377, 416
Jacobsen, Eletha, xv, 482n. 25
Jacob's Pools, Arizona, 6, 16, 26, 27, 30, 32, 38, 39, 41, 42, 45, 58, 62, 120, 138, 187, 193, 195, 202, 203, 256, 258, 259, 266, 271, 272, 481n. 35
James, George Wharton, 155, *157, 158, 159*, 489n. 32
Jesús (Mexican worker), 124
Johann, Maud, 385, 408, 410, 411
Johnson, Adolpha, 281, 285, 288, 326–29, *330*
Johnson, Aaron, 69, 479n. 43
Johnson, Agnes, xv
Johnson, Annie Young, 143, 216, 495n. 3
Johnson bypass/cutoff, 102, 104, 110. *See also* Lee Hill, Lee's Backbone
Johnson, Earl, 423, *429*, 443
Johnson, Elizabeth "Lizzie," 32, 91, 97, 125. *See also* Carling, Elizabeth "Lizzie" Johnson; Colvin, Elizabeth "Lizzie" Johnson
Johnson, Frank Tilton, xiii, xv, 77, *109*, 120, *121, 135*, 141, 142, 224, 252, 254, 257, 261, *269*, 273, 280, 290, 312, 331, 332, 388, 476nn. 6, 27, 485n. 35, 487n. 59, 510n. 15
Johnson, Jeremiah "Jerry," x, xii, 61, 118, 138, 139, 141, 152, 216, *247*, 264, *264*, 268, *269*, 280, 312, 315, 319, 341, 349, 363, 372, 431, 477n. 80
Johnson, Jonathan, 103, 128, 486n. 44
Johnson, Joseph "Jody," xv, 131, 140, 143, 253, 264, 266, 267, 269, 288, 316, 332, 335, 431

Johnson, Laura, 128, 486n. 44
Johnson, LeRoy Sunderland, 108, 128, 131, *135*, 143, 233, 240, 251, 253, 260, 264, 266, 483n. 1
Johnson, Lola, 355, 358, 360
Johnson, Lydia. *See* Spencer, Lydia Johnson
Johnson, Marva, 326, 327, 329, 331, 503n. 37
Johnson, Mary Evelette, 108, 109, 118, 131
Johnson, Melinda, 60, 108, 111, 127–29, 486n. 44
Johnson, Millie, 128, 486n. 44
Johnson, "Captain" Neal, 353, 355–61, 363
Johnson, Neal, 420. *See also* Galloway Cave, Outlaw Cave
Johnson, Nephi, 25, 149
Johnson, Owen, 298, 310, 314, 447
Johnson, Pearly Simmons, 216, 231, 233, 238, 253–55, 261, *264*, 288, 311, 319, 321, 327, 333, 349, 357, 363, 369
Johnson, Permelia Smith, 55, 58, 84, 90, 91, 103, 105, 108, *109*, 115, 118, 119, 122, 124, 127, 129, 131, 133, *135*, 137, 140, 141, 143, 144
Johnson Point, Arizona, 481n. 17
Johnson, Price William, 103, 144, 237, 253, 260, 264, 267, 270, 281, 282, 284, 288, 290, 291, 294, 295, 298, 312, 314, 317, 318, 323, 325, 326, 333, 334, 335, 341, 347, 348–51, 365, 421, 429, 447, 504n. 1, 505n. 44
Johnson, Rhoda Young, 143, 144, 216, 225, 331
Johnson, Samantha, 60, 76, 91, 96, 103, 108, 115, 119, 124, 125, 127, 130, 139, 143, 144
Johnson, W. D., 28, 148, 478n. 33
Johnson, Warren Elmer "Elmer," 124, 233, 260, 290, 315, 359, 360, 373, 419
Johnson, Warren Marshall, xiii, xiv, 54, 56, 58, 61, 64, 76, 82, 86, 88, 90, 92–95, 97, 102, 105, *109*, 113, 117–20, *121*, 122–31, 133, 136–44, 152, 161, 166, 473n. 70, 474n. 6, 477nn. 13, 15, 485n. 24, 487nn. 77, 81, 488n. 88
Jones, Albert H., xv, 217–28, 232, 243, 245, 246, 259, 496n. 7
Jones, Charles Jesse "Buffalo," 205, 206, 210
Jones, Daniel W., 56, 58, 59, 68

Jones, Les "Buckethead," 436
Jones, William C. "Willie," 192
Jotter, Lois, 405
Judd, Asa W., 128, 129, 205, 358
Judd, Henry Eli, 131, 141
Judd, Zadok Knapp, Jr., 81, 82, 388
Julius F, 407

K

Kaibab deer drive, Arizona, 306
Kaibab Land and Cattle Company, 173
Kaibab Trail, Arizona, 298. *See also* trails, trans-Canyon
Kanab, Utah, 9, 13, 15, 29
Kane, Thomas L., 30, 32
kayaks, 407, 416
Kelly, Charles, 348, 394, 406, 407, 507n. 22, 510n. 15
Ketchene (Navajo chieftain), 20, 21, 46, 47
Keyhole Natural Bridge, Arizona, 464
King, John Aaron, 191, 464
Kitchen, John Green, 148, 150–51, 153, 160, 163–65; estate, 165, 169, 170, 172, 173, 183, 188, 189, 490n. 53
Kitchen, Martha G., 150–51, 153, 160, 164
Klohr, Christina "Chris," xv, 282–83, 289, 303, 311, 328, 424, 426
Klohr, James E., xv, 282–83, 286, 287, 296–98, 300–2, 305, 308, 309, 311, 312, *313*, 314, 320, 415, 424, 426, 427, 433
Knight, Samuel, 48
Knox, J. S., 167, 169
Kolb, Ellsworth, 243, 244, 282, 284, 498n. 42
Kolb, Emery, 243, 244, *247*, 284, 298, 301, 498n. 42

L

Lake Mead, Arizona-Nevada, 416, 422, 430–32, 434–37, 440, 441, 462
Lake Powell, Arizona-Utah, 3, 441, 445, 449, 454, 467
Lamb, Charlotte, 170
Lamb, Gladys, 170, 490n. 65
Lamb, William S., 167, 170, 172
Larabee, Charlie, 430
LaRue, Eugene C., xiii, 272, 278, 280, 291–94, 305, 316, 324, 332, 386, 433, 437, 438

Latter-day Saints. *See* Church of Jesus Christ of Latter-day Saints

launch, the. *See Canopy*

launches, 164, 178, 221–24, 228, 239

Layton, Judge N. G., 169, 172, 173, 186–89

LDS. *See* Church of Jesus Christ of Latter-day Saints

Leach, Albert E. "Bert" "Teddy," 240, 242, 246, 247, 249, 251, 254

LeBaron, Annie Spencer, 349

LeBaron, Grover Cleveland "Cleve," 349, 368, 369

Lee, Bill, 111–3, 126, 137; Billy, 30, 32, 41, 42, 56, 59, 61, 81–83

Lee, Bill Jr., 137

Lee cabin, xiii, 394, 507n. 22

Lee, Clara B. Workman, 126, 137, 489n. 31

Lee, Emma Batchelor, xiii, 23–25, 31, 32, 41–43, 46, 49, 52–55, 57–59, 61, 67, 69–72, 75, 78, 80–83, 143, 473n. 69, 474n. 6, 481n. 3, 489n. 31. *See also* French, Emma Batchelor Lee

Lee Ferry, Arizona, 500n. 22. *See also* Compact Point, Arizona

Lee Ferry Bridge. *See* Navajo Bridge

Lee, Francie Dell, 25, 49

Lee Hill, Arizona, 36, 62, 69, 70, 72, 76, 77, 80, 83, 88, 92, 93, 100, 102–4, 106, 107, 110, 166, 378, 390. *See also* Johnson cutoff, Lee's Backbone

Lee, Jim, 112

Lee, Joe, 388

Lee, John Doyle, xii–xiv, 11–14, *12*, 18, 19, 22–25, 39, 41, 47, 49, 52, 53, 55, 474n. 6, 475n. 45, 476nn. 55, 61, 68

Lee, Joseph Hyrum (son of John D. Lee), 74, 156

Lee, Joseph Hyrum (grandson of John D. Lee), 388

Lee, Lavina Young (wife of John D. Lee), 23, 24, 47, 52, 53

Lee, Lovina (granddaughter of John D. Lee). *See* Brinkerhoff, Lovina Lee

Lee, Polly Young, 23, 24, 52, 53

Lee, Rachel A. Woolsey, 23–25, 27, 30, 46, 49, 52, 53, 74

Lee, Sarah Caroline Williams, 23, 24, 52, 53

Lee's Backbone, Arizona, 36. *See also* Johnson bypass/cutoff, Lee Hill

Lee's Ferry cemetery, *129*

Lee's Ferry Bridge. *See* bridges, proposed; Navajo Bridge

Lee's Ferry Post Office, Arizona, 84, 161, 168, 232, 257, 297, 298, *313*

Lee's Ferry Ranger Station, Arizona, 445, 449

Lee's Ferry roads, *162*

Leigh, John David, 200, 201, 203

Leithead, James, 80, 81, 85, 87, 90, 91, 93

Lewis, Charlie, 271, 283, 288, 305, 310, 312, 366

Leydet, François, 463

Ligon, Waddy T., 316

Lint, Leigh, 512n. 6

Little Colorado River, Arizona-New Mexico, 34, 259, 303

Little Jean, 160, 178, 179; Stanton's flatboat, 95

Little Johnny (Navajo worker), 202, 206, 210–13

Litton, Martin, 463, 465, 513n. 10

Lonely Dell, Arizona, 8, 13, 23, 25, 27, 28, 31, 39, 43, 45, 51, 57, 76, 450, 473n. 69

Loper, Bert, 208, 244, 245, 276, 295, 410, 431, 432, 436, 440, 494n. 76

Lopp, Larry, 447, 510n. 15

Los Angeles Times, 276, 277, 279, 336, 338, 454

Lowrey, David, 325, 326, 331, 333, 378, 383, 384, 396, 397, 404, 407

Lowrey, David Crockett "Buck," 270, 308, 322–28, *325*, 332, 333, 335, 337, 338, 340, 343, 347, 354, 357, 361, 365, 366, *367*, 368–73, 381–84, 388, 389, 391, 392, 396, *396*, 399, 401, 404, 426, 504n. 52, 505n. 44

Lowrey, Florence, 324, 326, 339, 383, 426

Lowrey, Mamie, 333, 339, 340

Lowrey, Virginia, 331, 383

Lye (Hopi guide), 6, 7, 470n. 17

M

MacKay, Alex J., 186–88

Maid of the Cañon, 472n. 50

Mail Trail, Arizona, 141

Mangum, John, 10, 23, 24, 26, 27, 30, 44, 45

Mangum, Joseph, 21, 27

Mansfield, Eph, 232, 235, 238, 252, 254, 256–58, 261, 262, 266, 267, 268, 270–73, 279, 281, 295, 304

Marble Canyon, Arizona, 117, 322

Marble Canyon Bridge. *See* bridges, proposed; Navajo Bridge

Marble Canyon Dam, Arizona, 447, 453, 454

Marble Canyon Lodge, Arizona, *367, 403,* 418, 421, 427, 430, 433, 442, 443, 454, 504n. 52. *See also* Vermilion Cliffs Lodge, Arizona

Marble Canyon Post Office, Arizona, 324, 377, 440

Mariger, Lawrence C., 99, 110

Marshall, Edwin J., 209, 255, 256, 261, 266

Marston, Garth, 418

Marston, Otis Reed "Dock," xii, 418, 420, 422, 423, 432, 435, 461, 462, 496n. 10, 512nn. 3, 4, 5, 6

Martin, Phillip "Phil," 449, 511n. 20

Mayrant, Howard, *219,* 228, 229–31, 233, 235–38

McAllister, William James Frazier "Will," 105, 108

McArthur, Daniel D., 7, 8, 49, 50, 64, 147

McClurg, Archimedes, 139, 487n. 75

McConkie, Wayne, 418, 420, 422

McConnell, Jehiel, 10, 23

McCormick, George, 255, 306–8, 324, 325

McDaniels, Lafe, 332

McDonald, Alex F., 38, 42, 49, 69, 101, 476n. 55

McDonald, Charlie, 347, 352–56, 358–60, 363, 394

McDonald, Harry, *119,* 120, 122, 123, 130, 131, 485n. 31

McIntyre, Robert, H., 7–8

McKean, James B., 11, 22, 32, 43, 51

McKee, Edwin D., 401, 407, *461*

Mecham, Samuel Alvarus "Al," 167–70, 172, 176

Mesken Bar, Utah, 360, 431

Mesken, Ed, 134, 153, 154–156, 157, 159, 489n. 32

Mexican Hat, Utah, xii, 217, 392, 420; bridge, 217, 393

Mexican Hat Expeditions, 432, 450, 462

Mile Zero, Arizona, 301, 501n. 32

Moenave, Arizona, 5, 31, 59, 474nn. 21, 22

Moenkopi, Arizona, 5, 20, 31, 238, 474n. 21

Monett, Edwin R., 208, 410

Montéz, Ramon, 142

Monte Vista Hotel, Flagstaff, Arizona 345, 346, 350, 351, 406

Monument Valley, Arizona-Utah, 265

Moon, Chester A., 311, 316, 318, 321, 322, 328

Moon, "Sweeter," 311, 316, 321, 322

Moore, Elijah "Lige," 286, 287, 317, 318, 435

Morell, 37. *See also* Morell and Evans

Morell and Evans, 38, 39

Mormons. *See* Church of Jesus Christ of Latter-day Saints

Mortenson, "Brick," 463

Mountain Meadows, Utah, 145, 470n. 7; massacre at, xii, 4, 11, 13, 14, 18, 19, 22, 23, 27, 28, 52, 53, 71, 166, 470n. 4, 471n. 36, 472n. 43, 476n. 76; John D. Lee executed at, 53

Muerto Deambro. *See* Ketchene

Mullins Boat, 226, 227, 386

Muñiz, Andres (Domínguez-Escalante scout), 3

Muñiz, Lucrecio (Domínguez-Escalante scout), 3, 138

N

Nancy Lee, 160; Stanton's flatboat, 95

Nankoweap, Arizona, 124; basin, 123; Canyon, 298; Creek, 127; Trail, 307. *See also* Horsethief route

Naraguts (Southern Paiute guide), 3

National Park Service, xiii, xv, 306, 336–37, 416, 437, 441, 444, 446–52, 454–59, 464–66

Navajo, 282, 283, 285, 356, 357

Navajo Bridge, 322, 323, 326, 328, 331, 333, 334, *334,* 336, 337, *338,* 340, 379, 401, 442, 444, 457, 467, 510n. 7; old Navajo trail near, 401, 457; proposed, 90, 92, 289, 305

Navajo Spring, Arizona, 7, 37, 40, 73, 88, 91, 112, 139, 182, 228, 267, 300, 320, 322, 334, 391, 392, 394, 432, 433

Neal, John, 192, 195

Nebeker, Ashton, 14, 16, 186, 187, 205

Nellie, 115, 116, 118, 136, 142, 156, 160, 315, 448, 458, 507n. 22

Nellie Powell, xiii, 24, 29–31, 115, 406–7; replica, 406

Nelson, Charlotte Annie Tanner, 103–4

Nelson, Peter "Pete" (Nielson), 348, 354, 356, 364, 365, 389, 448

Nelson, Price William, 60, 61, 91, 103

Nevills, Doris, 416, 427, 432, 462, 512n. 6

Nevills, Joan, 420, 441

Nevills, Norman D., xii, 392, 393, 405, 410, *414*, 415–8, 420–23, 426–32, 434, 435, 441, 450, 461–63, 465, 467, 507n. 20

Nevills sadiron boats, 434, 461, 463

Nevills, Sandra, 512n. 6

Nielson, Frihoff G., 62, 68, 72, 84, 92, 104, 123, 478n. 24, 485n. 18

Nielson, John R., xiii, 114, 115, 118, 448; floating placer mining boat *(see Nellie)*

Nims, Franklin, 119, 119, 120, 121, 122, 123, 140, 485n. 32

Nipple Ranch, 150, 151, 153, 160, 165, 170–72

Nuttall, L. John, 64, 65, 67, 73, 77, 80–84, 93, 94, 98–100, 127, 148

O

Oljeto, Utah, 218, 222–25, 231. *See also* trading posts

Olson, Ed, 418

O'Neill, William O. "Bucky," 112, 113

Oraibi, Arizona, 3–6, 9, 16, 18, 21, 31, 33, 34, 186, 218

O'Sullivan, Timothy, *40*, 41

Outlaw Cave, Utah, 420, 427, 487n. 66. *See also* Galloway Cave; Johnson, Neal

Owens, Jim "Uncle Jimmy," 206, 210, 256

P

Page Land and Cattle Company, 457

Pahreah, x, 1, 28, 474n. 14. *See also* Paria

Pahreah, 33, 40

Pahreah Canyon, Arizona-Utah, 16, 24, 25, 219, 366, 473n. 70

Pahreah Ferry, Arizona, 87, 98, 102, 103, 110

Pahreah Ranch, 281, 295, 297, 328, 356, 404, 416

Pahreah Reservoir project, 268, 282, 287

Pahreah Riffle, Arizona, 120, 173

Pahreah River, Arizona-Utah, xiii, 16, 24, 25, *40*, 219, 252–53, 366; bridge, 446, 447, 498n. 6

Pahreah, Utah, 25, 113, 511n. 33

Palmer, John, 231, 253, 241, 249

Palmer, William J., 89

Paradise Canyon Ranch, 378, 379, 382, 386, 387, 390–93, 395, 397, 400, 402, 404, 406, 409–11

Paria, x, 28, 474n. 14. *See also* Pahreah

Parker, Earl W. "Daddy," 329, 331

Parker, Walter, 272, 282

Parkyn, Harold, 228–30, 232, 235, 236, 241, 248, 267

Parkyn, Herbert A. "Bert," 217, 228, 242, 253, 272, 282

Pathé-Bray party, 324, 353, 503n. 31

Pearce Ferry, Arizona, 71, 72, 74, 75, 83, 386, 434

Pearce, Harrison, 70, 71, 72, 88

Petty, Nate, 215, 216, 258

Phantom Spring, Arizona, 91–2, 123, 333, 407, 481n. 16

Pierce, Irving C., 194–96, 201, 204, 205

Pierce, Matthew, 457

Penny, Tillie Mary, 211, 212

Pipe Spring, Arizona, 7–9, 15, 19, 20, 22, 36, 37, 64, 110, 111

Pipe Spring Ranch, 89, 147, 148, 152

plural marriage. *See* polygamy

Pole Bayestewa. *See* Bayestewa, Pole

Poli Hungavi. *See* Hungavi, Poli

polygamy, 10, 11, 22, 25, 80, 95, 100–4, 106, 113, 117, 125, 130, 152, 166, 191, 216, 259, 260, 264, 288, 290, 294, 312, 315, 318, 319, 327, 331, 349, 351, 355, 356, 358, 362, 363, 368, 371, 373, 376–78, 381. *See also* Edmunds Act; Edmunds-Tucker Act; Woodruff Manifesto

pontoon boats, 436, 437. *See also* rafts

Portola, 463

Powell, Walter Clement "Clem," 27, 29–31

Powell, Major John Wesley, 13–18, 20–31, 115, 117, 141, 441, 472nn. 41, 43, 50, 51

Power, Rhoda, 385, 395, 397, 400, 402

Pratt, Lorum, Jr., 308

punts. *See* San Juan punts

Pure Gold claim, Utah, 136–38, 218

Q

Quist, Goddard, 260

R

rafts: driftwood, 3, 6, 7, 9; inflatable, 427, 429, 430, 431, 435, 436, 445,

452, 455, 457, 462, 465; wood, 26. *See also* pontoon boats

railroads: Atchison, Topeka, and Santa Fe Railroad, 123, 185, 191, 197, 163, 336; Atlantic and Pacific Railway, 92, 132; Denver & Rio Grande Railway, 89, 92, 96, 289; Northern Arizona Railway, 89; Sevier Valley Railway, 89, 90, 273; Southern Pacific Railroad, 276, 277; Union Pacific Railroad, 89, 332; Utah Southern, 89

Rainbow Bridge, Utah, xii, 235, 255, 293, 300, 314, 345–47, 353, 354, 360, 386, 406, 420, 422, 428, 429, 440, 443, 434, 504n. 8

Reilly, Elizabeth M. "Susie," ix–x, xv–xvi, 460–62, 464, 465, 467, 468, 510n. 1, 511n. 20, 512n. 6

Reilly, P. T., ix–x, *429*, 460–68, *461*, 469n. 1, 476n. 72, 474n. 4, 481n. 17, 485n. 22, 486n. 47, 492n. 30, 508n. 2, 508n. 12, 509nn. 24, 27, 510nn. 1, 4, 16, 511nn. 20, 23, 512nn. 1, 2, 3, 8, 513nn. 10, 11, 12, 15, 16, 17, 20

Rescuer, The, 67, 479n. 35

Richards, Henry, 117, 464, 465

Richardson, Hubert, 263, 328, 405, 423, 442

Rider, Dave, 215

Rider, Rowland, 215

Riddle, Isaac, 5, 6

Rigg, Bob, 434

Rigg, Jim, 432, 434, 435, 461, 462, 509n. 37, 512n. 4

Roemer, Charles, 430

Rogers, Buck, 456

Roosevelt, Archie, 255, 257, 338

Roosevelt, Nicholas, 255, 257, 338

Roosevelt, Quentin, 255, 257

Roosevelt, Theodore, 190, 191, 202, 205, 255–57, 257, 261, 276

Rosenfelt, Herman, 240, 242, 246, 448

Roundy, Lorenzo W., xiii, 7, 15, 19, 33–36, 39, 40, 58, 64, 65, *66*, 67, 68, 70; rock, 388, 475n. 45, 478n. 32

rowboat, 40, 90, 134, 164, 177, 190, 197, 202, 203, 206, 254, 261, 279, 280, 329

Russell, Bill, 366, 389

Russell, Blanche, 366, 389

Russell, Charles S. "Charlie," 208, 260, 410, 499n. 19

Rust, David D., 156, 159, 193, 210, 215, 235, 244, 255, 256, 314, 405, 406,

410; tram, 197, 200, 204, 210, 215, 255, 256

S

sadiron, Nevills. *See* Nevills sadiron

Salton Sea, California, 276

Salton Sink, California, 275–76

Sand Trail, Arizona, 3, 4, 27, 50, 89, 218, 219, 221, 224, 287, 356, 501n. 28

Sandra, 427

Sandslide Trail, Arizona, 218, 300, 501n. 28. *See also* Buzzard's Highline Trail

San Francisco Peaks, Arizona, 14, 33, 34, 57, 59, 72, 74, 81, 259, 263, 268, 307, 442,

Sanger, Arthur Randall, 191, 464

San Juan punts, 421

San Juan River, Colorado-New Mexico-Utah, 39, 43, 216, 218, 227, 265, 284, 340, 345, 420, 426, 438, 461; bridge, 217, 393

Saunders, Benjamin Franklin, 151, 152, 174, 185, 186, 192–96, 198–200, 203–5, 207, 209, 213

Schenck, Harry A., 274, 279, 280–2, 285, 288

Scott, Marion B., xv, 347, 367, 380

scow, 16, 33, 80, 85, 95, 265, 300, 331, 334–35

Seegmiller, Daniel "Dan," 53, 92, 110, 126, 133

Separation Canyon, Arizona, 435

Separation Rapid, Arizona, 13

Shelton, Marion, 5

Shinumo Trail, Arizona, 210, 472n. 51

Short Creek, Arizona, 147, 257, 258, 260, 264, 329, 360, 365, 377, 399

Simmons, Pearly. *See* Johnson, Pearly Simmons

skiffs, 5, 6, 31–33, 39–42, 55, 57, 59, 61, 63, 64, 67, 68, 70, 71, 75, 76, 77, 88, 90, 91, 93, 96, 97, 99, 101, 106, 107, 112, 113, 115, 137, 154, 155, 176, 177, 182, 197, 224, 226, 227, 254, 273, 284, 300, 302, 329, 346

Simms, Al, 303

Skutumpah, Utah, 15, 18–20, 23, 24, 52, 134

Smith, Dick, 320–22, 328

Smith, George A., Jr., 6, 9, 20, 23, 46, 52, 54, 58, 73, 470n. 15

Smith, Jesse N., 77, 78, 88, 100, 117, 118, 127, 137, 138, 262, 351
Smith, Joseph, 11, 19, 30, 127, 145, 260
Smith, Lot, 60, 61, 62, 74–78, 82, 87–90, 100, 101, 103, 113, 118, 167, 388
Smith, Shine "Preacher," 320, 324, 325, 336, 340, 344, 346, 366, 388, 393, 397, 401, *402*, 403, *403*, 404, 430
Smith, "Uncle Tommy," 32, 33, 35, 42
Snow, Erastus Beamon, 8, 9, 18–23, 33, 34, 42, 64, 65, 68, 75–78, 80–82, 84, 85, 88, 89, 92–94, 98, 102, 104, 147, 148
Soap Creek, Arizona, 26, 29, 45, 61, 62, 91, 120, 122, 127, 193, 209, 210, 214, 243, 263, 272, 301, 333, 335, 344, 348, 361, 366, 389, 398, 404, 432, 433, 442, 443
Soap Creek Rapid, Arizona, 156, 332, 335, 474n. 4
Southern California Edison Company, xiii, xv, 273, 274, 279, 281–83, 285, 287–79, 292, 293, 296, 297, 301, 303, 310, 317, 331, 356, 357, 374, 425
Spencer, Annie, 318. *See also* LeBaron, Annie Spencer
Spencer, Charles Harvey "Charlie," x, xiii, 216–55, *219*, *250*, *255*, 257–60, 263–64, 267–68, 271–72, 279–82, 285–88, 290, 293–95, 297–98, 300, 302–3, 308, 311, 314–18, 320, 323, 326–17, 333, 341, 344–56, 358, 360–64, 366–70, 373, 376–78, 380–82, 420, 471n. 27, 496nn. 4, 7, 497n. 33, 511n. 33
Spencer, Eugene E., 232–34, 242, 243
Spencer, George, 217, 221, 222, 231
Spencer, Isaac Carling, 288, 315–17, 320, 323, 326, 341, 344, 347, 349–52, 356–58, 362, 363, 365, 368, 369, 373, 377
Spencer, Lydia Johnson, 288, 315, 344, 349
Spencer, Merrill F., 401
Spencer, Sylvia Allred, 344
Spencer Trail, Arizona, 229, 232, 253, 259, 280, 294, 298, 314, 318, 389, 396
Spicer, Wells, 55, 56, 57, 59
Staker, Joseph S., 163, 167, 168, 170, 171
Staker, Sadie, 161, 164–77, *171*, *175*, 187, 490nn. 53, 64, 68, 491n. 73
St. George, Utah, 3, 6, 9, 15, 19, 22, 23, 38, 47, 49, 52, 54, 57, 70, 265, 455;

Temple, 23, 69, 71, 104, 105, 131, 143
Standifird, John H., 73, 98, 100
Stanton boat, 227
Stanton, Robert Brewster, 116–20, *119*, *121*, 122, 134, 156, 159, 160, 164, 167, 169, 172, 177–80, 184, 186, 219, 226, 227, 233, 485nn. 19, 27, 489n. 34
Stanton Road, Arizona, 300, 393
Staveley, Gaylord L., 441, 450
Staveley, Joan Nevills. *See* Nevills, Joan
Steele, John, 470n. 17
Stephenson, Henry S., 209, 213, 219, 220, 222, 223, 231, 232, 251, 255, 256, 260–3, 265, 266, 271, 273, 295, 303, 304, 309–11
Steward, L. L., 194
Stokes, William, 51, 52
Stone, Julius F., 167, 169, 170, 215, 406, 407, 495n. 1, 497n. 41
Stewart, Levi, 13, 15, 43, 48
Styles, M. V., 354–56
Sumner, Jack, 134
Sunset, Arizona, 53, 62, 68, 69, 72, 74, 76, 84, 87, 92, 93, 96, 100, 103, 189, 193; Crossing, 62, 70; dam, 92
Susie Too, 463
Swapp, Alex, 127, 141, 142
Swapp, Ben, 124, 485n. 35
Swett, Joshua, 484n. 15
Switzer, Bill, 231, 235, 236, 238, 240, 242, 245, 248, 249, 351

T

Taltee (Hopi leader), 41
Tanner, Charlotte Annie. *See* Nelson, Charlotte Annie Tanner
Tanner Crossing, Arizona, 186, 196, 206, 223, 230, 235, 238, 240, 251, 336
Tanner, George S., xv
Tanner, Henry M., 72, 101
Tanner, Seth Benjamin, 58, 59, 103, 139, 167
Tanner Tank, Arizona, 211
Tanner Trail, Arizona, 307. *See also* Horsethief route
Taylor, John, 73, 74, 76–78, 80–82, 84, 94
Telesnimki (wife of Tuba), 18–21, 37, 48, 473n. 61
Temple Bar, Arizona, 436, 450
Tenney, Ammon M., 16, 48, 56, 68, 100

Terry, Paul B., xvi
Thomas, Richard William. *See* Watson, Frank D.
Thompson, Almon H., 14, 22, 27, 28
Thompson, Nellie Powell, 28, 29
Tibbetts, James L., 56, 57, 59
Tipton, John C., 218–21, 226–28
Tipton's boat. *See Mullins Boat*
Toquerville, Utah, 14–16, 21, 22, 38, 47, 56, 182
trading posts: Babbitt, Cedar Ridge, Arizona, 331, 335; Tuba City, Arizona, 351; Coppermine, 423; Gap, Arizona, 316, 320, 322, 365, 382; Hubert Richardson, Cameron, Arizona, 263; Oljeto, Utah, 218, *219;* Rust's, Navajo Bridge, Arizona, 325; Wetherill, Kayenta, Arizona, 256, 345, 346, 423; Wetherill and Colville, Oljeto, Utah, 218
trails, 9, 92, 471n. 27, 481n. 17, 501n. 28; trans-canyon, 185, 191–94, 197, 198, 200, 204, 210, 215, 298. *See also under specific name*
Tsinnie, Lewis (Nez), 329, 331
Tuba (Tuvi), 5, 18–21, 31, 32, 34, 35, 37, 38, 41, 43, 47–49, 475n. 41
Tuba City, Arizona, 105, 117, 163, 220

U

Udall, David K., 89, 90, 100, 453
U. S. Geological Survey (USGS), xv, 274, 278, 279, 283, 291, 296, 302, 305, 311, 315, 321, 326, 342, 348, 353, 355, 358, 366, 370, 377, 412, 415, 424, 425, 428, 438, 448, 449, 457
Underhill, Karen, xi
United Order, 51, 54, 55, 59, 74, 105, 132, 189, 350, 371, 476n. 72, 477n. 5
United Effort Plan, 483n. 1. *See also* Johnson, LeRoy Sunderland; McAllister, William James Frazier
Ute Crossing, Utah. *See* Ute Ford, Utah
Ute Ford, Utah, 1, 3, 6, 8, 9, 16, 18, 20, 21, 43, 49, 50, 55, 154, 159, 184, 214, 356, 406, 410, 470n. 17. *See also* Ute Crossing, Utah
Ute Trail, Utah, 1, 2, 3, 15

V

Vermilion Cliffs, Arizona, 2, 28, 138, 333, 364, 434

Vermilion Cliffs Lodge, Arizona, 337, 366, *367,* 396, *403,* 412, 418, 433, 504n. 52. *See also* Marble Canyon Lodge, Arizona
Violet Louise, 238, 239, *239,* 246, 282
V. T. Cattle Company, 110, 117

W

Wahweap, Utah, 9, 189, 285, 317, 439, 440, 441, 444, 445, 452, 453; Creek, 113, 221, 284, 415, 427, 439, 445
Walker, Pres, 418
Waller, Arthur C. "Art," xv, 218, 220, 223–29, 231, 235, 253, 259
Warner, Matt, 114, 484n. 15
Watson, Frank D. (Richard William Thomas), 225, 226, 232–35, 240, 242, 244, 245, 249, 496n. 14
Weaver, Billie, 345, 346, 377, 378, 392, 398, 402, 406, 407
Weaver, Hazel Barbeau, xv, 345, 346, 351, 352, 373, 374, 376–79, 381, 385, *385,* 386, 390–93, 397, 399, 402–11
Weaver, Leo, x, 345, 346, 350, 351, 352, 373–82, *375,* 385–87, *385,* 389–400, 402–11, 415, 419, 434, 442
Weaver, Nellie Foerster, 345, 376
Wells, Daniel H., 22, 53, 58, 63–65, 67–69, 73, 74, 94
Wetherill, John, 218, 345, 346, 403, 504n. 8
Wetherill, Richard, 345, 403, 416
Wheeler, George, 32, 41, 182
White, Albert, 384
White Canyon, Utah, bridge, 449
White, Georgie, 435
Whitmore, James M., 7–8
Widtsoe, John A., 293, 294
Wilkinson, Joseph T., 333, 342, 344
Wilkinson, Mary W., 351, 359, 366, 377
Williams, Sarah Caroline. *See* Lee, Sarah Caroline Williams
Wilson, Frank, 104, 107
Wilson, George, 364, 367, 381, 382–384, *383*
Wilson, Mary, 271, 283, 302
Wilson, Neill C., 418
Wilson, Sidney "Sid," 251, 273, 279–87, 292, 295, 298, *299,* 302, 308, 311, 314, 317, 319–21, 328; buildings, 348, 435; cabin, *402;* ranch, 281, 344, 356, 433, 499n. 35

Winburn, Mr., 41, 43

Winsor Castle Stock Growing Company, 147, 151, 488n. 3

Woodruff, Arizona, 263, 340, 352; dam, 263

Woodruff, Halbert E., 340

Woodruff, Mamie Lowrey, 333, 339, 340

Woodruff Manifesto, 125, 259; opposition to, 259, 260, 264, 312, 371

Woodruff, Wilford, 73, 80, 81, 87, 88, 90, 107, 109–11, 124, 125, 127, 130, 143, 152, 167, 168

Woods, George L., 11, 18, 21, 22, 32, 51

Wooley, Ed, 189, 190, 193, 201, 211, 212, 491n. 3

Wooley, Sarah Ellen. *See* Emett, Sarah Ellen Wooley

Woolley, Edwin D. "Dee," 106, 110, 111, 124, 126, 133, 139, 140, 143, 148, 150, 152, 168, 173, 176, 177, 181, 185, 188, 191, 194, 197–200, 204, 205, 207, 211, 214, 491n. 3

Woolley, Edwin G., 8

Woolley, Elias Benjamin "Hum," 191, 464, 492n. 30

Woolley, Emma B., 128, 133

Woolley, Royal B. "Roy," 176, 178, 181, 182, 487n. 57

Woolsey, Rachel A. *See* Lee, Rachel A. Woolsey

Workman, Clara B. *See* Lee, Clara B. Workman

Wrather Arch, Utah, 452–53, 511n. 31

Wrather, William Emery, 511n. 31

Wright Bar, Utah, 137, 215, 218–21, 225, 227

Wright, George M., xiii, 134–139, 215, 218, 356, 487nn. 59, 72

Wright, Frank, 432, 435, 461, 462, 509n. 37

Wright, J. B., 265, 273, 289, 331

Y

Young, Annie. *See* Johnson, Annie Young

Young, Brigham, 4, 10, 11, 13–15, 17–20, 22, 23, 30, 32, 34–40, 42, 43, 46–52, 54, 58–61, 63, 64, 69, 71, 73

Young, Brigham, Jr., 64, 73–4, 92, 95

Young, Brigham S., 388

Young, Howard O., 82

Young, John R., 9, 48, 49

Young, John W., 71, 73–6, 78, 80–84, 88, 92, 94, 105, 110, 111, 132–34, 138, 173, 486n. 56

Young, Joseph A., 48

Young, Joseph W., 15, 20, 23, 32, 34, 35, 37–39

Young, Polly. *See* Lee, Polly Young

Young, Lavina. *See* Lee, Lavina Young

Young, Rhoda. *See* Johnson, Rhoda Young